Readings for the History of the English Language

Readings for the History of the English Language

CHARLES T. SCOTT
Associate Professor of English

JON L. ERICKSON
Assistant Professor of English

UNIVERSITY OF WISCONSIN, MADISON

ALLYN and BACON, INC.
BOSTON

LIBRARY OF CONGRESS CATALOG CARD NO. 68-20532

PRINTED IN THE UNITED STATES OF AMERICA

Preface

This collection of readings is intended as a supplement to the standard textbooks for courses in the history of the English language. The volume is an anthology of articles dealing with topics directly concerned with various aspects of the historical development of English, as part of a more general examination of the principles and procedures underlying historical linguistics. The book is meant for use in graduate level courses in the history of English.

The papers included have been selected to reflect what we consider should be the principal emphasis in courses in the history of English, viz. internal or linguistic history. It is our feeling that a supplementary text such as this should be devoted entirely to matters of internal history, since the social, political, and cultural forces which have had some bearing on the development of the English language have already been well documented in the standard handbooks. Such information, therefore, is readily available to the student. An adequate and consistent linguistic history of English, however, has yet to be written, although numerous scholarly studies of various aspects of this history have appeared in widely scattered professional journals. This text is an effort to bring together some of this scholarship in an orderly and pedagogically useful way. Articles dealing with such familiar topics as the history of English spelling reform, sources of vocabulary, and questions of usage and correctness have not been included, since these matters are also amply treated in the handbooks.

The articles have been chosen to represent modern research in the linguistic history of English, and in general historical linguistics, where the latter is relevant to an understanding of historical change in English. The essays introducing each section are intended to provide a general framework within which the individual articles may be read. The arrangement of the selections is not meant to prescribe a sequence of topics for the instructor, since there are a number of equally profitable ways in which topics for a course in the history of the English language may be ordered. The selections in the anthology, therefore, may be used by the instructor in whatever sequential arrangement best suits his purposes.

The volume is divided into five parts. Part I *(Linguistics and the Historical Perspective in Language)* consists of articles devoted to certain principles underlying descriptive and historical linguistics, since the latter cannot be properly understood without attention to the former. Part II *(Phonetics, Phonemics, and Diachronic Phonology)* includes articles which focus the student's attention on the relationship between phonetic and phonemic description, and the relevance of this distinction to the study of change in the phonological structure of a language. Part III *(Phonological Change in the History of English)* deals specifically with the structural changes that have taken place in the English sound system. The selections in Part III represent both the traditional and the diasystemic approaches to the analysis of historical English phonology. Part IV *(Grammatical Change in the History of English)* presents articles concerned with features of paradigmatic and syntagmatic structure in English and the changes which these structures have undergone. The articles are meant to introduce the student to serious and systematic studies of certain aspects of historical English grammar and to counteract many of the facile generalizations which are often made about the characteristics of historical English morphology and syntax. Part V *(Linguistic Variation and Language Contact)* is concerned with the problem of regional and social variation in English during its various historical stages, and with the patterns of alteration which result, and have resulted, when linguistic systems come into contact. Such an examination is essential to a discussion of the history of English, since the principles of social and regional dialectology are vital to the determination of the direction of change in language and to the subsequent propagation of linguistic innovation.

We recognize that not everyone will be satisfied with the selections we have made. Limitations of space have made it impossible to include many excellent studies relevant to the history of English—especially in the area of historical phonology. We feel, however, that the selections presented will offer a sufficiently wide range of material to illustrate the scope and vigor of research in English historical linguistics.

C. T. S.
J. L. E.

Madison, Wisconsin
June, 1968

Contents

PART I

Linguistics and the Historical Perspective in Language

The basic tenet of modern linguistics is to be found in Ferdinand de Saussure's conclusion that "the true and unique object of linguistics is language studied in and for itself." When viewed in and for itself, a language, de Saussure found, is "a system of pure values which are determined by nothing except the momentary arrangement of its terms." A language is a system of components (linguistic units) in stable relationships to one another, and such relationships can be abstracted from the actualities of sound.

This interpretation of language establishes the proper focus of linguistic investigation, but it does not divorce language entirely from its social context. The system of a language can be approached only through its physical realization. The system can never be observed directly. The linguistic elements which make up the system cannot be determined without examining actual differences in the sounds of language, and correlating these differences with the responses of speakers. But it is only by starting from the hypothesis that the system itself is autonomous and capable of being abstracted from the circumstances of its realization that the true nature of language as system can be understood.

De Saussure proposed that a language must be thought of as a self-contained whole. As such, it is amenable to analysis as a structured system, and not merely as an aggregate of independent entities. Thus, linguistics as a science is concerned with the study of the structure of language—with the identification of the linguistic elements and with the relations which govern the parts as members of a system. In cooperation with other disciplines like ethnology, sociology and psychology, linguistics may also seek to describe the relations of such a linguistic system to other aspects of society, but this is peripheral to the main objectives of linguistics.

Individual languages may be described either in terms of their structure at any given point in their history or in terms of their evolution through time. One of de Saussure's most important contributions to the development of linguistic science was his recognition of the importance of distinguishing between these two points of view, and his further insistence that priority must be given to the former, the *synchronic* view, rather than to the *diachronic*.

For de Saussure, an appropriate analogy for elucidating the two points of view is to be found in a game of chess. The progress or evolution of the game can be thought of as a succession of spatial arrangements of chessmen on the board, as a series of static events. At any point in the course of the game the arrangement of chessmen is a structured system and the significance of any piece on the board is derived from its position relative to the other chessmen in the system—no piece has any significance in and of itself. Each move by one of the players results in a rearrangement of the system, and because each piece has value only in terms of the system, there is a redistribution of the value of each piece in the game. A historical account of the game is, therefore, a series of static descriptions of the systematic arrangement of the pieces at succeeding points in time. Similarly, the history of a language may be described as a succession of portraits of the system of the language at successive points in time. At any given point in the history of a language, the system can be interpreted as a self-contained whole, the elements of which have a value dependent upon the relations which exist in the language at that point in time. The function of synchronic linguistics, therefore, is to describe the structural relations which exist at any given moment; the function of diachronic linguistics is to describe the differences in the structure of a linguistic system between two or more synchronic points. A satisfactory diachronic description of such differences depends on the adequacy of the juxtaposed synchronic descriptions.

De Saussure expressed the distinction between synchronic and diachronic linguistics in terms of the axes along which the subject matter of each aspect of linguistics can be aligned. In the following illustration, AB represents the synchronic axis, where time is excluded; CD is the diachronic axis, which represents a sequence of synchronic states related through time.

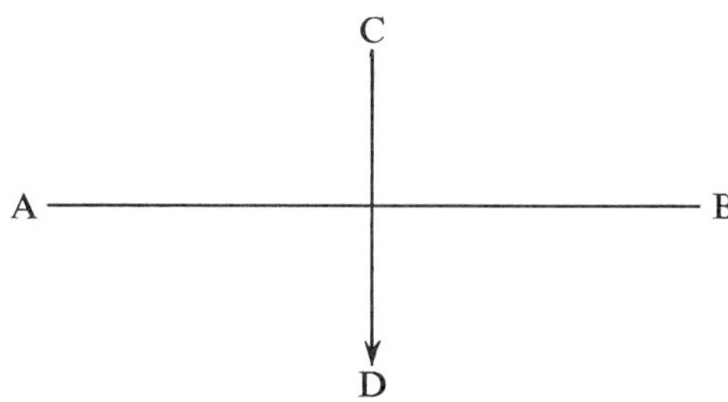

Diachronic linguistics is concerned, not with the history of linguistic elements in isolation, but with the history of such features only in so far as they are members of successive systems. Thus, diachronic linguistics presupposes synchronic description, since investigation along the diachronic axis CD cannot profitably be carried on without prior synchronic descriptions like that represented by AB. For example, an adequate historical description of the grammatical category of 'gender' in English depends primarily on the adequacy of successive synchronic descriptions of gender in the systems—and as part of the systems—of Old English, Middle English, Early Modern English, and New English.

The 'system of values' of the chessmen on the board, on the one hand, and of the elements of language, on the other, is determined by the arrangement of the appropriate elements relative to each other and to the system as a whole. Differences in the structures of these systems at rearrangement of the elements. The description of the changes which various historical stages result principally from the addition, deletion, or bring about structural differences is the province of diachronic linguistics; the explanation of the motivation for the changes, however, is the responsibility of other disciplines such as psychology, anthropology, and sociology.

The historical dimension in language is discovered by the comparative study of two or more linguistic systems. Linguistic features which are shared by several languages often emerge from such comparison, and it becomes the task of diachronic linguistics to explore the nature of the relationships between these shared features to determine whether they are purely accidental, whether they are the result of linguistic contact and hence borrowed from one system to the other, or whether they are systematic, thus offering evidence for the genetic relationship of the systems under comparison.

Evidence of genetic relationship between languages comes both from observed similarities in corresponding linguistic features and from systematic differences. The essential feature of comparative description is the formulation of rules of correspondence which demonstrate that two or more linguistic systems are mutually convertible. When it is possible to demonstrate, as the nineteenth century comparativists succeeded in doing, that the Latin phonemes /p t k/ systematically correspond to the Germanic phonemes /f θ x/, then such rules of correspondence may be said to demonstrate genetic relationship; both systems may be said to have been derived from a common source.

The establishment of rules of correspondence between linguistic systems not only provides convincing evidence that the systems are derived from some common system, thus enabling linguists to classify the respective languages as members of the same group, but it also provides the data from which aspects of the source or 'proto-' language can be reconstructed. Proto-languages can be reconstructed through a 'triangulation' procedure, back from the evidence of the later, attested languages. Such reconstructions are generally understood to be hypothetical in the sense that they are structural summaries of linguistic features shared by the related languages. From the attested evidence of languages like English, Dutch, Frisian, and German, for example, a hypothetical proto-West Germanic can be reconstructed, just as a proto-Indo-European can be reconstructed on the basis of the evidence offered by such language groups as Germanic, Romance, and Balto-Slavic. Since there are no records to reveal anything of the life of this earlier Indo-European speech community, the reconstructed evidence provides the chief information available about the early ethnic and social history of the people.

To express the systematic relationships between different language systems, diachronic linguistics has generally adopted the terminology of kinship. The language of an earlier speech community is commonly referred to as the 'ancestor' or 'parent' language from which later languages are 'descended'. To portray such relationships, a 'family tree' is often constructed. Thus proto-Indo-European may be regarded as the parent language from which such modern languages as English, German, French, Russian, Persian, and Hindi are ultimately descended. Questions, however, have been raised about the appropriateness of using analogies with biology to describe linguistic relationships, since languages do not behave like living organisms, passing through successive cycles of birth, maturity, decay, and death. The metaphors of kinship, if taken literally, may tend to obscure, rather than clarify, the realities of linguistic changes and relationships through time. Linguistic models must, therefore, be employed with a realization of both their metaphorical basis and their inherent limitations.

Since the objective of diachronic linguistics is the study of modifications in linguistic systems through time, it follows that formal linguistic criteria must be used to define the historical stages in the history of a language. The English spoken at the time of the Viking invasions, for example, was different from that spoken in the fourteenth or nineteenth centuries. Such differences are amenable to formal description, making it possible to delineate the features which distinguish Old English, for example, from New English. In actual practice, however, the designation of periods in the history of a language is usually made on the basis of political, social, or cultural criteria, rather than linguistic criteria. For the Germanic languages, the terms 'old', 'middle', and 'new' generally correspond to a three-way chronological partition of the Christian era. These distinctions correspond in a broad way to social developments in western Europe between the decline of the Roman Empire and the present. It is not demonstrable, however, that important political or social events are directly reflected by linguistic changes or that periods of rapid political or social change are, as well, periods of rapid linguistic change. It is, therefore, preferable to attempt to establish historical stages of a language without reference to non-linguistic events. Since, at any point in time, a language is a system, the evolution of a language must be viewed as a succession of linguistic systems, each of which is a modification of the previous system, brought about through the addition, deletion, or rearrangement of elements. The description of changes which result in structural modifications will therefore serve to define the differences between systems in succeeding periods, and serve as well to define the demarcation points between successive periods.

The articles which follow are intended to introduce the student to some of the fundamental notions of linguistic science and to the more general areas of interest in historical linguistics. The first article by Joseph H. Greenberg has been selected as a useful and reasonably comprehensive introduction to the views and methodological procedures of those who have worked within the framework of 'structural' linguistics and also to the range of interests in linguistics in both its synchronic and diachronic aspects. Martin Joos's article is, historically, an important one for its more formalized view of linguistic description as a type of discrete mathematics, i.e. for its conception of language design as a 'code' consisting of structural units in oppositional relationships to one another. The second article by Joseph H. Greenberg provides a general formulation of the methodological procedures in comparative linguistics. The article serves as a valuable theoretical orientation to the specific problems and conclusions involved in the genetic classification of the Indo-European and Germanic language groupings, from which English derives. The papers by Ernst Pulgram and Robert D. Stevick consider the difficult problem of attempting to describe language history by means of adequate models to represent that history. It has been well understood that, of methodological necessity, the comparative approach, when used alone, leads inevitably to an incomplete statement of language history because of factors such as dialect mixture and language contact. As a result, the earliest models of genetic relationship among languages have had to be supplemented by additional models to express the realities of linguistic variation. Pulgram endeavors to relate the conclusions of dialectology to a proper interpretation of both the 'family tree' and the 'wave theory' models of historical relationship. Stevick reconsiders the utilitarian value of biological models in the light of an updated theory of evolution, pointing out that such models need not be dismissed as lightly as they have been in recent years. Finally, W. P. Lehmann's article attempts to provide a linguistic, rather than cultural, definition of one particular stage in the chronological history of a language, and, in doing so, provides the theoretical argumentation for such definitions.

The Linguistic Approach

JOSEPH H. GREENBERG

AS DISTINCT FROM PSYCHOLOGY, which is concerned with verbal behavior in the context of events occurring within the organism, and from the other social sciences, which analyze the contents of verbal behavior insofar as it consists of shared cultural beliefs and actions (e.g., religion, philosophy, economic and political norms), linguistic science has as its traditional subject matter the signal system as such. Its orientation tends to be social rather than individual, since the use of speech in communication presupposes a group of intercommunicating people, a speech community. In general, therefore, it has dealt with the speech of individuals merely as representative of the speech of a community. The interest in an individual's speech as such, his *idiolect,* in relation to his personality structure constitutes a relatively new, marginal, and little explored area. The distinction between language as a system and its actual employment has been variously phrased as *langue* vs. *parole* (de Saussure), syntactic vs. pragmatic (Morris) or code vs. message (information theory).[1] However stated, it marks in general the boundary between what has traditionally been considered the province of linguistic science and what lies outside it.

The Field of Linguistics

The primary subject matter of the linguist is spoken language. Writing and other systems partly or wholly isomorphic with speech are viewed by most linguists as secondary systems. Speech has both ontogenetic and phylogenetic priority. There are even now peoples with spoken but not written languages (so-called primitives), but the reverse situation has never been obtained. Moreover, written systems are rela-

---

Reprinted by permission from *Psycholinguistics: A Survey of Theory and Research Problems* (Bloomington: Indiana University Press, 1965), pp. 8-18.

[1] [*Eds.:* See Ferdinand de Saussure, *Course in General Linguistics,* trans. Wade Baskin (New York, 1959) and Charles Morris, *Signs, Language and Behavior* (New York, 1946).]

tively stable while spoken language, by and large, changes more rapidly. It is always the written language which must make the readaptation, when it is made, by way of a new orthography. The effect of, say alphabetic writing on speech, in the form of spelling pronunciations, is a real but quite minor factor in the change of spoken language. The linguist views writing, then, as a derivative system whose symbols stand for units of the spoken language.

Linguistic science is divided into two main branches, the *descriptive* and the *historical.* Historical interests presided at the inception of modern linguistic science (ca. 1800) and have predominated until fairly recently. Within the last few decades the focal point of linguistics has shifted to problems of description. These two chief areas of study complement each other. The degree of success of historical inquiry is largely dependent on the adequacy of descriptive data. On the other hand any particular stage of a language, while it can be completely described without reference to its past, can be more fully understood if the time axis is also taken into account. A cardinal and generally accepted methodological principle, however, is the clear distinction between synchronic and diachronic investigations. In particular, descriptive grammars were, and sometimes are, so replete with historical interpretations, that the locus in time of individual linguistic facts is obscured and observed phenomena are not distingushed from inferences, so that no clear picture of the structure of the language at any one time emerges.

The aim of a scientific language description is to state as accurately, exhaustively, concisely, and elegantly as possible, the facts concerning a particular language at a particular time. It is assumed that the changes which are inevitably proceeding during the period in which the linguistic informant's speech is being studied are negligible and can be safely disregarded. It is also assumed that the speech of the informant is an adequate sample of some speech community. This concept is applied rather vaguely to any group within which linguistic communication takes place regularly. Minor cleavages within a group of mutually intelligible speech forms are called *dialects.* The maximal mutually intelligible group is a *language community,* as defined by scientific linguistics, but the term is often loosely applied on a political basis. Thus Norwegian is usually called a language although it is mutually intelligible with Danish, while Low German is considered a form of German, although objectively the difference between Low and High German is greater than that between Danish and Norwegian. The phrase 'mutually intelligible' is itself vague.

The speech of an informant is normally characteristic of that of a dialect community along with some idiosyncrasies. Language is so standardized an aspect of culture, particularly in regard to those structural aspects which are of chief concern to the linguist, that a very small number of informants usually proves to be adequate. If necessary, the linguist will even be satisfied with a single informant in the belief that systematic divergence from the shared habits of the community as a whole are likely to be of minimal significance. However, the sampling problem must eventually be faced in a less makeshift manner. The systematic mapping of speech differences on a geographic basis, through sampling at selected points, is known as *linguistic geography* and is a well-established subdiscipline of linguistics. Far more remains to be done with non-geographic factors of cleavage within the language community, on sex, occupational and class lines. Such study is a prerequisite for adequate sampling.

Units of Linguistic Analysis

Linguistic description is carried out in terms of certain fundamental units which can be isolated by analytic procedures. The two key units are the *phoneme* and the *morpheme,* of which the phoneme has a somewhat more assured status. The phoneme is the unit of description of the sound system (phonology) of a language. Many widely differing definitions have been offered, some of which are objects of doctrinal differences between various linguistic 'schools.' Fortunately, the actual results in practice of the applications of these divergent approaches are surprisingly similar.

The *phoneme* was foreshadowed by the pre-scientific invention of alphabetic writing. An adequate orthography of this kind disregards differences in sound which have no potential for the discrimination of meaning. Moreover, unlike syllabic writing, alphabetic writing selects the minimal unit capable of such differential contrast. The naive speaker is generally unaware of sound variations which do not carry this function of distinguishing different forms. For example, speakers of English have usually never noticed that the sound spelled *t* in 'stop' is unaspirated as contrasted with the aspirated *t* of 'top.' Yet this difference is sufficient to differentiate forms in Chinese, Hindustani, and many other languages. Phonemic theory is necessary because if we approach other languages naively we will only respond to those cues as different which are significant in our own language. On the other hand, we will attribute significance, and consider as indicative of separate elements, those differences which have a function in our own language, although they may not have such a function in the language we are describing.

For example, in Algonquian languages distinctions of voicing are not significant. A naive observer with an English linguistic background will carefully mark all *p*'s as different from *b*'s. The reaction of an Algonquian would be similar to that of an English speaker if he were presented with an orthography devised by a Hindu in which the *t* of 'top' was represented by a different symbol from the *t* of 'stop.' The arbitrariness of such a procedure comes out when we realize that an untrained Frenchman would describe the sound system of a particular language in different terms than a naive Englishman or German. As a matter of fact, this has often occurred. Equally unsatisfactory results are obtained by a phonetically trained observer, unaware of the phonemic principle, who indicates all kinds of nonessential variants because his training permits him to distinguish them. Here also there is a certain arbitrariness based on the particular phonetic training of the observer. The logical outcome of such a phonetic approach would be to carry discriminations even further by instrumental means, and the result would be that every utterance of a language would be completely unique, for no two utterances of the 'same' sequence of phonemes is ever acoustically identical with any other.

The procedure of the descriptive linguist, then, is a process of discovering the basic contrasts which are significant in a language. Since he cannot know *a priori* which particular features of an utterance will prove to be significant, he must be prepared to indicate them all at the beginning by a phonetic transcription. Instrumental aids, though useful, are not essential to the preliminary research. The linguist gradually eliminates those sound differences from his transcription which prove to be non-significant so that the phonetic transcription becomes a phonemic one. In doing this, he makes use of the two principles of *conditioned* and *non-conditioned variation*. If the occurrence of one or another of a set of sounds may be predicted in terms of other sounds in the environment, this variation is said to be conditioned. If either of two sounds may be used for the other and still produce a meaningful utterance, the variation is called free, or non-conditioned. Such variant sounds grouped within the same phoneme are called allophones. In English, *k̯*, a front velar sound is found before *i, I, e, E* and other front vowels (e.g., the initial sound of 'key') . A sound different enough to be a separate phoneme in many languages, *ḳ*, a back velar sound, is found before *u, v, o, ɔ* and other back vowels (e.g., the initial sound of 'coat') . Since the particular variant can be predicted by reference to the following vowel sound, *k̯* and *ḳ* are in conditioned allophonic variation and are members of the same English /k/ phoneme.

The number of potential phones (sounds) in a language approaches infinity. The great virtue of the phonemic principle is that it enables the linguist to effect a powerful reduction from this complexity to a limited number of signals that constitute the code, and this represents a great economy in description. For languages so far investigated, the number of phonemes runs about 25 to 30 (the English system tending toward the higher figure) . It is possible to effect a still greater economy in description. This is achieved by the analysis of phonemes into concurrent sets of *distinctive features.* Since the features which distinguish certain pairs of phonemes are found to be identical with the features which distinguish certain other pairs, the number of entities necessary to describe the significant aspects of the sound matter is thus further reduced. For example, in English /p/ is distinguished from /b/, /t/ from /d/, /k/ from

/g/, and /s/ from /z/ on the basis of the same feature, the former being unvoiced and the latter voiced. Other distinctive features, such as tongue position or nasalization, produce other sets of contrasts. By contrasting every phoneme in the language with every other phoneme, each phoneme comes to be uniquely identified in terms of the set of contrasts into which it enters, this 'bundle of distinctive features' being the definition of that phoneme. The distinctive oppositions that occur in languages studied so far run about 6 to 8. These are perhaps the minimal discriminanda in language codes.

Analysis into distinctive features is a development within the past two decades, associated with the Prague School but not universally accepted. Jakobson and his associates go one step further still, by imposing upon the entire phonemic material *binary opposition* as a consistent patterning principle, but this needs much further exploration.[2] Whereas American linguists usually say that sounds must be phonetically similar to be classed as members of the same phoneme, members of the Prague School state that members of the same phoneme class must share the same set of distinctive features. These criteria will generally lead to the same classificatory structure.

For example, *k̯* and *ḳ* would be said by members of the Prague School to share the following features in common: velar articulation, non-nasality and lack of voicing. These would be the relevant features shared by all varieties of the /k/ phoneme while, in this instance, back or forward articulation is irrelevant. The /g/ phoneme shares velarity and non-nasality with /k/ but not lack of voicing. The /ŋ/ phoneme (as in 'sing') shares velar articulation but not non-nasality or lack of voicing. The /t/ phoneme shares non-nasality and lack of voicing with /k/ but not velar articulation. Thus /k/ is uniquely determined by these three relevant features. Certain recent American analyses employ a methodology nearly identical with that just described.

Phonemes are sometimes distinguished as being either *segmental* or *prosodic*. The former proceed in one dimensional time succession without gap. The latter are intermittent and necessarily simultaneous with segmental phonemes or successions of segmental phonemes. Examples of prosodic phonemes are phonemes of tone (sometimes called tonemes), stress, etc. In principle, we should sharply distinguish prosodic phonemes simultaneous with a single segmental phoneme from those which are distributed over a grammatically defined unit such as a phrase or sentence. The former can always be dispensed with in analysis, though they often prove convenient. For example, in a language with three vowel phonemes /a, i, u/ and two tone levels high /´/ and low /`/ we might

[2] [*Eds.*: See Roman Jakobson, C. G. Fant, and Morris Halle, *Preliminaries to Speech Analysis: The Distinctive Features and their Correlates*, Acoustic Laboratory, Massachusetts Institute of Technology, Technical Report No. 13 (Cambridge, Mass., 1952).]

analyze /à/, /á/, /ì/, /í/, /ù/ and /ú/ as six separate segmental phonemes or we might make /a/, /i/ and /u/ segmental and /′/ and /‵/ prosodic. This particular analysis has no doubt been largely determined by our traditional orthography which uses separate marks for pitch. The carrying through of this procedure to its logical conclusion is called *componential analysis* and results in the resolution of each phoneme into a set of simultaneous elements equivalent to the distinctive features mentioned above. The other type of prosodic element is illustrated by question or statement intonation in English. Unlike the elements just discussed, it cannot be dispensed with.

Still another type of phoneme is the juncture or significant boundary, whose status is much disputed in contemporary linguistics. The conditioning factor for phonemic variation is sometimes found to be the initial or final position in some grammatical unit such as a word, rather than a neighboring sound. For example, unreleased stops *p, t, k* are found in English in final morpheme or word position. Unless we indicate the boundary in some fashion we must nearly double the number of phonemes in English. Spaces, hyphens and other devices are employed to indicate the presence of these modifications. For example, the *n* of 'syntax' is shorter than the *n* in 'sin-tax.' Either we posit two different *n* phonemes or we describe the longer *n* as *n* plus juncture, transcribing /sintaks/ and /sin-taks/ respectively (or we deny the existence of the phenomenon altogether).[3] The agreement as to the boundaries of grammatical elements is almost never perfect, and some linguists assume that if such boundary modifications exist in some cases they must exist in all, even though they have not actually been observed to occur.

In addition to the enumeration of phonemes and their allophonic variants, the phonological section of a description usually contains a set of statements regarding permitted and non-permitted sequences of phonemes, frequently in terms of the structure of the syllable. In this as in other aspects of linguistic description it is not usual to give text or lexicon frequencies. Statements are limited to those of simple occurrence or non-occurrence. Only such quantifiers as some, none and all occur in most linguistic description.

Corresponding to the minimal unit of phonology, the phoneme, we have a unit of somewhat less certain status, the *morpheme,* which is basic for grammatical description. Bloomfield states as the fundamental assumption of linguistic science that in a given speech community some utterances show partial formal-semantic similarity.[4] For example, in the English-speaking community the utterances 'the dog is eating meat' and

[3] Actually there is also a louder stress on the second syllable of 'sin-tax' and some would maintain that it is merely the stress difference which is phonemic. Even if this is true for English, the question arises in other languages.

[4] [*Eds.:* See Leonard Bloomfield, *Language* (New York, 1933) and "A Set of Postulates for the Science of Language," *Language* 2.153-64 (1926).]

'the dog is eating biscuits' are partially similar in their sequence of phonemes and refer to partially similar situations. The linguist, through the analysis of these partial similarities, arrives at the division of utterances into meaningful parts. The analytical procedure as applied to individual utterances must eventually reach a point beyond which analysis becomes arbitrary and futile. The minimum sequence of phonemes thus isolated, which has a meaning, is called a morpheme. The morpheme is a smaller unit than the word. Some words are monomorphemic, e.g. 'house.' Others are multimorphemic, e.g. 'un-child-like.' There is some uncertainty as to the point up to which such divisions are justified and the rules of procedure may be stated in several alternate ways. Thus all would concur in analyzing 'singing' as having two morphemes 'sing-' and '-ing' and there would likewise be general agreement that to analyze 'chair' as containing two morphemes, say 'ch-' meaning 'wooden object' and '-air' meaning 'something to sit on' is not acceptable. But there is an intermediate area in which opinions differ. For example, 'deceive' contains two morphemes 'de-' and '-ceive' according to some but not according to others. In such borderline cases it becomes impossible to specify the meaning of each morpheme without some arbitrariness.

Morphology and Syntax

The work of the descriptive linguists in this area is not exhausted by the analytic task just described. Having arrived at his units he must describe the rules according to which they are synthesized into words, phrases, and sentences. In somewhat parallel fashion to the situation in phonology, having isolated minimal units, he must describe their variation and their rules of combination.

In regard to the first of these problems, it is not sufficient to consider each sequence of phonemes which differs either in form or meaning as a different unit from every other. For example, the sequence 'leaf' /lijf/ is different in form from 'leav-' of the plural 'leaves' /lijv-z/ but we cannot consider them as units without relation to each other. We call /lijf/ and /lijv-/ morphs rather than morphemes and consider them allomorphs of the same morpheme because: (1) they are in complementary distribution, /lijv-/ occurring only with /-z/ of the plural and /lijf/ under all other conditions; (2) they have the same meaning; (3) there are other sequences which do not vary in form and which have the same type of distribution, e.g., 'cliff' for which we have /klif/ and /klif-s/.[5] Such variation in the phonemic composition of allomorphs of the same morpheme is called morphophonemic alternation, and systematic statements of such alternations comprise the portion of grammar known as *morphophonemics.* Some alternations occur in all instances in a language regardless

[5] This is too simple a formulation. Many problems arise at this point which cannot be discussed here.

of the particular morphemes in which the phonemes occur. Such alternations are called automatic. There are others which are unique. These are called irregular. Others are intermediate in that they apply to classes of morphemes of various sizes. In English, morphemes which have *s, z* and *əz* as variants exhibit automatic alternation, *əz* occurring after sibilants (and affricates), *s* after unvoiced non-sibilants and *z* after voiced non-sibilants. Thus the same rule applies both for the third person singular present of the verb and the nominative plural. On the other hand, the variation between /čajld/ 'child' and /čildr-/ of the plural 'childr-en' is a unique irregularity. Psychologically, there would seem to be a real difference between these extremes.

Having distinguished morphemic units, there remains the basic task of grammatical description—the setting up of rules of permitted combinations of morphemes to form sentences. Generality of statement is here obviously a prime requirement. Languages vary widely in number of morphemes, from some hundreds to many thousands. Their possible sequences in constructions can only be stated in practice by the setting up of classes whose members have the same privilege of occurrence. In setting up such classes, modern linguistics characteristically uses a formal, rather than semantic approach. Classes of morphemes or classes of sequences of morphemes (word classes, phrase types, etc.) are defined in terms of mutual substitutability in a given frame. Any utterance and the morpheme or morpheme sequence within it, for which substitutions are made, defines a class. Thus, in English, among other criteria, substitution of single words for *house* in the frame 'I see the house' determines the class of nouns. This contrasts with the traditional *a priori* semantic approach according to which all languages have the same basic grammatical categories (actually based on Latin grammar) and a noun, for example, is defined as the name of a person, place, or thing. Actually, formal criteria have always been used in grammars, although often tacitly. 'Lightning' is a noun in traditional English grammar also, although it names an event. because it functions in the same constructions as other nouns.

It is customary to regard sentences as the largest normalized units,[6] and these are successively decomposed into clauses, phrases, words, and morphemes. These units constitute a hierarchy which is also reflected in the speech event by *configurational features,* which, like the distinctive features of phonemic analysis, are assumed to operate on a strictly binary, 'yes-no' basis. Configurational features include such distinctions as those of pitch, stress, rhythm, and juncture, and provide appropriate signals

[6] However, discourse analysis, being currently developed by Zellig S. Harris, carries linguistic techniques beyond the boundary of the sentence, and Thomas A. Sebeok has attempted to study the construction of sets of whole texts of folkloristic character in this manner. [*Eds.*: See Harris, "Discourse Analysis," *Language* 28.1-30 (1952) and Sebeok and Ingemann, "Structural Analysis and Content Analysis in Folklore Research," in *Studies in Cheremis,* Vol. 2: *The Supernatural,* Part II (New York, 1956).]

as to construction. The sentence is so complex a unit that it cannot be described directly in terms of morpheme constructions. Rather, the description is built up in layers. On any particular level, the combinations are practically always accounted for in terms of *immediate constituents.* In the sentence 'unlikely events may actually occur,' the morpheme *un-* and the morpheme sequence *-likely* are the two immediate constituents which make up the word *unlikely.* In turn, *likely* has as immediate binary constituents the morphemes *'like-'* and *'-ly.'* On a higher level *unlikely* enters as a whole in a construction with *events* while *events* itself has *event-* and *-s* as immediate constituents.

It is usual to distinguish as primary divisions of grammar all constructions of morphemes to form words as *morphology* and all constructions using words as units to form phrases, clauses, and sentences as *syntax.* Although no generally accepted definition of the word-unit exists, in fact very nearly every grammar written makes use of the word as a fundamental unit and describes morphological and syntactic constructions separately. In spite of traditional differences of terminology in morphology and syntax, it is generally agreed that the same fundamental principles of analysis apply.

Problem of Meaning in Linguistics

Besides specifying meaningful units and their constructions, a complete linguistic description must state the meanings of these units and of the constructions into which they enter. The status of meaning has been a crucial point in contemporary linguistic theory. The statements of Bloomfield concerning meaning in his influential book have sometimes been interpreted both by followers and opponents as indicating that the field of linguistic science only includes a logical syntax of language without reference to meanings. The definition of meanings, on this view, rests with other sciences which deal with the subject matters which speakers talk about. Thus, the definition of 'moon' is the business of the astronomer, not the linguist. The actual practice of linguists both here and in Europe, however, indicates that semantic problems are in fact dealt with and cannot well be excluded from scientific linguistics.

Without entering into the exegetical problem of what Bloomfield meant, which is irrelevant to the present purpose, it may be pointed out that Bloomfield coined the technical terms 'sememe' for the meaning of a morpheme and 'episememe' for the meaning of a construction, both of which are current in American linguistics. Moreover, problems of historical meaning change are discussed at length in his book. This would imply that scientific linguistics does not exclude semantics. It is evident that historical linguistics draws conclusions regarding relationships by comparisons of cognates, that is, forms with both formal and semantic resemblances, so that in this branch, at least, meanings must be dealt with. It is likewise clear that the compiling of dictionaries has traditionally fallen within the linguist's province and continues to do so. No linguist has ever written a grammar in which the forms cited were not accompanied by translations.

The linguist deals with meaning by the bilingual method of translation or the unilingual method of paraphrase, that is, by the apparatus of traditional lexicography. In keeping with the general orientation of linguistics as a social science, the linguist defines the socially shared denotative meanings. Avoiding as far as possible controversial issues in the domain of epistemology, it may perhaps be ventured that a distinction may be, and in practice is, drawn between definitions which embody our scientific knowledge about a thing and nominal definitions which are observed rules of use in a given speech community. The linguist practices the latter type of definition. His methods up to now have been the more or less rough and ready methods of lexicography based on the traditional logical concepts of definition. The difficulties involved in the vagueness of actual usage of all linguistic terms in a speech community (if we exclude some scientific discourse in a few societies) are in practice circumvented by the not altogether happy devices of translation and paraphrase, which, involving as they do, language in its everyday use, are equally as vague as the terms which are to be defined. Ambiguity is dealt with by multiple listings of separate meanings based primarily on common-sense analysis. The boundary between the same form with synonymous meanings and separate homonymous forms has never been clearly determined, since it has not been possible to specify *how* different meanings must be in order to justify treatment as homonyms. Nor, in this instance, does an approach in terms of purely formal differences in distribution prove more successful.

Historical Linguistics

Thus far all our consideration of linguistic topics has omitted the basic dimension of change in time. This is the field of historical and of comparative linguistics which form a single sub-discipline. The investigation of the history of a specific language may be considered as a comparative study of its sequential synchronic states, while one result of comparing related, contemporaneous languages is a reconstruction of their history. History and comparison are thus, for the most part, inseparable in practice, though a much less frequently employed nonhistorical comparative approach, the so-called 'typological,' will be considered below.

It was the recognition of certain facts about language change that ushered in the modern scientific period in linguistics. The most fundamental of these were (a) the universality of language change, (b) the fact that changes in the same linguistic structure when they occur independently, as through geographical isolation, always lead to different total end results, and finally (c) that certain of those changes, particularly in the area of phonology, show a high degree of regularity. The acceptance of these three principles—universality, differential character, and regularity of language change—add up to a historical and evolutionary interpretation of language similarities and differences which contrast with the older notion based on the Babel-legend that, as with organic species, languages were types fixed from the time of creation and only subject to haphazard, degenerative changes.

The second and third of these principles, those concerning the differential nature of independent changes and their regularity, in combination, lead to the concept of genetic relationship among languages. Whenever a language continues to be spoken over a long period of time, weaknesses in communication through migration, geographical and political barriers and other factors, result in a pattern of dialect cleavage as linguistic innovations starting in one part of the speech community fail habitually at certain points to diffuse to the remainder. As this continues, the dialects drift farther and farther apart until they become mutually unintelligible languages. However, they continue to show evidence of their common origin for a very long period. In fact, a number of successive series of cleavages may occur within a period short enough for the whole set of events to be inferred. For example, the Proto-Indo-European speech community was differentiated into a number of separate speech communities, one of which was the Proto-Italic. The Proto-Italic in turn split into the Latin, Venetic, Oscan, Umbrian and other separate language-communities in ancient Italy. One of these, Latin, survived, but it in turn developed into the various Romance languages, French, Italian, Spanish, etc. Sometimes, as in the case of Latin, the original speech from which the descendant forms branched off is attested from written records. In other cases we legitimately assume that such a language must once have existed although no direct evidence is available. Such an inferred language is called a *proto-language* ('Ursprache') .

Because of the regular nature of much linguistic change, it is possible under favorable circumstances to reconstruct much of the actual content of such extinct languages. In particular, the reconstruction of the ancestral language of the Indo-European family has been a highly successful enterprise which has occupied a major proportion of the interest of linguists up to the present day. Thus far, linguistic relationships are well-established only in certain portions of the world and reconstruction has been carried out for only a limited number of linguistic families, particularly Indo-European, Uralic, Semitic, Bantu, Malayo-Polynesian, and Algonquian. Reconstruction is most successful, probably, in phonology, somewhat less so in grammar, and least of all in semantics. Forms which resemble each other in related languages because of common origin from a single ancestral form are called *cognates,* e.g., English *foot* and

German *Fuss*. The history of such a particular cognate is called its *etymology* and it has both a phonological and semantic aspect.

The difficulties of semantic reconstruction may be appreciated from the following artificial example which illustrates, however, the real difficulties often encountered. If in three related languages, a cognate form means 'day' in A, 'sun' in B, and 'light' in C, here are some of the possibilities among which it is impossible to make a rational choice. (1) The original meaning was 'day' which remained in A, shifted to 'sun' in B and to 'light' in C. (2) The original meaning was 'sun' which shifted to 'day' in A, remained in B and shifted to 'light' in C. (3) The original meaning included both 'sun' and 'day.' It narrowed to 'day' in A, to 'sun' in B, while in C it narrowed to 'sun' and then shifted to 'light.' These and others are all possible, and, in the present stage of our knowledge, about equally plausible. On the other hand, various Indo-European languages do have cognates, all of which mean approximately 'horse,' which can therefore be safely reconstructed for the parent language.

The changes undergone by languages whether documented or inferred can be classified under various universally applicable processes such as sound change, borrowing and analogy. Such processes show a high degree of specific similarity. To cite an example from phonology, *au* has become *o* in many different languages independently. Similar highly specific parallel changes occur in grammar and semantics. In spite of this, our second postulate of differential change shows that there are always a number of possible changes from a given state and our knowledge is not yet sufficient to predict which one will ensue or indeed whether the system will change or remain stable in some particular aspect. Parallel changes within related languages, called 'drift' by Sapir, are probably especially frequent and presumably strongly conditioned by internal linguistic factors.[7]

Typological Comparison

The ascertaining of historic relationships and the reconstruction of processes of change is not the only possible motive for the comparison of languages. We can examine the languages of the world, comparing both related and unrelated ones, in order to discover language universals, the greater than chance occurrence of certain traits, and the significant tendencies of traits to cluster in the same languages. The isolation of such clusters leads to the setting up of criteria for classifying language types. The classical nineteenth century typologies rested primarily on considerations of the morphological structure of the word. Because of the relatively unadvanced state of descriptive theory, it suffered from lack of precise definitions for the units employed and was, moreover, tied to an ethnocentric outmoded type of evolutionism. Recently text ratios of

[7] [*Eds.:* See Edward Sapir, *Language* (New York, 1921) .]

more rigidly defined units have been employed in order to construct a more refined typology.

The problems of typology are of intimate concern to psycholinguistics. The universal or more than chance occurrence of certain traits is in need of correlation with our psychological knowledge. More data on languages in many parts of the world and some effort at cross-linguistic cataloguing are probably necessary prerequisites for any considerable advance in this area.

Description of Language Design

MARTIN JOOS

Physicists describe speech with continuous mathematics, such as Fourier analysis or the autocorrelation functions. Linguists describe language instead, using a discontinuous or discrete mathematics called 'linguistics'. The nature of this odd calculus is outlined and justified here. It treats speech communication as having a telegraphic structure. (Non-linguists normally fail to orient themselves in this field because they treat speech as analogous to telephony.) The telegraph-code structure of language is examined from top to bottom, and at each of its several levels of complexity (compared to the two levels of Morse code) its structure is shown to be defined by possibilities and impossibilities of combination among the units of that level. Above the highest level we find, instead of such absolute restrictions, conditional probabilities of occurrence: this is the semantic field, outside linguistics, where sociologists can work. Below the lowest level we find, instead of such absolute restrictions, conditional probabilities of phonetic quality: this is the phonetic field, outside linguistics, where physicists can work. Thus linguistics is peculiar among mathematical systems in that it abuts upon reality in two places instead of one. This statement is equivalent to defining a language as a symbolic system; that is, as a code.

THE WORD 'DESIGN' may be interpreted in at least two senses without violating engineering usage. First, there is the work of the engineer who is designing something, for example a telephone system. Second, there is the finished something, such as that same telephone system, considered now as something to be analysed and described. Our description of it, then, can also be called its 'design'. It is in this last sense that the word 'design' has to be understood when we are talking about the design of language and how it is analysed for description.

Engineers never have occasion to analyse a gadget the way linguists do a language. The nearest thing to it might be this sort of episode. A supplier had been asked to furnish a band-pass filter, single T section, with rather modest cut-off requirements. Instead of the expected classical constant-k filter—two series arms, one parallel arm, total three coils and

---

Reprinted by permission from *Readings in Linguistics,* Martin Joos, ed. (New York: American Council of Learned Societies, 1958), pp. 349-356.

three capacitors—he furnished a filter with three coils and four capacitors connected in an unexpected way. The writer was asked to analyse the design and report whether it was worth adopting for future routine construction of band-pass filters. It turned out that the odd design had two advantages: one of the coils could be a large stock-size coil used without trimming, and the design gave any desired impedance-transformation without a transformer. But—and here is the crucial point—it did not seem possible to arrive at these conclusions without taking into consideration the designer's intentions; and the experience seemed to show that a 'why' question has an answer only when intention is in the picture—when the presence of intention is given, so to speak, as a boundary-condition.

Linguists have described numerous languages, and have observed language design-changes through the centuries. But although quite a body of 'how' knowledge concerning these matters has been built up, we have so far nothing but a number of unconfirmable guesses concerning the 'why'. Hence most of us are now pretty sure about one thing: there is nothing conscious, nothing deliberate, about language-design. (Naturally we don't mean to study Basic English or Esperanto until we have first built up the theory of natural language-design.) Accordingly we do not present the design of any language as the result of intentions—we do not answer 'why' questions about the design of a language.

Having thus limited our problem, we proceed with greater confidence to look for answers to the 'how' questions of language-design. In other words, we try to describe precisely; we do not try to explain. Anything in our description that sounds like explanation is simply loose talk —deliberately loose, perhaps, for the sake of persuasion by analogy—and is not to be considered part of current linguistic theory.

We can allow other people—telephone engineers or sociologists, for example—to speak artistically, imprecisely, about language. But as linguists we lay upon ourselves the condition that we must speak precisely about language or not at all. We can do that, of course, only under two conditions, of which the first has already been hinted at. First, we must limit our field, leaving outside it certain things to be treated precisely by engineers or by sociologists, while we speak of them more or less artistically. Second, within our field we must adopt a technique of precise treatment, which is by definition a mathematics. We must make our 'linguistics' a kind of mathematics, within which inconsistency is by definition impossible. True, miscalculations may occur through inadvertence. And different workers describing the same language may arrive at conflicting statements because they have started out from different sets of axioms. But in principle every possible statement of ours must be either true or false—nothing half-way.

Have linguists succeeded in setting up such a mathematical style for describing language designs? Well, not quite; but our science is still young. In its mathematical phase it is just a quarter of a century old, for we date it from Bloomfield's 'A set of postulates for the science of language' (in the journal *Language,* 1926). And even physics has not yet entirely resolved the conflict between quantum theory and the wave theory of light. But of all the sciences and near-sciences which deal with human behavior, linguistics is the only one which is in a fair way to becoming completely mathematical, and the other social scientists are already beginning to imitate the strict methods of the linguists.

Presenting only 'how' statements without regard to 'why', we of course have no assurance that we are 'right' in any sense that would satisfy a theologian. And we feel that our descriptive statements fit actual speech-behavior, but we have no right to claim that they are 'correct' in the sense that they fit the neural events in the brains of the speaker and listener. Such arrogant modesty is not peculiar to linguists; it is simply the normal attitude of mathematicians confronting the real world. The mathematical description for reality has been most illuminatingly called a 'map'. Now when one holds a map (in the ordinary sense) in one's hands, one may say, "I feel that this is a map of the countryside around me here," but there is no way to prove logically that it is not instead a map of a piece of Australia or perhaps of some imaginary Treasure Island. Undeterred by the impossibility of logical justification, explorers use maps, scientists use mathematics, and linguists use the descriptive technique called 'linguistics'. All three have the same attitude toward the map. One proceeds across the terrain and simultaneously traces a line across the map; one notes discrepancies between one's reading of the map and the sense impressions from the real world, until the discrepancies seem to form a pattern themselves; then one corrects the map and starts all over again. All this is intuitive behavior, and logically unjustifiable. Nor does it need justification. The place for logic is inside the map, not between the map and the real world.

Ordinary mathematical techniques fall mostly into two classes, the continuous (e.g. the infinitesimal calculus) and the discrete or discontinuous (e.g. finite group theory). Now it will turn out that the mathematics called 'linguistics' belongs in the second class. It does not even make any compromise with continuity as statistics does, or infinite-group theory. Linguistics is a quantum mechanics in the most extreme sense. All continuity, all possibilities of infinitesimal gradation, are shoved outside of linguistics in one direction or the other. There are in fact two such directions, in which we can and resolutely do expel continuity: semantics and phonetics.

Every language has 'meaningful' molecules called 'morphemes', subassemblies which roughly correspond to subdivisions of the real world outside language. The word *nose,* for example, consists of one such morpheme; the word *noses* consists of two, the second having as its real-world correspondent the conventional category of numerousness, one of our customary subdivisions or categorizations of the real world. Now consider these facts. The English word *nose* may refer to a part (how much?) of an airplane. With a lipstick draw a loop on your own face to enclose your nose and nothing else; another person will say that you have enclosed either too much or too little. Say in English: "The councillors all put their glasses on their noses" and then get the sentence translated into German; for English *noses* you will get the singular noun-form *Nase,* not the plural *Nasen.* The German knows that numerous councillors have equally numerous noses, and he has a word for 'noses', but in this sentence he uses his word for 'nose' instead. In linguistic terminology we simply say that the form *Nase* belongs to the category which we have called 'singular'. We chose that name the way the physicist chose the name 'work', because in German the category most often refers to lack of numerousness in the things referred to; but this is not a logical reason, it is only a motivation out of convenience. High-school physics teachers often have good reason to regret the choice of the term 'work' for force times distance, and in expounding linguistic theory we often have the same reason for regretting the choice of terms 'singular' and 'plural'. The trained listener, the listening linguist in this case, is not deceived; he knows that in calling *Nase* 'singular' we have not said whether one nose or more than one nose was involved.

We keep on and say a few thousand things like this, but as long as we are talking about German or English we never place a noun-form in a third category side by side with 'singular' and 'plural', say a category which is neither singular nor plural, or is both, or is ambiguous as to number. The listening linguist, noting the absence of this other kind of statement, sooner or later decides that in German or in English every noun-form is either singular or else plural—*tertium non datur.* This may be called the tyranny of linguistic categories. It is found in every language. It is not a question of 'correctness' in the popular sense of the word, for every kind of speech, elegant or sub-standard, has its own categorical tyrannies. For example, in the writer's dialect the form *whom* can't follow a pause: it is permissible to say "To whom did you give it?" or "Who did you give it to?" but not "Whom did you give it to?" In situations where the normal language-design is not quite adequate, such as in the composition of a paper like this, we get amusing difficulties, such as finding it necessary to say either 'one nose or more than one nose was involved' or else 'one nose or several noses were involved.' The difficulty is just as severe if we say 'one sheep or more-than-one/several sheep was/were involved.' That is, it is the category that tyrannizes over us, not the form, and not the meaning either; and even a word like *sheep* must be, each time that it is used, either singular or else plural. We might like to replace *was/were* with a verb-form which was, like the Irishman's trousers, singular at the top and plural at the bottom, but we haven't got any such category in English. In fact, in every known language there is a limit to the kinds and numbers of its categories, a limit which may seem very low compared to the elaborations which philosophers and poets indulge in. Then when an unusual message is to be transmitted, the categories are never split or supplemented, but are instead used in unusual combinations. The listener's total reaction may or may not be as expected, but his detail reactions are predictable at least to this extent: For every form-class represented in the utterance ('noun' is one form-class, 'verb' is another) there are a certain number of dimensions of categorization (in the English noun there are two: possessive-vs.-common, and singular-vs.-plural) ; and now, for every dimension thus introduced into the utterance, the listener will react to exactly one of the categories in that dimension—he will not react to more than one, or to none, whether the utterance is ambiguous or not. The reader can check this fact easily. Without looking back to the sentence about the councillors, let him ask himself whether it referred to present time or to past time. He will find that he has made up his mind one way or the other; and yet, on checking the wording, he will find that he was not told. The English categorization, past-vs.-present, forced him to decide, even though the decision had to be made at random. Each language does this within the range of its own categories, WHICH WILL NOT BE THE SAME RANGE AS IN OUR LANGUAGE. In Chinese, for example, the translation lacks both the past-vs.-present dimension and the singular-vs.-plural dimension; these 'meanings' can be indicated on occasion, but when they are not, the Chinese listener leaves the question open—he says he is not even aware that it is a question.

The linguistic categories, then, are absolutes which admit of no compromise. They correspond roughly to favorite categorizations in the real world, and it is widely held that every community subdivides the phenomena in the real world according to the categories of its language, rather than the reverse. But the correspondence between the discrete categories of the language and the continuous phenomena of the real world is not and cannot be precise. Our reaction, as linguists, to this situation, is very simple: all phenomena, whether popularly regarded as linguistic (such as the tone of anger in an utterance) or not, which we find we cannot describe precisely with a finite number of absolute categories, we classify as non-linguistic elements of the real world and expel them from linguistic science. Let sociologists and others do what they like with such things—we may wish them luck in their efforts to describe them precisely in their own terminology, but no matter whether they describe them with discrete categories or not, for us they remain vague, protean, fluctuating phenomena—in a word, they represent that 'continuity' which we refuse to tolerate in our own science.

Have we ever had any choice? Could we have chosen to use a continuous rather than a discrete mathematics for describing language-design? Our experience with the analysis of a few hundred of the world's several thousand languages makes us very sure that we must answer negatively. We can, with some effort, begin to imagine a quasi-language used on some other planet by creatures unlike ourselves, in which a quasi-word [kul] (identical with the way I have just now pronounced English *cool*) signifies a temperature of +10° centigrade, and another one, [kold] , signifies —10°, while any intermediate temperature worth mentioning is precisely signified by an intermediate pronunciation, with a vowel between [u] and [o] at just the right proportionate distance from them both (phonetically a reasonable thing to say: [o] and [u] are phonetically neighbors, and continuous gradation of quality from one towards the other is a commonplace) and just the right strength of [d] (from zero strength, or lack of [d], at one end of that segment of temperature scale, up to that full strength which I used just now at the other end of it) to measure and signify just the temperature meant. But neither this sort of thing, nor indeed any other gradation or continuity IN EITHER FORM OR MEANING, has ever been found IN ANY LANGUAGE on this planet. True, the sounds (and thus all the forms) occurring in the use of the language are variable by continuous gradation, and so are not only temperatures but all things and phenomena spoken of. But IN THE DESIGN of the language we never find a trace of those facts! Messages are communicated in the language, both in speech and in writing, as if the forms (words, etc.) were invariants and as if the referents (things, etc.) were also invariants: that is, the only way the forms and meanings of a language are ever used is the way an accountant uses 'dollars' or 'shillings'—not the way a numismatist or even an economist uses them.

The accountant banishes two kinds of continuity from his debits-and-credits mathematics: the continuous variation in 'state' of a coin that interests a numismatist, and the continuous variation in 'real value' that interests an economist. Linguists do the same in describing language: from their linguistic calculus they banish the continuous variation in phonetic 'state' of the utterance, and the continuous variation in semantic 'real value' thereof. Now is this the right way to discuss language? Is it somehow adequate to the way languages work? Or is it instead a falsification, a Procrustean mistreatment? Let us consider the phonological half of it first.

Here we have 'phonemics' inside of linguistic science; and 'phonetics', which is not so very different from and may even be considered a division of the physicist's 'acoustics', in the realm of overt speech-behavior, which is not the realm of linguistics but belongs to the real world outside of linguistics. When a physicist analyses speech he finds a continuum of articulatory activity, of sound, and of events in the ear—at least until, working both ways from the sound, he comes to the all-or-none discharging of single nerve-fibers—and for describing any or all of this he uses a continuous mathematics, such as Fourier analysis or the autocorrelation function. On the other hand, linguists have found it appropriate always to describe every language so far studied as having, and every act of speech as corresponding to, combinations of an astonishingly small number of smallest signalling units called 'phonemes' which recur identically insofar as they can be said to occur at all. Thus the word *hotel* can't be spoken the same way twice, from the physicist's viewpoint, no matter whether the same person or different persons should utter it; and yet from the linguist's viewpoint it always has in the middle a phoneme /t/ which is identically the same every time. And it is not considered the same through neglect of unimportant variations in reality; rather, it is identical by definition, simply because it is a linguistic atom, a category, and these are either identically the same or absolutely different.

Here, then, linguistics insists upon being atomistic. Is this the right and only thing for a linguist to do? Telephone engineers have been known to protest at this point and say something like this: "When you were discussing linguistic discreteness and non-linguistic continuity in the semantic field you had me where you wanted me, for how should an engineer know anything about semantics? But now you are talking about sound, and here I am perfectly at home; I have even made extensive and precise observations upon normal speakers and listeners: for instance, I have gathered statistics about the variations in vowel qualities. Your mathematically identical phonemes are a delusion; what you've got are statistical norms, clusterings around averages which you take as norms and then arbitrarily make into absolutes. We are both talking about phonetics; and when you admit that I can prove continuity, you can't claim to prove discreteness.

"Let us agree to neglect the least important features of speech sound, so that at any moment we can describe it sufficiently well with n measurements, a point in n-dimensional continuous space, n being not only finite but a fairly small number, say six. Now the quality of the sound becomes a point which moves continuously in this 6-space, sometimes faster and sometimes slower, so that it spends more or less time in different regions, or visits a certain region more or less often. In the long run, then, we get a probability-density for the presence of the moving point anywhere in the 6-space. This probability-density varies continuously all over the space. Now wherever you can find a local maximum of probability-density, a place where the probability-density does not increase for short distances in any direction away from the place in question, I will let you call that place a 'phoneme'; and I expect, just as you do, that there will be not only a finite but a fairly small number of such points, say less than a hundred. Thus you see that there is no need to use a discrete mathematics to get a finite number of phonemes out of the phonetic continuum."

We could answer that our name for that would be, not 'phoneme', but 'allophone', and allophones belong to phonetics while phonemes belong to linguistics. But that would be evading the issue. The engineer's argument is a formidable one, and deserves to be met squarely. According to our view concerning the relationship between any mathematical map and the real phenomena to which it corresponds, it is not possible to argue logically in this field; therefore we have to argue by means of analogy. Fortunately a suitable analogy lies ready to hand.

Let us consider telegraphy, using Morse or Baudot coding. The units are the mark and the space; it doesn't matter whether the 'space' is an electrical impulse of opposite polarity to the 'mark', or an electrically neutral period. A Morse dash could be considered as three integrally sequent marks, and a letter-space as three spaces; then the units differ in only one dimension. Or the dash and the letter-space may be considered as independent signals; then there are four signals, differing from each other in two dimensions, namely electrical intensity (or polarity) and duration. Thus there are at least two ways of describing the Morse code, both discrete and both correct, each by its own axioms. They differ in their grammar, though. The first way requires the grammatical rule that each occurrence of mark after space (or of space after mark) is always followed by exactly two more of the same or else by one or three of the other. The second way requires the rule that either mark is followed by a space, and either space by a mark. This sort of interrelation between a set of axioms and a set of grammatical rules is a commonplace in linguistics. But now let us continue with telegraphy.

A Morse S is mark-space-mark-space-mark. A Baudot Y is mark-space-mark-space-mark—shall we say "also"? That depends; we can settle it later. At the far end of a long line, the marks and spaces are slurred together into a continuous smooth fluctuation so that on first inspection it may be far from easy to tell what the original signals must have been. Then a regenerative repeater is used to square up the marks and spaces so that they can be read or will operate an ordinary teletypewriter. But if the line is very long, not much noise will be needed to cause occasional errors in the repeater's operation. A regenerative repeater for Baudot signals will in general not handle Morse signals, nor vice versa. (We begin to see why we had better not say "also" as proposed at the beginning of this paragraph.)

Now let us find a telephone engineer who knows nothing about telegraphy, and give him the output of a long telegraph line. What does he do with it? He does Fourier analysis and autocorrelation and perhaps something else—at any rate, at first he works on it with continuous mathematics, for the material is obviously continuous. But as long as he does that, he can make no sense out of it. In desperation he next differentiates the output voltage, so that he has two data for every instant, the voltage and its first time-derivative. Now for each five milliseconds he averages each of these, and plots the two averages as a single point on a sheet of graph-paper. When he has put a few thousand points on his paper, he sees a continuous variation of point-density, with a number of local maxima—perhaps a few dozen of them. To each maximum he assigns a label, a letter or a number, arbitrarily. Now he interprets his original data, his voltage and derivative data, in terms of these labels: every time the line-output and its derivative come close to one of those maximum-density points, he will write down the label of that point, so that finally he has replaced the original data by a string of those labels. Now he can turn this result over to a cryptanalyst, who will be able to read the original plain-language text out of it—not quite completely on first reading, but probably he will be able to reconstruct a good text if he knows the language well. Ridiculous? Not at all. This is exactly what our telephone engineer wanted to do with phonetics and phonemics.

Now we also know what that same telephone engineer will do after we tell him of the existence of telegraph codes employing molecular signals made up of atomic units, each unit being identically one or another of a very small number of atoms. He will not use Fourier analysis or any other continuous mathematics at first. Rather, he will start out by looking for wave-trains that look nearly alike, their slight differences being explicable, as he can easily see, either as the effects of noise or as the effects of context. He will see many occurrences of a three-peaked wave-train, no two occurrences precisely alike. But when the first peak is rather low, then there will be a long hollow before it; when there is no hollow, the first peak is as high as the second or a bit higher. This is a context-effect. Once most of the context-effects have been spotted, the remaining variations will be ascribed to noise. In this fashion he will learn to identify the three-peaked wave for Morse S or Baudot Y, and also all the other common molecular signals.

Next he will set up the hypothesis that there are just *n* atomic signalling units, and that not only the inter-molecular context-effects but also the intra-molecular smoothings can be accounted for by low-pass filtering. Here he can use continuous mathematics for a while, and the result will be that this hypothesis works best if *n* equals two. Now it won't take him long to reconstruct the entire telegraphic code; quite easily if it is Baudot, not so easily or swiftly if it is Morse, but in either case with absolute certainty.

Finally he will describe the design of the telegraphic code, and he will describe it in terms of absolutely identical square-wave signalling atoms, even though he has never observed anything that could be called absolute identity, and even though he knows that square waves are impossible. And when he has thus finished his job, he will be able to convince his colleagues, the other telephone engineers who knew nothing about telegraphy, that this is the right way to do it. Convince them by logic? Not a chance. Nothing but the superior elegance of his results will speak for the rightness of his method, but that will be enough.

Linguists find themselves so successful in describing languages in this fashion that they have elevated their descriptive technique to the rank of a theory about the nature of language. They say, in effect, that the design of any language is essentially telegraphic—that the language has the structure of a telegraph-code, using molecular signals made up of invariant atoms, and differing e.g. from the Morse code principally in two ways: the codes called 'languages' have numerous layers of complexity instead of only two, and in each layer there are severe limitations upon the combinations permitted. This much, we find, all languages have in common. But the particular code is different from one language or dialect to another, as the Baudot and Morse codes differ. Those two telegraphic codes share, on the phenomenal level, this molecular signal among others: mark-space-mark-space-mark. Now suppose we find this signal in the output of one telegraph line, and find it again in the output of another telegraph line; are they the same or are they not the same? That depends. If they are both Morse or both Baudot, then they are identically the same signal, no matter whether or not they are distorted by different noises or different line characteristics, or are sent at different speeds, or by a well-adjusted or a badly-adjusted transmitter. If one is Morse and the other is Baudot, then they are not in the least the same signal, even when their oscillograms come out the same within the limits of instrumental error.

This is obvious to any telegraph engineer. But in the linguistic field it did not seem obvious or even credible to a certain engineer who said to the writer: "Surely you can tell when two men pronounce the word *father* alike!" The answer had to be: "On the data you have given me, the question has no meaning. First I have to find out whether they rhyme *father* with *bother*. If they both do, or neither does, then I must find out whether both of them or neither of them pronounces *cot* the same as he pronounces *caught*. Then I have a few more questions of the same sort, with which I explore their contrasts for some distance around the word *father* in all directions. If I always get the same answer from both of them, then I say, 'Yes, they pronounce *father* alike,' meaning 'identically the same,' even if they sound quite different when they say the word. But if, during this exploration, I find a discrepancy between their systems of phonemic contrasts before I have gone very far from the word *father* itself, then I shall have to say, 'No, they pronounce it differently,' meaning 'their pronunciations are incommensurable,' even if they sound so much alike that no difference can be heard." This statement was met with amazed incredulity, and a request to state honestly whether anybody else held similar views. It is to be feared that the answer to this request was not accepted at face value. The trouble was, of course, that no bridge had been built between the engineer's knowledge of telegraphy and the language experience of linguists.

Now let us go on with the design of language. We have dealt with the phonemes individually, and shown that the most important thing about them is that they are either absolutely the same or absolutely different. And yet, in another sense it is to be expected that two of them can be partly the same and partly different. This can be possible in this way. If it is possible to put phoneme /A/ into three categories x, y, and z (as the word *noses* simultaneously belongs to the three categories 'noun', 'common rather than possessive', and 'plural'), and to put phoneme /B/ into three categories v, w, and z (as the word *were* belongs to the three categories 'verb', 'past', and 'plural'), then /A/ and /B/ can be said to be similar, but of course only in the sense that they are partly identical: similarity can't be gradual, but only quantized, as in this instance, where /A/ and /B/ are identical to the extent of z and otherwise absolutely different, hence are called 'similar'. This is another way of stating the discrete nature of the descriptive method called 'linguistics': similarity is described as fractional identity. We naturally use quantized identity, wherever we can find it, to describe what we find in a language; and what has been described in that fashion has been rigorously described.

The Morse code uses two signalling units, 'mark' and 'space', differing in one dimension; or it can be considered as using four units, 'dot', 'dash', 'space', and 'letter-space' different in two dimensions, namely electrical intensity (or polarity) and duration. On the other hand, every known language uses more than a dozen (and less than a hundred) phonemes, different from each other in at least four, more probably at least five, dimensions. Spanish, for example, seems to have at least nine dimensions in its phonemic system (which some phonologists will reckon as fewer by the trick of identifying some dimension found in one area of the phonology with a dimension found only in another area) and English is known to have more than Spanish.

These are so many that a complete catalog would be confusing, but a sample may be helpful. One of the Spanish dimensions is 'vowel-vs.-consonant'. Among the five Spanish vowels, two more dimensions are clearly evident. In one dimension, the five are categorized as 'high, mid, low'; in the other, as 'front, central, back'. /i/ and /u/ are high; /e/ and /o/ are mid; /a/ is low; /i/ and /e/ are front; /u/ and /o/ are back; /a/ is neither, so it is called central. The six category-names were borrowed from phonetics into phonemics, just as the word 'work' was borrowed by physics, and as we borrowed 'plural' from other fields of discussion, where it was a synonym for 'numerous': in linguistics it is not! In phonetics, 'high, mid, low, front, central, back' refer to tongue-position in the mouth; in phonemics, of course, we have to strip away those denotations of the words, which have now become distracting connotations. Instead, the phonemic categories get whatever denotations may be useful in the further description of the language. The PHONETIC term 'labial' means 'articulated with a lip or lips'. The PHONEMIC term 'labial' means different things for describing different languages. In describing the Oneida language it would be a meaningless term. In describing English, it means 'forbidden after /aw/' (where /aw/ means what we spell *ou* in such words as *council*)—that is, after /aw/ without any sort of break (such as the /+/ break in *cowboy*) we never have any of the phonemes /p, b, f, v, m, k, g/ and perhaps certain others; now the first five of these are said to be forbidden after /aw/ because they are labials, and other reasons are found for the others that never occur after /aw/. Thus the term 'labial' is not USED in phonemics (though it might still be spoken or written casually) unless to make statements about what occurs, or, because it has not yet been found to occur, is taken to be impossible. Such statements are the characteristic statements of descriptive linguistics; and among them, the statements of non-occurrence are, oddly, of the greatest importance, as will appear again below.

A telegraphic 'mark' does not signal anything by itself. In principle, it takes an assembly of marks and spaces to make up a signal. Then the one-dot Morse E is a sort of accident, what mathematicians call a 'trivial' or 'degenerate' case; it is a molecule of only one atom, like a helium molecule.

The same is true of phonemes. Linguistic signalling is done, not with phonemes, but with morphemes, like either morpheme of the word *noses.* It is only when the coding has been built up at least to the morpheme level that it is permissible to talk of 'meaning'. The morphemes, when viewed from the phonemic level, are assemblies; viewed from levels of higher complexity, the morphemes appear as unanalysable units; viewed from the outside, the morphemes are sub-assemblies in engineering terminology. They combine into larger sub-assemblies, and these again and again into more and more massive ones, until a complete utterance has been built up, through a number of stages of assembly. In the English sentence about the councillors, at least seven stages of assembly can be found, at least seven layers of complexity in the coding of a fairly simple message. We shall discuss them only summarily.

If we start with the complete utterance and break it down by stages until we arrive at the phonemes, a pattern of analysis emerges which has interesting peculiarities. As a whole it belongs to the category 'sentence'; nothing less than all of it is classified thus; this classification is plainly marked by details of rhythm and intonation which the spelling does not indicate but which are essential structural details of English. Parts of it belong to different classes, as we shall see in detail; and the classes found early in the analysis are partly the same and partly not the same classes as those found later.

First analysis: cut it into *the councillors* and *all put their glasses on their noses.* The first part is a 'noun-phrase' because it fits into the sentence in the same way as a plain 'noun' might, such as the word *councillors;* its further analysis will of course agree with this, for example it contains the word *the* and a 'noun', and such combinations generally make up noun-phrases. It is an 'actor-expression', we might say "by default" (as so often in English) because of the absence of any other candidate for the job, while the rest of the sentence, the 'action-expression', can use one and will cause anything to be so classified which is not marked as having a different value: this one is rather marked as probably being an 'actor-expression' by the fact that it is a 'noun-phrase' and stands first (a position which signifies 'actor' in this language and certain others, not including German!), and its classification as an 'actor-expression' is not forbidden by any such mark as the *s* of *man's*. Hence it is 'common' rather than 'possessive', although it is not marked as such, as the words *man* and *men* are: the apostrophe of *councillor's* or of *councillors'* belongs to the spelling, not to the language. Therefore the final *s* here marks it as belonging to the 'plural' category; this is at least not forbidden by the form *put,* while *puts* would refuse to fit it; therefore, when we later analyse the 'action-expression' we shall classify *put* as 'plural'—whereupon it will be seen that *put* is not marked as either 'present' or 'past', while *puts* would have been marked as 'present'. It is marked as 'definite' by the presence of *the* in it; being 'definite', it will fit a 'plural' 'action-expression' containing the word *all* used as it is here, which at least some 'indefinite' 'actor-expressions' will not fit, for instance *some councillors.* In summary, this *the councillors* is a 'common definite plural noun-phrase' functioning as an 'actor-expression'; it will not do simply to call it a 'common definite plural noun-phrase actor-expression' because then 'common' would be made redundant by 'actor-expression'. On the other hand, 'actor-expression' is not made redundant by 'common', for 'common rather than possessive' will fit other categories besides 'actor-expression', as in *I met the councillors.* It is precisely such asymmetries, found everywhere in language, which makes our analysis possible and keeps our arguments from being circular. The reader may check through this paragraph for other asymmetries and see how they were taken advantage of.

Second analysis: cut *the councillors* into *the* and *councillors.* The reader can set up the discussion himself on the model of the preceding paragraph.

Third analysis: cut *councillors* into *councillor* and *s.* Now *councillor* looks like a word, but in this sentence it is not a word; we can call it a 'stem' here; to it is added the 'morpheme' *s.* Discussion of this would use up our space unprofitably.

Fourth analysis: cut *councillor* into *council* and *or.* Either one of these is a morpheme. The first of them looks like the one-morpheme word *council,* but here it isn't; a 'morpheme' is all we can call it. It belongs to that category of morphemes which is defined by the fact that each of them will combine with the morpheme *or*; and it belongs to other categories similarly defined by possibilities of combination: for example, it will combine with certain *s* morphemes, to make the possessive singular *council's* or the plural *councils* or *councils'*. It will be noted that these criteria of classification are essentially of the same sort as those used in our first analysis, but now the categories are different.

Fifth analysis: we may or may not choose to break *council* into two syllables, but it appears that we can never get any profit out of doing so in our language, so we cut it at once into seven phonemes—by an odd accident, the same as the number of letters in the spelling—by a single act of analysis.

Now we have arrived at the phoneme level, and no further analysis is called for by the kind of procedure we have been following. We can classify the phonemes into different categories of vowels and consonants, as was indicated above for Spanish and English. Then we could, if we chose, treat these intersecting categories as component parts, and this work, known as componential analysis or analysis into distinctive features, is done by some linguists. But although this procedure helps in settling arguments about the adequate phonemic analysis of a language, it doesn't often shed any light on the higher organization of the language. Hence we may as well stop here and say that we have reached the lowest level of analysis when we have split *council* into seven phonemes. Here it was called the fifth analysis; to get to the bottom of the second half of the same sentence would have required going to a seventh analysis. This is the reason why we prefer to start numbering from the bottom, and to speak rather of successive syntheses, from phonemes up to the complete utterance, reaching different heights in different parts of it.

Within an English morpheme some sequences of phonemes are forbidden. For example, what is commonly spelled *ou* (as in *council*) is never followed immediately by any of /p, b, f, v, m/. We have seen that analogous restrictions apply at every level of analysis up to the complete utterance. Above the level of the phonemic system, these restrictions define for us the 'grammar' of the language, and all without reference to what is popularly thought of as the 'meaning', namely the popular categorizations of continuous reality such as 'nose' or 'numerous', just as we find it expedient to define the phonemic system independently of the phonetician's categorizations of continuous speech (although borrowing some of his terms). Typically, the elements of a grammar are stated as possibilities and impossibilities of occurrence, especially the latter, for example the English elementary grammatical fact that *this* is not followed by *men* without at least a comma between: *this men* is not English, but *This, men, is what I want* is. (Statements of what CAN occur are more difficult.) And these possibilities and impossibilities are all *a posteriori*: they are based on observation only, not on logic, and thus not on meaning.

Could we perhaps do something further with 'meaning' inside linguistics? Yes, but only on condition that we distinguish sharply between the inside and the outside. Let the sociologists keep the outside or practical meaning; then we can undertake to describe the pure linguistic meaning. We can do it thus:

Among permissible combinations of morphemes, some are commoner than others. Thus there are conditional probabilities of occurrence of each morpheme in context with others. The conditional probability of a forbidden occurrence is of course ZERO and drops out of the picture. If we ever found a conditional probability of ONE, we should decide that we had made a miscalculation, and that what we thought was composed of two morphemes was really unanalysably one morpheme (perhaps a discontinuous one).

Now the linguist's 'meaning' of a morpheme is by definition the set of conditional probabilities of its occurrence in context with all other morphemes—of course without inquiry into the outside, practical, or sociologist's meaning of any of them. Of course we have no zero probabilities in the set, and in practice we should neglect all very small probabilities. So far we have done almost nothing with pure linguistic 'meaning' as so defined, for the obvious reason that its mathematics is of the continuous sort, which we are not accustomed to handling—continuous by statistical derivation from discreteness, but still unmanageable under our working habits. Still, a beginning has been made on a structural semantics by one linguist. He replaces all small conditional probabilities by ZERO, and all large ones by ONE, so as to get a discrete mathematics again, in which he can work with synonymy that is absolute by definition. (He makes no such claims for his procedure, incidentally: he calls it 'discourse analysis' and applies it to single texts.) This work is very recent, and is the most exciting thing that has happened in linguistics for quite a few years; in spite of its theoretical flaw as a semantic analysis, it has produced some very elegant and illuminating results.

We can close with a general characterization of linguistics and language. Most well-known mathematical maps are connected with the real world by a single intuitive bridge; linguistics is connected with reality by two of them, so that a language makes a correspondence between a real noise and a real thing or the like (between an utterance and its referents). This defines language as symbolic. Overt acts of speech alter reality in that changes in listener's behavior correspond to them. This defines speech as communication. The technique is organized, patterned, as disclosed by linguistic science. This defines language as systematic. Altogether, then, we have defined a language as a symbolic communication system, or in one word, as a 'code'.

[*Eds.:* The author has pointed out to us that the fourth, third, and second paragraphs from the end of the above essay have been superseded by his paper "Semology: A Linguistic Theory of Meaning," *Studies in Linguistics* 13.53-70 (1958), in which a subsequently developed theory of meaning is presented which is indeed of the discrete kind, contrary to his expectations at the time the paper reprinted here was composed.]

Genetic Relationship Among Languages

JOSEPH H. GREENBERG

The establishment of valid hypotheses concerning genetic relationships among languages is a necessary preliminary to the systematic reconstruction of their historical development. The appropriate techniques cannot be applied to languages chosen at random but only if preliminary investigation has already indicated the likelihood of the success of such an enterprise. Correct hypotheses of relationship are also of very real significance to the archeologist, the physical anthropologist, the ethnologist, and the culture historian, even in those instances in which systematic linguistic reconstruction has not yet begun and may, indeed, in our present state of descriptive knowledge be of only limited feasibility. The considerations advanced in this chapter are intended as a realistic analysis of the factors involved in the formulation of reliable hypotheses of such relationships. It should be possible, through clarification of the assumptions involved, to resolve the conflicting classifications found in certain areas. It is likewise hoped that a sufficient basis will be presented so that the non-specialist can intelligently evaluate alternative classifications through an independent examination of the linguistic evidence itself.

Hypotheses concerning genetic relationship among languages are established by comparing languages. But languages are complex wholes which exhibit many facets, and the question which inevitably arises at the outset is one of relevance. Are all aspects of language equally germane for comparison? A language contains a set of meaningful forms (morphemes), themselves composed of meaningless sound types (phonemes) and entering into various combinations in accordance with the rules of its grammar. The meaningful forms (morphemes) may themselves be roots, in which case they are normally assigned to the lexicon, or non-roots (affixes) with derivational or inflectional grammatical function, in which case their description is part of the grammar. In either instance they involve both sound and meaning.

Reprinted by permission from *Essays in Linguistics* (Chicago: University of Chicago Press, 1963), pp. 35-45.

It is clear that, in principle, the connection between sound and meaning is arbitrary, in the sense that any meaning can be represented by any combination of sounds. A dog may as easily be called *Hund, cane, sabaka,* or *kalb* and, in fact, is—in German, Italian, Russian, and Arabic, respectively. Moreover, the thousands of meaningful forms of any language are basically independent. Except for the occasional avoidance of homonyms, which involves an exceedingly small limitation, the principle holds in general that, just because you call a dog a "dog," it does not mean you have to call a cat a "cat." It is unlikely, however, that you will call it a "dog." From these two principles of the arbitrariness of the sound-meaning connection and the independence of meaningful forms, it follows that resemblances beyond chance in both form and meaning require a historical explanation, whether through borrowing or through common origin.

By "lexical resemblance" will be meant similarity in sound and meaning of root morphemes—e.g., English *ˈhænd* and German *ˈhant,* both meaning "hand." By "grammatical resemblance" will be meant similarity of both sound and meaning in non-root morphemes, e.g., English *-ər* and German *-ər,* both indicating the comparative of adjectives. Both lexical and grammatical resemblances thus defined are relevant as evidence for historical relationships. On the other hand, similarity in meaning not accompanied by similarity in sound or similarity in sound without corresponding similarity in meaning may be considered of negligible value. Thus the presence of sex gender expressed by morphemes without phonetic resemblance or the existence of tonal systems without specific form-meaning similarities in the forms employing tones should be excluded as arguments for historical connection.

The order of meaningful elements may be considered a formal characteristic, like sound. In syntactic constructions only two possibilities usually occur in the arrangement of forms, A either preceding or following B, as contrasted with the numerous possibilities of sound combinations. Hence arguments based on word order are of minor significance. This is all the more so because the kinds of constructional meaning which may be significant are necessarily small, e.g., dependent genitive or actor-action. Historically unconnected occurrences of such resemblances are therefore extremely likely and heavily documented.

The order and meaning of morpheme classes within complex words in certain cases offer far greater combinational possibilities. The meaning possibilities involved are more numerous than for syntactic construction, though less than for sound-meaning resemblances. For example, within the verb complex we may have such meaning categories as pronominal subject, direction of action relative to speaker, tense, transitivity or non-transitivity, etc. This method can be used with real effect only in polysynthetic languages, those with complex internal word structure. Moreover, lack of agreement in such matters is not significant where sufficient specific sound-meaning agreements in morphemes are found. For example, the verb structures of Russian and Hindustani are quite different; once the periphrastic construction based on the participles became established, the whole elaborate inherited inflectional mechanism of the Indic verb was eliminated at one stroke. Even where such agreements are found among polysynthetic languages, it would seem to provide merely confirmation, however welcome, of results also attainable by the more generally applicable method of morpheme comparison.

Granted that sound-meaning similarities of morphemes weigh most significantly in determining historic relationships, it is evident that not all such resemblances need stem from historic factors. Thus Didinga, a language of the Anglo-Egyptian Sudan, has *badh* in the meaning "bad" and *man* means "man" in Korean. Moreover, although, as stated previously, the connection between sound and meaning is arbitrary, that is, unpredictable, there does exist in certain instances a well-marked tendency far greater than chance association between certain sounds and meanings. Examples are the nursery words for "mother" and "father" and onomatopoetic terms. This factor will increase slightly the number of sound-meaning resemblances between any two languages. If we call this source of resemblance "symbolism," then there are four classes of causes for sound-meaning resemblances, two of which—chance and symbolism—are non-historic, while the remaining two—genetic relationship and borrowing—involve historic processes.

The two basic methodologic processes then become the elimination of chance and symbolism leading to hypotheses of historic connections and the segregation of those instances in which borrowing is an adequate explanation from those on which genetic relationship must be posited.

The most straightforward method of eliminating chance would be the calculation of the expected number of chance resemblances between two languages, taking into account their respective phonemic structures. In practice, this proves extremely difficult, and no satisfactory technique for its accomplishment has yet been devised. Moreover, it requires, in addition to consideration of the possibilities of phonemic combination, a frequency weighting of phonemes. If both languages show, as is normal, considerable variation in the frequency of the various phonemes and if similar phonemes are among the most frequent in each language, the over-all expectation of chance coincidences is increased. More practicable would be a percentage count of resemblances among large numbers of pairs of presumably unrelated languages. This would also have the advantage of taking into account resemblances due to symbolism also. Where the percentage of resemblance between languages is very high, say 20 per cent or more, some historic factor, whether borrowing or genetic relationship, must be assumed. Where the proportion of similarities is significantly lower, a consideration of the qualitative characteristics of the sound-meaning resemblances found and the broadening of the basis of comparison to other languages, usually numerous, which show resemblances to the pair being considered (mass comparison) bring into play factors of the highest significance which should always insure a decisive answer. These factors quite overshadow the mere percentage of resemblances. In many instances this, if small, may be approximately the same between several pairs of languages, yet in some cases there will be certainty of historic relationship beyond any reasonable doubt and in some others no compelling reason to accept such an explanation.

Qualitatively, not all sound-meaning similarities are of equal value as evidence for a historical connection. For example, the longer a form, the less likely does it become that chance is an explanation. From this point of view, *\\intər\\našənəl* in language A and *intərnatsjo\\nal* in language B is far more likely the result of historic factors than are *-k,* "locative," in language A and *-g,* "locative," in language B.

The natural unit of interlingual comparison is the morpheme with its alternant morphs. The presence of similar morph alternants in similar environments is of very great significance as an indication of historical connection, normally genetic relationship. This is particularly so if the alternation is irregular, especially if suppletive, that is, entirely different. The English morpheme with alternants *gud-, bet-, be-,* with the morph alternant *bet-* occurring before *-ər,* "comparative," and the alternant *be-* before *-st,* "superlative," corresponds in form and conditions of alternation with German *gu:t-, bes-, be-,* with *bes-* occurring before *-ər,* "comparative," and *be-* before *-st,* "superlative." We have here not only the probability that a similar form is found in the meaning "good" but that it shows similar and highly arbitrary alternations before the representatives of the comparative and superlative morphemes. The likelihood that all this is the result of chance is truly infinitesimal.

Similar rules of combinability, even without alternations in form, are also of considerable significance. In Niger-Congo languages, not only are forms similar to *to* in the meaning "ear" found widely, but they are also found in construction with the same classificational affix *ku.*

Such indications of historical connection founded on morphological irregularities of form and combinability may not always be found. Many languages of isolating or of highly regular structure will have few or no morph alternants. Even where originally present, they are subject to constant analogical pressure toward replacement by regular alternations. Hence their chance of survival in related languages is not great. Where they are found, however, they are precious indexes of historical relationships.

Another factor bearing on the value of particular resemblances is semantic plausibility. This is greatest where the meanings are similar enough to have been given as translation equivalents for the same term in some third, usually European, language or for translation equivalents in two other languages. Semantic plausibility likewise attaches to comparisons involving single-step, widely attested shifts in meaning, e.g. "moon" and "month." The more intermediate semantic steps allowed, the larger the chance of obtaining form-meaning similarity, some of which may indeed stem from historical connection. But the greater the methodological latitude permitted, the less plausible is each individual comparison.

Considerations derived from the extension of comparison beyond the pair of languages initially considered are of fundamental importance. The problem as to whether the resemblances between two languages are merely the result of chance plus symbolism can then be subjected to further and decisive tests. Let us say that, as is usually the case, one or more other languages or language groups resemble the two languages in question. The following fundamental probability considerations apply. The likelihood of finding a resemblance in sound and meaning in three languages is the square of its probability in two languages. In general, the probability for a single language must be raised to the (n — 1th) power for n languages. Thus if five languages each showed a total of 8 per cent sound-meaning resemblance to one another, on a chance basis one would expect $(0.08)^4$ or 0.00004096 resemblances in all five languages. This is approximately 1/25,000. In other words, were one to compare sets of one thousand forms from all five languages, one would have to do this twenty-five times before a single instance of a resemblance in all five languages would occur. Even recurrence in three languages would be rare on a chance basis, 0.0064, that is, less than 1 per cent. Hence the presence of a fair number of recurrent sound-meaning resemblances in three, four, or more languages is a certain indication of historical connection.

Finally, there are considerations based on the phonetic form. The presence of recurrent, i.e., non-unique correspondences, adds greatly to the value of the comparison. In this area, also, mass comparison is of significance. Are the forms found in a number of languages such as to suggest that they are changed forms of a common original? The bringing-in of closely related languages on each side will then show tentative reconstructions converging as we go back in time. This procedure is not possible where only two languages are being compared.

Assuming that the factors just cited lead to the establishment of a historical connection, there still remains the problem of whether the resemblances in question can be explained by borrowing. While in particular and infrequent instances the question of borrowing may be doubtful, it is always possible to tell whether a mass of resemblances between two languages is the result of borrowing. A basic consideration is the a priori expectation and the historical documentation of the thesis that borrowing in culture words is far more frequent than in fundamental vocabulary and that derivational, inflectional, and pronominal morphemes, and morph alternations are the least subject of all to borrowing.

While it cannot be said that any single item might not on occasion be borrowed, fundamental vocabulary is proof against mass borrowing. The presence of fundamental vocabulary resemblances and resemblances in items with grammatical function, particularly if recurrent through a number of languages, is a sure indication of genetic relationship. Where a mass of resemblances is due to borrowing, they will tend to appear in cultural vocabulary and to cluster in certain semantic areas which reflect the cultural nature of the contact, and the resemblances will point toward one or, at most, two or three languages as donors. The forms will be too similar to those found in these particular languages, considering the great differences in other respects and the consequent historic remoteness of the relationship, if it really existed. Thus the Romance loanwords in English are almost all close to the French forms, in addition to hardly penetrating the basic vocabulary of English. Were English really a Romance language, it would show roughly equal similarities to all the Romance languages.

The presence of recurrent sound correspondences is not in itself sufficient to exclude borrowing as an explanation. Where loans are numerous, they often show such correspondences; thus French loanwords in English often show Fr. *š* = Eng. *č*, Fr. *ã* = Eng. *æn* (*šãs:čæns; šãt:čænt; še:z:čejr,* etc.) .

All these principles are well illustrated from Thai, whose resemblances to Chinese are the result of borrowing rather than genetic relationship, as is being realized more and more. Most of the resemblances usually cited between Thai and Sino-Tibetan languages, such as the existence of a tonal system, involve sound only or meaning only and are therefore irrelevant. The specific resemblances found with Sino-Tibetan languages always occur in forms found in Chinese, usually to the exclusion of other Sino-Tibetan languages. The specific form, even when found elsewhere, is always very close to Chinese. Moreover, the resemblances cluster in a few semantic spheres, the numerals from 2 to 10 and a few names of metals and domestic animals. In contrast, the Thai resemblances to the Kadai languages and Malayo-Polynesian tend to recur throughout the family, not just in some single language; are basic; do not concentrate in any particular semantic area; and exhibit an independence of form which excludes any particular Kadai or Malayo-Polynesian language as a source.

Borrowing can never be an over-all explanation of a mass of recurrent basic resemblances in many languages occurring over a wide geographical area. It is sometimes adduced in this *ad hoc* fashion. Since we find independent sets of resemblances between every pair of languages, among every group of three languages, and so on, each language would have to borrow from every other. A thesis of borrowing to account for resemblances must be specific, pointing out which peoples have borrowed from which, and it must be plausible in terms of the factors just cited. It may be added that the vast majority of languages do not display mass borrowing, and, where it does occur, it is easily detected.

The method for discovering valid relationships described here may be summarized as resting on two main principles—the relevancy of form-meaning resemblances in morphemes to the exclusion of those based on form only and meaning only and the technique of group comparison of languages. Some of the reasons for this latter emphasis have been adduced earlier. There are further considerations which recommend this procedure. Instead of comparing a few or even just two languages chosen at random and for linguistically extraneous reasons, we proceed systematically by first comparing closely related languages to form groups with recurrent significant resemblances and then compare these groups with other similarly constituted groups. Thus it is far easier to see that the Germanic languages are related to the Indo-Aryan languages than that English is related to Hindustani. In effect, we have gained historic depth by comparing each group as a group, considering only those forms as possessing the likelihood of being original which are distributed in more than one branch of the group and considering only those etymologies as favoring the hypothesis of relationship in which tentative reconstruction brings the forms closer together. Having noted the relationship of the Germanic and Indo-Aryan languages, we bring in other groups of languages, e.g., Slavonic and Italic. In this process we determine with ever increasing definiteness the basic lexical and grammatical morphemes in regard to both phonetic form and meaning. On the other hand, we also see more easily that the Semitic languages and Basque do not belong to this aggregation of languages. Confronted by some isolated language without near congeners, we compare it with this general Indo-European rather than at random with single languages. It is a corollary of the considerations advanced here that if a language has no close relatives, it is more difficult to find its distant relatives. Therefore, we should begin with well-defined groups of more closely related languages and leave such isolated cases to be considered after more widespread families have been constituted. Table 1 will show that it is not mere percentage of resemblances between pairs of languages which is decisive, except for quite close relationships, but rather the setting-up of restricted groups of related languages which then enter integrally into more distant comparisons.

TABLE 1

	A	B	C	D	E	F	G	H	I
Head	kar	kar	se	kal	tu	tu	to	fi	pi
Eye	min	ku	min	miŋ	min	aš	min	idi	iri
Nose	tor	tör	ni	tol	was	waš	was	ik	am
One	mit	kan	kan	kaŋ	ha	kan	kɛn	he	čak
Two	ni	ta	ne	kil	ne	ni	ne	gum	gun
Blood	kur	sem	sem	šam	i	sem	sem	fik	pix

In examining the forms in Table 1, the hypothesis immediately arises that A, B, C, and D form a related group of languages. We will call this "Group I." It is also apparent that E, F, and G constitute another related group (Group II), and that H and I are likewise connected (Group III). The hypothesis will also suggest itself that Groups I and II are related. On the other hand, the material cited offers no real support for the relationship of Group III to Groups I and II. If we look more closely, however, we will see that languages B and E show no likely cognates, whereas E has a form for "one," *ha,* closely resembling *he* in language H. E therefore shows a higher percentage resemblance to H than to B on the basis of isolated comparison. Yet the hypothesis that E is related to H rather than to B would hardly occur as a realistic one when all the relevant evidence from languages more closely related to E, B, and H is taken into consideration. The tables of percentages of resemblances among pairs of languages which are sometimes cited as evidence can at times be quite misleading, nor can elaborate statistical manipulations of these quantitative data add to their validity.

There is the further consideration that isolated hypotheses are less significant in their culture-historical implications and may even, on occasions, lead to erroneous conclusions. Thus it is no doubt true that Albanian, Bengali, and Swedish are related; but if all the intervening languages are unclassified or stated to be independent, some rather questionable historical deductions would be made. In addition, isolated hypotheses may lead to fruitless controversies, in which both parties have correct but only partial answers. Thus in aboriginal South America, where widespread relationships on a scale hitherto unrecognized actually exist, there are controversies which, transposed in terms of the Eurasian area, might run somewhat as follows. One investigator states that Albanian is related to Greek. The other disagrees and maintains, on the contrary, that it is related to Italian. Both present fairly convincing cases, since their hypotheses are correct, though, of course, a far stronger case could be presented for Indo-European as a whole, with the positions of Greek, Italian, and Albanian defined within it. Other linguists viewing the controversy either come to the cynical conclusion that, with sufficient effort, you can present a convincing case for any relationship, real or fancied, or decide that we need several more generations to gather the data necessary to decide the controversy.

As a heuristic principle, the swiftest and surest method of bringing into play many of the considerations discussed here is the compilation of comparative fundamental vocabularies of all the languages of an extended area. This accomplishes a number of purposes simultaneously. It involves the aspect of language least subject to borrowing outside grammatical elements. The forms are generally of fair length. Semantic straightforwardness is attained by using the translation equivalent of the same term in English or whatever language is used as the language of translation.

The tendency of similar forms to appear in a number of languages, as well as the plausibility of descent from a common original, can easily be noted. The presence of recurrent phonetic correspondences can be seen without great difficulty. If, as is often the case, word lists or dictionaries include noun plurals or other morphological facts, even details of morphological combinations and alternations can be taken into account. Most important of all, perhaps, is that, where more than one family is represented, as is always the case when the languages examined are from an extensive area, the contrast between the relatively numerous and qualitatively superior resemblances among related languages, compared to the sporadic and qualitatively poorer resemblances among unrelated languages, becomes readily apparent. In this way the presence of unrelated languages provides a control for distinguishing mere chance from genetically significant resemblances.

A relationship may sometimes be first suggested by agreement in some strikingly irregular morphological alternation or very full agreement in some set of grammatical affixes. For example, I was first led to entertain the hypothesis of the relation of Zaghawa to Kanuri and Teda, to form the Central Saharan family, by a remarkable agreement in a conjugational paradigm in which the morphemes of the first two persons were suffixed while those of the third person were prefixed. All the personal affixes were, moreover, phonetically similar. An examination of the fundamental vocabulary of these languages, which followed, amply confirmed the result. As a general procedure, however, the great advantage of vocabulary is the large number of essentially independent items it furnishes which are comparable from language to language and which are always present. Moreover, where little information is available about languages, the data are far more likely to be lexical than grammatical. All available grammatical information should be systematically examined but vocabulary leads most swiftly to the correct hypotheses as a general rule. The effectiveness of mass comparison of basic vocabulary, for all its apparent simplicity, is illustrated in Table 2 by only a few forms from all the contemporary languages of Europe.

Note that, even by the time the second word has been examined, the correct hypothesis emerges. The subsequent words fully confirm the initial hypothesis again and again. I believe that it is not generally realized how great is the number of different ways in which a given number of languages can be genetically classified. If, for example, there are four languages, A, B, C, and D, the following classifications are possible: (1) into one family in one way /ABCD/; (2) into two families, seven ways, /ABC/D/, /ABD/C/, /ACD/B/, /BCD/A/, /AB/CD/, /AC/BD/, /AD/BC/; (3) into three families, six ways, /AB/C/D/, /AC/B/D/, /AD/B/C/, /CD/A/B/, /BD/A/C/, /BC/A/D/; (4) into four families, one way, /A/B/C/D/. This makes a total of fourteen ways. With the increasing number of languages, the number of distinct ways of classifying increases at a tremendous rate. For eight languages the number is

	One	Two	Three	Head	Eye	Ear	Nose	Mouth	Tooth
Breton	ünan	dau	tri	penn	lagad	skuarn	fri	genu	dant
Irish	ö:n	dɔ:	tri	kjan	su:lʲ	kluəs	srɔ:n	bjal	fjakəlʲ
Welsh	ɨn	dai	tri	pen	hləgad	klɨst	truɨn	keg	dant
Danish	en	to:ʔ	tre:ʔ	ho:dhə	ɔjə	o:rə	nɛ:sə	monʔ	tanʔ
Swedish	en	tvo	tre	hüvud	öga	öra	näsa	mun	tand
Dutch	e:n	tve:	dri:	ho:ft	o:x	o:r	nö:s	mont	tant
English	wən	tuw	*th*rij	hed	aj	ihr	nowz	maw*th*	tuw*th*
German	ajns	tsvaj	draj	kopf	augə	o:r	na:ze	munt	tsa:n
French	œ̃, yn	dö	trwa	tɛ:t	œ̃l/jö	orɛ:j	ne	bu:š	dɑ̃
Italian	uno, una	due	tre	tɛsta	əkkjo	orekkjo	naso	bokka	dɛnte
Spanish	un, una	dos	tres	kabesa	oxo	orexa	naso	boka	diente
Rumanian	un	doj	trej	kap	okiu	ureke	nas	gurə	dinte
Albanian	n'ə	du	tre	kokə	sü	vesh	hundə	goja	dhəmp
Greek	enas	dhjo	tris	kefáli	máti	aftí	míti	stóma	dhóndi
Lithuanian	vienas	du	tri:s	galva	akis	ausis	nosis	burna	dantis
Latvian	viens	divi	tri:s	galva	atss	auss	deguns	mute	zobs
Polish	jeden	dva	tši	glova	oko	uxo	nos	usta, gẽba	zõp
Czech	jeden	dva	tři	hlava	oko	uxo	nos	usta	zup
Russian	adʲin	dva, dvʲe	trʲi	galavá	óko	úxo	nos	rot	zup
Bulgarian	edin	dva	tri	glava	oko	uxo	nos	usta	zəb
Serbo-Croatian	jedan	dva	tri	glava	oko	uho	nos	usta	zub
Finnish	üksi	kaksi	kolme	pä:	silmä	korva	nenä	su:	hammas
Estonian	üks	kaks	kolm	pea	silm	wilja-pea	nina	su:	hammas
Hungarian	ed	ke:t	ha:rom	fö:, fej	sem	fül	orr	sa:j	fog
Basque	bat	bi	hirür	bürü	begi	belari	südür	aho	orts

already 4,140. For twenty-five, the number of languages in Table 2, the possible ways of classifying are 4,749,027,089,305,918,018, that is, nearly 5 quintillion or 5×10^{18}. Otherwise put, the method of vocabulary comparison, after the examination of two words, has already selected out of nearly 5 quintillion possibilities exactly that one which is, by universal consent and much other evidence, accepted as the correct one! There must be good reasons for this result. It has been the purpose of this chapter to explain what they are.

The correct hypothesis may not appear quite so quickly in every case, but even supposedly distant relationships, e.g., Algonkian-Ritwan, Austroasiatic, appear fairly soon and are confirmed again and again.

The methods outlined here do not conflict in any fashion with the traditional comparative method. They may be viewed rather as an attempt to make explicit the first step in that method itself, for we cannot begin systematic reconstruction until we know which languages to compare. The application of the comparative method is a continuous process, and, in principle, there is no sharp break between its initial and its more advanced stages. Thus at the very beginning, under the guise of the apparently synchronic concept of sound resemblance, what is being considered by the experienced observer is the diachronic probability that the compared sounds are independent continuations of the same original sound. This, on the whole, coincides with synchronic similarity on an articulatory basis, since sound changes normally involve the change of a single feature of articulation at a time. Such judgments are further guided by our accumulation of knowledge of attested sound changes in other language groups.

Indeed, the very act of noting form-meaning resemblances involves notions of correspondence and reconstruction. If we compare English *ˈhænd* and German *ˈhant,* we do so on the assumption that the *h* in both forms corresponds, that English *æ* corresponds to German *a,* etc., and not to *h* or to *n.* Moreover, however incompletely, reconstruction of an original sound system is involved. If I equate English *æ* and German *a,* this is on the assumption of a common origin; and the original form, while not precisely determined, is strongly limited to those sounds which could have given rise to both *æ* and *a.* It was very probably some low, unrounded vowel like *a,* far less likely *i,* and certainly not *k.* Moreover, the procedure of mass comparison advocated here helps to make the conjecture regarding the ancestral sound ever more precise by the addition of further forms from additional languages. The test provided by the tendency to converge backward in time as each form is compared within its own subgroup of the larger family which was earlier stated as an integral part of the method determining genetic relationship involves this type of preliminary reconstruction.

The further application of the comparative method resulting in more precise reconstruction is built on a systematic utilization of the etymologies disclosed by preliminary comparison. These etymologies are of varying strength, depending on the following factors: phonetic resemblance, semantic plausibility, breadth of distribution in the various subgroups of the family, length, participation in parallel irregular alternations, and the occurrence of sound correspondences found in other etymologies which are strong on these same grounds. More advanced reconstruction will add some new etymologies and/or invalidate some of the weaker original ones. Those etymologies that are strong on the basis of the criteria mentioned cannot, I believe, be invalidated by the later reconstructions of the sound system. It is rather the efficiency of such reconstructions in explaining these etymologies that is the touchstone by which such reconstructions are tested. Unless etymologies of this degree of strength existed, we would not have been justified in drawing a conclusion of genetic relationship in the first place.

This is clear from actual practice. The Latin form *quattuor,* "four," is a first-rate etymology because it is long, exhibits recurrent correspondences in most of its parts, occurs in every branch of Indo-European, and is semantically straightforward. However, the double *t* remains unexplained. The Indo-Europeanist does not therefore reject *quattuor* as a valid etymology. He seeks rather to explain it by other recognized historical processes, such as the analogical influence of other numerals. In other words, reconstruction of an original sound system has the status of an explanatory theory to account for etymologies already strong on other grounds. Between the **vaida* of Bopp and the **γwoidxe* of Sturtevant lie more than a hundred years of the intensive development of Indo-European phonological reconstruction. What has remained constant has been the validity of the etymologic relationship among Sanskrit *veda,* Greek *woida,* Gothic *wait,* all meaning "I know," and many other unshakable etymologies both of root and of non-root morphemes recognized at the outset. And who will be bold enough to conjecture from what original the Indo-Europeanist one hundred years from now will derive these same forms? Thus reconstruction is in itself a continuous process, although the human effort may be discontinuous and pause after the first stages through lack of refined descriptive data or qualified and interested specialists; and this process goes onward indefinitely into the unknown future.

Family Tree, Wave Theory and Dialectology

ERNST PULGRAM

AT ONE TIME OR ANOTHER, practically all linguists, including those whom no one could accuse of holding antiquated views, employ such terms as 'parent language', 'daughter languages', *'Ursprache'*, 'langue-mère', 'related languages', 'language families', 'inherited (as opposed to borrowed) features', and similar ones. They generally give explicit warning, or consider it implicitly understood, that these kinship terms are used metaphorically; that in calling the Romance languages 'descendents' or 'daughter languages' of Latin, one must not forget that they still are Latin, albeit in a modern, much altered form. Yet to say that French, Italian, Spanish, etc. *are* Latin, or neo-Latin, amounts to an equally metaphorical figure of speech, or else reflects such an overextension of the term 'language' as to make it inoperative: for if a language proposes, by definition, to facilitate cooperation among its speakers, then Latin and French cannot lightly be called one and the same language, since Cicero and Voltaire would not be able to communicate successfully with one another if each used his native tongue. True, it is impossible to say at what point exactly between 500 A.D. and 1000 A.D. Latin ceases and French begins. Yet such philosophical considerations of classification must not deter us from pragmatically classifying languages.

The idea of 'kinship' is as old as William Jones' discovery, in the eighties of the eighteenth century, that certain languages which he knew and compared and whose resemblances could not to such a degree be fortuitous, must have sprung from some common origin. Jones' successors, Bopp, Rask, Grimm, and Pott continued on this assumption of kinship and descendence, and considered the reconstruction of the mother-language their principal task. When Schleicher finally devised his genealogical tree, he was not at all promulgating any new theory of Indo-European relationships, but he simply presented schematically the method of comparative philology as practiced by his predecessors, him-

Reprinted by permission from *Orbis* 2.67-72 (1953).

self, and, indeed, largely though not exclusively, by ourselves.[1] For if we list, or seek, an etymon in an etymological dictionary, our aim is in effect to determine the older form of which the later or present form is a development. (This does not mean, by the way, at least nowadays, that the reconstruction of so-called Indo-European etyma necessarily constitutes an endorsement of the theory of a single Indo-European uniform proto-language, rather than several dialects which had a number of isoglosses in common). Yet since we establish that, barring an overextension of the term 'language', the older and the newer form ought to be referred to as belonging to two different languages, the indication of a relationship of these two languages in metaphorical terms of kinship is, it seems to me, quite appropriate and useful. The statement that '. . . if Sanskrit, Greek, Latin and Germanic are sister languages, Hittite is only a cousin . . .'[2] is picturesquely intelligible, whether you think it factually true or not.

It must be conceded to those who today refute completely the validity of the family tree scheme, that Schleicher himself, unlike ourselves, did not think of his *Stammbaum* and *Ursprache* and *Tochtersprachen* as metaphorical terms but as natural facts. Departing from the view that languages are natural organisms independent of their speakers, he concluded, as did his contemporaries in the natural sciences, that each specimen is derived by progenation from some predecessors, and ultimately all from some prototype. Here Schleicher was wrong, because language is no such organism. If he furthermore ever thought that his genealogical tree could furnish evidence on the relative location of the various dialects and on their subsequent geographic spread, if he ever meant to indicate any local or chronological measurements by the length of the branches of his tree, he was also wrong. The Stammbaum shows schematically the lines of descent and a relative chronology of languages: Sanskrit was spoken before Serbian, and the two languages, no matter how dissimilar, are provedly—and there is no better way of putting it—related. But to show that much, the tree is a good schematic device, though no more. Schleicher and his followers were equally wrong if they ever claimed that the genealogical tree in any manner represented any physical realities of the peoples and tribes which spoke these languages, such as their origins, their migrations, their blood relationship, and their racial history and peculiarities. It has often enough been said that 'language' may, but need not necessarily, coincide with 'nation' or 'race', and that no extra-linguistic statement can be correctly made on the basis of linguistic evidence alone, or vice versa.

[1] Cf. Leonard Bloomfield, Language (New York, 1933), 311: 'The earlier students of Indo-European did not realize that the family-tree diagram was merely a statement of their method . . .'.

[2] E. H. Sturtevant, The prehistory of Indo-European: a summary, *Language*, 28 (1952), 177-181, 177.

To remedy these shortcomings Schmidt devised his wave scheme which turned out to be remarkably illuminating and successful. But in their enthusiasm over this memorable restatement of Indo-European developments, scholars proceeded too ruthlessly in chopping down the family tree: the old trunk was still solid in the core, and a radical pruning would have preserved its usefulness. In their eagerness to correct and forestall various historical, geographical, ethnological, and indeed linguistic pseudo-corollaries emanating from the genealogical tree, many linguists also denied its purely schematic and metaphoric value for indicating linguistic relationships. Since the tree, stripped of all other pretensions, visualized, as I said, the very method of contemporary comparative philology, the Schmidt-reformers should also have felt obligated, for the sake of consistency, to swear off comparative philology as a method of research. This, inconsistently though luckily, they did not do. But it remains a pity that the family tree has ever since been in ill repute, so that students nowadays are taught to shun it in favor of the wave theory.

Yet Schmidt's protests against, and his rejection of, Schleicher's Stammbaum had really deeper roots, I believe, though Schmidt himself might not have immediately realized this. While his quarrel was ostensibly with the family tree and especially its overreaching implications, the true source of trouble lay in fact with the comparative method as until then commonly practiced. For the truth was that the pure, unadulterated comparative philology had reached an impasse, since it did not 'allow for varieties within the parent language or for common change in the related languages'.[3] It could no longer persist in its attempts to explain all linguistic facts in purely diachronic comparative terms of historic sequence and descent, but it had to learn to answer satisfactorily such questions as these: When linguistic agreements in two families cannot be accounted for through inheritance from a parent speech, how can they be explained? Why is common-Indo-European not necessarily equivalent with proto-Indo-European? How can one explain such resemblances as are inconsistent with those upon which a hypothesis of closer relationship between two language families has been founded?

Wherever two Indo-European linguistic families, say, Italic and Keltic, are shown by virtue of their position on the family tree to be more closely related to one another than each is to the other families, the implication according to the family tree is that they together continue a trait or traits of the Indo-European mother language. However, we know now that this can be factually true only with the proviso that they have not passed together, separate from the others, through a period of common development. For if they have passed through such a period of common development, the agreements between them cannot furnish any evidence as to the state of proto-Indo-European. If, therefore, a family

[3] Bloomfield, *op. cit.*, 314.

tree is faultily designed, one will of necessity infer from it the wrong answers to questions on linguistic relationships.

Here Schmidt's wave theory provided appropriate theoretic and visual corrections by showing that linguistic areas may overlap, and that in these overlaps dialect features may spread as waves do on a quiet pool, so that linguistic agreements may be not inherited but acquired. The pure comparative method, and with it the family tree simile, presupposes a 'clear-cut splitting off of successive branches, but the inconsistent partial similarities show us that later changes may spread across the isoglosses left by earlier changes'.[4] It was the great merit of Schmidt's wave theory to provide a visual scheme, entirely different from the family tree, which could plainly and correctly account for the overlapping of isoglosses and explain inconsistent partial similarities.

Now if the family tree device corresponds to one aspect of the modern comparative method, the wave theory presents the other principal aspect of linguistic investigation, namely dialectology, dialect geography. Schmidt perhaps never thought of himself as a dialectologist; the term was not fashionable in his day. But it may be significant that the beginnings of scientific linguistic geography and the incorporation of its methods and results into comparative linguistics fall in the same period.[5] Thus it was Schmidt's wave theory which supplemented and completed Schleicher's genealogical tree, even as dialect geography opened new paths in Indo-European linguistics and provided a method for clearing up the residue of problems which a theory committed to the definite, clean cleavage of daughter languages from an ideally uniform parent language could not successfully handle.[6]

There is no question but that the designs of the spreading waves and of the spreading branches are nothing but visual devices, schematic sketches, with all the shortcomings and advantages of such pictures. The misleading implications of the family tree have already been pointed out. The wave picture is of course not innocent of pitfalls either. It can only be used to show graphically how at any given moment (and that is important!) the relative geographic position of various dialects is

[4] Bloomfield, *op cit.*, 318.

[5] Schmidt's wave theory was published in 1872. In 1876 George Wenker began an investigation of the dialects of the Düsseldorf area; in 1881 he published the first of six maps of what was to become a dialect atlas of Germany. He was followed by H. Fischer with an atlas for Swabia in 1895, then by Gilliéron and Edmont who started publishing their French atlas in 1896.

[6] Cf. Bloomfield, *op. cit.*, 321: 'The conflicting large-scale isoglosses in the Indo-European area . . . show us that the branches of the Indo-European family did not arise by the sudden breaking up of an absolutely uniform parent community. We may say that after the break-up various sets of daughter communities remained in communication; both statements amount to saying that areas or parts of areas which already differ in some respects may still make changes in common. The result of successive changes, therefore, is a network of isoglosses over the total area. Accordingly, the study of local differentiations in a speech area, *dialect geography,* supplements the use of the comparative method'.

responsible for the fact that contiguous dialects may possess in common linguistic features which only one of them inherited directly from the parent speech. No single map of intersecting and overlapping linguistic areas (i.e. isoglosses) can furnish evidence, beyond directional clues for a forecast, as to the historical linguistic developments; these can only be gleaned from a series of sketches in which the successive dislocations and the shifting of areas become apparent.[7]

Both the wave and the tree diagram have their limitations. No scholar could divine the existence of Hittite and Tocharish before their discovery merely by contemplating a family tree or a wave picture, for no such design can of and by itself suggest the existence of a hitherto unknown tongue: there is in them no structural force, no *Systemzwang*, of the kind which, in a correctly devised and mathematically unobjectionable celestial map will lead an astronomer to postulate the existence and fix the location of a hitherto unseen heavenly body. (The planet Pluto was thus theoretically discovered before it was actually seen.) Not even today, long after the discovery of Hittite and Tocharish, can scholars quite agree on the place of the two dialects on either the family tree or the wave diagram. In terms of the genealogical tree, there is no agreement whether Hittite is a branch of proto-Indo-European like Sanskrit, Germanic, Keltic, etc., or a descendent of an earlier Indo-European form of speech, that is, a sister language of proto-Indo-European.[8] And in terms of the wave scheme the question arises how one should on a map accommodate Tocharish which is a western, a *centum* dialect, although its known documents of the 7th and 8th centuries of our era were found in eastern Turkestan. We shall in fact have to resign ourselves to more than one family tree and more than one wave diagram for the moment, at least until these questions have found irrefutable answers, unless our partisanship or our convictions are strong enough to reject all but one right now.

If it is true, as I hope to have shown, that the family tree and the wave diagram are usable not for the illumination of uncharted areas but merely for the illustration of the known or what is believed to be true, that they are representations of our two primary methods of investiga-

[7] Cf. Hermann Hirt, *Die Indogermanen* (Strassburg, 1905) 1.95: 'Die Wellentheorie ist also im Hinblick auf die historischen Tatsachen wenig glaublich, sie ermöglicht uns nur, soweit sie zu Recht besteht, die ursprünglichen Lageverhältnisse der indogermanischen Sprachen einigermassen zu bestimmen'.

[8] Cf. the reference to footnote 7. Vittore Pisani, La question de l'indohittite et le concept de parenté linguistique, *Archiv Orientální* 17, part 2 (1949), 251-264, thinks, however, that Forrer and Sturtevant, in dealing with the classification of Hittite, '. . . ont eu recours à l'expédient le plus usé et le plus suranné de la méthodologie Schleicherienne, c'est-à-dire à l'arbre généalogique, et ils ont enrichi la mythologie linguistique d'une nouvelle 'langue-mère' dont on n'avait pas le moindre besoin.' (257) It is interesting to note that Pisani has since suggested another simile or schematic design to visualize linguistic relationship, namely that of a river-system with its various sources and tributaries, in an article entitled Parenté linguistique, *Lingua* 3 (1952) 3-16.

tion in accord with the principal types of linguistic differentiation, that they are complementary and no more exclude one another than do comparative linguistics and dialect geography, then it may be agreeable to use both types of visualization of linguistic processes as legitimate didactic devices, though always with due warning as to their figurative nature and their impermanence in the face of new discoveries and insights.

The Biological Model and Historical Linguistics

ROBERT D. STEVICK

BAD LUCK WITH BIOLOGICAL MODELS has left historical linguistics with such a heritage of confusion and specious explanations as to condition linguists to reject or ignore all putative parallels between languages and living organisms. Traditional textbooks for the history of the English language, though they show vestiges of biology-patterned language history, make regular protests that a language, after all, is not really an organism. Sapir charged 'the evolutionary prejudice' with being 'probably the most powerful deterrent of all to clear thinking', and offered a devastating, memorable comparison:[1] 'A linguist that insists on talking about the Latin type of morphology as though it were necessarily the high-water mark of linguistic development is like the zoölogist that sees in the organic world a huge conspiracy to evolve the race-horse or the Jersey cow.' A few years ago Charles F. Hockett attacked the shoddy terminology of historical linguistics,[2] demonstrating that, from both the pedagogical and the professional point of view, ' "evolution" and "progress" certainly ought to be avoided', that 'law', a long-time troublemaker, was distorted by deterministic biology as well as by physics, and that the use of kinship terms 'must be modified in order to render them fit for use in discussing language'. Henry M. Hoenigswald's *Language change and linguistic reconstruction*[3] treats language so unbiologically that the few traditional terms employed for language relationships—'ancestor', 'daughter', and 'sister'—are as startling as if they were bold, fresh metaphors. Quite recently Winfred P. Lehmann declared on behalf of historical linguists:[4] 'We now view language as a set of social conventions so complex that a simple biological or geometrical model is totally inadequate. Rather than force one on language, we attempt to understand it in its complexity.'

Reprinted by permission from *Language* 39.159-169 (1963).

[1] Edward Sapir, *Language* 123-4 (New York, 1949; 1st ed. 1921).

[2] 'The terminology of historical linguistics', *SIL* 12.57-73 (1957). See also Hockett's *Course in modern linguistics* 369 (New York, 1958).

[3] Chicago, 1960.

[4] *Historical linguistics: An introduction* 142 (New York, 1962).

Resistance to analogies from biology has been justified at nearly every turn. It is certainly time we had done with valuational views of language development established on 'progress',[5] human mental evolution, racial and cultural preferences, orthogenetic patterns, and anterior or future perfections. It is time that confusion between biological and linguistic situations be removed once for all. It is time to leave behind inaccuracies of oversimplification. And now, although it will take some years yet to supersede the earlier errors still circulating in many books and teachers, the time appears finally to have come when we may assume that the worst is over. Historical linguistics seems to be about free from the contaminations of biology. The charter of independence, however, in its near-final draft, lists several responsibilities that historical linguistics must assume on its own: if terminology has been as much handicap as help, if classification has been haphazard, if explanations have been specious under the influence of biology (among other things), still we must continue to name, sort, and offer rational constructs of data. The job ahead is a very large one, and a model, if one can be found, should be welcome.

I shall urge in this paper that old prejudice be set aside and the scientific model of organic evolution be given scrupulous and exhaustive attention for its potential assistance in reconstituting historical linguistics. This is not a reactionary proposal. For just as historical linguistics has eliminated many of its errors and deficiencies, so evolutionary biology has brought itself a long way beyond the mistakes and gaps of its earlier stages. Just as language history has excised false formulations, many of them from biology (and its enthusiastic imitators), so evolutionary theory has purified itself from the crudities of extrascientific notions. If complexity is a criterion, evolutionary biology more than qualifies as a model for language history. More than this, evolutionary theory has recently achieved, in its biological application, a 'new synthesis' that seems to have put the formulation of organic evolution securely on the way to the continuously self-corrective and expansive development that marks it as a mature historical science. It is in some ways perhaps beyond the present stage of development in language history. Whatever its worth for language history turns out to be, the new biological model is different from the older ones that we properly reject. It should be judged independently. Some reasons for proposing the biological model are the substance of what follows.

Strategy, aside from substantive considerations, justifies exploring systematically the relationships between organic and linguistic evolution. There hardly appears to be a better way of guaranteeing a scientific his-

[5] Even in his final effort to sustain 'progress in language', in *Efficiency in linguistic change* (København, 1941; reprinted in *Selected writing* 381-466), Otto Jespersen could not make 'energetics' a convincing basis for declaring that linguistic change generally results in progress.

tory of language against further contamination from this source than a thorough understanding of these relationships. If the correlation is in fact negligible, or if the similarities and dissimilarities are hopelessly tangled, we will have the better reason for a final rejection of evolutionary linguistics. A thorough attempt to define the relations, whatever the attendant conclusions may be, would be a more effective strategy for keeping clear of past errors than sporadic forays against them. Detailed investigations of the relation between languages and living forms (historically viewed) can also assure a significance of findings not possible to fragmentary comparisons. It will make unavoidable the proper use of analogy and make any other use manifestly inappropriate: it will demonstrate plainly—and within historical linguistic discourse—that biological analogies are not sources of proof but sources of hypotheses. Or they may be convenient resources in the rhetoric of exposition.

The nature of the analogy between historical linguistics and historical biology asks first consideration. At the highest level of abstraction there is little reason to expect them to lack parallels. On the contrary, since both analyze persistence with modification of systems ('descent with modification'), we should expect some resemblance in their methodologies. More than that, we can say that if the two methodologies have nothing in common, then at least one of them cannot be scientifically sound. Some territories of similarity in methods will be mentioned below. For the moment I assert only that so far as they both analyze modifications in persisting systems, and hold similar purposes, historical linguistics and historical biology should be specific instances of the same general model of evolution.[6]

The attempt to apply the methodology of the one discipline to the content of the other is at once to test the hypothesis of shared methods and to get down to the practical business of assessing specific analogies which are suggested by considering the two historical subjects together. Perhaps the most pointed protest against biological and linguistic analogies is, in Hockett's words,[7] that 'in biology we have INDIVIDUATION, lacking in language'. 'A language does not reproduce: it simply CONTINUES.' The differences between organisms and languages, in this view, are absolute, and preclude significant analogies. Failure to realize the absolute differences lay behind the errors that Hockett is here attacking. But the formulation of this protest (which is typical) is not quite accurate. For if we draw out its implications,[8] we should have to say that organisms change, or modify, or evolve—organisms in the sense of the individuals that do the reproducing. This, of course, is bad biology. It is not the

[6] And if they are, some analogies between their parts should be close, hence potentially useful in either direction.

[7] Hockett, 'Terminology'.

[8] Not only in the immediate context of the sentences quoted, but in the article as a whole. Again the implications are those of typical protests.

organisms (in this sense) that evolve:[9] species or (better) populations evolve. So that while it is true that a language does not reproduce, it is also true that a species does not reproduce. Again, as a language is said to continue, so a species (and not an organism) is said to continue. And we can immediately add the other side of this: languages change in the course of persisting (continuing), and species evolve in the course of persisting. Whether we are justified in making a complete parallel in this last assertion by resolving 'change' and 'evolve' under the same term is to restate the principal question.

Obviously, this does not require that languages and species be equated. One is made up of utterances and the other of organisms, and no word-magic should be worked on them to obscure their differences: we are dealing with an analogy and attempting to establish its dimensions. If we have put aside the mistaken analogy of language and organism, we can now consider what correspondences may be recognized, for linguistic and biological science and history, between utterances and organisms, between languages and species.

Linguists and biologists may well feel a certain kinship and mutual sympathy if they compare notes on the practical tasks and the theoretical problems they both face in classifying the subjects treated in their respective fields. The basis for this feeling of kinship can be stated by analysing and enumerating procedures and 'fields'; but it is more strikingly presented by indirect statement in the form of paraphrase. Below is an extended adaptation to linguistic interests of a biologist's statement about classification. The adaptation is achieved simply by substituting linguistic for biological terms and examples; the 'fit' of the altered statement is objectionable where historical development of the two sciences is involved, but hardly elsewhere.[10]

> The scientific classification of speech materials is founded on the discontinuity and the hierarchy of variation, or to put it more precisely, these properties of variation have been used for the purpose of making a classification. The fact that this is not the only possible kind of classification should not be lost sight of. . . .
>
> The concept of a 'natural' system of classification is far from being always made clear. Being told that a language belongs to the branch 'Germanic' we may safely predict that its grammatical machinery is inflectional in nature, that it has a two-way tense system, that this tense system is carried by both 'strong' and 'weak' inflections, that it has fixed stress-accent, that certain of its consonants differ in regular ways from consonants of other European languages, that certain lexical items will be common to all members of the branch, and so on. The position of a sample corpus in earlier classifications would not define

[9] They do not evolve in the sense of 'evolve' and 'evolution' used in this context. In an older and quite different sense, similar to that of 'develop', individuals are said to evolve.

[10] Theodosius Dobzhansky, *Genetics and the origin of species*² 362 ff. (New York, 1941).

so many of its characteristics. This seems to be the reason why our system is more natural than that of earlier classifiers. A knowledge of the position of a corpus in an ideal natural system would permit the formation of a sufficient number of deductive propositions for its complete description. Hence, a system based on the empirically observed discontinuities in materials to be classified, and following the hierarchical order of the discontinuous arrays, approaches most closely to the ideal natural one. Every subdivision made in such a system conveys to the student the greatest possible amount of information pertaining to the language materials before him. The modern classification of language materials uses the principles on which an ideal system could be built, although it would be an exaggeration to think that the two are consubstantial.

On the other hand, since the time of Sir William Jones and his early successors the 'genetic classification' has meant in language study one based on the hypothetical common descent of language materials. The features united together in a dialect, language, branch, or family were supposed to have descended from a single common ancestor (language), or from a group of very similar ancestors. The lines of separation between the systematic categories were, hence, adjusted, at least in theory, not so much to the discontinuities in the observed variations as to the branching of real or assumed phylogenetic trees. And yet the classification may continue to be based chiefly on structural studies of the existing language materials rather than on the phylogenetic series of written records. The logical difficulty thus incurred is circumvented with the aid of an hypothesis according to which the similarity between language samples is a function of their descent. In other words, it is believed that one may safely base the classification on studies of the structure and meanings of the utterances existing at our time level, in the assurance that if such studies are sufficiently complete, a picture of the phylogeny will emerge. The validity of this hypothesis can evidently be tested only through data of older written records, by comparing the theoretically constructed phylogenies with the actual ones. Such a comparison seems to show that in general the structurally similar language materials existing at our time level have derived from more similar or identical ancestors. In some groups no appreciable structural convergence is, however, observed if one compares more and more remote attested ancestral forms of a given complex of forms. Rather, the development takes place along parallel lines, in such a way that several genealogical strains pass in the course of time through a certain sequence of stages; analogous stages may, however, be reached at different time levels in the different lines of descent. The result is that if one makes a structural comparison of the entire series of forms regardless of their age, the consecutive stages of development with a genealogical line may be less similar than analogous stages in different lines. Two classifications become possible: a 'vertical' one uniting all types with a genealogical line, and a 'horizontal' one combining analogous stages of different genealogical lines. . . .

Fortunately, the difficulty just stated is more abstract than real. The fact is that the classification of language materials that exists independently of genetic theories must undergo surprisingly little change in the adaptation of it to genetic classification, and such changes as must be made depend only to a small extent on the elucidation of the actual genetic relationships. . . .

Before proceeding further our discussion of languages as natural units, it may be useful to make a short digression to consider certain prolegomena on which this discussion must be based. Let us examine first an imaginary situation, a linguistic world in which all possible combinations of linguistic elements are represented by equal numbers of utterances. Under such conditions no discrete groups and no hierarchy of groups could occur, since the single difference of linguistic feature, producing distinct effects within utterances, would be the sole remaining source of discontinuity. Disregarding these, the variability would become a perfect continuum. The most 'natural', although not the only possible, classification would be a sort of multidimensional periodic system, with a number of dimensions equal to that of the variable features.

Clearly, the existing world of speech is unlike the above imaginary one . . . Only a small fraction of the possible combinations of linguistic features is, or has even been, realized among speech utterances . . . The existing combinations of linguistic features are grouped into more or less compact arrays attached to one or to several related 'adaptive peaks' in the field. The arrays are therefore complexes of fairly similar combinations of features that make their carriers fit to survive in the cultural situations into which they must fit, in real life. The 'adaptive valleys' intervening between the peaks correspond to discordant combinations of linguistic features, most of which would be nearly or completely inviable. A promiscuous formation of language-feature combinations would give mainly a mass of freaks. . . .

The discontinuous variation in the world of language is therefore not a superficial appearance, but the consequence of a fundamental discontinuity in the structural make-up of languages. The discontinuity and the hierarchical character of the empirically observed variation may be viewed as a response of language (or its users) to the pressure of the cultural environment. Each dialect, language, branch, or any other group embraces a certain array of language-feature combinations attached to an 'adaptive peak,' or to several neighboring peaks. The fact that one group may be distinguished from the related one implies that the combinations of language features lying in the field between the peaks are formed rarely or not at all. Now, if the representatives of the different groups were to combine or merge at random, all the structural-lexical-semantic combinations that are now rare or absent would be produced—given a sufficient number of utterances—within a few generations from the start of the random mergers. That would mean a breakdown of the separation of the groups, and an emergence of continuous variability over a part of the field. If all the utterances were to amalgamate freely, a perfect continuum would result, as postulated above.

The conclusion that is forced on us is that the discontinuous variation encountered in natural speech, except that based on single feature differences, is maintained by means of preventing the intercommunication of representatives of the now discrete language groups. This conclusion is evidently applicable to discrete groups of any rank whatever, beginning with languages and up to and including branches and families. The development of isolating mechanisms is therefore a *conditio sine qua non* for emergence of discrete groups of forms in linguistic development . . . This conclusion is certainly not vitiated by the well-known fact that the isolation between groups may be complete or only partial. An occasional exchange of language materials, not attaining to the frequency of random interchange, results in the production of some intergrades, without, however, entirely swamping the differences between the groups.

Paraphrases of this kind can be constructed easily and in great number. Significantly, one of the statements most readily adaptable to linguistic discourse is Felix Mainx's theoretical groundplan of biological classification, 'The foundations of biology'.[11] I offer a brief example.

> Every classificatory approach is based on the concept of languages. The differences of opinion about the definition and use of this concept in linguistics are indicative of the great difficulties of this group of problems. The concept of a language is used in very different senses by different linguists, according to their point of view and the problem in hand. Nevertheless, most linguists are of the opinion that 'language', in contrast to the higher systematic units, is to be regarded as a primary natural unit of human speech. The contradiction which seems to occur here is in some degree understandable in view of the present state of linguistic knowledge but still often leads to misunderstandings. The pure systematist understands by 'language' a type, a 'language model', which is defined by the enumeration of a series of structural, possibly also semantic and utilization features. Utterances found in the field can be recognized as 'members of this language' for the most part with certainty by comparison with this language model. It is left to the tact of the specialist, schooled by experience, to regard certain deviatory types as dialects or jargons within a language or as another language, or, in particular cases, as an aberration or anomaly. When we say that 'within this branch so and so many languages (or dialects) have so far been described', we are using the word 'language' in this purely systematic sense. That this use of the language notion has persisted for the practical purposes of defining individual utterances and assigning them a place in the given multiplicity is for us a proof of the finiteness and discontinuity of this multiplicity and of the constancy—at least relatively—of its ordering structure. In the view of 'language' as an elementary unit of just this order there lies a weighty argument for its estimation as a natural unit.

The parallelism of historical linguistics and biology implied by the ease of paraphrase is reassuring. Let us turn now to aspects of these two fields for which the parallelism is less obvious and in which may lie some assistance to extending the formulations of language history.

Both disciplines distinguish variation and change: variation consists in differences viewed without respect to time, change consists in differences viewed as occurring in temporal succession. The two are found to be interdependent. Also, in both fields it is possible to explain mechanisms and processes of change with some assurance. But just as it is not possible to predict what particular changes will in fact occur (or when change of any kind will occur) in life forms, so we cannot predict the occurrence of linguistic changes—phonological, morphological, syntactic,

[11] *International encyclopedia of unified science* 1:2.567-654 (Chicago, 1955).

or semantic. The reason is perhaps the same in both instances: the incidence of variation remains entirely a matter of chance. If we had precise knowledge of the occurrence of variations and complete information regarding the conditions into which a variation was introduced, we could presumably predict (in principle, at least) modifications of either species or languages throughout the time for which our data were complete. Predictions in biology would probably be more reliable, simply because the methodology of evolutionary biology has become the more refined. Historically this is attributable to the more extensive and persistent requirement of facing the problems of dealing with variations; classification of individual living forms has never ceased to require the attention of biologists, while many linguists (earlier, philologists) did not take full notice of dialectal and idiolectal variation. Consequently biologists had a head start in recognizing and working with the dimensions of variation and with its attendant factor of chance. By the time regularity of sound change was established—by the time the tenets of the 'neogrammarians' were refined into acceptable form—historical biologists not only understood regularity in evolutionary change, together with chance variation, but had formulated some of its conditions as well. Meantime, both linguists and biologists have come to view historical change in their respective fields as explicable without teleological assumptions. The development of methodology in both fields continues parallel though not contemporaneous.

Thus, in providing a model for explaining the occurrence, the regularity, and the extent of language change, evolutionary biology may have great potential value for historical linguistics. Let us sketch one use of the model.

In language study, variation is now well understood, including the element of chance in its occurrence: there are degrees of precision in articulation, degrees of precision in perception, degrees of allowable variation in sound and timing defined by the phonemic system of the language, combinations of sounds in which the articulation of one is conditioned (varied) by another, and so forth. The distribution of variations is treated as random, as evidenced by the bell-shaped curves used to represent the distribution of allophones. Furthermore, phonetic change is observed to be regular. And when one stage of a language is replaced by another, it is found that both stages are systematic, that as a language instrument neither is inferior to the other. Language change is considered as well to be gradual, taking place by shifts in norms among variations, whether by phonetic drift, by analogical reformation, or by other means; sudden change in an idiolect is only a datum in the statistical description of gradual change in a language. Finally, the mechanisms and processes of change are scientifically formulable.

The bridge between evolutionary results in language and the known mechanisms of change, however, is conspicuously absent, or, at best, somewhat shaky. If both occurrence and distribution of variations are in any appreciable degree random, how is it that change is orderly and that language is at all times systematic? Although 'conditioned' sound change implies regularity and order, 'unconditioned' sound change has no built-in regulating factor to account for orderly variation and orderly change. If the occurrence of variation in speech sounds is random, and if some changes (those called 'unconditioned') are not regulated, what is it, besides chance, that produces order? Apparently there is a factor of selection. 'Chance in combination with selection produces order' is one of the axioms of evolutionary methodology. Selection is the factor which, in linguistic history, seems to be most needed, even as it was necessary in biology to bridge the gap between genetics and paleontology.

Formulation of selective factors and their role in language history may proceed from knowledge already at hand. At the level of the individual speaker there is the existence of expectation patterns which, especially with respect to phonemes, are highly inflexible. Probably the clearest example is that a child has his language under thorough control by the time he is six, and that the whole of his experience before and after that age is to sort variations in speech sounds into the categories of his phonemic system. The number of phonemes is quite limited, and the phonemes combine in clusters of even fewer significant features; features of a non-distinctive variety or in unaccustomed combinations are discarded or extinguished, and the absence of expected features or combinations is compensated for. At the societal level the same expectation patterns exist, reinforcing and stabilizing the individual's productive and receptive speech habits. The selective function of these expectation patterns does not readily manifest itself in the traditional lists of sound changes for a language (especially when arbitrarily arranged by alphabetic sequence, lengthening vs. shortening, etc.) ; but it appears quite clearly in successive structural arrangements of sets of phonemes or other elements.

I take an illustration from English morphology. Variations occurred at random in the inflectional suffixes of Old English nouns: some of these resulted in leveling the vowels of the endings, some involved analogical substitution; it is possible, though perhaps not provable, that some depended on the development of a fourth (weaker) degree of phonemic stress. The occurrence of analogic change, again, must be regarded as random, even if the particular changes were correlated with (partly caused by) frequency. What must be accounted for, in addition to how changes occurred, is the regularity of the changes in the morphological apparatus—the paradigmatic order of the replacing inflections. Between Old and Middle English the restructuring of noun paradigms presents a striking problem which has not yet been satisfactorily solved, or even stated: why, out of all the variations and heterogeneous causes of variations, did ME noun inflections develop as they did—orderly and with a new basis? OE nouns, with the several paradigms for inflections indicating number, case, and gender, became ME nouns with a plural suffix (whatever differences in dominant allomorphs there may have been in the various dialect groups); Old English had no merely plural morpheme for nouns. The change cannot be attributed to the prominence (by frequency) of the model of masculine *a*-stem nouns, since the *-as* inflections designated case and gender as well as plurality. Though many nouns went over to this dominant declension, this fact alone cannot account for the development of the plural morpheme *-es* in Middle English.

Again we need a selective factor if we are to explain the changes. In this instance the factor, so far as we treat it as a habit of expectation among English speakers, can be traced in the overall morphological and syntactic patterns of the language, together with the kinds of meaning carried by the inflectional suffixes and their paradigmatic distribution. The OE inflections carried grammatical meaning of case and gender; the first was also carried in the redundant or secondary devices of word order, intonation, and prepositional constructions, while the second had no semantic reference and no essential grammatical function. The inflections also carried number meanings—singular and nonsingular—which were both grammatical and meaningful. Number was further expressed in personal pronouns and verbs, even after it was obscured and lost in adjectives, determiners, and relative and interrogative pronouns. The singular-plural distinction, like other linguistic habits, was learned early; it was recognized or expressed by several devices, and it had correlates in experience outside the language. More important perhaps was the habit of always specifying in utterances whether a noun or nominal is single or multiple in reference. The habit persisted, the expectation continued. The narrowing range of variations in shapes and the frequent phonetic features of noun inflections came to be sorted according to expectation habits that were not satisfied in other aspects of utterances: the persisting habit of specifying things as either singular or plural, reinforced by pronouns and verbs, was the selective factor that produced the new order in place of the random variations of inflectional noun suffixes.

The *-es* plural was not, of course, the only possible morpheme that could have developed, nor was *-es* the only suffix that could have provided a regular plural morpheme. In Southern dialects the *-en* plural became frequent, forming in fact a productive class. But the point is that a plural morpheme did in fact develop. Another possible solution, which has occurred under different circumstances, is the development of a plural-indicating particle after the noun in the Jamaican Creole dialect of English. Its source is the pronoun *them,* which carries, among other things, the meaning 'plural': *de bwai-dem, de pickny-dem, de gyal-dem* are plural, with corresponding singulars *de bwai, de pickny, de gyal.* In this dialect there are no other plural indicators for nouns, nor are there any in determiners, adjectives, or even verbs; they occur only in pronouns and (as postposed *dem*) in nouns. In effect, English nouns in this dialect have lost all inflection, yet the result is a perfectly regular system which retains a plural morpheme for nouns. The selective factor is the only means we have for satisfactorily accounting for this change.

The same principle of the operation of selection could be illustrated as well in the history of English phonotactics, where habits seem to have been even more rigid than phonemic or morphological habits. The distribution of /š/ and /č/ in Modern English continues to correspond closely to the distribution of their OE correlatives, even though both are new phonemes.

The illustrations make it clear that the function of selection is not merely to eliminate variations. It is also creative. For this reason selection is potentially a powerful concept in historical linguistics; without the scientific means to account for the appearance of new factors in language systems, no historical account of a language can be complete. The creative aspect of selection will not be described here. It need only be said that historical biology has discovered how to deal with the creative function of selection without falling back into teleological explanation.

Another concept in evolutionary theory prominent in biology but not in linguistics is that of isolative factors. Drift occurs both in the genetic make-up of populations of organisms and in the structure of the speech systems of language communities. But this kind of change modifies only the collective unit—the species or the language; no differentiation can occur. Isolation of organic or linguistic populations is the only factor by which differentiation can occur: Isolation combined with drift produces differentiation, to paraphrase the axiom stated earlier. The important thing here is that isolation is not just a sufficient condition for differentiation: it is a necessary condition. Linguistic isolating factors require more careful definition and more judicious use than they now receive if the differentiation of languages is to be fully accounted for.

I consider only one more aspect of historical linguistics and the biological model—the rate and nature of change in complex natural systems. The old expository analogy between linguistic conservatism and botanical transplanting hardly qualifies as scientific or otherwise significant; it is embarrassing, too, unless linguistic conservatism is at the same time detached from the condition of permanent location of a continuing speech community. Biological models for variations in the rate of linguistic change are to be found, however, in the study of population structure. The size of populations provides the simplest examples. If a small group is detached from a relatively large speech community, say by migration ('transplanting'), the variations in language will probably be reduced in number in the small community. Within a generation they will probably be diminishing, particularly if, at the same time (as we may believe for most historical instances), the members of the small speech community have less time and circumstance than the larger community for variety and frequency of linguistic interchange. Fewer variations are available to spread, the frequency of new variation will be less, and hence the relative frequency will be greater for any one variation. Differences between the large and the small community (population) are now partially definable as divergent developments in their experience of code noise and their tolerance for it: the tolerance diminishes in the smaller community. Over an extended period—say four generations—certain additional differences between linguistic change in the small and the large population may then occur. Where there had been several alternants in the elements of expression, a single alternant may come to dominate or even to occur exclusively in the smaller population but not in the larger. This phenomenon is perhaps most easily traceable in allomorphs: which allomorph happens to dominate is not so much a consequence of population size as of frequency, liability to confusion through developing homophony, and the like; but the rate at which the single allomorph rises to dominance may be a function of the population structure. The rate at which one change is completed will also necessarily have an effect on other changes under way at the same time, and on the initiation of related changes. Potential collapse of two or more grammatical elements, any one of which requires a further change in the language system, may combine in a small population to produce grammatical change that calls for no further adjustment; at the least, grammatical change in a small community is likely to be different from change in a larger one.

If there is a significant parallel between biological and linguistic rates and conditions of change, that parallel suggests that the formulae of glottochronology are based on inapposite analogies, such as the change rate of carbon 14. While the processes studied in physical sciences may take place at fixed and calculable rates, in biological (and perhaps linguistic) history they do not seem to. At least, they do not seem to by any system of measurement so far devised for defining rate of change. A genetic change will spread through a small population in a relatively short time; if it is the kind which produces easily observed effects, the phenotypic average shows a relatively rapid alteration. The phenomenon is similar to that described above for linguistic change in a small speech community. But the same kind of change takes longer to spread through a larger population, with the species norm showing a correspondingly slower rate of alteration. Furthermore, if the change tends to produce isolation, it can spread through part of a large population without reaching the rest. In this case, rates of change of a specified kind will be characteristic of a segment but not the whole of the population. To extend the example: if one change begins to spread from one part of the population, and a second change begins to spread from another part of the same population, the two changes can have several possible effects. These depend on the interval between the incidence of the changes; on their relation (reinforcing, destructive, or merely combining); on the 'dominance' of one change over another; and, again, on the size of the population. The distribution of isoglosses in linguistic geography provides abundant examples of this phenomenon in language change.

All in all, the biological model seems to be more appropriate than a physical one for constructing a dating technique. Both biological and linguistic populations are more complex than physical entities, and their complexities show a great many more correspondences. The biological model points to lexicostatistical techniques for dating that require closer definitions and attention to population size, the interrelation of segments of the population (degrees of isolation or intercourse), and changes in size and relation of the populations and their subgroups during the entire period of change in question.

This paper has urged exploration of the analogies between historical linguistics and biology as a means to extending and refining the methodology of the former. Its strategy concentrates on similarities between the two fields, not on differences. The differences, besides those mentioned earlier, include the fact that linguistic change belongs to cultural evolution, which is superimposed on biological evolution. But these two evolutions, however different, are in no way contradictory: they are particular developments of the general model of persistence with modification of complex systems. If this paper has shown that linguistic change, like biological change, occurs as modification in persisting systems through selection combined with chance variation and the attendant factor of isolation, the whole conditioned by population structure, then it has established linguistic and biological histories as closely similar particular examples of the general evolutionary model. In this circumstance lies the potential value of the biological model to historical linguistics.

A Definition of Proto-Germanic: A Study in the Chronological Delimitation of Languages

W. P. LEHMANN

IT MAY SEEM OBVIOUS that when we set out to write a grammar of a language, the definition of that language is one of our first tasks. Further, that since we are dealing with language, the criteria used in our definition should be linguistic. These criteria should delimit the language geographically, that is, from other languages, and chronologically, that is, from earlier and later stages of the same language. Yet in spite of these minimum requirements for an adequate definition, our handbooks are not precise in their definitions or explicit in regard to criteria used for the definitions they give.

Though we are here concerned with the definition of Proto-Germanic, the problem applies to all languages. Handbooks often delimit a language through the use of social or political changes rather than linguistic changes. Middle High German, for example, has been defined as that stage of German which was spoken between the period of the great medieval German poets and the Reformation. The Norman Conquest and the introduction of printing have been used to define Middle English. While linguistic changes may coincide with other social changes, the coincidences are interesting correlations rather than defining features for the language. We can determine them only after we have selected those differences in language structure which distinguish successive periods of any language, such as Middle English in contrast with Old English and Modern English, or different languages, such as Italian in contrast with French and Sardinian or Low German in contrast with High German and English.

Imprecise definitions are objectionable in part because they permit unnecessary disputes to arise regarding the description of a language. Two inadequate definitions from grammars in general use may indicate

Reprinted by permission from *Language* 37.67-74 (1961).

the need for improved definitions.[1] Prokosch, *CGG* 26, contents himself with indicating the location of the Germanic speakers and adding:[2] 'Shortly before the beginning of our era, the Germanic group appears to have been a fairly homogeneous linguistic and cultural unit. This is the period that is termed Urgermanisch, Primitive Germanic.' Mossé, also a clear and careful writer, makes a similar statement, *MIG* 19: 'Les langues germaniques sont les formes diverses prises, au cours de l'évolution historique et du morcellement géographique, par une langue commune parlée jusque vers le début de l'ère chrétienne dans le Sud de la péninsule scandinave, le Danemark et la plaine de l'Allemagne du Nord et que l'on appelle le proto-germanique (all. *Urgermanisch*) réservant le terme de germanique commun (all. *Gemeingermanisch*) pour désigner les faits postérieurs communs à toutes les anciennes langues germaniques.' Neither Prokosch's definition nor Mossé's meets the requirements I have set, for each is little more than an impressionistic suggestion. Yet other handbooks have failed to give better definitions. After several decades of Germanic study it seems desirable to define Proto-Germanic precisely. Upon proposing such a definition I will note some disputed problems in Proto-Germanic grammar and suggest how my definition may aid in clarifying them.

For linguistic purposes, establishing the relative chronology of Proto-Germanic is more important than determining the location of its speakers. For both aims our only usable evidence to the present is linguistic; until we find inscriptions which enable us to relate prehistoric cultures of northern Europe with prehistoric linguistic communities, attempts to locate the speakers of pre-Germanic or post-Indo-European dialects in northern Europe are completely speculative, if intriguing. Only on the basis of the available linguistic evidence can we make reliable statements about the location and the dates of the community of Proto-Germanic speakers.

[1] Since the bibliographical material on Proto-Germanic is easily accessible and well known, I refer only to a few of the standard texts; further bibliography is listed in them. E. Prokosch, *A comparative Germanic grammar* [*CGG*] (Philadelphia, 1939) lists bibliography 300-302; F. Mossé, *Manuel de la langue gotique*[2] [*MIG*] (Paris, 1956) lists a small set of works important especially for Gothic studies 15-17. F. van Coetsem, *Das System der starken Verba und die Periodisierung im älteren Germanischen* (Amsterdam, 1956) lists bibliography 83-86. Recent bibliography is available in the pertinent sections of the *Bibliographie linguistique* and the annual bibliographies of the Modern Language Association.

[2] For 'primitive', it is now the convention to use Proto-, to avoid the connotation carried by the nontechnical use of 'primitive'. The prefix pre- is used to indicate a prior stage to any given language when the prior stage is not capable of more precise definition, or when more precise definition is not pertinent for the moment. As in the quotation from Mossé the term 'common' (Germanic) has often been used in dealing with features found in all dialects which have developed from a given language but which may not have a distinct etymon in that language. Handbooks label umlaut Common Germanic but not necessarily Proto-Germanic. Since the label is confusing in suggesting a further distinct phase of a language, I avoid it entirely; if necessary we may describe a feature as *common to* various segments of a linguistic group, such as Germanic.

In framing our chronological definition of Proto-Germanic we use a technique similar to that which is used to distinguish Germanic from other Indo-European dialects.[3] Rather than choose natural boundaries—rivers, seas, mountains—to bound Proto-Germanic and separate it from neighboring dialects such as Baltic, Celtic, Greek, Italic, Slavic, we choose linguistic data, of which the following are samples which can easily be supplemented.

Phonetically we can distinguish German from Baltic, Celtic, Italic, Greek and Slavic by the presence of [f þ x], which correspond to [p t k] in those dialects and in Proto-Indo-European (or to clearly definable structural points in certain environments, such as zero for PIE *p* in the Celtic dialects).

Phonemically we can distinguish Germanic by the loss of contrast between reflexes of Indo-European voiceless stops and voiced aspirated stops after unaccented vowels, its preservation elsewhere. A pair illustrating the loss of contrast is Goth. *sibun* 'seven' with reflex of PIE *p* and Goth. *giban* 'give' with reflex of PIE *bh*; a pair illustrating its maintenance is Goth. *faihu* 'cattle' with reflex of PIE *p* and Goth. *bairan* 'bear' with reflex of PIE *bh*. In Celtic, Baltic, and Slavic the contrast between PIE *b* and *bh* was completely lost; in Italic it was partially maintained; and in Greek it was maintained except when a reflex of another aspirate occupied a syllable contiguous with that having a reflex of PIE *bh*. A complex realignment like that of PIE *p* : *bh*, *t* : *dh*, *k* : *gh* in Germanic provides excellent means for geographical definition, for even the varied developments in Italic and Greek fail to coincide with it, not to speak of the simple changes in Celtic, Baltic, and Slavic.

Morphologically we can distinguish Germanic by the development of two adjective declensions and of a weak preterite marked with *d*.

Such data for distinguishing Germanic geographically we find in our handbooks, although since our handbooks dealing with Proto-Germanic are based on neogrammarian theory they fail to make use of the strongest distinguishing criteria at the phonological level, which are structural. Data like those cited here so clearly distinguish Germanic from neighboring Indo-European dialects that questions rarely arise in identifying Germanic material of any extent as distinct from that in other Indo-European dialects. To ensure a satisfactory description of Proto-Germanic we need to use similar means for delimiting it chronologically.

[3] The terms *geography* and *geographical* in their linguistic usage are to be taken as indicating relative distribution of a segment of speech. In spite of possible misunderstandings I maintain these terms with other terminology based on 'the study of the earth' because they are established. Yet terminology based on language distribution or linguistic distinctiveness would be less likely to mislead than that based on the concrete classifications of a physical science. An example is the persistence of the classification into North, East, and West Germanic, and the positing of proto-forms with these labels in spite of the absence of proof for such subgroups subsequent to Proto-Germanic. The attractiveness of a favored tripartite grouping based on the points of the compass seems to outweigh more complex classification based on available data.

In defining a language chronologically, we should also rely on structural differences, but now the differences we select are carried out within a given territory and a given linguistic tradition. Again the usefulness of our definition depends on the significance of our criteria. One measure of their significance is the differentiating effect they have had on the language at the time of their occurrence and on its subsequent stages. Accordingly we choose criteria which affect more than one of the systems in a given language.

The criteria I choose for defining Proto-Germanic in its inception and in its conclusion are changes in its suprasegmental system and their results. The inception of Proto-Germanic I place at the completion of its shift from free pitch accent to a stress accent fixed on the initial or stem syllable of words. This accent shift entailed a major shift in the segmental system, the first major structural change among the phenomena associated with Grimm's law. For as the accent shift was completed, the distinction between two of the three orders of Indo-European stops was broken down medially, under certain accentual conditions, as in Goth. *giban* of the Indo-European *bh*-order and *sibun* of the *p*-order.[4] Moreover, the new alignment in the Proto-Indo-European voiceless stop order was exploited morphologically. Its possibilities may be illustrated by the contrast between the medial consonant of the infinitive in OE *cweþan,* OS *quethan,* OHG *quedan* and that of the past participle, OE *cwedan,* OS *quedan,* OHG *quetan;*[5] these were also available in word formation, e.g., OE *dēaþ* 'death' versus OE *dēad* 'dead'. Since the shift in accent entailed structural shifts in the various systems of Proto-Germanic, it constitutes a major break in the history of Germanic and merits recognition as the essential dividing mark between pre-Germanic and Proto-Germanic.

The structural shift I choose to define the conclusion of Proto-Germanic is a result of the accent shift: the loss of the final short low vowels /e a/ when they did not have primary stress. Their loss is the only one finally among that of the Germanic short vocalic segments [i e a u] which is general to all the Germanic dialects. Runic *-gastiR* and *magu* indicate retention of *-i* and *-u* to the time of North Germanic; OE *wine* vs. *giest, sunu* vs. *feld* show reflexes of PGmc. [i u] preserved even into the dialects.

[4] For the traditional terms *order,* referring to classes determined by manner of articulation, and *series,* referring to classes determined by place of articulation, see C. D. Buck, *A comparative grammar of Greek and Latin* 33 (Chicago, 1933) .

[5] More significant morphologically was the coincidence of the past participle marker, from Proto-Indo-European *t,* and the preterite tense marker, from Proto-Indo-European *dh,* in weak verbs. Only after these fell together can the Germanic verbal system have developed as a tightly knit subsystem with nominal forms included in the paradigm. But since some scholars still seem to favor theories which derive the preterite marker from PIE *t* rather than *dh,* ascription of a single preterite and preterite participial marker in weak verbs to one of the results of the Germanic accent shift would not be universally accepted and is therefore omitted from the body of the text here.

With the loss of weakly stressed final [e a] the distribution of Germanic vocalic phonemes was greatly altered. Moreover, morphological categories were modified, such as the first and third persons preterite of strong verbs, which coalesced as a result of this phonological change, e.g. Goth. *wait* 'I know, he knows' in contrast with Gk. *oîda* 'I know' and *oîde* 'he knows'. Again the selected structural change affects various systems of the language.

Proto-Germanic I then define as that stage of Germanic which was spoken between the time of the Germanic accent shift and the loss of /e a/ when final and weakly stressed. A grammar of Proto-Germanic will be a description of this stage of Germanic. Even a short sketch of the various systems of Proto-Germanic would be unduly long. Here I note briefly some disputed questions which my definition may clarify.

One of these questions is determination of the reflexes of PIE /e/ from position to position. Throughout the history of Germanic studies there have been suggestions that PIE [e] and [i] coalesced in Germanic.[6] We may cite evidence that at least in some positions they did not.

When weakly stressed and final, [e] did not become [i] in Proto-Germanic. For if final weakly stressed [e] had become PGmc. [i], it would have remained after short root syllables, as did the reflex of PIE [i], in Old English, Old Saxon and Old High German, e.g. in OE *meri,* later *mere 'sea',* OS OHG *meri* < PIE [$m_e$ri], cf. Lat. *mare,* gen. pl. *marium.* If PGmc. *-e* had become *-i,* the imperative 2d sg. of *faran* in Old English should have been **færi.*

Moreover, *-e-* of root syllables did not become *-i-* before final unstressed *-e* (as it should have, if *-e* had become *-i*) ; cf. ONorw. *mek,* OE *mec,* and Gk. *(e)mége* 'me'.

Though this evidence is negative, the absence of any final *-i* in Old English, Old Saxon, or Old High German which could be a reflex of pre-Germanic *-e* is completely convincing on the loss of final *-e* before weakly stressed *-e* became *-i* in Germanic. Accordingly by my definition of Proto-Germanic, final *-e* remained unchanged and in contrast with final *-i* throughout the Proto-Germanic period.

Although proper names must be used with caution, they comprise our only Proto-Germanic material and they can serve to support conclusions based on reconstructions. The oldest proper names preserve *-e-* in stressed syllables, even before vowels which subsequently became *-i-* and caused change of *e* to *i,* e.g. Tacitus' *Venedi* as compared with OHG *Winida, Erminones* as compared with OHG *Irmin-sul, Gepidos* as compared with OE *Gifeðas.* Forms which we can reconstruct with assurance, such as PGmc. *meke,* and names preserved in classical materials therefore support the conclusion that throughout Proto-Germanic stressed *e* was maintained distinct from *i.*

[6] For two discussions of the problems see W. F. Twaddell, The prehistoric Germanic short syllabics, *Lg.* 24.139-51 (1948) , and J. W. Marchand, Germanic short **i* and **e*: Two phonemes or one, *Lg.* 33.346-54 (1957) .

Yet since the evidence in stressed syllables has been interpreted both for and against a four-vowel system, the crucial evidence is from unstressed syllables. There is little question that *-i* was preserved in the Proto-Germanic etymon of Goth. *mari-,* OE *meri* 'sea', etc., which we may reconstruct PGmc. [mari]. On the other hand, *-e* must have been maintained in such 2d sg. imperative forms as PGmc. [gebe], the etymon of Goth. *gif,* OE *gef, gife,* etc. PGmc. [i] and [e] then contrasted, and must be assigned to separate phonemes.

A second disputed question is the allophonic position of PGmc. [i]. Previously I have stated that, while the Proto-Germanic short vowel phonemes were /e/ and /a/, [i] was a member of the /y/ phoneme, which like the five other Indo-European resonants was maintained into Proto-Germanic with the threefold allophonic variation of Proto-Indo-European, *Lg.* 31.355–66 (1955). Arguments presented against this view have been weakened by not being made in a proper chronological frame. We may recall how Streitberg failed to note the relevance of chronology in discussing the Proto-Germanic *e* : *i* situation. He assumed that the inclusion of Goth. *bidjan,* OIcel. *biðia,* OE *biddan* among strong verbs of the fifth class was an argument for the coalescence of *e* and *i* in Proto-Germanic; for he interpreted its root as a reflex of PIE *bhydh-* not *bhedh-*. The inclusion of a Gmc. *bid-* in the fifth class, and the formation of a preterite *bad* seemed to him an indication that PGmc. *i* was an allophone of *e, Urgermanische Grammatik* 53 (Heidelberg, 1896). Yet *bad-* may have developed subsequently in the various dialects because of its root structure CVC, as the preterite of the Germanic form of Lat. *scrībere* was made on the basis of a root structure *s*C*r*V*y*C. Accordingly the realignment of *bid-* is of little significance for understanding the status of Proto-Germanic *e* : *i*; it indicates however the intricacies of Germanic vocalic and morphological development, and the necessity of viewing Proto-Germanic as a language with the complexities of languages we know in greater detail.

To my earlier suggestion that the Indo-European allophonic variation of resonants, in the patterns described under Sievers' law, survived into Germanic, Marchand raised a vigorous objection, *Lg.* 32.285–7 (1956). Dealing with only a part of the evidence, he contended that Sievers' law was not operative in Proto-Germanic; he reconstructed etyma of Gothic first class verbs in Proto-Germanic and Proto-Indo-European, of which I reproduce only the third singular:

**-ye/o-*		**-eye/o-*	
LONG STEMS	SHORT STEMS	LONG STEMS	SHORT STEMS
PIE **sāgiyeti*	**kapyeti*	**gouseyeti*	**logheyeti*
Gmc. **sōkiyid/þi*	**hafyid/þi*	**kausiyid/þi*	**lagiyid/þi*
Goth. *sokeiþ*	*-hafjiþ*	*kauseiþ*	*lagjiþ*

By my point of view, the post-root vocalism in these forms was rearranged in accordance with Sievers' law; by Marchand's, it was rearranged by analogy, and the Sievers'-law variations were no longer in operation.

As an argument that he considers to be in his favor, Marchand cites minimal contrasts between Proto-Germanic infinitives and participles which were etyma of Goth. *beidan* etc. and *bidan* etc.; he reconstructs the Proto-Germanic forms **biydana*^{n} and **bidana*^{n}, labeling the vocalic nucleus of the infinitive stem the PGmc. reflex of PIE *ey*. He goes on to assert that if the allophonic situation described under Sievers' law had been in operation in Proto-Germanic the two forms would have fallen together. At the time that Marchand published his view, van Coetsem stated at some length his opinion that *-ey-* remained unchanged until late in Proto-Germanic. But even if he did not accept van Coetsem's statement, the difficulty is a figment of Marchand's. The *-iy-* he posits in the infinitive stem is his own construction; actually PIE *-ey-* as syllabic nucleus coalesced in Germanic with the reflex of PIE *ī*, not with *iy*. Like the other 'long' vowels PGmc. *ī* is analyzed as a gemmate vowel, *-ii-*, by Hamp in his article on Germanic final syllables, *Studia linguistica* 14.29–48 (1960). The third allophone of PIE /y/, [iy], like those of the other resonants, never occurred except at syllable boundaries. Accordingly, whether we posit the generally assumed PGmc. /ī/ or Hamp's /ii/, the contrast between the vocalism of infinitive and participle in Proto-Germanic has nothing to do with the allophonic variation of /y/ in Proto-Germanic or with the suffix of the first class weak verbs. In the third singular of weak verbs the forms were PGmc. [káusiyidì] and [lágyidì]; the infinitive stem of Goth. *beidan* in Proto-Germanic was /bīd-/ or /biid-/ from /beyd-/ from PIE *bheydh-*. Accordingly there is no conflict between the allophonic situation in [káusiyidì] and the vocalic development of PIE *bheydh-*.

There is further no obstacle to assuming that weakly stressed *-e-* of the Proto-Indo-European suffix *-eye-*, as in **gouseyeti* and **logheyeti*, had become *-i-* before *y*. Marchand stated that if [e] before [y] had become [i], this change would have disrupted the allophonic variation of /y/, bringing about a phonemicization of [y] and [i]. This statement cannot be supported by observation of change in historical linguistics. As an instance of Marchand's supposed rule we might cite the allophonic structure of the allophones of American English /d/ initially and intervocalically after strongly stressed vowels. Intervocalically an allophone of /t/ is coalescing with an allophone of /d/, as in *latter* and *ladder*. Yet the two phonemes are being kept distinct elsewhere, and no new *D* phoneme has arisen between vowels. For a set of allophones in a phoneme may be enriched by the addition of merging members and still maintain its relationship to another set of allophones in that phoneme. We may also then assume that PGmc. *-e-* > *-i-* before *-y-* with no disruption of the /y/ phoneme. Accordingly by the 'converse of Sievers' law' in short stem verbs like *lagjan,* the expected *iy* from PIE *ey* would have become [y], giving rise to the forms we find in the dialects, such as Goth. *lagjiþ.*

Since the objection which Marchand raised to the Germanic allophonic variation of /y/ has proved groundless, there is no point in restating here evidence for positing the retention into Germanic of the Indo-European variation of resonants in other surroundings. Yet the demonstration, given above, of the continued contrast in Proto-Germanic between final [e] and [i] (probably even after PIE *-ey-* > PGmc. *-ii-*) supports the assumption that [i] maintained into Proto-Germanic its allophonic position as a member of the /y/ phoneme. The two problems discussed are then intricately allied, and must be carefully examined within a chronological frame.

Defining Proto-Germanic as we have permits a description of it comparable to those of attested languages in rigor, if not in depth. Its phonological structure I have sketched elsewhere, *JEGP* 52.140–52 (1953). In accordance with the definition given here we must posit for its morphological system full endings, since final vowels were preserved to the end of the Proto-Germanic period. The dative plural forms, *Vatvims* and *Aflims,* attested in Latin materials—F. Kluge, *Urgermanisch* 197 (Strassburg, 1913)—indicate the extent of preservation of nominal endings. Verbal endings were similarly preserved, as in the first and third singular of the preterite. Throughout Proto-Germanic, morphological categories were clearly marked phonologically. Only after Proto-Germanic do we find a falling together of forms, with greater reliance on syntactic devices to indicate distinctions which earlier were morphologically marked. Our definition therefore assists us in determining the morphological and syntactic structure of Proto-Germanic, and in clarifying our description at its various levels, not only the phonological.

Besides assisting us in clarifying problems in any stage of a language, chronological definitions will also enable us to set up stages of prelanguages rather than treat them as huge amorphous masses. Proto-Germanic is scarcely to be dated before 500 B.C., yet a very conservative estimate of Proto-Indo-European would set for it a final date of at least 2500 B.C. The intervening period of two thousand years during which some species of Germanic was spoken is generally shrugged off with the label pre-Germanic, although in the two thousand years after Proto-Germanic at least three subclassifications are posited for English, German, and the other Germanic dialects. With structural analyses we can propose subclassifications of prehistoric languages too; such more detailed classification is one of the most useful and interesting tasks of contemporary historical linguistics. It will enable us to gain a clearer idea of the development of any given language, and of language generally, in accordance with the last section of Otto Jespersen's *Language* (London, 1922). To deal satisfactorily with 'the development of language' in general, to decide whether Jespersen's view of a progression in language from complex sentence-like entities to individual word-like entities is to be preferred to Whitney's view of precisely the opposite progression, we will have to analyze in detail, and with great care, the prehistory of numerous languages.

Three stages in the pre-history of Germanic were proposed by F. van Coetsem in his capable monograph, *Das System der starken Verba und die Periodisierung im älteren Germanischen*: 1. Urgermanisch, which 'loses itself in Proto-Indo-European'; 2. Gemeingermanisch; 3. the individual dialects. To the first stage, characterized by free accent, like that of Proto-Indo-European, he assigned the changes described by Grimm's law and Verner's law. Yet the strong stress accent on the first or stem syllable he ascribed only to the second stage. Although further developments which he places in each period are acceptable, the basic criteria that he proposes are not, for the sound change described by Verner affected the structure of Germanic only when the accent was fixed. Moreover, it is something of a simplification to say that Proto-Germanic loses itself in Proto-Indo-European, for in the interval between Proto-Indo-European and Proto-Germanic important changes have taken place at the morphological level. More compact inflections have been developed, for substantives as well as verbs, but especially for verbs; for adjectives on the other hand two basically different inflections have been developed. Further, the basis of inflection has changed, in the verb from an indication of aspect to tense, in substantives from an indication by case forms of relating a substantive to a given situation, primarily local, to indication of relationship with other components of the sentence. When these and other changes are associated with the phonological changes which took place in early Germanic, we will have a more precise and complex statement of the history of pre-Germanic. The greater complexity will lead us to recognize that the two thousand years of pre-Germanic were not empty of change; the greater precision will enable us to provide a more balanced history from Proto-Indo-European to contemporary Germanic dialects.

Chronological delimitation of languages, based on linguistic criteria, must be stated or implicit in all future grammars. The possibility of defining languages structurally has made obsolete the vague statements given formerly in delimiting languages such as English or German, dialects such as Bavarian or West Saxon, or poorly specified stages of either such as Middle English, Old High German, or Proto-Germanic. Our definitions may be minute or broad. We may choose to deal with a span of several centuries or several millennia, just as geographically we may restrict ourselves to a single dialect of English or deal with the whole range of modern English. Whether the scope of our treatment is small or great, in the future it must be precisely specified. Such precise techniques have been evolved for the description of language that we have no further excuse for poorly supported definitions, including those of prehistoric languages like Proto-Germanic.

Suggested Additional Readings for Part I

LEONARD BLOOMFIELD, "A Set of Postulates for the Science of Language," *Language* 2.153-64 (1926).

________________, *Language* (New York, 1933), esp. chapters 1, 2, 3, 4, 18.

FRANCIS P. DINNEEN, S. J., *An Introduction to General Linguistics* (New York, 1967), esp. chapters 1, 6, 7.

CHARLES C. FRIES, *Linguistics: The Study of Language,* Chapter II of *Linguistics and Reading* (New York, 1964).

H. A. GLEASON, JR., *Linguistics and English Grammar* (New York, 1965), esp. chapters 2-4.

CHARLES F. HOCKETT, *A Course in Modern Linguistics* (New York, 1958), esp. chapters 16, 44, 45, 57.

OTTO JESPERSEN, *Language: Its Nature, Development, and Origin* (London, 1922), esp. chapters 1-4. Also Norton N229.

WINFRED P. LEHMANN, *Historical Linguistics: An Introduction* (New York, 1962), esp. chapters 1, 2, 3, 5, 9.

BERTIL MALMBERG, *Structural Linguistics and Human Communication* (Berlin, 1963), esp. chapter 1.

EDWARD SAPIR, *Language: An Introduction to the Study of Speech* (New York, 1921). Also Harvest HB7.

FERDINAND DE SAUSSURE, *Course in General Linguistics,* trans. Wade Baskin (New York, 1959). Also McGraw-Hill Paperbacks.

JOHN T. WATERMAN, *Perspectives in Linguistics* (Chicago, 1963). Also Phoenix P106.

PART II

Phonetics, Phonemics and Diachronic Phonology

Diachronic, or historical, phonology is the study of modifications which have taken place in phonemic systems through the course of time. Such study involves both the description of change in entire networks of phonological oppositions and the tracing of changes in individual phonemes, insofar as these changes result in new relationships with the other phonemes in a system.

The contemporary view of languages as systems of phonological, grammatical, and semantic units which derive their value only from their interrelations with one another has led to a reinterpretation of diachronic studies. This reinterpretation has been most fully developed in the area of historical phonology, but its effects are also beginning to be felt in both grammar and semantics. Thus, for example, there is a tendency today to abandon traditional etymological investigations because they have been judged to be too limited and atomistic for a proper consideration of semantic change. It now seems preferable to treat lexical items not in terms of their individual meanderings through history, but in terms of their relationship to other lexical items in associative and oppositional sets. In this way, semantic change, like phonological and grammatical change, can be viewed as the study of modifications between systems of linguistic entities. Bloomfield's analysis of the change of OE *mete* 'food' to NE *meat* as part of a relational shift within an associative set which also included the lexical items *food* and *flesh* is an early example of this point of view.

In diachronic phonology, the change of PIE /p/ to Gmc. /f/ is now seen to be of less structural importance than was formerly realized. Indeed, any change of the generalized form /x/ > /y/ is structurally insignificant unless the change results in the addition or loss of phonemic units (i.e. changes in number of oppositions), or in the rearrangement of previous allophonic structurings. One must examine the entire obstruent systems of Proto-Indo-European and of Germanic to determine the full implications of the First Consonant Shift for the historical development of the Germanic languages. If the changes PIE /p t k/ > Gmc. /f θ x/, PIE /b d g/ > Gmc. /p t k/, and PIE /b^h d^h g^h/ > Gmc. /β ð γ/ had resulted in no modifications in the *number* of phonemic oppositions, and in no reassignment of allophones from one unit to another, but only in phonetic changes in the distinctive features which maintained the oppositions, then from the phonetician's point of view, these differences would be considerable, but from the linguist's point of view, they would be inconsequential.

In language change, therefore, it is useful to distinguish between modifications in linguistic systems themselves and changes in the details which 'express' these systems. The outward manifestations of phonological, grammatical, and semantic systems change more rapidly than the systems themselves. Again, the obstruents of Proto-Indo-European and of Germanic are illustrative. With respect to phonetic modifications, PIE voiceless stops /p t k/ became Gmc. voiceless fricatives /f θ x/, PIE voiced stops /b d g/ became Gmc. voiceless stops /p t k/, and PIE voiced aspirated stops /b^h d^h g^h/ became Gmc. voiced fricatives /β ð γ/. In spite of these phonetic changes, however, the basic 3 x 3 obstruent system (leaving out of consideration the problem of the PIE labio-velars) was not modified in terms of *number* of oppositions; in both cases the system involved intersections of a three-way contrast in type of articulation with a three-way contrast in position of articulation. Whatever systemic changes occurred took place as a result of the redistribution of allophones from one phonological unit to another (e.g. PIE /p t k/ after /s/ remained stops, and therefore fell in with the reflexes of PIE /b d g/).

Since the basic oppositional relations which characterize systems appear to show greater persistence than the details that 'express' these systems, it is sometimes argued that, of two or more competing phonemic solutions for an earlier stage in a language's history, the solution which departs least from the prevailing analysis of the current system is the one which is preferable, providing the solution does not contradict available evidence. This assumption is not indisputable, but it has considerable bearing on efforts to provide adequate phonemic descriptions of Old and Middle English (especially with reference to the vowel systems), and consequently, on the overall description of historical English phonology.

The variety of phonetic changes which have been recorded in the history of languages may be described with greater consistency and economy when treated within the theory of the phoneme. Since the principal concern in diachronic phonology is with those modifications that result in systemic changes, the linguist is primarily interested in the basic patterns of phonological realignment. These patterns are referred to as splits and mergers, and are the fundamental processes underlying the loss, addition, or rearrangement of phonemic units. The reinterpretation of phonetic modifications in phonemic terms serves to distinguish significant from nonsignificant changes in phonological systems.

Earlier stages in the history of a language may either be totally unattested or attested only in documents. In the former case, phonemic systems must be reconstructed from the evidence afforded by historically later dialects which show demonstrable genetic relationships to one another. For example, the phonemic system for Proto-Indo-European is reconstructed on the basis of evidence from IE dialects such as Indo-Iranian, Greek, Italic, Celtic, and Germanic. In the second case, phonemic systems are posited principally on the basis of graphemic analysis of available documents—an analytical procedure which necessarily introduces a number of complex problems, including the possibility of scribal influences from linguistically unrelated communities. The analysis of orthographic practices from which phonemic conclusions may be derived is discussed more fully in the introduction to Part III, where these problems are directly related to alternative phonemic solutions for Old and Middle English. Here it is sufficient to call attention to the necessity of graphemic analysis of documents, since such materials usually represent the primary evidence for the phonological systems of earlier stages in the history of a language.

Because the sound system of an earlier stage of a language is not directly accessible, precise phonetic reconstruction of phonemes is impossible. Such reconstructions, however, can be reasonably accurate due to inferences which may be drawn from phonetic studies of contemporary dialects. Thus, while phonetic conclusions cannot be reached directly in diachronic phonology, the role of phonetic investigations, especially in present-day dialectology, should not be underestimated. The data which such investigations yield serve to verify the probabilities of phonetic modifications which have been proposed to account for historical phonological changes.

The articles in this section are meant to introduce the student to the descriptive goals of diachronic phonology, i.e. the historical statement of change or modification in phonemic systems. Although the article by Archibald A. Hill might be revised in some of its details in the light of numerous advances in our understanding of phonological structures, it still provides an important and unchanged insight into the necessity of distinguishing between phonetic and phonemic change in historical description. Hans Kurath's article is a statement urging caution in the drawing of historical conclusions, directed particularly at those who would view phonemic systems and changes in those systems too abstractly, with the result that undue attention to 'overall patterns' of phonological structures and their historical modifications tends to obscure the more accessible evidence of phonetic change as evidenced particularly in the examination of modern dialects. In the important paper by Herbert Penzl, the various kinds of evidence of historical phonemic changes, especially those of an orthographic nature, are classified and discussed in the light of the types of phonemic change which may be described. W. Freeman Twaddell's structural restatement of the assimilating process of umlaut in Old High German provides a strong argument for the distinction between phonetic and phonemic change in its clear application of this principle to an historical sound change whose results are still attested in both Modern German and Modern English. Finally, W. P. Lehmann re-examines the phonological system of Primitive Germanic in the light of a revised statement of Proto-Indo-European phonology, and demonstrates that, in its phonemic structure, Germanic reveals less systemic change from Proto-Indo-European than many of the other Indo-European dialects. All of the articles in this section point towards the validity and economy of historical description restated in terms of the phoneme theory rather than in terms of isolated phonetic modifications.

Phonetic and Phonemic Change

ARCHIBALD A. HILL

THE THEORY OF PHONEMES has received a great deal of attention from linguists within the last few years, and the applications of the theory to descriptive linguistics have become reasonably clear, though there still remain problems in need of further study. However, there has been less interest in the theory on the part of students of the history of language, many of whom practically ignore the theory altogether; or assume, on the other hand, that the sound changes which we can prove to have taken place in the past were practically coextensive with phonemic shifts.[1] It seems, therefore, worth while to attempt a tentative examination and classification of the relations between sound change and phonemic change in the hope that the applications of the theory of phonemes to the historic study of language may be to some extent clarified.

In the first place it is clear that the shifts in the pronunciation of a whole set of phonemes, which leave the phonemes as far apart as at the start of the change, involve no shift in the phonemic pattern. This is usually clearly recognized by all scholars, and involves no particular difficulty. A simple example is the fact that most phoneticians who visit the Southern United States for the first time, or after a stay in New England, are struck by the fact that the whole Southern vowel scheme is a notch higher than that of other parts of the country. Aside from individual differences in the pattern of vowel phonemes due to other causes there are, however, no striking differences in phonemic pattern in the two dialects. Historically, also, the first consonant shift did not result in extensive phonemic changes, since the three groups of IE sounds remained separate in PGmc., though on a new basis.

Reprinted by permission from *Language* 12.15-22 (1936).

[1] This seems to be the attitude of Bloomfield, *Language,* N.Y., 1933. In his chapters on Phonetic Change and on the Comparative Method he makes quite clear that in general the formulae in which historic states of language are summed up indicate historic phonemic rather than narrowly phonetic structure. He does not, however, give any detailed discussion of the exceptions to this rule, or of the relations of the two types of change.

Allied to this principle is a second, less often noticed. Phonetic shifts can result in a change in what constitutes the significant element in a phoneme or set of phonemes. This likewise produces no change in the phonemic pattern, though, as in the type of change cited above, the individual phonemes affected are all altered. An example of this type of change is found in the history of English long and short vowels. Originally the long and short vowels of English seem to have had the same quality; thus the significant feature of the two sets must have been length; and that the difference was phonemic is proved by such OE pairs as *fullīce* 'fully, completely', and *fūllīce* 'foully, basely'. However, in the late 13th century in the North, and a little later in the Midlands,[2] a change set in the quality of the short vowels, whereby the natural tendency toward relaxation in short sounds resulted in open quality, eventually giving rise to the distinction that exists between such modern phonemes as [u] and [ʊ]. The gradual result of this sound change has been that quality has replaced quantity as a mark of distinction between phonemes in Modern English. The phonemes remain at equal distance from each other, but the nature of the difference has changed. It is interesting that this change has indirectly contributed to a new treatment of length. Since length has become a non-distinctive feature the way has been left open for a regrouping of long and short quantities in rigid correspondence with the phonetic situation.[3] In fact I think most of the puzzling changes in the quantity of Modern English vowels can be referred to this general tendency, rather than to elaborate 'laws' describing the treatment of individual long and short vowels in special situations, as was the method of many older grammarians.

A third type of phonetic shift which need not involve phonemic readjustment is combinative sound change. Combinative sound change does not necessarily produce a phonemic shift so long as the sound causing the change remains. The simplest example of this sort of assimilation, not resulting in phonemic difference, is to be found in the almost universal American treatment of the vowels of *pat* [pæt] and *pan* [pæ̃n]. In spite of the nasalization of *pan,* the two vowels are still members of the same phoneme, and it usually requires training in phonetics for an American speaker to perceive the phonic difference. If, however, the two final consonants should disappear, while the nasality persisted, the two vowels [æ] and [æ̃], would then automatically become members of different phonemes.

An almost exactly similar assimilation which does not affect the phonemic pattern occurs in the speech of Spaniards, who often nasalize the first vowel of a word like *notario* without recognizing any difference

[2] Cf. Luick, *Historische Grammatik der Englischen Sprache* 374-9, Tauchnitz, Leipzig, 1921.

[3] The best description of the phonetic rules governing NE vowel length is to be found in E. A. Meyer, *Englische Lautdauer,* Uppsala, 1903.

between it and the last vowel of the word. A further example is the velarization of the nasal consonant of Spanish *cinco* [θiŋko], which is still felt to be a member of the *n* phoneme. Another case is the French unvoicing of the final *m* of words like *rhumatisme* [ʁymatism̥].

A more complicated example of the principle that as long as the sound which causes the assimilation remains, the phonemic pattern is not affected, is found in Modern English. Thus in my own speech the Early Modern English open [o] before [r] has resulted in a long [ɔ]-like phone. Since I use this phone in all words of the [o + r] type, and since the [r] is always preserved, I make no distinction between pairs like *coarse* and *course, morning* and *mourning*. This open phone is therefore still a member of the [o] phoneme, though the change which produced the variant phone is of considerable antiquity. In the speech of Virginians and New Englanders who do not pronounce final and preconsonantal *r,* on the other hand, the loss of the sound which brought about the lowered variant of the phoneme has resulted in the setting up of a new phoneme, since *foe* and *for* now contain significantly different sounds, not phonetically controlled variants. In a phonemic transcription of such a type of speech *foe* and *for* would have to be distinguished by some such symbols as [fo] and [fɔə].

The difficulty of determining whether a historic sound change represented a mere phonic shift, or is one involving phonemic difference, is sometimes considerable. Thus the OE change of 'breaking' is a case in point. OE *æ* was 'broken' to a diphthong, written *ea,* and presumably pronounced [æə], before double *ll* as in [*fællan] > [fæəllan]. The generally accepted cause of this breaking was the development of a glide vowel before a 'dark' variety of *l* in the same syllable. If the [æə] had continued to occur only before such dark sounds, it would clearly have remained only a subsidiary member of the [æ] phoneme, in spite of the different spelling. There were, however, other varieties of *ll,* particularly a brighter *ll* from WGmc. *lj,* before which breaking often did not take place.[4] The occurrence, however, of occasional forms like Northern *sealla* from WGmc. **saljan* suggests that perhaps the diphthong was carried over to the bright varieties of *ll* as well, in which case phonemic readjustment of either the vowel or the consonant must have taken place.

Occasionally we are more fortunate in being able to determine the phonemic standing of an ancient sound change. Thus the Gothic lowering of Gmc. *u,* represented in Gothic by the spelling *au,* occurs only before *r, h,* and *hw*. There is, therefore, no evidence that it was not still a member of the *u* phoneme, since it is obviously phonetically controlled.

Even without the loss of the sound which brings about change in the members of a phoneme placed in its neighborhood, phonemic shifts

[4] Sievers-Cook, *Grammar of Old English* 51, Ginn and Company, N.Y., 1903.

may, however, occur. Such phonemic shifts nevertheless do not result in the setting up of new phonemes. Their sole result is to bring about a redistribution of already existent phonemes in the words affected. What happens in such a case is that the combinative sound change produces a phone which is closer to a member of some other phoneme than it is to the original phoneme, with the result that attraction sets in, assimilating the aberrant phone to this new close neighbor. This is what has happened in forms like [kæpm̩] for older [kæptən]. On a larger scale it is illustrated by those people who, while still preserving final and preconsonantal *r*, refer the [o + r] words to the same phoneme as *law,* making no distinction between *war* and *wore*. An instructive example of phonemic regrouping of this sort is cited by Grammont.[5] He points out that in the French phrase *robe courte* the final *b* of the first word is unvoiced, but remains a member of the *b* phoneme, since it is still a lenis. In *obtenu,* on the other hand, the following voiceless sound is a constant part of the environment, not a mere accident of the phrase. Here, therefore, the unvoiced *b* goes completely over to the *p* phoneme, since it loses its lenis quality.

To turn to phonetic shifts which involve shifts in the phonemic pattern. The most obvious of these is a shift in the direction of some already existent phoneme. Such a change results in the falling together of two phonemes, eliminating one from the total number. A well known example of such a falling together is that of ME [e:] as in [kwe:nə] and [ɛ:] as in [hɛ:θ] which have both given rise to NE [i:] as in *queen* and *heath*. A type resulting in an increase of the number of phonemes by means of a split in what was once one phoneme has already been discussed; that is, the splitting of a phoneme because of the loss of a sound which caused a combinative change, as in [fo], [fɔə], above.

Here it is only necessary to add that it is sometimes difficult to determine when the change-causing sound can be called lost. This is particularly true when complete assimilation takes place. Thus it was mentioned that WGmc. *lj* resulted in a double *ll* as in WGmc. **taljan* > OE *tellan*. Can one speak of this *j* as being lost if the second *l* is still its representative? The answer should be in the affirmative, since we have essentially one sound, though long, as the representative of the two earlier ones. Moreover it is probable that this *ll* was different in character (perhaps palatalized?) from the common Germanic *ll,* since the geminated *ll* did not produce breaking in OE. As long, therefore, as the difference in character persisted, the two *ll*'s constituted separate phonemes.

No less important than these purely phonetic changes are changes in the phonemic pattern resulting from dialect mixture. Thus if a given local dialect shifts a whole phoneme in a new direction (without thereby bringing about a collision with some other phoneme) no phonemic shift

[5] Grammont, *Traité de Phonétique* 186-7, Delagrave, Paris, 1933.

occurs. However, if the speakers of that dialect thereafter come in contact with another dialect, or a standard language which they imitate, phonemic changes almost certainly result. If phonemic changes occur, the result may be either the setting up of a new phoneme, or a redistribution of already existent phonemes. The only instance in which such dialect mixture does not produce phonemic changes is when a true variphone is set up, each speaker using either of the dialectically variant phones in all of the words in question. Such cases would seem to be rare. A more common state of affairs is fixation of the variants, either in different ones of the affected words, or in different senses of the same word. An interesting example of the setting up of a new phoneme by fixation of the second type is found in the speech of a subject from eastern Maine. This speaker comes from a region in which the [o] phoneme is strongly centralized, giving a phone which can be written [ɵ]. However, this particular subject belongs to a family in which local dialect has long been abandoned for Standard English. Thus *coat* has the [ou] phone of the Standard English phoneme. But in the special, and more homely, sense of *coat of paint* the local phone [ɵ] occurs. Thus there has been a phonemic split, actually in two senses of the same word.

The type of shift which results in the redistribution of already existent phonemes can be exemplified from the speech of many Virginians. The local dialect of eastern Virginia has the [a] phoneme in words of the *aunt, dance* type. However, the [æ] phoneme characteristic of General American occurs in the special use of *aunt* or *auntie* as a title for an old colored woman. It now seems probable that the puzzling divergences in the history of ME [a] and [ᴜ], resulting respectively in NE [a] as in father and [æ] as in *rather,* [ᴜ] as in *put* and [ʌ] as in *but,* but with fixations in individual words, are the result of dialect mixture of the types described above; the first resulting in redistribution of existent phonemes, the second giving rise to a new phoneme.

The case of genuine variphones is unknown to me in personal experience of dialect investigation. However, I am acquainted with speakers who vary separate phonemes in a way almost exactly similar. Thus one subject who has lived both in Virginia and the middle Atlantic states uses either [æ] or [a] phonemes in words of the *aunt, dance, ask,* type, according to what sort of speakers he is addressing. Also the borderline cases in which some words occur with either phone, but some are limited to one or the other, is known to me from subjects in Maine. Thus one speaker can say either [stoun] or [stɵn], but always says [bout]. In such types of distribution it seems closest to the truth to say that there are two phonemes, but that some words can be pronounced with either one.

There remain fairly numerous examples of change in pronunciation where there is a phonemic shift without any general sound change. This is the type of change found in individual words, in which the change is not supported by a similar drift in other words of the same history. An example of this kind of individual change is found in the speech of some localities in Virginia where the single word *say* has undergone lowering in the stressed position so that it appears with the phoneme of *bed.* This is in contradiction to the general tendency in this region, which is to raise rather than lower vowels in stressed syllables. Another similar example is found in Maine where at least one speaker says that an ox is driven with a [gɔəd], using the phoneme of *board.* It is highly improbable that such an individual change, of whatever origin, should result in the setting up of a new phoneme, occurring only once in the speaker's language, since it can usually be assumed that the attraction of existent phonemes will be too strong for a single word to resist it. Only in the more or less isolated and sub-linguistic forms of interjections and similar highly colored words can phones not found in the general phonemic pattern easily maintain themselves. The origin of such individual changes as the two cited above is extremely various, and must always be explained out of a knowledge of the history of the individual word in question. Thus, though I cannot prove it, I suspect that the first change is due to the analogy of the third singular *says,* and the preterite *said.* As to the second example, the explanation would more probably be found in the existence of the words *gore, gored, gourd,* which have somehow become blended with *goad,* always a word of limited application in folk speech. Thus analogy, folk-etymology, and the restoration of worn-down forms all play an important part in such individual changes.

Closely allied to the phenomena of individual phonemic attraction are certain other phenomena that result from closely similar or overlapping phones within two separate phonemes. In English, a characteristic change is the reduction of many unstressed vowels to [ə]. When any of those reduced vowels are restressed, an 'incorrect' form, i.e. not belonging to the original phoneme, may be the result. Such a form is the Louisiana [ˈpʌkɔn] for *pecan.* More interesting, and less widely known, however, are cases of individual attraction resulting from contiguity of two whole phonemes. Thus in many parts of New England there are raised and fronted variants of the [a] phoneme, producing a phone, [a$^{\wedge}$], which is extremely close to the lower limits of the [æ] phoneme. In general the two phonemes are kept quite distinct, but in occasional words attraction between the two phonemes has produced confusion. A clear instance of this kind of confusion is found in the speech of a subject from southern Massachusetts, who pronounces the first syllable of *clapboard* with the [a$^{\wedge}$] phone, which is a member of the [a] phoneme, not the [æ] phoneme.[6]

[6] The pronunciations [kætrɪdʒ] for *cartridge,* and [pæsl̩] for *parcel,* common in New England, are not examples of the reverse confusion, but of early loss of [r] before dentals.

From the preceding discussion it seems possible to deduce a few general principles which govern phonemic change in its relation to phonetic change. The most important of these is that when phonetic change brings two phonemes close together, attraction may set in. This attraction may manifest itself more strongly in some words than others, thus appearing at first as a confusion between phonemes of individual words, though the two similar phonemes may elsewhere remain distinct. Later the attraction may extend to the whole group, in which case we say that 'two sounds have fallen together'. Indeed, I think it may safely be assumed that no two phonemes ever fall together without passing through such a transition stage, in which the attraction manifests itself sporadically in ever increasing numbers of words.

However, attraction is not the only possibility when phonetic change brings two phonemes close to each other. A second possibility is phonemic repulsion, which results in the selection by the speaker of variants which offer less overlapping, and so tend to increase the distance between the phonemes, rather than to lessen or eradicate it. An instance of phonemic repulsion seems to have taken place in the history of British English in early modern times. We know that at one time some varieties, at least, of London English had a voiced intervocalic *t*, which we can assume was probably the same phone as the flapped, voiced *t* so common in America at present.[7] We also know that at some time, presumably fairly recent, British English must have developed the flapped intervocalic voiced *r* which is characteristic of Standard British English today. These two phones are extremely close to each other, differing principally only in length. Consequently if they existed as members of separate phonemes at the same time, we should expect confusion to have arisen. Evidence of this confusion, and so of the contemporaneity of the two phones is found in *porridge*, the by-form from *pottage*. But at present British English *t* is unvoiced, and even slightly aspirated, medially, so that there is no longer the slightest danger of confusion with *r*. I know of no explanation other than habitual selection of variants farther removed from *r* than is the flapped *t* to account for this drift.

As to whether attraction or repulsion will result from the overlapping or contiguity of two phonemes, it seems to me that we must resort to the principles of dangerous as against unimportant confusion laid down by the French linguistic geographers to account for the disappearance or preservation of homonymous words. Thus it is demonstrably more important to keep consonant phonemes clear and distinct in English as it is at present organized, than it is to do the same for vowel phonemes. It is thus not strange that confusion in consonants

[7] Cf. the spellings collected by Wyld, *A History of Modern Colloquial English* 312-13, E. P. Dutton, N. Y., 1920.

should be rarer than in vowels, where several ME sounds have been confused in NE.

In conclusion, the theory of phonemic attraction and repulsion, if accepted, should modify considerably our notions of how linguistic change takes place. Where the neo-grammarians held that the individual speaker was without control over sound drift, the theory of phonemes emphasizes that many more things than inexorable phonetic law can control the non-distinctive features of utterance. The selection of those phones within a given phoneme which offer least likelihood of confusion may often spring from a necessity for clearness which has too often been ruled out of court by students of language.

Phonemics and Phonics in Historical Phonology

HANS KURATH

MY PURPOSE IN THIS ARTICLE is to discuss the interplay of phonemic and phonic data in historical phonology, and to demonstrate by examples chosen from the collection of the Linguistic Atlas the importance of giving adequate attention to phonic data not only in historical phonology but also in synchronic linguistics.

To achieve my purpose, I must first outline my view of the field of linguistics, even at the risk of making the tail wag the dog. As I see it, linguistics has two major fields: pure linguistics, whether synchronic, diachronic, areal, or social, which deals with usage without reference to the history of the speaker or the speech community; and historical linguistics, which undertakes to account for usage, or change in usage, by correlating purely linguistic data with the character and the history of the speaker or the speech community.

Pure synchronic linguistics (glottotechnics) proceeds on the assumption that in a given society, at a given time, the sounds of the current language constitute a system. Operating on this theory, the descriptivist establishes the functional units of sound (the phonemes) and formulates the system of sounds of the language in question. Focusing his attention upon systematics, he stands the best chance of finding all the systematic features peculiar to it. In this pursuit he sets aside, quite properly, all historical considerations and the culture of the community in which the language is used. The feasibility of abstracting from historical and social realities is, indeed, one of the crowning features of this method of dealing with language.

To say that language is essentially systematic at any given time, and therefore amenable to the descriptive technique, is not to admit that it is ever wholly systematic. The findings of diachronic and of area linguistics sharply contradict any such assumption. Relics of older usage that no longer fit into the current system and piecemeal innovations not yet systematized are ever present. Moreover, the descriptivist cannot ignore

Reprinted by permission from *American Speech* 36.93-100 (1961).

the patent fact that systems do change, and that a change in the system of a language is not conceivable without a temporary breakdown of certain structural features.

The proper procedure in synchronic linguistics is, therefore: (1) to identify all the systematic features; and (2) to isolate those features that are no longer, or not yet, systematized. To invent ingenious formulas in order to make irregularities look regular is a futile exercise, to say the least, since it is based upon a misconception of the nature of language, which is a historically created system of communication.

Pure diachronic linguistics employs essentially two techniques in its efforts to trace the changes in a language, to determine the genetic relationship between languages, and to reconstruct a prehistoric parent language of a linguistic stock.

Proceeding on the theory that changes in the phonemes of any language occur with regularity, the diachronist undertakes to establish the historically corresponding phonemes of two or more chronological stages of one language, or of two or more related languages. In reconstructing a prehistoric parent language, he utilizes the corresponding phonemic units thus established as a basis of inference. All such operations can be performed without reference to the peoples who speak, or spoke, these languages.

The theory of the regularity of phonemic change thus serves the purpose of identifying all regularities and of sorting out apparent irregularities. It is a heuristic device of diachronic linguistics parallel to that of the theory of essential systematization in pure synchronic linguistics; and, like the latter, it need not take account of the culture and the history of the speech community. It can be applied abstractly.

Just as pure synchronic and diachronic linguistics have methods of dealing with language without reference to the speaker or the speech community, so does pure areal and social linguistics—an aspect of linguistic research more widely known as linguistic geography or dialectology.

Using a sampling technique, the linguistic geographer undertakes to establish the regional and social dissemination of heteroglosses—differences in pronunciation, morphology, syntax, and vocabulary—within an area. He maps separately the variants of each feature investigated, making separate entries for each speaker. If the regional dissemination of heteroglosses warrants it, he draws isoglossic lines setting off the heteroglosses within the area; if the heteroglosses exhibit a social dissemination, he tabulates them in some way. After handling each item in this manner, he compares the regional dissemination patterns as exhibited by the heteroglossic lines, and finds that the heteroglosses (lexical, morphological, and phonetic) form bundles of various sizes in some sections of the area investigated but not in others. These bundles he takes to be indicative of the existence of major and minor dialect boundaries within the total area, and hence also of the existence of major dialect areas and their subdivisions.

All these operations and inferences are purely linguistic. They do not, and should not, take into account the history of the speech communities at this stage of the investigation. The historical interpretation of the dialect areas in terms of settlement areas, political and economic subareas, dominant cultural centers, and so forth, is an independent subsequent enterprise.

To summarize: the techniques of pure synchronic linguistics, pure diachronic linguistics, and pure area linguistics are effective scientific devices applicable to language without reference to the culture and the history of the speech community.

However, the synchronist must be aware of the fact that language is a historical product shaped by complicated cultural and social processes, and therefore it cannot be wholly systematic at any time. The diachronist will want to relate the changes in language to the history of the speakers whenever possible; and the linguistic geographer should not stop short of interpreting heteroglosses, dialect boundaries, and speech areas in terms of demographic areas and forces of one kind or another.

Pure linguistics achieves its immediate ends without reference to the culture or the history of the speech community. Thus the system of phonemes and the distribution of the units can be described, in the abstract, for any given time. Changes in the system of a language can be established and described simply by comparing two or more chronological cross sections. A parent language can be reconstructed by comparing the phonemic systems of two or more genetically related languages and the incidence of the phonemes in the shared vocabulary (etymology), even though the history of the peoples speaking these languages may not be known. Speech areas can be delineated and subdivided on the basis of heteroglosses without reference to settlement history, population centers, or lines of communication. For certain purposes this is enough, and under certain circumstances this is all that can be achieved.

But historians of language, comparativists, and dialectologists understandably want to relate their purely linguistic findings to the culture and the history of the peoples who use, or have used, the language, and in matters of pronunciation to known facts concerning habits of articulation. They want to know how phonemes split or merge, how allophones of one phoneme come to be subsumed under another phoneme, how native phonemes are replaced by foreign phonemes, how foreign phonemes are adapted to the native system, and under what conditions foreign phonemes are adopted.

For all these problems the phonemic point of view is essential. But for most of them a careful consideration of the phonic character and range of the several phonemes is of crucial importance. In dialectology (areal and social linguistics), positional and prosodic allophones are directly observable. In diachronic linguistics they must be inferred from phonemic splits and mergers for which dialectology and instrumental phonetics furnish the clues.

Relying upon the findings of the Linguistic Atlas of the Atlantic States, one can illustrate the way in which new phonemes arise or are lost, how the incidence of phonemes in the vocabulary changes, and how the phonic character of phonemes is modified. In some instances, the immediate drive for a change can be safely inferred from the regional and/or social dissemination of the variants; in others, a probable source of the change can be pointed out by considering demographic factors such as settlement, migration, population and cultural centers, the British background, and so on.

My illustrations are necessarily brief and simplified. A fuller account will be found in *The Pronunciation of English in the Atlantic States.*[1] The unitary phonemicization of diphthongal vowels I use is fully described in that publication.

To make my points, I have introduced a number of clear examples from earlier English and from Primitive Germanic.

THE ADDITION OF PHONEMES

New phonemes arise, or are introduced, in various ways:

1. The PGc back vowels have fronted allophones before the high-front vowels /ī i/ and the palatal semivowel /j/ in WGc. With the loss of these position markers, rounded front vowels become separate phonemes, as in OE *mȳs* (pl.) vs. *mūs* (sg.), *fœ̄t* (pl.) vs. *fōt* (sg.). This process has been well described by W. Freeman Twaddell.[2]

2. OE had only one set of short fricatives, /f þ s h/, voiceless in all positions except between voiced sounds. In intervocalic position, short /f *þ* s/, pronounced as voiced [v ð z], contrasted with long /ff þþ ss/, pronounced without voice. Through the loss of phonemic length in the consonant system (*c.*1200 in the North Midland, *c.*1400 in the South Midland), the intervocalic voiced allophones [v ð z] were raised to phonemic status, contrasting henceforth with voiceless /f *þ* s/ in this position, as in /bɑ̄ðən, rīzən/ *vs.* /wrɑ̄*þ*e, kisen/. In initial position, voiced /v z/ became established in ME through the adoption of words from OF and L.

In an earlier article, I have described the development of contrastive voiced and voiceless fricatives in ME.[3] They came into being partly as a native development, partly through borrowing from OF.

[1] Hans Kurath and Raven I. McDavid, Jr., *The Pronunciation of English in the Atlantic States* (Ann Arbor, 1961).

[2] 'A Note on Old High German Umlaut' (1938) in *Readings in Linguistics,* ed. Martin Joos (Washington, D.C., 1957), pp. 85-87.

[3] 'The Loss of Long Consonants and the Rise of Voiced Fricatives in ME,' *Language,* XXXII (1956), 435-45.

3. In several subareas on the Atlantic coast, the postvocalic /r/ of *ear, care, four, poor,* and so on, articulated as a constricted [ɚ] elsewhere, developed into an unconstricted mid-central semivowel [ə̯]. Since this phone has nothing in common with the prevocalic /r/ of *read, road,* and so on, in articulation or acoustic quality, it must in my opinion be taken as a separate phoneme. If the incidence of this semivowel /ə̯/ is restricted to certain positions, the same is true of the consonants /ŋ ž/ of *sing, pleasure;* and the semivowels /j w/ of *yes, well* are restricted to prevocalic position, if one treats diphthongal vowels as units, as I do.

The gradual phonic shift from fully constricted [ɚ] to unconstricted [ə̯] is well documented on the periphery of the areas that now have the semivowel /ə̯/ in *ear, four,* and so on. Other speakers, of course, simply replace postvocalic /r/ by /ə̯/, as in the lower Hudson Valley, under the influence of metropolitan New York.

4. In the areas on the Atlantic seaboard that have the semivowel /ə̯/ after high and midvowels, as in *ear, care,* and so on, this /ə̯/ has merged with the low checked vowel /ɑ/ of *hot* to create a new free vowel, as in *car, far, garden* /kɒ, fɒ, gɒdən/. Here *hard, barb* and *hod, bob* have contrastive vowels, which differ in quality but not in length. However, some speakers on the periphery of these areas, in adopting that distinction, substitute for the free vowel a prolonged variant of the checked vowel /ɑ/ of *hod, bob.* This usage is clearly in transition.

THE LOSS OF PHONEMES

The loss of phonemes by merging is too well known to need extensive illustration. Thus the three IE vowels /o ɑ ə/ coalesce in PGc /ɑ/, IE /ō ɑ̄/ in PGc /ō/; OE *ēa* and *ǣ* (<PGc ai/j) are merged in ME /ū/, ME *ai* and *ā* in MnE /e/; and so on.

Two examples from American English will serve to show how complicated this type of process can be.

1. In eastern New England some words that had a long /ǭ/ in ME have a checked vowel /ɵ/, e.g., *stone, coat, road.* This phoneme is most common in rural areas (especially from Maine to the upper Connecticut Valley) and more common in rustic words than in other expressions. It is relatively rare in cultivated urban speech, though some cultured speakers take pride in retaining it in *the whole thing* and *wholly.* Relics of /ɵ/ survive in the New England settlements along the Great Lakes.

The areal and social dissemination of this phoneme, and its peculiar incidence in the vocabulary, provides valuable insight into the complicated gradual recession of a unique regional phoneme in American English. Though the social forces behind the replacement of this checked /ɵ/ by the free /o/ of *know* are complex, it is nevertheless clear that New England is in this instance bowing to national usage.

Walter S. Avis has described this process in great detail.[4] It is perhaps not inappropriate to point out that one of the nine vowels in the Trager-Smith 'over-all' system hangs by this frail thread.

2. The merging of the free vowel /ɔ/ of *law* with the checked vowel /ɑ/ of *lot* in a free vowel /ɒ/ in eastern New England and in western Pennsylvania is treated by Thomas H. Wetmore in his University of Michigan dissertation.[5] The British background of this phenomenon is so complex, and the situation in the Eastern states so fluid, that it would be foolish to attempt a description of the process before the English dialect atlas is published.[6]

It is clear, however, that the merger has taken place in the two areas mentioned above and, at least in part, in the Great Lakes and the Pacific Northwest.

CHANGES IN INCIDENCE

1. In America, *mood, good,* and *blood* now regularly have three different vowel phonemes, all derived from the same ME vowel /ǭ/ in one and the same position, that is, before /d/. In other words, these three derivatives of ME /ǭ/ occur in varying regional dissemination: *(a) broom* and *room* often have the checked /ʊ/ of *full* in eastern New England, eastern Virginia, and the Low Country of South Carolina, the free /u/ of *fool* elsewhere; *(b) coop* has the vowel of *full* in the South and the South Midland, that of *fool* in the North Midland and the North; *(c) roof* as /rʊf/ is common in New England, on Delaware Bay, and in northern West Virginia, /ruf/ predominating everywhere else; *(d) soot* as /sʊt/ predominates on all social levels in the North and in much of Pennsylvania, whereas in the South it is largely confined to cultivated speech. The variant /sʌt/ is regular in Southern folk speech and in middle-class speech but is uncommon farther north. The variant /sut/ occurs in the New England settlement area, rarely elsewhere, and has the earmarks of a prestige pronunciation.

This chaotic regional and social incidence of the three derivatives of ME /ǭ/ defies formulation in phonetic rules. However, from the social dissemination of the variants in the several focal dialect areas present trends in usage can be inferred; and on the margin of these areas phones can be observed that cannot be definitely assigned to one phoneme rather than another, as in the case of *room* and *broom*. Such 'compromise' pronunciations (unsystematized phones) are a reality, and must be reckoned with in synchronic and diachronic linguistics.

[4] 'The Mid-back Vowels in the English of the Eastern United States: a Detailed Investigation of Regional and Social Differences in Phonic Characteristics and in Phonemic Organization' (University of Michigan dissertation, 1955).

[5] *The Low-central and Low-back Vowels in the English of the Eastern United States,* Publication of the American Dialect Society, No. 32 (University, Ala., 1959).

[6] Harold Orton, director of the English atlas, tells me that the fieldwork has been completed.

The situation in Standard British English is no less confused than in American English. Blending of regional derivatives of ME /ọ̄/ in England appears to be at the root of the matter. At any rate, the incidence of /u/, /ʊ/, and /ʌ/ in *room, roof, soot, root,* and *hoop* varies just as much in English folk speech as in American English.

2. In the greater part of the Eastern states Early Modern English short /o/ and long /ō/ before an /r/ of the same syllable have remained distinct. But in a wide belt extending from the lower Hudson Valley westward through New Jersey and Pennsylvania and southward to the Potomac, the two phonemes have coalesced in this position. In this belt *four* and *forty, hoarse* and *horse* have the same vowel phoneme (as also in Standard British English). The lowering effect of postvocalic /r/ upon high and midvowels is well known. Thus the old long midvowels of *poor* and *ear* fail to be raised in some regional dialects of American English (which have /poə̯, eə̯/), the high vowel of *pure* is lowered to /o/ in the South and in northeastern New England, and the midvowel of *care* is lowered to the /æ/ of *cat* in parts of the South and of New England. The merging of the vowel of *four* with that of *forty* must therefore be attributed to the same cause.

The history of the vowels before an /r/ of the same syllable points up the importance of dealing with subphonemic (phonic) features adequately. In diachronic linguistics we usually have no *direct* evidence of the phonic range of phonemes, that is, of their positional and prosodic allophones. We infer their existence and their approximate phonic character from mergers and splits in the phonemes as evidenced by changes in the spelling, by rhymes, and so forth. In dialectology, phonic recording of living speech gives us direct evidence of the phonic range of the phonemes (their positional and prosodic allophones), evidence that leads to a realistic treatment of phonemic mergers and splits.

3. In Virginia, North Carolina, and the upcountry of South Carolina, the vowel in *aunt, half,* and *ashes* is extensively articulated as an upgliding [æᶦ]. This regional allophone of [æ] is especially common in *can't,* which is so frequently heavily stressed. In some sections of this extensive area, notably in North Carolina and in the Appalachians south of the Kanawha, *can't* has the vowel of *cane.* Though avoided by the cultured, /kent/ is here common among the middle class and all but universal among the folk.

Since /kent/ is confined to the area in which the vowel of *aunt, half,* and *ashes* is articulated as an upgliding [æᶦ], the origin of /e/ in *can't* is quite clear: as an upgliding vowel, articulated with raised tongue position under heavy stress, it fell in with the normally upgliding /e/ of *cane.*

In similar fashion the upgliding positional allophone of checked /ɛ/ in *egg* is often phonemicized as the free /e/ of *plague* in folk and common speech of the South and the southern Appalachians, and of eastern New England.[7]

Changes of all these types are documented in areal and social linguistics, based upon the observation of living speech. When the areal and social dissemination of features of pronunciation is established by systematic sampling, the manner in which changes occur in a given regional or social dialect can often be pointed out with a high degree of probability.

Areal and social linguistics, therefore, make a substantial contribution to our understanding of historical processes in phonology—not that such discoveries are entirely new or revolutionary. Traditional historical phonology has for more than a century undertaken to account for changes by distinguishing indigenous changes from borrowed features, by adducing positional variation in the articulation of the phonemes in dealing with splits and mergers, and by pointing out parallel phonemic developments (as in the development of the long high and midvowels of ME in Early MnE).

However, while the historical interpretation of phonological events in diachronic linguistics is achieved by inference from the events, the processes themselves are directly observable in areal and social linguistics. Having fuller and more precise data at his disposal, the dialectologist is often in a position to pinpoint changes and to document the complexity of changes that ultimately lead, or may lead, to uniform results in a given dialect. Knowing not only the phonemic data—the only data directly accessible in diachronic linguistics—but also the phonic range of the several phonemes in the system, he can observe directly how phonemic splits and mergers, whether partial or comprehensive, come about. The dialectologist will therefore attach great importance to an exact phonic record of the speech of his informants.

He has no reason to fear that the phonic record will prevent him from setting up the phonemic system for each speaker, always provided that the record is ample. He will be skeptical of facile schemes that fail to make allowance for unsystematized items and fluctuations in idiolects and dialects. He will not accept an 'over-all' phonemic scheme for all varieties of American English as a scientific statement. Whether it has some pedagogical value or not is another question.

[7] The terms *North, Midland, South Midland, South,* and so forth, refer to the speech areas of the Atlantic seaboard as defined in Hans Kurath, *A Word Geography of the Eastern States* (Ann Arbor, 1949).

The Evidence for Phonemic Changes

HERBERT PENZL

I. TYPES OF PHONEMIC CHANGE

IN DIACHRONIC LINGUISTICS a great variety of phonetic changes can be observed. Scholars seem to be agreed, however, that there are only very few types of phonemic change. Prehistorical, i.e. reconstructed changes cannot be treated in the same manner as historically attested changes. Only a careful consideration of historical changes enables us to draw any conclusions regarding prehistorical changes. The problems of reconstruction should not be prematurely linked and added to the specific problems of diachronic phonemics.

§ 1.1 *Phonemic Change.* A number of changes affect only the shape of certain morphemes but not the phonemic stock. Among them we notice the loss or replacement of certain phonemes in morphemes (assimilation, dissimilation), e.g. *Tölpel* 'bumpkin' (MHG *dörpære, dörper* > *dörpel*); *Pfennig* (OHG *pfenning*); *Welt* (MHG *werlt, welt*); *Hoffart* 'arrogance' (MHG *hochvart*); *Elle* (OHG *elina*). The sequence of phonemes in a morpheme can be reversed (metathesis): *Wespe* (MHG *wefse, webse, wespe*), *Erle* 'alder' (OHG *erila, elira*). A phoneme can be added to a morpheme: *Obst* 'fruit' (MHG *obez*), *Habicht* 'hawk' (MHG *habech*), *albern* 'foolish' (MHG *alwære*), *niemand* (MHG *nieman*). All these changes could be called distributional; they do not constitute sound-change in the regular sense. Some of them may occur almost with the regularity of a sound-change at a given time in a given language, but they are not gradual, even if possibly produced unconsciously. They seem often sporadic, involving some morphemes but not others with the same structure. Analogical remodeling is a common factor in their occurrence. They may be a factor leading to a phonemic change, however, since any change in incidence or distribution may also

---

Reprinted by permission from *Studies Presented to Joshua Whatmough on His Sixtieth Birthday,* Ernst Pulgram, ed. (The Hague: Mouton and Co., 1957), 193-208.

result in a change in pattern and stock. The evidence for such distributional changes is usually plentiful and unambiguous; it does not differ from the evidence for phonemic changes which we will consider here. All observable phonetic changes in the history of a language may have some phonemic significance.[1] Thus a phonemic change is any sound-change that gradually affects the contrastive features of the phonemes, their general incidence and patterning, or their allophonic variation.

The phonemic principle makes it necessary for us to view each and every change from the point of view of the entire pattern. This is perhaps the most important new methodological demand in historical linguistics that at the same time presents a distinct advance over an earlier approach that appears too atomistic now. If we thus isolate in this paper certain phonemic changes and do not analyze their pattern impact in detail, we are aware that we are not offering an adequate description of the change. After all, we do not indicate its absolute and relative chronology, its regional origin and spread, and its probable causes either. We are concerned here with its typological classification and the evidence for its occurrence, not with any other pertinent factors.

§ 1.2 *The Phonemic Shift.* All phonemic changes may either occur in all positions or only in specific ones; the latter changes are usually called 'conditioned', the former 'unconditioned'. What is conditioned change diachronically, corresponds synchronically to conditioned allophonic variation.[2] André Martinet[3] subdivides phonemic change into (1) those that do not affect the number of distinctive features within the language, (2) those that reduce them, (3) those that increase them. Daniel Jones' 29 types of phonemic change are partly based on phonetic criteria.[4] Among attested phonemic changes we distinguish six different types: shifts, mergers (§ 1.3), splits (§ 1.4), monophonemization (§ 1.5), diphonemization (§ 1.6), phonemic loss (§ 1.7). The phonemic shift consists of the change of a phoneme of one sound-type to a phoneme of another sound-type. Any such shift may result in a whole series of interconnected changes, but the pattern adjustment may also not exceed some allophonic variation which is not recoverable historically. The change from the high back rounded vowel phoneme /u/ to a high front rounded vowel phoneme /ü/ in French, *tu, dur, duc* is an example of a

[1] R. Jakobson, "Prinzipien der historischen Phonologie," *TCLP* 4.247 ff. (1931) labeled sound-changes as 'phonologisch' or as 'ausserphonologisch'. N. van Wijk, *Mélanges van Ginneken* 94 ff., rejected this dichotomy.

[2] Charles E. Osgood and T. E. Sebeok, *Psycholinguistics* 148 (1954).

[3] *Économie des changements phonétiques* 175 (1955). Henry M. Hoenigswald, "Sound change and linguistic structure," *Language* 22.138 (1946), differentiated between: phonemic change without loss of contrast; unconditioned and conditioned mergers with loss of contrast; secondary rearrangements induced by a primary loss of contrast; borrowed contrasts.

[4] D. Jones, *The phoneme: its nature and use,* chapter 32, pp. 233-252 (1950).

shift. Another example is the change from an apical lenis spirant /þ/ to an apical lenis stop /d/ in Old High German: *ther* or *dher,* later *der*; *thing,* later *ding.* In both cases the 'terminal' phoneme is of a different type than the 'initial' one and not identical with any phoneme already in the language: neither /ü/ in French (Latin) nor /d/ in most Middle and Upper German dialects of Old High German existed before the phonemic change. In a shift the number of phonemes remains the same, since the loss of one or more units of the initial pattern seems compensated by the addition of one or more units in the terminal pattern. The formula to express a phonemic shift is: /A/ > /*x*/.[5] A. Martinet considers all phonemic changes that affect the pattern as part of a chain, which, from the point of view of the change in question, would either seem to be a 'drag-chain' or a 'push-chain'.[6] Most shifts represent what R. Jakobson called 'Umphonologisierung', i.e., a change from one phonemic distinction between two phonemes to another phonemic distinction between them.[7]

§ 1.3 *The Phonemic Merger.* Another important and most frequent type of phonemic change is the merger, the coalescence of two phonemes. This can either occur in all positions (unconditioned change) or only in some special phonetic environment (conditioned change). The result of the merger may be the exclusive occurrence of either one of the two contrasting units or the emergence of a new, possibly intermediate type. Two well-known examples for merger in the history of German are the medial and final coalescence of the two sibilants /s/ and /z/ in late Middle High German, e.g. *es* from earlier *ez* 'it' and *es* 'of it, of him', and the coalescence of the allophones of /a/ and /e/ before *i* sounds in Old High German (primary umlaut of /a/), e.g. OHG *gesti,* plural of *gast.* The phonetic identification of the initial sibilant phonemes /s/ and /z/ has been a moot question, but at any rate a single terminal phoneme /s/ results, in contrast with the other new sibilant /š/ which developed from the cluster /sk/ in Middle High German (see below § 1.5). The Old High German [e] allophones of /a/ before *i*-sounds and the [e] allophones of /e/ in its rare occurrences before *i*-sounds, e.g. in *felis* (NHG *Fels*) 'rock', *krebiz* (NHG *Krebs*) 'crab', *pelliz* (NHG *Pelz*) 'fur', merged; thus a suspension of the contrast between /a/ and /e/, in the terminology of the Prague school a 'neutralization', resulted in that position. The /e/ phoneme prevailed however. Our formulas for merger will have to be:

$$\begin{matrix} /\mathrm{A}/ \\ /\mathrm{B}/ \end{matrix} > /A/\,; \qquad \begin{matrix} /\mathrm{A}/ \\ /\mathrm{B}/ \end{matrix} > /B/\,; \qquad \begin{matrix} /\mathrm{A}/ \\ /\mathrm{B}/ \end{matrix} > /x/$$

[5] We use Roman capitals for the phoneme in the initial pattern (AB), Italic capitals for the corresponding more or less identical phonemes in the terminal pattern (*AB*), and lower case Italics (*x*) for a new terminal phoneme which is not identical with any initial phonemes.

[6] A. Martinet, "Function, structure, and sound change," *Word* 8.1ff. (1952).

[7] *TCLP* 4.255ff.

This indicates that the terminal phoneme may be either one of the two initial phonemes or a phoneme that is different from them.[8] Partial or limited merger (neutralization), e.g. before a phoneme /X/, we can express as follows:

/AX/ > /*BX*/; /BX/ > /*AX*/

This indicates the merger of /A/ and /B/ only before /X/ with the terminal prevalence of /*B*/ or /*A*/, respectively. Most mergers represent what R. Jakobson called an 'Entphonologisierung' of some distinctive feature.[9]

§ 1.4 *The Phonemic Split.* A third most important type of phonemic change is the split, a bifurcation of two phonemes out of the allophones of one initial phoneme. Striking examples are provided by the results of umlaut in late Old High German, when all rounded back vowel phonemes developed rounded front vowel phonemes from their allophones before former *i*-sounds:[10] /a/ and /ä/, /ā/ and /ǟ/, /ō/ and /ȫ/, /o/ and /ö/, /ū/ and /ǖ/, /u/ and /ü/, /au/ and /eu/, also /ë/ and /e/, e.g. MHG *maht,* pl. *mähte* (OHG *mahti*), *nāmen* (OHG *nāmun*) 'they took', *næmen* subj. (OHG *nāmin*), *schōne* adv. 'beautifully' (OHG *scōno*), *schoene* adj. 'beautiful' (OHG *scōni*), *hūt* 'skin', pl. *hiute* (OHG *hūti*), *übel* (OHG *ubil*) 'evil'. Our formula for a phonemic split is as follows:

/A/ > /*A*/
/*x*/

/*x*/ in this formula designates the new phoneme, which is often /*A'*/ from an allophone [A'] of /A/. All splits represent what R. Jakobson (see footnote 9) calls a 'Phonologisierung' (a phonemization or phonemicization).

§ 1.5 *Monophonemization.* Another phonemic change consists of the change from a cluster to a single phoneme. This often resembles a phonemic shift (§ 1.2). As examples we quote the development of a groove sibilant /š/ from an earlier cluster consisting of a slit sibilant and a velar stop (/sk/) in Middle High German and in Middle English: MHG *visch* (OHG *fisk*), ME *fish, fissh* (OE *fisc*) (see § 3.4). In English and in German the cluster /ng/ developed into a single velar nasal

[8] See Osgood-Sebeok, *loc. cit.*, for factors determining the likelihood of merger between two phones.

[9] *TCLP* 4.250ff.

[10] Herbert Penzl, "Umlaut and secondary umlaut in Old High German," *Language* 25.233ff. (1949).

phoneme /ŋ/: *singen, to sing*. The formula for such a change is as follows:

/AB/ > /*x*/

The new phoneme /*x*/ may represent /*A'*/ or /*B'*/, i.e. be the reflex of allophones [A'] or [B'] appearing in the initial cluster: e.g., /ŋ/ developed from the allophone [ŋ] of /n/ appearing before /g/ (or /k/); thus /ng/ ([ŋg]) > /ŋ/ is an example for /AB/ > /*A'*/.

§ 1.6 *Diphonemization.* A single phoneme can develop into a cluster of two phonemes: /A/ > /*XY*/. Also this change resembles a phonemic shift (§ 1.2). The terminal cluster can contain two phonemes already found in the pattern. An example for this change is the New High German diphthongization where Middle High German /ī/ became /ai/, /ū/ became /au/, /ǖ/ became /oi/: *Wein* (MHG *wīn*), *Haus* (MHG *hūs*), *Leute* (MHG *liute*) (§ 3.4).

§ 1.7 *The Phonemic Loss.* Another phonemic change is the loss of a phoneme either in some positions only or everywhere: /A/ > 0. It could be labelled 'merger with zero'.[11] As examples we can cite the Old High German loss of the phoneme /h/ in clusters as /hl/ /hr/ /hw/ /hn/, e.g. *laut* (OHG *hlūt*), *Ross* (OHG *hros*), *wer* (OHG *hwer*), *neigen* (OHG *hnīgan*), or the loss of /h/ in intervocalic position in late Middle High German: e.g. in *sehen* (§ 3.5).

The rise of a new phoneme by borrowing, e.g. the appearance of nasalized vowels in French loan-words in German (*Cousin, Bonbon*), or the adoption of /f/ in Russian, cannot be considered a counterpart to phonemic loss because the borrowing of foreign phonemes is not a sound-change from initial zero.[12]

II. EVIDENCE FOR SYNCHRONIC AND DIACHRONIC ANALYSIS

§ 2.1 *Orthographic Evidence.* In historical linguistics diachronic analysis must be preceded by synchronic analysis. The former can only be based on the comparison between two or more successive stages of a language that have been analyzed synchronically. The evidence for the synchronic and diachronic analysis is the same. There are several types of such evidence. Their careful consideration, which seems to have been somewhat neglected, is of great importance for the methodology of historical linguistics.

Orthographic evidence (§ 3) must be mentioned first. The relationship between symbol and sound, between the graphemic and the phonemic system is a basic problem in historical linguistics. Alphabetic writ-

[11] Hoenigswald, *Language* 22.139.
[12] R. Jakobson, *TCLP* 4.254,261; D. Jones, *The phoneme* §§735-739.

ing itself in its inception used to involve a certain 'phonemic' interpretation of the sounds on the part of scribes and authors, particularly if they wrote their own native language or dialect, when they would attempt to render the essential units of their phonemic system and would not be aware of allophones. Thus the use and distribution of graphemes is important evidence in synchronic analysis. The known derivation of the symbols and their original values can be used for general phonetic identifications (§ 2.5). Occasionally recorded transliterations into another alphabet, e.g. into the Cyrillic, Arabic, or some phonetic alphabet, may be helpful. Diachronic interpretations are facilitated by the observation of changes in the orthographic system, of internal orthographic fluctuation or of a modern discrepancy between symbol and pronunciation.[13] Not every change in spelling implies a change in pronunciation; e.g., the Middle English use of 'ou' for Old English 'u' is simply due to the different spelling-practice of the Anglo-Norman scribes. Not only the analysis of orthographic systems, but also the study of all deviations from them, namely of occasional spellings ('naive spellings'), provides evidence. Their synchronic analysis reveals the discrepancy between the traditional orthography and the phonemic system of its user.

The term 'occasional spellings' suggests a minority-type of orthography which occurs together with the majority-type in identical or contemporaneous texts. Occasional spellings may represent just graphical errors, e.g. dittography, mistakes in copying, or only graphical variants, which are determined by the orthographic system with which the scribe or naive writer is familiar. They may reveal historical or dialectal variants for individual words: e.g. *jest* 'just', *gould* beside *gold, loom* beside *loam*. Synchronic analysis has to screen these spellings carefully within a given text and separate them from spellings that reveal the writer's or scribe's phonemic distribution or phonemic changes (see below § 4).[14] Diachronic analysis centers on the relevant differences between the conventional orthography and the observed individual deviations.

§ 2.2 *Orthoëpic Evidence.* Statements by grammarians at different times offer one type of evidence to the synchronic and diachronic analyst that orthography itself cannot supply (§ 5): phonetic identifications of the values designated by the symbols. Certain characteristics of Latin, Greek, Sanskrit sounds can be ascertained from the descriptions of native grammarians.[15] With the notable exception of the First Grammatical Treatise written about Old Icelandic phonemes in the middle of the twelfth cen-

[13] C. L. Wrenn, "The value of spelling as evidence," *TPS* 1943, 14ff. speaks of the 'diachronicness' of English orthography (p. 16).

[14] Herbert Penzl, *Language* 18.148-151 (1942). R. E. Zachrisson, *Pronunciation of English vowels 1400–1700* 52ff. (1913) distinguished between "phonetic doublets" (historical variants), "irregular spellings due to miswriting, analogical transference, mechanical transference of symbols", and "phonetic spellings", which he defined as "deviations from the traditional spelling by which a sound-change is denoted."

[15] E. H. Sturtevant, *The pronunciation of Greek and Latin*[2] § 5 (1940).

tury, evidence of this kind is not found for the Germanic languages until we reach early modern times. Then grammarians describe foreign sounds in terms of their native language; they describe the correct pronunciation and dialectal usage as to spelling and pronunciation; they describe the correlation sound : symbol to facilitate the teaching of reading and spelling. They are often interested in normalizing or reforming the orthographic evidence mentioned above (§ 2.1). They are usually themselves decisively influenced by the orthography.

Occasional and systematic representations of speech or dialect characteristics by deviant spellings in literary works can provide evidence equivalent to the observations of grammarians, e.g. the rendering of rustic American English in Lowell's *Biglow Papers.* The German schoolmasters' transcriptions of German dialects in conventional orthography for the Deutscher Sprachatlas as well as scholars' phonetic or phonemic field-notes or the phonetic recordings of a speech-atlas can also be interpreted by what Charles F. Hockett[16] called the analyst's 'philological method'.

§ 2.3 *Metrical Evidence.* Evidence is supplied by the structure of lines of poetry, either by the appearance of stressed or quantitatively marked syllables in a determined sequence, by the pattern of alliteration, or by the demands of assonance and rime (§ 6). Synchronic analysis of texts provides a description of these metrical patterns; diachronic analysis compares their observed differences at different times.

Similar to the evidence of alliteration, assonance, and rime is that furnished by puns in literary works. Puns may be homonymic or only show a partial correspondence in pronunciation.[17]

§ 2.4 *Comparative Evidence.* Comparative data provide important evidence for the analyst. Internal comparison considers distributional and structural facts, or other parallel sound-changes of the language itself. We often assume a symmetrical structure of the phonemic pattern and draw inferences from correlated features.[18]

The comparison may also concern the corresponding historical values of other dialects of the same language or of related languages within the same branch or within the same language family. We can call this 'syncomparative' analysis. The comparison may involve a contrastive treatment of later attested stages of the same or related languages: this constitutes 'diacomparative' evidence. It may pertain to the values that could have developed out of a reconstructed system of protophonemes and thus be 'protocomparative', which is actually COMPARATIVE in the narrowest sense. Also all modern dialectal values in their present areal

[16] *Language* 24.119f. (1948).

[17] H. Kökeritz, *Shakespeare's pronunciation* 53-157 (1953); Sturtevant, *Pron.* § 10.

[18] Sturtevant, *Pron.* § 11: "Having discovered, therefore, that Latin ē was closer than ĕ, we expect to find ō closer than ŏ."

distribution can be interpreted diachronically as 'neocomparative' material. Significant alternations at a later stage will often provide comparative evidence for an earlier stage of the same language or dialect. All diachronic interpretation implies a comparison, of course. The comparative evidence reveals that diachronic considerations can be fruitful also for supplementing or revising synchronic analyses. The terminal value can be used to determine the initial values. All historical comparative data consist in turn of orthographic, orthoëpic, metrical, and contact material. The method of direct contact or field-work can only be applied to neocomparative data.

§ 2.5 *Contact Evidence.* While syncomparative evidence concerns simultaneous or roughly simultaneous correspondences in related languages, further data for analysis are provided by the actual interchange, the loan and borrowing of words from one language to the other. The adoption of the alphabet or single letters of another language yields important evidence for the initial values linked to the letters. Accurate transliterations of words or sentences into different writing systems provide a welcome key to the corresponding values of the symbols (see above § 2.1). Loans based partly or totally on the written form or presumably provided by a third language as an intermediary must, of course, be interpreted differently from direct borrowings based on the spoken form in the contact between speakers of the two languages. The actual borrowing of foreign phonemes is a rare occurrence (§ 1.7). Ordinarily, we can observe in such direct loans the rendering of the foreign phoneme by corresponding native phonemes. In historical linguistics, of course, the graphic reflexes of the correspondences have to be subjected to synchronic analysis. Under favorable circumstances both the initial and the terminal values of phonemic changes that are involved in the borrowings can be isolated by diachronic interpretation of such reflexes in a foreign pattern.

III. ORTHOGRAPHIC EVIDENCE AND PHONEMIC CHANGES

§ 3.1 *Orthography and Shifts.* The orthographic system expresses all distributional changes, since they concern the incidence of phonemes, for which symbols are available (§ 1.1). It often indicates phonemic shifts (§ 1.2). The Old High German change from /þ/ to /d/ is clearly rendered, particularly in initial position, by the replacement of 'th' or 'dh' by the letter 'd': *der* for earlier *ther* or *dher.* Originally the digraph which Latin scribes used to transliterate the Greek theta was employed to render the OHG apical spirant unknown to Latin; the prompt rendering of the new OHG value may be due to the convenient availability of the symbol 'd' which agrees more or less with its Latin value. The French phonemic shift from /u/ to /ü/ in *tu, dur*[19] is not reflected by any orthographic change: the initial symbol 'u' remains constant.

[19] A. G. Haudricourt and A. G. Juilland, *Essai pour une histoire structurale de phonétisme français* 100-113 (1949).

§ 3.2 *Orthography and Mergers.* Orthography indicates phonemic mergers and their results, e.g. by noncontrastive use of two formerly contrasting symbols or by the use of one symbol instead of two initial ones. The terminal use of one symbol only indicates the prevalence of the phoneme initially designated by it. The OHG spellings *gesti* 'guests' (sing. *gast*), *eltir* 'older' (*alt* 'old') with the 'e' symbol as found in *herza* 'heart', *helfan* 'help' indicate the merger of /e/ and /a/ before *i* and the replacement of /a/ in that position. The merger of /s/ and /z/ in medial and final positions in late MHG was first shown by the indiscriminate use of 's' and 'z' and their graphic variants.[20] Reverse or inverse spellings ('umgekehrte Schreibungen') always indicate a phonemic coalescence (see § 4.2).

§ 3.3 *Orthography and Splits.* Orthography gives often belated recognition to a phonemic split (§ 1.4) by the creation of new symbols derived from the old ones or by consistently contrastive use of two available symbols. In Middle High German most scribes use special diacritics or digraphs to render the new umlaut phonemes: e.g. *ä æ oe ü* in *mahte, næmen, schoene, übel.* The late OHG merger of the diphthong /iu/ and the umlaut of /ū/ provided a digraph symbol 'iu' for /ǖ/: *hiute* (OHG *hūti*) 'skins' like *hiute* (OHG *hiutu*) 'today'. This practice is already found in the orthographic system of Notker III. The phonemic split of Old English *k* was expressed by a contrastive use of the two available symbols 'k' and 'c' in some manuscripts, e.g. in that of the Rushworth glosses to the gospel of St. Mathew; *kining, cild,* since 1200 by the symbols 'k (c)' and 'ch', respectively: *king, child.*[21]

§ 3.4 *Orthography and Cluster Changes.* The development of clusters into single phonemes and of single phonemes into clusters is often indicated by a change in orthographic practice. Middle English spellings *s ss sch sh ssh* for historical /sk/ indicate its change to a single phoneme, similarly such Middle High German spellings as *sch sg sh ss* (*s*): e.g. *sharp* (*sarp, ssarp, scharp*), *fissh* MHG *scharpf* (OHG *scarpf*).[22] The change from /ng/ to /ŋ/ is not expressed by the orthography; the digraph 'ng' remains in German and in English. The New High German diphthongization is indicated by the replacement of 'i' 'u' 'iu' symbols from the 12th century on by the digraphs 'ei' 'ou (au)' 'eu', respectively:[23] *wein* MHG *wīn*), *hous, haws, hauss* (MHG *hūs*), *leute* (MHG *liute*) (§ 1.6). A similar development in Early Modern English is not reflected

[20] O. Behaghel, *Geschichte der deutschen Sprache*[5] § 380.7 (1928); V. Michels, *Mittelhochdeutsches Elementarbuch*[3,4] § 184 (1921); V. Moser, *Frühneuhochdeutsche Grammatik* 3.3 §. 146 (1951; Friedrich Kauffman, *Geschichte der schwäbischen Mundart* 210 (1890).

[21] Herbert Penzl, "The phonemic split of Germanic *k* in Old English," *Language* 23.34-42 (1947).

[22] R. Jordan, *Handbuch der mittelenglischen Grammatik* § 181 (1934); V. Michels § 109; Karl Weinhold, *Mittelhochdeutsche Grammatik*[2] §§ 206, 210 (1883).

[23] K. Weinhold §§ 105ff., 118; Michels § 91; Kauffmann §§ 76, 82.

by any change of the orthography: *wine* (ME *wīn*), *house* (ME *hous, hūs*). The French change from clusters of vowel plus nasal to nasalized vowel phonemes is not shown by the orthography, which still retains the digraph spelling: e.g. *danser, pain, bon.*

§ 3.5 *Orthography and Phonemic Loss.* The orthography usually reflects the loss of a phoneme. The OHG loss of initial /h/ is indicated by spellings without 'h' (§ 1.7): *nigan, lut, ros, wer.*[24] The MHG phonemic loss of intervocalic /h/ is not reflected by a regular orthographic loss, only by occasional spellings (§ 4): *sehen* (MHG *sehen*), *Vieh* (MHG *vihe*), *Stahl* (MHG *stahel*).[25] But the Modern German 'h' with the value zero signifying vowel-length, e.g. in *gehen* (MHG *gēn*), *mahlen* (MHG *maln*) 'grind', indicates this postvocalic 'merger with zero' orthographically. It constitutes a reverse spelling (§ 3.2). The Late Latin loss of /h/ in all positions is also reflected by the alternation of the symbol 'h' and zero: e.g. *onurem, hedernam.*[26]

The borrowing of foreign phonemes is usually accompanied by the adoption of foreign orthographic symbols: e.g. *Cousin, Bonbon* in Modern German with French orthography.

IV. OCCASIONAL SPELLINGS AND PHONEMIC CHANGES

§ 4.1 *Occasional Spellings and Shifts.* Occasional or naive spellings (§ 2.1) render most readily all distributional changes found in colloquial speech: e.g. such Early Modern English and American English spellings as *nex* 'next', *husbon* 'husband', *myssomer* 'midsummer', *wrytyn* 'writing', *orphants* 'orphans', *meten* 'meeting', *of* 'have'.[27] Some of these spellings show loss (or addition) of phonemes in fast, unstressed forms. The *-en, -yn* spellings indicate the change of /ŋ/ (/ng/?) to /n/ in the suffix *-ing*. The traditional orthography usually reflects the forms of slow, careful speech.

Medieval scribes or copyists sometimes unintentionally, sometimes intentionally but inconsistently, substitute symbols either representing their own phonemes or at least their usual orthographic practice for those found in the original text. We find substitutions of the symbol 'd' for a presumable 'th' or 'dh' in the OHG Monsee Fragments, the Freising MS of Otfrid, in the MS of 'Christ and the Samaritan Woman'. This reveals the diffusion of the phonemic shift from /þ/ to /d/ in OHG dialects: e.g. *thaz, ther* and *daz, der* (Christ and the Samaritan Woman); *dhuo* and *duo* 'da' (Monsee).

[24] W. Braune and W. Mitzka, *Althochdeutsche Grammatik*[8] § 153 (1953).

[25] Moser, *Frühnhd. Gramm.* 1.1 § 10 (1929).

[26] R. L. Politzer, "The phonemic interpretation of Late Latin Orthography," *Language* 27.151-154 (1951).

[27] H. C. Wyld, *A history of modern colloquial English*[3] 69f., 289f. (1937); George Ph. Krapp, *The English language in America* 2.215, 232 (1925).

§ 4.2 *Occasional Spellings and Mergers.* Occasional spellings indicate general (unconditioned) or limited (conditioned) phonemic merger. They may do this preceding a general orthographic change. They may reveal the phonemic change the orthography does not show through any adjustment. They may reveal a dialectal change that is not reflected by the established spelling, which rather shows the phonemic pattern of another dialect or of the standard language. Graphic confusion of the symbols 's' and 'z' in late Middle High German and Early New High German manuscripts preceded the orthographic readjustment by the general adoption of 's' symbols (§ 3.2). All reverse spellings are really occasional at first (§ 3.5). Such spellings as OHG 'hr' for /r/ indicate the loss of the /h/: e.g. *hrinnit* for *rinnit* 'flows'.[28] Occasional spellings readily show the merger with already existing phonemes: e.g. the merger of /sj/ and /š/ in Modern English is shown by such 15th century spellings as *conschens* 'conscience', *ishu* 'issue', *condishon* 'condition', *pashens* 'patience'.[29] Such 1st century forms in inscriptions indicate an early substandard merger of *ae* and *e* in the Latin of Rome and Pompey: *etati* 'aetati', *maeae* 'meae', *saenatus* 'senatus', *Clarie* 'Clariae' (dat.).[30] Numerous occasional spellings indicate the merger of the rounded front vowels /ö/ /ü/ and their unrounded counterparts /e/ /i/ in High German dialects since the middle of the 12th century. 'e' 'i' are written for the historical umlauts: *werter* 'Wörter', *gresser* 'grösser', *yber* 'über', *vnglick* 'Unglück', *anzinden* 'anzünden.' Also reverse spellings are numerous: *bösser* 'besser', *moer* 'Meer', *schüff* 'Schiff', *kürche* 'Kirche'; some of the 'ö' and 'ü' spellings may indicate new roundings or hyperforms.[31]

Phonemic splits are not as readily reflected by occasional spellings, since no contrastive symbols are ordinarily available, but they must have preceded a general orthographic adjustment wherever it took place (§ 3.3).

V. ORTHOËPIC EVIDENCE

Certain morpheme-bound (distributional) changes such as additions, omissions, or substitutions of phonemes are described in the statements of grammarians, and illustrative forms are often quoted as vulgarisms or dialectal. Elphinston (1765, 1787), e.g., 'generally' heard *Lunnon* for *London;* he called *proddestant* 'protestant', *pardner* 'partner' London vulgarisms. Noah Webster in *Dissertations on the English Language* (1789) attacked the New England pronunciation *kiow* for *cow*.[32]

Orthoëpic evidence reveals the occurrence of the various types of phonemic changes. The statements of grammarians in the Early New

[28] Braune-Mitzka § 153, Anm. 1.

[29] H. C. Wyld, *HMCE,* pp. 69, 293.

[30] Sturtevant §§ 4, 132; F. Sommer, *Handbuch der lat. Laut- und Formenlehre* § 61 (1948); Max Niedermann, *Historische Lautlehre des Lateinischen*[3] § 31 (1953).

[31] V. Moser 1.1 § 65f., F. Kauffmann 79, 81; H. Penzl, *Language* 32.354f. (1956).

[32] Wyld, *HMCE* 302, 313; Krapp 2.210.

High German period reveal that the Middle High German contrast between /s/ and /z/ has survived medially after long vowels and diphthongs in some dialects as one between a lenis written 's' and a fortis written 'ss' 'sz': e.g. Standard German *reisen* 'travel', *reissen* 'tear'.[33] The phonemic development of the cluster /ng/ into a velar nasal /ŋ/ is confirmed by Valentin Ickelsamer in his *Teutsche Grammatica* (1537), who deplores the orthography 'ng', since neither sound is completely heard in *Engel angel franck* but rather a fusion ('zusammen schmeltzung').[34] Orthoëpic evidence is obviously of particular importance, whenever the orthography fails to indicate a phonemic change. The Early Modern English change of Middle English /ī/ and /ū/ into diphthongs is also not expressed by the orthography but attested by descriptions of British grammarians like Salisbury (1547, 1567), Hart (1569), Gill (1621), and of French grammarians like Bellot (1580), Mason (1622), Festeau (1693).[35] Some of the latter sources clearly indicate a merger of Middle English /ī/ and Middle English /oi/ during their time (see below § 6).

VI. METRICAL EVIDENCE

The synchronic analysis of the distribution of stress and quantity is aided by the rigid pattern of some verse lines (§ 2.3). For the recognition of phonemic changes the analysis of rime is of particular importance. Even assonances may yield some phonemic information. Such Otfrid rimes as *quad*: *sprah* and *ward*: *tharf* have been interpreted as indicating that his final 'd' still represents a spirant rather than a stop; thus the shift from /þ/ to /d/ has not been completed finally in spite of the misleading orthography.[36] The impure rime *hart*: *anbracht* of the Nürnberg poet Jakob Ayrer (1543-1605)[37] probably indicates a uvular *r*. The rime *zit*: *geleit* by Heinrich von dem Türlin (1215) may still be impure but it reveals the diphthongization of /ī/.[38]

On the whole, only poetry with predominantly pure rimes can reveal phonemic shifts, mergers, and splits, since only their occurrence or nonoccurrence in rime position can indicate sameness or difference. The nonoccurrence of certain types of rimes indicates, if statistics make mere chance unlikely, a phonemic split or a phonemic distinction; the occurrence of rimes indicates phonemic merger. Rimes may not always reflect the pattern of the poet's own dialect. Isolated rime-words may represent historical variants. Some rimes may reflect an earlier phonemic stage

[33] Moser 3.3 § 146, Anm. 9.

[34] Johannes Müller, *Quellenschriften und Geschichte des deutschsprachlichen Unterrichts bis zur Mitte des 16. Jhd.* 139 (1882).

[35] Zachrisson, *Pron. of Engl. vowels,* 129ff., 205ff.

[36] Braune-Mitzka § 167, Anm. 4; J. Franck, *Altfränkische Grammatik* § 92 (1909); but see W. Wilmanns, *Deutsche Grammatik*³ 1. § 83, Anm. 1 (1911).

[37] Herbert Penzl, *Language* 18.299-302 (1942): review of W. A. Kozumplik, *The phonology of Jacob Ayrer's language based on his rhymes.*

[38] Michels § 91.

of the language (traditional rimes), particularly if the orthography still provides rimes for the eye: e.g. Modern English *hand*: *wand*. The results of more recent splits or coalescences may be rarely reflected by rimes if the orthography seems to disagree: such French rimes as *nous:loup, talent:grands* are considered incorrect; rimes of the *water:quarter* type are very infrequent in Modern British English.[39] Another type of rime may reflect the phonemic pattern of another, presumably more prestigious dialect or the standard language (literary rimes). The analyst will have to decide whether any given rimes of a poet are genuinely dialectal or just traditional or literary. Middle High German rimes of the classical period reveal what the orthography with its uniform symbol 'e' does not indicate: there are two short *e* phonemes in the language which do not rime. Only in certain dialects and in certain positions, e.g. in Bavarian before *b d g t,* do /e/, the result of the historical umlaut, and /ë/, the old Germanic *e* sound, merge, as rimes show: *heben* 'lift': *lëben* 'live'; *stete* 'place': *bëte* 'prayer, request'.[40] Classical Middle High German shows no rimes of final *-z* and *-s;* they appear in the 13th century, e.g. Meier Helmbrecht shows *hūs* 'house': *ūz* 'out'.[41] This indicates the merger of the two sibilants in final position. Rimes confirm the orthographic and orthoëpic evidence for a merger of the reflexes of ME /ī/ and ME /oi/ since the 16th century: *swine:groin* (Shakespeare); *smile:coil* (Suckling); *toil:isle* (Waller); *join:divine:line* (Pope).[42]

VII. COMPARATIVE EVIDENCE

§ 7.1 *Proto-Comparative Data.* All prehistoric reconstructed phonemic changes are exclusively based on proto-comparative evidence, e.g. the Germanic Consonant Shift or the Old High German Consonant Shift. The initial values of a phonemic change, e.g. of 'th' in Old High German (which became /d/), can sometimes be established by comparative evidence. Syncomparative evaluation reveals the existence of an interdental or postdental, nonsibilant, voiceless spirant in cognate morphemes in Old Icelandic, Gothic, Old English, Old Frisian, Old Saxon, Old High German: e.g. OIc. *þjōfr,* Go. *þiubs,* OE *þēof,* OFrs. *thiāf,* OS *thiof,* OHG (Franc.) *thiob* 'thief'. This evidence can be used for the reconstruction of a proto-phoneme *þ, a voiceless, nonsibilant, interdental or postdental spirant. The umlaut variation of velar vowels in the Germanic languages can be compared, and postulated for the prehistoric stage. The feasibility of such a reconstruction confirms by its consistency the assumption of initial palatal allophones of long or short *a o u* before *i*-sounds in

[39] O. Jespersen, *A Modern English grammar* 1.13.27 (1909); C. L. Wrenn, *TPS* 1943, 34-37; H. C. Wyld, *Short history of English*³ § 214 (1927).

[40] K. Zwierzina, *ZfdA* 44.249ff. (1900).

[41] A. Schirokauer, *PBB* 47.97-100 (1922).

[42] Wyld, *SHE* § 270; *HMCE,* pp. 224, 249-251.

the Germanic languages. Reconstructed proto-phonemes can support the results of historical synchronic and diachronic analyses.

§ 7.2 *Diacomparative and Neocomparative Data.* Diachronic analysis presupposes 'diacomparative' data from different periods, preferably within the same dialect or language but by no means excluding available allotopic evidence. Other phonemic changes can furnish evidence. The common dialectal change of *-ing* to *-in* makes the initial value [ŋ] more likely than [ŋg], thus provides evidence for the change from the cluster to a single nasal phoneme.

Evidence from modern dialectal conditions and from modern areal distribution, i.e. 'neocomparative' material (§ 2.4) is of special importance, since it can be directly observed in the field, not only through its written reflexes. We can compare the modern sounds and their relation to modern orthographic symbols to the earlier symbols and their presumable sound-values. We find, e.g., that Modern French orthography still has the symbol 'u' in *tu dur,* which is pronounced as [ü]: this definitely proves the completion of the phonemic shift from /u/ to /ü/. The fact that Modern German 's' is pronounced like a dorsal or like an apical sibilant at the present time has been used for phonetic identification attempts of the respective values of OHG and MHG 'z' and 's'. Modern German and Modern English 'ng' are pronounced like a single velar nasal in final position: *sing.* But English shows a morphophonemic variation between the single sound and the cluster in such sets as *long* [ŋ], *longer* [ŋg], and it contrasts *finger* with the cluster and *singer* from *sing* with the simple nasal. Thus modern pronunciations confirm the assumed terminal values of phonemic changes, while sometimes their relation to the modern orthographic symbols or an internal phonemic alternation throws light on earlier or initial values. Neocomparative evidence can show the completion of phonemic shifts, splits, and mergers, also the presence of foreign phonemes of marginal status (§ 1.7). The modern areal distribution can also sometimes indicate which values are terminal and which initial or, as it is usually stated, which are archaic and which innovations. This modern dialectal diffusion and differentiation has been used to postulate intermediate stages of a sound-change, but this seems more of a problem of historical reconstruction, which we shall not take up here.

VIII. EVIDENCE FROM CONTACT BETWEEN LANGUAGES

It is tempting to look for proof of a completed shift of French /u/ to /ü/ among French loan-words in Middle High German and Middle English, since the orthography does not indicate the phonemic shift. MHG forms like *natiure* (OF *nature*), *aventiure* (OF *aventure*), *creatiure* (OF *creature*), *hürten* (*hurten*) (OF *hurter*) 'attack, push forward', *kabütze* (OF *capuce*) 'monk's hood' reveal by the spellings 'iu' (for /*x*/) and 'ü' rounded palatal vowels. Only the western dialects of Middle English had a sound phonetically identical with the French sound. The diphthong /iu/ written 'ew' 'eu' renders French 'u' in *glew, mewe, deuk*;[43] early ME *hurten, hirten, herten* renders French *hurter,* and Modern English /i/ is found in unstressed syllables in *minute, lettuce, conduit,* /ī/ in *pedigree* from *pied de grue.* Thus also the English evidence points to a rounded palatal vowel, and indicates the completion of the shift to /ü/ in French.

The adoption of certain orthographic symbols (§ 2.5) can throw light on the values in both languages. The use of the OHG symbol 'z' to render the Old Slovenian sibilants *s z,* but of the symbol 's' to render Old Slovenian sibilants *š ž* in the Freising documents[44] proves that the phonetic differences between the OHG sibilants /z/ and /s/ did not consist in voice participation or fortis and lenis articulation but rather in the manner and place of articulation. The MHG reflexes 's' and 'z' of Old French *s* and *c* in loan-words reveal the phonemic contrast between the two sibilants but admit of no specific phonetic identifications or conclusions because of the ambiguity of the MHG 'z' symbol: *birsen* (OF *berser*) 'to hunt', *garzûn* (OF *garçon*) 'page'.

Sometimes we can be more specific in our synchronic and diachronic analyses. E. H. Sturtevant[45] has pointed out that OE *stræt, strēt* from Latin *(uia) strāta* has preserved the dental stop *t* better than most Romance languages and reveals the long quantity of the Latin stem vowel. OHG *keisur* from Latin *caesar* suggests a late diphthongal pronunciation of 'ae' as the basis for the OHG sound value. Thus, evidence through contact between languages can be valuable for phonetic identifications, which other evidence supplies even less readily.

IX. CONCLUSIONS

The innumerable phonetic changes found in the history of languages represent not more than six types of phonemic change, which could even be further reduced to these three major types: phonemic shift (including cluster changes); phonemic merger (including phonemic loss); phonemic split. All reconstructed sound-changes and their special problems have been excluded from our consideration here, since we are at first concerned with methodological clarification, which must come from the synchronic analysis of both the initial and the terminal values of historical phonemic changes and their diachronic interpretation. Only one major aspect of phonemic change has been dealt with: its evidence. The various types of evidence have been analyzed as to how they can reveal the various types of phonemic change. Orthography and its deviations

[43] Karl Luick, *Historische Grammatik der englischen Sprache* § 412 (1921); Jespersen *MEG* 1.3.815; Karl Brunner, *Die englische Sprache* 1.156f., 241 (1950).

[44] W. Braune, *PBB* 1.527-534; also Primus Lessiak, *Beiträge zur Geschichte des deutschen Konsonantismus* 83ff. (1933).

[45] *Pronunc.* § § 3c, 130e.

(the occasional spellings) reveal shifts and mergers but they indicate often only belatedly phonemic splits. Orthoëpic evidence is often tied to the orthography but can reveal all phonemic changes, even specific phonetic values. Evidence from rimes is sometimes particularly useful in detecting phonemic mergers and splits. Among the comparative evidence not proto-comparative reconstruction, but rather data from the structure of the language and from other sound-changes as well as from present-day dialects or the standard language (neo-comparative data) throw light on historical shifts, mergers, and splits. The evidence from loan-words can sometimes reveal shifts where orthography and orthoëpic evidence fail to provide satisfactory data.

We cannot expect that all types of evidence can be found for each phonemic change within the history of a language. It is necessary, however, to make use of all available evidence and to correlate its data. Interpretation and even speculation has often taken the place of the missing data. It is imperative that the description of each assumed phonemic change should contain a discussion of the evidence, its type, scope, and conclusiveness.

A Note on Old High German Umlaut

W. FREEMAN TWADDELL

IT IS GENERALLY AGREED that a group of modifications of vowels and diphthongs known collectively as umlaut occurred in connection with a following palatal element, *i, ī,* or *j*; and that the modifications begin to be represented orthographically in MHG, but not in OHG, except for the mutation of short *a*.

A difficulty arises from the fact that, in large measure, the *i, ī,* or *j* which 'caused' the umlauting was no longer present in MHG. We are faced with two alternative interpretations: either the umlaut occurred after the disappearance of the condition which caused it—a patent absurdity—or the umlaut occurred in OHG times but for some reason was not recorded orthographically until centuries later.

There is general agreement that the differences caused by umlaut existed in OHG, that however only the umlaut of short *a* was represented in the writing.[1] And there have been attempts to answer the question: Why, if the umlaut changes occurred in OHG, were they not represented until MHG, except in the case of short *a*? It has been suggested[2] that the phonetic differences due to umlaut were inconsiderable in OHG times, too inconsiderable to call for orthographical representation. This suggestion leaves the essential problem unsolved, for it entails as a corollary the unsupported and inherently improbable assumption that the difference became considerable only after the disappearance of the factor which had caused the original 'slight' differences. A variant of this type of answer is an explanation in terms of a delayed mediate

---

Reprinted with permission of The Regents of the University of Wisconsin, from *Monatshefte für deutschen Unterricht* 30.177-81 (1938), the University of Wisconsin Press.

[1] Cf.: Behaghel, *Gesch. d. d. Spr.* (5) §253; Braune, *Ahd. Gram.* (3) §51; Paul, *Mhd. Gram.* (10) §40. a 1; Priebsch and Collinson, *The German Language* II. I B.8; Prokosch, *Outline of Germ. Hist. Gram.* p. 51; Schade, *Ahd. Gram.* §§47,63; Sütterlin, *Nhd. Gram.* I. 1. 5. a. A concise account of the history of investigation is presented by Jellinek, *Die Erforschung der indogermanischen Sprachen,* II. *Germanisch* (Streitberg, Michels, Jellinek), 1936, pp. 381-395.

[2] E.g., Braune, Paul, *op. cit.*

palatalization through intervening consonants: The *i, ī,* or *j* is supposed to have palatalized the preceding consonant or consonants, which, having acquired a palatal articulation, subsequently palatalized the preceding vowel. This explanation has several serious weaknesses: It implies that the palatalization of the consonants, originally dependent upon the following *i, ī,* or *j,* became an independent phonetic characteristic (though never indicated orthographically), and survived the depalatalization or loss of the following *i, ī,* or *j.* The allegedly palatalized consonants would have to retain their palatalization long enough to palatalize the preceding vowel; and then they would have to lose their palatalization, since the phonetic history of German shows no traces of a differential treatment of palatalized and non-palatalized consonants. This is in itself a highly improbable sequence of combinatory charges. There is the further difficulty of imagining any chain of combinatory changes which involves a succession of regressive palatalizations in *trahani, aruzzi,* or *hawi.* The most serious practical objection is of course the complete lack of any evidence for such mediate palatalizations; the only reason why anyone should have thought of such a rationale was the need to explain the delay in orthographical representation of umlaut. It is, in short, an explanation with no basis in objective evidence—a purely *ad hoc* hypothesis. Another suggested answer[3] is the argument that the Latin alphabet did not supply the required symbols. But the MHG scribes were able to invent symbols; and they knew the same Latin alphabet as the OHG scribes, so far as the number of symbols is concerned. If the Latin alphabet was inadequate in the 9th century, it was similarly inadequate in the 13th; if new symbols were invented in the 13th, they could have been invented in the 9th.

Let us consider the umlauts which are not regularly indicated in OHG, taking *u* as a paradigm. We note the following phonetic developments:[4]

Uxi — [yxi]
Uxxi — [uxxi]
Uxa — [uxa]

Then [y] is the phonetic form of sound-type U, when followed by -xi. [y] always represents U before -xi, and never represents any other sound-

[3] E.g., Behaghel, Schade, *op. cit.*

[4] A capital letter is used to represent a sound-type, which is that of the stressed vowel to be considered in connection with umlaut. Thus U represents OHG *u* at the beginning of the divergent developments due to umlaut; x represents a consonant or consonant group which permits phonetic mutation of the preceding vowel; xx a consonant group which inhibits umlaut, temporarily or permanently; -i represents the umlaut-inducing elements *i, ī, j;* -a represents any other suffixal element. Vowel-symbols in square brackets indicate the actual phonetic form of a given sound-type in a given phonetic environment.

type. Hence [y] and [u] can never occur in a similar phonetic environment; they are the two complementary representatives of the general sound-type U. [y] and [u] represent two aspects of U, dependent upon the phonetic environment. If the phonetic environment is orthographically indicated, the phonetic representative of U (either [y] or [u]) is automatically indicated. When the OHG scribe wrote *uxi,* the OHG reader had to pronounce the vowel as [y], for the written symbol in this -xi environment had to be interpreted as indicating the fronted variety of U.

It is indeed conceivable that the speaker of OHG was unaware of the phonetic difference between [y] and [u], or at most regarded them as slightly different forms of the 'same vowel', U.

In this earlier phase, the nature of the vowel and the phonetic environment were so correlated that the environment was the determining, primary factor, the independent variable; and the nature of the vowel was secondary, the dependent variable. It was the difference between -xi and -xa which determined the difference between [y] and [u].—This is the definition of the conditions of umlaut.

But when the post-tonic vowels fall together to [ə][5] then an entirely new set of relations obtains. In this later phase, the old relationships between [y] and -xi, between [u] and -xa, can no longer exist. For both -xi and -xa have been replaced by -xə. We have accordingly arrived at a state in which our three formulae must be represented:

Uxi — [yxi] — [yxə]
Uxxi — [uxxi] — [uxxə]
Uxa — [uxa] — [uxə]

As between the first and third of these formulae, the difference [y/u], which had originally been dependent upon and secondary to the difference [-i/-a], has now become an independent and autonomous difference. In the terminology of the Cercle Linguistique de Prague, the phonetic opposition [y/u] has been 'phonologized'. The result is a new sound-type, Y. Instead of the earlier status, in which [y] and [u] were representatives of two aspects of U, dependent upon phonetic environment, [y] and [u] are now representatives of two different sound-types, Y and U, which occur independently of phonetic environment.

In this phase, then, our formulae must be interpreted as

[yxə] representing Yxə
[uxxə] representing Uxxə
[uxə] representing Uxə

The application to our problem is plain. In the earlier phase, as long as -i [that is: *i, ī, j*] remained distinct from other suffixal vowels, then there

[5] Or, for that matter, to [i].

would be no need, indeed no occasion, to record the phonetic difference between [y] and [u]. For, in that phase, the difference between [y] and [u] was not the significant difference; it was a secondary difference, dependent upon and induced by the difference between -i and -a.

As soon as the difference between -i and -a has ceased to be significant then (and not until then) does the difference between [y] and [u] become a significant difference, which must be represented orthographically. What is here paradigmatically and over-simply referred to as the dephonologization of the difference -i/-a was in reality of course a series of processes: [-j] was lost or assimilated earlier than the weakening of [-i] to [-ə]; many of the [ī] suffix vowels were long maintained. There must have been a period in which the opposition [y/u] was in part independent (where [-j] had been lost) and in part dependent (where [-i] remained). The failure to record immediately the [y/u] opposition in the former cases was a natural orthographical conservatism, since such cases constituted a minority of the occurrences of [y], and were pretty completely restricted to certain morphological classes and functions,[6] with related forms still displaying [-i]: e.g., infinitive of weak verbs I and related finite forms. Further, the loss of [-j] and the weakening of [-i] occupied appreciable periods of time, and we must assume fluctuations of usage, local, individual, and probably even within the speech of one individual. Not until a considerable majority of the occurrences of [y] were definitely independent of phonetic environment was the phonologization of [y/u] sufficiently valid to call for orthographical representation.

According to this rationale of OHG umlaut, there is nothing surprising about the absence of orthographical representation of [y, ø], etc. in OHG. Indeed, the failure to represent these conditional variants of the sound-types U, O, etc. is entirely natural. To have represented them would have been an act of supererogation, of orthographical pedantry, parallel to an attempt at representing orthographically the various phonetic forms of the sound-type K in modern English and German, or of the sound-type CH in German *Frauchen: rauchen.*[7]

In following this line of argument, we encounter however one major difficulty, which is the reverse of the usual one. For, if we account for the failure to represent the umlauts of *u, o,* etc. as above, we are faced with the necessity of accounting for the fact that the umlaut of short *a* is represented in the OHG orthography.

In dealing with the umlaut of short *a*, we have to distinguish three lines of development:

[6] Similar to the status of *ch* in *Frauchen / rauchen:* see L. Bloomfield, "German ç and x," *Le maître phonétique* (1930) 27f.

[7] A similar phonological process (though with a different orthographical outcome) in Russian is described by Trubetzkoy, *Archiv für vergleichende Phonetik* 1.144.

Axi — [exi]
A*x*i — [æ*x*i][8]
Axa — [axa]

As between the second and third formulae here, with [æ] and [a], we have a relation analogous to that between [y] and [u]. The difference [æ/a] is merely phonetic in the earlier phase, but is phonologized subsequently, and appears as the so-called 'secondary' umlaut.

With respect to the first formula, Axi, however, a different relation exists. The [e]-aspect of sound-type A was phonetically rather similar to a phonetic aspect [ɛ] of a different sound-type, E. Further, this [ɛ]-representative of sound-type E appeared in another phonetic environment, as in *erda*.—This is the only phonetic environment in which sound-type E can historically be expected, because of the earlier shift of *e* to *i* before *i*, etc.

The phonetic similarity of [ɛ] (from E) and [e] (from A) would then have had a surprising consequence. It must be remembered that the [e] of *gesti* was a closer vowel than the [ɛ] of *erda*. The complex of sounds representing the old E and A sound-types would then have assumed this form:

[exi] from A
[ɛxa] from E
[æ*x*i] from A
[axa] from A

Historically, three of these represented one old sound-type, one represented the other. But the speakers of OHG knew their language functionally, not historically. And functionally, there would have been a neat pairing-off, resulting in a new and symmetrical distribution of sound types:

[exi] representing Exi
[ɛxa] representing Exa
[æxi] representing Axi
[axa] representing Axa

The preponderant OHG orthography represents such a new distribution of E and A. The functional unity of the new sound-type E is confirmed by the cases in which OHG [ɛ], occurring exceptionally before -i in new formations, was replaced by [e].[9]

Thus we arrive at a formulation for OHG in which there were two phonetic forms for each of the vowel-types, with the exception of the palatal vowels and diphthongs. But in each case these two phonetic forms

[8] *x* represents such combinations as *-ht-*, etc.; cons.-vowel-cons.

[9] Cf. v. Bahder, *Grundlagen d. nhd. Lautsystems* 132 f.

are substantially complementary, dependent upon the phonetic environment; and therefore no orthographical representation is called for. Subsequently, when the environmental differentiation is eliminated, the phonetic differences are phonologized. Orthographical evidence of this is found in MHG for every vowel but *e;* and for *e* the rime-usage of the poets is conclusive evidence.

It goes without saying that the actual historical shiftings of orthographical usage were often tentative and inconsistent, with all the fumblings that a change in craft tradition can entail. This discussion is not concerned with them, nor with subsequent disturbances of umlaut-relations through operations of analogy. It is presented as a sketch of the main trends of the earlier stages of umlaut in High German, viewed as a phonetic and phonological (therefore orthographical) phenomenon.

The Conservatism of Germanic Phonology

W. P. LEHMANN

1. GERMANIC is generally characterized as one of the Indo-European dialects that have undergone the greatest changes from Proto-Indo-European (PIE). Among the changes considered most striking are those in phonology. Meillet concludes his discussion of Gmc. phonology by stating that "all the elements of the Indo-European phonetic system were changed or greatly modified in Gmc."[1] He bases this statement not only on spectacular changes like those of PIE /p/ to PGmc. /f/, PIE /b/ to PGmc. /p/, and the others described in Grimm's Law, but also on changes in function, such as those of PIE /r/ and /l/; though PGmc. /r/ and /l/ closely resemble their PIE etyma /r/ and /l/ in pronunciation, they differ from them in function because they no longer alternate with vocalic *r* and *l*.

Hirt's belief that the changes are very marked led him to conclude that Gmc. must have been transferred to a people that previously spoke a different language;[2] for he assumed that the home of the Indo-Europeans was near the earliest known location of the Germanic speakers, a situation which favors conservatism rather than marked innovation. Transference of the Gmc. language to a people who did not speak it

---

Reprinted by permission from *Journal of English and Germanic Philology* 52. 140-52 (1953).

[1] *Caractères généraux des Langues Germaniques* 90 (Paris, 1917).

[2] *Handbuch des Urgermanischen* I, 8-9 (Heidelberg, 1931). Prokosch considers such a transference probable, though he holds that "the common Indo-European element seems to predominate more definitely in the Germanic group than anywhere else," *A Comparative Germanic Grammar* 23 (Philadelphia, 1939). Many other scholars have dealt with the relationship of PIE and PGmc., some like Prokosch holding that the changes between PIE and PGmc. were relatively minor; see, for example, various essays of *Germanen und Indogermanen, Festschrift für Herman Hirt* (Heidelberg, 1936). Whatever the views propounded on the degree of relationship, when they have been based on linguistic evidence, they have lacked conviction because the PIE used as basis of comparison is outmoded, and the criteria selected are haphazard rather than a total structural element of the languages, such as their phonological or morphological systems.

natively seemed the best explanation of the supposed radical changes in Germanic. Feist too assumes such transference, though he places the home of the Indo-Europeans far from the location of the Gmc. speakers; to this he ascribes the fundamental difference of the Gmc. "phonetic system" from that of PIE.[3]

If we followed Meillet and Hirt in their principles of characterization and their description of PIE we should indeed have to consider Gmc. one of the least conservative IE dialects, and might feel obliged to provide some explanation from the culture of the Gmc. speakers or their change in physical environment for the many phonological changes. Change of physical environment offers little hope of explanation. Even if the Gmc. speakers had wandered from the area north of the Black Sea to present-day Germany or Scandinavia the change in environment would be minor when compared with that of the Italic speakers or that of the Indo-Iranians. Since we have no evidence for a striking change in culture, we would be left with the rather desperate explanation of Hirt for which there is no evidence.

2. I suggest, however, that in its phonological system Gmc. has undergone less radical change from PIE than have many of the other IE dialects. This conclusion is based on a revision of PIE phonology. Our description of PIE phonology has recently been modified by improvements in linguistic methodology, and by new phonological evidence which has been provided primarily by Hittite. The phonological system of Brugmann and his followers was drawn up before this evidence was available, and must be revised at least in part to account for the new data. Since the evaluation of Gmc. as a radically innovating dialect is based on the former description of IE phonology, a revision of this description entails also a revision of the evaluation of the position of Gmc.

Unlike the former phonological description of PIE that of PGmc. has not been modified in its essentials by recent work in historical linguistics. On the one hand the various Gmc. dialects, that is the reflexes of PGmc., are closer to one another than are the IE dialects; consequently the reconstructions of PGmc. have had more foundation than have those of PIE. And when these reconstructions were made they could be checked from cognates in other IE dialects, and even from etyma in PIE. As a result few changes are likely in our phonological analysis of PGmc. Actually our description of PGmc. is so complete that it may now be subjected to a process of refinement; we may now deal with PGmc. as with a language based on actual texts, ascribing to it variations in dialect and allophonic structure.[4] Our description of PGmc. is therefore in a category with that of Greek and Indo-Iranian, though we have extensive written materials from these languages but none from PGmc.

[3] "The Origin of the Germanic Languages and the Indo-Europeanizing of North Europe," *Language* 8, 245-54 (1932).

[4] See W. F. Twaddell, "The Prehistoric Germanic Short Syllabics," *Language* 24, 139-151 (1948).

The results of a revaluation of PGmc. have other linguistic importance besides that of reshuffling the IE dialects by degree of conservatism. If PGmc. resembles PIE we no longer have to look for striking cultural changes in the pre-history of the Gmc. peoples. Moreover we may be able to arrive at a more accurate description of PIE than that now held; for this is based on the nineteenth century evaluation of the conservatism of the various dialects.

3. The PIE of Brugmann and Hirt resembles a composite of Sanskrit and Greek, and its structure reflects the history of IE studies in the nineteenth century. The beginning of Indo-European studies dates from the discovery of Sanskrit in Europe. Since Sanskrit shows a great variety of inflections, and since these inflections can readily be analyzed into various elements—roots, suffixes, endings—it seemed to the early Indo-Europeanists, such as Bopp, to be very close to the parent language. The parent language of the first stage of Indo-European studies was then a close image of Sanskrit.

Schleicher attempted to remove Sanskrit from this position of preeminence in work on the parent language, and to take into equal account evidence from the other IE dialects. His chief method for this was the introduction of reconstructions. By using reconstructions rather than Sanskrit forms to illustrate the etyma of the various dialect forms Schleicher hoped to dissociate Sanskrit from its identification with the parent language and to show that Sanskrit too underwent many changes from the parent language as had the other IE dialects. Unfortunately his reconstructed Indo-European strongly resembled Sanskrit.[5]

Sanskrit lost some of its position of preeminence in the reconstruction of PIE phonology only after Indo-Europeanists in the eighteen-seventies and eighties discovered that Sanskrit itself contained evidence that its vocalic system was less original than was that of the other dialects, especially Greek. Consistent palatalization before some Skt. /a ā/ where these had /e ē/, e.g. Skt. *jāni* 'woman,' Goth. *qēns* 'woman,' and absence of palatalization before other Skt. /a ā/ where these had /a ā/ or /o ō/, e.g. Skt. *gaús* 'cow,' OHG *chuo* 'cow' showed that Sanskrit too had once distinguished between /e ē/, /a ā/, and /o ō/. Sanskrit perfect forms in which palatalization is found before the /a/ from PIE /e/ of the reduplicated syllable, but not before the /a/ from PIE /o/ of the stem syllable furnish clear illustrations of the Skt. developments, e.g. *cakára* 'I have done,' *jagáma* 'I have gone.' In subsequent reconstructions of PIE the single /a ā/, as found in Sanskrit, was replaced by the threefold /a e o ā ē ō/ as found in Greek. Henceforward the PIE vowel system was based primarily on that of Greek, but Sanskrit still formed the basis for the PIE consonant system. This PIE based on Sanskrit and Greek was revised and refined through a tremendous amount of work

[5] See H. Pedersen, *Linguistic Science in the Nineteenth Century,* English translation by J. Spargo, 278-79 (Cambridge, 1931).

in the last quarter of the nineteenth century, and the results of this work are found in Brugmann's *Grundriss.* Brugmann's phonological system of PIE became the standard system. It was adopted in essence by Hirt, and is that used today by most Indo-Europeanists and in most handbooks.

3A. Only recently has there been a departure from the PIE system used by Brugmann. This has been brought about by a change in phonological theory, and an increase in the data on which the PIE phonological system is based.[6] The change in theory is the application of structural linguistics and the phonemic theory to the study of PIE. The increase in data is the evidence in our Hittite records for sounds not directly attested in any of the other IE dialects; these sounds are generally referred to as laryngeals, and the attempts to account for them in the IE phonological system are called the laryngeal theory.

The PIE phonological system that Brugmann proposed was based primarily on phonetic criteria.[7] Brugmann assumed a velar nasal in his system even though it was found only before velars, and never in an environment where the dental *n* was found. By current linguistic theory we should assume one phoneme with dental and velar allophones. For in arriving at the units of our system, at the phonemes, we take into account distribution as well as phonetic characteristics.

On the basis of current linguistic theory then Brugmann's system is markedly reduced. The most striking reduction is in the resonants (semi-vowels). Edgerton has pointed out that the consonantal and vocalic resonants, e.g. [w u], [y i], [m m̥], occur in complementary distribution, cf. Goth. nom. f. *midja* 'middle,' nom. nt. *midi,* thus reducing from Brugmann's fourteen to six the number of PIE resonants.[8] The obstruent system is similarly reduced; Brugmann's *z* is an allophone of the /s/ phoneme. His spirants *sh, zh,* and *j* have long been dropped from the system for want of evidence. And when we apply the phonemic principle to Brugmann's three series of palatovelar stops, *k̑*, *k*, k^w, etc., we can assume two series, *k* k^w, etc.; Brugmann's palatal stops are found notably in the neighborhood of front vowels, and of *o* which had developed from a front vowel; they were thus allophones of the velar phonemes in PIE. When we treat Brugmann's inter-dental spirants, *þ þh ð ðh,* as cluster phenomena, we can reduce Brugmann's entire consonan-

[6] Numerous articles have been published which suggest revisions of Brugmann's system, but until recently no comprehensive study; a convenient list of them may be found in E. H. Sturtevant's *The Indo-Hittite Laryngeals,* 20-22 (Baltimore, 1942). Sturtevant himself maintains Brugmann's system, ascribing the changed phonology to pre-IE. An attempt at a comprehensive study dealing with the segmental phonemes of Indo-European may be found in W. P. Lehmann's *Proto-Indo-European Phonology* (Austin, 1952).

[7] This emphasis on phonetic criteria has persisted into recent times; Feist, for example, used such criteria in his article in *Language* 8, in which he characterized Germanic as fundamentally different from PIE.

[8] "The Indo-European Semivowels," *Language* 19, 83-124 (1943).

tal system (except for the voiceless aspirated stops) to thirteen obstruent phonemes, and six resonant phonemes.

Brugmann's vocalic system can be similarly reduced. With a phonemic analysis of the PIE vocalic system we are left with no diphthongs. There are numerous reasons for this conclusion of which the more important are the following. a) We find *e*:*o*:- ablaut variation in roots of various structures, e.g. /teg-/, in which obstruents precede and follow /e/, /terp-/, in which a resonant follows /e/, and /trep-/, in which a resonant precedes /e/. Roots like /terp- bheydh- bhewg-/ are generally said to contain diphthongs. If /er ey ew/ were diphthongs the parallelism in ablaut change is remarkable; the assumption is much more plausible that they, like /et edh eg/, patterned as sound sequences. The validity of this assumption is supported by roots in which we find some ablauting forms with vowel preceding resonant, e.g. /werp-/, others with resonant preceding vowel, e.g. /wrep-/. Such variations would be unlikely for 'diphthongs.' b) We find further evidence for assuming clusters rather than diphthongs in reflexes in various dialects. The Sanskrit nom. pl. of *agni-* 'fire' is *agnáyas,* the gen. sg. *agnés;* in the nom. pl. the cluster /ey/ became Skt. *ay* and was maintained before a vowel, in the gen. sg. it was contracted before a consonant. Greek *k*ʰ*éō* 'I pour,' aor. 1st sg. *ék*ʰ*eua* shows a similar development: in the present /w/ was lost before a vowel, in the aorist it was maintained before an /s/ (which was later lost). If PIE had had diphthongs in these words, we should expect less variation in their developments. I conclude that diphthongs developed only in the dialects, and that PIE itself had clusters of vowel plus resonant, e.g. /ew/, resonant plus vowel, e.g. /we/. Thus the numerous diphthongs which Brugmann and others assume for the PIE vocalic system must be removed from the list of phonemes.

3B. The resultant simplification in the phonemic system of PIE does not account for all of the developments from PIE to the various dialects. To these we must add the developments for which Brugmann could not find a satisfactory explanation, such as the apparently twofold development of PIE initial /y/ to Gk. rough breathing, as in *hós,* Skt. *yás,* 'who,' and zeta, as in *zugón,* Skt. *yuga-* 'yoke.' Many such developments are found where on the basis of Hittite we should assume laryngeal consonants. Only Hittite gives us orthographical evidence for laryngeals. But from a comparison of Hittite and the IE dialects it is apparent that some of the elements of Brugmann's system were combinations of one element with laryngeal.

A group of these are the voiceless aspirated stops, *ph th kh.* Brugmann assumed these for PIE on the basis of Sanskrit; the other dialects do not have them as distinct phonemes. It is clear that *ph th kh* developed in Sanskrit from combinations of voiceless stop and laryngeal, for they are found where we expect voiceless stop plus laryngeal, as in Sanskrit ninth class verbs, e.g. *mathnā́ti* 'shakes,' from PIE /met-X-/. We must ascribe the development of *ph th kh* to the post-IE period, for if *kh* had been a unit phoneme in early Skt. we should expect it, like *k g gh,* to have undergone palatalization before front vowels. Since it did not, I assume that *ph, th,* and *kh* became phonemes only in Indo-Iranian, and are not to be posited for PIE. For PIE we must assume a system of three classes of stops: voiceless, /p t k k^w/, voiced, /b d g g^w/, and voiced aspirated, /bh dh gh g^wh/. Here again it is not Sanskrit which maintained the PIE stop system.

Another group of elements which resulted from combinations with laryngeals are Brugmann's so-called "long semi-vowels." Hirt had already rejected these. When we compare available cognates of these in Hittite we find there a laryngeal, e.g., Lat. *plānus* 'flat,' Hitt. *pal-ḫi-i-iš* 'broad.' Instead of Brugmann's "long semi-vowels" we must posit for PIE short vocalic resonant plus laryngeal.

Accordingly when we analyze PIE on the basis of current linguistic theory and the added data that Hittite gives us we are left with a system much smaller than that of Brugmann, but with some additional phonemes. Although their distribution and allophones remain to be clarified we may assume four laryngeal phonemes; since we often cannot identify the laryngeal in question cover symbols are used; I use /X/ as symbol for any larnygeal.

This PIE phonemic system falls into four classes which we may set upon the basis of the syllabic structure.

a) Phonemes which may not occur at the peak of the syllable may bc callcd obstrucnts; these are:

p b t d k g k^w g^w
bh dh gh g^wh
s

b) Phonemes which occur only at the peak of the syllable, vowels; these are:

e a o ₑ
e• a• o• i• u•

c) Phonemes which may occur either at the peak of the syllable, on its slopes, or at its limits, resonants; these are:

m n w r l y

d) Phonemes which may not occur at the peak of the syllable, but unlike obstruents may either precede or follow resonants on the slope of the syllable, laryngeals; these are:

x γ h ʔ

4. This then is the phonemic system from which that of PGmc. and the other IE dialects developed. When we compare with it the phonemic system of the various dialects we find that of Gmc. among those closest to it.

4A. In its obstruent system PIE had a threefold distinction in manner of articulation in each of four positions, e.g. for the labial position voiceless, /p/, voiced, /b/, and voiced aspirated, /bh/.[9] PGmc. maintained this threefold distinction although it changed the manner of articulation. Where PIE had two stops, /b p/, and one aspirated stop, /bh/, PGmc. had one stop, /p/, and two spirants, /f ƀ/. These were striking changes from a phonetic point of view; and it was phonetic changes that the nineteenth century linguists considered significant. From a structural point of view they were minor.[10] The changes described in Grimm's Law modified the structure of PGmc. little more than did the change of English /t/ and /d/ from dentals to alveolars in the past few hundred years. In both instances we find substitution of phonetically different units, with maintenance of the linguistic system. Oddly enough, the only real PGmc. changes in structure were those with which Grimm could not cope, the so-called exceptions to Grimm's Law. The chief instances of these were the alternation of voiceless and voiced spirants, as in the Old High German past 3d sg. *zōh,* past 3d pl. *zugum* 'pulled,' where PIE had one phoneme, /k/, as in Lat. *dūcere* 'lead.' Stated differently, the major changes in the obstruent system from a structural point of view are the falling together of reflexes of voiceless stops after unaccented syllables with the reflexes of aspirated voiced stops, and the development of *z* as a separate phoneme, i.e., those exceptions to Grimm's Law which were explained by Verner. Retention of the unshifted phonemes /p t k/ after spirants /s f þ χ/, e.g. Goth. *ahtau,* Lat. *octo* 'eight,' were only minor disturbances of the structure.

Such a maintenance of the PIE obstruent system is found only in Greek. Greek maintained a threefold distinction between voiceless stop, e.g. /p/, voiced stop, e.g. /b/, and aspirated stop, e.g. /p^h/. Although Armenian maintained the threefold distinction, though undergoing a phonetic shift as extensive as Gmc., positional changes there disrupted the PIE system, e.g. PIE /p-/ becoming Armenian /h-/ or /-/, PIE /-p-/ becoming Armenian /-w-/. Of the other chief dialects, Slavic, Lithuanian, and Irish introduced a twofold distinction, e.g. /p b/, abandoning that between voiced stops, e.g. /b/, and voiced aspirated stops, e.g. /bh/.

[9] Examples can be found in the various handbooks.

[10] After the publications of the past few years it is hardly necessary to dwell on this observation. To my knowledge the first treatment differentiating between the phonetic and phonemic changes of the Germanic consonant shift is W. F. Twaddell's brief account in *On Defining the Phoneme,* 60-61 (Baltimore, 1935). J. Fourquet presents a fuller discussion in *Les mutations consonantiques du germanique* (Paris, 1948), and on page 74 he states his conclusion on the basis of his study of the obstruents alone that Germanic must be considered a conservative IE dialect.

Latin gave up the PIE threefold distinction in part, with /bh/ and /dh/ becoming /f/ initially, but /b d/ intervocalically, and /gh/ becoming /h/. Sanskrit expanded the PIE obstruent system to one with fourfold distinction, e.g. /p ph b bh/. Avestan shows a twofold distinction like that of Slavic; the realignment here is apparently a reduction of the fourfold system found in Sanskrit.

A far-reaching structural change in the obstruent system was the development of the labio-velars to two phonemes in Gmc. Although this was a major change in the system it is one which is shared by all other IE dialects. None of them keep labio-velars distinct from the inherited velars, or from other phonemes, such as labials and dentals in Greek. In losing the labio-velars Gmc. shows no decided innovation, or conservatism; it shares with the other dialects one of the chief distinctions between PIE and its dialects.

In addition to maintaining the PIE obstruent system structurally, Gmc. has been more conservative than much older dialects in several areas. One such is the velar stops. These developed in the so-called satem dialects to two phonemes which were conditioned by the following vowel —spirants before front vowels, e.g. Skt. /ś/ from PIE /k/, stops before back, Skt. /k/ from PIE /k/. Gmc. was also conservative in maintaining the phonemic structure of PIE syllables with two successive voiced aspirated stops, e.g. Goth. *ga-digans* 'kneaded' from PIE /dheygh-/. Here Skt. and Gk. were less conservative, for both lost the aspiration of the first stop; Skt. *déhmi* 'spread over' and Gk. *têik*^{h}*os* 'wall' developed from PIE /dheigh-/.

We may conclude that in maintaining the structure of the PIE obstruent system Gmc. was very conservative.

4B. In the vocalic system Skt. introduced radical changes, Greek was remarkably conservative, Gmc. like Baltic and Slavic occupies a middle position. It maintained PIE /e e•/ but combined the two back vowels, /a a•/ and /o o•/; the Gmc. phonemes are traditionally written *a* and *ō* but structurally the opposition is one of front versus back vowels.

Although few IE dialects, only Greek, Italic, Armenian, maintained the IE /a e o a• e• o•/ distinction, the greatest rearrangement of PIE phonemes was in the sphere of resonants and laryngeals. Their developments are intimately connected with those of the vowels. The PIE vocalic system was asymmetrical phonemically; three of the long vowels, /a• e• o•/, were paired with short vowels, two of them, /i• u•/, were not, and a short vowel, /$_{e}$/, was unaccompanied by a paired long vowel. Phonetically, however, this asymmetry did not exist; the vocalic allophones of the resonants, /y w/, that is, [i u], provided pairs for the long vowels, /i• u•/. This symmetrical system was then as follows: the allophones are enclosed in brackets, the phonemes are unmarked.

[i] i• [u] u•
e e• $_{e}$ o o•
a a•

We should expect such a potentially symmetrical system to develop into a symmetrical one, and we find that this has happened in all of the IE dialects. All of them show a tendency to complete symmetry in the vocalic system. /i· u·/ are maintained as separate phonemes in all dialects, and [i u] become phonemes, thereby rounding out the system. When however this tendency is actualized the IE resonant system is disrupted; two of the resonants, /y w/, lost their vocalic allophones, [i u]; as a result an environment in which only allophones were admitted in PIE permitted phonemes in all of the dialects. Thus all of the vocalic resonants were potentially phonemes. The consonantal allophones remained as the most important, and almost exclusive representatives, of the resonants, becoming phonemes in all dialects. Of the vocalic allophones only [i] and [u] became unit phonemes without undergoing phonetic change, except for PIE [r] becoming /r/ in Skt. The others for the most part developed into clusters of vowel plus consonantal resonant, e.g., PIE [r̥ l̥ m̥ n̥] becoming PGmc. /ur ul um un/, or they coalesced with other phonemes, e.g. PIE [n̥ m̥] becoming Skt. /a/, Gk. /a/.

The PGmc. vowel system has a contrast of front and back, and high and low vowels, thus showing a development from a five-vowel to a four-vowel system. No vowel is found characteristically in unaccented syllables. The simple vowel system is as follows:

i	i·	u	u·
e	e·	a	o· .

In addition the low short vowels form the diphthongs /au eu ai/ with the high short vowels, leaving vacant the potential *e* plus *i* diphthong. Here the lack of symmetry was removed by the development of a high front vowel, generally written $\bar{e}^2$: this developed when *e* was lengthened upon loss of a following spirant, usually before *i*. Though this is a development towards a completely symmetrical system, the symmetry was lost upon the development of PGmc. /a·/ from /a/ plus *ŋ* before /χ/.

A second result of the disruption of the PIE resonant system was the formation of diphthongs. These are found in the phonemic systems of all IE dialects, including Gmc., as noted above. Their development is a further characteristic dividing the dialects from PIE.

Since the resonant system is everywhere disrupted, it is only the speed of the disruption and the relative maintenance of the resonant system which enable us to determine the conservatism of the various dialects in this part of the phonological system. The essential characteristic of the PIE resonants was their threefold function as vowel, e.g. [i], consonant, [y], or vowel plus consonant [iy], as conditioned by the preceding phonemes; the description of this variation is generally known as Sievers' Law. It is most clearly apparent in our Vedic Sanskrit documents. But it had not been given up completely at the time our Gmc. documents were written down, a time when it is no longer maintained in the Indic dialects. Its maintenance in Gmc., as reflected in the Goth. genitives singular *harjis* and *hairdeis,* led Sievers to his original description of the allophonic variation of the PIE resonants, *PBB* 5.129ff. Gmc. therefore was apparently no less conservative than was Vedic in preserving this characteristic of PIE; most of the other dialects have maintained few traces of it. Moreover the vocalic allophones of the resonants, which no dialect has maintained completely, are preserved as to position of articulation in Gmc.; Gmc. represents PIE [i u r̥ l̥ m̥ n̥] by /i u ur ul um un/, while Skt. has reduced them to /i u r̥ a/, Greek to /i u ar al a/.

4C. The IE resonant system was apparently maintained as long in Gmc. as in any other dialect; the vocalic system too underwent relatively few changes there. But what of the laryngeals? Have we any evidence for their preservation in Gmc.? There is considerable such evidence, especially in the neighborhood of resonants.

A notable characteristic of the Gmc. dialects is the lengthening of -*j*- and -*w*- in certain words, e.g., OIcel. *skugge* 'shadow,' *Frigg,* the name of Odin's consort; the description of this phenomenon is generally known as Holtzmann's Law. Various Germanists have tried to explain the lengthening on the basis of the position of the accent, both the PIE accent and the Gmc. None of these attempts has been successful. Only the assumption of laryngeals in the PIE, and PGmc. phonemic system has led to a solution. Gmc. -*w*- was lengthened directly before laryngeals, -*j*- directly before or after laryngeals. OIcel. *skugge* is cognate with Sanskrit *skunā́ti* 'covers,' from which we can assume PIE /skew^{x}-/; *Frigg* is cognate with Sanskrit *priṇā́ti* 'pleases,' from which we can assume PIE /prey^{x}-/. Similar evidence for the presence of laryngeals may be found in most of the other words with lengthening.

Another Gmc. development without explanation until the laryngeal theory was proposed is that of *g* and *k* in certain words from PIE /w/. An example is OE *naca* 'ship.' This and its cognate forms, OIcel. *nǫkkue,* OS *naco,* OHG *nacho,* are obviously related to Lat. *nā̆vis,* Gk. *nâus* 'ship'; the PIE /w/ is preserved in OIcel. *naust* 'boat-house' and OHG *ver-nawun* 'boats that carry wood.' The *ā* of Lat. *navis* and cognates has long been derived from a PIE "original long vowel," that is, by the laryngeal theory, a combination of vowel and laryngeal. Again in Gmc. the laryngeal was preserved sufficiently long to undergo a peculiar development, not found elsewhere.

Still other developments in Gmc. may be explained from preservation of laryngeals in the neighborhood of resonants. One such is the development of the so-called PIE long semi-vowels into Gmc. Only Gmc. and Armenian fail to distinguish between reflexes of 'long' and short vocalic resonants other than *i* and *u*. When Indo-Europeanists assumed 'long resonants' for IE this lack of distinction was very difficult to explain. By the laryngeal theory instead of long vocalic resonants, e.g., Brugmann's l̥̄ for the etymon of Lat. *plānus* 'flat,' combinations of short resonants and laryngeals were assumed, e.g. [l̥^{x}], thus accounting for cognate forms like Hittite *pal-ḫi-i-iš* 'broad.' We may explain the Gmc. and Armenian lack of distinction between vocalic resonants and vocalic resonants followed by laryngeals, e.g., [l̥] and [l̥^{x}], by assuming that in these dialects the laryngeals were maintained sufficiently long in this position so that upon their loss they had no effect on the preceding resonant.

Accordingly the laryngeals too were long preserved into Gmc. We have considerable evidence for their survival into Vedic Skt. and PGreek, but little evidence for them in later stages of Sanskrit or Greek or in other dialects. Gmc. again exhibits a marked conservatism.

4D. As a final conservative feature in its phonological system we may note the preservation of the IE free accent. Verner showed that this was preserved into Gmc. even after the time of the first changes in the obstruent system; for to root accent may be ascribed the preservation of the voiceless spirant in Gmc. prt. sg. forms, e.g. OHG *zeh,* to accent on the ending the voiced spirant in the prt. pl., e.g. OHG *zigum.* Further evidence for relatively late preservation of the IE accent may be adduced from Gmc. verse; prosodic features such as the lack of accent on finite verbs indicate that the same principles of accentuation were observed here as in Indic verse.

5. It is clear that, far from having modified radically the PIE phonological system, PGmc. has been remarkably conservative. Apart from developments shared by all the dialects the PIE obstruent system was preserved in Gmc. with only two significant disruptions—unshifted /p t k/ after spirants, and the coalescence of some PIE voiceless stops with voiced aspirated stops; the PIE vocalic system was reduced; the PIE resonant and laryngeal system were rearranged, though not so radically, nor so early, as in many other dialects. When we add to these conservative features the preservation of the IE free accent we find a conservatism of phonological structure equalled only by the oldest records in Sanskrit and Greek. Some dialects have maintained certain archaic features, to be sure; such are the labio-velar /qu/ in Latin, and the intonation of some Baltic and Slavic dialects. In spite of such particular archaisms these dialects have departed much more than Gmc. from the PIE phonological pattern.

5A. Because of this conservatism Gmc. should be taken into greater consideration than it has been in the past for reconstruction of PIE; on the other hand less emphasis may be laid on some other dialects. This principle may apply not only to phonology. From Hittite we have learned that the elaborate systems of forms in Skt. and Greek have largely been built up in these dialects, not retained from PIE. The PIE morphological system was apparently rich and flexible, not neatly systematized. It was systematized in all of the dialects, perhaps most rigorously in Skt. and Greek. The Sanskrit expansion and regularization of the PIE phonemic system seems typical of the development of the morphological system there. In the verb the present and aorist, which to be sure developed from phonetically and semantically differentiated IE forms, were widely expanded and organized; we find in Skt. presents with sub-classes, primarily of mood, which grammars generally label indicative, subjunctive, optative, imperative, imperfect, and participles. Aorists have but one sub-class less. This type of systematization is no more characteristic of PIE than is the type found in Greek, in Germanic, or Hittite. All of them have forfeited the flexible IE system. Our knowledge that Gmc. was conservative in phonology may help us to a better description of PIE morphology; for if Gmc. was conservative in one branch of grammar it may also have been so in others.

5B. We may further abandon the fanciful attempts to account for the "changes" into Gmc. For the changes between PIE and PGmc. were relatively negligible. Those between PGmc. and the various Gmc. dialects were more extensive, but not extreme when compared with the changes found in other branches of the IE family. There is no need to look for unusual cultural developments to explain the Gmc. changes.

Suggested Additional Readings for Part II

[See additional readings for Part I for works cited by author and date only.]

BLOOMFIELD 1933, esp. chapters 5-8, 20, 21.

YUEN-REN CHAO, "The Non-uniqueness of Phonemic Solutions of Phonetic Systems," in Martin Joos, ed., *Readings in Linguistics* I, 4th ed. (Chicago, 1966), 38-54.

J. FOURQUET, *Les mutations consonantiques du germanique* (Paris, 1948).

MORRIS HALLE, "Phonology in Generative Grammar," *Word* 18.54-72 (1962). Also in Jerry A. Fodor and Jerrold J. Katz, eds., *The Structure of Language* (Englewood Cliffs, 1964), 334-52. This paper should be read as an example of how the descriptive approach of generative phonology may be applied to historical data.

R-M. S. HEFFNER, *General Phonetics* (Madison, Wis., 1952).

HOCKETT 1958, esp. chapters 2-13, 52-54, 58.

CHARLES F. HOCKETT, "A System of Descriptive Phonology," *Language* 18.3-21 (1942). Also in *Readings in Linguistics* I, 97-107.

HENRY M. HOENIGSWALD, *Language Change and Linguistic Reconstruction* (Chicago, 1960), esp. chapters 1, 2, 8, 9.

——————, "Sound Change and Linguistic Structure," *Language* 22.138-43 (1946). Also in *Readings in Linguistics* I, 139-41.

LEHMANN 1962, esp. chapters 4, 10.

MALMBERG 1963, esp. chapters 4, 12.

KENNETH L. PIKE, *Phonemics: A Technique for Reducing Languages to Writing* (Ann Arbor, 1947).

EDUARD PROKOSCH, *A Comparative Germanic Grammar* (Philadelphia, 1939).

N. S. TRUBETZKOY, *Principes de phonologie,* trans. J. Cantineau (Paris, 1964).

W. FREEMAN TWADDELL, "On Defining the Phoneme," *Language Monograph* 16 (1935). Also in *Readings in Linguistics* I, 55-79.

PART III

Phonological Change in the History of English

The most reliable evidence for phonological change in the history of English comes from an examination of the orthography used at the various stages in the development of English. From the OE period to the present, the language has been written with adaptations of the roman alphabet. If it could be assumed that this alphabet were adjusted to reflect the actual structure of each of the succeeding phonemic systems in the history of its use as an English orthography, the pattern of oppositions which constitutes the phonemic system at any given point in time could be established with a high degree of probability. The actual phonetic realization of each of the phonemes within the system of a stage of a language no longer spoken, however, could only be conjectured. Thus, on the basis of the roman system used for the writing of Old English, it could be demonstrated that the elements represented by *t* and *d* are phonemically distinct (cp. *tūn* 'village, enclosure' and *dūn* 'down, hill'), but there is little evidence for determining if these were alveolar stops as in modern English, dental stops as in modern German, or articulations differing from both.

The historical orthography of English is not always unambiguous in its representation of the phonemic systems of earlier periods in the history of the language. Scribal traditions, once established, tend to be conservative of change. Even if a writing system has precise phonological reference at its introduction—as is usually assumed in the case of Old English orthography—scribal traditions may not adapt to reflect subsequent phonological changes unless the traditions are undermined. Such undermining took place with the introduction of the Norman-fostered scribal reforms after 1066. Scribal reforms do not alter the structure of a language when they are introduced, but they usually reflect changes which have taken place since the stabilization of the traditions they supersede, thus giving the appearance of sudden or very rapid change. The Norman scribal reforms are, therefore, of great interest since they provide important information about the phonological changes which had taken place since the establishment of the conservative OE system. The textual differences between Old English and Middle English reflect both differing scribal traditions (though each was based on the roman alphabet) and the changes which had taken place in Old English by the latter part of the eleventh century. It is also significant, however, that these differing scribal traditions may conceal—at least superficially—a number of the similarities in the two systems they represent.

Once it is possible—on the basis of orthographic evidence—to establish the structure of the phonological systems of earlier periods in the language, it is then possible to construct rules (or sound laws) to delineate the relationships which hold between historical periods—for if phonological systems are related, they must be related in precisely definable ways. If such rules can be established, therefore, they both prove that the systems are related and specify how they are related. For example, such pairs as OE *tūn,* NE *town,* OE *tīd,* NE *tide* are instrumental in establishing the relationship: OE /t/ = NE /t/. Such rules prove that Old English and modern English are related by establishing how they are related.

If there were but a single analysis possible for the phonological system at each of the various periods in the history of English, then there would also exist a single uniform set of sound laws relating any two periods. As in the case of the data for modern English, however, the linguistic material available for earlier periods is amenable to analysis in a number of defensible ways, depending upon the assumptions and goals of the analysis. In historical study, the linguist must therefore attempt to insure that the assumptions and goals of his analysis are comparable for each of the stages he is analyzing so as to formulate sound laws which have the widest generality and which require the fewest qualifications (exceptions). If the related stages are not analyzed on comparable bases, the rules (sound laws) relating them will be at best unnecessarily complex and at worst completely lacking in explanatory power.

For English, there is a good deal of controversy about the nature of the phonemic systems of the old, middle, and modern periods and about the rules relating the systems. With respect to the historical consonantal systems, the disagreement tends to center on such problems as the interpretation of the OE graphic sequence *sc* (as a single phoneme /š/ or as a phonological cluster) and on the allophonic structure and subsequent development of OE /x/. With respect to the vocalic systems, the most significant disagreement is concerned with how the OE vowel graphs are to be interpreted. There are two major points of dispute. The first concerns the determination of the distinctive feature or features differentiating the two subsets of the vocalic system, which are generally distinguished through the use of the macron in edited texts. In the Old English scribal tradition, these subsets were written identically, but since the two have separate reflexes in modern English (cp. OE *bid(dan),* NE *bid*: OE *bīd(an),* NE *bide*), they may be presumed to have been phonemically distinct in Old English as well. Assuming that such a distinction did exist, some analysts would interpret the distinction as one of quantity (with or without concomitant distinctions of quality). Thus the first vowel in *biddan* would be said to differ from that in *bīdan* in that the latter would be marked by phonemically-relevant prolongation: /ɪ/ vs. /ɪ:/ or /i:/. Other analysts would interpret the distinction as being marked by the presence or absence of a phonemic glide equivalent to /y/: /i/ vs. /iy/. The second analysis is patterned on the Trager-Smith analysis for modern English.

The second point of dispute revolves about the interpretation of the Old English digraph spellings *ie, eo, ea.* These spellings often represent the reflexes of Germanic diphthongs (cp. Goth. *biudan,* OE *bēodan* 'command'). In other cases, the spellings correspond to Germanic short vowels (cp. Goth. *giban,* OE *giefan* 'give'). The two are distinguished editorially through the use of the macron to mark the former.

The more traditional interpretation analyzes the digraph spellings as representing phonological diphthongs, and the distinction between those corresponding to Germanic diphthongs and those to Germanic short vowels is interpreted as a quantitative distinction similar to that which would be postulated for the non-diphthongal sub-sets. Other analysts question the phonemic significance of those digraphs not representing the reflexes of Germanic diphthongs. They point out that the 'short' digraphs tend to occur in two basic environments—after palatal consonants on the one hand, and before /l/ or /r/ plus consonant, before *h,* and before consonant plus back vowel on the other. Since /k/ and /c/ are both written *c,* and /g/, /j/, and /y/ are all written *g,* the digraph spellings often appear to be diacritics indicating that the vowel is preceded by a palatal rather than a velar consonant—otherwise the spelling would be ambiguous in indicating the palatal quality of the consonant. Examples of digraph spellings after palatals are: *giedd* 'song', *geong,* 'young', *ceaster* 'city'. The other 'short' digraphs would be interpreted as allographs representing the front vowel phonemes, since they appear to be in complementary distribution with the more common symbols representing the front vowels: *i (ie), e (eo), æ (ea).* Examples of digraph spellings in the second environment are: *healf* 'half', *fierd* 'militia', *feoht* 'battle', *heofon* 'heaven'.

The traditional interpretation allows for little ambiguity in the relationship between orthography and vocalic system, since the spelling system is argued to represent the vocalic system directly. The second interpretation attempts to bring the principles of distributional analysis to bear in the examination of the orthography, but there remain certain ambiguities in the interpretation of spellings like *ceorl* 'churl'. The spelling may be interpreted as representing either /corl/ or /cerl/ depending on whether *eo* is argued to represent /o/ preceded by a diacritic, thus indicating the palatal quality of *c,* or to represent /e/, which would usually be spelled *eo* before /r/ plus consonant.

Since the primary evidence for English historical phonology rests upon orthographic evidence, such problems of interpretation are of great significance, because the structure of the sound laws relating historical periods will vary according to the interpretation of the orthographical-phonological relationships at any given period. Thus, before it is possible to account for the changes which have taken place between periods, it is necessary to establish a point of departure and a point of termination. Problems like those of interpreting the Old English graphic system are not limited, therefore, to the study of any particular period of English—they have ramifications for the interpretation of the whole history of English.

The selections which follow are concerned with some of the important problems in the analysis of English historical phonology and with the problems of interpreting textual evidence for phonological change. The often conflicting views presented reflect the difficulties involved in accounting for textual evidence. The introductory article, by Robert P. Stockwell, presents an analysis of OE phonology employing a model similar to the Trager-Smith diasystem for modern English. This model differs significantly from earlier analyses which would interpret the textual evidence more literally. The following article, by Sherman M. Kuhn, presents the evidence for a more conservative analysis of the OE vocalic system. The selection by William G. Moulton examines in detail the textual evidence for the OE consonantal system; his conclusions differ in several respects from those presented by Stockwell. The articles by Herbert Penzl and Hans Kurath are concerned specifically with the analysis and evaluation of two important structural changes which have taken place in the history of English phonology—the first in the pre-OE period, the second in the pre-ME period. These articles illustrate both the systemic changes which may result from regular sound change and the techniques which must be employed in the use of textual evidence to substantiate such changes. The second article by Robert P. Stockwell is an attempt to account for one of the major problems in ME phonology within a model like that presented for Old English in the first selection. The final article presents the general argument for the use of such a diasystemic model in the analysis of English historical phonology.

The Phonology of Old English: A Structural Sketch

ROBERT P. STOCKWELL

O. THIS ANALYSIS of the phonemic structure of the West Saxon dialect of Old English is posited without any description here of the evidence which one normally expects for the justification of so considerable a departure from the tradition. It has been made as concise as is consistent with a reasonable intelligibility. Since the evidence is not cited at this time, it should be read as A POSSIBLE ANALYSIS proposed by one structuralist. It is not a unique phonemic solution of the manuscript and etymological data. Nevertheless, it is, at least at this time, unique in the ease with which it accounts for the complexities of dialect variation and prepares the ground for an economical diachronic statement of the subsequent history of the language.[1]

1. The simple syllabic nuclei of Old English in the earliest recorded period were /i e æ ü ö u o ɔ/. Before the literary period, /ö/ had been unrounded and had fallen in with /e/ except in Northumbrian, where it was retained after labial consonants. In phonetic terms, the eight vowels may be approximated as [ɪ ɛ æ ʏ ö ᴜ oˠ ɔ]. In order as listed, these are the vowels of Mid-Western American English *bit, bet, bat,* Modern High German *müssen, wörter,* Mid-Western American English *put,* Eastern New England *coat, cot.* These vowels are arranged in the diagram below to show the structural oppositions:

HIGH	i	ü	u
MID	e	ö	o
LOW	æ		ɔ
	FRONT UNROUND	FRONT ROUND	BACK ROUND

Reprinted by permission from *Studies in Linguistics* 13.13-24 (1958).

[1] In this sketch, phonemes are enclosed between slant lines, phonetic symbols are enclosed between square brackets, graphemes are enclosed between broken brackets, and items given in traditional orthography are italicized. The paper was originally written in 1952 and was discussed in a faculty seminar at the Linguistic Institute at the University of Indiana that summer.

Thus the system is arranged as a set of intersecting categories consisting of three dimensions: high—low, front—back, round—unround. The system was imperfectly symmetrical at one point, since the low front round vowel /ɔ̈/ did not develop in any Old English dialect; in West Saxon, /ö/ had been lost, leaving seven vowels for that dialect.

Mossé, in the original French edition of his manual, described the three digraphs *ĕa ĕo,* and *ĭe* as representing simple vowels.[2] Marjorie Daunt had earlier described them similarly.[3] Neither Mossé nor Daunt adequately delimited the conditions of complementary distribution which make their interpretation phonemically valid. This has since been attempted for *ĕa* by the present writer and C. Westbrook Barritt.[4] Abstracting the three front unround vowels from the complete system of simple vowels, one may schematize the allophonic relationship of the phones represented by the short digraphs in this fashion:

/i/	*i*	[ɨ]	*io, ie*
/e/	*e*	[ə]	*eo*
/æ/	*æ*	[ɑ]	*ea*

The phones [ɨ ə ɑ] are then to be described as the central allophones of the front unround vowels. There were some differences among dialects in the distribution of these central allophones, but for West Saxon the distribution seems to be reasonably clear: [ɨ ə ɑ] occur before /l/ plus consonant, /r/ plus consonant, and /x/ (spelled *h*). The phonemic norms of /i e æ/ occur elsewhere, including those situations where *ie, eo, ea* appear as spellings to indicate a preceding palatal.

Using typical West Saxon spellings, the following lists furnish instances of the eight simple nuclei (including the non-West Saxon /ö/ for the sake of completeness):

/i/: *bill* 'bill', *bind* 'bind', *biter* 'bitter', *hlid* 'lid', *licgan* 'lie', *pricel* 'prickle', *wittig* 'witty', *giefan* 'give'.[5]

[ɨ]: *bierce* 'birch', *bierhtan* 'to illuminate', *fierran* 'far', *wierð* 'becomes', *siehð* 'sees', *fieht* 'sheepskin, wool'.[6]

[2] *Manuel de l'anglais du moyen âge des origines au XIVe siècle,* 1.30-32. An English edition was at one time (I do not know whether it still is) under preparation by James Walker, who did the excellent translation of the second part of the manual, the *Handbook of Middle English* (Baltimore, Johns Hopkins, 1952).

[3] "Old English sound-changes reconsidered in relation to scribal tradition and practice," *Trans. of the Philological Society* 108-37 (1939).

[4] *Some Old English graphemic-phonemic correspondences:* æ, ea, *and* a. *SIL:OP4* (1951).

[5] *ie* spellings here indicate palatals; in *giefan* the phoneme represented is /i/; in *gielpan* it is /e/. Since /i/ and /e/ are very stable nuclei in the history of English, their modern reflexes will generally reveal the Old English shape.

[6] The exact distribution of [ɨ] has not yet been fully delimited, but it is apparently somewhat more limited than that of [ɑ]. This limitation is also true of [ə]. The underlying conditions of complementary distribution seem to be identical, with subsequent re-shifting of the allophones in some distributions.

/e/: *bedd* 'bed', *helpan* 'help', *hecg* 'hedge', *lettan* 'let', *gieldan* 'yield', *gielpan* 'yelp', *geostra* 'yesterday'.[7]

[ə]: *meolcan* 'to milk', *eorðe* 'earth', *heorte* 'heart', *cneoht* 'boy', *georn* 'yearn'.[8]

/æ/: *bæc* 'back', *fæst* 'fast', *græft* 'graven image', *ðæcc* 'thatch', *ceaster* 'city', *sceaft* 'shaft', *ceafl* 'jaw'.[9]

[ɑ]: *healt* 'halt', *stearc* 'strong', *eald* 'old', *gearn* 'yarn', *sceald* 'shallow', *scearfian* 'scrape'.[10]

/ü/: *ðynne* 'thin', *cynn* 'kin', *cyssan* 'kiss', *dysig* 'dizzy', *dyne* 'din', *gryllan* 'grill'.

/ö/: Does not occur in literary West Saxon. Instances in early documents and Northumbrian include *œxen* (WS exen) 'oxen', *œle* (WS *ele*) 'oil', *cwœllan* (WS *cwellan*) 'kill'.

/u/: *cruma* 'crumb', *cunnan* 'can', *dumb* 'dumb', *geong*[7] 'young', *nunne* 'nun', *sculan* 'shall'.

/o/: *bolt* 'bolt', *crop* 'crop', *botm* 'bottom', *geolca*[7] 'yolk', *locc* 'lock'.

/ɔ/: *man* 'man', *crabba* 'crab', *fanu* 'fane', *gada* 'companion', *glades* 'glad' (gen. sing.).

2. The complex syllabic nuclei of Old English consisted of any one of the above simple nuclei followed by any one of three semivowels, /y w h/. In phonetic terms, /y/ represents an off-glide in the direction of high front position; /w/ represents an off-glide in the direction of high back rounded position; and /h/ represents an off-glide in the direction of central position. Allophonically, /h/ may show only a lengthening of the simple nucleus with slight relaxation of tenseness. It is very important to recognize that the DIRECTION of off-glide is the phonemically significant phonetic fact.

A full statement of the phonetic characteristics of /y w h/ in Modern English has been given by George L. Trager and Henry Lee Smith, Jr., in their *Outline of English structure*.[11] Some comprehension of their analysis is necessary in order to understand the present analysis of Old English. Without attempting to reproduce their full exposition, the following illustrations of complex nuclei in Mid-Western American English are given to help the reader make the proper phonetic realization of these phonemic interpretations: /bíyt/ *beat,* /béyt/ *bait,* /báyt/ *bite,* /búwt/ *boot,* /bówt/ *boat,* /báwt/ *bout,* /lɔ́h/ or /lóh/ *law,* /yéh/ *yeah*

[7] *ie* and *eo* after palatals are often interchangeable; sometimes *eo* after palatal is /e/, as in *geostra,* also spelled *giestra;* sometimes it is /u/, as in *geong* (*o* here being the 'scribal *u*'); sometimes it is /o/, as in *geolca.* Such confusion is to be expected in instances where a graph is used in several significations, and only the later history will separate them.

[8] *eo* in double signification—both to indicate palatal and central allophone of /e/.

[9] *ea* spellings here indicate palatals.

[10] *ea* in double signification in the last three items—to indicate palatal and central allophone of /æ/.

[11] *SIL:OP3* (1951).

(not *yow*), /fáhr/ *far*, /šúhr/ *sure*, /bíhr/ *beer*. This is not a complete listing, since Modern English has nine simple nuclei and twenty-seven complex nuclei of the sort illustrated above.

Returning to Old English, one may analyze the 'long vowels' and 'long diphthongs' as complex nuclei similar, structurally, to those of Modern English. The complex nuclei which the writer has settled upon for the West Saxon dialect, after careful study of the earlier and later history of the items which contain these nuclei,[12] are these: /iy, üy, iw, ew, æw, uw, ɔw, eh, æh, ɔh, oh/. After the date of the sound change traditionally referred to as '10th century lengthening clusters', /ih, üh, uh/ were also present. The following lists furnish instances of the complex nuclei which appeared in West Saxon before 10th century lengthening:

/iy/: *bîtan* 'bite', *blîðe* 'blithe', *cîdan* 'chide', *dîc* 'dike', *glîdan* 'glide', *rîdan* 'ride'.

/üy/: *cŷta* 'kite', *drŷge* 'dry', *fŷlan* 'defile', *fŷr* 'fire', *hŷd* 'hide'.

/iw/: *bîetel* 'beetle', *cîegan* 'shout', *cîese* 'cheese', *dîers* 'dear', *dîofol* 'devil', *frîo* 'free'.

/ew/: *brêost* 'breast', *clêot* 'cleat', *fêorða* 'fourth', *hêofan* 'lament', *sêoðan* 'seethe', *bêo* 'be'.

/æw/: *bêam* 'beam', *dêaf* 'deaf', *flêah* 'flea', *lêap* 'leap', *nêar* 'near', *scêaf* 'sheaf'.

/uw/: *fûl* 'foul', *hû* 'how', *mûð* 'mouth', *nû* 'now', *rûst* 'roust', *sûr* 'sour'.

/ɔw/: *clawu* 'claw', *strawu* 'straw'.[13]

/eh/: *grêne* 'green', *sêkan* 'seek', *fêt* 'feet', *hêr* 'here', *mêd* 'meed'.

/æh/: *hǣlan* 'heal', *hǣte* 'heat', *mǣnan* 'mean', *rǣdan* 'read', *sǣd* 'seed', *slǣpan* 'sleep'.

/ɔh/: *âðe* 'oath', *bân* 'bone', *lâm* 'loam', *stân* 'stone', *tâ* 'toe'.

/oh/: *dôm* 'doom, judgment', *gôd* 'good', *scôh* 'shoe', *môna* 'moon', *pôl* 'pool'.

Further examples of the /Vw/ nuclei may be included among the above listings after the distribution of the allophones of /w/ has been described.

[12] The study here referred to is in the writer's dissertation, *Chaucerian graphemics and phonemics: a study in historical methodology*, University of Virginia, 1952. It is hoped that this study in revised and extended form may be published reasonably soon.

[13] Items of this type are rare, since they are all rebuilt nominatives where /æw/ is expected but /ɔw/ appears from the oblique cases. Thus *clêa* and *strêa* are the expected forms here (and they do occur). *Clawu* and *strawu* are by analogy with the dative plural.

The allophones of /w/ were these: (1) a consonantal on-glide, and (2) a vocalic off-glide. The consonantal allophone occurred in three positions: (1) after pause or any juncture phoneme (for juncture see section 5, Suprasegmental phonemes); (2) after a consonant; and (3) after a semivowel (i.e. after a complex nucleus except before juncture). The vocalic allophone occurred elsewhere (i.e. after any simple nucleus and before juncture). Of the three semivowels /y w h/, only /w/ had both consonantal and vocalic allophones in Old English. In Modern English, all three have both allophones, distributed as were the Old English allophones of /w/. In the older period, /y/ and /h/ each had the vocalic off-glide as its only allophone; the consonantal allophone of /y/ developed during the Middle English period from Old English /j/, and the consonantal allophone of /h/ developed late in Middle English or perhaps even as late as the 15th century from the initial allophone of Middle English /x/.

The pertinence of the description of the two allophones of /w/ rests in the fact that there were a large number of items in Old English which had the shape /Vww-/, i.e. contained a complex nucleus consisting of simple vowel plus the vocalic allophone of /w/ followed in turn by a SECOND /w/ which was the consonantal allophone functioning as the initial consonant of another syllable. These items have a history which is different from the history of straight /Vw/ nuclei; the second /w/ of the /Vww-/ nuclei seems to have had a kind of holding power over the shape of the /Vw/ nucleus which it followed, with the result that these nuclei strongly resisted the tendency to change in the direction which other /Vw/ nuclei took. Whatever the explanation may be, the /Vww-/ items are among the most stable in the language. And besides holding a preceding /w/ stable, whenever the consonantal allophone of /w/ appeared after a complex nucleus of *any* shape, the semivowel of the nucleus was assimilated to /w/, resulting in a great many new /Vww-/'s during the Old English period.[14] Thus OE *stîward,* which had earlier been /stíywɔrd/, must be interpreted as /stíwwɔrd/ by the date of recorded documents. The following lists furnish instances of the occurrence of /Vww-/ nuclei in West Saxon:

/iww-/: *stîward* 'steward', *brîwan* 'cook, *boil',* gîw 'hawk', *hîewere* 'hypocrite'.
/eww-/: *êowu* 'ewe', *hêowe* 'hew', *fêower* 'four'.
/æww-/: *fêawe* 'few', *mǽw* 'mew', *êawan* 'point out'.
/uww-/: *cnûwian* 'break', *rûwe* 'cover'.
/oww-/: *flôwan* 'flow', *grôwan* 'grow', *stôwan* 'stow'.
/ɔww-/: *sâwan* 'sow', *blâwan* 'blow'.

[14] While it is not a pertinent matter to the student whose primary interest is in Old English without regard to its later history, the same kind of assimilation occurred before OE /j/ which became ME /y/.

To the list of eleven complex nuclei one may now add /ow/ as having been a nucleus contained in /oww-/ nuclei. Thus there were two /Vy/ nuclei, six /Vw/ nuclei, and four /Vh/ nuclei in the West Saxon dialect from the total potential of twenty-four.

3. The total West Saxon system of syllabic nuclei is arranged schematically below:

/V/	*/Vy/*	*/Vw/*	*/Vh/*
/i/ *i, ie*	/iy/ *î*	/iw/ *îe, îew*	—
/e/ *e, eo*	—	/ew/ *êo, êow*	/eh/ *ê*
/æ/ *æ, ea*	—	/æw/ *êa, êaw, æw*	/æh/ *æ̂*
/ü/ *y*	/üy/ *ŷ*	—	—
/u/ *u*	—	/uw/ *û, ûw*	—
/o/ *o*	—	/ow/ *ôw*	/oh/ *ô*
/ɔ/ *a*	—	/ow/ *aw, âw*	/ɔh/ *â*

The other dialects of Old English may be shown to complete this structure by filling in certain ones of the blanks above, and by including an eighth vowel, /ö/. Each dialect in turn may be described in terms of the appropriate set of syllabic nuclei selected from this total vocalic structure. The identifications of these particular nuclei for West Saxon are made only after careful examination of the later history of the system; they are not simply arbitrary assignments.

4. The Old English consonant structure was this:

	Labial	Dental	Palatal	Velar
Voiceless stop	/p/	/t/	/c/	/k/
Voiced stop	/b/	/d/	/j/	/g/
Spirant	/f/	/θ/	/s/	/x/
Nasal	/m/	/n/		
Lateral		/l/		
Apical		/r/		
Semivowel		/y/ /h/ /w/		

Of these consonants, not including /y w h/ (discussed under 2. above), each had the phonemic norm indicated; the phonemic norm was the unique allophone of all the phonemes (at least as far as the allophonic details can be recovered) except in the following instances:

/f/: [f] in all positions except not doubled between voiced sounds, where [v] occurred. Always spelled <f>.

/θ/: [θ] [ð], same distribution. Spelled *þ, ð* without distinction (one grapheme <ð>).

/s/: [s] [z], same distribution. Always spelled <s>.

/g/: [g] everywhere except not doubled between vowels, where [γ] occurred. Spelled <g>.

/x/: probably had less friction initially than elsewhere, but was a velar spirant in all positions. Spelled <h>.

/c/: voiceless palatal, or palatalized, stop. May have been phonetically very close to Modern English /č/ (also structurally a stop). Spelled *ċ* by modern editors; *sċ* was /sc/, *ċċ* was /cc/, phonetically the affricate [tš] with lengthened hold on the stop component.

/j/: voiced palatal, or palatalized, stop. Phonetically close to the palatal spirant of North German /g/ in *liegen*. When doubled /jj/, it was phonetically close to the Modern English affricate /ǰ/. Assumption of different developments justified by subsequent divergent history. OE /jj/ > NE /ǰ/, OE /j/ > NE /y/. Spelled *ġ* by modern editors.

/n/: [n] everywhere except before /k/, /g/, and /x/, where [ŋ] occurred. Spelled <n>.

Except for /k/, spelled <c>, and except where noted differently above, the consonants were spelled with the symbols used here to represent the phonemes.

5. Suprasegmental phonemes were of three types: stress, pitch, and juncture. Since these have only recently begun to be studied within an adequate phonemic frame, their reconstruction in this particular shape is tentative at this time. Their presence in Old English is beyond question, but one may legitimately question distributional statements about them until more data are available.

Although Modern English has four stress phonemes, primary, secondary, tertiary, and weak, symbolized by /´ ˆ ` ˘/, there is doubt about whether more than three were significant in Old English. These may be labeled primary, secondary, and weak, symbolized by /´ ˆ ˘/, with the observation that the Old English weak stress was phonetically approximately the equivalent of the Modern English tertiary.[15] These stress phonemes are illustrated in the sample transcription given under section 8.

Pitch phonemes account for significant relative pitch. Numbering from the lowest to the highest, in Modern English they are /^{1} ^{2} ^{3} ^{4}/. The pitch phonemes must be assumed, in Old English as in Modern English, to have been arranged in contours which combined with the terminal junctures described below to form intonation morphemes. They may be reconstructed with considerable assurance in view of their phonemic status as far back into the history of the Germanic languages as the time of the split between Germanic and Slavic. The details of their distribution are not recoverable.

The juncture phonemes are of two types: internal juncture, and terminal juncture. Internal open juncture is symbolized by /+/ and, for convenience, labeled 'plus juncture'. The phonetic nature of /+/ in Old

[15] This is not to suggest that OE /˘/ was the ancestor of NE /`/. The history appears to be a complex one and is left for full description at another time and place.

English can only be guessed at, and any really full formulation must await the outcome of the attempts at formulation in Modern English which are now being carried on. As a purely tentative formulation, even though it is one which the writer realizes may well be upset by subsequent study, the following is offered. It is pragmatically a useful one at the present stage of historical investigation. In their normal sequential arrangement in utterance, the segmental phonemes of English characteristically at all periods may be stated to have had two shapes: one which they assume contiguous with pause, and one which they assume contiguous with other segmental phonemes. /+/ is assumed to be present when one hears the characteristically final shape of one segmental phoneme followed by the characteristically initial shape of the next one. /+/ is, then, the phonemic shape of potential pause, and it is believed to have been a real phonetic entity. The shape of segmental phonemes contiguous with each other is their shape in normal transition. The reconstruction of this phoneme for Old English is one of the most important steps to be taken in an adequate descriptive statement of Old English structure, since only in terms of juncture are such statements of allophonic distribution as were earlier made for consonants meaningful on the phonological level. Thus when one describes the initial allophone of /x/ as having less friction than the other allophones, he is really saying that /x/ has less friction when it immediately follows juncture than it has elsewhere.

As in Modern English, it seems necessary to assume that there were three terminal junctures in Old English, which can be symbolized by /| || #/ and labeled 'single bar', 'double bar', and 'double cross'. Double cross juncture represents the diminishing intensity of utterance, with or without a falling pitch contour, and the substantial retardation of tempo, which occur at the end of an English utterance such as 'I'm going home'. Phonemically, this is: /^{2}àym+gôwiŋ+^{3}hówm^{1}#/. The double cross juncture is not to be confused with the /^{3} ^{1}/ fall of pitch which precedes it. Double bar juncture represents the retardation of tempo (less than for /#/) and pitch rise after the last pitch in an utterance such as 'Is he going?' Phonemically, this is: /^{2}ìziy+^{3}gówiŋ^{3}||/. Single bar juncture, unlike the other two, is not normally found, in Modern English or in Old English, as utterance final; it represents a slight retardation of tempo (less still than for /||/), but it has no diminution of utterance intensity, nor a characteristic rise nor fall; it is accompanied by a freezing of pitch level between the final pitch phoneme of one phrase and the initial pitch phoneme of the next; thus, 'If I wanted to, I'd do it'. Phonemically, this is: /^{2}if+ày+^{3}wɔ́hntid+tùw^{2}|^{2}àyd+^{3}dúwɨt^{1}#/. Until there is evidence to the contrary, this analysis presumes a high degree of similarity between the distribution of terminal junctures in Modern English and their distribution in the older stages of the language. Their presumed distribution in West Saxon is illustrated by the sample transcription under 8.

6. Although students of Old English are principally interested in reading the literary monuments which appear in the West Saxon dialect, it may be pointed out that the type of dialectal variation which characterizes Modern English, Modern German, and the other living Germanic languages is not an innovation in their modern periods, but was characteristic of the older periods as well. A description of Old English dialectal variation requires nearly every counter in the full structural frame of eight simple nuclei and twenty-four complex nuclei. A few, as far as the evidence of the documents goes, are not required; one may suspect, but of course never be able to prove, that some of these lacunae are in the documentation, not actually in the structure of the language.

7. There are several respects in which this analysis differs from the traditional one. It assumes a minimum of systemic change between Old and Modern English. It includes the suprasegmental phonemes as a necessary condition of completeness in the description. It furnishes a tool for describing dialect variation in terms of the differing commutations which go on within a unified structural frame for the entire language. It avoids setting up a structure for Old English of a type which seems excessively far removed from the demonstrable structuring habits of the living dialects. And in every respect of which the writer is aware at this time, it accounts for the data completely and consistently as well as economically and symmetrically.[16] This is not to say that it is more than a hypothesis; it is only to point out that the traditional analysis is ALSO a hypothesis which is perhaps rather too often mistaken for a proved theorem.

[16] Since this was written (1952), further discussion of some of the issues has appeared in print. In "Some recent interpretations of Old English digraph spellings" (*Lang.* 29.143-56, 1953), Sherman Kuhn and Randolph Quirk argued that Barritt and I (see fn. 4) had not proven our case with regard to the phoneme /æ/. We answered in "The Old English short digraphs: some considerations" (*Lang.* 31.372-89, 1955) and they submitted further objections in "The Old English short digraphs: a reply" (*Lang.* 31.390-401, 1955), to which a long footnote at the end of ". . . some considerations" attempted further reply. In that footnote, certain citations were erroneously given (388) with initial /h/ rather than initial /x/, (/hǽw/ for /xǽw/, /hǽww/ for /xǽww/, /hǘjd/ for /xǘjd/, /hǘyd/ for /xǘyd/), and these errors became the basis for a paper read by Kuhn before the Linguistic Society of America (Summer, 1956). I was not present to hear the paper, so that my only information about it comes at second-hand (Kuhn declined to send me a copy of the manuscript). The mimeographed sheet that accompanied his presentation seems to accomplish no more than to point out the obvious error in our writing of /h/ rather than /x/ word-initially, though I assume his argument was concerned with more fundamental questions. Finally, in volume 1 of *Litera* (1954), C. E. Bazell reviewed *OP*4 (see fn. 4) very unfavorably, offering some remarkable conclusions of his own about OE phonological structure ('The whole point of the old system [i.e. traditional analysis of OE vowels] was that the "diphthongs" behaved like simple vowels . . . they were . . . *simple phonemes*. . . . When West Saxon *eo* became a monophthong towards the ME period, there was no phonemic change; quite simply, the diphthongal rendering of a unit-phoneme became a monophthongal rendering.' 'The late West Saxon system was:

i y u
e eo o
æ ea a').

In my opinion, Bazell has not grappled with the issues at all, and without hurting us he throws no light on the problem by referring to our reasoning as 'eminently stupid'.

8. The following transcription is from one of the more famous prose passages, the 'sparrow analogy' in the Alfredian Bede. It is a 9th century West Saxon text.[17] All phonemes are symbolized except weak stress, which is left unmarked. Note that in the orthography, circumflex represents a long vowel, but in the phonemic transcription, it represents secondary (i.e., medial) stress.

*þyslîc mê is gesewen, þû cyning, þis andweard*e

/^{3}θûs+liyc+mêh+is+je+^{2}séwen^{1}|^{2}θûw+kǘning^{2}||^{2}θis+ɔ̂nd+wæ̂rde+

lif manna on eorðan tô wiðmetenesse þǣre tîde

^{2}líyf^{2}||^{2}mɔnnɔ+on+^{2}érθɔn^{2}||^{2}toh+wîθ+mête+nêsse+θæ̂hre+^{2}tíyde^{2}||

þe ûs uncûð is, swycle þû æt swǣsendum sitte

^{2}θe+ûws+un+^{3}kúwθ+îs^{3}|^{3}swǘlce+θûw+æt+^{2}swǽhsendum+sîtte^{2}||

mid þînum ealdormannum ond þegnum on wintertîde,

^{2}mid θîynum ^{3}ǽldor+mɔ̂nnum+ond+
θêjnum^{2}|^{2}on+^{3}wínter+tîyde^{1}#

ond sîe fŷr onǣled ond þîn heall gewyrmed,

^{2}ond+sîw+fü̂r+on+^{2}ǽhled^{2}||^{2}ond+θîyn+xæ̂l+je^{2}wǘrmed^{2}||

ond hit rîne ond snîwe ond styrme ûte;

^{2}ond+xit+^{3}ríyne^{3}||^{2}ond+^{3}sníwwe^{3}||^{2}ond+^{3}stǘrme+ûwte^{1}#

cume ân spearwa ond hrædlîce þæt hûs þurhflêo,

^{2}kûme+ɔ̂hn+^{3}spǽrwɔ^{2}|^{2}ond+^{3}xrǽdliyce+θæ̂t+xûws+θûrx+flêw^{1}#

cume þurh ôþre duru in, þurh ôþre ût gewîte.

^{2}kûme+θûrx+^{3}óhθre+dûru+în^{3}||^{2}θûrx+^{3}óhθre+ûwt+je+wîyte^{1}#

Hwæt! he on þâ tîd hê inne bið

^{4}xwǽt^{4}||^{3}xéh^{3}||^{2}on+θɔ̂h+^{2}tíyd^{2}||^{2}θe+xêh+înne+^{2}bíθ^{2}||

ne bið hrinen mid þŷ storme þæs wintres;

^{2}ne+bîθ+^{3}xrínen+mid+θüy+stôrme+θæs+wîntres^{1}#

ac þæt bið ân êagan bryhtm ond þæt lǣste fæc,

^{2}ɔk+θæ̂t+bîθ+ɔ̂hn+^{3}ǽwgɔn+brü̂xtim^{3}|^{2}ond+θæ̂t+^{2}lǽhste+fæ̂k^{1}#

ac hê sôna of wintra on þone winter eft cymeð.

^{2}ɔk+xêh+sôhnɔ+^{3}óf+wîntrɔ^{3}||^{2}ôn+θone+^{3}winter+êft+kü̂meθ^{1}#

Swâ þonne þis monna lîf tô medmiclum fæce ætŷweð;

^{3}swɔ́h^{3}|^{3}θónne^{3}|^{2}θîs+^{3}mónnɔ+lîyf^{2}|^{2}toh+^{3}méd+mîklum+fǽke+
ætü̂yweθ^{1}#

hwæt þǣr foregange, oððe hwæt þǣr æfterfylige,

^{2}xwæ̂t+^{3}θ ǽhr+fôre+gɔ̂nge^{2}||^{2}ôθθe+xwæ̂t+^{3} θǽhr+ æfter fü̂lije^{2}||

wê ne cunnun.

^{3}wéh+ne+kûnnun^{1}#/

[17] The text used here is from p. 49 of *An Anglo-Saxon Reader,* ed. by Alfred J. Wyatt (Cambridge, 1948) . A free translation is this: 'Thus it seems to me, oh king, this present / life of man on earth in comparison with the time / that is unknown to us, as if you were siting at a banquet / with your aldermen and thanes in winter time / and your fire aflame and your hall warmed / and it were raining and snowing and storming outside; / there comes a single sparrow and quickly flies through the house, / comes in through one door, departs out through the other. / What! He, in the time that he is inside, / is not touched by the storm of the winter; / that is but a twinkling of an eye and the least amount of time / and he soon from winter again comes into the winter. / So, then, this life of man appears like a little time; / what went before it or what follows after it, we do not know'.

On the Syllabic Phonemes of Old English

SHERMAN M. KUHN

1. THE PHONEMIC SYSTEM OF OLD ENGLISH has become a matter of increasing interest to linguists in recent years. Twenty years ago, structural linguists seldom concerned themselves with the phonemes of a 'dead' language, while traditional linguists and philologists generally regarded phonemes as something exotic, something outside the purview of normal language activities and studies. Since 1939, however, we have seen a fair number of publications dealing with the Old English phonemic system or portions of it, written either from a structural viewpoint or in a manner which indicates an awareness of the structural problems of the language.[1]

Reprinted by permission from *Language* 37.522-38 (1961).

[1] Marjorie Daunt, Old English sound-changes reconsidered in relation to scribal tradition and practice, *Transactions of the Philological Society 1939* 108-37 (1940); J. W. Watson, Northumbrian Old English *ēo* and *ēa*, *Lg.* 22.19-26 (1946); id., Non-initial *k* in the North of England, *Lg.* 23.43-9 (1947); Herbert Penzl, The phonemic split of Germanic *k* in Old English, *Lg.* 23.34-42 (1947); W. F. Twaddell, The prehistoric Germanic short syllabics, *Lg.* 24.139-51 (1948); Norman E. Eliason, Old English vowel lengthening and vowel shortening before consonant groups, *Studies in philology* 45.1-20 (1948); A. S. C. Ross, Old English *æ* ∼ *a*, *English studies* 32.49-56 (1951); R. P. Stockwell and C. W. Barritt, Some Old English graphemic-phonemic correspondences—*ae, ea,* and *a*, *Studies in linguistics: Occasional papers,* No. 4 (Washington, D. C., 1951); Karl Brunner, The Old English vowel phonemes, *English studies* 34.247-51 (1953); Sherman M. Kuhn and Randolph Quirk, Some recent interpretations of Old English digraph spellings, *Lg.* 29.143-56 (1953); Alfred Reszkiewicz, The phonemic interpretation of Old English digraphs, *Biuletyn Polskiego Towarzystwa Językoznawczego* 12.179-87 (1953); M. L. Samuels, The study of Old English phonology, *TPS 1952* 15-47 (1953); Daunt, Some notes on Old English phonology, *TPS 1952* 48-54 (1953); C. E. Bazell, rev. of Stockwell and Barritt (1951), *Litera* 1.75-7 (1954); W. G. Moulton, The stops and spirants of early Germanic, *Lg.* 30.1-42 (1954); Stockwell and Barritt, The Old English short digraphs: Some considerations, *Lg.* 31.372-89 (1955); Kuhn and Quirk, The Old English digraphs: A reply, *Lg.* 31.390-401 (1955); Gerd Bauer, The problem of short diphthongs in Old English, *Anglia* 74.427-37 (1956); Hans Kurath, The loss of long consonants and the rise of voiced fricatives in Middle English, *Lg.* 32.435-45 (1956); The binary interpretation of English vowels: A critique, *Lg.* 33.111-22 (1957); Seymour Chatman, The *a*/*æ* opposition in Old English, *Word* 14.224-36 (1958); C. F. Hockett, *A course in modern linguistics* 372-9 (New York, 1958); J. A. Nist, Phonemes and distinctive features in *Beowulf*, *SIL* 13.25-33 (1958); James Sledd, Some questions of

Very few of these studies deal with more than a small segment of the Old English phonemic system; most of them attack some portion of something which is described as the 'traditional interpretation' or the 'traditional view'. To my knowledge, no one has yet given us an account of all the Old English phonemes from the viewpoint of the traditional linguists. There are several reasons for this silence. In the first place, there is no single 'traditional view', because traditional linguists differ concerning many details of Old English phonology; and if a scholar takes sides on any point against one of the better known grammars or handbooks, many of his fellow-traditionalists will conclude at once that his work is unsound. Many of the structuralists, on the other hand, will be inclined to view him with suspicion merely because he defends traditional views. A more important reason is probably that the traditional linguist has little to say that is new or startling. For the most part, he can only restate well known facts and interpretations in phonemic terminology.

I believe, nevertheless, that such a restatement is desirable, if only that we may have a better understanding of what is being attacked. In the sections that follow, I shall first attempt to reconstruct the Old English syllabics as they were about 700 A.D., shortly before the appearance of the first written records. I shall then show the development of this system in each of the OE dialects in which any writings survive: Mercian (Merc.), Northumbrian (Nhb.), West Saxon (WS), and Kentish (Kt.).[2] An account which is as inclusive as this must necessarily be general. Only a small part of the evidence on which it is based can be given. Many facts which concern the incidence of phonemes rather than their existence in a given dialect must be passed over briefly or omitted. Individual works and scholars can be mentioned only when they are especially pertinent to the discussion.[3]

OLD ENGLISH SYLLABICS ABOUT 700

2. [Table I] presents the OE phonemes at a period for which we have no written records. The phonemes must be inferred from data in later MSS and from developments in cognate languages. The system is an

English phonology, *Lg.* 34.252-8 (1958); Stockwell, The phonology of Old English: A structural sketch, *SIL* 13.13-24 (1958); Hockett, The stressed syllabics of Old English, *Lg.* 35.575-97 (1959); Kemp Malone, Diphthong and glide, *Mélanges de linguistique et de philologie: Fernand Mossé in memoriam* 256-66 (Paris, 1959); Stockwell and Rudolph Willard, Further notes on Old English phonology, *SIL* 14.10-13 (1959); Stockwell and Barritt, Scribal practice: Some assumptions, *Lg.* 37.75-82 (1961).

[2] Linguistic analysis normally proceeds from the individual and specific to the general. The order of the analysis itself is reversed here for clarity of presentation.

[3] For the earlier studies, see A. G. Kennedy, *A bibliography of writings on the English language from the beginning of printing to the end of 1922* (Cambridge, Mass., and New Haven, 1927). For more recent work, see the various annual bibliographies and those in recent grammars, such as K. Brunner's *Altenglische Grammatik nach . . . Eduard Sievers*[2] (Halle, 1951) and A. Campbell's *Old English grammar* (Oxford, 1959).

abstraction—as though the living language had been frozen at a particular point in time. In some ways it may be inexact; for example, it shows an independent phoneme /ɔ̈/, although in the year 700 the sound in question may have been further advanced in the direction of /e/ than the table suggests.

	FRONT VOWELS UNROUND	FRONT VOWELS ROUND	BACK VOWELS	DIPHTHONGS	UNACCENTED VOWELS
HIGH	/i/ [ɪ]	/y/ [ʏ̈]	/u/ [ʊ]	/io/ [ɪɒ, ɪɛ]	
	/ī/ [i:]	/ȳ/ [ü:]	/ū/ [u:]	/īo/ [iɒ:, ɪɛ:]	[ɨ]
MID	/e/ [ɛ]	/œ/ [ɒ]	/o/ [ɒ]	/eo/ [ɛɒ]	
	/ē/ [e:]	/œ̄/ [ö:]	/ō/ [o:]	/ēo/ [eɒ:]	/ə/
	/æ/ [æ, æ˔]	/ɔ̈/ [ɔ̈]	/a/ [ɑ̈, ɔ]	/æa/ [æɑ̈, æɒ]	[ə]
LOW	/ǣ/ [æ:, ɛ:]		/ā/ [ɑ̈:]	/ǣa/ [æɑ̈:, æɒ:]	

TABLE I—*About 700*

The principal texts used in this reconstruction are three early Latin-English glossaries: the *Epinal Glossary* (8th century), the *Corpus Glossary* (8th), and the *Erfurt Glossary* (early 9th).[4] The first is most conservative in its spellings and seems to be the earliest linguistically, although it may not be the earliest MS. The second represents a revision, with additions and much modernization, of the original glossary (now lost) from which *Epinal* was derived. The third is closely related to *Epinal* and very similar, but was copied by a scribe familiar with High German and shows a few un-English features. Some additional evidence will be found in three early Northumbrian fragments *(Caedmon's Hymn, Bede's Death Song, Leiden Riddle)* and in the proper names of the earliest MSS of Bede's history.[5] For much of our understanding of these earliest surviving texts, we are indebted to H. M. Chadwick, whose *Studies in Old English* appeared in 1899.[6] By comparing items common to two or more of the early glossaries, he was able to reconstruct most of the scribal practices[7] of the original (Archetype I), which is generally thought to have been written late in the seventh century. Although Arch. I, like the three glossaries derived from it, was basically Mercian, the dialect was much less differentiated from other dialects of Old English than it later became.

[4] Henry Sweet, *The oldest English texts* = *EETS OS* 83.35-121 (1885); W. M. Lindsay, *The Corpus Glossary* (Cambridge, 1921).

[5] Sweet, *OET* 132-47, 149-51; A. H. Smith, *Three Northumbrian poems* (London, 1933); E. V. K. Dobbie, *The Anglo-Saxon minor poems* 104, 107, 109 (New York, 1942); Charles Plummer, *Venerabilis Baedae historiam ecclesiasticam* (Oxford, 1896).

[6] *Transactions of the Cambridge Philological Society* 4.87-265.

[7] I agree with Hockett 578 (1959) that any analysis of OE phonemes must account satisfactorily for scribal practices. To be more specific, I am certain that the OE writing system (or any other alphabet system used for a language before the invention of dictionaries) was roughly phonemic; otherwise it would have been like an elaborate cipher, unintelligible to anyone who did not possess a special key. I am equally certain that the graphemes were roughly phonetic; otherwise how would anyone identify the phonemes?

This table obviously owes something to Hockett 576 (1959). I use one symbol, /ɔ̈/, for a phoneme outside the scope of his article. In place of some of his other symbols, I prefer symbols somewhat closer to the graphs used for them in Old English texts: /œ/ for his /ø/; /a/ for his /ɒ̈/ (although there are several shapes of this grapheme in the MSS, modern printed texts have settled upon the one I use); /io, eo, æa/ for his /ɨ, ə, a/; and /ə/ with allophones [ɨ, ə] for sounds in unaccented syllables. I prefer a macron to Hockett's dot for the phoneme of length, partly because it is used in the printed texts, partly because it makes possible the indication of stress within a vowel cluster, as /ēo/ (falling) versus /eō/ (rising). I do not treat long vowels as self clusters, or use /h, w, y/ for either length or glide, for reasons that will appear below. I treat vowel plus length as a complex phonemic unit in order to avoid certain difficulties which arise when the phonemic system must be treated diachronically;[8] thus, /ǣ/ is not merely /æ/ plus length, but a higher and more fronted sound, which became /ē/ (long open *e*) in Middle English while the /æ/ without length became a lower, more retracted sound commonly written *a* in Middle English. There was a similar qualitative difference between the members of most short–long pairs; the difference is important historically but was not sufficient to keep the scribes from writing both sets of phonemes with one set of graphemes.

2.1. It should be clear from the table that the short syllabics of prehistoric English about 700 had advanced well beyond the prehistoric Germanic stage outlined by Twaddell (150). The allophones [æ, a], [y, u] and [ø, o] had become separate phonemes, and a new series of diphthongal phonemes had arisen. Some of the new phonemes in their turn had developed allophones which would later become significant. There were also dialectal differences, in the incidence of phonemes and the preference for certain allophones, which do not show up in the table but which will be noted in the discussion of individual phonemes.

2.2. /i/ < Gmc. /i/ in *fisc, biden* (p.ppl. of *bīdan*), etc.; Gmc. /e/ before nasal plus consonant in *bindan,* etc.; Gmc. /e/ before /m/ in *nimen* (pr. opt. pl. of *niman-nioman*), etc.; Lat. or Gk. /i, y, e/ in *ċiriċe, ġim,* etc. There was already a tendency to diphthongize /i/ in an open syllable followed by a back vowel (velar umlaut); this would later produce an allophone [ɪɒ], which would fall together with /io/ and ultimately with /eo/. But the tendency cannot have been far advanced by 700; cf. Epinal *sifun-,* Corpus *sibun-,* later OE *siofon, seofon.*[9] Only after /w/ was the change noticeable enough to be reflected in spelling; e.g. Corpus *uudu-,* Epinal *uuidu* (but also *uudu*), Erfurt *uuydu,* later OE *wudu, wiodu.*

2.3 /ī/ < Gmc. /ī/ in *bīdan,* etc.; Gmc. /im, in/ in *fīf, swīþe,* etc.; Lat. /ī, ē, oe/ in *wīn, pīn,* etc. Before /h/, this sound had developed in

[8] I agree with Kurath 114 (1957).

[9] Chadwick 226-8, 250.

the WS and Kt. dialects a diphthongal allophone [iu:] or [iɒ:], falling together with the reflex of Gmc. /iu/. Very likely, the same 'breaking' took place in the Anglian dialects (i.e. Merc. and Nhb.); but if so, the diphthong had been reduced to a monophthong by 700 ('smoothing'); cf. Ep. *bituicn,* Erf. *bituichn,* later WS *bĕ̄tweoh, bētweonum.*

2.4. /e/ < Gmc. /e/ in *weġ, sweltan,* etc.; Gmc. /a/ with fronting and *i*-umlaut in *bed, hebban,* etc. Like /i/, this vowel tended to diphthongize in an open syllable followed by a back vowel, but velar umlaut had scarcely affected scribal practices by 700; cf. Ep., Corp., Erf. *bebr* (later OE *beofor*) and early Nhb. *hefen-, hefaen-,* later OE *heofon, heofen.*[10]

2.5. /ē/ < Gmc. /ē/ in *hēr* adv., etc.; Gmc. /e/ final under the accent in *sē* pron., etc.; Gmc. /iz/ in *mē,* etc. This phoneme existed in all of the dialects but was relatively infrequent in WS.[11] In the other three dialects, Gmc. /æ/ (WGmc. /ā/, WS /ǣ/) had become /ē/ in words like *dēd, lētan, wēpen* (WS *dǣd, lǣtan, wǣpen*); cf. Ep., Erf. *meeġ,* Corp. *meiġ,* etc. Similarly, Latin /ā/ had become /ē/ in *strēt* (WS *strǣt*), etc.[12] In Merc. and Nhb., /ē/ had also resulted from smoothing of Gmc. /eo/ before /c, ċ, g, ġ, h/; e.g. Merc. *flēge, þēh,* WS (and Kt.) *flēoge, þēoh.* This process was advanced but not yet complete in the basically Merc. Archetype I.[13]

2.6. /æ/ < Gmc. /a/ in closed syllable or in open syllable followed by an originally front vowel ('fronting'), cf. WS, Nhb. *dæġ, dæġes, fæder, fæt, æfter,* etc.; Gmc. /a/ with secondary *i*-umlaut, cf. WS *æþeling, hærfest, gædeling* (< **aþyling, *harybist, *gadyling* < **aþuling, *harubist, *gaduling*), etc. A raised and fronted allophone, a sound somewhere between [æ] and [ɛ] which I now indicate [æ˔],[14] existed in Merc., in Kt., and to a limited extent in Nhb.; cf. Merc. (*Vespasian Psalter*) *deġ, deġes, feder, fet, efter,* etc. The evidence of the early glossaries indicates that this allophone was of minor importance, certainly not yet a phoneme, in the Merc. of Arch. I.[15] The spelling in this MS must have been normally *ae,* occasionally *e;* cf. Ep. *uuaeter-,* Corp. *uuęter,* Erf. *uaeter* (and at least twenty-nine other instances in which all three have some allograph of *ǣ*), but Ep., Corp., Erf. *reftras* (and eight other instances in which all three have *e*). Another source of /æ/ in Anglian

[10] Ibid.; see also Hilmer Ström, *Old English personal names in Bede's history* 117 (Lund, 1939).

[11] This must be inferred from later WS, for there are no surviving WS texts comparable in date to the glossaries and early Nhb. texts.

[12] Chadwick 206-10, 250.

[13] Ibid. 219-20, 225.

[14] I once tried using Bülbring's [æᵉ] for this, but I find this symbol often misinterpreted as a diphthong.—The diacritic here is intended to indicate a vowel simultaneously raised and fronted.

[15] Chadwick 190-5.

was the [æ] from smoothing of /æa/, dealt with under that diphthong. Although /æ/ originated as an allophone of /a/, it was certainly an independent phoneme in Old English.[16]

2.7. /ǣ/ < Gmc. /ai/ with *i*-umlaut in *hǣlan, hǣþ,* etc. The incidence of this phoneme was greatly increased in WS by the reflex of Gmc. /æ/ in that dialect (see /ē/ above). In Merc. and Nhb., /ǣ/ also arose from the smoothing of Gmc. /au/ before /c, ċ, g, ġ, h/. This change was well advanced but not yet complete by 700, and the resulting monophthong was commonly spelled *æ* in Arch. I; cf. Ep. *-bēag,* Corp., Erf. *-bǣg* (later Merc. *bēg,* WS *bēag,* later *bēah*) and Ep. *-lēc,* Corp. *-leec,* Erf. *-lēc* (WS *lēac*).[17] There was also a tendency for /ǣ/ (< Gmc. /ai/) to become raised and fronted to [ɛ:] in the Anglian dialects, especially before dentals; and this sound later fell together with /ē/; cf. Ep. *taenil,* Erf. *tēnil,* Corp. *tāēnil* (but elsewhere *-tēnil*), later OE *tǣnel, tēnel.* In Kt., the shift of /ǣ/ to [ɛ:] to /ē/ went further than in Anglian. This tendency was probably present but still in its earliest stages when Arch. I was written.[18]

2.8. /y/ < Gmc. /u/ with *i*-umlaut in *cyning, byċġan,* etc.; Latin /o/ before nasal with *i*-umlaut in *mynstre,* etc.; Lat. /u/ with *i*-umlaut in *pyt,* etc. This sound was clearly distinct from /u/ by 700. It was still relatively stable if the spellings of the early glossaries are to be trusted. There is no evidence of unrounding to /i/ or of the Kt. shift to /e/ before the ninth century.

2.9. /ȳ/ < Gmc. /ū/ with *i*-umlaut in *mȳs, fȳr, ontȳnan,* etc.; Gmc. /un/ with *i*-umlaut in *cȳþan; ȳst,* etc.; Gmc. /wō/ with *i*-umlaut in *cȳe,* etc. This sound, like the preceding, was an independent phoneme and relatively stable around 700.

2.10. /œ/ < Gmc. /o/ with *i*-umlaut, cf. Merc. *doehter* dat. sg., etc.; Lat. /o/ with *i*-umlaut in Anglian *oele,* etc. This must always have been a rare phoneme because Proto-Gmc. /u/ did not become /o/ before /i, j/, and the umlaut could take place only when an /o/ was introduced into umlaut position through analogy or borrowing. There was a tendency to unround /œ/ to /e/ in all dialects. The evidence of Archetype I is not clear as to how far the unrounding had gone, but the survival of *soęrgęndi* in Ep., *ðroehtig* in Corp., *doehter* and *oexen* in the *Vespasian Psalter,* suggests that there was probably such a phoneme around 700.

2.11. /œ̄/ < Gmc. /ō/ with *i*-umlaut in *fōēt* nom. pl., *dōēman,* etc.; Gmc. /am, an/ with *i*-umlaut in *sōēfte, tōēþ* nom. pl., *gōēs* nom. pl., *ōēhtan,* etc.; Gmc. /æ/ before nasal with *i*-umlaut in *cwōēn, wōēnan,* etc. This phoneme eventually unrounded to /ē/, but much more slowly than

[16] For WS, see Ross 49; Stockwell and Barritt 37-8 (1951). For Merc., see Chatman 229-36. The proofs for WS can be extended to Nhb., those for Merc. to Kt.

[17] Chadwick 223-5.

[18] Ibid. 212.

its short counterpart. It was spelled *oe* in Arch. I; cf. Ep. *ġirōēfan,* Corp., Erf. *ġerōēfan,* later WS *ġerēfan.* It was spelled either *oe* or *oi* in early Nhb.; cf. *Cōēnrēd, Cōīnrēd* in Bede.[19]

2.12. /ɔ̄/ < Gmc. /a/ before nasal with *i*-umlaut; cf. Ep., Erf. *dopaenid,* Corp. *doppaenid* (later OE *dopenid*), Ep., Erf. *aemil,* Corp. *emil,* etc.; *Haengest* beside *Hengist, Middilaengli* beside *Middilengli,* etc., in the early Bede MSS.[20] The regular spelling in Archetype I was probably *ae.* During the course of the eighth century, this phoneme fell together with /e/, except in a part of the Southeast Midland area (Essex and part of Middlesex), where it held its ground until some time in the Middle English period.[21] It is a question whether this sound should be regarded as a phoneme in prehistoric Old English. It began as an allophone of /a/ and ended in most dialects as an allophone of /e/; hence, there is a period in which it belonged to neither of these phonemes. It could be regarded as an allophone of /æ/ during the transition, but it did not develop like /æ/. The latter normally became WS, Nhb. /æ/, Merc., Kt. /ɛ/; /ɔ̄/ became /e/ in all the dialects except the small subarea already mentioned. On the whole, the analysis of OE phonology is simplified for us if we treat /ɔ̄/ as a phoneme about 700.

2.13. /u/ < Gmc. /u/ in *hund, dulfun, -on* (pt. pl. of *delfan*), etc.; Gmc. /o/ in *fugul, -ol, hunig,* etc.; Lat. /o/ before nasal in *munt,* etc. In unaccented syllables, there was a tendency to lower /u/ to /o/ in all of the dialects.

2.14. /ū/ < Gmc. /ū/ in *mūs, brūcan,* etc.; Gmc. /un/ in *ūs, mūþ, þūhte,* etc.; Gmc. /u/ in *fūre* (gen. sg. of *furh*), etc.; Gmc. /wō/ in *cū, hū,* etc.

2.15. /o/ < Gmc. /o/ in *dohtor, morgen,* etc.; Lat. /o/ in *offrian,* etc.; Gmc. /ō/ shortened in *godspel,* etc.

2.16. /ō/ < Gmc. /ō/ in *dōm, grōwan,* etc.; Gmc. /am, an/ in *fōn, gōs, sōfte, tōþ,* etc.; Gmc. /o/ in *hōles* (gen. sg. of *holh*), etc.; Gmc. /æ/ before nasal in *mōna,* etc.

2.17. /a/ < Gmc. /a/ in open syllable before back vowel in *faran, dagas* nom. pl., *fatu* nom. pl., *clawan,* etc.; Gmc. /a/ in closed syllable before certain long consonants in *habban,* etc.; Gmc. /a/ before nasal in *man, ram,* etc.; Lat. /a/ in *carcern, salm,* etc. Phonetically, this sound was probably low back unround. Stockwell and Willard, although using the symbol /ɔ/, say that it may have been 'phonetically . . . low back unround [ɒ]'.[22] Hockett represents it as /ɑ/, places it among the rounded vowels, but says that it was not necessarily 'rounded in the physiological sense'.[23] The treatment of borrowed words containing Lat. /a/ and /o/ seems to

[19] Ström 97.

[20] Chadwick 204-6, 250; Ström 93.

[21] K. Luick, *Historische Grammatik der englischen Sprache* 349-50 (Leipzig, 1921); cf. ME *pani* 'penny', *pans* 'pence', etc.

[22] Page 10 (1959).

[23] Page 576 (1959).

me significant. The earliest borrowings with Lat. /a/ develop like words with Gmc. /a/; e.g. *condel, candel,* and *ceaster, cæster, cester.* Late borrowings are spelled with *a,* as though OE /a/ were identical with Lat. /a/; e.g. *capellān, caric, cat, catte, castel, cwatern* 'four-spot', *canceler, canon, cantere, cantic.* Lat. /o/, certainly a rounded vowel, is commonly *o* (not *a*) in late borrowings; e.g. *ācordian, coliandre, columne, corōna, copel, comēta, consolde, consul.* Lat. *chronica* appears in late WS as *cranic,* but this *a* precedes a nasal and may merely indicate that the allophone [ɔ] survived in late WS, although generally spelled *a.*

There were probably dialectal differences in the incidence of /a/ as early as about 700. This phoneme was more frequent in Merc. and Nhb., where it occurred before /l/ plus consonant; e.g. *ald* (WS, Kt. e*ald*). It was most frequent in Nhb., where it seems to have occurred also before /r/ plus consonant; e.g. *arm* beside *earm, eorm* (Merc., WS, Kt. *earm*).[24]

There were two important allophones of /a/ in all of the OE dialects: [ɔ] before nasal, [a] elsewhere. The former must have existed from very early times, for when lengthened it fell together with /ō/ in all dialects, as in *gōs,* etc. In metathesized forms like *orn* 'ran', it eventually fell together with /o/ in most dialects of Middle English. The [ɔ] was much more important in Anglian than in WS and Kt.; cf. Merc., Nhb. *mon, rom,* etc., early WS *man, mon, ram, rom,* late WS *man, ram.* In Anglian /ɔ/ became phonemic for a time in the ninth and tenth centuries but later (probably early in the ME period) fused with /a/. The early glossaries vary in spelling practices: Ep. shows nearly all *a* before nasal, while Corp. has *o* about five times as often as *a.* Arch. I apparently had *a* rather consistently.[25] The early Bede MSS fluctuate between *a* and *o.*[26] We may conclude, I think, that [ɔ] was still an allophone at the end of the seventh century.

2.18. /ā/ < Gmc. /ai/ in *hāl, hātan,* etc.; Gmc /æ/ before /w/ in *cnāwan,* etc.; Gmc. /a/ final under the accent in *swā* (but also *swē* in Anglian), etc. In WS, Gmc. /æ/ before /p, g/ plus back vowel also became /ā/; e.g. *slāpan, māgas* nom. pl., etc. This phoneme was rounded to /ō/ in ME (long open *o*),[27] but in OE and early ME it is spelled *a* with no suggestion of rounding.

2.19. Length in OE vowels calls for additional comments. Length was clearly phonemic, as Reszkiewicz has demonstrated by means of minimal pairs.[28] Doubling of the vowel is also an indication of length in some OE texts, e.g. in the *Corpus Glossary.* Although a long vowel is not invariably doubled in Corp., the following instances may be noted: *briiġ, criid, fiil, liim, miil, piic, tiiġ, wiin-; breer, -leec, eil, deid; bruun, cuu,*

[24] For *a* and *ea* in the early Bede MSS, see Ström 92, 103-4.

[25] Chadwick 200-3.

[26] Ström 92.

[27] Except in the Northern dialect.

[28] Page 181. His sets of minimal pairs are all WS, but similar pairs can be adduced for all dialects except Kt., in which the surviving texts contain insufficient materials.

ġebuur, luus, muus, tuun; ānmood, boog, flooc, flood, foor, fornoom, forsooc, ġemoot, good, goor, goos, hood, hool, loob, roopnis, stool, wooð; aac, aam, aar, baan-, baar, baat, braad-, faag, faam, flaan, gaad, gaar-, ġemaad, haal-, haam, laac, laam, paad, waar. Length was rarely indicated by doubling when the vowel or diphthong was spelled with a digraph, but it was phonemic here also. Malone notes minimal pairs in WS: *heoru* 'sword' : *hēoru* 'pleasant', *sċeat* 'money' : *sċēat* 'corner'.[29] One may add *heofon* 'heaven' : *hēofan* 'to lament' : *hēofon* 'lamentation', *ġear* 'creaked' : *ġēar* 'year', *steor-* (in *steorglēaw* 'clever at astronomy') : *stēor-* (in *stēorlēas* 'uncontrolled'), *mæġ* 'can' : *mǣġ* 'kinsman'.

The OE 'lengthening' of Gmc. /æ iu, eo, au/ is sometimes misunderstood. In Gmc., this series stood alone, there being no corresponding series, either longer or shorter; hence, these phonemes were neutral, neither long nor short.[30] In prehistoric OE, they became /æ, io, eo, æo/, the last > /æa/; e.g. **dæd, *þiustru, *ċeosan, *heafud.* Through fronting, breaking, and other sound changes, a parallel series arose; e.g. **dæġ, *iorrja, *heorte, *bearn.*[31] The new sounds were shorter than the old; hence, quantity became significant. Without any phonetic change in themselves, the older series became phonemically /ǣ, īo, ēo, ǣa/.

The fact that long vowels in OE are often doubled in writing should not lead us to suppose either that they were self clusters or that a long vowel was necessarily equal in quantity to two short vowels. The self-cluster concept is precluded by the later history of the sounds; e.g. WS /a/ became southern ME /a/, but WS /ā/ became ME /ǭ/ (long open *o*); WS /æ/ fell together with ME /a/, but WS /ǣ/ became ME /ę̄/ (long open *e*); WS /e/ became ME /e/, when lengthened (in ME) /ę̄/, but WS /ē/ became ME /ẹ̄/ (long close *e*). There was clearly a qualitative as well as a quantitative difference, although it was not great enough in OE to prevent the scribes from writing both long and short vowels with the same set of graphemes. As for absolute quantity in OE, this is something which we do not know and may never know. The metrical evidence of OE poetry indicates that a long vowel (or a long diphthong) was longer than a short vowel (or a short diphthong), but it does not tell us how much longer.[32] Hitherto, most attempts to solve this problem have been based on introspection rather than evidence.

2.20. /io/ < Gmc. /i/ before /r/ plus consonant in *iorre, iorsian,* etc. This phoneme (complex phonemic unit, if you prefer) appears to have been distinct from /eo/ at the end of the seventh century. It fell together with /eo/ in Merc. during the ninth century, in Nhb. and Kt.

[29] Page 260.

[30] They are customarily left unmarked, as though short.

[31] According to Samuels 43, the short diphthongs became phonemic in the seventh century. /æ/ must have become a phoneme considerably earlier through the loss of inflectional endings, etc.

[32] See also Samuels 24.

late in the OE period or early in the ME period. In early WS, its [ɪɒ] allophone fell together with /eo/, while its [ɪɛ] allophone became phonemic. Originally, /io/ is thought to have been phonetically [ɪʊ], and this pronunciation may be reflected in early Anglian *iu*-spellings;[33] cf. *uuiurthit* in *Bede's Death Song*. This allophone has been omitted from Table I because it was probably rare at 700 and because it has little importance for the later history of OE.

The allophone [ɪɛ] was due in some instances to the weakening of the second element of /io/ to [ɛ], perhaps to [ə]. There are occasional *ie*-spellings in the early glossaries and in later Anglian texts, which suggest that this allophone existed in Anglian. In early WS it became the dominant allophone; hence, I write the early WS phoneme /ie/ rather than /io/. In late WS, /ie/ monophthongized to /i/, and then rounded to /y/ unless prevented from rounding by a palatal consonant; e.g. *ierre, iersian, siehþ,* etc. (later *yrre, yrsian, sihþ,* etc.). Another source of early WS /ie/ was Gmc. /a/ with breaking and *i*-umlaut (Angl. /æ/ or /e/) in *ierfe, fiellan, hliehhan, sleihþ, ġiest,* etc. A further source was Gmc. /e/ with diphthongization by initial palatal in *ċiele, ġiefu, sċieran,* etc. There is no WS text comparable in date to the early glossaries, and the evidence of the latter does not suggest that [ɪɛ] was as yet an important allophone when Archetype I was written. We should probably assume, however, that [ɪɛ] was important in WS as early as about 700; for palatal diphthongization and *i*-umlaut had certainly taken place before this date.

2.21. /īo/ < Gmc. /iu/ in *þīostru, ġeþīodan,* etc.; Gmc. /ī/ by breaking in *līoht,* etc.; Gmc. /ijō, iju/ in *þrīo,* etc. The diphthong in words like *līoht* was generally smoothed to /ī/ in the Anglian dialects by 700; it survived in Kt., fell together with /ēo/ during the ninth century in WS. The phoneme /īo/ was originally [iʊ:] phonetically, and this pronunciation may be reflected in occasional *iu*-spellings of the eighth century; e.g. Corp. *ðīustra* (later Nhb. *ðīostro,* later Merc. *ðēostru,* WS *ðīestre*). The pronunciation [iɒ:] was undoubtedly dominant about 700. The phoneme fell together with /ēo/ in OE, but more slowly than its short counterpart fell together with /eo/. An allophone [iɛ:] existed in all dialects and is reflected in later Merc. by spellings like *sīe* (nom.sg. fem. of *sē*), in WS, [iɛ:] was, or soon became, the dominant allophone; hence, in early WS, the phoneme must be written /īe/ rather than /īo/. In this dialect, the phoneme (like its short counterpart) had several sources: Gmc. /iu/ with *i*-umlaut in *līehtan,* Gmc. /au/ with *i*-umlaut in *hīeran,* etc. Like the short diphthong, it was rounded in late WS to /ȳ/.

2.22. /eo/ < Gmc. /e/ before /r/ plus consonant in *heorte,* etc. In Anglian this phoneme also resulted from /e/ before /lf/ in *seolf* (late Nhb. *solf, sulf;* WS *self, sylf*). In Nhb., /eo/ was confused with /æa/ from an early period; cf. *Earpualdo* (for *Eorp-*) in the Moore MS of

[33] Chadwick 216-8; Ström 106-7.

Bede, etc.[34] In the tenth-century Nhb. gloss of the *Lindisfarne Gospels, ea* is frequently written for /eo/, as in *hearte*. In the Nhb. portions of the gloss to the *Rushworth Gospels,* the opposite is true, and *eo* frequently appears for /æa/. The confusion of the short diphthongs may have been purely orthographic and due to the parallel confusion of their long counterparts.

2.23. /ēo/ < Gmc. /eo/ in *þēof, ċēosan,* etc.; Gmc. /ew, eww/ in *trēo* 'tree', *trēow* 'trust', etc.; Gmc. /e/ in *fēores* (gen. sg. of *feorh*), etc.[35] Falling together of /īo/ with /ēo/ was just beginning when Archetype I was written.[36] An [eu:] allophone in early OE may be reflected in a few *eu*-spellings of the eighth and early ninth centuries: *Hrēutford,* etc., in the Bede MSS,[37] *flēutas* in the *Erfurt Glossary.*

The orthographic confusion of /eo/ and /æa/ in Nhb. has already been mentioned. A similar confusion of /ēo/ and /ǣa/ appears in the late Nhb. texts; e.g. *behēald* (for *-hēold*), *ēade* (for *ēode* pt. sg.), *ðēafas* (for *ðēof-*), etc., in the Lindisfarne gloss; *fīcbēome* (for *-bēam-*), *dēode* (for *dēad-*), *hēonissum* (for *hēa-*), etc., in the Nhb. portions of the Rushworth gloss. The early Bede MSS show this confusion to some extent; e.g. *Eodbaldo* (beside *Ead-, Aeod-*), *Strēanæshalch* (beside *Strēonæs-*).[38] Without more evidence, we cannot say whether Nhb. /ēo/ and /ǣa/ had fallen together phonemically by the beginning of the eighth century.

2.24. /æa/ < Gmc. /a/ before /r/ plus consonant in *heard, bearn,* etc.; Gmc. /a/ before /h/ in *seah* pt. sg., etc. Breaking before /h/ probably took place in all dialects; it is difficult otherwise to account for Merc. *slēan* (Nhb. *slēa,* beside *slǣ, slā*) from Gmc. **slahan* and other contracted forms. In noncontract forms, /æa/ before /h/ was smoothed to /æ/ in the Anglian dialects; cf. *sæh* pt. sg. (WS, Kt. *seah*). This Anglian smoothing was not complete until some time in the eighth century, but was well under way by 700. In WS and Nhb., the incidence of /æa/ was increased by palatal diphthongization, which must have preceded 700; e.g. *ċeaster, ġeat, sċeaft* (also spelled with *æ, e,* in Nhb., with *e* in late WS as compared with Merc., Kt. *ċester, ġet, sċeft.* There is no real evidence of palatal diphthongization in Archetype I.[39] The early Bede MSS show *Ceadda* but *cæstir.*[40] In WS and Kt., /æa/ also resulted from Gmc. /a/ before /l/ plus consonant; e.g. *eald, healtian* (Anglian *ald, haltian*).

[34] Ström 104.

[35] There is doubt, however, about the lengthening of vowels after loss of /h/ in the clusters /lh, rh/; see Randolph Quirk and C. L. Wrenn, *An Old English grammar* 137 (1955).

[36] Chadwick 216-8.

[37] Ström 101.

[38] Ibid. 99-101, 147. Similar confusion of /eo, ǣa/ and /ēo, ǣa/ occurs to a limited extent in the *Vespasian Psalter* gloss and other Merc. texts.

[39] The apparent examples given by Chadwick 228 are actually due to velar umlaut.

[40] Ström 107-8.

2.25. /ǣa/ < Gmc. /au/ in *hēafod, ċēas* pt. sg., etc., Gmc. /a/ in *slēan, mēares* gen. sg., etc.; Gmc. /aw, awu, aww/ in *clēa, hrēa, hēawan,* etc. In WS, Gmc. /æ/ broke to /ǣa/ before /h/; e.g. *nēah* (Merc., Nhb. *nēh*). The diphthong was further augmented in WS by palatal dipthongization of Gmc. /æ/ in *ċēace, ġēar, sċēap,* etc.; cf. Anglian *ċēce, ġēr,* Merc. *sċēp,* Nhb. *sċīp.*

2.26. /ə/. The vowels and diphthongs of unaccented syllables are very difficult to pin down. If long, they were usually but not invariably shortened. If short, they were weakened in various ways, sometimes apparently to /ə/. Variation in spelling (*heofon, heofan, heofen*) suggests the existence of /ə/. Alternations like *stefn* ~ *stefen, heofnas* ~ *heofenas* are a further indication. The /ə/ must also be assumed in prehistoric English as an intermediate stage between **cwiþiþ* and *cwiþ* (pr. sg. 3 of *cweþan* ~ *cweoþan*) and similar forms. Parasitic vowels must have begun as /ə/; cf. *berct, berect, berict* (WS *beorht*) in the early Bede MSS. At the present time, it would be rash to generalize about the distribution of /ə/ in OE, but its existence as a phoneme seems certain. It probably varied considerably in pronunciation, but I have been content with suggesting two allophones: [ɪ], inclining to high front articulation and generally derived from front vowels in unaccented syllables, and [ə], inclining to a lower, more retracted articulation and generally derived from back vowels in unaccented syllables.

2.27. The OE diphthongs require further comment. As far as the diphthongs of OE about 700 are concerned, I find myself in rather close agreement with Hockett. The sounds represented by *io* (or *ie*), *eo, ea,* long and short, were phonemically distinct from the other syllabics of OE; they were certainly no mere allophones of the phonemes represented by *i, e, æ.*[41] Germanic had diphthongs /iu, eo, au/ (Hockett's /iw, ew, aw/), which entered early OE as phonetic diphthongs /īo, ēo, ǣa/ (Hockett's /iw, ew, æw/).[42] In view of his argument for parallel development of the long and short syllabics, Hockett would perhaps agree that the short *io, eo, ea* also represented phonetic diphthongs in the early period. If so, there is, thus far, no disagreement between Hockett's views and those of the traditional type.

Hockett believes that later (perhaps by the time the *Vespasian Psalter* was glossed) the diphthongs of early OE were phonetically [ɪ, ə, a], long and short. I can see no possibility, at present, of reconciling this view with the findings of traditional linguistics or comparative linguistics.[43] If we agree (as Hockett does, 596) that OS *liudi,* OHG *liuti,*

[41] Hockett 575-7 (1959). This view is attacked by Stockwell and Barritt (1961).

[42] Hockett 596 (1959). The spellings cited by Hockett as reflections of early pronunciation are from the eighth-century glossaries and the early Bede MSS.

[43] I do not have space to discuss Hockett's five orthographical principles (590-1). They are admirably set forth, but I see no necessity for explaining *io, eo, ea* by principle 5; his principle 4 would explain them equally well.

OFris. *liōde* contained diphthongs, why should we assume that OE *līode* (later *lēode*) contained a monophthong? If the digraphs in OS *diop*, OHG *tiof*, OFris. *diāp*, OIc. *diūpr* represented diphthongs, why should the digraph in OE *dēop* be interpreted differently? If OHG *stroum* and OIc. *straumr* have diphthongs spelled as though diphthongal, and OS *strōm*, OFris. *strām* have monophthongs spelled as though monophthongal, why should OE *strēam* have a monophthong spelled as though diphthongal? English missionaries had a large share in converting all of these other peoples and in transmitting to them the written Scriptures and the art of writing. One would expect more parallelism in the development of scribal practices.

The development of twin forms in ME is hard to explain except on the assumption that there were diphthongs and that stress shift could occur in those diphthongs; i.e. there existed twin pronunciations in OE, [éɒ:] beside [ɛó:] etc. Hockett notes OE *ċēosan* > ME *chēsen, chōsen* (597). Further examples are OE *lēosan* > ME *lēsen, lōsen;* OE *sċēawian* > ME *shēwen, shōwen;* OE *fēawe* > ME *fēwe, fōwe;* OE *ġeond* > ME *yēnd, yōnd;* WS, Kt. *weald* > *wēald, wōld;* WS *ġēomor* > southern ME *yēmer, yōmer;* WS *sċēadan* > sth. ME *shēden, shōden;* WS *ċeald* > sth. ME *chēld, chōld;* WS *ġeong* > sth. ME *yeng, yo(u)ng.*[44]

Finally, I do not venture to use /h, w, y/ to represent the second elements of diphthongs or to indicate vowel length. Even experts in the use of these symbols frequently err when introducing them into OE phonemic transcriptions.[45] How could a traditionalist like myself hope to use them correctly? I am also deterred by the objections raised by Hans Kurath,[46] even though these are partially met by James Sledd.[47]

THE SYLLABICS OF MERCIAN

3. The *Corpus Glossary* represented a mid stage between Chadwick's Archetype I (*c*700) and the full development of Mercian in the gloss of the *Vespasian Psalter* (*c*825). In Corp., some of the newer allophones noted in Table I are better reflected in the spellings, but there is no apparent change in the phonemic structure of the dialect.[48] The syllabics of ninth-century Merc. are presented in Table II. The analysis is based on the gloss to the *Vespasian Psalter* and a contemporary fragment called the *Lorica Prayer.*[49]

[44] Malone distinguishes between true diphthongs and 'glides' (256). He holds that OE *io, eo, ea, ie* represented true diphthongs until almost the end of the OE period (258-61).

[45] See Stockwell and Barritt 388 (1955); Stockwell 23 (1958).

[46] Pp. 111-2, 121 (1957).

[47] Pp. 253-4 (1958).

[48] My article, The dialect of the Corpus Glossary, *PMLA* 54.1-19 (1939), presents the data, which can readily be interpreted in structural terms.

[49] Both are available in Sweet's *OET* 174, 188-420. Errors, chiefly in Sweet's Latin text of the Psalter, do not materially affect the general phonemic analysis.

	FRONT VOWELS				BACK				UNACCENTED
	UNROUND		ROUND		VOWELS		DIPHTHONGS		VOWELS
HIGH	/i/	[ɪ]	/y/	[ʊ̈]	/u/	[ʊ]	/io/	[ɪɒ]	[ɨ]
	/ī/	[i:]	/ȳ/	[ü:]	/ū/	[u:]	/īo/	[iɒ:, iɛ:]	
	/e/	[ɛ]	/œ/	[ɒ̈]	/o/	[ɒ]	/eo/	[ɛɒ, ɛə]	
MID	/ē/	[e:]	/œ̄/	[ö:]	/ō/	[o:]			/ə/
	/ɛ/	[æ⊥]			/ɔ/	[ɔ]	/ēo/	[eɒ:, eə:]	[ə]
LOW	/æ/	[æ]			/a/	[ɑ]	/æa/	[æɑ, æə]	
	/ǣ/	[æ:, ɛ:]			/ā/	[ɑ:]	/ǣa/	[æɑ:, æə:]	

TABLE II—*Mercian*

Changes in the incidence of phonemes can be dealt with briefly, since most of the allophones, as well as the sound changes which produced them, have already been described. The incidence of /æ/ had been greatly reduced by the operation of the second fronting in the eighth century. Except in a few positions, e.g. before /h/ in *mæht,* [æ] had moved to [æ⊥] and was a new phoneme. The short /œ/ was a relic phoneme, having almost completely fallen together with /e/. The long /œ̄/ was more stable, but this also was beginning to unround. The incidence of /a/ had been reduced by the splitting off of /ɔ/ and by the combined operation of velar umlaut and the second fronting, which caused /a/ in open syllable followed by back vowel to become /æa/. The diphthong /io/ was by this time a relic, surviving only in velar-umlaut position (*nioman,* etc.). Breaking-/io/ had fallen together with /eo/. The long /īo/ was rapidly falling together with /ēo/.

3.1 /ȳ/ was no longer a phoneme, having unrounded to /e/ in *ende, wemman,* etc.

3.2. /ɛ/ is a misleading symbol for the new phoneme from the second fronting of /æ/ from Gmc. /a/. Phonetically, the sound must have been somewhere between [æ] and [ɛ], for in ME times it coalesced with the reflexes of /æ/, /ɔ/, and /a/, not with the reflex of Merc. /e/.[50] It is spelled *e* too regularly in the Vespasian gloss to be regarded as an allophone of /æ/, from which Hockett correctly separates it. A few minimal pairs contrasting /e/ and /ɛ/ are probably concealed by the *e*-spelling: *wes* (imp. sg. of *bīon*) : *wes* (pt. 1 and 3 sg.), *cweð* (imp. sg. of *cweoðan*) : *cweð* (pt. 1 and 3 sg.), *bed* (nom. sg.) : *bed* (pt. 1 and 3 sg. of *biddan*), *hel* (nom. sg.) : *hel* (pt. 1 sg. of *helan*). Pairs to illustrate the distinction /æ/ ~ /ɛ/, which no one appears to question, are much rarer, but perhaps *æt* (prep.) : *et* (adv.) will serve.

3.3. /ɔ/ < Gmc. and Lat. /a/ before nasal is consistently written *o,* and Hockett rightly separates it from /a/. That /ɔ/ was no longer a mere positional variant in Merc. is indicated by the shape of Late Lat. borrowings in the Vespasian gloss: *plant, geplantade,* (?) *organe,* etc. More-

[50] Hockett would not use later historical evidence in a synchronic article. Since this article is both synchronic and diachronic, I have no scruples about using any valid evidence that I can find.

over, /ɔ/ can appear before a consonant other than a nasal; cf. *born* (pt. 3 sg. of *beornan*), *orn* (pt. 1 sg. of *eornan*). That /ɔ/ did not fuse with /o/ is indicated by its falling together with /a, æ, ɛ/ in ME.

3.4. In later Merc. of the tenth century, /œ, œ̄, io, īo/ fell together with /e, ē, eo, ēo/ respectively. In the late tenth and eleventh centuries, /eo, ēo, æa, ǣa/ monophthongized to /ö, ȫ, æ, ǣ/. These appear in early ME: /ö, ȫ/ spelled *eo, oe, o, u, ue,* etc.; /æ/ spelled *a, æ, ea;* /ǣ/ spelled *e, æ, ea,* etc. They became /e, ē, a (æ), ē/ earliest in the eastern parts of the old Merc. area. The late Merc. texts, of which Farman's gloss to portions of the *Rushworth Gospels* is the most important, are difficult to analyze because of the strong influence of WS, the standard dialect in the tenth and eleventh centuries. But much can be learned from them if due precautions are taken.[51]

THE SYLLABICS OF NORTHUMBRIAN

4. The Nhb. dialect closely resembles Merc. in some respects, probably because the two kingdoms were closely associated from the fifth century to the seventh. Mercia seems to have been a dependency of its northern neighbor until the rise of King Penda in the second quarter of the seventh century. The early Nhb. fragments have been mentioned. The principal texts of later Nhb. are the ninth-century *Liber Vitae* of Durham,[52] and the tenth-century glosses of the *Lindisfarne Gospels,* the *Durham Ritual,* and portions of the *Rushworth Gospels.*[53] The vowels and diphthongs appear in Table III.

	FRONT VOWELS UNROUND	FRONT VOWELS ROUND	BACK VOWELS	DIPHTHONGS		UNACCENTED VOWELS
HIGH	/i/ [ɪ]	/y/ [ü]	/u/ [ʊ]	/io/	[ɪɒ, ɪə]	
	/ī/ [i:]	/ȳ/ [ü:]	/ū/ [ü:]	/īo/	[iɒ:, iə:]	[ɨ]
MID	/e/ [ɛ]	/œ/ [ɒ̈]	/o/ [ɒ]	/ɛɒ/	[ɛɒ, ɛə, æa, æə]	/ə/
			/ō/ [o:]			
	/ē/ [e:]	/œ̄/ [ö:]	/ɔ/ [ɔ]	/ɛ̄ɒ/	[ɛɒ:, ɛə: eɒ:, eə:]	[ə]
LOW	/æ/[æ, æ⊥]		/a/ [ɑ]			
	/ǣ/[æ:, ɛ:]		/ā/ [ɑ:]			

TABLE III—*Northumbrian*

Most of the sound changes affecting Nhb. syllabics have been mentioned in connection with the prehistoric period. We may note here the survival of /y, ȳ, œ, œ̄/ as phonemes until the tenth century. In the Northern dialect of ME, they appear unrounded to /i, ī, e, ẹ̄/. The phonemes /io, īo/ remained distinct from /eo, ēo/ in the tenth century.

[51] *E* and *Æ* in Farman's Mercian glosses, *PMLA* 60.631-69 (1945).

[52] Sweet, *OET* 153-66.

[53] W. W. Skeat, editions of the four Gospels in WS, Merc., and Nhb. (Cambridge, 1871-87); Uno Lindelöf, *Rituale Ecclesiae Dunelmensis,* Surtees Society, Vol. 140 (1927).

In ME of the fourteenth century, however, the same fusion appears as that which we have noted in Merc.

4.1 /ɔ̄/ fell together with /e/, as in most OE dialects.

4.2. /ɔ/ became phonemic in Nhb., as in Mercian. [æ⊥], however, remained an allophone.

4.3. The spellings *ea* and *eo* are confused in late Nhb., as already noted. I have indicated phonemic fusion with a wide range of variant pronunciations as one means of reconciling the scribal practices of the tenth century with the various and inconsistent developments of later times. Unfortunately there are no further texts from the old Nhb. area until the fourteenth century, and by that time several sound changes had occurred which make the evidence hard to interpret. The short diphthongs /eo, æa/ apparently split between 1000 and 1300 A.D. (or perhaps they were not truly fused in the tenth century), for they appear generally to be /e/ and /a/ in the *Cursor Mundi*.[54] The long diphthongs show more evidence of fusion than the short. There are several views as to what happened.[55] Watson points out a Northern dialect of modern English in which the reflexes of OE /ēo/ seem to have fallen together with those of OE /ǣa/.[56] There are rimes in the *Cursor Mundi* which suggest that fusion had taken place: *leme* (OE *lēoma*) : *bem* (OE *bēam*) ; *leue* (OE *lēaf*) : *leue* (OE *lēof*) ; *leue* (OE *lēaf*) : *thef* (OE *þēof*) ; *ded* OE *dēad*) : *yede* (OE *geēode*) ; etc.[57] In general, the reflexes of OE /ǣa/ in the *Cursor Mundi* show a tendency to rime with ME /ē/ (long close *e*): *dede* (OE *dēad*) with *red* (Anglian *rēd*, WS *rǣd*) , etc. This might suggest that Nhb. /ǣa/ fell together with /ēo/, rather than the reverse. With our present knowledge, it seems to me hazardous to say anything more positive. The frequency with which expected ME /ē/ and /ẹ̄/ rime in the *Cursor Mundi* led Strandberg to assume that northern ME /ē/ had become close /ẹ̄/ in a number of contexts in which we should not normally expect this change. Possibly the rimes of this text are not dependable as evidence for the reflexes of OE /ē, ǣ, ēo, ǣa/. The modern dialects, also, are in need of further clarification, which may come with the publication of the linguistic atlases of England and Scotland now being prepared by Harold Orton and Angus McIntosh. For the present, I believe that my phonemicization can serve as a working hypothesis.

THE SYLLABICS OF WEST SAXON

5. As the dialect in which most of OE literature has survived, WS is well known and can be treated briefly. The principal texts in early WS are

[54] The MSS are of the late 14th century, and some of the spellings probably reflect the late ME shift of /er/ > /ar/.

[55] For a summary, see Watson 19-20 (1946) ; see also Campbell 117-20.

[56] Op.cit. 21-6.

[57] Otto Strandberg, *The rime-vowels of Cursor Mundi* 106-7, 118, 145, etc. (Uppsala, 1919) . I omit studies of later Northern texts for lack of space.

the Parker MS of the *Anglo-Saxon Chronicle* (as far as A.D. 901) and King Alfred's translations of Orosius' history and of Gregory's *Pastoral Care.*[58] The MSS used were written about 900 and are basically early WS, although some of their spelling practices suggest Merc. influence and others point to the onset of sound changes which are regarded as characteristic of late WS.[59] The vowels and diphthongs of early WS are given [in Table IV].

	FRONT VOWELS		BACK			UNACCENTED	
	UNROUND	ROUND	VOWELS	DIPHTHONGS		VOWELS	
	/i/ [ɪ]	/ȳ/ [ü]	/u/ [ʊ]	/ie/	[ɪɛ, ɪə]		[ɨ]
HIGH	/ī/ [i:]	/y/ [ü:]	/ū/ [u:]	/īe/	[iɛ:, iə:]		
	/e/ [ɛ]		/o/ [ɒ]	/eo/	[ɛɒ, ɛə]	/ə/	
MID	/ē/ [e:]		/ō/ [o:]	/ēo/	[eɒ:, eə:]		
LOW	/æ/ [æ]		/a/ [ɑ, ɔ]	/æa/	[æɑ, æə]		[ə]
	/ǣ/ [æ:]		/ā/ [ɑ:]	/ǣa/	[æɑ:, æə:]		

TABLE IV—*West Saxon*

Most of the phonetic features of early WS have already been noted. As in the other dialects, the second elements of diphthongs tended to become [ə]. The question whether the short *ie, eo, ea* represented diphthongs has been rather fully discussed elsewhere.[60] The incidence of /eo/ and /io/ was reduced in WS by the manner in which dental consonants, palatals, velars, and nasals hindered velar umlaut; e.g. WS *cweþan* (Merc. *cweoðan*), *niman* (Merc. *neoman,* Nhb. *nioma*), *WS brecan* (Merc. *ġebreocan*), etc.

5.1 The phonemes /œ, œ̄/ had probably disappeared from the spoken dialect by the late ninth century, although sporadic *oe*-spellings occur in the early WS texts.[61]

5.2. As in Merc. and Nhb., the phoneme /ɔ̈/ fused with /e/.

5.3. The phonemes /ie, īe/ were rapidly becoming monophthongs at the close of the ninth century, as is indicated by spellings like *fird, irfe, ġehīran, ġestīran,* and by reverse spellings like *briengan, ġegrīeþð.*

5.4. The late WS phonemes were the same as those in Table IV, with a few exceptions. /i, ī/ had a tendency, at least in some parts of the WS area, to round to /y, ȳ/ except in the neighborhood of palatal consonants. /y, ȳ/ tended to unround to /i, ī/ before palatal consonants. /ie, īe/ monophthongized to /i, ī/ and then rounded to /y, ȳ/ except

[58] C. Plummer and J. Earle, *Two Saxon chronicles parallel,* 2 vols. (Oxford, 1892, 1899); Sweet, *King Alfred's Orosius = EETS OS* 79 (1883); Sweet, *King Alfred's West Saxon version of Gregory's pastoral care = EETS OS* 45, 50 (1871-2; repr. 1909).

[59] For a useful analysis, see P. J. Cosijn, *Altwestsächsische Grammatik,* 2 vols. (The Hague, 1883-6).

[60] Daunt, Samuels, Stockwell and Barritt, Barritt, Bazell, Reszkiewicz, Malone, Kuhn and Quirk; see fn. 1.

[61] Cosijn 1.71, 76.

in the neighborhood of palatal consonants. Thus the older phonemes /ie, īe/ probably disappeared from the spoken dialect, although occasional *ie*-spellings occur as archaisms in the late WS texts.[62] The other diphthongs remained and even survived in early ME with a diphthongal pronunciation, at least in some parts of the Southern area.[63] The effects of palatal umlaut *(meaht > miht)* and other late WS sound changes are dealt with in all of the standard grammars and handbooks of OE. The late WS texts are too numerous to list even selectively. Generally, the works of Aelfric and Wulfstan and the *West Saxon Gospels* are regarded as major texts.

THE SYLLABICS OF KENTISH

6. The Kt. dialect of the OE period survives only in a few fragments, and these are mixed with other dialects, the early ones with Merc., the later with WS. Only by comparing their features with those of Kt. texts of the ME period[64] can one arrive at any conclusions as to the sounds of Kt. in the older period. The following table fairly represents the views of many traditional linguists.

	FRONT	BACK	DIPHTHONGS		UNACCENTED
HIGH	/i/ [ɪ]	/u/ [ʊ]	/ɨɒ/	[ɨɒ, ɛɒ, ɪɒ, ɨə]	
	/ī/ [i:]	/ū/ [u:]			[ɨ]
MID	/e/ [ɛ]	/o/ [ɒ]	/ɨ̄ɒ/	[ɨɒ:, eɒ:, iɒ:, ɨə:]	
	/ē/ [e:]				/ə/
	/ɛ/ [æ˔]	/ō/ [ö:]			
LOW	/æ/ [æ]	/a/ [ɑ, ɔ]	/æa/	[æɑ, ɨɑ, æə]	[ə]
	/ǣ/ [ǣ:, ɛ:]	/ā/ [ɑ:]	/ǣa/	[æɑ:, ɨɑ:, æə:]	

TABLE V—*Kentish*

The tendency of /ǣ/ to develop a higher, more fronted allophone in Anglian is paralleled by a similar development in Kt., but the tendency was stronger in Kt., shifting /ǣ/ toward /ē/ in almost any context. The allophone [ɔ] did not become phonemic. The first elements of the phonemes /æa, ǣa/ underwent some degree of raising and fronting in late Kt. Frequently they are spelled with *ia* or other digraphs suggesting this pronunciation, and even in middle Kentish we find spellings like *dyaþ, dyeaþ,* which suggest the survival of a diphthongal /īə/ or /ɨ̄ə/ as late as the fourteenth century.

[62] According to Brunner 249-50 (1953), /ie/ acquired a 'palatoguttural pronunciation' in late WS. Although not actually rounded, the sound was often confused with /y/ and hence written *y*. He concedes that 'a rounded [y] may have been substituted for it by some speakers or in some areas'.

[63] Henning Hallqvist, *Studies in Old English fractured ea* 9-77 (Lund, 1948).

[64] Especially *Dan Michel's ayenbite of inwyt,* ed. by R. Morris, = *EETS OS* 23 (1866); and *William of Shoreham's poems,* ed. by M. Konrath, = *EETS ES* 86 (1902).

6.1. The new phoneme /ɛ/ arose in Kt., as in Merc. The fact that Merc. and Kt. share this and some other features may be due to the fact that Kent was under Merc. rule during most of the eighth century and the first part of the ninth.

6.2. Kt. was the first dialect (of those in which any writings have survived) to lose all of its front rounded vowels. /y, ȳ/ shifted to /e, ē/ during the ninth century. /œ, œ̄/ unrounded to /e, ē/, as in Merc. and WS. /ɔ̈/ unrounded to /e/, probably at the same time as in Merc.

6.3. Spelling evidence suggests that /eo, ēo/ fell together with /io, īo/ in late Kt. The middle Kt. evidence is not clear, but some of the spellings suggest a raised and fronted articulation of the first element (cf. *chiese* < OE *ċēosan*, etc. in *Ayenbite*). On the other hand, *heuene* (OE *heofon*), etc., in the same text suggest that /eo/ did not completely fall together with /io/ in late Kt. of the OE period. As with the Nhb. diphthongs, I have chosen a compromise phonemicization.

7. This discussion has been an attempt at description rather than argument. It represents the views of many traditional linguists, but by no means all. To introduce all the theories which conflict with my schematization would swell the article to great length and defeat its purpose, which is to present the OE syllabics structurally in a form easily grasped and understood. If there is any one inference which might be regarded as a structural conclusion, it is that the OE dialects were surprisingly alike in their structure. The differences produced by the numerous sound changes affected chiefly the incidence of phonemes and the variety of allophones. The early loss of the old front rounded vowels in Kt. only anticipates a similar loss in the other dialects. The new phonemes /ie, īe/ in WS resulted from the rise to dominance of allophones which were present in the other dialects also. The new phonemes, /ɔ/ in Merc. and Nhb., /ɛ/ in Merc. and Kt., were comparatively short-lived. The latter is probably the source of the modern English [æ] pronunciation of the sound written *a*, but that is a matter too complicated to be introduced here.

The Obstruent System of Old English

WILLIAM G. MOULTON

THE OLD ENGLISH EVIDENCE, as presented in Table 4, shows two changes that are reminiscent of Pre-Old-Icelandic: a voicing of medial voiceless spirants (indicated by the downward arrows in Table 4) and an unvoicing of final voiced spirants (indicated by upward arrows).[1] Although the dentals illustrate only the former of these changes, we may begin with this order because the resulting phonemic structure is entirely clear.

The dentals present a special structure because of a familiar phenomenon that is common to all the West Germanic languages: the spirantal allophones of PGmc. /d/ became stops, so that /d/ showed stop allophones in all positions. We may therefore assume a stage in Pre-Old-English during which the contrast [t-þ-d] existed through columns 1-10 except after nasal (where /Vnþ/ > /V:þ/, cf. Gothic *kunþs* but OE *cūþ* 'known') and after /l/ (where /lþ/ > /ld/, cf. Gothic *-gulþ* but OE *gold* 'gold'). This structure was phonologically ambiguous, since either voice (as in Gothic and runic Norse) or occlusion (as in Old Icelandic) could be considered the primary distinctive feature. That is to say, because of the absence of [ð], the system could be analyzed either as (t : þ) : d, or as (t : d) : þ.

The elimination of the spirantal allophones of /d/ of course opened the way for /þ/ to develop voiced allophones.[2] When this change took

---

Reprinted by permission from "The Stops and Spirants of Early Germanic," *Language* 30.1-42 (1954). Of Moulton's article, only the section dealing with the Old English evidence (pp. 21-29) is reprinted here. The reference to Table 4 has been retained, but the footnotes have been re-numbered.

[1] See Karl Luick, *Historische Grammatik der englischen Sprache* (1914 ff.) §639 (voicing of medial [f þ s], §656 (loss of medial [h]), §651 (unvoicing of final [ƀ g]).

[2] It might also be assumed that the spirantal allophones of /d/ became stops because /þ/ began to develop voiced allophones. For two reasons, however, this alternative analysis is unlikely. First, the change of [ð] to [d] presumably occurred before the Anglo-Saxon migration from the continent, since it is common to all the WGmc. dialects; whereas the voicing of medial voiceless spirants was apparently not completed at the time of our earliest OE documents. (See below under the discussion of the labials.) Secondly, final [ð] became a stop just like medial [ð], even though final [þ] did not become voiced and thereby 'push' [ð] into becoming a stop.

TABLE 4—*The Old English Evidence*

		1. C—	2. CC	3. NCV	4. NC+	5. lCV	6. lC+	7. rCV	8. rC+	9. VCV	10. VC+	11. VCS	12. VCT
/p/	[p]	pæþ	uppan	gelimpan	gelamp	helpan	healp	weorpan	wearp	grīpan	grāp	grīpst	cēpte
/f/	[f]	fisc	woffian			↓	wulf self	↓	þearf swearf	↓	hōf geaf	swīfst drīfst	æfter
	[b]					wulfas selfa	↑	? sweorfan	↑	hōfas giefan	↑		
/b/	[b]	burg	crabba	lambes	lamb						crib(b)		
/t/	[t]	tunge	sceattes	winter	brant	sealtan	sealt	heorte	sweart	hātan	þæt	bletsian	(see 2)
/þ/	[þ]	þanc	moþþe	mōnþe	winþ	hǣlþe	fielþ	↓	wearþ	↓	cwæþ	cwiþst	
	[ð]							weorþan		cweþan			
/d/	[d]	dæg	coddes	landes	land	scylde	scyld	wordes	word	bēodan	bēad		
/ċ/	[ċ]	cēn	strecc(e)an	drenc(e)an	benc	gefylce	swelc	wyrc(e)an	wyrc	stice	pic		
/ġ/	[ġ]		licg(e)an	seng(e)an	feng						wecg		
/k/	[k]	cēne	hnecca	drincan	dranc	folces	folc	weorces	weorc	ēacen	ēac	oxa	īęcte
/x/	[x]		cohhettan				sealh swealg		mearh bearg		scōh drōg	nīehsta stīhst	meaht
	[g]					swelgan	↑	beorgan	↑	dragan	↑		
/g/	[g]	gēs	dogga	springan	sprang								
/h/	[h]	horn				↓		↓		↓			

place (see columns 7 and 9), the ambiguity of the phonological structure was removed. The primary feature was now one of occlusion, which distinguished the stops /t d/ from the spirant /þ/; the secondary feature was one of voice, which distinguished voiceless /t/ from voiced /d/. Since voice was not a distinctive feature of /þ/, it could (and did) show voiced allophones. The structure was now clearly (t : d) : þ.

The voicing of medial voiceless spirants affected those following a stressed vowel, but not those following an unstressed vowel.[3] Thus the [þ]'s of dative *[mó:naþæ, há:liþæ] 'month, health' remained voiceless, and when the medial vowels were syncopated, the new medial clusters [nþ lþ] arose: *mōnþe, hǣlþe* (columns 3 and 5). Final [nþ lþ] also arose through syncope in such forms as *winþ, fielþ* 'wins, falls' and nominative *hǣlþ* 'health' < */wínniþ, fǽlliþ, há:liþu/ (columns 4 and 6). Syncope also brought about the new clusters /ts þs/ in *bletsian* (beside *blessian*) 'bless', *blīþs* (beside *bliss*) 'bliss', and *cwiþst* 'sayest' < */bló:diso:jan, blí:þisi, kwíþis(t)/ (column 11).

In the labial order we find evidence for the same voicing of medial voiceless spirants, whereby [wúlfas, hó:fas] > [wúlƀas, hó:ƀas] 'wolves, hooves' (columns 5, 7 [no extant examples], 9), and also for an unvoicing of final voiceless spirants, whereby [sélƀ, swéarƀ, jǽƀ] > [sélf, swéarf, jǽf] 'self, swerved, gave' (columns 6, 8, 10). Whatever the exact phonetics of these changes may have been, we can date them phonemically as being in the process of completion during the first half of the 8th century, since a few of the earliest documents still distinguished PGmc. medial and final /f/ and /b/ as *f* and *b*.[4]

Before these changes, [ƀ] was in contrast with [f] (columns 5–10) but not with [b]; hence it belonged with [b] to a phoneme /b/. After these changes, the phonological structure per se was ambiguous: [ƀ] was no longer in contrast with [f], but it was also still not in contrast with [b]. Given the relationship of [ƀ] and [f] in columns 5–10, any modern analyst would probably assign them both to the same phoneme in order to keep the morphophonemics as simple as possible, i.e. analyze the singular and plural forms as /wúlf, wúlfas/ rather than as /wúlf, wúlbas/, etc. More important, however, is the fact that in the dental

[3] For the following, see Luick, *Hist. Gram.* §639.2. Other examples of voiceless [þ] following an unstressed vowel are the ordinal numerals *sēofoþa, eahtoþa, nigoþa,* etc.

[4] E.g. *Epinal Glossary* 223 *giroefa* 'officer', 183 gen. *uulfes* 'wolf', 142 *uuf* 'owl', 192 *obaer* 'over', 51 *halbae* 'halves', 577 *staeb* 'staff'; Henry Sweet, ed., *The oldest English texts* (1885 = *Early English Text Society,* Vol. 83). Cf. Eduard Sievers, Altangelsächsisch *F* und *B, Beiträge z. Gesch. d. dt. Spr. u. Lit.* 11.542-5 (1886), and *Anglia* 13.15-6 (1891). Luick, *Hist. Gram.* §639 Anm. 4, §658, dates the voicing of medial [f s þ] as 'spätestens im 6. Jahrhundert', and interprets the *f–b* spelling contrasts of the early documents as representing labiodental vs. bilabial voiced spirants. However this may be, it is clear that the phonemic merger of /f/ and /b/ had not been completed at the time of these documents, but that it was completed shortly thereafter. This point is nicely made in Herbert Penzl, A phonemic change in early Old English, *Lg.* 20.84-7 (1944).

order the voiced spirant [ƌ], corresponding to labial [ƀ], necessarily belonged with [þ] rather than with [d]. As was the case with the OIc. labials, it is therefore the analogy of the dentals which leads us to assign [ƀ] and [f] to the same phoneme, and to assume that the older structure (p : f) : b had changed to (p : b) : f. This is of course the analysis made by the OE scribes, as is shown by their spellings *wulf—wulfas, self—selfa,* etc.

A number of minor points need special mention. The inherited cluster /fs/ perhaps became /ps/ in the Pre-OE period: cf. *ræpsan* 'reprove', though early documents also show *ræfsan.*[5] The clusters /ps pt fs/ (columns 11 and 12) also arose through vowel syncope: *grīpst, cēpte, swīfst, drīfst* 'graspest, kept, sweepest, drivest' */grí:pis(t), kó:pidæ, swí:fis(t), drí:bis(t)/.

One further form needs interpretation: column 10 *crib(b)* 'crib' < */kríbbu/ < PGmc. */kríbjo:/. When the earlier [bb] in forms of this type came into final position through the apocope of the final vowel, the long stop seems to have been shortened but to have kept its stop articulation, thus introducing [b] into a new environment. In all words of this type the OE scribes wrote indiscriminately in final position both single and double letters (though always *cg;* see below). The double spellings were almost certainly taken from forms where the consonant really was phonemically long (*cribbe* etc.); the single spellings therefore represent the actual phonemics: *crib* = /kríb/ = [kríb].[6]

PGmc. /k g h/ underwent even more extensive restructuring in Pre-OE times than did the labials and dentals. The most striking development was the palatalization of /k/ and /g/ in the neighborhood of front vowels.[7] This change must have begun phonetically before the migrations from the continent, since it is shared by continental dialects (Frisian). For Pre-Old-English we may assume a phoneme /k/ with palatal allophones in such forms as */strákkjan, dránkjan, bánki; ké:na/ 'stretch, submerge, bench, torch', but velar allophones in such forms as */hnékko: drínkan, dránk, kó:ni/ 'neck, drink, drank, bold'. Still in Pre-OE times, after umlaut had taken place, postconsonantal /j/ and final /i/ were lost, so that the palatal and velar allophones came to contrast with one another and hence split into two separate phonemes: in the environment /V( )V/ as /stréċċan/ vs. /hnékka/; in the environment /C( )V/ as /drénċan/ vs. /drínkan/; and in the environment /C( )+/ as /bénċ/ vs. /dránk/. Cf. OE *strecc(e)an, hnecca, drenc(e)an, drincan, benc, dranc.* In early OE times, after /o/ and /o:/ had been umlauted to /ö/ and /ö:/ and then unrounded in most dialects to /e/ and /e:/, /ċ/ and

[5] Cf. Luick, *Hist. Gram.* §634.2; Eduard Sievers (ed. Karl Brunner), *Altenglishe Grammatik* §193.3 (1952). For a different view (*ræfsan* < */rafisjan/, *ræpsan* < */rábisjan/*), see Albert Morey Sturtevant, *Lg.* 7.191 (1931).

[6] This is the usual interpretation; cf. Sievers-Brunner, *Ae. Gram.* §231.1. Luick, *Hist. Gram.* §§625.2, 631.1, 644.1, states that geminates which came into final position thereby lost their geminate quality, but still remained long.

[7] For details, see Luick, *Hist. Gram.* §637.

/k/ came to contrast also in the environment /+( )V/ as /ċé:n/ vs. /ké:ne/, OE *cēn* 'torch' and *cēne* 'bold'.[8]

The development of Pre-OE /g/ was more complicated than that of /k/ because it had both stop and spirant allophones. The evidence indicates that it was a stop in only three positions: initially before consonants and back vowels,[9] in gemination, and after /n/. In the latter two positions we can assume for Pre-Old-English a palatal stop allophone in such forms as */líggjan, sángjan, fángi/ 'lie, singe, grasp', but a velar stop allophone in such forms as */wiggo:, sprîngan, spráng/ '(ear)wig, jump, jumped'. As in the case of the voiceless stop, it was the loss of postconsonantal /j/ and final /i/ which later brought the palatal and velar allophones into contrast with one another and hence split them into two separate phonemes: in the environment /V( )V/ as /líġġan/ vs. /wígga/; in the environment /C( )V/ as /sénġan/ vs. /sprîngan/; and in the environment /C( )+/ as /fénġ/ vs. /spráng/. Cf. OE *licg(e)an, (ēar)-wicga, seng(e)an, springan, feng, sprang.*

In all other environments Pre-OE /g/ was a spirant. We can assume a palatal allophone in such forms as */wǽ:gi/ 'wave' (OE *wǣg*) and a velar allophone in such forms as */dá:ga/ 'dough' (OE *dāg*). What apparently caused them to split was not that they came to contrast with one another (though this would eventually have happened), but rather that the palatal allophone merged with inherited /j/: OE *wǣg* /wǽ:j/ < */wœ́:ġi/ 'wave' like *wǣg* /wǽ:j/ < */wá:ju/ 'wall', or initially *gēafon* /jǽ:fon/ < */gǽ:bun/ 'they gave' like *gēar* /jǽ:r/ < */jǽ:ra/ 'year'. The velar allophone continued as [ɡ̧] in Old English, but was of course unvoiced in final position: pl. *dāgas* [dá:ɡ̧as], sg. *dāg* [dá:x] 'dough'. That [ɡ̧] and [j] were in contrast is clear from such forms as *beorgas* 'hills' with [ɡ̧] but *hergas (herias, herigas, herigeas)* 'armies' with [j].

We have seen how the stop allophones of PGmc. /g/ split into OE palatal /ġ/ and velar /g/, and how the spirantal allophones split when the palatal one merged with inherited /j/. We must now ask: was the

[8] To indicate the OE palatal stops, I use the traditional symbols *ċ* and *ġ*; the exact phonetic quality is uncertain. For an excellent analysis of palatalization in Old English, see Herbert Penzl, The phonemic split of Germanic *k* in Old English, *Lg.* 23.34-42 (1947). Penzl says that the 'crucial innovation' in the phonemic split of /k/ into /ċ/ and /k/ was 'the appearance of velar [k] before the new palatal vowels developed through *i*-umlaut' (42). This would mean that the phonemic split did not take place until early OE, when /ö/ and /ö:/ were unrounded in most dialects and thus merged with inherited /e/ and /e:/. However, if my own analysis is correct, the 'crucial innovation' was the loss of /j/ and final /i/, which put the [ċ] of [stréċċan, bénċ] in contrast with the [k] of [hnékka, dránk]; and this happened before the time of the earliest documents.

[9] E.g. Pre-OE */gró:nja, gó:si/ > *grēne, gēs* 'green, geese'. The evidence that OE initial *g-* plus back vowel or consonant represented a stop is inconclusive; it could conceivably have been a velar spirant. I assume stop articulation because that is what we find as far back as we can trace the pronunciation from modern times. Luick's assumption (*Hist. Gram.* §§633, 696) that both velar AND palatal *g*, including *g* </j/ (!), were stops initially, leaves me quite unconvinced. For the more generally accepted view (which I follow), see Sievers-Brunner, *Ae. Gram.* §206.8.

original complementary distribution of stop and spirant allophones also destroyed? That is, can we demonstrate a contrast between [g] and [ǥ], and between [ġ] and [j]?

Let us examine first [ġ] and [j]. We find [ġ] in gemination, between nasal and vowel, and finally after a nasal (columns 2, 3, 4). Since [j] did not occur in any of these positions, it would be possible to analyze *licg(e)an, seng(e)an, feng* as /líjjan, sénjan, fénj/. On the other hand, both [ġ] and [j] seem to have occurred finally after a vowel (column 10) and to have contrasted in this position: *wecg* /wéġ/ 'wedge' vs. *weg* /wéj/ 'way'. The only question about this contrast in the interpretation of the spelling *cg*: should it perhaps be analyzed as long [ġġ], so that *weg* could be /wéj/ and *wecg* could be /wéjj/? The answer to this question has already been given, I believe, in the discussion of such spellings as *crib(b)*: Old English had no long consonants in final position. The spellings *cribb, mann, eall* 'crib, man, all' could alternate freely with *crib, man, eal,* since neither spelling created any ambiguity. On the other hand, a spelling such as *wecg* could not alternate with *weg,* since this latter form would be ambiguous. Hence *cg* was retained in final position. It did not indicate a long consonant, but merely the phone [ġ] as opposed to [j]. The loss of final vowels and the subsequent shortening of long final consonants were therefore the changes which brought [ġ] and [j] into contrast with one another.

There remains the relationship between [g] and [ǥ]. As Table 4 shows, they were nowhere in contrast with one another and could therefore be analyzed as allophones of a single phoneme. But for a proper understanding of their structural relationship we must first examine the history of [x] and [h] in Old English.

Whatever the status of [x] and [h] may have been in Proto-Germanic, Pre-Old-English seems to have had velar [x] finally and before voiceless consonants (/s/, /t/, and later /þ/), but to have had glottal [h] initially and between voiced phonemes medially.[10] The proof of glottal (or at least non-velar) articulation medially is the same as in Pre-Old-Icelandic: the voicing of medial voiceless spirants changed [f þ] to their voiced counterparts [ƀ ð]; it did not change [h] to velar [ǥ], but caused its loss; therefore [h] was not velar but something else—presumably glottal. The same early documents which show medial *f* in contrast with *b* also show medial *h*: Epinal Glossary 3 *thohae* 'clay', 1066 dat. pl. *uulohum* 'ornaments', 884 dat. pl. *furhum* 'furrows', etc.; therefore /h/ still occurred at this time, either as voiceless or—if voicing had already taken place—as voiced [h]. By the time of the later documents it had been lost: *þō, wlō(u)m, fūrum.* In initial position we find the same development: Pre-OE */frí:+hàls/ > */frí:hals/ > OE *friols* 'freedom'.

[10] Cf. Luick, *Hist. Gram.* §636; Sievers–Brunner, *Ae Gram.* §§217-23. It is possible that a medial [x] still existed at the time of 'breaking', but changed to glottal [h] afterwards. This would give the following sequence of changes: *[séxan > séoxan > séohan > se:on], OE *sēon* 'see'. However, this is slim evidence indeed, since there is no reason why 'breaking' could not have taken place before both [x] AND [h].

Here also the spirant cannot have been [x], but was presumably the same [h] that survived through Middle English into Modern English.

The proof of velar rather than glottal articulation in other positions is easily given. In gemination and before /t/, OE *h* survives as [x] in Middle English: OE *cohhetan, hlæhhan, dohtor, meaht,* ME *coughen, laughen, doughter, might* 'cough, laugh, daughter, might'. In final position it not only survived as ME [x], but merged in OE times with final unvoiced [g̊]: OE *rūh* and *rūg, þurh* and *þurg,* ME *rough, thurgh* 'rough, through'. Whether [x] or [h] occurred before /s/ we cannot know, since it was dissimilated to /k/: Gothic *auhsa,* OE *oxa*/óksa/ 'ox'.[11]

Having established the approximate sound values of these phones, we may now turn to their phonemic status. Since [h] was not distinguished by the feature of velar articulation, it was a separate phoneme /h/. It occurred only in the environments of columns 1, 5, 7, 9. In position 1 it survived through Old English: *horn* 'horn'; in positions 5, 7, 9 it was lost during early OE times, apparently as part of the general voicing of medial voiceless spirants: OE genitives *sēales, mēares, scōs* 'willow, horse, shoe' < */séalhes, méarhes, scó:hes/, cf. the nominatives *sealh, mearh, scōh.*

Before the unvoicing of final [g̊], we may assume a stage during which [x] and [g̊] were in contrast: *[séalx, méarx, sċó:x] 'seal, horse, shoe' vs. *[swéalg̊, béarg̊, dró:g̊] 'swallowed, protected, drew' (columns 6, 8, 10). Since [g̊] was in contrast with [x] but not with [g], it clearly belonged with [g] to a phoneme /g/, and [x] was a separate phoneme /x/. The Pre-OE phonological structure of the velars was therefore (k : x) : g. After the unvoicing of final [g̊], however, the phonological structure per se was (as with the labials) ambiguous: [g̊] was no longer in contrast with [x], but it was also still not in contrast with [g]. Again, given the relationship of [x] and [g̊] in columns 5–10, any modern analyst would probably assign them to the same phoneme in order to keep the morphophonemics as simple as possible. He could not avoid the morphophonemic alternations of /sé:ales—séalx, mé:ares—méarx, sċó:s—sċó:x/; but he could certainly choose the analysis /swélxan—swéalx, béorxan—béarx, dráxan—dró:x/ in preference to /swélgan—swéalx, béorgan—béarx, drágan—dró:x/. Even more important than this, however, would be the fact that in the dental order the voiceless and voiced spirants [þ ð] necessarily belonged together as allophones of a phoneme /þ/. It is again the analogy of the dentals which leads us to assign [x] and [g̊] to the same phoneme, and to assume that the older structure (k : x) : g had changed to (k : g) : x. All three orders then show the same structure: a primary feature of occlusion, distinguishing the stops /p b, t d, k g/ from the spirants /f þ x/; and a secondary fea-

[11] The cluster [xs] was later restored in such forms as *nīehsta* 'next' and *stīhst* 'climbest' (column 11); cf. Sievers-Brunner, *Ae. Gram.* §214.1 Anm. 2, §222. The cluster /kt/ in column 12 also arose as a result of vowel syncope: */é:akidae/ > *īecte* 'increased'.

ture of voice, distinguishing voiceless /p t k/ from voiced /b d g/. The three spirantal phonemes, not having voice as a distinctive feature, can and do show both voiceless and voiced allophones.

Our structural analysis of the labials and dentals agrees with the analysis of the OE scribes as shown by their choice of symbols. With the velars this is no longer true. For one thing, the scribes used an alphabet that was hopelessly inadequate: it had only the three symbols *c, g, h* (disregarding the rare uses of *k*) to use for the seven phones [ċ ġ k x ᶃ g h] which we have analyzed into the six phonemes /ċ ġ k x g h/. Then too, the lack of contrast between [g], [ᶃ], [x], and [h] in columns 3–12 of our table made it possible to use either *g* or *h* quite unambiguously for any of these four phones in any of these ten positions, and the scribes took full advantage of this opportunity.[12] The stop [g] was written quite consistently with the letter *g*, but the spirants [ᶃ] and [x] were written with both *g* and *h*. For a while *g* predominated for [ᶃ], and the choice of *h* or *g* for [x] was governed largely by morphophonemic convenience. *ealh, mearh, scōh* usually with *h*, but *swealg, bearg, drōg* usually with *g* because of the related *swelgan, beorgan, dragan,* etc. Later on the scribes began to write [x] more or less consistently with *h,* regardless of morphophonemics, and continued the use of *g* for [g] and [ᶃ].

With the phonemic status of [ᶃ] established, we can rapidly complete our analysis of the OE stops and spirants. The PGmc. contrast /s–z/ was of course lost when /z/ merged with inherited /r/: Gothic *maiza* but OE *māra* 'more'. The way was then open for /s/ to develop voiced allophones, and it did this at the time of the general voicing of medial spirants. This is indicated by the modern reflexes of /s/, and also by the *-de* of such forms as *līesde,* preterit of *līesan* 'set free', as against the *-te* of *cyste,* preterit of *cyssan* 'kiss'. Thus all of the OE spirant phonemes (except /h/, which had been lost in voiced surroundings) showed both voiceless and voiced allophones, in complementary distribution.

Our analysis has led us to set up /ċ/ and /ġ/ as some sort of palatal phonemes (palatal or palatalized stops or affricates), with no spirantal counterpart; and to set up /s/ as a spirant with no stop counterparts. If we could group these together as (ċ : ġ) : s, we would have a perfect parallel to the labial, dental, and velar orders. To do this, however, it would be necessary to establish some distinctive feature (say, palatal articulation) common to all three of them. Since the subsequent development of these phonemes indicates that there was no such feature, we cannot assign them to a single order. The OE stops and spirants therefore seem to have had the following structure: (p : b) : f, (t : d) : þ, (k : g) : x, ċ : ġ, s, h. . . .

[12] The following description gives only the broad outlines; no attempt is made to trace the detailed usage of *g, h, gh, hg, ch* for the spirants, and *g, c, cg, gc* for the (palatal and velar) stops. Cf. Sievers–Brunner, *Ae. Gram.* §211-23. I use the letter *g* to represent the special OE symbol.

The Phonemic Split of Germanic k *in Old English*

HERBERT PENZL

[Two allophones of Germanic *k* became separate phonemes after the *i*-umlaut had changed the distribution of palatal vowels in Proto-Old-English. Not the phonetic development of palatal [k′], but the distributional change involving velar [k] caused the completion of the phonemic split.]

CHANGES IN THE PHONEMIC SYSTEM of a language, e.g. the development of new distinctive units or the coalescence of old ones, are the most important events in its history. It is often difficult to interpret the evidence for such phonemic changes in the older stages of languages, because it consists exclusively of indications in orthography and spellings. It is still harder to interpret such evidence if the phonemic change in question preceded our earliest written sources in the language. Fortunately, orthographic evidence and occasional naive spellings lend themselves primarily to phonemic, hardly ever to a purely phonetic interpretation,[1] because they show essential sound-contrasts and distinctions but never specific sound-values. We shall deal here with the circumstances of the phonemic split of Germanic *k,* of which we find the results now in such Modern English word pairs as *chin* and *kin, chill* and

---

Reprinted by permission from *Language* 23.34-42 (1947).

[1] See *Lang.* 20.84 ff.

Abbreviations: AB = *Anglia Beiblatt;* Bülbring = K. D. Bülbring, *Altenglisches Elementarbuch* (Heidelberg, 1902); Bülbring II = K. D. Bülbring, Was lässt sich aus dem gebrauch der buchstaben *k* und *c* im Matthäus-Evangelium des Rushworth-Manuscripts folgern?, *Anglia Beiblatt* 9.289-300 (1899); Dieter = F. Dieter, *Laut- und Formenlehre der altgermanischen Dialekte* (Leipzig, 1898; Jordan = Richard Jordan, *Handbuch der mittelenglischen Grammatik*[2] (Heidelberg, 1934); Kluge = F. Kluge, *Geschichte der englischen Sprache,* Paul's *Grundriss*[2] 1.926-1151 (Strassburg, 1900 sqq.); Ley = Hermann Ley, Der Lautwert des altenglischen c (Diss. Marburg 1914); Luick = K. Luick, *Historische Grammatik der englischen Sprache* (Leipzig, 1914 sqq.); Sievers = E. Sievers, *Angelsächsische Grammatik*[3] (1898); Viëtor, = W. Viëtor, *Die northumbrischen Runensteine* (Marburg, 1895); Wyld = H. C. Wyld, Contributions to the history of the guttural sounds in English, *Transactions of the Philological Society* 1899.129-260.

kill, batch and *back.* First, we shall take up the evidence for the split in Old English and Middle English.

1. OLD ENGLISH EVIDENCE FOR THE PHONEMIC SPLIT

1.1 All words with initial *c* alliterate with one another in Old English poetry. This fact is not conclusive evidence against a phonemic split, because it may have been due to a poetic tradition of the kind that is responsible for Modern English 'eye-rhymes'.[2]

1.2. *c* is the almost universal spelling for Germanic *k* in Old English manuscripts. But a second symbol, *k,* is occasionally used. Such *k* spellings appear e.g. in the Cotton and Hatton manuscripts of the Cura Pastoralis: *kyninʒ, kyþan, kynn, kenninʒ, markien. k* spellings occur frequently in the Rushworth glosses to the Gospel of St. Matthew: *kasere, unklene, Krist, kneu, kempe, kennisse, kyninʒ, bokere, ʒebroken, ek, eknisse, ciken, kælic, kæʒen.*[3]

1.3. Germanic *k* is rendered by the so called cēn-rune in Old English runic inscriptions: it appears e.g. on the cross of Lancaster in *Cuþbereh(t), Cynibal(þ).*[4] The poet Cynewulf writes his name with the cēn-rune. The Old English alphabet shows several adjustments to phonemic changes;[5] thus a second symbol for Germanic *k,* the so-called calc-rune, was formed from the cēn-rune.[6] The calc-rune in its simplest form is nothing but a cēn-rune symmetrically supplemented. The cross of Bewcastle shows a slightly varying form. The cross of Ruthwell has a sign consisting of the ʒār-rune with a vertical shaft through it for the sound of the calc-rune. The cēn-rune appears on the cross of Ruthwell in *ic, kyniqc, licæs, riicnæ;* probably on the cross of Bewcastle in *Alcfriþu.* The calc-rune appears at Ruthwell in *Crist, cwomu,* at Bewcastle in *Cyniburug, Cristtus,* on the third stone of Thornhill in *becun.* The ʒār-rune with the shaft, which Viëtor transliterates by *k,* appears at Ruthwell in *kyniqc, uqket;* at Bewcastle perhaps in *kyniq.*[7]

1.4. In some Old English manuscripts *e* or *i* is written after *c,* mostly before velar vowels. We find the spellings *ce* for *c* in *ciricean, tæcean, strecceane; ci* for *c* in *drencium, ecium, birciae, ciae.*[8] Spellings with this

[2] Cf. G. Hempl in *Anglia* 22.382; Bülbring, *AB* 9.102 ff.; Ley 64; A. Pogatscher, *Zur Lautlehre der griechischen, lateinischen, und romanischen Lehnwörter im Altenglischen* 185 f. (Strassburg, 1888). As to the alliteration of ʒ see fn. 18.

[3] Cf. Wyld 138-41; Kluge 990 (§65b); Bülbring II.

[4] Viëtor §33, Anm. 1; also §73, where he states that the *cēn*-rune 'offenbar den gutturalen Laut mitbezeichnet'; Bülbring, *AB* 9.77 f.

[5] Out of the original a-rune were created signs for /æ/ (the æsk-rune), for /a/ (the āc-rune), and for /o/ (the ōs-rune). This happened after the allophones of original /a/ had developed into separate distinctive sound units (phonemes). The original symbol for /o/ became the symbol for the umlauted sound /ö/, later of /e/. A runic sign for /ü/ was formed by combining the characters for /u/ and /i/. Cf. Helmut Arntz, *Handbuch der Runenkunde* 146 ff. (1935); O. von Friesen. *Runorna* 55 ff. (1933).

[6] Friesen 58; Th. v. Grienberger, *Arkiv för Nordisk Filologi* 15.22 (1899).

[7] See Viëtor; A. B. Webster in G. Baldwin Brown, *Arts in Early England* 5.21,25.264 ff.; Zupitza–Schipper, *Alt- und mittelenglisches Übungsbuch*[6] 3 ff. 1902).

[8] Sievers §206.3b; Bülbring §499, Anm. 4.

intrusive *e* are particularly common, also initially, after *c* in the cluster *sc: sceacan, sceomu, sceond, sceop, sceoh* occur beside *scacan, scomu, scond, scop, scoh.* In late West Saxon, spellings like *sceucca, sceocca* are found beside *scucca; sceufan, sceofan* beside *scufan; sceaþ* beside *scæþ.*[9]

1.5. *cea-* and *cie-*spellings in West Saxon have been interpreted to indicate a special change of the palatal vowels *æ, e* after the palatal *c* sound: *ceaf* (**æ* > *ea*) 'chaff', *sceap* (**ǣ* > *ēa*), 'sheep', *scield* (**e* > *ie*) 'shield'. Some scholars—e.g. ten Brink,[10] Kluge,[11] Dieter,[12] V. Rehm, and E. Prokosch[13]—assumed this apparent 'diphthongization' to be merely orthographic, only an expression of the palatal quality of the preceding *c,* as in the forms *ciricean, sceacan* quoted above: *e* or *i* after *c* was to them just a diacritical mark on the line, a 'Palatalzeichen'.[14] Already Sievers[15] pointed out that *ea* and *ie* written after *c* seem, on the whole, to follow the development of the diphthongs *ea, ie* in the dialect: instead of *ea* we find later the spelling *e (scep* 'sheep', *cerf* 'carved'); instead of *ie* we find the spellings *i, y* (*cyse* 'cheese'). Whether we are dealing with actual changes of palatal vowels or merely with spelling variation, in either case we have evidence for the palatal quality of sounds written *c.*

1.6. Certain naive spellings reveal a phonetic change involving *c.* The spelling *orceard* for *ortʒeard* appears in the Cura Pastoralis, *feccan* for *fetian* in Alfred's writings. Other spellings include *wicca* for *witʒa, witeʒa; cræftca* for *cræftʒa, cræfteʒa.*[16] The use of the symbol *c* for a cluster of dental plus palatal consonants indicates a frequent similar sound-value of *c* elsewhere. Sievers[17] quotes an Old English loan-word where *c* corresponds to Old French *ch,* a sibilant: *kæcepol* 'catchpoll', from Old Northern French *cachepol.* This indicates a sound-value for *c* resembling that of Old French *ch.*

1.7. Like all *c*'s, all *ʒ*'s alliterate together in most of Old English poetry.[18] Germanic *g* is almost exclusively rendered by *ʒ.* But in runic writing a special velar ʒār-rune was developed from the ʒifu-rune. The

[9] See Kluge 993 f. (§66); Sievers §76.2; V. Rehm, *Die Palatalisierung der Gruppe* sc *im Altenglischen* (Heidelberg, 1901). Luick, §254, thinks of genuine diphthongs but assumes a 'flüchtige erste Komponente'; cf. also §691.

[10] *Anglia* 1.518 ff.

[11] *Anglia* 5, Anzeiger 83.

[12] §57.

[13] Rehm 53; E. Prokosch, *A Comparative Germanic Grammar* 77, §148 (Baltimore, 1939).

[14] Kluge, 990 (§65b), suggests in a footnote 'eine eingehende Geschichte des *e* als Palatalzeichen'. This remark inspired V. Rehm's study. Ley, 39 ff., assumes the Palatalzeichen to indicate the assibilation of *c*—[kx] or [kj].

[15] §75 f. and Anm. 5; Dieter §57; Luick §§171 ff., 263, 279; Bülbring §315.

[16] See Luick §667, Anm. 2 and 4; Kluge 993 (§65g); Sievers §§196.3, 416, Anm. 15b; G. Hempl, *Anglia* 22.376 f.

[17] *Anglia* 13.314.

[18] But see Kluge 1000 (§68); R. Loewe, *Germanische Sprachwissenschaft* 73 (1933); Luick §§633, 696 and Anm. 1; Prokosch 76 f. Alliteration offers no evidence for such specific sound-values as Prokosch's [g] for ʒ before velar vowels, Luick's [gj] for ʒ before palatal vowels.

latter appears e.g. on the cross of Ruthwell in *gistoddun, gidrefid;* the former occurs in *galgu, god.* There is ample evidence that the reflex of the palatal [g′]-allophone merged with the reflex of Germanic *j.*[19] *ȝea-* and *ȝie*-spellings have been interpreted exactly like the cases of *ea, ie* after *c* discussed in §1.5, as diphthongizations of palatal vowels or as orthographic variation.[20] A special development of the cluster *g′g′* < *gj, gi,* and of *ŋg′* < *ŋgj* in Old English is indicated by the use of the symbols *cȝ.* The writing of *e* after *c, cȝ* as in *lecȝean, secȝean, strenȝeo, ȝemenȝean* resembles the *ce*-spellings for *c.*[21] Occasional spellings show *cȝ* instead of *dȝ,* e.g. *mićȝern* for **midȝern, Muncȝiu* for *Muntȝiof;*[22] they provide more evidence for a sound-value of *c* that resembles that of a cluster of dental plus palatal.

1.8. The Old English use of a second symbol *k* in manuscripts, as well as the development of the calc-rune out of the cēn-rune in runic inscriptions, is evidence for a phonemic split of Germanic *k.* The variations *cea/ca* and *cie/ce* provide additional evidence for the split, whether they indicate an actual change of palatal vowels or are only orthographic. The appearance of *c, cȝ* instead of *tȝ, dȝ* in naive spellings, and the substitution of *c* for Old French *ch* in a loan-word reveal that *c* sometimes has a sound-value far removed from original [k] or [k′], probably close to [tj] or [tš]. The evidence for a phonemic split of Germanic *g* partly parallels and confirms the evidence for the split of Germanic *k.* But initially, this split of *g* led to a phonemic merger, since the reflex of the palatal allophone [g′] coalesced with Germanic *j.* The phonetic development of the allophone [g′] in medial clusters to the sibilant [dž] offers a parallel to the phonetic change of the allophone [k′] to [tš].

2. MIDDLE ENGLISH AND MODERN ENGLISH EVIDENCE FOR THE PHONEMIC SPLIT

2.1. Middle English orthography, with its departure from the Anglo-Saxon scribal tradition, indicates the phonemic split of Germanic *k* even more clearly. The symbols *ch* on the one hand, and *c k* on the other hand came to be generally used for the two phonemes. *ch* has the value [k] only in some texts of the late Old English and earliest Middle English period.[23] Its normal Middle English sound-value is based on the Anglo-Norman value of *ch,* which is [tš]. *ch* is in general use around 1200;[24]

[19] See Viëtor; A. B. Webster, loc. cit. 5.213 f.; Sievers §212, Anm. 2; Bülbring §492 and Anm. 1.

[20] Sievers §§74 ff.; see also fn. 15.

[21] Hempl, *Anglia* 22.375 ff.; Bülbring §499, Anm. 4.

[22] Sievers §§192.2, 196.3, 216.1, Anm. 2.

[23] See Wyld 140; Jordan §178, Anm. 1; Bülbring, *AB* 9.75; E. Ekwall, *AB* 32.157 f.; W. Schlemilch, *Beiträge zur Sprache und Orthographie spätaltenglischer Sprachdenkmäler der Übergangszeit* 48 (1914).

[24] Wyld 142; Kluge 990.

tch does not occur with great frequency even in the 15th century.[25] Both *c*[26] and *k*[27] are used with the value [k]; *k* becomes frequent before *e, i* in the 11th and 12th centuries: *kepen, kei.* It is common before *n*: *knee, knowen;* before unstressed *e*: *maken, drinken. c* is common before velar vowels: *can, corn;* before consonants other than *n*: *clene, crepen.* In final position, *c* is used until the 14th century, then *k* becomes more common: *bok, folk.*[28]

2.2. Middle English orthography not only indicates the split of Germanic *k;* it also reveals the change of the Old English cluster /sk′/ into the unit phoneme /š/, with the spellings *s, ss, sch,* later *sh*: *scharp, ship.* The phonemic split of Germanic *g* into /j/ and /g/ is indicated by the use of spellings with *ȝ* (later *y*) and with *g* respectively: *ȝellen, yellen, girden, gilden.* The change of [g′] in the clusters *g′g′* and *ŋg′* to [dž], however, is not clearly expressed by Middle English orthography: *egge* 'edge', *sengen* 'singe'. *dg* is very rare before the 15th century.[29]

2.3. Spelling and pronunciation of words with initial *ch* and with initial *c* or *k* in Modern English throw light on the corresponding forms in Middle English and Old English: we pronounce [tš] in *child, cheese, cheer,* [k] in *can, cool, clean, kill, ken.* Phonemicists are still debating whether [tš] in *child* should be considered a unit-phoneme /č/ or a cluster of /t/ and /š/;[30] but this descriptive problem of Modern English phonemics has no immediate bearing on our historical study. As for the split of Germanic *g,* Modern English spelling and pronunciation clearly confirm the values of Middle English *y* and *g*: *yell, yolk, gird, gild.*

3. THE DISTRIBUTION OF VELAR AND PALATAL ALLOPHONE REFLEXES

3.1. We must assume that Proto-Old-English /k/ had two main types of positional variants: a palatal allophone [k′] before palatal vowels, and a velar allophone [k] before velar vowels. The occurrence

[25] Jordan §179; Wyld 146.

[26] *c* beside *ch* with the sound-value [tš] is found in some texts of the early 12th century. *c* was also used in French loan-words with the sound-value [ts], which became [s] in the 12th century. In the latter part of this century, marks in Old English mss. show that *c* was ambiguous: a *k* is written over the *c* in *swylce, stearce, ceas,* an *h* over the *c* in *rica, ceald, wyrcan.* See S. J. Crawford, The Worcester Marks and Glosses of the Old English Manuscripts in the Bodleian, *Anglia* 52.1 ff.

[27] After 1135, *k* is used more frequently in the Peterborough Chronicle. See Wyld 140 f.; Jordan §178, Anm. 1.

[28] Jordan §178.

[29] Jordan §§192, 194; Kluge 998; Wyld 154 f.

[30] N.S. Trubetzkoy, *Grundzüge der Phonologie* 50 ff. (1939), discusses 'monophonematische Wertung' and 'polyphonematische Wertung'. See also L. Bloomfield, *Language* 120 (1933) and *Lang.* 11.98, fn. 3 (1935); Bloch and Trager, *Lang.* 17.229 (1941) and *Outline of Linguistic Analysis* 49 (1942. Phonetic differences between the cluster [t] plus [š] as in *courtship* and the cluster [tš] as in *child* have often been pointed out, e.g. by W. L. Thompson, *Le Maître Phonétique* 1914.46. ff; Daniel Jones, id. 1931.64 and *Outline of English Phonetics* §608 (1932). Cf. also J. S. Kenyon, *American Pronunciation*[8] §207.4 (1940).

and distribution of the derivatives of these two allophones in Old English is important for the understanding of the phonemic split of Germanic *k*. The symbol *k* in Old English manuscripts expresses everywhere the reflex of the velar allophone. There is, however, not a single document where *k* is used exclusively for the derivatives of the velar, and *c* exclusively for the derivatives of the palatal allophone. Farman in his Rushworth glosses uses *c* more often than *k* before velar vowels, before consonants, and even before *y*. He differentiates, however, almost without exception between initial *ce* and *ke, ci* and *ki* where the distinction is really important: *ceke, kempe, cild, kininȝ*.[31] *c* appears before Germanic *e* and *i; k* appears before *e* and *i* that originated through the *i*-umlaut of Germanic velar vowels.

3.2. The calc-rune is found in runic inscriptions before consonants (*r, w*) and velar vowels (*u*); the modified ȝār-rune that is assumed to be identical with the calc-rune, appears after a nasal and before *y*, the *i*-umlaut of *u*. The cēn-rune, however, mostly appears after Germanic *i* (see above §1.3). The runic texts have no example of Germanic *k* before Germanic palatal vowels.[32] But the cēn-rune does not exclusively indicate the reflexes of the palatal allophone [k′]; it occurs also before Gemanic *u* and its umlaut *y*, e.g. in *Cuþbereh(t), Cynewulf*. The calc-rune indicates only reflexes of the velar allophone [k].

3.3. After *s* or medially before original *i*, spellings with *ce* and *ci* are frequent. In words like *ceaf, sceap, scield,* original palatal vowels are written *ea* and *ie*. These *c*'s represent reflexes of the palatal allophone [k′]. No such spellings with *ce* and *ci* for *c* ever occur before velar vowels (as in *calan, corn, cuþ*) or palatal vowels that originated through the *i*-umlaut of velar ones (as in *cepan, cynn*).

3.4. Middle English orthography reveals velar /k/ in the following positions: initially before the Old English velar vowels *a ā o ō u ū* and their umlauts *ǣ æ ē e (oe) y ȳ (i)*, and before consonants, e.g. *care, corn cocc, cu (ku, kow), kennen, kempe, keie* (Old English *cæȝe*), *kissen* (Old English *cyssan*), *clene, knee, knowen;* in medial position before original velar vowels, e.g. *maken, token, naked;* in final position after Old English velar vowels, e.g. *bok, milk*. The Middle English spelling *ch* and the Modern English pronunciation [tš] indicate that the descendant of the palatal allophone [k′] of Germanic *k* occurs in the following positions:[33] initially before the Proto-Old-English palatal vowels *æ ǣ e ē i ī ea ēa eo (io)*, e.g. *chaff* (OE *cealf*), *chest* (OE *cest*), *chep* (OE *ceap*), *cheke* (OE *ceace*), *chesen* (OE *ceosan*), *chin* (OE *cinn*), *chiden* (OE *cidan*); in medial position before original *i ī j* or after original *i*, if not followed by velar vowels, e.g. *beche* (OE *bece*), *eche* (OE *cee*), *techen*

[31] See Bülbring II.
[32] Viëtor §73, Anm. 1. On *c* in *kyniqc* see Bülbring, *AB* 9.74.
[33] Jordan §179; Kluge 991 f.

(OE *tæcan*), *strecchen* (OE *streccan*), *wicche* (OE *wicce*); in final position after *i ī* or before original *i*,[34] e.g. *picche* (OE *pic*), *hwich* (OE *hwelc, hwilc, hwylc*), *bench* (OE *benc* < **banki*).

3.5. The Middle English spellings *s, ss, sch, sh,* which indicate /š/ for the Old English cluster /sk′/, occur initially before all vowels; medially before palatal vowels; finally after palatal vowels. The spellings *sc* and *sk,* which indicate /sk/, appear medially before originally velar, also finally after velar vowels: *asken, tusk*.[35] Middle English *g,* indicating /g/, the reflex of the velar allophone [g] of Germanic *g,* occurs before the Old English velar vowels *a ā o ō u ū* and their umlauts, e.g. *galwes* (OE *ȝalȝa*), *gyrden, girden* (OE *ȝyrdan*), *gilden* (OE *ȝyldan*). The spelling *ȝ* or *y* indicating /j/, the reflex of the palatal allophone [g′] of Germanic *g,* appear before Proto-Old-English palatal vowels, e.g. *ȝellen, yellen* (OE *ȝellan*), *ȝolke, yolke* (OE *ȝeolca*). The distribution of the derivatives of the velar and palatal allophones of Germanic *g* thus corresponds to that of the derivatives of the allophones of Germanic *k*.

3.6. The description in §3.4 of the distribution of /k/ and /tš/ does not take into account the results of analogical transfer. Variation between /k/ and /tš/ even within the forms of one paradigm would have to be expected, because the inflectional endings contained both velar and palatal vowels or had lost their vowels at an early date. Within the nominal declension the plural endings *-as, -a, -u, -um,* and the weak ending *-an* contrasted with the singular endings *-es, -e,* e.g. *ȝelic, ȝelices, ȝelice,* but *ȝelica, ȝelicum*: the singular forms must originally have contained the palatal allophone [k′], the plural forms the velar allophone [k]. Middle English actually has both *liche* and *like,* of which the latter prevailed in Modern English.[36] The first, second, and third classes of the strong verbs must originally have had a [k′]/[k] variation according to the vowel in the stem, e.g. *cīnan* [k′], *cinon* [k′], *cinen* [k′], but *cān* [k]; *cēosan* [k′], *cēas* [k′], but *curon* [k], *coren* [k]; *ceorfan* [k′], *cearf* [k′], but *curfon* [k], *corfen* [k]. Later, analogical leveling of this variation took place.[37] Such leveling would bring reflexes of the palatal allophone [k′] into positions where only derivatives of the velar allophone formerly occurred *(chosen),* and the velar allophone [k] into positions where only the palatal allophone formerly occurred (ME *kerven*). The /k/ of such forms as *secst, secþ, þyncst, recþ, wyrcþ,* where a velar [k] had developed before the consonants after an early loss of *i,*

[34] Luick says §685.3: 'Ob auch nach anderen hellen Vokalen, etwa auf kleinerem Gebiet, ähnliches eintreten konnte, ist zweifelhaft.' See also Jordan §179, Anm. 2; Kluge 992; E. Ekwall, *AB* 32.160 ff.

[35] Luick §691; Jordan §181; H. Weyhe, *Englische Studien* 39.161 ff.; Kluge 993 f. (§66); V. Royce West, *Der etymologische Ursprung der neuenglischen Lautgruppe* [*sk*] (Heidelberg, 1936).

[36] Luick §688; Sievers §240, Anm. 3.

[37] Luick §637, Anm. 6. On the leveling of a variation between [sk] and [sk′] in paradigms like that of Old English *fisc,* see Luick §691.2; Weyhe loc.cit.; Jordan §181.

was transferred to the infinitives in Middle English *seken, þinken, rekken, wirken.*[38]

3.7. The assumption that the phonemic split of Germanic *k* had not taken place in the North and the Northeastern Midland turned out to be false. It is a general English development.[39] Since there are dialectal differences in the analogical transfer of /k/ or /tš/ to the various forms, Middle English as well as Modern English dialects often show a double development, e.g. *teken* and *techen, benk* and *bench, birk* and *birch,* Modern English *dike* and *ditch.* A number of the /k/ forms are probably due to Scandinavian influence: *kirk* 'church'; *casten, kesten; ketel.* Some may be forms directly borrowed from Scandinavian, some may be hyperforms due to false analogy.[40] Romance loan-words also introduced forms with /k/ and /tš/ in positions that differed from the native development: *chasen, chaumbre, chalengen, escapen.*

4. THE PHONETIC CHANGE OF THE PALATAL ALLOPHONE

4. The phonetic development of the palatal allophone [k] to [tš] and the intermediate stages of this change were formerly widely discussed by scholars. It seemed the most important problem in regard to the development of Germanic *k.* Hempl[41] assumed a development from velar stop to palatal stop to palatal affricate to dental affricate; Jordan[42] and Luick[43] assumed a development from [k] to [kχ] to [tχ] to [tš]. Some scholars asserted that the [tš] stage had been reached in Old English, e.g. Bülbring[44] and Sievers.[45] Sweet[46] assumed the [tj] stage for Old English; H. C. Wyld[47] agreed, and thought that [tš] had been reached in the middle of the 13th century. The phonetic development of palatal [g′] in the clusters *g′g′* and *ŋg′* to [dž] was assumed to have been parallel to and simultaneous with the change of palatal [k′] to [tš].[48] Ortho-

[38] Jordan §179; Luick §689.

[39] Wyld 142 f.; A. Ritter, Die Verteilung der *ch-* und *k*-formen im Mittelenglischen (Diss. Marburg 1904); O. Gevenich, *Die englische Palatalisierung von* k *zu* č *im Lichte der englischen Ortsnamen* 159 (Halle, 1918). Jordan, §179, Anm. 1, calls the change 'lautgesetzlich gemeinenglisch'.

[40] See Gevenich, op.cit, 15; Jordan §179; Erik Björkman, *Scandinavian Loan-Words in Middle English* 139 ff. (1900); Luick §§687, 701. On the dialectal variation between forms with /g/ and /dž/, see Jordan §192; Luick §690 and Anm. 1.

[41] *Anglia* 22.376.

[42] §177.

[43] §685, also §687; Max Förster, *Idg. Forschungen,* Anz. 12.105 ff.

[44] *AB* 9.102; §493.

[45] §206.4; *Anglia* 13.312 ff.

[46] *History of English Sounds* §§496, 737; *An Anglo-Saxon Primer*[8] 3 (1905).

[47] 136 f. See also Kluge 993 (§65g). Joseph and Elizabeth Wright, *An Old English Grammar* §309 (1908), call [tš] for Old English 'an assumption which cannot be proved'.

[48] Jordan §§192, 194; Luick §685, on an assumed change from [g′] to [gj] to [dj] to [dž]; Hempl, loc.cit.

graphic evidence in support of either [tš] or [tj] for Old English is inconclusive, of course, because orthography never lends itself to detailed phonetic interpretation: such spellings as *orceard, feccan* do not prove any specific sound-value;[49] *micȝern* does not prove [dž];[50] *c* in *kæcepol* does not necessarily indicate [tš] simply because it corresponds to Old French *ch*. However, the specific phonetic values at any particular time are not as important as the distinctive sound units and their contrasts. Old English has satisfactory evidence for the phonemic split of Germanic *k* itself, but only the general sound-types of the historical phonemes can be ascertained on the basis of the available evidence.

5. THE COMPLETION OF THE PHONEMIC SPLIT

5.1. We have assumed the existence of velar and palatal allophones of Germanic /k/. Positional variation within the /k/ phoneme, i.e. the fact that a palatal [k′] is pronounced before front vowels like [e] and [i], and a velar [k] before back vowels like [o] and [u], cannot by itself lead to a phonemic split, even if the difference between the allophones comes to be phonetically quite large. As long as the phonetic quality of the allophones is determined by their phonetic surroundings, we are not yet dealing with two distinctive sound units, two phonemes. But the moment that we find two different sounds in the same phonetic position with a difference in meaning, we can tell that the phonemic split has been completed and that two phonemes have developed out of allophones of one. Old English orthography already indicates the split; Middle English orthography and Modern English pronunciation confirm it. We find clear indications in Middle English inflectional paradigms of transfers of /k/ forms into original /tš/ positions and conversely, through the working of analogy. Scandinavian and Romance loan-words introduced /k/ and /tš/ into positions where the sounds were not found in their regular native development. But all this has nothing to do with the change of two allophones into separate phonemes. No analogical transfer took place; no foreign loan-words introduced /k/ and /tš/ into unusual positions before the two allophones had reached phonemic status. Transfers and loans only affected the internal distribution of the phonemes; they did not create the contrastive units.

5.2. Scholars have noticed, in the historical distribution of forms with /k/ and with /tš/, that these sounds developed differently before Germanic palatal vowels (Sievers' and Luick's 'primäre Palatalvokale') and before palatal vowels developed by Proto-Old English *i*-umlaut from velar vowels ('sekundäre Palatalvokale'). A typical explanation is that 'the process of palatalization had ceased' by the time of the *i*-umlaut, so that the velar allophone [k] was no longer affected by the new palatal

[49] See Luick §687; Ley 49 ff. (§44).
[50] Wyld 149.

vowels.[51] No further inferences were ever drawn from this striking distribution. Actually, the phonemization of [k] and [k′] is a direct result of the Proto-Old-English *i*-umlaut. Twaddell[52] has shown that the *i*-umlaut in the Germanic languages presupposes the existence of positional variants of velar vowels before *i ī j* in a following unstressed syllable. We must assume, therefore, that certain Proto-Old-English vowels had special allophones before unstressed *i ī j*; these are listed here, with an indication of the probable phonetic values of the allophones: /a/ : [æ], /æ/ : [e], /ā/ : [ǣ] or [ē], /ea, eo/ : [ie] or [ē], /u/ : [ü], /ū/ : [ǖ] /o/ : [ȫ], /ō/ : [ȫ].[35] For example, the variation between the allophones [ō] and [ȫ] in Proto-Old-English **fōtu-* and **fȫti-* was determined simply by the following unstressed vowels *u* and *i* respectively. When final *u* and *i* were lost, the vowels /ō/ and /ȫ/ in *fōt* and *fȫt* (later *fēt*) were brought into contrast as two separate phonemes. Thus, the two allophones of original /ō/ at first created new independent contrastive values. The /ö/ sounds that were written *oe* in the oldest Old English documents (e.g. Cod. Epinal *coempa*) soon developed into /e/, except in the Northumbrian dialect, where [ö] was preserved until the 11th century. The /ü/ sounds were written *y* in Old English (e.g. *cyþan, ʒylden, cyninʒ*), but later Old English sources frequently write *i*, indicating the value /i/ (e.g. *cininʒ, cinn*).[54] Proto-Old-English velar [k] was not affected by this *i*-umlaut. If all the new palatal vowels had remained phonetically distinct from the old palatal vowels, the velar allophone [k] and the palatal allophone [k′] would not have been brought into contrast, because they would have continued to occur only in complementary, mutually exclusive positions. But since the new palatal vowels merged with the old ones—since for example the new allophones [e] and [æ] merged with the old phonemes /e/ and /æ/ respectively—both the velar and the palatal allophones came to stand before identical palatal vowels: the sounds [k] and [k′], formerly mere variants of a single phoneme /k/, were now in contrast, and had thus become separate phonemes. The phonemic split was complete.

The phonemic status of /k/ and /k′/ can be understood without knowing exactly how the two sounds differed phonetically at the time that they were brought into contrast. We have no evidence to determine whether /k′/ had the sound-value [kj] or [tj] or [tš] or something intermediate.

5.3. The great and exclusive interest hitherto shown in the change [k] > [tš] has probably prevented the recognition of the fact that it was

[51] Ley states (31), 'die Vermutung läge nicht fern, dass eine richtige Erkenntnis des Wesens des i-Umlauts mit seiner Wirkung und Gegenwirkung auch die hier bestehenden Schwierigkeiten aufhellen würde.'

[52] A Note on Old High German Umlaut, *Monatshefte für deutschen Unterricht* 30.177-81 (1938).

[53] See Luick §§182 ff.; Bülbring §§158 ff.

[54] Luick §281; Bülbring §307.

the velar, not the palatal allophone of Germanic *k* that was responsible for the phonemic split. The crucial innovation was the appearance of a velar [k] before the new palatal vowels developed through *i*-umlaut. All the Old English evidence points clearly in that direction: the special *k* symbol is used for the velar sound, while *c* indicates the reflexes of Germanic *k* in general, not merely the palatal ones; the calc-rune was created specially for the velar sound, while the cēn-rune often represents Germanic *k* in general.

It was not the phonetic change of the palatal allophone [k′], but the persistence of the velar allophone [k] in a changing environment that caused the phonemic split of the Germanic *k* to be completed.

The Loss of Long Consonants and the Rise of Voiced Fricatives in Middle English

HANS KURATH

1. IN OE,[1] long consonants are fully established in one and only one position: between a fully stressed or a half-stressed SHORT vowel (or diphthong) and a following unstressed vowel, as in *clyppan, settan, reccan, ebba, middel, hycgan, frogga, fremman, spinnan, spillan, steorra, siþþan, missan, hliehhan (hlæhhan),* and (after a half-stressed short vowel) in *bliccettan* 'glitter', *oretta* 'challenger', *faranne* (inf.), *wēstenne 'wilderness'*.[2]

In MSS of the 10th century, double letters are written with great consistency in such words, whereas in other words single letters appear with equal consistency in the same position, e.g. in *witan* 'know', *sunu* 'son', *stelan* 'steal'. The consistent writing of double letters in some of these words and of single letters in others makes it clear that between a short stressed or half-stressed vowel and a following unstressed vowel long and short consonants are in phonemic contrast in OE. To support this inference from the spelling, one may cite such minimally differentiated pairs as *sittan* 'sit' : *witan* 'know', *sellan* 'sell' : *stelan* 'steal'.

In OE, double consonants are also written at the end of stressed monosyllables whose dissyllabic forms have long consonants after short

---

Reprinted by permission from *Language* 32.435-45 (1956).

[1] The substance of this paper was presented in the Linguistic Forum at the University of Michigan in the summer of 1953. The results are briefly stated in H. Kurath and S. M. Kuhn, *Middle English dictionary: Plan and bibliography* 6 (Ann Arbor, 1954).

[2] Most long consonants in this position result from the assimilation of /j/ to the preceding consonant, as in *settan* < **satja-nam;* a few are inherited from Proto-Germanic, as in *fulle* < **fullai.* Since /j/ was assimilated to a consonant without lengthening it if the consonant was preceded by a long vowel, a diphthong, or a short vowel plus consonant (as in *sēcan* 'seek', *hwǣte* 'wheat', *sendan* < **sōkja-, *hwaitja-, *sandja-*), long consonants occur only after short vowels in OE (as also in continental West Germanic; NHG *weizen* has /ts/ from /t/ in syllable-initial position, as in *wälzen*).

vowels, as in *bed(d), cyn(n), eal(l),* infl. *beddes, cynnes, ealle,* but without consistency. From this inconsistency in spelling we may safely draw the inference that long consonants were no longer phonemic in this position; for if OE had preserved long consonant phonemes at the end of words, they would be written with the same consistency as long consonants between vowels. We must therefore regard such spellings as *bedd, cynn, eall,* beside *bed, cyn, eal* as analogical to the spellings of the inflected forms, i.e. as instances of standardized spellings of the morphemes in question, each of which had two stem variants (allomorphs) in the paradigm.

Double writing, of stops and fricatives only, occurs furthermore between a short stressed vowel and a following sonorant, as (1) in *ap(p)las* 'apples', *bet(t)ra* 'better', *bit(t)re* (infl.) *offrian* 'sacrifice' (from Latin), and (2) in *at(t)re* (dat.) 'poison', *æt(t)rig* 'poisonous', *æd(d)re* 'vein', *næd(d)re* 'adder', *maþ(þ)um* 'treasure'. All native words in these two groups had stem variants (allomorphs): in group (1) e.g. *æpel/æppel/æp(p)l-/ap(p)l-, biter/bitter/bit(t)r-;* in group (2) e.g. *nǣdr-/nǣder-/næd(d)r-/nædder-, māþm/maþþum.*[3]

It is generally assumed, and properly so, that in such words stops and fricatives were lengthened in those forms in which they were immediately followed by a sonorant, e.g. in dat. pl. *applum* < **aplo-miz,* but not in nom. and acc. sg. *æpel* < **apl̩* < **apla-z, *apla-m,* whereupon either stem variant could be extended to the entire paradigm.[4]

Apparent inconsistencies in the OE spelling should, I believe, be interpreted as follows. (1) Since consonant length in other historical types was unquestionably phonemic between vowels, we must take the spelling variants *biter* ~ *bitter, æpel* ~ *æppel, māþm* ~ *maþþum* at face value and admit the existence of variations (unsettled or regional usage) in this position. (2) On the other hand, the variation in the spelling of the consonants between a SHORT vowel and a following sonorant, as in *bittre/bitre, æppla/æpla, nǣdre/næddre,* should be taken as reflecting the phonemically ambiguous status of phonically long stops and fricatives in a position in which phonically short consonants did not occur.

This interpretation is not in conflict with the historical observation that long stops and fricatives actually developed before sonorants in prehistoric Old English (West Germanic) and were secondarily extended to the intervocalic position, e.g. from pl. *æppla* to sg. *æppel,* which occurs in historic Old English alongside the old sg. *æpel.* The shape of the older sg. form, it may be noted, survives in ME *āker* (OE *acer*), whereas all

[3] Since in one and the same morpheme OE did not have long vowels before long consonants in other positions, it must certainly be assumed that long vowels were shortened when a following consonant before a sonorant was lengthened.

[4] Corresponding developments occurred in the other West Germanic languages, which display similar variation; e.g. OHG *affal* beside *apfal* 'apple', *ahhar* beside *ackar* 'field'. See K. Luick, *Hist. Gram.* §631.3 and Anm. 7; W. Wilmanns, *Deutsche Gram.* 1.192 (1911).

other words in this group have short vowels in ME in accordance with the normal development of OE short vowels before long consonants and before consonant groups, as in *appel, ap(p)les* from OE *æppel, æp(p)la(s)*.

In summary we may say that c1000 Old English had contrastive long consonant phonemes only in the sequence /v́ccv/, i.e. between a stressed or half-stressed short vowel and a following unstressed vowel, as in *settan, hycgan, spinnan,* etc. and in *bitter, æppel*.[5]

Before turning to ME, brief comments on relevant aspects of OE spelling will be appropriate. (1) In accordance with Latin spelling, phonemically long and short vowels are not identified in OE, but phonemically long and short consonants are. (2) Although double consonant symbols stand for long consonants, they also indicate indirectly the quantity of the preceding vowel, which is always short in this position. (3) We may therefore expect, especially in view of the defective spelling of phonemically long and short vowels, that the double writing of consonants will be retained as a diacritic of vowel quantity after its primary function is lost with the loss of phonemically long consonants. It is this adaptation of double consonant symbols to a new function—the retention of the spelling for a new purpose—that conceals from us the sweeping changes in the consonant system of Middle English. Hence, spelling alone will be of little help in our problem. We must look to other clues.

2. The most important lead for tracing the history of the long consonants comes from a consideration of the structure of sound sequences and the development of the sounds in these sequences in ME. Since the long consonants of OE occur only between vowels, we shall consider those sequences of OE in which a single consonant, long or short, is flanked by vowels. These sequences are three in number:

(1) /v́ccv/, as in *sittan, sunna, tellan, frogga, bannan*;
(2) /v́cv/, as in *witan, sunu, brecan, brocen, bana*;
(3) /v́vcv/, as in *wītan, brūcan, blēdan, sōna, stānas*.[6]

It should be clear that here both vowels and consonants have functional (phonemic) length, since any SHORT consonant can be preceded by either a short or a long vowel (e.g. *wītan* 'blame' but *witan* 'know'), and any short vowel can be followed by either a short or a long consonant (e.g. *witan* 'know' but *sittan* 'sit'). It must further be granted that both vowels and consonants will retain phonemic length as long as these three se-

[5] It should be noted that this statement refers only to the occurrence of /v́cc-v/, in which both consonants belong to the same morpheme. Complex forms such as the preterits *rǣd-de* 'advised', *mēt-te* 'met', do not have long consonants, but sequences of identical short consonants; i.e. such forms must be taken as /v́vc-cv/. Here OE retains long vowels, which in late OE or early ME are shortened before these consonant clusters. The derivative ME *red-de, met-te,* /vc-cə/, are also complex; they become *red, met* in late ME.

[6] For convenience, long vowel phonemes are presented by /vv/, long consonant phonemes by /cc/.

quences are preserved, whereas the coalescence of any two of the sequences would result in complementary distribution of long and short vowels, long and short consonants, or both. In either event contrastive quantity would be lost either in the vowel system or in the consonant system.

From these preliminary observations we shall now turn to a consideration of the history of long consonants in Middle English, which in the transition period from OE to ME occurred unambiguously only in the sequence /v́ccə/.

There is general agreement among scholars that in the Northeast Midland and in parts of the North, apparently from Norfolk northward to Yorkshire (or beyond), the sequence /v́cə/ changed to /v́vcə/ in words of two syllables, through the lengthening of ALL short stressed vowels in this position, some time before 1200. Thus OE *talu, brecan (ge)brocen, witan, sunu* became ME *tāle, brę̄ken, brǭken, wī̜ten > wē̜ten, sū̜ne > sǭne,* coalescing in type with ME *bǭnes, rē̜den,* etc. from OE *bānes, rēdan* (Anglian), etc.

The elimination of the sequence /v́cə/ in these dialects of the East Midland left only two sequences, in which PHONICALLY long and short consonants as well as PHONICALLY long and short vowels were in complementary distribution. How are the two PHONIC sequences [v́vcə] and [v́ccə] to be interpreted in phonemic terms? Are both the vowels and the consonants PHONEMICALLY long?

The answer, it seems to me, is perfectly clear. (1) Since phonic vowel length is phonemic in the sequences /v́vc/ versus /v́c/, as in *bǭk, fīn* vs. *buk, fin,* it is also phonemic in the sequences [v́vcə] vs. [v́ccə] despite complementary distribution. (2) On the other hand, since contrastive phonemically long consonants are restricted to the sequence /v́ccə/ before the coalescence of /v́cə/ with /v́vcə/, the resulting complementary distribution of phonically long and short consonants in the two remaining sequences, [v́ccə] and [v́vcə], deprives the long consonants of their phonemic function; that is, the phonic sequences [v́ccə] and [v́vcə] have become /v́cə/ and /v́vcə/, in which only vowel length is phonemic (functional).

The changes brought about by the lengthening of all short vowels in the sequence /vcə/ in these Northeast Midland and Northern dialects of ME can be conveniently summarized as follows:

	1000	a1200
(1)	/v́vcv/	phonically [v́vcə], phonemically /v́vcə/
(2)	/v́cv/	falls together with (1)
(3)	/v́ccv/	phonically [v́ccə], phonemically /v́cə/

This loss of phonemically long consonants in intervocalic position inevitably entailed the loss of phonemically long consonants before sonorants, as in *apples, bittre, offren,* whose phonemic status depended upon the contrastive consonant length in the sequences /v́cv/ : /v́ccv/. Remaining phonically long, stops and fricatives in this position became allophonic.

It is interesting to observe that a PHONIC change in the vowels of the sequence /v́cə/ subverts the PHONEMIC status of the long consonants in the sequences /v́ccə/ and /v́ccr, v́ccl/ without changing them phonically, and thus eliminates phonemic length from the consonant system of these dialects of ME.

The loss of phonemic length in the consonant system of the dialects of the Northeast Midland and parts of the North resulted (1) in the elimination of the long sonorants /mm, nn, ll, rr/ and the long stops /pp, bb, tt, dd, čč, ǰǰ, kk, gg/ of older English as separate phonemic entities, and (2) in the regrouping of the voiced and the voiceless allophones of the fricatives /f, þ, s/.

Since in older English the long sonorants and stops contrasted with their short counterparts only in length, the long and the short simply coalesce into one set of sonorants and stops, namely /m, n, l, r/ and /p, b, t, d, č, ǰ, k, g/, all of which occur before, after, and between vowels.

The development of the fricatives is more complicated. The older English short fricative phonemes /f, þ, s/ had voiced allophones [v, ð, z] between vowels, and contrasted in this position with the voiceless long fricatives /ff, þþ, ss/ both in quantity and in vocalization. Since quantity was the sole distinctive feature between the short and long sonorants and stops, the quantitative difference between short and long fricatives of OE must be regarded, from the point of view of the system, as their primary distinctive feature, and the difference in vocalization as a secondary, concomitant feature. With the loss of quantity as a distinctive feature in the stops and the sonorants, and hence also in the fricatives, voicing becomes the distinctive feature of the fricatives in intervocalic position. Thus, although between vowels the phonemes /f, þ, s/ and /ff, þþ, ss/ of older English continue to be pronounced as [v, ð, z] and [ff, þþ, ss] respectively, undergoing no PHONIC change, they now contrast PHONEMICALLY as /v, ð, z/ vs. /f, þ, s/.

The shift from length to vocalization as the distinctive feature entailed a regrouping of the allophones of the fricatives. Intervocalic [ff, þþ, ss], derived from the older phonemes /ff, þþ, ss/, join the initial and final allophones [f, þ, s] of the older phonemes /f, þ, s/ to constitute the new phonemes /f, þ, s/, while the intervocalic allophones [v, ð, z] of the phonemes /f, þ, s/ of older English come to function as the separate phonemes /v, ð, z/.

At this stage in the development of the English consonant system the voiced fricatives /v, ð, z/ occurred only between vowels, as in *liven, bathen, risen.* Initial /v/ became established later through the adoption of French words, such as *veile, venim, vertu*; initial /z/, through the slow adoption of such words as *zele* 'zeal', *zodiac* (usually *sodiac* and always *senith, cenith* 'zenith'). Initial /ð/ arises at a later date from a native development in such normally (or frequently) unstressed words as *the, there, than,* starting as a prosodic allophone.

Not until final /ə/ was lost, beginning c1300 in the North Midland and the North, did the voiced fricatives /v, ð, z/ also occur in final position, e.g. *live, bathe, rise.*

The fricative /š/, as in *ship, fish, fishes,* has no voiced counterpart in ME. It is derived from the OE cluster *sc,* which yielded long /šš/ between a short stressed vowel and a following unstressed vowel, and a short /š/ in all other positions—in accordance with the restrictions governing the occurrence of long consonants in late OE. Evidence for this development is scant, but quite unambiguous. OE *flǣsces* (gen.) appears in ME either as *flę̄shes* /vvcə/, with shortening of the consonant, or as *flesshes* /vccə/, presumably in regional distribution. Southwestern ME *eschen* 'ask' /vccə/, from OE *āscian,* clearly shows the shortening of *ā* to *ă* > *e* before the rounding of *ā* to *ō*. For examples see Kurath and Kuhn, *Middle Engl. dict.* under *flesh* and *asken.*

A voiced partner of /š/ arises in MnE through the assimilation of medial /zj/ to /ž/, as in *measure, azure.*

From this brief sketch it should be clear that the fricatives of English have a rather complicated history in ME. As has been pointed out above, the contrast between voiceless and voiced fricatives arose in medial position before 1200 through a native development in the dialects here discussed. This development must have facilitated the acceptance of this contrast in initial position in French and Latin loanwords during the 13th century. When, with the loss of final /ə/ during the 14th century, the voiced fricatives came to stand also in final position, the voiced–voiceless contrast had been extended to all positions, a situation that has persisted to this day.[7]

The loss of long consonants as phonemic entities in the Middle English dialects of the Northeast Midland and the Northern areas as a consequence of the lengthening of all short vowels in the sequence /v́cə/ before 1200 is only sporadically reflected in the spelling of the manuscripts, since the double writing of the formerly long consonant phonemes is retained to indicate short vowels.

Clear evidence for the changes in the consonant system may be expected only in unconventional spelling systems, such as that of Orm, who uses double consonant letters with remarkable consistency to indicate that a preceding vowel, stressed or unstressed, is short. He does this not only where older English had long consonants but also where it had short consonants. Thus Orm writes *mann, forr, þatt; fissk, rihht; manness, fillenn,* etc.; *bedd, beddess,* but *bede; wittness,* but *witen; summ,*

[7] In the Southern dialects of ME, which had only [v, ð, z] in initial position, the introduction of /f, s/ in French and Latin loanwords created the contrast in this position.

but *sume; godd, staff,* but *godes, stafes; little,* but *litell,* etc. On this interpretation of Orm's use of double consonant letters scholars are in complete agreement; but no one appears to have drawn from his practice the conclusion that Orm would not have used this spelling device if long consonants had still been phonemic in his dialect (Lincolnshire, a1200). It is, however, quite certain that in his dialect Orm has only the two phonemic sequences /v́cə/, as in *mannes, wittes, sunne,* and /v́vcə/, as in *godes, witenn, sune.*

It should be pointed out that the adoption of this spelling device did not remove the ambiguity of the vowel letters in Orm's orthography, but it reduced their burden from three phonemes to two, by identifying the short vowels.[8] Also, it leaves the quantity of word-final vowels unmarked, as in *clene, temmple,* which end in /ə/; in *se, be* (sbj. of *sen, ben*), which have /ẹ̄/; in the pronouns *he, we,* and the preconsonantal variants of the prepositions *i* 'in' and *o* 'on', which probably had two allomorphs each, ending in a long and a short vowel respectively. Of more serious consequence is the resulting ambiguity of the spellings *ff* and *ss,* which in Orm's system represent both /f, s/ and /v, z/, as in *offrenn, blisse* and in *heffne, grissli* respectively. Since, however, *ff* and *ss* between vowels always stand for voiceless fricatives in Orm's spelling, the ambiguity is confined to the relatively few words in which the fricative is followed by a sonorant, as in *offrenn* /ofrən/ and *heffne* /hevnə/.

3. It has been shown above that the loss of long consonant phonemes in the Northeast Midland and parts of the North resulted from the elimination of the sequence /v́cə/, which, on the evidence of Orm's spelling, occurred no later than 1200. This theory implies that long consonant phonemes would persist as such in dialects of Middle English that preserve the sequence /v́cə/ along with the sequence /v́ccə/, the only sequences in which /cc/ contrasts with /c/.

Such a situation is generally assumed, though not presented in these terms, for the South Midland dialect and for Southern. In these dialects the mid vowels /e, o/ and the low vowel /a/ were lengthened in the sequence /v́cə/, as in the North Midland and the North, but the high vowels /i, u/ remained short. Since, as a result of this change, the sequences /ecə, ocə, acə/ became /ę̄cə, ǭce, ācə/, falling in with the old sequence /v́vcə/, the sequence /v́cə/ came to be restricted to /icə/ and /ucə/.

[8] In Orm's spelling of the long vowels (identified as long by a following single consonant letter) only *æ* is unambiguous, as in *hæte* (OE *ǣ* < **ai/j*), *dæþ* (OE *ēa*), *ærd* (OE *eard*). *e* and *o* represent both close /ẹ̄, ọ̄/; and open /ę̄, ǭ/; *i* and *u* stand for close /ị̄, ụ̄/ and for open /į̄, ų̄/ (later/ẹ̄, ọ̄/, as in *min* (OE *ī*), *fir* (OE *ȳ*), *hus* (OE *ū*), and in *witen* (OE *i*), *sune* (OE *u*), respectively; *a* spells a low back vowel /ɑ̄/ (later /ǭ/) in *stan* (OE *ā*), and a low front vowel /ā/ in *name* (OE *a*). The open high vowels of this dialect later coalesced with the close mid vowels, the low back vowel with the open mid back vowel, as in *wẹ̄ten, sọ̄ne* and in *stǭn* respectively. It should also be pointed out that the letter *e* has a third value, standing for /ə/ in unstressed syllables.

Henceforth the sequences /eccə, occə, accə/ contrast only with /ę̄cə, ǭcə, ācə/; but /iccə, uccə/ contrast both with /icə, ucə/ and with /īcə, ūcə/. That is to say, after the low vowels /a, ā/ and the mid vowels /e, ę̄, ẹ̄; o, ǭ, ọ̄/, long and short consonants occur in complementary distribution (a long consonant only after a short vowel, a short consonant only after a long vowel), and might therefore be regarded as positional allophones rather than as separate phonemes. However, since both long and short consonants occur in these dialects after short /i, u/, as in *sittan* 'sit', *sŏnne* 'sun' vs. *witan* 'know', *sŏne* 'son', long consonants clearly remain phonemic in the sequences /iccə, uccə/ vs. /icə, ucə/. Hence the phonetically long consonants after short /a, e, o/ must be taken as phonemically long also, though they never contrast with short consonants in these positions.

How long do phonemically long consonants persist in these dialects, including the literary dialect of the London area? The generally accepted view is, that phonemically long consonants disappeared c1400, with the loss of final /ə/ in the sequence /vccə/; but that is only part of a rather complicated story, which is initiated by the loss of final /ə/.

The loss of long consonants in these dialects, we may feel sure, occurred in three or four stages:

(1) The word-final sequence /vccə/ became /vc/, as in *sitten, frogge, sunne, tellen, missen, laughen* > *sit, frog, sun, tel, mis, laugh.* At this stage, the inflected forms *sitteth, frogges,* etc. still had long consonants, so that such words had variant allomorphs, e.g. /sit/ ~ /sitt-/, /frog/ ~ /frogg-/.

(2) Some word-final sequences of the type of /vcc-əc/ became /vc-c/, as in *sittes* (replacing *sitteth*), *frogges* > *sits, frogs*; but others retained /ə/, and hence also the long consonants, as *misses, wasshes.* At this stage, such inflected words as *sit* : *sitting, mis* : *misses, missing* still had allomorphs with phonemically short and long consonants respectively. Variant allomorphs occurred at this time also in the dissyllabics *bitter* ~ *bit(t)r-e, appel* ~ *ap(p)l-es, adder* ~ *ad(d)r-es, letter* ~ *let(t)r-es.*

(3) The allomorphs with phonemically long consonants were eliminated within the paradigms of inflected words and in derivational sets, under pressure of the great majority of words that had no such allomorphs.

(4) At this stage, these dialects of English had given up contrastive length in the consonants, except for a residue of plurisyllabics, such as *shilling, fissūre,* in which only long consonants occurred within the paradigm. Here the phonically long intervocalic consonants after a short vowel are interpreted as consonants pure and simple, since the phonic length of consonants had become allophonic in the vast majority of words current in English—short consonants after long vowels, long consonants after short vowels.

Steps (1) and (2) in the history of the long consonants are the result of a well documented phonemic change, the loss of /ə/; step (3) is an instance of stem-leveling, a common process in Middle English and in early Modern English (cf. *dai* ~ *dau-es* > *dai, dai-es; liǧǧ-en* ~ *lī-eth* > *lī-en, lī-eth; whīt* ~ *whit-re* > *whīt, whīt-er*) ; step (4) results from the pressure of the dominant pattern (Systemzwang)—here the lack of contrastive consonant length in the bulk of the English vocabulary.

Between steps (2) and (3) the phonemic status of phonically long consonants must have fluctuated, as the extreme instability of their spelling c1400 betrays. A language cannot pass from one system to another without temporary disorganization.[9]

4. In what precedes we have undertaken to show (1) that phonically long consonants had lost their phonemic status by 1200 in the dialects of the Northeast Midland and parts of the North, as the result of the lengthening of ALL short vowels, including /i, u/, in the sequence /v́cə/; (2) that phonically long consonants retained their phonemic status until c1400 in the Southeast Midland dialect, and in all other dialects in which the sequences /ícə, úcə/ survived unaltered and thus contrasted with the sequences /íccə, úccə/; and (3) that the elimination of the long consonant phonemes in these dialects was initiated by the loss of /ə/ in the sequence /v́ccə/, which was thus reduced to /v́c/.

In Chaucer's London the Southeast Midland type predominated; but it seems safe to assume that the Northeast Midland type was also current to some extent. Other Northeast Midland features, such as the leveled stem of the ablaut preterit, the extension of the *s*-plural in nouns, the regularized forms of the 2nd and 3rd singular of the present, the *n*-plural of the present, and the pronoun *thei,* were widely current in London in Chaucer's time. Still other features, such as *theim* and the 3rd sg. in *-(e)s,* intruded later from the same direction. Whatever the explanation in terms of economic, social, and cultural history for this persistent intrusion of North Midland features in the London area may be, its reality cannot be doubted.[10]

In view of this dominant trend, the currency in Chaucer's London of the North Midland derivatives /ē̹cə, ō̹cə/ from earlier /icə, ucə/ can hardly be questioned. (1) Spellings such as *reden* 'ridden', *to wete* 'to wit', *dede* 'did', *stodes* 'studs', *sholen* 'shall' are not uncommon in the Brewers' Records (1422–5) .[11] (2) The Midland type became established

[9] Some American structuralists are reluctant to admit this obvious fact. The aim of the structural analysis is, after all, to discover the extent of systematization in a language at a given time, not to impose a system on it.

[10] For an important recent statement concerning the influx, beginning c1300, of prominent merchant families from Norfolk, Lincolnshire, and other East Midland counties into London, see Eilert Ekwall, *Two early London subsidy rolls* 69-70 (*Skrifter utgivna av Kungl. Humanistiska Vetenskapssamfundet i Lund,* Vol. 48; 1953) .

[11] R. W. Chambers and Marjorie Daunt, *A book of London English, 1384-1425* 140-91 (Oxford, 1931) .

in Standard English *beetle* (OE *bitela*), *creek* (cf. OIcel. *criki*), *week* (OE *wicu*), *weevil* (OE *wifel*), *wood* (OE *wudu*), and must therefore have been current in London at a rather early date. (3) The common spellings *rody* (OE *rudig,* MnE *ruddy*), *rode* (OE *rudu*), *wouke* (OE *wucu,* from *wicu*) in early-15th-century MSS also point to the currency of the North Midland type in London English at the turn of the century.

In view of the great probability that alongside the South Midland type the North Midland type of the features under discussion had some currency in London during the latter part of the 14th century, Chaucer's rime practice, and the reasons for it, call for reconsideration.

Chaucer keeps the ME derivatives of the OE contrastive sequences /íccv : ícv : ẹ̄cv/ and /úccv : úcv : ọ̄cv/ strictly apart. He never rimes /icə/, as in the ppls. *riden, writen,* with /iccə/, as in the infs. *bidden, sitten,* or with /ẹ̄cə/, as in *fẹ̄den, grẹ̄ten.* Correspondingly, /ucə/, as in *sŏne* 'son', never rimes with /uccə/, as in *sŏnne* 'sun', or with /ọ̄cə/, as in *sọ̄ne* 'soon'. This rime practice mirrors the phonemic features of the South Midland dialect to perfection: both vowels and consonants have phonemic length.[12]

Although Chaucer's rime practice clearly conforms to the South Midland dialect of the latter part of the 14th century, must we assume that he was unfamiliar with the divergent situation in the North Midland type? Should we not consider an alternative motivation for his deliberate practice? I think we should. If words like the ppls. of *rīden* and *wrīten* had two different pronunciations in London, riming with *fẹ̄den* and *grẹ̄ten* in the speech of some of his contemporaries but not in that of others, Chaucer might well avoid such rimes for that very reason. For the same reason he would forgo riming *sone* (OE *sunu*) with *sone* (OE *sōna*). Moreover, he would then also avoid riming *riden, writen, sŏne,* etc. with *bidden, sitten, sŏnne,* etc., whether the latter still had PHONEMICALLY long consonants or not. By adhering to self-rime he could satisfy all of his readers, whatever their dialect.

5. The brief comments offered below on several texts representing different literary dialects written in rather consistent and largely unique orthographies should serve to point up the types of evidence that are relevant to the problem under discussion, and to illustrate the types of ana-

[12] Since the sequences /icə/ and /ucə/ occur only in a small number of words, Chaucer's ingenuity in finding suitable rimes for such words was severely taxed. For instance, *love* (n. and v.) occurs more than 700 times in verse, but only 44 times in rime (38 times with *abŏve,* 3 times with the ppl. *shŏve,* and once with *Lŏve*); *sŏme* occurs more than 300 times, but only 13 times in rime (12 times with *cŏme); sŏne* occurs about 120 times, only 8 times in rime (invariably with *wŏne* n. and v.); *wode* 'wood' occurs 21 times, but never in rime; *dide* 'did' occurs about 180 times, but only once in rime. On the other hand, the ppl. *(i)nŏme* occurs only in rime (8 times with *cŏme,* once with *sŏme*). Here Chaucer uses the 'Southern' verb, which had been replaced by *taken* in contemporary London speech, for the sake of the rime. There could be no clearer evidence for his determination to use only self-rime.

logical and phonic changes that resulted in eliminating long consonants in certain words or positions prior to the loss of phonemically long consonants, or on the other hand, in introducing them on such models as *bed* : *beddes*. When the evidence of rimes is not available, a systematic analysis of spelling habits and a tabulation of consistent vs. sporadic deviations from the 'historically' normal spelling offer the only hope for tenable inferences. Since the double writing of originally long consonants —which occurred only after short vowels even in the oldest English known to us—remained orthographically functional after the loss of long consonant phonemes, serving as an indicator (diacritic) of short vowels, the spelling evidence, scant as it is, demands extremely cautious handling.

ANCRENE RIWLE. A rapid reading of pp. 101–26 of Mabel Day's edition of the Nero MS of the *Ancrene Riwle* (London, 1952), written in an orthography devised to render a Southwestern (Southwest Midland) literary dialect of c1225, and rather consistently applied, leaves no doubt that between a stressed short vowel and /ə/, contrastive long and short consonants of older English are preserved. The only clear deviations observed in a rather cursory reading of the 25 pages are these: (1) *dredfule, gledfule, seoruhfule, wunderfule* (but *fulle*); *leofmone* (also 47/34 *leofmones*); (2) *ʒichinge* (cf. OE *giččan*), *grime* (also *grimme*); (3) *summe, summe-cherre* (3×); *schullen, schallen; troddeþ;* (4) *luddere* 'louder', *schennure* 'brighter', *woddre* 'angrier'; *sliddrie* 'slippery'; (5) *nammore* (2×) 'no more'.

In group 1 the originally long consonants are shortened under weak stress, a purely phonetic process that occurred also in other dialects. In group 2 we may simply have aberrant spellings. In group 3 long consonants may have been introduced on the model of such sets of allomorphs as *bed* : *bedd-es,* unless the doubled letters merely indicate that the preceding vowel is short. In group 4 the double letters probably show that the preceding vowel is short, though *d* (hardly *n*) may actually have been lengthened phonically before *r*, as in *woddre* (< *wod-re* < OE *wōd-re*). *Nammóre,* stressed on the second syllable, may have a spelling patterned on Old French, a spelling that appears in many words taken into Middle English, such as *af(f)órcen, al(l)óuen, as(s)ī́gnen,* in which the spelling of the consonant BEFORE the stressed vowel varies in English as well as in French.

AYENBITE OF INWIT. Even a casual sampling of short passages (150–4, 172–83) of the *Ayenbite,* written in 1340 in a fairly consistent orthography created to render a Southeastern (Kentish) literary dialect, makes it perfectly clear that long consonants between vowels are kept apart from short consonants, for example in *habbeþ, nette, zeþþe, nesssse* (: *ulesse*), *beginne, conne, alle, uolle,* as opposed to *betere, biter, nime, siker, loue, ynome, come, zome, wones.*

But there are some troublesome problems. (1) Under secondary stress, long consonants seem to have been sometimes shortened, as in *to comene,* from OE *cumanne* (with which compare the inconsistent treatment in *to done, to zyenne*), sometimes preserved, as in the suffix *-nesse.* (2) *Eddre, little* (:*litel*), *gratter* 'greater' (beside *grater*) pose the same problem as in the *Ancrene Riwle* above. (3) The spelling of *onneaþe* (7×), with *nn* preceding the stressed vowel, seems to be modeled on that of words taken from Latin or OF, such as *commun* (6×). (4) The *tt* in *abbotte(s)* (3×) is puzzling. Obviously, a systematic study of the spelling of this important MS is needed to deal with such peculiarities.

THE GAWAIN POET. The rime practice of the *Gawain* poet largely agrees with Chaucer's, which is not surprising in the literary dialect of a contemporary of Chaucer. Nevertheless, there are several interrimes in the *Pearl* that point to an infusion from the Northeast Midland dialect: *gome, com, innome* (OE *u*) in lines 697–703 rime with *dome* (OE ō), and *won* (OE *u*) in line 918 rimes with *done, mone* (OE ō), the vowel being /ọ̄/. Though there is no rime evidence for [ẹ̄] from OE *i,* the spelling *e* in *smeten* (ppl. of *smīten*) in *Gawain* 1763, and *glede* 'kite' in *Cleanness* 1696 may be taken to represent /ẹ̄/.[13]

6. My object has been to sketch in outline the history of phonemically long consonants from OE to late ME times, from a structural point of view. I hope to have shown (1) that the loss of functionally long consonants occurred in some dialects of ME before 1200, in others not until c1400; (2) that in these two dialectal types the loss of phonemically long consonants resulted from very different causes; and (3) that the loss of phonemic length in consonants entailed the rise of voicing as a distinctive feature of intervocalic fricatives. These developments have not been treated adequately, if at all, by earlier students of English, although they produce rather revolutionary changes in the English consonant system.[14]

[13] Mabel Day and Mary S. Serjeantson, p. xlvi of their edition of *Gawain* (London, 1940), regard this as 'unlikely'; and R. Menner, p. lx of his edition of *Cleanness* (New Haven, 1920), points out that the spelling *e,* which occurs in *þeder* (64, 461) beside *i* (45, 61) also turns up along with *i* in *wekked* (855), *wykked* (570), where the vowel is certainly short. However, the clear rime evidence for /ọ̄/ from OE *u,* supports the view that /ẹ̄/ from OE *i,* a parallel feature of the Northeast Midland dialects, had a degree of currency in this literary dialect.

[14] The only fairly detailed treatment of long consonants in Old English is given in Karl Luick, *Historische Grammatik der englischen Sprachen* 797-932, edited from Luick's notes by F. Wild and H. Koziol. Although the structural point of view (analogous patterning) was not at all foreign to Luick—witness his treatment of the sweeping quantitative changes in the vowels of late OE and early ME (§§203-206, 352) and his presentation of the Great Vowel Shift of late ME and early MnE (§§479 ff), his treatment of the long consonants is plainly nonstructural. Hence my interpretation of double consonant letters written at the ends of words and before sonorants differs sharply from that of Luick and his editors.

The Middle English "Long Close" and "Long Open" Mid Vowels

ROBERT P. STOCKWELL

THE RELATION BETWEEN a linguistic structure at a given date and a derived linguistic structure at a later date can be stated as a series of rules by which the later structure can be generated from the earlier, plus exceptions. The generating rules are called sound laws, but exceptions do not invalidate laws of this type: they merely require that stronger generalizations be sought that will permit a shorter list of exceptions.

One of the strong generating rules of traditional historical English phonology is that short vowels, when lengthened, appear in the quality of the matching long vowels, and that long vowels, when shortened, appear in the quality of the matching short vowels.[1] The rule may be written in some such form as this:[2]

Reprinted by permission from *Texas Studies in Literature and Language,* II (1961) 529-38.

[1] This rule is implicit not only in modern grammars and phonologies, from Luick to Brunner to Quirk and Wrenn, but also in all earlier grammars of OE and of comparative Gmc., back to at least the first quarter of the nineteenth century. I have not been able to determine who first stated it as an explicit assumption. It is, in fact, rarely made explicit down to the present day, since the traditional interpretation of OE phonology adheres so closely to OE spelling that this crucial assumption is not often described for what it actually is, namely a hypothesis that has great explanatory power, in that without further specification it will generate many later forms of English from earlier forms.

[2] I leave the front-round vowels /ü/ and /ö/ unlisted, since they unrounded and fell in with /i/ and /e/. The fact that the latter coalescence (/e/ and /ö/) occurred relatively early, and the former (/i/ and /ü/) relatively late, is irrelevant to the present argument, though it is significant indeed in a more inclusive statement of English vocalic history. I also ignore, for this purpose, the graphic diphthongs, short and long, since a one-to-one relationship of nucleus *vs.* nucleus-plus-length clearly does not hold between the short and long members of the class.

OE {ĭ, ĕ, ǣ̆, ă, ŏ, ŭ} plus length ⟶ LOE {ī, ē, ǣ, ā, ō, ū}

OE {ī, ē, ǣ, ā, ō, ū} minus length ⟶ LOE {ĭ, ĕ, ǣ̆, ă, ŏ, ŭ}

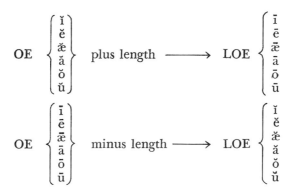

Examples to prove that lengthened vowels (lengthened, for instance, before certain clusters in the tenth century) behaved just like the inherited long vowels may be cited at greater length for some vowels than for others. One of each will serve:

OE *wĭlde*	like	OE *wīs*
OE *fĕld*	like	OE *grēne*
OE *ǣ̆*	like	(see discussion below)
OE (Ang.) *ăld*	like	OE *stān*
OE *gŏld*	like	OE *fōd* (i.e., ⟶ *Gould*)
OE *grŭnd*	like	OE *hūs*

/ǣ̆/ had earlier broken in many of the environments which later caused lengthening. In the remaining environments that later caused lengthening (i.e. those that consisted of nasal plus voiced stop), the following nasal had maintained the quality of WGmc. /ă/ as low central or back in opposition with the shift to low front that otherwise occurred under Frisian influence.[3] It is therefore difficult, perhaps impossible, to cite examples of /ǣ̆/ *vs.* /ǣ/ which are revealing in their subsequent history in the same way that examples from the other five vowels are. No problem exists in establishing the essential validity of the generalization, however; we merely reverse it, and examples are numerous. /ǣ/, with shortening, has the subsequent history that the generalization predicts: OE *blǣdre,* shortened, is *blǣ̆ddre,* becoming MnE *bladder,* with the normal history of any OE /ǣ̆/. Similarly for the other five vowels: *hid* (OE *hȳdde*), *kept* (OE *cēpte*), *soft* (OE *sōfte*), *hussy* (OE *hūswīf*), *lamb* (OE *lāmbru*).

This generalization, then, is one of very considerable power, and any apparent exceptions to it should be studied carefully before either

[3] David DeCamp, in "The Genesis of the Old English Dialects: A New Hypothesis" in *Language,* XXXIV (1958), 232-244, has so convincingly argued the role played by Frisian in the initiation and spread of certain key dialectal features of Old English that I have here adopted a manner of speaking that implies my confidence in DeCamp's arguments, whatever doubts others may still have.

throwing it out (which, as far as I know, no one has suggested) or setting up additional subsidiary generalizations for data that are thought to be unaccountable under the primary one. It is on a generalization of precisely the latter type that I wish to focus our attention, one that is to be found in every standard reference book on the subject of historical English phonology.

This subsidiary generalization can be stated as follows: /ē/ (long close *e*) and /ō/ (long close *o*) when shortened during ME times fell in with /ĭ/ and /ŭ/, and, conversely, /ĭ/ and /ŭ/ when lengthened during ME times fell in with /ē/ and /ō/.[4] Examples:

Shortening[5]

OE *rēdels*	⟶ ME, MnE *riddle*	
OE *sēc, sēoc*	⟶ ME, MnE *sick*	
OE *hrēc*	⟶ ME, MnE *(hay)rick*	
OE *brēc*	⟶ ME, MnE *breeches*	
OE *sēlig*	⟶ ME, MnE *silly*	
OE *blōd*	⟶ LME *blŭd,* MnE *blood*	
OE *flōd*	⟶ LME *flŭd,* Mne, *flood*	

Lengthening

OE *wicu*	⟶ ME *wēke,* MnE *week*	
OE *bitel(a)*	⟶ ME *bētel,* MnE *beetle*	
OE *wifel*	⟶ ME *wēvel,* MnE *weevil*	
OE *yfel*	⟶ EME *ivel*	⟶ ME *ēvel,* MnE *evil*
OE *wudu*	⟶ ME *wōde,* MnE *wood*	
OE *duru*	⟶ ME *dōre,* MnE *door*	
OE *lufu*	⟶ ME *lōve,* MnE *love*	

[4] As far as I can determine, the earliest statement *in essentially this form* is Luick's, in his *Untersuchungen z. engl. Lautgesch.*, 1896 (pp. 209 ff). Earlier discussions of the same material are cited by Luick and hence need not be cited here.

[5] The problem of what forms to cite in lists like these two is acute. Wyld (*Short Hist. Eng.*, §174) and Brunner (*Die eng. Spr.*, p. 221) cite OE *bitul, wifol* instead of *bitela, wifel.* Bosworth and Toller cite *bītela, wifel,* and Toller's supplement cites *bitela* with short *i.* Luick (*Hist. Gram.*, §393) cites instances of regular morphophonemic alternation between long and short vowels: *sun—sōnes, gum—gōmes, dur—dōres, wud—wōdes, cum—cōmes, gif—gēves, lif—lēves, wit—wētand, crik—crēkes,* and others like these in which one form would normally be lengthened, the other would not. Similar pairs, arising from the fact that one form has three syllables so that the first remains short (or if originally long, becomes short), but the other form has only two syllables and so may have a long vowel in the first, include *sōmer—sumeres, thōner—thuneres, ēvel—iveles, crēpel—cripeles, wēdow—widowes, bēsi—bisily,* and others like these. It is obvious that in the subsequent history of such pairs EITHER form may be analogically extended throughout the paradigm, so that a list which shows a late ME singular with /ē/ may, in fact, have the length from analogical extension of the plural. These morphophonemic alternations can be cited at much greater length than can examples of the direct-derivation type shown above. Even if every example of the type of *wifel* ⟶ *wēvel* (*weevil*) could somehow be accounted for without assuming that

Examples of shortening in the above pattern are a good deal scarcer than examples of lengthening, since lengthening in the open syllable is a regular occurrence in the thirteenth century. The lengthening occurred after OE /ē/ and /ō/ had become what are ordinarily called "long close *e* and *o*," i.e. ME /ē/ and /ō/, in contrast with "long open *e* and *o*," i.e. ME /ę̄/ and /ǭ/. The long open vowels are never the reflexes of OE /ē/ and/ō/. They come from ME /ĕ/ and /ŏ/ lengthened in the open syllable, or from OE *ēa* and *ā* (examples: ME *mę̄te* from OE *mĕte,* ME *stę̄len* from OE *stĕlan,* ME *smǭke* from OE *smŏca,* ME *hǭpe* from OE *hŏpa,* ME *dę̄th* from OE *dēað,* ME *stǭn* from OE *stān*). But whereas lengthening in the open syllable was a regular occurrence, there was no comparable regular and widespread pattern of shortening at the same date: shortening before two syllables under weak stress, and before certain consonant clusters, was earlier, whereas that before dentals was later. If this chronology did not hold, then forms like ME *wĕpte* (OE *wēpte*), ME *frĕndschip* (OE *frēondscipe*), ME *gŏsling* (OE *gōsling*), ME *sŏfte* (OE *sōfte*) would be inexplicable counter-examples to the pattern seen above. So long as these shortenings occur at a time *before* the open-close contrast arises, however, they present no problem (since they follow the primary generalization about the matching of vowel quality in long *vs.* short sets).[6]

Since we seek always the simplest set of rules that will generate later forms from earlier ones, we are faced with the question of just what is the simplest way to account for this breakdown in our fundamental—and I think both powerful and necessary—generalization about the matching of vowel quality in long *vs.* short sets.

The solution offered by Luick and now, as far as I can determine, the only solution widely accepted by scholars in the history of English, is as described above, namely to write in an exception to the otherwise powerful generalization about the matching of long *vs.* short vowels as to quality. The phonetic logic that justifies the exceptional rule is solid but not inescapable. Since /ē/ is phonetically intermediate between /ī/ and /ę̄/, and since there existed only *two* short vowels in the same range, a

---

/ĭ/ plus length became /ē/, the morphophonemic alternants cited by Luick would still have to be explained by some such assumption. That is, Luick's hypothesis that /ĭ/ and /ē/, /o/ and /ō/ are related as long and short matched pairs would stand unaltered by the loss of any examples in the cited lists.

[6] Alan S. C. Ross, in *Etymology* (London, 1958), is the most recent of several scholars who would reverse the whole direction of English sound change by assuming that OE /ĕ/ and /ŏ/ were close vowels that became open vowels at the beginning of the thirteenth century, so that when lengthened after that date they gave /ę̄/ and /ǭ/ (p. 125), though they had earlier given /ē/ and /ō/. Thus, whereas in the Luick tradition—with which I agree on this detail—it was necessary to assume a *raising* of OE long mid vowels, resulting in a contrast between the raised inherited long mid vowels and the newly generated long mid vowels, Ross assumes a *lowering* of OE short mid vowels, resulting, by a different route, in the same contrast, but describable rather as between the inherited long mid vowels and the long mid vowels newly generated from *lowered* short mid vowels.

shortening of /ē/ must necessarily fall in either with the higher quality or with the lower—if, of course, it did not generate a third short phoneme, for which there is no evidence at all.

But suppose we have a different hypothesis about the structure of long vowels. Instead of assuming that they were structured as short vowel plus a phonemically relevant element of length, suppose we assume that length was a property of glide vowels (i.e., semivowels) of two or even three types. It makes no difference what symbols are attached to phonemic length in the traditional view: length may about equally well be viewed (1) as vowel clustering (so that /ī/ would be transcribed as /ii/), (2) as a unit phoneme that can occur after any segment, vowel, or consonant (so that /ī/ would be transcribed /i:/), or (3) as a set of long vowels in opposition with a set of short vowels (the length being viewed as inherent in the vowel itself). Nor does it make any difference what symbols are attached to the interpretation of length as being a property of a cluster made up of a vowel plus a semivowel. A front glide may, for purposes of this argument, equally well be written with /y/ or /i/; a back glide with /w/ or /u/; and a central glide with /h/ or /ə/ or /˙/ or /ˇ/ or /ʜ/ or whatever suits the convenience of one's typewriter and the conditioning of his theoretical training or disposition. In short, I am not discussing symbols but structure.

If we assume that length was a post-nuclear glide of any one of three kinds, front /y/, back-round /w/, or relaxed central /h/ (which should not to be confused with the OE and ME fricative /x/, spelled *h, ȝ,* and later *gh*), we have a good deal of evidence immediately in our favor. For instance, OE *–ig* comes to be spelled *i, y,* and *ii,* i.e. /ī/—a spelling which is entirely reasonable if the palatal fricative originally symbolized by *g* had lost its friction, thus falling in with /y/: OE *stig* becomes ME *stye.* Likewise OE *–ug* comes to be spelled *u, ou, ow,* i.e. /ū/—reasonable if the velar fricative had lost its friction, thus falling in with /w/: OE *sugu* becomes ME *sow.* That is, if /ī/ and /ū/ were structurally /iy/ and /uw/, then a sequence like OE /ij/ (in which /j/ represents the voiced palatal fricative written *ġ* by modern editors) easily becomes /iy/ merely by loss of friction, and OE /uȝ/ (in which /ȝ/ represents the voiced velar fricative) easily becomes /uw/ in the same way. There is a good deal more evidence that falls into place in this hypothesis: without detailed specification, we may mention that tenth-century lengthening before certain clusters is readily interpretable as the achieving of phonemic status of a previously allophonic centralizing glide toward the dark-vowel coloration of /LC_v/ and /NC_v/ (L for /l/ and /r/, C_v for voiced consonant, N for nasal); that the long-term stability of a vowel like OE /ō/ before /w/ as in OE *grōwan* is easily explained if /ō/ was assimilated from an earlier /oh/ to /ow/ in the environment of a following /w/ in *–wan;* and that the perplexing problem of the so-called great vowel shift, in which the crucial change is the diphthongization of the high front and high back vowels /ī/ and /ū/ to MnE /ay/ and /aw/, is much more readily formulated as

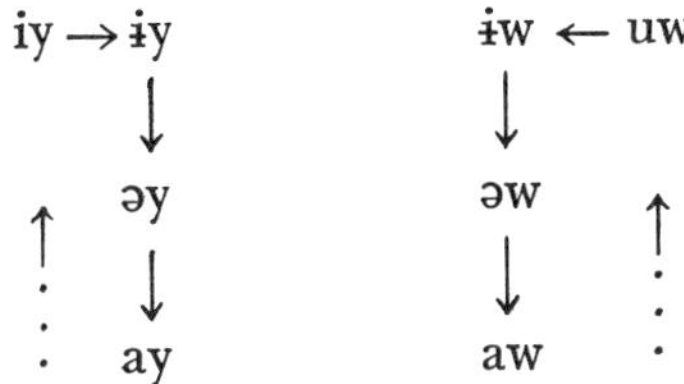

All this is only to say that the glide-vowel interpretation of length is not *ad hoc,* not limited to the explanatory power it has for the phenomena of the long close and long open mid vowels of ME, even though the detailed discussion of this paper is limited to an explication of the latter.

Turning back now to the evidence that shows /ĭ/ and /ē/, /ŭ/ and /ō/ to behave in ME as though paired with respect to quality, but seeking to re-analyze their structure in such a way as to eliminate an exception from the primary generalization about the matching of paired long and short vowels, we find that the crux of the problem is that there were three long vowels in front and three in back, but only two short vowels:

/ī/ }	/ĭ/	/u/	{ /ū/
/ē/ }			{ /ō/
/ę̄/	/ĕ/	/ŏ/	/ǭ/

But if "length" is of more than one type, then two short vowels in front and two in back are quite enough counters to account for all the contrasts:

/iy/ }	/i/	/u/	{ /uw/
/ih/ }			{ /uh/
/eh/	/e/	/o/	/oh/

Indeed, we have one counter left over in each area: /ey/ and /ow/. Both leftover slots are, so to speak, already occupied: /ey/ from the inherited /æj/ and /ej/ with loss of the friction in /j/, and /ow/ by assimilation from /oww/. The remaining unused combinations—/iw/, /ew/, /uy/, and /oy/—are taken up in French loan words and a few inherited forms (OE *fēawe* becomes ME /few/, /fiw/). So while the analysis of ME /ē/ and /ō/ as /ih/ and /uh/ is offhand somewhat startling, we are in fact forced to it by our primary hypothesis. We must then look again at the evidence to see whether we have been forced into a corner that we might well wish to be out of.

We saw earlier that /ē/, when shortened, gave /ĭ/. Now if we rewrite /ē/ as /ih/, when it is shortened it must yield /i/—and no exception to our primary generalization is needed to explain why it does. Similarly /ō/, if it is /uh/, must give /u/ when shortened—as it does. Conversely, if an /i/ is lengthened, it must fall in with /ih/, and /u/ with /uh/—as they do. That is, by formulating the structure of Old and Middle English vocalism in different terms, we do not at all require that the most powerful generalizations about the history be revised, but we *do* eliminate a difficult set of exceptions and show that they in fact behave exactly as the primary generalizations predict they ought to behave. The fact that they do behave in conformity with the most general rules is very strong corroboration of the revised formulation of Old and Middle English vocalism: so strong that it then becomes necessary for an alternate interpretation, no matter how well established by tradition and usage, either to demonstrate that the revised formulation is not in fact simpler or, if it fails, then to accept this formulation.

The examples cited earlier may be briefly recapitulated in the revised formulation:

Shortening

OE *rēdels*:	OE /réhdel(s)/	⟶	ME /ríhdəl/, shortened /rídəl/, *riddle*
OE *sēc*:	OE /séhk/	⟶	ME /síhk/, shortened /sík/, *sick*
OE *hrēc*:	OE /xréhk/	⟶	ME /xríhk/, shortened /(x)rík/, *—rick*
OE *brēc*:	OE /bréhkj/	⟶	ME /bríhč(əs)/, shortened /bríčəs/, *breeches*

[/kj/ is one possible phonemicization of the OE palatal /k/, written *ċ* by modern editors]

OE *sēlig*:	OE /séhlij/	⟶	ME /síhliy/, shortened /síliy/, *silly*
OE *blōd*:	OE /blóhd/	⟶	ME /blúhd/, shortened /blúd/, *blood*
OE *flōd*:	OE /flóhd/	⟶	ME /flúhd/, shortened /flúd/, *flood*

Lengthening

OE *wicu*:	OE /wíku/	⟶ ME /wíhkə/, *week*
OE *bitel*:	OE /bítel/	⟶ ME /bíhtəl/, *beetle*
OE *wifel*:	OE /wífel/	⟶ ME /wíhvəl/, *weevil*
OE *yfel*:	LOE /ífel/	⟶ ME /íhvəl/, *evil*
OE *wudu*:	OE /wúdu/	⟶ ME /wúhdə/, *wood*
OE *duru*:	OE /dúru/	⟶ ME /dúhrə/, *door*
OE *lufu*:	OE /lúfu/	⟶ ME /lúhvə/, *love*

It is clear that all other shortenings and lengthenings, both later and earlier, are in the same pattern, but they have never required a revision in formulation because they could, in each instance, readily be paired with a matching vowel in the appropriate quality. Thus OE *wēpte* /wéhpte/ ⟶ ME /wéptə/, OE *sōfte* /sóhfte/ ⟶ ME /sóftə/, because such shortenings occurred before OE /eh/ ⟶ /ih/, /oh/ ⟶ /uh/.

The spellings of ME /ih/ and /uh/ as *e, ee* and *o, oo* remain to be accounted for. The dilemma facing the scribe was simply that he had only two symbols for front vowels and two for back: *i, e* and *u, o*. Given three front vowels of the long variety, he had little choice but to write two of them alike. Similarly in the back. That he should file /ih/ and /eh/ in the same folder, leaving /iy/ in a separate one, suggests that /ih/ and /eh/ seemed more nearly alike than /ih/ and /iy/. Similarly /uh/ and /oh/ *vs.* /uw/. It is of course always difficult to account for spelling practices, but lest anyone should feel that this particular difficulty is damaging to the case, I must emphasize that no account of ME vowel structure has any *less* difficulty in explaining the fact that *ē* and *ę̄* were spelled alike but have consistently different subsequent histories. Similarly *ō* and *ǭ*. The tradition which writes both the higher and the lower entities with the same letter modified by different diacritics perhaps makes it appear to be less of a problem by using the same letters, but it does not thereby escape the problem. Any phonemicization must presumably postulate phonetic shapes for *ē* and *ō* that are nearer to *ę̄* and *ǭ* than they are to *ī* and *ū*, respectively. I offer the following suggestions:

[i̇˰̂ î̯] /iy/ ī; [iᵛ ə̯̂] /ih/ ē; [eᵛ ə̯̂] /eh/ ę̆;
[u˰̂ û̯] /uw/ ū; [iᵛ ə̯̂] /uh/ ō; [oᵛ ə̯̂] /oh/ ǭ.

Whatever the phonetic facts may have been (they are, after all, unrecoverable: only contrasts and cognate relationships are recoverable, so that those rules that generate the latter two most simply must be assumed to provide the soundest basis for speculating about phonetic shape), we are not wholly without evidence that long close *e* /ih/ and long close *o*

/uh/ were in fact often identified with *i* and *u* rather than *e* and *o*. There are many instances from the fourteenth and fifteenth[7] centuries of spellings of /ih/ and /uh/ words with *i, y* and *u, ou* rather than *e* and *o*. These spellings have previously been taken[8] as evidence that, among some speakers, that part of the great vowel shift in which the OE mid vowels were raised to their modern quality occurred quite early. I see no reason why they cannot equally well be taken as instances where /ih/ and /uh/ were heard as closer to /iy/ and /uw/, respectively, than to /eh/ and /oh/. In this way, the early spellings that appear to wreck any general chronology for the details of change in the great vowel shift can be viewed simply as additional corroboration for this revised formulation.

To sum up, then: viewed through the traditional phonological frame of reference, the relationship between ME short *i* and long close *e*, and that between ME short *u* and long close *o*, requires that a special rule be written which contradicts a much more general rule about the phonetic quality of long *vs.* short pairs. Viewed through a different formulation of the structure of long *vs.* short vowels, in which length is assigned to one of three glide phonemes, the general rule is seen to hold without exception.[9] In addition, it is apparent that certain related rules imposed by the traditional analysis can either be eliminated or stated more simply with the revised formulation.

[7] Wyld, *Hist. Mod. Coll. Eng.* (p. 67), cites *myte* 'meet', *dyme* 'deem', *agryed* 'agreed', *wyping* 'weeping', *slyves* 'sleeves', *stypylle* 'steeple'. He also cites *must* for ME *mōste, Munday, suthly* 'truly', *forsuk, stude.* Unhappily, Professor C. E. Bazell writes me that in his experience of checking the spellings cited by Wyld, he has found little reason to have confidence in their reliability. I have no independent evidence on this matter, and I must leave the validation or invalidation to later study. It would be surprising if study of informally written documents of the fourteenth and fifteenth centuries did not turn up a small but significant number of items with /ē/ spelled *i, y,* and of items with /ō/ spelled *u, ou.* The doubt that Bazell casts on Wyld leaves me temporarily without convincing examples, nonetheless. I am not sure that such spellings are a *necessary* consequence of my hypothesis, but they are probably a likely one. The reason why they may not be necessary is that by the beginning of the fifteenth century ME /iy/ was almost certainly well on its way to becoming MnE /ay/. That is, it was perhaps /ɨy/ by this date. If so, then the identification of the letters *i, y* with a diphthong approximating /ɨy/ would make it unlikely that /ih/ could be spelled with the same symbols. The same argument of course holds for the high back area.

[8] Wyld concludes from the *y*-spellings cited in the preceding footnote that they "show that the Mod. sound had already developed out of the old ē . . ." (67). From the *u*-spellings he concluded that they "show that [ū], or this sound shortened, was already pronounced." (67) Kökeritz states flatly (*Shakespeare's Pron.*, p. 190) that "The raising of ME *ē* in *he, see,* etc., to [i:] occurred at least as early as the beginning of the fifteenth century, and the new vowel has remained virtually unchanged in an independent position ever since." Since this is the starting point of his discussion of *ē*, one cannot object that he finds no evidence to contradict it. Yet, as I see it, every citation (the most striking one: *miter* for *meter*) can equally well be explained by /ih/, without having to push the chronology of the great vowel shift back to an unreasonably early date.

[9] One objection has already been raised to the views I have presented here, and since it is important, it must be dealt with. Professor C. A. Bazell, in personal correspondence about this problem, has pointed out that it is easier to formulate rules which will generate a later phonological structure from an earlier one, if the later structure is, as it were, built into the earlier one. The point is a strong one, and amounts to an

accusation of circularity. Yet I think that it is possible to avoid both the accusation and the danger, if the position I have been developing is a little clarified. There are two theories of the nature of "long vowels" in Modern English: that they are to be analyzed as vowel and length, or as vowel and semivowel. The same two theories exist for Old English. It would be wasteful to say that English had developed from a language with vowels and length to one with vowels and semivowels. It would be equally wasteful to assume that vowels and semivowels had become vowels and length. Either assumption would involve a theory of maximum rather than minimum change, and no one seriously proposes either theory. The assumption of this paper is that Old English and Modern English are characterized by vowel and semivowel sequences. The alternate hypothesis is that both are characterized by vowel and length. What I have done is test which of these two alternate hypotheses gives a simpler and more powerful statement for dealing with changes in vowel quantity. Since the traditional view requires a set of exceptions, whereas the revision suggested here does not, it would seem that there is some gain in revision.

If, then, I am right in assuming that such a simplification represents a genuine gain, the result is one of the reasons for carrying on what Voegelin has called "structural-restatement linguistics" (Review of Bloomfield-Hockett's *Eastern Ojibwa,* in *Language,* XXXV [1959], 109-125). From this kind of activity we expect to reach insights that we did not possess before the restatements, and we expect the insights to emerge from the statements, rather than to be built into them. The test which was applied suggested that Old English was like Modern English in the structure of its vowel nuclei. If this is a reasonable conclusion, it carries with it a further suggestion which certainly was not visible at the start of the investigation. Since some stage of pre-Modern English must have been more like the structure of other Indo-European languages than Modern English is, there must have been a change. Reorganization of vowel structure is shown to have required vastly more time than has elapsed since the reign of Alfred. The reorganization of vowels could very well have been a change of the order of magnitude and time depth represented by Grimm's law, which separates Germanic from the Indo-European line.

On the Utility of an Overall Pattern in Historical English Phonology

ROBERT P. STOCKWELL

THE OVERALL PATTERN CONCEPT[1] has met with a variety of responses.[2] I will try first to clarify what its characteristics are, and then try to see whether it provides anything useful to the investigator who wishes to introduce a degree of reason and pattern into the story of how English pronunciation came to its present state.

The strongest form of the concept holds that there exists in a language an inventory of phonemes from which speakers select a subset in producing utterances. It asserts that mutual intelligibility between dialects results from an awareness of the system as a whole on the part of speakers who themselves utilize one subset but are capable of interacting with speakers who utilize another subset. That pattern is assumed to be implicit within the linguistic awareness of any speaker of the language, whether or not he himself in fact utilizes more than some indeterminate fraction of the system. This strong form of the concept is untenable, asserting that because there are dialects of English in which a centralizing glide in phonemic (*can* /kéə̯n/ "container" vs. *can* /kǽn/ "be able"), then all dialects must have such a glide transcribed phonemically wherever it occurs phonetically, even if it is never contrastive (i.e. even if it is always predictable). It is useful to compare two dialects and to find, for example, that one of them *has* such a contrast and the other does not; to discover that in spite of this difference, and presumably others, speakers

Reprinted by permission from Horace G. Lunt, ed., *Proceedings of the Ninth International Congress of Linguists* (The Hague, 1964), 663-9.

[1] G. L. Trager and H. L. Smith, Jr., *Outline of English Structure* (= *Occasional Papers No. 3* of *Studies in Linguistics*) (1951).

[2] For reasonably full bibliographical notes, see my "Structural Dialectology: A Proposal" (*American Speech*, 34.4, 1959, 258-68), or James Sledd's review of Trager and Smith in *Language*, 31.3 (1955), 312-45.

of the two dialects communicate with each other efficiently; to seek to explain *why* the difference in structure does not inhibit communication. But the explanation is to be found in such facts as syntactic coincidence, lexical coincidence, contextual probability, and the practice that speakers have had in making appropriate adjustments. Of the many hypotheses that might explain why the gap is easy to bridge, surely the least verifiable is the speculation that the speakers share an awareness of the entire phonological pattern, in terms of which each can place the other's phonological habits appropriately.[3] There is a weaker form of the concept[4] which does not make the mistake of treating the units in the pattern as indivisible particles (phonemes), from which inventory a selection is made in each dialect. The weaker form instead views the units of the pattern as convenient labels for intersecting categories of distinctive features. In this view, one aspect of the vowel system which is "overall" for English is merely a set of features—*high, mid, low* intersecting with *front, central, back*—assuming that no dialect of English has a vowel system that is adequately characterizable by fewer than these six features. The features may be labeled in other ways, as with terms which are applicable to the feature analysis of consonants also. The other aspect of the system which is "overall" for English is that three of the categories of the system of simple nuclei—*front, central, back*—are distinctive features among the glides also. One of the most debated properties of the system has been the insistence on three such glides, since it is demonstrable that only two of them are distinctive in numerous dialects. But there is no *need* to insist on this: some dialects exploit the set of six features more fully than others, and whereas *central* is distinctive among the simple nuclei of all dialects, it is not distinctive among the glides in all dialects.

In this weaker form, it may be argued that nothing has been gained; we must still examine an adequate sample of tokens from each dialect and demonstrate what the system of contrasts and their distribution is. It may turn out that all English dialects, shorn of phonetic differences and reduced to a set of minimal feature oppositions, in fact are not reducible

[3] This is not to suggest that I disapprove of the notion that the grammar is a kind of Platonic ideal lying behind actual instances of speech, in terms of which slips of the tongue, grammatical deviation, reduced constructions, etc. can reasonably be explicated. On the contrary, I see no very satisfactory approach to the characterization of utterance tokens other than in terms of underlying abstract rules to which the tokens conform in varying degrees and manners. But this notion, and the overall pattern notion, though in some surface ways similar, are notions sharing nothing that is really distinctive. Abstract rules of the types found in a transformational grammar or a stratificational grammar are quite explicit about the structure of the sentences they characterize; an overall pattern of vowel phonemes is explicit only about potential contrasts—not about the system of contrasts that characterizes a set of utterance tokens from a single dialect.

[4] Found in A. A. Hill's exposition of the Trager-Smith nine vowels (*Introduction to Linguistic Structures,* New York, 1958), and in my "Structural Dialectology: A Proposal" (*loc cit.*).

below this particular set of features—even though some exploit the set more fully than others. But we have gained nothing in explicitness, which resides in the detailed sub-rules that describe the phonetic exponents of the feature bundles, and in the differentiation of the bundling habits of different dialects. We have not gained any power to describe the phonological system of English as a whole until we have seen the results of several linguistic atlases now in progress to determine whether the feature analysis has any general validity. Dialect geographers have attacked the system in its stronger form, but they have not considered it in its weaker, but testable and more general, form.

So it is not immediately clear that for purely synchronic purposes anything has been gained. But I should like to remain cautious: it is generally the case that an analysis which appeals to so many linguists has elements of truth, though they may await correct formalization.

For diachronic purposes a good deal more has been gained. For one thing, only sets of oppositions are recoverable from historical documentation; there is no way at all to test the physical realization of these oppositions in the speech of any individual; there is no way to defend historically the assertion, common in synchronic discussion, that John has a contrast that James lacks. Documents from one area may consistently distinguish two items that are not distinguished in documents from another area or another period. But there is very little chance, except with an Orrm or a Wilkins, that such distinctions are assignable to a single individual's awareness of his own speech habits. A very considerable degree of generalization about what oppositions were consistently maintained over a wide range of documents is required. Furthermore, the internal symmetry of alternative formulations of these oppositions counts for vastly more than it does in synchronic description. And finally, descriptions of phonological change cannot rest merely on synchronic descriptions of periodic slices through the time continuum, since the synchronic descriptions of historical systems depend not only on documents (a description of graphic contrasts is not a phonological description but the starting point for one), but also on the internal consistency of the transitional rules that link one slice with the next.

I hold that the laws of sound change are the simplest set of general rules, plus exceptions, which with earlier forms as input yield later forms as output; the most insightful analysis of the structure of the most investigable state of the language—contemporary speech—is evidence of a high order for the structure of earlier states. This does not mean that the phonological structure of OE or ME was identical with that of MnE. A simple untenable form of this assumption was made by R. F. Weymouth in his long forgotten dispute with A. J. Ellis.[5] He assumed there had been no change at all from OE vowels to MnE vowels, that the graph ⟨ii⟩ or ⟨ī⟩ was as reasonable a way to write [ai] or [əi] then as now.

[5] R. F. W., *On Early English Pronunciation* (London, 1874); A. J. E., *On Early English Pronunciation,* EETS 1867-1889.

The assumption as I wish to state it is not that the vowels remained unchanged, but that the *system* did; I believe this assumption should be overruled by only the most convincing evidence of systematic change, as, e.g., between IE and Gmc. By the *system* I mean the set of features and their bundling potential; even more generally, I mean the *types* of features and the *types* of bundles. I would differentiate four types:

(1) Vowel plus length (i.e. oppositions of short vs. long vowels) : a/ā, e/ē, i/ī, etc. This system also requires a small number of diphthongs: ai/au/ɔi. [Jones, Kökeritz, Dobson, etc.]

(2) Vowel plus vowel (where, to be justifiable, a significant variety of the potential clusters must be shown to occur): a/aa, e/ee, i/ii, a/ai, a/ae, e/ea, etc. [Sledd, Jakobson, Lamberts.]

(3) Vowel plus glide (where only direction of glide is significant, with a range of variation as to the extent of the glide) : a/ay, e/ey, i/iy, a/aə, i/iə, a/aw, u/uw, u/uə̥, etc. [Trager, Smith, Hill, Bloomfield, Sweet, etc.]

(4) Vowel quality (where such features as height, tenseness, and offglides are considered to be inherent in the qualitative distinction) : i/ɪ, e/ɛ, u/ʊ, etc. Like (1), this system requires additionally ai/au/ɔi. [Pike, Kurath, Fries, Kenyon, etc.]

Within each of these types, certain features are taken as distinctive and others as redundant. All of them agree, for English, that at least three grades on the vertical axis (height) are distinctive, and three grades on the horizontal axis. But no two agree as to what *other* features are distinctive. For (1), length is distinctive, but off-glides (except in ai/au/ɔi) and tenseness are redundant. For (2), nothing is distinctive but vertical-horizontal categories and clustering. For (3), off-glides are distinctive, but length, tenseness, and grades of height beyond three are redundant. For (4), at least five grades of height are distinctive, but length, off-glides (except in ai/au/ɔi), and tenseness are redundant. (1) is the least realistic in terms of the phonetic facts of MnE, since length need not occur acoustically in the instances where it would have to be transcribed as distinctive, and it does occur acoustically across a spectrum of conditioning environments. (2) is the most economical of symbols but it provides for far more contrasts than can be shown to occur, and at the same time requires drastic *ad hoc* adjustments to account for non-contrastive variation in the system (such as the variability of the extent of the glides in *bite, boat, bout,* etc.) (3) requires that two symbols (*y* and *w*) be utilized which are not required by (2), but it allows for variation in extent of glide, and it is just as economical in terms of the features required for its specification. (4) is, in my view, the most acceptable competition for (3), though it is the most wasteful of symbols and of features required for specification. Synchronically, I view (3) and (4) as about equally defensible in terms of dialect studies, psychological validity, pedagogical application, and so on. Diachronically, I think the case for (3) is much stronger.

In historical studies of English it has always been assumed that (1) is the strongest of the four types.[6] If it could reasonably be demonstrated that (1) is best for MnE, then, since it certainly corresponds best, on the surface, with OE and ME spelling practices, I should be less inclined to question the traditional analysis of English historical phonology.[7] But (1) is not considered the best analysis for MnE by most investigators.[8] The assumption that it is best for OE and ME must therefore be put aside until it can be shown that there is no reasonable alternative to the conclusion that OE-ME were type (1) and that they changed, not only in details within the type, but changed from type (1) to some other type altogether. We *must* seek alternatives to this conclusion, since it is inherently more complex than an analysis which shows changes within a system, but no change of systemic type.

(2) is the type that has been proposed for MnE by James Sledd,[9] and for the history of English phonology in a still unpublished account of the Great Vowel Shift by J. J. Lamberts. Since Lamberts' work is not generally accessible, I cannot properly comment on it here beyond observing that on certain essential points he and I are evidently in agreement, though having arrived at them independently.[10] The only advantage of (2) over (3) is that it provides for an enormously larger inventory of potential contrasts, at the cost of complicating allophonic statements and of having no dialect whatever realize more than a tiny fraction of the potential. It is less a systemic analysis than a grid for transcription of data to be systematized.

(4), while very popular as an analysis of MnE, has been proposed by no one that I know of as the basic type from OE down. Whatever the "long/short" contrasts of earlier English were, evidently no one thinks they were distinctively qualitative.

[6] I believe we can reject quite flatly, however, Sherman Kuhn's assertion ("On the Syllabic Phonemes of Old English," *Language* 37.4, 522-38) that in OE "Length was clearly phonemic, as Reszkiewicz has demonstrated by means of minimal pairs" (528). What R. demonstrated was only that there was a contrast, of undetermined nature, between two types of vowels. The contrast may equally well have been of any one of the four types, or perhaps of some combination of two or more types.

[7] There would still remain certain exceedingly perplexing aspects to the Great Vowel Shift, such as [ī] ⟶ [ai], aspects that do not seem so perplexing within an analysis of type (3).

[8] Key references basic to documentation are the following: Einar Haugen and W. F. Twaddell, "Facts and Phonemes," *Lang.*, 18.3 (1942) 228-37; R. M. S. Heffner, "Notes on the Length of Vowels," *Am. Sp.*, 12.2 (1937), 128-34, with continued study through six parts up to 1943.

[9] *A Short Introduction to English Grammar* (Chicago, 1959).

[10] Particularly we agree on setting up, instead of length, three kinds of 'length' (i.e. three kinds of non-simple nuclei), which he writes /-i/, /-ɨ/, /-u/, which I have elsewhere written /-y/, /-h/, and /-w/. We agree on positing stages /ɨy/ and /ɨw/ as the first steps in the changes *ī* ⟶ [ai] and *ū* ⟶ [au].

What, then, are the strengths of (3) as a type of phonological structure within which not only is MnE reasonably describable but also as a type within which the diachronic changes may be simply accounted for?

(a) In the OE spelling *-iġ* (in *bodiġ, stiġ,* etc.[11]), *ġ* is generally assumed to have represented a voiced palatal fricative, roughly a front-gliding [i] plus friction. In ME *-iġ* falls in with the reflexes of inherited *ī*. If *ī* by this time represented /iy/, the collapse of *ī/iġ* is fully accounted for merely by loss of friction in *-ġ*. In this way it appears to be precisely parallel with such developments as *hæġl* ⟶ *hail, dæġ* ⟶ *day, weġ* ⟶ *way,* etc., where the assumption that *-ġ* ⟶ /-y/ is fully borne out by ME spelling and MnE pronunciation.

(b) In the OE spelling *-ug* (in *fugol, sugu, bugan,* etc.), *g* is generally assumed to have represented a voiced velar fricative with strong lip rounding (by assimilation to the preceding rounded vowel). In ME *-ug* falls in with the reflexes of inherited *ū*. If *ū* by this time represented /uw/, then the collapse of *ū/-ug* is fully accounted for merely by loss of friction and velarity—the voiced lip rounding components remaining as /-w/. The /-w/ which is present in *fowl, sow,* etc. now may thus be traced in a direct line to *-g,* without the complication of *-ug* ⟶ *ū* ⟶ /aw/, which posits total assimilation of *-g* to *ū* and then generation of a new /-w/ subsequently.

(c) The assumption that one of the three types of "long" vowel was V + /ə̣/ (or simply /ə/, or even /h/) makes at least reasonable, an account of the phenomenon known as lengthening in the 10th century before certain clusters (liquids or nasals plus homorganic voiced consonants, shown consistently in Orrm, but more generally restricted to the groups *-ild, -eld, -uld, -old, -ald, -ind, -und, -imb,* and *-omb*). The mid-central resonance of /l/ in English is well-known. I know of no contemporary instances where a simple vowel falls in with a complex nucleus under this influence, probably because MnE complex nuclei are predominantly out-gliding, whereas those of OE were predominantly in-gliding. Instances of analogous phenomena in MnE include the influence of velar stops in Southeast Midland American where e/ey have coalesced in *leg, egg, beg,* etc., or of palatal fricatives in Southwest Midland American where ɔ/ɔy have coalesced in *wash,* u/uy in *push, bush.*

(d) The curious relation of ME *ē* to *ĭ*, and of *ō* to *ŭ*, such that 13th century "lengthening" of *ĭ* yields *ē*, *ŭ* yields *ō*, is readily accounted for without special *ad hoc* sound laws. The change OE ⟶ ME includes the series given below. Since I have presented elsewhere[12] the argument for this interpretation, I will omit further details of it here.

[11] I use the dot over the *g,* as is the practice of modern editors, to distinguish the palatal fricative from the velar.

[12] "The Middle English 'Long Close' and 'Long Open' Mid Vowels," *U. of Texas St. in Lit. and Lang.,* 2 (1961), 529-38.

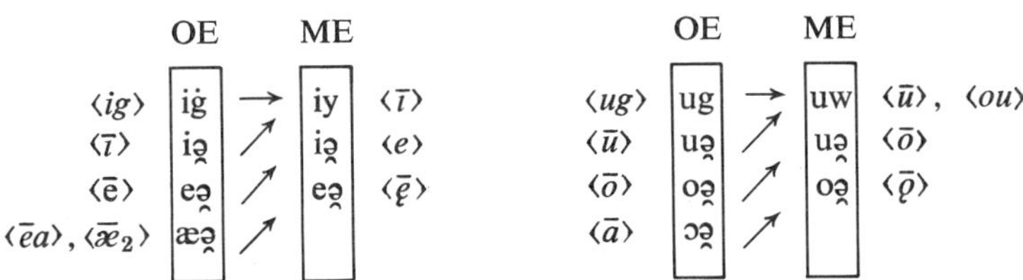

(e) The "first step" in the Great Vowel Shift, which has been the subject of argument through hundreds of pages of the journals since the time of Ellis, becomes reasonably clear—at least as to *what* it must have been, if not why. Leaving the question of dating aside for the moment, we ask where ME *ī* /iy/ might "go," so to speak, without intersecting and coalescing with other units with which it was in opposition.[13] For the vocalic element to lower, yielding /ey/, was impossible without coalescence (which did not occur) with the existing /ey/ from a variety of sources, including Norse loans (*they,* etc.). For the glide to become centralizing or backing rather than fronting, yielding /iə̯/ or /iw/, would result in coalescence with the existing /iə̯/ (long close *ē*) or /iw/ (from such sources as OE- *-īew*), and would be unlikely in any case since the glide is still /-y/. The only possible change that would maintain the oppositions already in existence was for the vocalic element to centralize, yielding /ɨy/, subsequently /əy/ and finally /ay/. The widespread present-day alternation between /iy/ and /ɨy/ (Cockney, Philadelphia, etc.) gives dialectal support to this suggestion. Support for the parallel series /uw/⟶/ɨw/⟶/əw/⟶/aw/ is even stronger: all four stages still exist, in the same words, in present-day dialects (Scots /huws/; Tidewater Virginia /hɨws/; Piedmont Virginia and Eastern Canada /həws/; /haws/ ~ /hæws/ elsewhere).

(f) The OE features distinctive in the vowel system were *high, mid, low* and *front, round,* and *back*. Loss of the front rounded vowels (which were, in any case, structurally *central* as between front and back) left a gap which was filled by the splitting off of the central allophones of high and mid front vowels (i.e. the OE system /i e æ ü ö u o ɔ/ had become /i e æ ɨ ə u o/ by ME). In some dialects (Southwestern), the front round vowels fell in with the new central vowels rather than with front unround. The assumption of a high central vowel is more defensible in late ME than is the assumption of a high front rounded vowel at that time.

(g) Finally, the question of chronology. By some investigators the GVS has been assigned an almost cataclysmic timing (roughly 1400-1500), and a more generous spread by others (roughly 1350-1650). It is my contention that the series of changes of which the GVS is a part have

[13] I take *ī* simply for exemplification; *ū* would do as well, since it is completely parallel.

been going on at a remarkably steady rate for more than 1500 years, and that the GVS part of that series was in no way more abrupt or sudden than the rest of the changes—which, one can demonstrate, are still going on in the same pattern. The pattern consists in two main types of change: (1) raising of the vocalic element in complex nuclei toward the extremes, and centralizing followed by lowering of the extremes; (2) alternation between out-glides and in-glides. Thus:

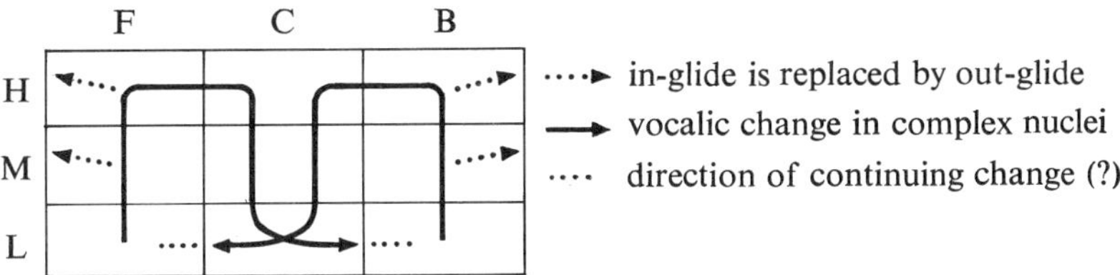

Limitations of space do not permit me to fill in the details of this chart, nor to list the pre-GVS and post-GVS changes that belong in the same series. I have tried only to show that the notion "overall pattern" is a useful and stimulating one in diachronic phonology.

Suggested Additional Readings for Part III

Footnote 1 of Kuhn's paper in this Part provides an excellent bibliographical summary of recent research on the problems of historical English phonology. Note that Daunt's paper, "Old English Sound ^ Changes Reconsidered in Relation to Scribal Tradition and Practice," is reprinted in Part V of this volume for reasons given in the Introduction to that Part.

PART IV

Grammatical Change in the History of English

The significance of morphological or syntactic elements, like that of phonological entities, is determined by structural opposition. Each element has significance only in terms of the system to which it belongs. If the oppositional relations between members of the system are altered, the new relations which are established constitute a different system. Historical grammar is concerned with the description of such systemic alterations as they have taken place in time. The systemic changes which are studied in historical grammar involve alterations in the patterns of morphological opposition which make up the paradigms of the language, and also alterations in the composition and ordering of elements which form the syntactic units of the language.

Underlying the study of historical grammar is the assumption that it is possible to determine the synchronic structure of at least two periods in the history of a language, e.g. those of Old English and of modern English. With two such descriptions, it is then possible to examine the similarities and differences in the two systems, and to formulate diachronic statements (i.e. rules) for relating the two periods. If these diachronic statements are to be representative of the relationships between the two systems, however, the synchronic descriptions of both periods must be equally complete, and each description must be formulated in terms of the system it describes, without reference to the descriptions of earlier or later systems. A disregard for these conditions generally leads to the pitfalls of antiquarianism and relic hunting, on the one hand, and to retroaction, on the other. Both undermine the effective formulation of accurate diachronic rules. In the first case, the description of a later system is not fully undertaken because of the attempt to see in it only the remnants of an earlier system; in the second case, the description of an earlier system is distorted because of the temptation to view it merely as a foreshadowing of the later system. In either situation, the synchronic descriptions are inadequate, and as a result, the diachronic statements based upon them will also be inadequate. In the historical grammar of English, influence from earlier systems is the more important potential source of distortion, because of a traditional tendency for descriptions of early English to be influenced by the analyst's knowledge of the structure of Proto-Germanic and of Proto-Indo-European.

Viewed historically, the grammatical systems of Old English and modern English differ most extensively in the degree to which grammatical categories (*person, number, case,* etc.) are marked inflectionally, and in the relative flexibility of word-order patterns. The inflectional differences stand out, for example, in the respective categories for which the finite verb may be inflected. The Old English verb can be marked for two distinctions of tense—*past* or *non-past*. Correlated to tense, there are two modal distinctions, generally designated *indicative* and *subjunctive,* the latter usually being found only in certain types of dependent constructions. A third modal category—the *imperative*—is also marked by inflection, but is not correlated to tense (i.e. there are no past imperatives). All forms of the verb are marked for number, and the indicative singular is marked for person. The paradigm can be illustrated with the verb *sing(an)*, NE *sing*:

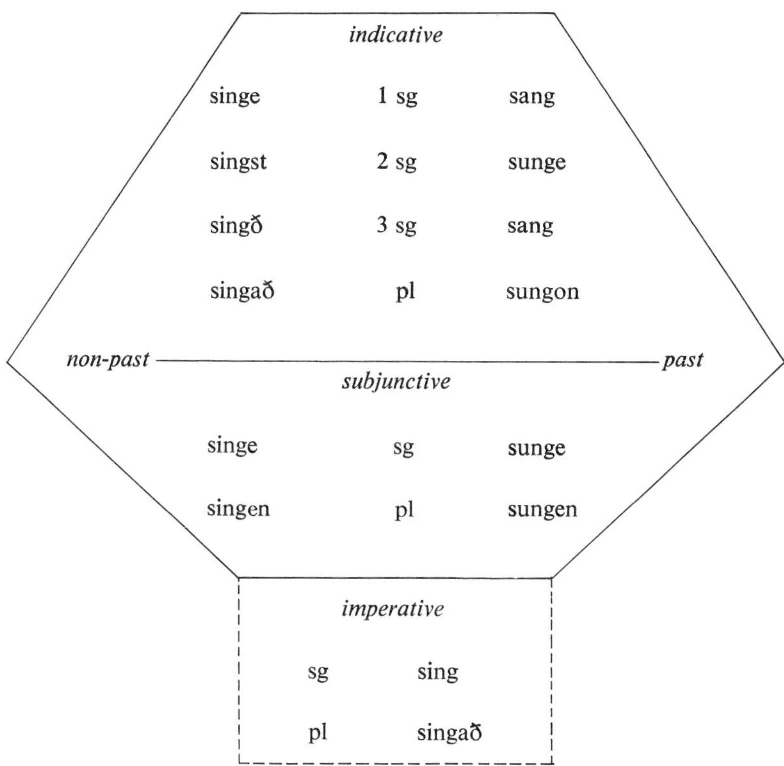

In modern English, by contrast, there is only the distinction of tense—*past* vs. *non-past*—with the non-past marked either by no overt inflection or by an *-s* inflection which coincidentally marks the third-person singular:

non-past	*past*
sing sings	sang

Changes in morphological systems like those that have taken place between Old English and modern English are generally the result of a number of related factors. Two of the most significant of these factors are phonological change and the analogical extension of grammatically dominant patterns into environments where they were historically absent. In the history of English, phonological changes like the reduction of nonstressed vowels to [ə], the loss of inflection-terminal nasals, and the reduction of terminal [ə] to Ø tended to eliminate many of the overt distinctions within the verbal paradigm—as they did within all of the other paradigms in the language. Analogical processes also served to extend the statistically more prominent indicative inflections (where these remained) to the former subjunctive and imperative environments. The result was not merely the loss of subjunctive and imperative categories of inflection, but the loss of mood itself as a grammatical category in the verb system —for, since categories exist only by virtue of opposition, a single distinction (in this case, the indicative) constitutes no distinction.

The comparatively large number of inflectional categories in Old English in contrast to the fewer distinctions in modern English has traditionally been used as an explanation for the syntactic differences between the same two periods. In modern English, the order of syntactic units is highly stable within the clause. In Old English, however, overt morphological marking of syntactic functions like *subject, verb, object* made it possible to vary the order of elements within the clause without obscuring the syntactic relationships. Because of the absence of case inflection in modern English, variations on the characteristic SVO order *(the man opened the door)* change the syntactic relationships between the elements as well. Thus, such permutations of the normal order of syntactic elements as SOV and VSO (both potentially possible in Old English as well as SVO) are much less likely in modern English. Statement patterns other than SVO are so rare in modern English that they call attention to themselves as stylistic variations for poetic or rhetorical effects. Since each of these syntactic functions could be marked inflectionally in Old English (the subject can be recognized as the subject whether it occurs before or after the verb), intelligibility did not limit the possibilities of permutation. As morphological distinctions were eliminated through historical change, however, dominant syntactic patterns were extended to the point where flexibility in the order of syntactic units was virtually eliminated, since deviation from predictable order tended to lead to unintelligibility.

The rigidity of the order of function units is demonstrable for modern English. The permitted flexibility of word order in Old English, however, despite the high degree of inflection, is less clear-cut than was formerly believed. Various permutations of word order can be found in Old English texts, but modern scholarship has largely discredited traditional assumptions about the syntactic 'freedom' of Old English. In his monumental work on Old English syntax (*La structure de la phrase verbale à l'époque alfrédienne,* Strasbourg, 1962), Paul Bacquet presents the case against the long-held notion that word order in Old English prose is indiscriminately variable. Bacquet argues that Old English order is unpredictable only if one fails to recognize the fundamental distinction between normal word order *(ordre de base)* and word order which calls attention to itself rhetorically *(ordre marqué),* precisely because it deviates from the normal order. Thus, while variation in word order is possible, it is not employed indiscriminately, and an examination of normal word order not only demonstrates a high degree of stability in the ordering of elements, but it also shows that there exists a relatively high degree of similarity between the word order of Old English and that of modern English—despite the disparity in the inflectional paradigms. Compare, for example, Old English *se cyning seah his cwen* with modern English *the king saw his queen,* or *he sealde Alexandre his dohtor* with *he gave Alexander his daughter.* (The Old English forms are cited by Bacquet as *ordre de base.*) Pronominal objects, however, precede the verb in Old English. Compare Old English *he hit dyde* with modern English *he did it.*

Bacquet maintains that the notion of structural freedom in Old English syntax arose because investigators "have not taken the trouble to separate the different levels of style and have thus confounded normal and marked word order" (p. 754) . To make such a separation, he notes, one "must take into account not only the rhetorical conventions and style-consciousness of medieval writers, but their didactic intentions as well," and this can be done "only if one pays strict attention to the context in which the sentence under scrutiny is found."

Once again, this emphasizes the problems inherent in the interpretation of texts and the care which must be taken in interpreting them. In the study of historical morphology, a conservative orthography may conceal morphological changes which have taken place since the stabilization of the spelling conventions, just as it may hide those which have taken place in phonology. In historical syntax, the problems of interpretation may be even more sophisticated, for it may be necessary to evaluate each construction in terms of its environment—a much more difficult problem than evaluating the more restricted occurrence of an orthographic symbol or an inflectional form. It is a problem that touches upon the very complex area of stylistics.

The first four selections which follow are concerned with problems of historical English morphology, the remaining with problems of historical English syntax. The introductory article, by Samuel R. Levin, is an analysis of one aspect of Old English grammar—the variation in the stem structure of strong verbs—in descriptive terms, without reference to systems which existed at earlier periods. Levin illustrates the distinction between descriptive analysis and analysis modified to accord with what is known of earlier periods in the history of a language. The article by Samuel Moore is a detailed examination and evaluation of textual evidence for morphological change in the late OE period. Such an examination reveals the difficulties inherent in the use of textual materials for determination of morphological change. The article by Robert B. Stevick applies the tools of modern linguistics to the explanation of the historical development of modern English *she*—a member of a small morphological subset, the personal pronouns. The following article, by Robert J. Menner, is a theoretical discussion of the influence of one factor, homophony, on the historical development of morphological and semantic sets in English. The Menner discussion illustrates the complexity involved in analyzing the changes which may have taken place in the morphological structure of a language and of the interrelationship between phonological and morphological changes.

Of the three articles on syntax, the first, by Charles R. Carlton, is an illustration of the application of descriptive techniques to the analysis of the syntax of earlier periods in the history of English. Like the Levin article discussed above, it is an example of the type of descriptive statement which can be used as the basis for sound historical statements. The article by Charles C. Fries makes use of statistical evidence to describe the historical development from the stylistically variable OE word-order to the comparative rigidity of that of modern English. The final article, by Elizabeth Closs Traugott, is an application of the transformational model of grammatical description to one important aspect of historical English syntax—the development of English verbal auxiliary constructions. The Traugott article is indicative of the potential power of transformational grammar for the description of historical change in grammatical systems.

A Reclassification of the Old English Strong Verbs

SAMUEL R. LEVIN

THE TRADITIONAL CLASSIFICATION of the Old English strong verbs is crucially influenced by historical considerations. This is obvious; it is less obvious that the description is thereby distorted. It will be the purpose of this paper to show that a strictly synchronic approach results in a different analysis.

The strong verbs are traditionally presented as in the following list. Subclasses are included only so far as they bear on the discussion; the 7th class will be dealt with later. For comparison I cite the Gothic cognates.

TABLE 1. *First six classes of Old English and Gothic strong verbs*

	Old English				Gothic			
I	bīdan	bād	bidon	biden	beidan	baiþ	bidum	bidans
II	lēogan	lēag	lugon	logen	liugan	laug	lugum	lugans
IIIa	bindan	band	bundon	bunden	bindan	band	bundum	bundans
IIIb	helpan	healp	hulpon	holpen	hilpan	halp	hulpum	hulpans
IVa	beran	bær	bǣron	boren	bairan	bar	bērum	baurans
IVb	cuman	cōm	cōmon	cumen	qiman	qam	qēmum	qumans
IVc	niman	nōm	nōmon	numen	niman	nam	nēmum	numans
V	metan	mæt	mǣton	meten	mitan	mat	mētum	mitans
VI	faran	fōr	fōron	faren	faran	fōr	fōrum	farans

Table 1 shows certain similarities between members of different classes. The preterits of classes IVb and IVc are similar in their vocalism to the preterits of class VI; the preterits of class IVa are similar to those of class V. In part, the reason for separating these similar classes is that

Reprinted by permission from *Language* 40.156-61 (1964).

there are differences of vowel grade in the remainder of their paradigms. Even more significant is that the different classes reflect Indo-European and Germanic root formations of different types. Three criteria enter into the traditional analysis: the particular distribution of resonants and consonants in the original root structure, the original ablaut alternation, and reduplication.[1] The function of the first two criteria is seen most clearly in the first three classes, whose root structure in Pre-Germanic is set out in Table 2.[2]

TABLE 2. *Pre-Germanic root structure of classes I-III*

	PRES.	PRET. SG.	PRET. PL.	P. PTC.
I	CeiC-	CaiC-	CiC-	CiC-
II	CeuC-	CauC-	CuC-	CuC-
IIIa	CenC-	CanC-	C(v)nC-	C(v)nC-
IIIb	CelC-	CalC-	C(v)lC-	C(v)lC-

Class I reconstructs to a root with the resonant *i* followed by a consonant; class II to a root with *u* followed by a consonant; class III to a root with a nasal or a liquid followed by a consonant.[3] With full grade, the resonants are consonantal (second members of diphthongs); with zero grade, the resonants are originally vocalic, assuming syllabic status; at a later stage, a svarabhakti vowel develops here.

Classes IV–VI have the Pre-Germanic structure shown in Table 3.

TABLE 3. *Pre-Germanic root structure of classes IV-VI*

	PRES.	PRET. SG.	PRET. PL.	P. PTC.
IVa	Cel-	Cal-	Cǣl-	C(v)l-
IVb, c	Cen-	Can-	Cǣn-	C(v)n-
V	CeC-	CaC-	CǣC-	C(v)C-
VI	C(v)C-	CōC-	CōC-	C(v)C-

Class IV reconstructs to a root ending in a nasal or a liquid resonant, and class V to a root ending in a consonant (stop or spirant); class VI is less determinate: the phoneme with which it ends is a stop, a spirant, a nasal, or a liquid.[4]

[1] See Jacob Grimm, *Deutsche Grammatik*[2] 1.756-57 (Berlin, 1870).

[2] Pre-Germanic reconstructions are chosen for convenience and effectiveness. Indo-European reconstructions would require a consideration of laryngeals or reduced-grade vowels or both; Proto-Germanic reconstructions would obscure the original ablaut alternations.

In the tables *C* denotes a consonant or cluster, *n* a nasal, *l* a liquid. A small *v* denotes an obscure or reduced vowel which develops as Proto-Germanic *u* in the zero-grade forms of classes IIIa and IIIb. In Table 3, *v* denotes Germanic *a* (< IE *a* or *ə*) in the present of class VI, and a still more diverse vocalism in the participles of IV, V, and VI.

[3] This applies to most roots in class III; but the class includes also verbs like *feohtan* 'fight', *stregdan* 'strew', *frignan* 'ask'. In the discussion that follows, some of these and other rare types will be incorporated into the analysis.

[4] Class VI includes a few roots ending in more than one consonant, e.g. *wascan* 'wash', *standan* 'stand'.

From the historical point of view, classes IV–VI are distinctive also in that the regular alternation *e* ~ *o* ~ zero of the first three classes is not consistently carried through. The discrepancies occur in the preterit plurals of classes IV and V and throughout class VI.[5] The vowel *ǣ* in the preterit plurals of classes IV and V reflects an IE lengthened grade *ē*, as in Latin perfects of the type *vēxī* (*vehō* 'I carry'). In class VI the vowel of the present stem probably reflects an old weak-grade present;[6] the vowels of the preterit go back to various sources.[7]

The historical basis for segregating the seventh class of Germanic strong verbs is that their preterits were originally formed by reduplication.[8] Of all the Germanic languages, however, only Gothic systematically retains this formation: the preterits of Gothic *haldan* 'hold' are sg. *haihald,* pl. *haihaldum;* of *lētan* 'let', sg. *lailōt,* pl. *lailōtum.* In Old English, except for a few vestiges, the seventh class shows no reduplication.[9]

Notice, in the Gothic forms just cited, that the same vocalism is found throughout the preterit. Uniformity of preterit vocalism is true in general of the seventh class. In Old English, two major subtypes are distinguished, according as the preterit vowel is *ē* or *ēo*. In their uniform preterit vocalism, verbs of the seventh class correspond to Greek perfects of the type *léloipa* 'I have left', *leloípamen* 'we have left' (*leípō* 'I leave).

TABLE 4. *Seventh class of Old English strong verbs*

VIIa	hātan	hēt	hēton	hāten	'call'
	lǣtan	lēt	lēton	lǣten	'let'
VIIb	blāwan	blēow	blēowon	blāwen	'blow'
	bēatan	bēot	bēoton	bēaten	'beat'

[5] The *æ* for expected *a* in the preterit singular of classes IV and V is regular in Old English. The *i* of *niman* results from a Germanic sound-change; the *u* of *cuman* is that of a weak-grade present.

[6] The type with reduced or zero grade is more clearly seen in presents like class I *rīpan,* III *murnan,* IV *cuman.* It is also seen, with lengthening of the original short vowel, in the rather large subclass of class II that includes *brūcan* and *lūcan.*

[7] Cf. for instance E. Prokosch, *A comparative Germanic grammar* 173-4 (Philadelphia, 1939).

[8] Reduplication is one of the regular ways of forming the Indo-European perfect; the other way is exemplified in Greek *oída* 'I know', *ídmen* 'we know'. The latter forms lack reduplication, and retain the alternation of *o* grade in the singular and zero grade in the plural. Sanskrit reduplicating perfects reflect the same alternation: *riṇákti* 'he leaves' : *riréca* 'he has left', *riricimá* 'we have left'. But the corresponding Greek formations generalize the vowel grade of the singular: *leípō* 'I leave' : *léloipa* 'I have left', *leloípamen* 'we have left'.

Since Germanic shows a conflation of the Indo-European perfect and aorist, we speak instead of the preterit when dealing with Germanic verbs.

[9] Only traces of the original reduplication exist in Old English. A. Campbell, *Old English grammar* 320 (Oxford, 1959), lists the following as the only sure instances: *heht* or *hēht* from *hātan; leolc* from *lācan; ondreord* from *ondrǣdan; leort* from *lǣtan;* and *reord* from *rǣdan.* These forms are archiac in Old English; they occur chiefly in poetry and the old Anglian glosses.

Great changes have intervened between the reconstructed root structures of the Germanic strong verbs and their forms in Old English. In classes I and II the articulation of the resonants *i* and *u* with the other elements of the root has been largely obscured by subsequent sound-changes: the preterit plural and the past participle continue to show the reconstructible form, but the present and the preterit singular do not. In class III there is even less retention of the reconstructible forms: svarabhakti vowels have been developed in the preterit plural and past participle to prop up the zero-grade nasals and liquids, and the original *e* and *o* (Gmc. *a*) of the present and the preterit singular have also, in some cases, undergone sound-change.

The Old English classes IV-VI retain the original consonant structure, but show irregularities in the original ablaut alternation. Class VII shows, in addition, a drastic modification of the structure of the preterit: the original reduplication has been, for all practical (i.e. synchronic) purposes, lost.

The changes suffered by Old English in the period (more than a millennium) of its divergence from Pre-Germanic are not the main reason that the traditional classification of the Old English strong verbs is faulty. The reason, rather, is that the criteria for classification, which were perfectly appropriate for Pre-Germanic, are no longer functional in Old English. Thus, classes I–III of Old English, while still distinct, are distinct for reasons other than the original presence of different resonants in their roots. Likewise, while the seventh class of strong verbs in Old English is still distinct from the other classes, it is not because the preterit has a reduplicating syllable. In the same way, while differences of vocalism continue to distinguish some classes from others, the system of Indo-European ablaut alternation can no longer be regarded as a significant criterion of classification.

Discarding the original historical basis of the classification of Old English strong verbs, and using synchronic features as criteria, I propose the reclassification summarized in Table 5. Most of the subclasses are included; 4a belongs to IV of the traditional scheme, 4b-d belong to V; 5a-e to VI; 5f-g to IV; and all forms in 6 and 7 to VII.

The new arrangement, like the old, comprises seven classes. The criterion for class assignment is the vocalism of the preterit. By this cri-

TABLE 5. *Reclassification of the Old English strong verbs*

1a	ī	ā	i	i	bīdan	bād	bidon	biden	'await'
b	ēo	ā	i	i	wrēon	wrāh	wrigon	wrigen	'cover'
2a	ēo	ēa	u	o	bēodan	bēad	budon	boden	'command'
b	ū	ēa	u	o	brūcan	brēac	brucon	brocen	'use'
3a	i	a	u	u	bindan	band	bundon	bunden	'bind'
b	e	ea	u	o	helpan	healp	hulpon	holpen	'help'
c	eo	ea	u	o	weorpan	wearp	wurpon	worpen	'throw'
d	u	ea	u	o	spurnan	spearn	spurnon	spornen	'spurn'
e	e	æ	u	o	stregdan	strægd	strugdon	strogden	'strew'

(Table 5 continued)

4a	e	æ	ǣ	o	beran	bær	bǣron	boren	'bear'
b	e	æ	ǣ	e	metan	mæt	mǣton	meten	'measure'
c	ēo	ea	ǣ	e	sēon	seah	sǣgon	segen	'see'
d	i	æ	ǣ	e	biddan	bæd	bǣdon	beden	'pray'
5a	a	ō	ō	a	faran	fōr	fōron	faren	'go'
b	ēa	ō	ō	a	slēan	slōg	slōgon	slagen	'strike'
c	e	ō	ō	a	hebban	hōf	hōfon	hafen	'raise'
d	ie	ō	ō	ea	scieppan	scōp	scōpon	sceapen	'create'
e	æ	ō	ō	æ	stæppan	stōp	stōpon	stæpen	'step'
f	u	ō	ō	u	cuman	cōm	cōmon	cumen	'come'
g	i	ō	ō	u	niman	nōm	nōmon	numen	'take'
6a	ā	ē	ē	ā	hātan	hēt	hēton	hāten	'call'
b	ǣ	ē	ē	ǣ	lǣtan	lēt	lēton	lǣten	'let'
c	ō	ē	ē	a	fōn	fēng	fēngon	fangen	'seize'
7a	a	ēo	ēo	a	bannan	bēonn	bēonnon	bannen	'summon'
b	ea	ēo	ēo	ea	fealdan	fēold	fēoldon	fealden	'fold'
c	a	ēo	ēo	ā	blāwan	blēow	blēowon	blāwen	'blow'
d	ēa	eo	ēo	ēa	bēatan	bēot	bēoton	bēaten	'beat'
e	ō	ēo	ēo	ō	blōtan	blēot	blēoton	blōten	'sacrifice'

terion, the system falls into two divisions: in the first (1–4) the vowel of the preterit is different in the singular and the plural; in the second (5–7) it is the same. The vowels of the preterit, for the revised classes, are shown in Table 6. (The forms *strægd, strugdon* of 3e, and *seah, sǣgon* of 4c fall outside this scheme.)

TABLE 6. *Vowels of preterit singular and plural*

1	ā	i	5	ō	ō
2	ēa	u	6	ē	ē
3	a/ea	u	7	ēo	ēo
4	æ	ǣ			

Three major changes from the traditional classification follow from the selection of preterit vocalism as the criterion of class membership: (1) classes IVb and IVc *(cuman, niman,* and their prefixed congeners) are combined with class VI *(faran)* to yield the new class 5; (2) class IVa *(beran)* is combined with class V *(metan)* to yield the new class 4; (3) the former subtypes of class VII are now separate classes, 6 and 7.

It is clear from Table 5 that if the principal parts of a verb are given, the class is determined. But what are the chances of uniquely classifying an individual form? If the form is a preterit of class 1 or 5–7 there is no problem.[10] The preterit singular of 3a and the preterit plurals of 4 are also distinctive. Preterit vocalism alone, however, will not distin-

[10] When the vowel is the same as that of a present or past participle in another class, the ending will show that the form is preterit, except when the like vowels occur in a preterit singular and an imperative singular (3 *band* 'he bound', 5 *far* 'go'). Even then, the root structure will solve the ambiguity.

guish between the singulars of 3b–d and 4c or of 3e and 4a, b, d, or between the plurals of 2 and 3. In these cases we make use of a subsidiary criterion, the root structure: the historical changes affecting the root structure of Old English verbs have, as it happens, preserved a difference here. Verbs of class 3 have roots ending in a nasal or liquid followed by a consonant; verbs of classes 2 and 4 do not have this structure. Thus the preterit singulars *healp, wearp, spearn* (3b–d) are distinguishable from *seah* (4c), the preterit plurals *bundon, hulpon, wurpon* (3) from the preterit plurals *budon, tugon, curon* (2).[11]

Among the past participles unique determination is possible in all but a few cases. Often the vowel is enough to show the class; thus in classes 1, 4b, 4c, 4d, 5e, 6b, 7d, and 7e. The remaining classes have the vowel *o, u, a, ea,* or *ā* in the past participle. *o* occurs in 2a, 2b, 3b, 3c, 3d, 3e, and 4a. The root structure will distinguish class-3 forms from those of classes 2 and 4. 4a contains a liquid in the root (*boren, holen*), 2 ordinarily does not. The exceptions are a few class-2 verbs whose past participles (and preterit plurals) show *r* as a result of the operation of Verner's Law, e.g. *coren* (*cēosan*), *froren* (*frēosan*). (Note that in the traditional classification it is also not possible to distinguish between *boren* and *coren.*)

The vowel *u* occurs in the past participles of 3a, 5f, and 5g. Here again root structure is decisive: *bunden* as opposed to *cumen, numen.* When the vowel is *a,* in classes 5a, 5b, 5c, 6c, and 7a, root structure is usually determinative. In the last two classes the *a* is followed by either a geminate nasal (7a) or nasal plus consonant (6c); of the verbs in class 5 only *standen* has this structure.

The vowel *ea* of class 5d is distinguished from that of 7b in that the latter is followed by a consonant cluster, the former never.[12] The vowel *ā* of 7c occurs before *w,* that of 6a does not.

Present stems of class 1a are distinctive. Whereas the *ū* of 2b is also distinctive, the *ēo* of 2a is found also in 1b and in 4c; but verbs of 1b and 4c are contract verbs, e.g. *wrēon* 'cover', *tēon* 'accuse' (1b), *sēon* 'see', *plēon* 'risk' (4c), and those of 2a are not, e.g. *bēodan* 'command', *cēosan* 'choose'. There is no way short of listing, however, to distinguish the contract verbs of 1b from those of 4c.

In class 3, the vowel *eo* of 3c is distinctive; the *i* and *u* of 3a and 3d are distinguished from their counterparts in 5g and 5f by root-structure.

[11] 3e *stregdan* represents a small group of verbs in class III with roots that do not end in nasal or liquid plus consonant; others are *bregdan* 'brandish', *berstan* 'burst', *frignan* 'ask'. All such verbs have roots ending in a consonant cluster, which distinguishes their preterit singular forms (*strægd, bærst, frægn*) from those of 4a, b, d (*bær, mæt, bæd*).

[12] In 5d the *ea,* like the *ie* of the present stem, is conditioned by the preceding palatal consonant. The same sound-change might have occurred before a consonant cluster in the past participle, but there seem to be no verbs of this class where the change has in fact taken place.

(The *i* of 4d is followed by a geminate consonant, the *i* of 3a and 5g is not.) The *e* of 3b and 3e is similarly distinguished from the *e* of 4a and 4b, and from the *e* of 5c (*hebban, sceþþan, swerian*) by the lack of root-final geminate or *-ri-*.

Class 5d is unique, as are 5e and 7b. Class 5a is similar to 7a in that both have *a*. In 7a the *a* is always followed by a geminate nasal or by nasal plus consonant (*spannan, blandan*), in 5a only in *standan*. The *ēa* of 5b occurs in a contract form (*slēan, flēan,* etc.) and is thus distinguished from the *ēa* of 7d (*bēatan* etc.).

The *ǣ* of 6b is distinctive. The *ā* of 7c is always followed by *w* (*cnāwan, blāwan*), that of 6a never. The *ō* of 6c occurs in contraction (*fōn, hōn,* etc.), that of 7e does not (*hrōpan, grōwan*).

If we ask how the traditional classification and the new scheme compare in making possible the unique determination of individual forms, we see that in this they are exactly alike. Neither enjoys an advantage in its ability to assign individual forms. If I nevertheless regard the reclassification as superior, it is only in part because it uses purely synchronic criteria. The use of vowel gradation as the primary criterion, with root structure a subsidiary marker, greatly simplifies the system. By modifying the role of root structure as a class index, and by abandoning reduplication altogether, we achieve classes much more uniformly differentiated. There is little motivation, aside from diachronic considerations, for separating *beran* and *metan, cuman* and *faran,* verbs with such similar vocalism in their paradigms; at this point the traditional classification is overdifferentiated. On the other hand, only their common origin as reduplicatives could justify grouping in one class verbs with such different vocalism as *hātan, hēt* and *blōtan, blēot*; this is a clear case of underdifferentiation. The reclassification, by disregarding historical differences and focusing on synchronic evidence, presents a system of Old English strong verbs which is properly motivated; the result is neater and more adequate than the traditional scheme.

Earliest Morphological Changes in Middle English

SAMUEL MOORE

THE HISTORY OF ENGLISH SINCE 1050 may be regarded as consisting of two periods with the year 1300 as a very rough *terminus ad quem* for the first and *terminus a quo* for the second. The period from 1300 to the present has been characterised by very extensive changes in the phonetic form of English and by important syntactic changes but not by correspondingly great changes in the morphological pattern of English speech. The morphological changes in nouns and adjectives have been almost wholly the result of the loss of final *e* and to a very small extent the result of analogical processes. Analogical processes have resulted in important changes in the inflectional pattern of verbs but in verbs also changes in morphological structure have been to a much greater extent the result of other causes, especially the displacement of forms ending in *-en* by forms ending in *e* and the subsequent loss of final *e*.

The period from 1050 to 1300, on the other hand, was characterised by very extensive morphological changes that transformed English from a rather highly inflected language to one having the relatively few and simple inflections of late Middle English. All distinctions of case were lost except the genitive singular of nouns and the distinctions of grammatical gender were lost altogether. And even the grammatical categories that remained were more simply expressed, for in late Middle English the single ending *-es* had replaced the variety of endings that had expressed the genitive singular and plural of nouns in Old English.

The rapid and extensive morphological development that took place between 1050 and 1300 was the result of a highly complex cooperation of sound changes, syntactic changes, and analogical changes. To identify these several factors in the successive stages and various phases of the

Reprinted by permission from *Language* 4.238-50 (1928).

morphological development is an extremely important problem. It seems obvious, however, that the cooperation of these factors must have become increasingly intricate as the development proceeded and as the results of sound changes, syntactic changes, and analogical changes themselves continually provided more varied material for analogical processes to work upon. It is therefore the purpose of the present paper to examine only the very earliest morphological changes that took place within this period, to establish the relative chronology of these changes, to identify the parts played by sound change and analogy in bringing about the development, and to show *what* analogical processes operated and why they should have operated at this period rather than earlier.

The documents that we must depend on for a knowledge of the earliest stages of the morphological development of Middle English are not the literary texts of the thirteenth century (such as Layamon's *Brut,* the *Moral Ode,* the *Owl and the Nightingale,* and the *Ancren Riwle*) or the twelfth century transcriptions of eleventh century texts (contained in such MSS as Cotton Vespasian D 14, Bodley 343, and Hatton 38) but eleventh century MSS containing texts composed for the most part early in the eleventh century or in the tenth. The MSS of the eleventh century were written under the influence of a very strong literary and orthographic tradition. None of them probably reflect accurately the speech habits of the scribes who wrote them. The written form of all of them is more or less archaic. The very great majority of the inflectional forms, even in the MSS written in the latter part of the century, are the normal Late West-Saxon forms of (say) the year 1000. But alongside of the forms of the year 1000 we find occurring, to a small extent in the early eleventh century MSS and to an increasing extent in MSS of the later eleventh century, forms that were not Old English but Middle English. These forms are only occasional, not normal, even in the texts in which they are most numerous. They are 'slips', errors, in the sense of being departures from the orthographic tradition to which the scribes were intending to conform. But they are errors in that sense only, for they reveal the speech habits of the scribes which the 'correct' forms conceal. These occasional 'incorrect' forms are our best (and almost our only) evidence of the actual speech of the period from about 1050 to 1100.

In practically all the texts (109 out of 110) used as the basis of the present paper there occur examples of inflectional changes that are very much more frequent or normal in the twelfth century MSS. These changes are as follows:

1. The unaccented post-tonic vowels *a, e, o,* and *u* are levelled to a vowel written *e;*
2. Final *m* in unaccented syllables becomes final *n;*

3. Final *n* in unaccented syllables is subject to loss;[1]
4. Feminine *jō*-stems and long feminine *ō*-stems, which ended in a consonant in Old English, end in *e*.

In addition to these changes there occur in 30 of the texts a few examples of inflectional forms which, tho much more frequent in the twelfth century MSS, did not attain their maximum displacement of historical forms until the second half of the thirteenth century or even later.[2] These forms, in spite of their sporadic occurrence in eleventh century MSS, belong really to a later period in the morphological development of Middle English than that to which the present paper is devoted.

Of the four changes noted above, the first change, levelling of unaccented vowels, affected by far the greatest number of inflectional forms and resulted in the greatest modification of inflectional patterns. Yet it is this change that is least consistently evidenced by the written forms of the eleventh century MSS. In only thirty of the texts used is the evidence of levelling at all conclusive and even in those texts the historical vowels *a, o,* and *u* are far more frequently retained than written *e*. The nature of the evidence is such that the relative chronology of this change can best be considered after the relative chronology of the other three changes has been established.

The relative chronology of the change of *m* to *n* and the loss of final *n* is indicated, I believe, by the distribution of the forms in the texts studied. The details of the evidence (the examples and the texts used)[3] are presented in the Appendix to this paper [see *Language* 4.251-66 (1928)]. The data may be very concisely summarised as follows:

106 texts out of 110 show evidence of the change of final *m* to *n;*

[1] For the history of this change in the eleventh and twelfth centuries and for much of the evidence used in this paper see my former paper, *Loss of Final* n *in Inflectional Syllables of Middle English,* published in *Language* 3.232-59 (hereafter referred to as LFn).

[2] These forms are:

þe and *þeo* for the demonstrative and definite article *sē* and *sēo* (Nos. 6, 19, 37, 38, 66, 67, 68, 77, 78, 82, 89, 103, 106)

Analogical *n*-plurals (Nos. 5, 24, 45, 65, 76, 80)

Use of the dative forms of the third personal pronoun instead of the accusative forms (Nos. 65, 68, 80, 83)

Analogical *s*-plurals (Nos. 24, 38, 65)

The numbers in parenthesis refer to the texts as listed in the Appendix. [Eds.: Appendix not reprinted here.] It should be understood that my statement as to the period at which these forms attained their maximum displacement of historical forms applies to the Southern dialect, not to the Midland.

[3] The material I have used does not exhaust the eleventh century material that is in print but includes the great majority of prose texts available in fairly modern editions. Considerably more material is available in Liebermann's *Gesetze der Angelsachsen,* for I restricted myself there (somewhat unwisely, I think) to the texts composed fairly late in the Old English period. I have used only a few of the interlinear texts and have made no use of the poetical texts. Included among the eleventh century texts are a few written early in the twelfth century.

46 texts show evidence of the change of final *m* to *n* but contain no examples of loss of final *n*;[4]

60 texts show evidence of the change of final *m* to *n* and also contain examples of loss of final *n*;

3 texts contain examples of the loss of final *n* but show no evidence of change of final *m* to *n*.[5]

This distribution seems to me explainable only on one hypothesis: that the change of final *m* to *n* in unaccented syllables was earlier than the loss of final *n*. If the loss of *n* had preceded the change of *m* to *n* we should expect that very few texts or none would show evidence of the change of *m* to *n* without also showing evidence of the loss of *n* and that a large number of texts would show evidence of the loss of *n* but would show no evidence of the change of *m* to *n*. In other words, the distribution would be the reverse of what we actually have. If the change of *m* to *n* had been contemporaneous with the loss of *n* we should expect that the majority of the texts would show evidence of both the change and the loss and that the number of texts showing evidence of the loss of *n* but no evidence of the change of *m* to *n* would be approximately equal to the number of texts showing evidence of the change of *m* to *n* but no evidence of the loss of *n*. The relative number of examples occurring in the texts that showed evidence of both the change and the loss also indicates the priority of the change of *m* to *n*. For altho unaccented syllables ending in *n* are very much more numerous in Old English than those ending in *m*, the number of examples of the change of *m* to *n* is much greater in the 60 texts than the number of examples of loss of *n*.[6]

If the change of final *m* to *n* preceded the loss of *n* in unaccented syllables the secondary final *n*'s resulting from this change must have been as subject to loss as the primary final *n*'s. That they were equally subject to loss is shown by the fact that in the twelfth century MSS the loss of final nasals is as great in the strong adjective as in the weak adjective and as great in the dative plural of strong nouns as in the plural of weak nouns.[7] It is indicated also by the fact that the eleventh century MSS already show some loss of the nasal in the dative singular and dative plural of the strong adjective and in the dative plural of

[4] Of these 46 texts, 7 contain examples of final *e* in the nominative singular of feminine *jō*- or long feminine *ō*-stems and really belong, I believe, to a later period of morphological development than the other 39 texts.

[5] These three texts are numbers 13, 34, and 77. The possibility of their showing evidence of the change of *m* to *n* is greatly restricted by their brevity, for all are less than 1000 words in length. Moreover, two other texts in the same MS (tho not in the same hand) as 13 contain examples of the change of *m* to *n* and number 76 in the same MS as 77 contains examples of the change; number 34 is the only text I have from the MS in which it occurs.

[6] A mere inspection of the material in the Appendix [see eds. note on page 230] is sufficient to verify this statement.

[7] See Table I in LFn 238.

strong nouns (all of which were *-um* forms in Old English).[8] In the eleventh century MSS, however, the loss of the final nasal is much less frequent relatively in the dative singular and dative plural of the strong adjective than in the weak adjective. This fact might be interpreted as evidence that the change of *m* to *n*, tho beginning earlier, may have partly overlapped the loss of *n*. As I have already argued in a former paper, it makes very little practical difference whether the change of final *m* to *n* was completely carried out before the loss of final *n* began or whether the change partly overlapped the loss; the important fact is that the secondary *n* resulting from the change was subject to loss.[9]

The hypothesis of partial overlapping would be difficult, perhaps impossible, to actually disprove, but I believe the totality of evidence is against it. I would call attention in particular to the following facts. (1) Altho the number of forms showing the change of *m* to *n* is much smaller in the great majority of our texts than we should expect to find on the hypothesis that change of *m* to *n* was completed before the loss of *n* began, there are at least two texts, containing no evidence of loss of *n*, in which the number of *-um* forms spelled with the final *m* is less than twice that of the number of *-um* forms spelled with the final *n*.[10] (2) In a number of eleventh century texts, including two that contain few or no *-um* forms spelled with final *n*, we find forms that ended in *n* in Old English spelled with final *m*.[11] (3) Altho the change of *m* to *n* was certainly completed by the year 1100 at the latest, the Old English *-um* forms are at least occasionally spelled with final *m* in all but two of fifteen twelfth century texts that I have studied and are spelled with final *m* more often than with final *n* in seven of the fifteen texts.[12] I infer from these facts that the apparent stability of final *m* in the eleventh century MSS as in the twelfth century MSS is a graphic rather than a linguistic phenomenon and that the change of *m* to *n* not only began but was completed before the loss of *n* began.

The relative chronology of the loss of final *n* and the addition of final *e* in the nominative singular of the feminine *jō*-stems and the long

[8] See Table II in LFn 243.

[9] See LFn 246f.

[10] These texts are numbers 4 and 92.

[11] In two homilies of Aelfric printed from MS Corpus Christi College Cambridge 188 by Assmann (*Bibliothek der angelsächischen prosa* 3.24-64) I found only one example of the change of *m* to *n* but five examples of *-um* for *-an;* Aelfric's *Letter to Wulfsige* printed from MS Corpus Christi College Cambridge 190 by Fehr (*Bibliothek der angelsächsischen prosa* 9. 1ff.) contains no clear case of the change of *m* to *n* but at least two examples of *-um* for *-an*. The other texts containing examples of final *m* used instead of final *n* are numbers 9, 10, 12, 17, 31, 37, 46, 67, 68, 71, 81, 82, 84, 89, 95. Most of the examples are *um*-spellings for the masculine and neuter dative singular of the weak adjective but there are also examples of infinitives and oblique forms of weak nouns spelled with final *m*.

[12] Of the twelfth century texts used for Table I in LFn (listed in LFn 235f.), *um*-spellings predominate, with some *n*-forms, in numbers 3, 6, 7, 8, 9, 12, 15; *n*-forms predominate, with some *um*-spellings, in numbers 1, 2, 4, 10, 11, 13; there are very few or no *m*-spellings in numbers 5 and 14.

feminine ō-stems is also indicated, I believe, by the distribution of the forms in the texts. The distribution (as shown in detail in my Appendix) [see eds. note above] is as follows:

40 texts out of 110 show no evidence either of the loss of *n* or of the addition of *e* in the feminine nominative singular;
63 texts show evidence of the loss of final *n;*
30 texts show evidence of the loss of *n* but no evidence of the addition of *e* in the feminine nominative singular;
33 texts show evidence of loss of final *n* and also of the addition of *e* in the nominative singular of feminines;
7 texts (7, 27, 47, 52, 54, 58, 91) show evidence of the addition of *e* in the feminine nominative singular but contain no examples of the loss of final *n*.

If the addition of *e* in the feminine nominative singular had preceded the loss of *n* we should expect that very few texts or none would show evidence of the loss of *n* without also showing evidence of the addition of *e* in the feminine nominative singular but that a large number of texts would show evidence of the addition of *e* in the feminine nominative singular but no evidence of the loss of *n*. That is, the distribution would be the reverse of what we actually find.[13] The evidence therefore seems clearly to indicate that the loss of final *n* preceded the addition of *e* in the feminine nominative singular.

The chronological relation of loss of final *n* and addition of *e* in feminines was not the same, however, as the chronological relation of change of *m* to *n* and loss of *n*. Change of *m* to *n* was completed before loss of *n* began but loss of *n* was not completed before the addition of *e* in the nominative singular of feminines began. For loss of final *n* began (at least according to the conclusions reached in my former paper)[14] as a combinative sound-change whose primary result was that each word affected by the change had two forms, with and without *n*. The original distribution of the forms with and without *n* depended on the phonetic environment of the word. This original distribution was later modified,

[13] The evidence of the texts that have examples of the loss of *n* but not of the addition of *e* in the feminine nominative singular is of less weight than their number might seem to indicate. Numbers 7, 27, and 58 (containing about 1000, 600, and 400 words respectively) are so short that the possibility of their showing evidence of the loss of *n* is considerably restricted. (Moreover, numbers 29 and 30, in the same MS and hand as 27, and numbers 55, 56, and 57, in the same MS and hand as 58, show evidence of the loss of *n* tho 27 and 58 do not). With respect to the longer texts, number 48 in the same MS as 47, number 51 in the same MS and hand as 52, and number 53 in the same MS and hand as 54 show evidence of the loss of *n* tho 47, 52, and 54 do not. The distribution of forms in number 91 (which is partly prose and partly verse) is not paralleled in any other of the 110 texts. The verse contains 5 examples of the addition of *e* in the nominative singular of feminines but no example of either change of *m* to *n* or loss of *n*. The prose parts of the text (and also texts 89 and 90 in the same MS) contain examples of the change of *m* to *n* but no examples of the loss of *n*.

[14] See LFn 248f.

however, by the operation of analogical processes that eventually resulted in establishing an entirely different distribution that depended on grammatical categories and was independent of phonetic environment. Loss of final *n* preceded the addition of *e* in the nominative singular of feminines only in the sense that it began first. In another sense, however, the two changes were contemporary, for the period during which the forms with and without *n* were being redistributed thru the operation of analogical processes included the period during which *e* was being added in the nominative singular of feminine nouns that ended in a consonant in Old English.

The levelling of unaccented post-tonic *a, e, o,* and *u* to a vowel written *e* is, as I have stated above, less clearly reflected in the written forms of the eleventh century MSS than the other three changes we have examined. It is evident that the orthographic and literary tradition of the historical vowels was very strong, for retention of the historical vowels is characteristic even of many of the twelfth century MSS. In that part of MS Laud 636 containing the *Chronicle* up to 1121, in MSS Harleian 6258 and Corpus Christi College Cambridge 303, and in the greater part of MS Bodley 343 the historical vowels *a, o,* and *u* are much more often retained than written *e*. They are more frequently retained than written *e* even in MS Cotton Claudius D 3 written in the first quarter of the thirteenth century. The historical vowels are quite frequently retained but much more frequently written *e* in MSS Hatton 38, Cotton Vespasian D 14, and Cotton Vespasian A 22, in those parts of MS Laud 636 containing the 'Peterborough additions' and in the latter part of MS Bodley 343. In MS Lambeth 487 the historical vowels *a, o,* and *u* are written *e* about as frequently as they are retained.[15]

In view of this graphic stability of the historical unstressed vowels the spellings in eleventh century texts that are positively indicative of levelling are of more importance than the spellings that conform to tradition. It is difficult to believe that a scribe would even occasionally have written *e* for the back vowels *a, o,* or *u* unless Old English unaccented *a, e, o,* and *u* had been merged into one uniform vowel in his own speech. Yet we find the back vowels *a, o,* and *u* written *e* with more or less frequency in thirty of the texts we have examined. These texts are the following:

4 texts (14, 101, 104, and 108) that show evidence of the change of *m* to *n* but not of the loss of *n* or of the addition of *e* in the feminine nominative singular;

11 texts (22, 23, 39, 40, 43, 50, 51, 57, 78, 79, and 83) that show evidence of the loss of *n* but not of the addition of *e* in the feminine nominative singular;

[15] The MSS referred to are those containing the texts listed in LFn 235f. The *Fragments* in the Worcester MS is the only text in the list that has *e* almost exclusively for OE *a, o,* and *u*. My statements as to the relative frequency of the spellings are only a very rough estimate based on a sample of one or two pages in each text.

15 texts (12, 13, 20, 24, 25, 31, 37, 38, 41, 46, 56, 65, 66, 68, and 80) that show evidence of the addition of *e* in the feminine nominative singular.[16a]

This evidence is very far from being conclusive as to the chronological position of levelling relative to the other three changes. But if we accept the hypothesis that the change of *m* to *n* preceded the loss of *n* and that the loss of *n* preceded the addition of *e* in the feminine nominative singular the evidence I have cited indicates that levelling of the unaccented vowels did not precede the change of *m* to *n*. The evidence also seems to me difficult to reconcile with the hypothesis that levelling was contemporary with the addition of *e* in the feminine nominative singular, for there are too many texts that show evidence of levelling without showing evidence of the addition of *e* in feminines. The hypothesis that best fits the evidence cited would seem to be that levelling of unaccented vowels preceded the addition of *e* in the nominative singular of feminines and was contemporary with the earlier stages of the loss of final *n*.

Some additional evidence as to the relative chronology of levelling may be derived from the spellings of forms that show the change of *m* to *n* and of forms that show loss of final *n*, as given in my Appendix [see eds. note above].

The *-um* forms that show evidence of the change of *m* to *n* are spelled *un, on, an,* or *en*. The distribution of the different spellings in the three classes of texts is approximately as follows:

	uN	oN	aN	eN
Texts that show evidence of the change of *m* to *n* only	2	82	123	1
Texts that show evidence of loss of *n* but not of addition of *e* in feminines		75	118	3
Texts that show evidence of the addition of *e* in feminines	4	54	168	6
Total	6	211	409	10

This evidence again seems to show that levelling of unaccented vowels did not precede the change of *m* to *n* but to throw little or no light on the relative chronology of levelling and the other two changes. But the fact that the proportion of *an* spellings is so much greater in the third group of texts than in the first and second seems additional evidence that the loss of *n* preceded the addition of *e* in the feminine nominative singular. For the *on*-forms and the *an*-forms reflect successive stages in the processes of weakening of unstressed *u* and the ratio of *on* spellings to *an* spellings in the three groups is respectively .66, .64, and .32.

[16a] Number 24 is in MS Corpus Christi College Cambridge 303, the twelfth century text referred to in the preceding paragraph.

The forms that show evidence of the loss of *n* are variously spelled *u, o, a,* or *e*. The distribution of these different spellings of the Old English endings *um, on,* and *an* in the two classes of texts is approximately as follows:[16b]

	u	o	a	e
Texts that show evidence of the loss of *n* but not of the addition of *e* in feminines			30	17
Texts that show evidence of the addition of *e* in feminines	1	1	60	54
Total	1	1	90	71

The proportion of *e* spellings to *u, o,* and *a* spellings is decidedly greater in the texts that show evidence of the addition of *e* in feminines than in the texts that do not, the ratio being .87 and .57 respectively for the two groups. The substantially smaller proportion of *e* spellings in the texts that do not show evidence of the addition of *e* in feminines seems again to confirm the hypothesis that loss of *n* was earlier than the addition of *e* in the nominative singular of feminines. As to the relative chronology of levelling and the other two changes the evidence is still very far from being conclusive but seems harder to reconcile with the hypothesis that levelling was contemporary with the addition of *e* in feminines than with the hypothesis that it preceded that change.

It seems fairly clear that levelling of unaccented vowels was later than the change of *m* to *n*. And it seems rather probable that levelling was completed before the addition of *e* in the nominative singular of feminines. The evidence I have presented is not complete enough and not exact enough to make possible a more definite determination of the chronology.[17] For convenience, however, I shall assume as fact the probability that the completion of levelling was contemporary with the earlier stages of the loss of final *n* and preceded the addition of *e* in feminines and I shall point out in a footnote the modification that must be made in my argument if later investigation fails to confirm my assumption.

The change of *m* to *n* and the levelling of unaccented post-tonic *a, e, o,* and *u* were clearly sound-changes.[18] In its earlier stages the loss of final

[16b] I have not counted among the *e* spellings those that occur in present and preterit subjunctive forms and the past participles of strong verbs, which ended in *en* in OE.

[17] The evidence is incomplete because of the indefiniteness of the criterion that those texts show evidence of levelling in which the back vowels are written *e* 'with more or less frequency'. Some more objective criterion is needed, e.g. that two (or three) such spellings occur in 1000 words of text. I believe that the application of such a criterion to the texts I have used might show that there are rather more than 30 texts that show evidence of levelling. It would also make possible a crude quantitative treatment of the data that might very well show differences great enough to be significant.

[18] According to Luick (*Historische grammatik der englischen sprache* 303, 491) and Jordan (*Handbuch der mittelenglischen grammatik* 128, 152) the change of *m* to *n* in the dative ending *um* was not the result of sound-change but of analogy. Their

n was a combinative sound-change; in its later stages analogical processes cooperated with sound-change in establishing the distribution of forms with and without *n* that we find at the end of the twelfth century. The addition of *e* in the nominative singular of the feminine *jō*-stems and the long feminine *ō*-stems cannot have been the result of a sound-change but must be assumed to have resulted from the operation of analogical processes. It therefore remains for us to inquire *what* analogical processes operated and why they should have operated at this period and not earlier.

The nominative and accusative plural forms were identical in all the Old English types of noun inflection. The nominative and accusative singular forms were also identical in all neuter nouns and in all masculine nouns except the *n*-stems (e.g. nominative singular *hunta,* accusative singular *huntan*). But the nominative and accusative singular of the short feminine *ō*-stems, the long feminine *ō*-stems, the feminine *jō*-stems, and the feminine *n*-stems were distinctive in form (e.g. nominative singular *lufu, hwīl, synn, tunge*; accusative singular *lufe, hwīle, synne, tungan*). These four types of inflection included such a preponderating majority of all the feminine nouns that distinctiveness of form in the nominative and accusative singular was very stable in Old English. In fact even the feminine *i*-stems, whose nominative singular and accusative singular were identical in early Old English, tended in late Old English to conform to the pattern of the *jō*-stems and the long *ō*-stems as a result of an analogical process that may be expressed by the proportion:

---

argument is concerned solely with showing that the change was *not* sound-change, not with showing that it *was* an analogical development. Luick's treatment of the point is more discriminating than Jordan's. For Jordan cites as part of his evidence that *m* 'bleibt in allen stellungen lautgesetzlich erhalten, auch im auslaut' the words *bosom, bottom, fathom,* etc., which are obviously irrelevant to the discussion because the *m* was protected in the final position by its retention in the inflected forms. The only words offered as evidence in Luick's discussion are Middle English *hwilom* and the place-name *Downham* (Middle English *Dounum*). Now *hwilon* is much commoner in the eleventh century texts than *hwilum* (there are more than 25 examples of *hwilon* in my Appendix) and the earliest Middle English references for *hwilom* in Middle English in the *Oxford Dictionary* are Orm, and *Kentish Sermons.* There is therefore good reason for accepting Jespersen's view (*Modern English Grammar,* I. 2. 414) that the final *m* of *hwilom* does not come from the Old English dative plural ending but developed (like *m* in *venom, ransom,* etc.) from earlier Middle English *n.* Jespersen's discussion is well supplemented by Holthausen's note (*Anglia Beiblatt,* 31. 137f.), which points out that final *m* in all the words under discussion can be explained as due either to 'assimilation at a distance' (e.g. *pilgrim*) or to dissimilation in syllables that began and ended with a dental. The difficulties in the way of regarding the change of *m* to *n* as a sound-change are therefore chiefly imaginary ones. Even if there were real difficulties in the way of so regarding it they would have to be very serious indeed to justify us in attributing the change to analogy. The analogical change according to Luick was from *um* to *un* (or *on*), which was later weakened to *an;* according to Jordan it was from *um* to *on.* What analogical process could have displaced the ending *um* by an ending *un* which does not occur in Old English at all? Or by the ending *on* which occurs only as a plural ending of verbs? We have a right to ask that those who hold this theory shall explain *what* analogical process could have operated to produce this result.

dǣde (acc. sing.) : dǣd (nom. sing.) : : hwīle : hwīl
synne : synn[19]

After loss of final *n* had occurred in unaccented syllables, however, the nominative and accusative singular of the masculine *n*-stems became identical (e.g. *hunta-hunta* instead of the older *hunta-huntan*). And after the levelling of unaccented vowels the nominative and accusative singular of the feminine *n*-stems and the short feminine *ō*-stems also became identical (e.g. *tunge-tunge, lufe-lufe* instead of the older *tunge-tungan, lufu-lufe*). Thus the formal distinction between nominative and accusative singular in the feminine nouns ending in a consonant (the *jō*-stems and the long *ō*-stems) was no longer supported by distinctiveness of form in any of the other types of noun inflection and the analogy of the other inflectional types operated. This analogy may be expressed by the following proportion:

hwīle (nom. s.)	:	hwīle (acc. s.)	: :	lufe	(nom. s.)	:	lufe	(acc. s.)	
synne (nom. s.)	:	synne (acc. s.)	: :	tunge	" "	:	tunge	" "	[20]
				hunte	" "	:	hunte	" "	
				ēage	" "	:	ēage	" "	

synne (nom. s.)	:	synne (acc. s.)	: :	ende	(nom. s.)	:	ende	(acc. s.)	
				rīce	" "	:	rīce	" "	
				sune	" "	:	sune	" "	
				dure	" "	:	dure	" "	
				dǣd	" "	:	dǣd	" "	[21]
				wulf	" "	:	wulf	" "	
				lim	" "	:	lim	" "	
				word	" "	:	word	" "	[22]

[19] In the proportions given here and later the analogical formation is indicated by italics.

[20] I wish to point out here a formal contradiction between this proportion and the first proportion in LFn 253. In LFn the nominative singular form *hwīle* is used as one of the elements in a proportion that is intended to show that the *n*-less form of the dative and accusative singular *hunte* (and by implication *tunge*) was supported by the analogy of five other types of noun inflection and that this analogy tended to accelerate the loss of *n*. In the proportion given here the *n*-less forms of *hunte* and *tunge* are themselves used as elements of a proportion that is intended to account for *hwīle* itself. Obviously the nominative singular form *hwīle* was not available until it came into use. The *n*-less forms of *hunte* and *tunge* were available as part of the analogical material that favored the development of *hwīle,* however, for loss of *n* preceded the analogical change. And after the nominative singular form *hwīle* had developed, it still further strengthened the analogical support that favored the *n*-less form of *hunte* and *tunge*.

[21] The analogical accusative singular form *dǣde* (see above) did not completely displace the earlier form *dǣd;* both survived in late Old English. The older accusative form *dǣd* was one of the elements in the inflectional system that favored the development of the analogical nominative forms *hwīle* and *synne*. But on the basis of the later accusative singular *dǣde* there developed by analogy a new nominative singular form *dǣde*.

It is evident that these analogical processes could not have begun to operate until loss of final *n* occurred and that they could not have operated fully until levelling of unaccented vowels was completed.[23] It is also evident that the operation of these analogical processes was practically inevitable after the stability of the traditional inflectional patterns had become so radically modified by the sound-changes that had taken place in unaccented syllables.

[22] The words *lufe,* etc., represent the following types of noun inflection: short feminine *ō*-stems; feminine, masculine, and neuter *n*-stems; masculine and neuter *ja*-stems, masculine and feminine *u*-stems, feminine *i*-stems, masculine *a*-stems, short neuter *a*-stems, and long neuter *a*-stems. The very great majority of all the Old English nouns were declined according to one or other of the types of inflection included in the proportion and the nominative and accusative singular were identical in all the types not included except the feminine *wō*-stems, e.g. *sceadu* and *mæd*. The development of these is complicated by certain factors that do not enter into the development of the feminine *i*-stems, *jō*-stems, and long *ō*-stems but in principle is the same.

[23] If the addition of *e* in the feminine nominative singular began before the levelling of unaccented vowels was completed the analogical process would not have had the support of the types *lufe-lufe* and *tunge-tunge* but would have had that of all the other types included in the proportion.

The Morphemic Evolution of Middle English She

ROBERT D. STEVICK

To SEEK AGAIN FOR SOLUTION to the perennial puzzle of the origin of English *she,* it will be well to begin with the most certain fact in the historical context: the nominative feminine third person (singular) pronoun first appeared with a new initial consonant in the Northeast Midlands and adjacent areas, with the clearest evidence from Lincolnshire and Yorkshire. It is also certain that the pronoun did not undergo similar consonantal reshaping in other major dialect areas, and the presence of *she, sho* (and other forms) in other dialects—including the Standard dialect as it developed—is attributable to dialect borrowing. We have to do with a local development. Evidence is sufficient to indicate as well that the *she* or *sho* form was neither a reshaping of the feminine singular nominative demonstrative nor a hybrid development of the demonstrative and personal pronouns. The a priori improbability of either process is sustained especially by the continuous record of *The Peterborough Chronicle*: the *seo* form was obsolete before *scæ,* (Orm) *ȝho* and other forms occurred. Rather, the new [ʃ-] forms developed by modification of the personal pronoun form of prior stages of English. This is the position taken by most investigators since Flom's article in 1908.[1]

So far explanation of the change by which *she, sho* replaced *heo, hie* has been sought solely within the storehouse of phonological facts and processes: development of [ʃ-] forms replacing earlier [h-] forms has been accounted for by reconstructing a credible phonological sequence. Because this particular change in the pronoun occurred in an area known to have had heavy Scandinavian settlement from the latter part of the ninth century (with prominent lexical influence on English in that area), and because no other circumstance—including normal sound change of English—has been found to connect the change to, the change

Reprinted by permission from *English Studies* 45.381-88 (1964).

[1] G. T. Flom, 'The Origin of the Pronoun "She",' *JEGP,* VII (1908), 115-125.

is attributed to influence of Scandinavian pronunciation of English. Where English had falling diphthongs, it is pointed out, Old Norse had rising diphthongs. Assuming a stress shift *héo* > *heó, hío* > *hió,* or in some instances *híe* > *hié,* it can be argued—with support from place-names and a few other localisms—that [hέ-], [í-] > [hj́-], > [ḉ-], which was interpreted then as [ʃ-]. This 'Shetland' theory implies that Scandinavians heard English *héo* as *hjó,* and the English heard Scandinavian *hjó* as [ço:], and pronounced it as [ʃo:]. But the advocate's resolution is required to keep the argument intact, because the initial assumption about shifting of stress in diphthongs is not free from doubt.[2] Gordon,[3] for instance, places stress shift of diphthongs in Icelandic at 'c. 850-1000, though in some instances considerably later. The shift took place earliest in diphthongs at the beginning of a word.' (§ 48) Also, 'There was not much blending of Norse and English'—within the Scandinavian-settled areas of England—'during the OE period', (§ 230) when Danish settlements were made in the East Midlands (ninth century) and Norwegian settlements followed in Yorkshire and the northwestern counties (first half of the tenth century). (§ 228) Norse phonology changed little in England, and 'it is clear that the following [change] had not taken place: . . . Except initially, the stress had not been shifted in diphthongs', though *York* = OI. *Jork,* etc. (§ 230) To this uncertainty in the dialect and chronology of Scandinavian language features in England we may add the following. The phonologically credible sequence [h-́] > [hj́-] > [ḉ-], [ʃ́] implies an unusually complex social-linguistic sequence: The English said [h-́]; their Scandinavian conquerors-turned-neighbors, always keeping þ- forms for plural third-person pronouns, at some time began to give up their *h-n* feminine and masculine pronouns and used English forms; the English heard their own stress-shifted pronouns, but kept on for a while using their own pronunciation—long enough for Scandinavians to use English singular pronouns regularly; then, giving up their own pronunciation of the feminine singular nominative form, the English anglicized the Scandinavian pronunciation of their own form. This complicated sequence, though not inconceivable, is not readily credible. Throughout the period in which the two languages were in contact, English continued intact: the English dialects were never creolized. More particularly, the change took place in a word of high frequency of occurrence. That a few place-names and a few other nouns show Scandinavian [hj-] becoming English [ʃ-] is fully conceivable and probable, and there is evidence to show that change of this kind did in fact occur. But the difference between a normal one-step process, beginning with Scandinavian forms and limited to names, and the multi-step process, beginning with an English form—a pronoun—and involving only the one

[2] Cf. Eugen Dieth, '*Hips:* A Geographical Contribution to the "she" Puzzle', *English Studies,* XXXVI (1955), 209-217 (esp. p. 215).

[3] E. V. Gordon, *An Introduction to Old Norse* (Oxford, 1927).

(nominative) form of high frequency, is so great that the parallel of phonetic change in place-names does not qualify as full warrant to postulate the same causal factor (or perhaps the same phonological sequence) for the change in the pronoun.

The reconstructed phonological sequence to account for replacement of *heo* by *she, sho, ʒho,* etc. thus remains unsatisfactory because of uncertainty of concatenating evidence. One other significant attempt to reconstruct phonological circumstances to account for development of *she* also assumes stress-shifted *hjó, hjé,* and posits sandhi occurrences of a preceding dental or alveolar.[4] Besides sharing the questionable assumption of Scandinavian-influenced stress-shift in the diphthong, the theory requires acceptance of a change occurring through a low frequency circumstance. There is no evidence, however, to suggest that the pronoun ever ceased to occur commonly after juncture or, when it occurred without preceding juncture, regularly followed dentals and alveolars. To be satisfying, an historical account of language change must offer both a sequence of linguistic circumstances and data that is credible, and evidence confirming the actual existence of those language facts and their historical relations. If that evidence cannot be found either in attested patterns of phonological change within English or in potential (direct) foreign influences, perhaps it can be found in an area not yet explored for this purpose—in some structural features of those stages of English in which *she* evolved.

Besides occurring with high frequency, the feminine nominative personal pronoun was part of a closed morphological system, not an isolated lexical item like a place-name. The closed personal pronoun system was marked by prominent inflectional regularity—as it still is in modified form[5]—in the paradigmatic prefixes consisting of initial consonants: /h-/ carried the meaning 'third-person singular' (and, perhaps, 'third-person plural'), just as /m-/ and /θ-/ meant 'first-person singular' and 'second-person singular' respectively. From one point of view, then, we must regard replacement of *heo* by *she, sho,* etc. as quite remarkable: substitution of /š-/ for /h-/ disturbed the entire pattern of personal pronoun inflections. Feminine pronouns in case forms other than nominative did not change in this respect, retaining the third-person /h-/ inflection. Both frequency and paradigmatic factors demand therefore an historical account of this unusual change that observes the strictest conditions of unobtrusiveness for innovation.

The various spellings for the pronoun clearly indicate that prior to the [ʃ-]-status of the initial consonant there was a [ç-] stage.[6] The reason

[4] Cf. H. Lindqvist, 'On the Origin and History of the English Pronoun *she*', *Anglia,* XLV (1921), 1-50.

[5] See, for example, Archibald A. Hill, *Introduction to Linguistic Structures* (New York, 1958), pp. 145-150.

[6] See Flom and Dieth, cited above, and such others as Henry Cecil Wyld, *A Short History of English,* third edition (New York, 1927), §§302, 303, 307.

commonly offered for the change, that [ç-] came to be heard as [ʃ-], is probably only partly right. At any rate, the phonological circumstances can be restated precisely in phonemic terms and must be so stated if the explanation of *heo* > *she, sho,* etc. is to be improved. The pronoun had an *h*-element as its inflectional prefix, and initial inflection was never in process of 'decay'. The allophones of /h/ could vary in position over a wide range, because there were no other phonemes both acoustically and distributionally similar: the clustering characteristics of /h/ and the spirants /f θ s/ were similar in word-initial position, for example, but /h/ did not occur in postvocalic position; /x/, with allophones having some phonetic resemblance to some /h/ allophones, occurred only in postvocalic position. Thus, under conditioning by the following vowel (or consonant), /h/ occurred as voiceless spirant articulated as glottal, velar, or palatal. (It could even overlap acoustically with palatal allophones of /x/ and remain distinct because of their different distributional features.) In short, [ç-] would not be perceived as an aberration in the /h-/ structure of third-person pronouns.

That the same conditions may have existed in other dialects without producing the same ultimate result of /š-/ is not relevant, since orthogenetic progress in language is not a concept that can be sustained by language history. But the circumstances of unique shift in the initial consonant phoneme of the pronoun suggests that still other characteristics of the speech areas of its occurrence should be examined. The consonant system in Yorkshire, Lincolnshire, and adjacent areas seems to have been much the same as in other dialect areas prior to the change in the feminine pronoun from *h-* to *sh-*. Yet, if Scandinavian speech did not materially influence the number and phonetic manifestation of individual consonants, or the formal structure of English,[7] it did contribute many lexical items to English. The clearest types are those having *sk-*, because the divergence of OE and ON is complete in this respect—OE having regularly developed *sh-* /š-/. A large number of Scandinavian words entered English between 1050 and 1150,[8] with a sufficient number beginning in *sk-* to establish, within the areas of heavy Scandinavian settlement, a type of initial consonant cluster that had disappeared when OE /sk-/ merged to produce the new /š-/. Assimilation into English of the initial cluster /sk-/, through adoption of many words which were common and cognate with English words, caused significant reorganization of distributional features of spirant and palatal phonemes. Earlier /spr- str- skr-/ had developed into /spr- str-/ and /šr-/, without any change in distribution of /šr-/; likewise, earlier /sp- st- sk-/ had had its third member replaced by /š-/, which also did not change in distribution. Meanwhile the clustering patterns of other consonants did not change in

[7] Joseph Wright and Elizabeth Mary Wright, *An Elementary Middle English Grammar,* second edition (Oxford, 1928), §162.
[8] *Ibid.,* §§159.5, 161.

general outline—Orm, for example, showing loss only of infrequent /fn- hn- gn-/ of OE and addition of only /šr-/. When, however, lexical borrowings from Scandinavian established /skr-/ and /sk-/ in English, these clusters patterned with the other three- and two-member initial clusters, with the results that /š-/ patterned with single consonants in prevocalic position—with /f θ s/—or with spirant + *r* clusters already established in the language. Postjunctural prevocalic /š/ began to be distributionally a spirant. The change in the assignment of [c-] from /h/ to /š/ in the feminine nominative pronoun could thus occur less obtrusively than in other dialect areas or at earlier times.

This restatement of the phonological circumstances within which *heo* > *she, sho* makes it plausible to regard the replacement of the initial consonant as change by allophone rather than, say, change by borrowing or analogy. It also connects the fact that the feminine nominative pronominal [ç-] was reassigned to /š/ rather than continuing as an allophone of /h/ to regional dialect facts of date, phonology, and distinct foreign influence. It shows why the change should have occurred when and where it did. But it in no way explains why it did in fact occur.

The cause of the change may be sought in morphological aspects of the dialects of LOE and EME. The paradigmatic frame of pronouns, though it was in process of modification for case distinctions (merger of accusative with dative forms), persisted without change of gender distinctions, as well as person and number distinctions. Gender distinctions had always been functional in English as indicating either the sex of the referent or the non-significance of sex-distinction of the referent; choice of personal pronoun form was referentially determined—i.e., it was based regularly on circumstances of the physical context; by contrast, choice of members of the *se, seo, þæt* paradigm, with parallel gender forms, had been only grammatically determined. Number and person distinctions also had functional relations with the context of utterances as well as with the patterns of the utterances themselves. It is the persistence of this paradigmatic frame—the structural pattern of distinctions among personal pronoun forms—that seems to have been the ultimate cause of the evolution of Middle English *she, sho.*

It was not, however, the inconvenience or confusion of homophony of some of the feminine singular and the plural forms that led to modification of the feminine nominative pronoun, as has sometimes been suggested. The potentional confusion of these forms probably did not occur nearly so often as comparison of abstracted paradigms may lead us to suppose. That *heo, hie,* etc. served in some dialects as nominative singular feminine and nominative plural would cause no difficulty so long as verb inflections showed number distinction. Dative forms were different, in *-r(e)* and *-m*. OE genitive forms had been different, in *-e* and *-a,* and as possessive adjectives in OE and ME, physical context or antecedents would usually keep them clearly apart; *hir* and *her* (e.g., in *Sir*

Orfeo) could have established the contrast; or confusion from homophony was prevented in many instances by the rapidly developing 'periphrastic genitive', in which object-case pronouns *h-r* and *h-m* (after *of*) contrasted. Potential confusion of plural and feminine accusative forms, if not prevented by context, either physical or grammatical, rapidly decreased as dative and accusative forms of all pronouns leveled under dative.

That the confusion of feminine singular and of plural personal pronouns was never serious could hardly ask better evidence than both the long persistence of *h*-forms and the unrelated way in which feminine and plural pronouns diverged from *h*-forms. The fact that only the nominative form of the feminine pronoun underwent change of initial consonant, with other case forms retaining inflectional *h-*, while all plural forms eventually developed /θ-/ *þ-*, *th-* forms (i.e., allomorphs, beside /h-/, later Ø-, allomorphs such as *'em* that persisted into NE) clearly shows that the causes of the respective changes were different. The processes were also different, in that the new plural forms were borrowed, while the feminine form was not. But whatever the process, development of new plural forms manifests the persistence of the singular-plural contrast alone. The change to /θ-/ forms was no more necessary when it occurred than it had been throughout the prior history of English; without altering the basic case (suffix) inflections /-Ø -r -m/, it merely provided an expression of number distinction in the initial (inflectional) phoneme, utilizing that inflectional position for number rather than solely for person (and incidentally regularizing first, second, third person inflectional patterns in this respect). The entire change is consistent with the tendency to develop a plural morpheme in nouns and nominals in this stage of English.

On the other hand, development of feminine /š-/ manifests the persistence of gender contrast alone. The earlier pronoun {he•o} had had a number of allomorphs; in most dialects the frequent form was /he•o/ but in Mercian and Northumbrian dialects it was /hi•o hi•w hi•e/ as well as morphs without lengthened /i/.[9] The following /i•/ or /i/ would have conditioned occurrence of the [ç] allophone of /h/ dealt with above. Also, the contrast between allomorphs of masculine {he•} and feminine {he•o} was always clear. The subsequent change by which /e•o/ (or perhaps /e•w/) > /ö•/ in Anglian (and West Saxon) dialects probably maintained the conditioning under which /h/ was phonetically [ç]. The fact that during the twelfth to fourteenth centuries both {šo•} and {še•} developed in West Midland and East Midland dialects supports this inference; so does survival of modern dialectal [ʃu:].[10] But monophthongization of *ēo* left a contrast between nominative masculine and feminine forms only in /e•/ *vs.* /ö•/, or, as was very soon the case in a few dialects,

[9] Cf. A. Campbell, *Old English Grammar* (Oxford, 1959), §703.
[10] Cf. Joseph Wright, *The English Dialect Grammar* (Oxford, 1905), §406.

the forms were left temporarily without regular contrast. Only two means were available to distinguish these two pronouns, short of borrowing a new form: contrast in the vocalic segment or contrast in the consonantal segment. Each method of differentiation was in fact followed in one dialect or another, and in the case of *sho* both were utilized. Vocalic contrast was already operative in some dialects to distinguish masculine *he* from plural *hi. The Peterborough Chronicle* (Second Continuation)[11] shows masculine *he,* feminine *scæ,* plural *hi.* Elsewhere, Orm has *he, ȝho, þeȝȝ; Bestiary* has *he, ge, he; Genesis and Exodus* has *he, she / sge / ge / ghe, he; Havelok* has *he, she / sho, þeī;* and so on. In short, once the masculine-feminine distinction by V *vs.* Vv was obscured, the /e•/ *vs.* /ö•/ contrast apparently was not sufficiently dependable to distinguish the two forms, and clearly contrasting allophones of /h/ and /š/ or /ė•/ and /o•/ (or in some instances both) were selected to keep communication efficient. That nominative morphs of pronouns often occur with light stress—certainly with less distinctness than citation forms—would have made potential confusion all the more likely, a circumstance under which more distinct allophones would tend to be selected.

Once the /š-/ forms were established, the analogical circumstances of nominative *he* and *þei/þeȝ* etc. and the increasing dominance of East Midland speech are sufficient to account for the displacement of *sho* by *she* wherever the two existed as allomorphs.

The empirical law of sound change occurring independently of morphological functions is in no way contradicted by the preceding hypothesis about the evolution of Middle English *she.* At the same time, the change in the English feminine nominative pronoun can not be referred to the attested regular patterns of phonological change in the language, a fact that sent philologists to Norse stress-shifts of diphthongs and models of blends or sandhi to try to account for the change. But explanations by the latter procedures, however exhaustively they are pursued, remain unsatisfactory, as we have seen. The final matter to consider, therefore, is whether the explanation developed above is superior to any offered heretofore.

The hypothesis is constructed from evidence that is unquestioned—the tested forms and the standard phonological interpretations of written records. In several ways, however, the evidence is analyzed differently. The phonemic and morphemic formulation is the first difference. A second is the extrapolation from the longer stretch of linguistic history of the kinds of change in progress in the entire system of personal pronouns (and nouns): the development of a plural (initial) inflectional morpheme, on the one hand, and the development of an acoustically distinct allomorph for the nominative feminine pronoun. A third is formulation of conditions of unobtrusiveness for the change, recognizing the frequency of the pronoun form and the initial inflectional morpheme /h-/

[11] Ed. Cecily Clark (Oxford, 1958).

that conditioned the shift by allophones. Fourth, identification—or assumption—of the persisting paradigmatic frame functioning as a selective factor for phonological and morphological variants and thus ultimately causing emergence of the distinctively new pronoun forms. The concept of an active selective function of what has been called a paradigmatic frame does not serve teleological explanation of linguistic history. On the contrary, its use allows us to explain the rise of either *she* or *sho* or *ho* or any other attested form. Neither is it formulated as an hypostatization that could equally well be labeled 'the will of the people' or 'the Genius of the Language'. In so far as its locus or substance can be described briefly, it is merely the linguistic habits of expectation and utterance of members of a speech community, the same conservative behavioral factor that accounts for continuity and coherence in any persisting language features. It is the same concept that must operate in explanation of other changes in the language, including that series of changes going on during the generations in which *she* evolved—the development of the distinct (segmentable) plural morpheme for nouns where there had not been one in OE, as well as to the short-lived plural morpheme /-e/ for adjectives.[12] Finally, the explanation here proffered does not require reference to the dubious intermediate step of Scandinavian *hjó* or the insufficient *was-hjó* type of circumstance. In sum, this hypothesis describes a credible linguistic sequence constructed from attested data, designates a causal factor, and avoids dependence on untestable assumptions.

If the conditions assumed by the 'Shetland' theory actually existed, or if sandhi conditions were influential, they may have supplied the cue, may have reinforced or modified the direction of a tendency, for the replacement of /h-/ by /š-/. But the evolution of Middle English *she* was caused and conditioned by the structure of the English dialects themselves.

[12] It was sufficient to differentiate demonstratives into singular and plural *this-these* and sustain the system to be filled by *that-tho/those*.

The Conflict of Homonyms in English

ROBERT J. MENNER

I

THE STUDIES OF GILLIÉRON and his followers in linguistic geography have made us familiar with the doctrine that two words of different origin which become homonyms by regular sound-changes may interfere with one another to such an extent that one is ultimately excluded from the vocabulary of a given dialect. The lack of a linguistic atlas of England has prevented the application of this principle, and likewise of others expounded by Gilliéron, to English dialects. For it was the comparison of maps which enabled Gilliéron and Roques to show, for example, that only in those French dialects where *mulgere* would have become homonymous with *molere,* is it replaced by other words for 'milk', such as *tirer, traire, ajuster, aria, blechi,* etc.[1] Although neat demonstration of this sort is seldom possible in English, conclusions about the conflict of homonyms may sometimes be reached, in the absence of an atlas, by more roundabout methods. Enough information for reasonable deductions may be obtained from the combined materials of the English Dialect Dictionary, which gives the distribution of a large part of the vocabulary in modern dialects, and the New English Dictionary, which gives a detailed semantic history and the approximate time of a word's disappearance from the language.

The studies hitherto made of the subject have been based almost exclusively on the NED. Several pupils of Holthausen have considered

---

Reprinted by permission from *Language* 12.229-44 (1936).

[1] Jules Gilliéron and Mario Roques, Études de Géographie Linguistique 10-18 (Paris, 1912).

the development of homonyms among other causes of the loss of words, such as the disappearance of the object or idea itself and the substitution of words from other languages of different or superior culture. More recently, Jaeschke, in a subtler analysis of the causes of obsolescence, included the conflict of homonyms, considering English words in the volumes of the NED (T-Z) which were not available to his predecessors.[2] In general, it may be said that most of those who have discussed the principle with reference to English have either rejected it too summarily, on the ground that it was disproved by the continued existence in English of such homonyms as *lie* 'prevaricate' and *lie* 'recline' and the two adjectives *light*;[3] or have applied it uncritically by assuming that when one of two homonyms was lost, it must have been lost because of homonymy. This is a dangerous method in a language that has suffered so many changes in vocabulary as English. There were, for example, four Old English words of the form *ār*: *ār,* masc. 'messenger', *ār* fem. 'honor', *ār* neut. 'bronze', 'copper', represented in modern *ore,* and *ar* masc. 'oar'. The first two words no longer exist in Modern English. Now if we examine the number of words that have disappeared from the Old English

[2] Holthausen in Germanisch-romanische Monatschrifte 7.184-96, summarises the results of four dissertations by his students: Emil W. Hemken, Das Aussterben alter Substantiva im Verlaufe der englischen Sprachgeschichte, Kiel, 1906; Johannes R. W. Offe, Das Aussterben alter Verba und ihr Ersatz im Verlaufe der englischen Sprachgeschichte, etc., Kiel, 1908; Wilhelm Oberdörffer, Das Aussterben altenglischer Adjektive, etc., Kiel, 1908; Friedrich Teichert, Über das Aussterben alter Wörter im Verlaufe der englischen Sprachgeschichte, Kiel, 1912. Teichert is more doubtful of the importance of 'lautlicher Zusammenfall' (46-7) than the others, and Holthausen (196) apparently shares his skepticism. Henry Bradley, whose work on the NED made him aware of certain conflicts, mentions the subject, On the Relations between Spoken and Written Language, 24-5 (Oxford, 1919) ; and Leonard Bloomfield, who treats several aspects of homonymy, gives some good English examples of interference, Language 396, 398 (New York, 1933) . Sir Robert Bridges, On English Homophones, Society for Pure English, Tract II, Oxford, 1919, is interesting, but unscientific; cf. Edwin B. Dike, 'Obsolete Words', JEGP 34.356-7. Kurt Jaeschke's Beiträge zur Frage des Wortschwundes im Englischen, Sprache und Kultur der germanischen und romanischen Völker, Anglistische Reihe 6, Breslau, 1931, is the best treatment; but most examples are discussed in summary fashion.

That the validity of Gilliéron's principle has been generally accepted by students of French dialects is evident from Karl Jaberg's Sprachgeographie, Aarau, 1908, and the discussions in such handbooks as Albert Dauzat's La géographie linquistique, Paris, 1922, and Ernst Gamillscheg's Die Sprachgeographie und ihre Ergebnisse für die allgemeine Sprachwissenschaft, Neuphilologische Handbibliothek für die westeuropäischen Kulturen und Sprachen 2, Bielefeld and Leipzig, 1928. For German dialects see Adolf Bach, Deutsche Mundartforschung, 108-10 (Heidelberg, 1934) . For criticism of the hypothesis and a not very successful attempt to explain the process of elimination in homonymic conflicts, see Elise Richter, Über Homonymie, Festschrift für . . . Paul Kretschmer 167-201 (Wien-Leipzig, 1926) . For Latin examples, see Roland G. Kent, "No Trespass" in Latin Linguistics, Classical Studies in Honor of John C. Rolfe 143-61, (Philadelphia, 1931) . B. Trnka's interesting Bemerkungen zur Homonymie. Travaux du Cercle Linguistique de Prague 4.152-6, I had not seen when this article was written, but I comment on it in two notes below.

[3] Cf. below [259].

vocabulary without any possible influence of homonymy, we find that it is well over fifty per cent. Thus of any four words, homonyms, or not homonyms, two might easily have disappeared for other reasons. Actually, in the case of *ār,* there would be little reason to suppose, as does Hemken,[4] that a noun denoting a person would be confused with an abstract noun, and neither is likely to succumb to the competition of two nouns denoting objects.

If one of two words that became or would have become homonyms has been lost, the loss should not be attributed to this fact without observing several rules of caution. The first is that two homonyms are unlikely to interfere unless they belong to the same part of speech: a verb is unlikely to conflict with a noun or a noun with an adjective. It is a priori improbable that OE *earm,* 'poor', 'wretched', disappeared because of *earm,* 'arm'. Usually the homonyms must also have the same syntactic function, and be capable of being used in the same construction. *Cleave* 'sunder' (OE *clēofan*) is usually transitive and *cleave* 'adhere' (OE *cleofian, clifian*) intransitive, but even when the former is used intransitively, as it sometimes is, it is distinguished from the second verb by the fact that the latter is always accompanied by a preposition, in Modern English *(un)to.* A second condition is that the words must fall within the same sphere of ideas and be likely to appear in similar contexts. An exception to this rule is the case of a word that would be avoided because its homonym was vulgar or in some way ludicrous; the avoidance of *ass,* because of the popular pronunciation of *arse,* cited by Bloomfield,[5] would be a case in point.

When these two conditions are fulfilled, it is possible for a combination of sounds representing two different words to become embarrassingly ambiguous, and the resultant confusion may be so marked as to lead to the elimination of one of the words. But even when a homonym has been lost under these conditions, it is hard to prove that homonymy was the determining cause. It is obvious that other and more usual causes of obsolescence must first be ruled out; and this is not easy because they are often obscure and elusive. Some indication of the probabilities may be obtained by a comparison of the chronology of sound-changes and the time of the disappearance of a word. If a word is lost or begins to be less frequently used after the sound-change resulting in homonymy takes place, this may confirm a suspicion that phonetic identity was a factor involved. Conversely, if one of two words which would have become homonymous in Modern English is proved by the NED's records to have disappeared as early as Middle English, the influence of homonymy is automatically eliminated. When all these cautions are observed, the influence of homonyms on the loss of words may sometimes be reasonably inferred. Actual proof, however, is possible only when it can be shown

[4] Page 30.
[5] Language 396.

that a word has disappeared in dialects where by normal sound-changes it became identical with another, but has been preserved in dialects where by normal development the two words remained different.

An illustration of the importance of consulting dialects may be seen in the homonyms *queen, quean.*[6] Modern English *queen* and *quean* (archaic, obsolescent) are, of course, two different words, though ultimately related by ablaut: OE *cwēn,* 'queen', 'princess'; and OE *cwene* 'woman', 'servant', 'harlot'. In Middle English, in spite of the lengthening of the short *e* in open syllables to [ɛ:], the two words are still easily distinguishable because close and open long *e* remain two different phonemes; the author of Piers Plowman can use the two words in the same line (C 9.45). A vocalic distinction was still maintained in the sixteenth century, when [e:] had been raised to [i:] and [ɛ:] to [e:]; and the word *quean* is still familiar to us from Shakespeare. But when, around 1700, the [e:] of *quean* (ME [ɛ:]) also became raised to [i:], it proved impossible for the same sounds [kwi:n] to continue to represent both a royal personage and the commonest kind of woman, and the word *quean* disappears from spoken Standard English. It might be suspected that *quean* 'low woman', 'harlot' is the kind of word which would be subject to replacement in any case because of euphemism. But a survey of the distribution of *quean* in English dialects clearly corroborates the view that confusion with *queen* is the cause of its disappearance. *Quean,* according to Wright's Dialect Dictionary, does not occur in the larger part of the Midlands, especially the East Midlands, and the Southeast, the territory in which ME [e:] and [ɛ:] fell together as they did in Standard English. In a Southwestern area which includes Somerset and Devon the two Middle English sounds remain distinct;[7] and, according to Wright, we find that *quean* 'low woman', 'harlot' is still a living word in Somerset and Devon. The evidence in the North, where initial *wh-* is often substituted for *qu-* in *quean,* and in Scotland, where *quean* has lost its evil meaning, is too complicated for presentation here, but it confirms the other evidence.[8]

When dialectal variants are not available, the case for the conflict of homonyms is less clear; but it may sometimes be reasonably inferred from the history of words in Standard English. In Middle English there were three verbs of the form *aleg(g)e* and three of the form *alaye.* Their interactions may be summarized in Table 1 on the basis of the NED's material.

Alegge[3] would probably have disappeared of itself, just as *lay* and *say*

[6] Bradley 24, said that 'when *queen* and *quean* came to be pronounced alike, it was inevitable that the latter should become obsolete as a spoken word.' He was considering only Standard English.

[7] Karl Luick, Hist. Gram. §497.2.

[8] Edna R. Williams in an unpublished dissertation on the conflict of homonyms now provides maps showing the development of *quean-queen* in various dialects, and discusses the interference of the two words more fully.

ETYMOLOGY	ME FORM	ME MEANING
VL **exlitigare* (?) > OF *esligier,* infl. by AN *alegier* < *allegare*	ALEGE[1]	plead, declare
Lat. *alleviare* > OF *aleg(i)er*	*alege*[2]	alleviate
OE *alecgan*	*alegge*[3]	put down, repress
OE *alegð,* 3 sg.pres.ind. of above	ALAYE[1]	put down, repress
Lat. *allegare* > OF *aleier*	*alaye*[2]	allege, declare
Lat. *alligare* > ONF *aleier*	*alaye*[3]	alloy, temper
Lat. *alligare* > OCF *aloier* > Mod F *aloyer*	[*alloy*]	

TABLE 1

triumphed in late Middle English over the less common forms *legge* and *segge* from the infinitive. Before *alegge*[3] disappeared, both the forms *alegge* and *alaye,* from different parts of OE *alecgan* and apparently interchangeable in meaning, took over the meaning of *alege*[2], 'alleviate', which is thus preserved in modern *allay.* Then both *alegge*[3] and *alege*[2] went out of use, the latter in the sixteenth century probably because of conflict with *alege*[1]. *Alaye*[2] disappeared (last quoted in 1470), chiefly because of the triumph of the common legal form *allege,* but partly because of confusion with *alaye*[1] and *alaye*[3]. *Alaye*[1] and *alaye*[3] persisted side by side, though sometimes confused, as the NED shows, because of such a figurative meaning of *alaye*[3] as 'temper', (last quotation 1769) which was very similar to that of *alaye*[1], until *alaye*[3] was replaced in the nineteenth century by *alloy* from Modern French. One can hardly look at the fate of these words without suspecting that phonetic identity played a part in eliminating some of them and left us with distinct forms for different ideas. Only one of the three verbs *alege* survives from Middle English, and only one of the three verbs *alaye.*[9] The survivors are indicated by small capitals in the table.

II

It would not be difficult to multiply examples of the types just given; but my present purpose is not so much to demonstrate the validity of Gilliéron's principle by illustration from English as to suggest various possible applications of the principle which students of English have neglected.

The relation of homonymic interference to the borrowing of French words in English is worth considering. The very abundance of French

[9] I am not here considering how far there was consciousness of separate words in these cases. *Alaye*[1] and *alaye*[3] were apparently sometimes apprehended as two meanings of one word in the eighteenth century. The difference between the lexicographer's and etymologist's conception of the word and that of the ordinary speaker and hearer has, of course, an important bearing on the interference of homonyms, and is touched on below [260-1].

loan-words and the great variety of causes which brought about their introduction[10] make it difficult to be sure of any real conflict among native homonyms that have been lost. Still, when the influence of law, war, religion, cuisine, and other fields in which the political and social dominance of the Normans facilitated borrowing, is not apparent, the reasons for the replacement of common English words by French is often hard to find. Jespersen has a list of common words for the introduction of which he finds no other explanation that that it was considered fashionable to interlard one's speech with French: this includes such words as *cover, cry, turn, use.*[11] Plainly fashion often played a part in the elimination of native words, but it seems quite possible that homonymy at least aided the substitution of French and Latin words for English in some of these cases. Take *cover.* The three commonest words for 'cover' in Old English were *wrēon, helan* and *ðeccan. Đeccan* became limited in early Middle English to a specialized sense of 'cover', i.e. 'thatch', which it was already developing in Old English. *Wrēon* may have been started on its decline by the fact that it was a contract verb, all but the commonest of which have perished. Still, it was used in Middle English, and occasionally survives in modern dialects; but in Middle English it attained the same form as another verb with a variety of meanings, OE *wrīgian,* intr. 'proceed', tr. 'twist', 'turn aside', etc. (the two are discussed in the NED under *wry* v.[1], and *wry* v.[2]). Other words for 'cover', both the strong *helan* and the weak *helian,* 'conceal by covering', likewise fell in with a verb and a very important one *hǣlan* 'heal'.[12] *Hele* is still used in gardeners' language of covering plants, but is no longer an ordinary word for 'cover'; the semantic fullness of ME [hɛːlə] must have proved inconvenient and facilitated the introduction and spread of *cover,* which first appears around 1300.

It is possible for words of French origin, after they have established themselves in the language, to interfere with native words, either because the French loan-word is first used in a specialized sense and only later comes into common use, or, more often, because, although differentiated from the native word at the time of its introduction, it becomes identical with the latter through phonological processes affecting one or the other.[13] Even a slight difference in the endings of two words may be sufficient to prevent confusion for a time. Thus, the commonest native word for 'use'

[10] On this subject see Otto Jespersen's Growth and Structure of the English Language, Chap. V; Robert Feist, Studien zur Rezeption des französischen Wortschatzes im Mittelenglischen, Leipzig, 1934, Beitr. zur engl. Philologie 25; Mary S. Serjeantson, Foreign Words in English, London, 1935, Chap. V.

[11] Growth and Structure[4] 91-2.

[12] Cf. Offe 25.

[13] An illustration of the elimination of a French loan-word, once well established in the language, by a native word which became homonymous with it is the case of archaic *strait* (OF *estreit*) and *straight* (OE *streht*), discussed by Miss Williams. I do not agree with Trnka's contention, Bemerkungen 153, that foreign words in English occupy a peculiar position and do not conflict with homonymous words of native origin.

in early Middle English was *notie* (OE *notian*) which, in the present forms with *-ie* and preterite forms in *-ede,* was distinguished from *note* (pret. *noted*) 'mark', 'observe', from OF *noter,* Lat. *notare.* But when both the differentiating *i* of *notie* and the final *e* of *notede* disappeared in the fourteenth century (earlier in the North), *note* 'use' soon disappeared, while *note* 'mark', 'observe' which had now become a popular word, remained. *Use,* another French word, which was beginning to establish itself in the language in other senses now replaces *note* 'make use of' in this sense,[14] NED's earliest quotation for the meaning 'make use of' being dated 1303. OE *notian,* ME *notie,* 'note' was not the only native word for 'use', 'enjoy'. The related *nyttan* had, however, died out around 1250, probably because the descendants of *notian* were protected by the corresponding noun OE *notu,* ME *note* 'benefit', 'use', 'enjoyment'. Still another word, OE *brūcan,* 'enjoy', 'use', survived in Middle English, but except in the Northern dialect and Scottish, where it is still found today, it became limited in early Middle English to the specialized sense of 'make use of (food)'.[15] Thus neither the descendant of OE *nyttan,* nor that of *brūcan* was in a position to become the ordinary word for 'make use of' at the beginning of the fourteenth century. Although proof is hardly possible in such a case, the combination of circumstances makes one suspect that the homonymy of the native and foreign *note* was one of the factors in establishing *use* as one of the commonest words in our language.

III

The disappearance of certain Old English forms of the personal pronoun provides a good illustration of homophonic conflict, because obscure preferences are much less likely to operate in the case of mere substitutes than in obsolescence of nouns, verbs, and adjectives. Many curious and difficult forms replace the normal descendants of the Old English pronouns. We might expect the development of a variety of forms due to lack of stress; but we find, in addition, the substitution of rare, sporadic forms for those which would have been regular by phonetic law, the occasional adoption of the demonstrative pronoun as the personal, and even numerous borrowings from the pronouns of a foreign language.

Thus, beside such forms for 'she' as *he,* which is a rare form of the Northeast Midland, *heo, ho* [hø:] in the West Midland, *hue* in the Southwest, and *hi* in Kentish, all of which might be considered regular

[14] Cf. Teichert, 49.

[15] Both the weak inflection and the phonology of *brook* in ME point to the existence of an OE **brucian,* beside *brūcan.* It is barely possible that the identity of the past participle *brocen* of the strong verb with that of the common verb *brecan,* 'break', helped to establish the weak verb. The NED finds no certain instance of either the strong preterite or past participle in ME.

dialectal developments from OE *hēo* or *hīo,* we have *ȝo, sho,* and *she.* *ȝo* [ço:] may be explained as a development of *hi̯ó* with a rising diphthong instead of the normal *hío, héo*; but the origin of *sho* and *she* has been much disputed, the older scholars attempting to derive them from the demonstrative *sēo,* and later students, with more probability, explaining *sho* by the combination of the third singular present indicative ending *-s* with descendants of *hīo*-forms, as in the inverted order *telles ȝo. She* would then be a blend of *sho* and *he.*[16] The important point for us is that *sho* and *she* become the regular pronominal forms in the North and Northeast Midland, where the nominative singular masculine and the nominative singular feminine would have become identical in the twelfth century; OE *hēo* here became *he* because of the unrounding of [ø:] (<OE *ēo*) to [e:].[17] In the West Midland and Southwest, where the representatives of OE *ēo* did not become [e:] but remained rounded until the fourteenth century or later, *h*-forms persist throughout the Middle English period, *hue* being a common spelling in the Southwest and *ho* the regular form in the West Midland and Northwest Midland, where it persists in some counties even in modern dialects as [hu:]. Here the fact that the vowel differentiated the form from the masculine *he* made the introduction of *sho* and *she* unnecessary. Where the customary dis-

	9th Cent.	10th Cent.	11th Cent.	12th Cent.
G.	*hiera, hiora, heora*	*hiera, hiora, heora*	*hira, hyra, heora, hiora*	*heora, hyra, hera, here*
D.	*him*	*him,* rarely, *heom*	*him, heom*	*heom, hem, him, hym*

TABLE 2. *West Saxon Plural Pronouns*

tinction between masculine and feminine was lost, Middle English made use of what would otherwise have remained mere nonce-forms or sporadic variants in order to maintain it.

Since I hope to treat other clashes among the pronouns more elaborately elsewhere, I will give only one other example here. The dative singular masculine and dative plural had in the earliest Old English texts, because of the loss of endings, both attained the form *him.* It is interesting to observe the beginnings of an attempt at differentiation in

[16] Martin B. Ruud, MLN 35.222-5; Harald Lindqvist, Anglia 45.1-50. NED, which adheres to the derivation of *she* from *sēo,* notes that the phonetic development which made *hē* and *hēo* undistinguishable in some dialects furnished 'a strong motive for using the unambiguous feminine demonstrative', but does not adduce the dialectal evidence given above for the influence of homonymy.

[17] Where the ONth. had *hīo,* this would, presumably, if the original diphthongal stress were preserved, become LOE *hēo,* provided *īo* here developed as did the *īo* from *i*-umlaut of *īu,* cf. Richard Jordan, Handbuch der mittelenglischen Grammatik §86.

Old English, and to find distinctive forms everywhere developed in Middle English. The easiest method of illustrating the gradual shift from *him,* plural, to the analogical *heom* will be to cite in Table 2 the West Saxon plural pronominal forms given by Bernhard Gericke.[18] I give the genitive forms because of their influence on the dative. *Heom* appears as a rare form in the tenth century, the diphthong arising by analogy with that of the genitive plural. By the eleventh century it has become common, and by the twelfth *heom* and the resultant *hem* have relegated the ambiguous *him* to the position of a secondary form. In Mercian the same development took place, though the paucity of early texts makes it impossible to follow the shift so clearly. In Middle English the descendants of *heom,* i.e. *hem, hom,* and *ham,* are the normal forms in the Midlands and Southwest. In the North *him* was still the plural form in the tenth century. At the beginning of the Middle English period, it has been replaced by *þaim* from the Old Norse. The ambiguous *him* has thus been everywhere ruled out.

It might be objected that the identity of pronominal forms could hardly be confusing, because the very fact that they must refer to persons previously mentioned would indicate clearly whether a pronoun was masculine or feminine, singular or plural. This theoretical objection, however, applies only to a carefully cultivated literary style. Both the difficulties that sometimes arise in interpreting *him* in Old English texts and the slovenly use of pronouns in popular spoken English indicate that there might occasionally be sufficient reason to prefer a distinctive form to an ambiguous one. Over a long period of time the occasional necessity of choosing a distinctive variant could easily lead to the establishment of the originally abnormal and infrequent form as the regular one. It is true that one may point to instances in several lanugages of the abandonment of a distinctive pronoun, especially when that of one person or number is transferred to another. The fact that Modern German has adopted the pronoun of the third person plural as the customary pronoun of the second person singular and plural shows that fashion and etiquette may sometimes triumph over ambiguity; but this, I believe, is a phenomenon that would be characteristic only of a language of culture consciously developed. Actually, as Prokosch points out to me, such a sentence as 'Ich habe [zi:] gesehen', with its three possible meanings, causes awkward ambiguities in spoken German. In any case, these possible objections to accepting the influence of homonymy in the choice of English pronominal forms seem to be outweighed by the striking historical evidence of Old and Middle English dialects. It is hard to find any other reason for the elimination of normal forms and the selection of various by-forms and other substitutes than the development of phonetic identity.

[18] Das Personalpronomen der 3. Person in spätags.- und frühmittelenglischen Texten, Palaestra 193.85-6 (Leipzig, 1934).

IV

A notable difference exists between the East Midland and the West Midland texts in forms of the preterite of the fourth and fifth ablaut classes. The East Midland dialects developed early *o* and *a*-forms in the stem of the plural: the *a*-forms are probably from the singular, the *o*-forms are a little difficult to account for, but may have arisen from

		PRESENT PLURAL	PRETERITE PLURAL
E Midland	OE	*berað*	*bǣron*
	ME	*b*[ɛ:]*re(n)*	*b*[ɛ:]*re(n)* replaced by *bore(n), bare(n)*
	ME	*berað*	*bēron*
W Midland	OE	*b*[ɛ:]*re(n)*	*b*[e:]*re(n)*

TABLE 3

some analogy with the past participle of class IV. These two types gradually tend to replace the early *e*-forms which would have been the regular development of OE *bǣron* (*bēron*), *spǣcon* (*spēcon*).[19] In the West Midland, however, the usual vowel of the preterite plural is *ē,* as in *spēken, bēren,* and such texts as The Pearl and The Chester Plays show by their rhymes that this is close *ē* [e:] from Anglian *bēron, spēcon,*[20] as we should expect. The analogical relationships in these classes are, of course, complicated, but no one has pointed out that if the East Midland texts had regularly preserved the Old English preterite plural vowel, the preterite plural would have been exactly the same as the present plural, i.e. *bēren, spēken* with [ɛ:], since the Midland endings are likewise the same. For, as the evidence of place-name shows, open *ē* [ɛ:] from OE *ǣ* not close *ē* [e:] from OE *ē,* is characteristic of East Anglia, as it is of Saxon territory, and even Orm in Lincolnshire has predominantly *æ,* indicating open *ē*. Table 3 shows the development in condensed form. In West Midland the close *ē* (OE *ē*) differentiated the preterite from the present. Here the characteristic *e*-vowel of the plural is even adopted in the singular, replacing *a,* and *bēr* becomes the usual preterite form for the singular. The contrast between the East Midland, where the regular phonological development of the plural is generally replaced, and the West Midland, where it is preserved, must be partly due to the fact that

[19] James F. Rettger, The Development of Ablaut in the Strong Verbs of the East Midland Dialects of Middle English, Language Dissertations, Ling. Soc. Amer. Chaps. III, IV, VIII, esp. 88 (Baltimore, 1934).

[20] Samuel O. Andrew, 'The Preterite in Northwestern Dialects', Review of English Studies 5.431-6. Though Andrew did not examine carefully the West Midland texts proper, which are mostly late, as opposed to the Northwest Midland, he cites *e*-forms from the early Katherine group.

the present and preterite plural would have been identical in the East and different in the West.[21]

Homophonic influence on the preterite forms of weak verbs may be seen in the case of verbs of the type OE *sende* (pres. 1 sg.), *sende* (pret. 1 sg.), which show two kinds of differentiation by Middle English times: *sēnde, send*; and *sende, sente*. Bülbring pointed out that in Robert of Gloucester the rhymes in *-ende* proved conclusively that the vowel of the preterite and past participle was short, while that of the present and infinitive was long: *sēnde, sende*.[22] That is, the Old English ninth-century lengthening before *-nd* either did not spread to the preterite, or a short vowel was reintroduced after lengthening had taken place. Bülbring attributed the differentiation to the analogical influence of verbs like *fēdan, fĕdde,* which normally shortened the *ē* of the preterite because of the double *d*; but it seems reasonable to suppose that the phonetic identity of the first and second persons singular of the present indicative (ending in *-e, -est*), and that of the whole present and preterite subjunctive facilitated the regularization of these analogical forms.[23]

Similarly, though Albert H. Marckwardt's careful study now shows clearly that homophony cannot explain the origin of the preterite form in *-ente*,[24] as had been suggested by Koch and Skeat, it is probable that the spread of such forms was to some extent governed by the factor of homophony. Marckwardt admits that this serves to indicate a condition which might have led to a preservation and perhaps an extension of the *-te* forms after they did originate.[25] It seems possible that some of the anomalies mentioned by him may be explained by the influence of homophony. He notes, for example, that *send,* although one of the first verbs to adopt the irregular weak inflection, seems to manifest in the texts of the fourteenth century, and particularly in the North, a tendency

[21] It may be noted that this explanation is somewhat similar to the principle of contrast expounded by Eduard Prokosch, JEGP 20.468-90, for the Germanic verb in older periods. A more exact parallel is the explanation of the OF preterite *valui* given by Friedrich Schürr, Zeitschrift für romanische Philologie 41.139-41; it replaces the **vail* which would have been identical with the present; cf. Gamillscheg, Die Sprachgeographie 45, and for a survey of the controversy concerning this and other forms, Über den Schwund des einfachen Praeteritums, Donum Natalicium Schrijnen 86-8 (Nijmegen-Utrecht, 1929).

[22] Englische Studien 20.149-54. The present and infinitive rhyme only with themselves and words of the type *hende, ende,* whereas the preterites rhyme only with themselves and French words in *-ende,* which never underwent OE lengthening. The difference was not inherited from the period when the preterite had *-dd-*.

[23] It must be admitted, however, that a similar analogical short vowel occasionally appears without this predisposing condition in cases where the verbal forms were already distinguished by the dental ending, as in *hēren-hĕrde* (the *rd* not causing shortening), as is shown by Orm's *herrde, ferrde.*

[24] Origin and Extension of the Voiceless Preterit and the Past Participle Inflection of the Irregular Weak Verb Conjugation, Essays and Studies in English and Comparative Literature, Univ. of Mich. Publ. in Lang. and Lit. 13.152-328 (Ann Arbor, 1935). Marckwardt finds that these are analogical forms first appearing in the Southeast.

[25] Page 160, note 21.

to return to the older inflection.[26] May it not be that the North abandoned the *sent* forms because in the Northern dialect the *-s* endings of the present indicative singular and plural made a differentiation of the tenses by other means unnecessary? To settle this problem satisfactorily one would, of course, have to make a detailed study of the texts involved. At any rate, it is plain that both in the strong and the weak Middle English preterites the factor of homophony cannot be disregarded even when analogy may explain the origin of forms produced.[27]

V

Another aspect of homonymy which deserves investigation is the kind of semantic interference that does not develop to the point of excluding one homonym from the language, but results only in a limitation of meaning or induces a new division of meanings in the homonyms involved. This possibility is seldom mentioned, presumably because proof of such an influence is difficult. A pair like the two adjectives *light* in English (German *licht* and *leicht*), which became hononyms in Old English (both LOE *lēht, līht*) and have existed as such in the language for over a thousand years, is sometimes cited as proof of the fallacy of Gilliéron's theory. Closer examination shows that their history, far from demonstrating the unlikelihood of homonymic confusion, really reveals its subtle operation in the gradual restriction of the meaning of one homonym to its less ambiguous senses. In Old English, *light* 'lucidus' had a much greater variety of meaning than at present: it often meant 'bright', 'brilliant', 'shining', and could be used of a bright fire and bright eyes. The author of Beowulf could speak of a *lēohtan sweorde,* but Shakespeare, if he desires to express the same idea must write 'put up your bright swords'. In Modern German the territory covered by *licht* is much more extensive than in Modern English. We cannot speak of a light fire, meaning 'ein lichter Feuer' (Goethe), nor use *light* in the sense of 'clear', 'lucid', as in 'diese Sätze sind mir nicht licht genug' (Kant), because of the co-existence of *light* 'levis'. Not only has *light* 'lucidus' suffered a considerable restriction of meaning because of *light* 'levis', but in contexts where the two are still likely to come into conflict, as in reference to materials, we continually resort to compounds to avoid ambiguity. Thus tailors speak of light-weight materials, and a man advertises 'a light-coloured gray overcoat' (NED's quotation), where of course 'light gray overcoat' would be ambiguous. It is possible that *light* as

[26] Page 313.

[27] B. Trnka explained the modern limitation of the idiom *use to* to the present tense by the development of homophony with the preterite, On the Syntax of the English Verb from Caxton to Dryden, Travaux du Cercle Linguistique de Prague 3.36 (Prague, 1930). For the Middle English and Early Modern English *I use to go* we are now obliged to substitute such periphrases as 'I usually go', 'I am in the habit of going', 'I am accustomed to go'.

applied to colors, 'pale', 'not dark', and *light* 'not heavy', are sometimes felt, by a kind of synesthesia, to be merely different meanings of the same word. *Light* in 'a light cloud' is presumably the antonym of *heavy,* but might easily be that of *dark.* This feeling has probably made it easier for the two homonyms to exist side by side. Certainly *light* 'lucidus' has become, since Old English times, less varied in meaning, less intense, and one might almost say 'less heavy', because it has been subjected to the influence of its homonym.[28]

The interaction of the two adjectives *light* shows how intimately the problem of homonymic conflict is connected with the problem of the limits of the word. The lexical distinctions of the etymologist may not exist for the majority of people, who have no knowledge of a word's history. As Bloomfield points out,[29] *ear* of corn (OE *ear,* Gmc. **aχuz*), has become a marginal (transferred) meaning of *ear* (OE *ēare,* Gmc. **auzō*). Most people who reflect on matters of language would probably feel that *ear,* an appendage to the stalk of corn, is a metaphorical transference from the *ear* of the body, just as is *head* of cabbage from *head* of the body. Here, then, we have an instance of the merging of two words into one from the point of view of the ordinary speaker; if, indeed, he reflects on the subject at all. Real confusion can hardly arise in the case of two words of this sort which are not used in the same context. But conversely, it is just as likely that one word may develop such different meanings as to seem to a person who is not an etymologist two or more different words, as in the classic instances *metal-mettle, flower-flour,* where we have marked the differentiation by the spelling. Often the development of a multiplicity of meanings or of sharply divergent meanings reaches such a point that some have to be abandoned. Students of the obsolescence of words have noted that this semantic 'plethora' is one cause of the disappearance of a meaning or of the word itself.[30] Thus the word *owe* (OE *āgan*) meant in earlier English 'own', 'possess', but, as the NED points out, the increasingly important legal and commercial sense of *owe* 'to have a thing to pay' brought about the abandonment of its old meaning, for which *own, possess, have* are now substituted. Holthausen believes that OE *ār* may have disappeared because it had come to mean too many things: honor, dignity, glory, reverence, mercy, favor, benefit, prosperity, revenue. It seems to me inconsistent to accept this kind of explanation for obsolescence and reject the hypothesis of the interference of homonyms. From the point of view of the speaker ignorant of origins, the

[28] It is perhaps worth noting that there were two OE verbs *līhtan,* 'to illuminate' and 'to make less heavy', and two verbs *lighten,* recorded from ME times. Though *lighten* 'illuminate' is still familiar to us from literature, as in 'lighten our darkness, O Lord', we tend to reserve *light* in transitive use, for 'illuminate' and *lighten* for 'relieve', though, occasionally, when *lighten* is unambiguous, we may say 'this wallpaper will lighten the room somewhat'.

[29] Language 436.

[30] Teichert 40 ff.; Holthausen 195.

embarrassment and confusion which is caused by multiplicity of meanings is likely to be as great when a form represents two or more etymologically distinct words as when it represents one. Most students of homonyms and most semanticists pay little attention to this fact, but Jespersen pertinently remarks that 'the psychological effect of those cases of polysemy, where "one and the same word" has many meanings, is exactly the same as that of cases where two or three words of different origin have accidentally become homophones'.[31] Because of this relationship, the conflict of homonyms should not be considered a merely curious and abnormal phenomenon, differing from other linguistic processes. The study of homonymic interference involves the whole problem of the word as an entity and illustrates some fundamental principles of semantics.

[31] 'Monosyllabism in English', Proceedings of the British Academy 14.28 (1928); cf. Jaeschke 60: 'Der Gleichklang ist gewissermassen das Gegenstück zur Mehrdeutigkeit'.

Word Order of Noun Modifiers in Old English Prose

CHARLES R. CARLTON

IT HAS OFTEN BEEN STATED that Old English had a free word order because of its inflections which indicate syntactic relationships. This has given the erroneous impression that Old English word order was completely unrestricted. A comparison of Old English with Modern English has placed the two on opposite ends of a scale: on the one hand, Old English having no requisite word order, and on the other hand, Modern English having strict syntactic word order. It is true that Old English had a somewhat freer word order in some instances than Modern English, but it had rules of its own (not necessarily those of Modern English) and these were rather rigidly followed. The application of the techniques of descriptive linguistics to an analysis of the simple, contiguous modifiers of nouns in Old English prose bears this out.

The corpus used for this analysis is a careful selection of fifty charters of varying lengths. They are *original* charters or copies *contemporary* with the events described in them and are dated from A.D. 805 to 1066. It should be emphasized that the corpus, although relatively small, is original Old English prose whose syntax has never been systematically studied before. By excluding prose manuscripts that exist today only as copies made sometimes considerably later than the original manuscripts, it is possible to avoid contamination due to scribal error, the influence of Latin and French when the scribes were no longer familiar with Old English as their native language, and historic change in the English language itself. This type of uncontaminated prose is definitely limited, so necessarily the examples are limited but numerous enough to establish the outlines of prose syntax.

Reprinted by permission from *Journal of English and Germanic Philology* 62. 778-83 (1963).

No poetry has been included because, just as in Modern English, the "real" language is reflected in prose literature more adequately than in poetry, which for its own purposes departs from the norms established and used in prose. Before one can see how and in what ways poetry has departed from the norms of prose, those norms in prose must be established; this can be done only by analysis of plain, pure, contemporary prose.

These charters are found in Birch's *Cartularium Saxonicum*.[1] All the recognized dialects of Old English are included, but there are no significant differences in the syntactic feature being investigated here which can be related to dialect or date.

The term *charters* is used to designate legal or semilegal prose documents. Included are not only land charters but also wills, manumissions, writs, declarations, etc., giving the term a broader meaning than usual.

In the charters, most noun modifiers immediately precede the noun but some may either precede or follow a particular noun. The modifiers have two types of structure: simple and complex. The complex modifiers (not to be discussed here) are longer and have an internal grammatical structure such as that of a prepositional phrase or a dependent clause. These always follow the noun they modify although they are not always contiguous to the noun.

Simple, contiguous modifiers are those which are adjacent to the noun modified and which are not composed of a complex grammatical structure. They are relatively short. In this corpus, nouns are most frequently modified by one word, less frequently by two or three words. Modifiers composed of four or more words involve immediate constituent levels which are not pertinent to this analysis. The simple modification structure usually precedes the noun, and its direct relation to the noun is shown by concord in case, number, and gender, with the exception of modifying nouns in the genitive case. The simple modifiers are words classified as nouns, adjectives, numerals, demonstrative pronouns, possessive pronouns, or participles.

Simple modifiers which precede the noun have an established position in relation to the other modifiers of the same noun; this order of precedence is called order class. There are six positions or order classes of modifiers which are numbered from right to left according to their proximity to the noun or headword: the first position is immediately in front of the noun, the second position immediately precedes the first position, the third position immediately precedes the second position, etc. The sixth position, which is farthest from the noun, precedes all other modifiers of the noun.

This is not to say that there are not or cannot be more such positions or order classes; it is possible that in other types of Old English

[1] Walter DeGray Birch, *Cartularium Saxonicum: A Collection of Charters Relating to Anglo-Saxon History*, 4 vols. (London, 1885-99) .

prose more positions can be found; however, only six positions are found in this corpus. Any of the six order classes may occur alone with a noun, but all six positions do not occur in any one example. When two or more modifiers occur, they precede the noun in the relative order described below.

The following noun phrases show the expansions of the noun modification structure and the order in which the items occur and can be used to illustrate the procedure of establishing the order classes of the noun modifiers. Many of the phrases are formula-like expressions which are frequently repeated; therefore I have selected a minimum number of examples containing different combinations of order classes to avoid monotonous and unnecessary repetition:

þære geættredan deofles lare 'the devil's poisoned teaching'
ænne blacne stedan 'one black stallion'
an oþer healf gear 'one other half year'
þæm þriim dælum 'the three parts'
þa oðoro lond 'the other land'
mænig oþer god man 'many another good man'
allum þæm halgum 'all the saints'
ealle his leofan halgan 'all his beloved saints'
sum þæt lond 'some [of] that land'
ealle mine freondum 'all my friends'
min twa wergeld 'my two wergelds'
oþrum sue miclum lande 'as much other land'

By placing all the noun headwords in one column and then spacing the modifiers in front of the noun column so that all forms of the same word or all words of the same part of speech fall in the same column according to position in front of the noun and other modifiers (maintaining the same relative position to the other modifiers), we obtain a six-position arrangement of the modifiers as shown below:

6th Position (*eall, sum, manig*)	5th Position (pron.)	4th Position (numeral)	3rd Position (*oþer*)	2nd Position (adj. and part.)	1st Position (noun in gen. case)	Head word (noun)
	þære			geættredan	deofles	lare
		an	oþer	healf		gear
		ænne		blacne		stedan
	þæm	þriim				dælum
	min	twa				wergeld
	þa		oþoro			lond
mænig			oþer	god		man
allum	þæm					halgum
ealle	his			leofan		halgan
sum	þæt					lond
ealle	mine					freondum
			oþrum	sue miclum		lande

The first position is occupied only by nouns in the genitive case.

The second position is occupied by past participles and adjectives except *oþer* (position 3) and those listed in position 6. The adverb *swa* is included in position 2 since it occurs only as an expansion of the adjective *micel* and never occurs alone as a modifier of a noun headword; it can be considered a complex modifier (adjective plus its own modifier) or an optional subdivision of the second position. When two adjectives of position 2 modify the same noun, they are joined by the conjunction *and.*

The third position is filled only by the adjective *oþer*. Usually this word has the characteristic occurrence of an adjective or numeral (meaning "second"), but since it occurs here after another numeral (*an*) and before an adjective (*healf*) it has been given a separate but intermediate position between the other two (numeral and adjective).

The fourth position contains only numerals.

The fifth position is occupied by demonstrative and possessive pronouns. In only one example these two types of pronouns occur together modifying the same noun:

his þære haligran unlu	'*his* saints' displeasure' or 'the displeasure *of those* saints *of his.*'

The sixth position is represented by *eall, sum,* and *ælc* (*ælces* þara monna), a special group of adjectives, occurring before position 5 (demonstrative and possessive pronouns).

In addition, it would appear that the words *manig, nænig,* and *æghwilc* should be assigned to position 6, even though they do not occur before a position 5 word, because they are more closely related to the other words already established in position 6 than they are to those of any other position before the headword. Examples illustrating these words are:

mænig oþer god man	'*many* another good man'
nænge oþre halfe	'*no* other half'
æghwilc Godes þiow	'*each* servant of God'

Therefore, position 6 includes a special group of adjectives—*sum, eall, manig, ælc, nænig, æghwilc*—which always precede all other modifiers of the headword and which are not preceded by other modifiers.

There are a few exceptions to the positional arangement of the order classes as given above. For instance, in the prepositional phrase . . . *an Godes libgendes naman,* there is inversion of the regular first and second position modifiers; although *naman* is ambiguous in case, it is probably dative case after this preposition; *libgendes* modifies the headword *Godes* and the two function as a unit or complex modifier of the headword *naman.* Therefore the translation of the phrase probably should be "in the *living God's* name" rather than "in *God's living* name." This, then, is an apparent rather than a real exception.

In the phrase *twægen mine mægas,* we find a reversal of position 4 (numerals) and position 5 (possessive pronouns). It is possible that the genitive pronoun has been drawn into position 1 with the genitive nouns by analogy and therefore tends to fluctuate between position 5 and position 1. If so, this is not an exception but an instance of the genitive pronoun following the pattern already established by the genitive noun. This phrase probably should be translated "two relatives of mine" rather than "my two relatives."

The expression *God Ælmihtig* "Almighty God" occurs frequently and seems to be influenced by the Latin expression *Deus Omnipotens* which it translates. When the expression is used with another noun headword, we find both word orders:

þæs almæhtigan Godes unhlis 'the Almighty God's displeasure'
on Godes Ælmihtiges naman 'in Almighty God's name.'

Simple modifiers infrequently follow the noun headword. However, in two instances the regular position of the modifier is after the noun: first, appositives regularly follow the noun:

And ic sello Æðelwalde *minum sunu* iii hida boclondes. 'And I give three hides of bookland to Æthelwald, *my son*.'

Second, titles of rank or position regularly follow the noun:

Eadward *kyning* gret Harold *eorl.* '*King* Edward greets *Earl* Harold.'

Adjectives follow the noun headword in the following instances:

1. The phrase *God Ælmihtig* has been mentioned above.

2. The adjective follows the noun when the adjective has a genitive complement:

mittan *fulne huniges* 'a mitta *full of honey*.'

3. The adjective sometimes follows the noun when the noun is preceded by another modifier:

in þissum life *ondwardum* 'in this *present* life.'

4. Modifiers which are genitives of specification or origin often follow the noun headword:

æfter regole *þæs halgan Benedictes* 'according to the rule *of St. Benedict*'
mid ten pundan *reodes goldes* 'with ten pounds *of red gold*.'

When there are two modifiers of the same noun object which are joined by *and* and which represent two different people or groups of people, the shorter (one word) precedes the noun and the longer (two or more words) follows:

æfter *minum* dege and *minra ærfewearda* 'after *my* and *my heirs'* life.'

Modifiers of two nouns joined by *and* functioning as object of the preposition may either precede or follow the nouns:

be *þæs cynincges* leafe and gewitnesse 'with *the king's* permission and testimony'
mid þafunge and leafe *Heardacnutes cynges* and *þæs arwurþan hiredes* 'with the consent and permission of *King Hardacnut* and *of the honorable brotherhood.'*

A prepositional phrase may be followed by *and* plus another preposition plus genitive modifiers without an expressed object; the preposition and modifiers refer to the object of the first preposition:

on Godes Ælmæhtiges noman and on *allra his haligra* 'In Almighty God's name and in *all his saints'*.'

The conclusions of this study are the following:

1. Word order is a syntactic feature of noun modification in Old English.
2. Old English allowed some modification structures which are not used in Modern English.
3. Although simple noun modifiers usually precede the noun, they sometimes follow or both precede and follow the noun; but in either case they keep a relative order arrangement according to the order class to which they belong.
4. There are six order classes for noun modifiers according to their position of occurrence before the noun; the reverse order holds when the modifiers follow the noun (position 6 is closest to the noun headword rather than farthest from it).
5. Descriptive (structural) linguistics is applicable to the study of historic stages of languages.

On the Development of the Structural Use of Word-Order in Modern English

CHARLES C. FRIES

[In the actor-action-goal construction and in the character-substance (or modifier-noun) construction, Old English used taxemes of selection (inflected forms) to distinguish between actor (subject) and goal (object), and to indicate the direction of modification. The development of English has been away from the use of taxemes of selection with non-distinctive and connotative word-order, toward the use of taxemes of order operating practically without the aid of other devices. The patterns of the Modern English use seem to have been established by the middle of the 15th century.]

'VIEWED FROM THE STANDPOINT OF ECONOMY, taxemes of order are a gain, since the forms are bound to be spoken in some succession; nevertheless few languages allow features of order to work alone; almost always they merely supplement taxemes of selection.'[1] In Present-day English, however, there are two 'grammatical forms' for which the taxemes of selection have been lost during the course of the historical development of English and the features of word-order do work practically alone.

The first of these is in the ACTOR-ACTION-GOAL construction, in which the substantive noun that forms the 'starting-point' (the so-called subject) of the action is distinguished from the substantive noun that forms the 'ending-point' (the so-called object) only by position. The difference between the sentences *The man struck the bear* and *The bear struck the man* rests solely on word-order. Such arrangements of the words as *The man the bear struck* and *Struck the man the bear* do not distinguish the starting-point from the ending-point of the action and are not the practice of Present-day English.

Reprinted by permission from *Language* 16.199-208 (1940).

[1] Leonard Bloomfield, Language (1933) 198.

In Old English, however, the order of the words in such sentences has no bearing whatever upon the grammatical relationships involved. Taxemes of selection do the work, and word-order is non-distinctive and connotative. The following Old English sentences, for example, would all express the same syntactic relationships between the two substantive nouns: that the bear is the goal or end-point of the activity and the man the starting-point.

Sē mann þone beran slōh.
Þone beran sē mann slōh.
Þone beran slōh sē mann.
Slōh sē mann þone beran.

In each of the four sentences, taxemes of selection—the nominative case form for *the man,* the accusative case form for *the bear*—signal the 'subject' and the 'object' relationships. It is true that in most Old English nouns there is no distinction of form between the nominative and the accusative; but with these nouns are used an inflected article and an inflected adjective, and these 'agreeing' words most frequently have distinct forms to separate the nominative from the accusative. As a matter of fact, in a count covering more than 2000 instances, less than ten per cent of the Old English forms which are syntactically nominative or accusative lack the distinctive case-endings. In respect to the actor-action-goal construction we are concerned with the shift from this grammatical situation in Old English, where taxemes of selection operate with only a non-distinctive and connotative word-order, to the grammatical situation in Present-day English, where distinctive features of word order operate without taxemes of selection.

The particular historical facts of significance for our purpose are (a) the position of those words which in Old English bear the accusative inflection—the 'accusative-object', and (b) the position of those words in Old English which bear the dative inflection—the 'dative-object'.[2] In both cases we are concerned only with those instances which do not involve the use of a preposition (function word).

(1) In Late Old English of about 1000 A.D., if the sermons of Ælfric can be taken as a fair representation of the language of that time, approxi-

[2] In examining the materials of Middle English and Early Modern English, where the distinctive inflectional syllables of both adjectives and articles have been lost, only those instances were counted as accusative-objects or as dative-objects for which there were clear inflectional parallels in Old English. I am indebted to a number of my students for contributions to my collection of instances upon which these figures are based, and especially to Dr. Frederic G. Cassidy (The Backgrounds in Old English of the Modern English Substitutes for the Dative-Object in the Group Verb + Dative-Object + Accusative-Object, University of Michigan Diss., 1938) and to Dr. Russell Thomas (The Development of the Adnominal Periphrastic Genitive in English, University of Michigan Diss., 1931).

mately 53% of the accusative-objects appear BEFORE THE VERB and only 47% after the verb. Typical examples are:

ælc man . . . þe . . . ðone oðerne hyrwde[3]
se man ðe hine sylfne godne talað
and Crist on ðære hwile to helle gewende and þone deofol gewylde
se Ælmihtiga God·ða dagas gescyrte
gif ðu þonne ðis lytle bebod tobrecst þu scealt deaðe sweltan
he ðone lyre anfealdlice gefylde
and ða ylcan lare eft ge-edlæhte

(2) The change from the Old English free position of the accusative-object (either before or after the verb) to the Modern English fixed position after the verb is indicated by the following figures:

	c. 1000	c. 1200	c. 1300	c. 1400	c. 1500
Acc-obj. before verb	52.5%	52.7%	40+%	14.3%	1.87%
Acc-obj. after verb	47.5%	46.3%	60—%	85.7%	98.13%

(3) If the sampling displayed in these figures is trustworthy, then the position following the verb had become the fixed position for the accusative-object probably by the beginning of the 15th century, certainly before 1500.

(4) In Old English the words with dative inflection, the so-called dative-objects, like those with the accusative inflection, are found in practically every position in the sentence. When a dative-object and an accusative-object appear in the same sentence, the order of these words in relation to each other and to the verb may be any combination, without doing violence to the ordinary patterns of Old English. Typical examples are:

Cartaginenses sendon fultum [acc.] *Tarentinum* [dat.] (Or. 162.8)
þam godan casere [dat.] *sende theodosie ærend-gewrit* [acc.] (Æl. Saints I.536.792)
he asende his apostlum [dat.] *þone halgan gast* [acc.] (Wulfstan 1.230.27)
Hi moston him [dat.] *beran unforbodene flæsc* [acc.] (Æl. Saints II.72.91)

(5) In the materials examined for Old English (900 A.D. to 1000) we find the following distribution of 2558 instances:[4]

[3] The practice of Old English of putting the verb at the end of subordinate clauses (similar to that of Modern German) accounts for the position of a large number of accusative-objects before the verb.

[4] Figures here summarized are from those given by F. G. Cassidy, op. cit.

	Dative-object before the verb		Dative-object after the verb		Dative-object before acc-obj.		Dative-object after acc-obj.	
	Number	Percent	Number	Percent	Number	Percent	Number	Percent
Nouns	95	27.6	249	72.4	249	64.0	140	36.0
Pronouns	495	48.7	518	51.3	674	82.8	141	17.2
Both together	587	43.4	767	56.6	923	76.6	281	23.3

In these figures three matters seem worth noting: (a) Even in Old English the dative-object usually appears before the accusative-object. This is especially true of the pronouns, with the dative-object coming first in 82.8% of the instances. (b) The position of the dative-object with respect to the verb is less certain in Old English. Of the pronouns, approximately half appear after the verb; of the nouns, nearly three-fourths appear after the verb. (c) In the case of nouns, a much larger percentage of dative-objects appears after the verb than of the accusative-objects (72.4% as against 47.5%).

(6) The materials examined for Early Middle English (c. 1200) show (a) practically the same pattern of the position of the dative-object in relation to the accusative-object as do the materials for Old English; but (b) a clear tendency to place the dative-object after the verb. The figures for (b) are as follows:

	Dative-object before the verb		Dative-object after the verb	
	Number	Percent	Number	Percent
Nouns	26	23.0	88	77.0
Pronouns	218	43.0	288	57.0
Both together	244	39.4	376	60.6

(7) By Early Middle English the position of the dative-object in relation to the accusative-object seems to have become a clear pattern. In about four-fifths of the instances the dative-object precedes the accusative-object. As the accusative-object comes increasingly to be placed after the verb, the dative-object also appears after the verb but before the accusative-object.

(8) The general situation at approximately the middle of the 15th century seems to have been as follows.

In the actor-action-goal construction the position for words expressing the goal (the ending-point or object) has become pretty thoroughly fixed as after the verb. Accusative- and dative-objects are distinguished by the fact that the dative-object, when present, precedes the accusative-object. This positional relation of the two classes of objects had existed for several centuries. Most important is the fact that by this time no nouns functioning as accusative-objects or as dative-objects precede their verbs.[5] The position before the verb, cleared of the presence of formally distinct accusative- and dative-objects, becomes in itself the distinguishing feature of the form-class of nominative expressions. The position before the verb becomes the territory of the actor (the starting-point or subject), the position after the verb becomes the territory of the goal (the ending-point or object); both exercise the 'pressure of position' upon the function of all substantives standing in each territory.

Nouns standing before the so-called impersonal verbs as dative-objects (earlier such dative-objects had clear dative-case inflectional forms) now, whenever the verb form permits, are interpreted as subjects; and nouns following these impersonal verbs—nouns which formerly had the clear inflectional characteristics of subjects—now, standing in object territory, are interpreted as objects.[6]

The knight liked it right noght (Tale of Gamelin 52)
This tale nedeth noght be glosed (Conf. Am. VII.3786)
Whan a wolf wanteþ [h]is fode . . . , of þe erþe he et (Alex. and Dind. 860)

The 'pressure of position' can perhaps most satisfactorily account for the changes in the pronoun forms in such sentences as these:

Me wæs gegiefan an boc = *I was given a book*
Hem nedede no help = *They needed no help*

and the 15th-century change of verb form in an old and common expression seems also to be connected with the development of this taxeme of order as the signal for the subject:

Habbað geleafan ic hyt eom (OE Gospels)
Wostow nought wel that it am I (Chaucer)
It is I that am here in your syth (Coventry Mysteries)

In general, then, in the actor-action-goal construction, in respect to the distinction between actor and goal, taxemes of selection which operated in Old English without relation to word-order have been displaced by taxemes of word-order working practically alone. These taxemes of

[5] Pronouns with distinct case forms did occasionally appear as dative-objects or as accusative-objects before verbs.

[6] The examples printed by Willem Van der Gaaf in his dissertation, The Transition from Impersonal to Personal in Middle English (1904), have been of great service. See also Otto Jespersen, A Modern English Grammar 3.11.2-3_5, and C. Alphonso Smith, Studies in English Syntax 66-86.

word-order seem to form a clear pattern in the 14th century and to be fully established by the middle of the 15th.[7]

The second of the grammatical forms in which taxemes of selection have been lost and features of word-order now work practically alone is the CHARACTER-SUBSTANCE (the MODIFIER-NOUN) construction.

In Old English, with taxemes of selection to show the direction of modification, modifiers appear either before or after their nouns or even separated from their nouns by other words. Some examples are the following:

Comon þær scipu six to Wiht (Chron. 897)
Æþelwulfes suna twegen (Chron. 855)
on ænium oþerum mynstres þingum (Ben. Rule 95.14)

[7] I have tried to describe the various aspects of the word-order pattern for the nouns of the actor-action-goal construction in the following ten statements:

(a) A single noun preceding the verb—a noun that has the full characteristics of a substantive (i.e. with possible determiners as well as inflection for number), that is not preceded by an accompanying function word, or inflected for genitive case—is the subject or the starting point of the actor-action construction.

(b) Two such nouns preceding the verb—nouns that are equivalent or refer to the same person or thing—are the subject and an appositive, the first in order being the subject.

(c) Two or more such nouns preceding the verb—nouns that do not refer to the same person or thing but which are levelled by similar accent and/or function words—constitute a compound subject (two or more subjects).

(d) If two nouns precede the verb, stand next to one another, and are not levelled by accent and/or function words, but with only one possible determiner and that before the first noun, the second noun is the subject and the first a modifier of the subject.

(e) A single noun following the verb—a noun that has the full formal characteristics of a substantive and is not preceded by an accompanying function word or inflected for genitive case—if this noun refers to the same person or thing as the subject noun, is an identifying noun—a so-called 'predicate nominative.'

(f) Such a single noun following the verb, if it does not refer to the same person or thing as the subject noun, is the end-point of the action or object.

(g) Two such nouns following the verb—nouns that do not refer to the same person or thing as the subject noun, but do themselves each refer to the same person or thing as the other, are a 'direct' object and a 'result' object or a so-called 'object complement,' after such verbs as *call, make, elect, appoint, consider*. After other verbs they are 'direct' object and appositive.

(h) Two or more such nouns following the verb—nouns that do not refer to the same person or thing as the subject noun and do not themselves each refer to the same person or thing as the other, but are levelled by accent and/or function words—are a compound accusative ('direct') object, i.e. several objects.

(i) Two such nouns following the verb—nouns that do not refer to the same person or thing as the subject noun, and do not themselves each refer to the same person or thing as the other, and are not levelled by accent and/or function words—are a dative-object ('indirect' object) and an accusative-object ('direct' object), the first in order being the dative or indirect object.

(j) If two nouns follow the verb, stand next to one another, and are not levelled by accent and/or function words, but with only one possible determiner and that before the first noun, the first noun is a modifier of the second and the second may be either (e) or (f) above.

and ealle þara nytena frumcennedan (Exod. 133.5)
Ge gesawon ealle þa mæran drihtnes weorc (Deut. 214.7)
an lytel sæs earm (Oros. 28.12)
to ðæm Godes huse (Oros. 94.18)
þone drihtnes þægen (Ælf. Hom. 184.249)

The progressive fixing of the word-order pattern for modification can be illustrated by the facts concerning the position of the inflected genitive modifying a noun. Adjectival in its function, the inflected adnominal genitive in Old English appears, like the adjective, either before or after the noun it modifies. Out of 2247 instances of this genitive from materials of c. 900 A.D., 1175 or 52.4% stand before the modified noun, and 1072 or 47.6% stand after it.[8]

The following figures show the developing change in this situation:[9]

	c. 900	c. 1000	c. 1100	c. 1200	c. 1250
Genitive before its noun	52.4%	69.1%	77.4%	87.4%	99.1%
Genitive after its noun	47.6	30.9	22.6	12.6	0.9

Before the end of the 13th century the post-positive inflected genitive has completely disappeared. By this time the general word-order pattern to express the direction of modification has become well established: single word modifiers of the noun or adjective class preceding the nouns they modify remain in that position, whereas single word modifiers in other positions are not so kept. As a matter of fact, in the materials examined for Present-day standard English, of the 1489 single word adjective modifiers there appearing, 94.9% immediately precede the nouns they modify and only 5.1% follow their nouns.[10] For single words of these classes the position immediately before a noun has become a taxeme of order signalling an adjunct relationship. In Modern English, position alone can indicate modification, and ever since the second half of the 17th century[11] nouns both singular and plural in form have with increasing frequency been made into modifiers by being placed before other nouns. The nature of such modification may be of the widest variety and is often extremely vague, but the direction of the modification is unmistakable.[12]

[8] An example from Ælfric is: *þæt he and eall Israhela folc sceoldon offrian Gode an lamb anes geares.*

[9] See Russell Thomas, op. cit. 65-70.

[10] Typical examples of those that followed are: *of the information available; the best physical condition possible; the best information obtainable from her; at some institution not familiar to me; for the time being; for the week following; two weeks ago.*

[11] I am indebted to Miss Aileen Traver for the collection of instances upon which this statement rests.

[12] Some typical examples are: *a school teacher; at sea level; the examination papers; beauty culture; a summer camp; a home visit; my household effects; the newspaper clipping; at government expense; the family physician; a funeral bill; the hospital*

The position immediately following a noun, however, has also become a taxeme of order indicating a similar modifying relationship for word groups—phrases introduced by the function words called prepositions, and clauses introduced by relative pronouns. The development of the so-called periphrastic genitive, 'the analytic genitive with *of*', is typical of this construction. This word group rose in frequency after the post-positive genitive had practically disappeared. The following figures show the details of the progress.

	Post-positive genitive	'Periphrastic' genitive	Pre-positive genitive
c. 900	47.5%	0.5%	52.0%
c. 1000	30.5	1.0	68.5
c. 1100	22.2	1.2	76.6
c. 1200	11.8	6.3	81.9
c. 1250	0.6	31.4	68.9
c. 1300	0.0	84.5	15.6

In Present-day Standard English the pressure of position is such that all word groups tend to modify the word immediately preceding. In the material examined for Present-day English, there appear 1258 of these 'prepositional phrases' as modifiers of nouns. Of these, only one (as the context proves) cannot modify the immediately preceding word:

The undersigned was given a physical examination for promotion by a medical board (9054)

In these same materials, of the 396 'clause' modifiers of nouns, 86% immediately follow the noun modified, and 14% have other words (invariably a 'phrase' modifier of some sort) intervening. Examples of those with intervening words are the following:

I purchased a new automobile from this company for which I paid cash (9033)
The family occupy a house consisting of six rooms and a bath which they own (8303)
The sister has made an affidavit to that effect which I am enclosing (8234)

---

gardens; labor conditions. The process of these noun-adjuncts seems to me to be the same as that underlying the formation of compounds. In fact it is hardly possible to draw a line bounding the compounds and separating them from these free syntactical groups. Accent and specialization of meaning set off many clear cases, but there is a wide band of borderline cases. Frequency of a particular combination often leads to the phonetic and the semantic features characteristic of a compound.

One other observation may be made in conclusion. Sapir distinguished between what he called the 'essential or unavoidable' grammatical concepts and the 'dispensable or secondary' concepts.[13] If, for example, we are to say anything about a bear and a man in connection with the action of killing, it is 'essential and unavoidable' that we indicate which one did the killing and which one was killed. If the qualities 'big' and 'fierce' are expressed in connection with the man and the bear, it is essential to know to which of these two the qualities are to be attached: one must know the direction of the modification. On the other hand, whether the killing took place in the past, the present, or the future, whether it was instantaneous or long drawn out, whether the speaker knows of this fact of his own first-hand knowledge or only from hearsay, whether the bear or the man has been mentioned before—these matters are of the 'dispensable or secondary' type and may or may not be expressed. Languages differ greatly in the extent to which their grammatical practices force the speakers to give attention to these points.

In Old English practically all the grammatical relationships to which the language gives attention—both the 'essential or unavoidable' and the 'dispensable or secondary' ones—can be expressed by inflections (taxemes of selection), and nearly all are so expressed. The development of English has been characterized by the loss of certain kinds of these inflections. It might almost be fair to say that the history of the English language in respect to its grammar has, in a large measure, been a movement away from the type of grammatical structure in which taxemes of selection (inflections or word forms) express both the essential and the dispensable grammatical concepts, toward a type of structure in which taxemes of selection are used only for the dispensable concepts and taxemes of order for the essential or unavoidable relationships.

[13] Edward Sapir, Language (1921) 99: 'We are thus once more reminded of the distinction between essential or unavoidable relational concepts and the dispensable type. The former are universally expressed, the latter are but sparsely developed in some languages, elaborated with a bewildering exuberance in others.'

Diachronic Syntax and Generative Grammar

ELIZABETH CLOSS TRAUGOTT

1. The problem [1]

THE OBJECTIVES of diachronic linguistics have always been to reconstruct the particular steps by which a language changes, and also to hypothesize about processes of language change in general. Recent discussion of the latter problem has frequently involved five closely related proposals.[2] First, language changes by means of a series of individual innovations. These innovations consist primarily in the addition of single rules to the grammar of the adult speaker. Second, these innovations usually occur at some point of break in a grammar; for example, 'before the first morphophonemic rule involving immediate constituent structure of the utterance . . . before the phonological rules that eliminate boundary markers from the representation'.[3] Third, these innovations are passed on to the next generation when the child imitates the adult. A child may internalize the adult's grammar; or, more probably, he will simplify it. This is because children have an ability, not shared by most adults, to construct by induction from the utterances to which they have been exposed, the simplest grammar capable of generating sentences. The simplification will give rise to a discontinuity in transmission from generation to generation. In the interests of preserving intelligibility, this discontinuity will be minimal. Fourth, whenever the discontinuity results in radical

---

Reprinted by permission from *Language* 41.402-15 (1965).

[1] I am deeply indebted to Morris Halle and Edward S. Klima for valuable criticism of an earlier draft of this paper. My thanks are also due to Sheldon Sacks, James Sledd, and Robert P. Stockwell for many helpful suggestions.

[2] For these proposals and their corollary, see especially Morris Halle, 'Phonology in generative grammar', *Word* 18.64-8 (1962), and the revised version in Jerry A. Fodor and Jerrold J. Katz, eds., *The structure of language: Readings in the philosophy of language* 334-52 (Englewood Cliffs, N. J., 1964).

[3] *Word* 18.66, ft. 12; *Structure* 346, ft. 13.

changes such as restructuring, a mutation occurs. Finally, these mutations, which affect the overall simplicity of the grammar, are rare.

The significance of the intelligibility criterion is summarized by Halle as follows:[4]

> Linguistic change is normally subject to the constraint that it must not result in the destruction of mutual intelligibility between the innovators—i.e. the carriers of the change—and the rest of the speech community . . . This restriction clearly affects the content of the rules to be added . . . the number of rules to be added must also be restricted, for very serious effects on intelligibility can result from the simultaneous addition of even two or three otherwise innocuous rules.
>
> It may be somewhat less obvious that the requirement to preserve intelligibility also restricts the place in the order where rules may be added. All other things being equal, a rule will affect intelligibility less if it is added at a lower point in the order than if it is added higher up.

A corollary of these various proposals is that the simplest rules in a synchronic grammar will mirror the relative chronology of those additions which do not affect the overall simplicity of the grammar. In other words, synchronic grammars reflect INNOVATIONS. They do not, however, reflect MUTATIONS.

These arguments have been presented mainly in connexion with phonological change. Ramification in all other areas of the grammar has been taken for granted, but has not been investigated in detail. Klima hints at the validity of the general claim that a synchronic syntax reflects historical change when he remarks in his article, 'Relatedness between grammatical systems',[5]

> Although motivated by a purely synchronic principle of simplicity (shortness of rules), the order in which the styles are considered does, in fact, recapitulate comparable aspects in the historical development of the pronouns.

No systematic attempt has, however, been made to investigate the five hypotheses cited above in the light of syntactic change. It is the purpose of this paper to make such an attempt, and to draw some minimal conclusions which any theory of language change must include.

2. *Representative data*

The investigation will be based on the history of the verbal auxiliary *Aux* in English. The relationship between one period of the language and another will be presented in terms of the relationships between

[4] *Word* 18.66; *Structure* 346.

[5] *Lg.* 40.2 (1964).

transformational generative[6] grammars of ninth-century Old English, mid-fifteenth-century Middle English, late-sixteenth-century Early Modern English,[7] and Modern English. By *Aux* I mean the tense marker, modals, the perfect and progressive helping verbs, and a few other helping verbs which will be specified in the course of this paper.

Attempts will be made to reconstruct the intermediate steps that account for the *Aux* structures and so to account for the types of innovations that can reasonably be assumed to underlie the observed mutations.

3. Modern English

Consider first Modern English *Aux* constructions as a type of control, since they are well known and have been accounted for in grammars that fulfill the strongest requirements of transformational generative theory.[8]

[6] The notion of grammar is developed by Noam Chomsky, *Syntactic structures* ('s-Gravenhage, 1957).

Questions have frequently been raised concerning the feasibility of using this notion of grammar in historical analysis, in particular concerning the appeal to intuition. A linguist theorizing about a living language ideally has as a control his own native intuition and that of the speakers around him, or at worst the native intuition of speakers of a language foreign to him. Against such intuition he can test, among other things, degrees of grammaticality and types of ambiguity. With dead languages, however, the linguist can rely only on the limited data available to him, and at best on a secondary 'native intuition' which can arise only after several years of close association with the language. He can find very few, if any, syntactically minimal pairs from which to set up paradigms of grammatical versus ungrammatical sentences. Deviation and ambiguity are even more elusive. If we take in its strongest terms the requirement placed on linguistic theory that it should characterize and predict all and only the sentences of the language and also account for the native speaker's competence in producing and understanding utterances of the language, we might ultimately conclude that a grammar can be written only by a native speaker, not a foreigner, and that grammars of dead languages cannot be written at all. The degree of accuracy will naturally vary according to the degree of acquaintance with the language. But this does not mean that all investigation of language not native to the linguist must de facto be abandoned, any more than any theory of history, whether cultural or geological, must be rejected because we cannot recapture all and only the characteristics of previous eras. We may quite legitimately put forward a theory of a dead language, in terms of a grammar which fulfills the requirements of descriptive adequacy and explanatory power. This theory will be based on all observable data, and also on unobservable data when necessary, i.e. when the logical consequences of the model would not match the observable data without this hypothesis. As in analysis of a living language, that model will be the simplest which will characterize the sentences of the corpus, and so the infinite set of unobserved sentences which pattern with them. Within such a framework, deviance as well as grammaticality can tentatively be made explicit.

[7] For fuller versions of these grammars, see Closs, *Syllabus for English 110, History of English* 11-6, 24-9, 34-7 (mim., University of California, Berkeley, 1964); *Deep and surface structure in Old English* (in preparation).

[8] See especially Chomsky, 'A transformational approach to syntax' in Archibald A. Hill, ed., *Third Texas conference on problems of linguistic analysis in English* 131-2, 144-7 (Austin, 1962); Klima, 'Negation in English' in Fodor and Katz, eds., *The structure of language: Readings in the philosophy of language* 251-3 et passim; Robert B. Lees, *A grammar of English nominalizations* 19-20 et passim (Bloomington, 1960). For a discussion of the criteria by which the set of auxiliary verbs is set up, see James Sledd, *A short introduction to English grammar* 106-9 (Chicago, 1959).

The set of optional Modern English auxiliary verbs is established according to the following criteria: position relative to other verbs, especially in passives, negatives, emphatics, interrogatives; use in tag questions and other reduced sentences; occurrence with *n't;* and possibility of occurrence under weak stress. These verbs include (1) the subset of modals *M* (*can, may, must, shall, will*), which all require a following verb in its base form, as in *I will go, I will have gone* where *go* and *have* are base forms; (2) the nonmodal operators: *have* requiring a past participle marker *PP,* and *be* requiring a present participle marker *PrP.* Any one or more of these subsets of auxiliary verbs may occur optionally, but only in the order described: *M – have – PP – be – PrP.*

In addition to these optional formatives, every verbal construction obligatorily carries one tense marker *T,* whether the helping verbs are present or not. *T* always occurs with the first member of the construction: *He would have come, *He will has come, *He will have comes.* For this reason, *T* is generated to precede the helping verbs and *MV* and every *Aux* is said to contain at least *T*. The formats can all be generated by the following rules. Only those elements relevant to *Aux* constructions are included here.

3.1 S $\longrightarrow$ NP – VP
3.2 VP $\longrightarrow$ Aux – MV
3.3 MV $\longrightarrow \begin{Bmatrix} \text{V}_t - \text{NP} \\ \text{V}_i \\ \vdots \end{Bmatrix}$
3.4 Aux $\longrightarrow$ T (M) (have – PP) (be – PrP)
3.5 M $\longrightarrow$ can, may, must, shall, will

A low-level affix switch rule assigns *T* to its correct position after the verbal base immediately following it.

Verbal constructions with *do* can all be accounted for by blocking the minimal auxiliary formant *T* from the main verb base in negatives, emphatics, interrogatives, tag questions, and imperatives, as in

(1) *He does not go*
(2) *He does go*
(3) *Does he go?*
(4) *What does she see?*
(5) *She went home, did she?*
(6) *Do be good*

In other words, *do* is automatically and obligatorily generated as a dummy carrier wherever *T* is blocked from a main verb base *MV*.

4. Old English [9]

The shape of the optional part of *Aux* was considerably different at other stages of the language, and this one factor to a very large extent accounts for the differences in structure of active statements, and also of passives, negatives, and interrogatives.

As at all other periods, *T* was obligatory in Old English. There is a subset of the optional helping verbs which functions very largely like the subset of modern modals, and whose members are actually their cognates: *cunn-, mag-, mot-, scul-, will-,* all requiring an infinitive marker *Inf.* These may be exemplified by

(7) *Or.*214.5: *Ac þær hie hit georne ongitan cuþen* 'But when they could readily understand it'
(8) *Or.*100.19: *Ic mæg eac on urum agnum tidum gelic anginn þæm gesecgan* 'I can also tell of a beginning similar to that in our own times'
(9) *Or.*30.33: *For ðon þe hio hyre firenluste fulgan ne moste* 'Because she could not satisfy her desires'
(10) *Or.*218.20: *Ic sceal eac niede þara monegena gewinna geswigian þe on eastlondum gewurdon* 'I shall also by necessity be silent about those many battles that took place in the East'
(11) *Or.*140.30: *a he & þa consulas hie attellan ne mehton* 'When he and the consuls could not count them'

In addition there is the cognate of the Modern English perfect helping verb, *habban* 'to have' which requires *PP,* provided that *MV* is transitive (V_t) :

(12) *Or.*172.18: *Ac him hæfdon Pene þone weg forseten* 'But the Carthaginians had blocked his way'

Occasionally *MV* may be one of a small set of intransitives (V_i), largely a set of verbs of movement, here classified as $V_{i\ move}$, as in

(13) *Or.*196.22: *a Scipia hæfde gefaren* 'When Scipio had gone'

The perfect auxiliary of intransitives is regularly, however, formed by the verb *wesan* 'to be'—*PP,* as in

(14) *Or.*4.17: *Hu Orosius sæde þæt he wære cumen* 'How Orosius said that he had come'
(15) Or.236.19: *ider hi þa mid firde gefaren wæron* 'To the place where they had then marched with the army'

There are also three progressive auxiliary verbs requiring *PrP* (realized in Old English as *-ende).* They are *wesan* 'to be', *beon* 'to be', and

[9] Quotations for Old English are derived from Henry Sweet, ed., *King Alfred's Orosius,* EETS 79 (London, 1883), abbreviated *Or.;* and from Henry Sweet, ed., *King Alfred's West-Saxon version of Gregory's Pastoral Care,* EETS 45, 50 (London, 1871), abbreviated *CP.* References are to page and line numbers.

weorðan 'to become', here classified as the subset *BE*. Examples of each of these progressives are

(16) *Or*.236.29: *& him æfterfylgende wæs* 'And was following him'
(17) *Or*.12.35: *þæt seo ea bið flowende ofer eal Ægypta land* 'So that this river floods all the land of Egypt'
(18) *CP*.405.25: *Ðin eagan weorðað gesionde ðinne bebiodend* 'Your eyes shall see your master'

Progressive but apparently not perfect auxiliary verbs may occur with *M*. In (19), for example, we find *M* and progressive. Sentences like (20) with *M* and progressive would be possible, but not (21) with *M* and perfect auxiliary; nor would (22) with *M* – perfect – progressive:

(19) *Or*.110.10: *Nu ic wille eac þæs maran Alexandres gemunende beon* 'Now I shall also consider Alexander the Great'
(20) *Ic sceal feohtende beon* 'I shall be fighting'
(21) **Ic sceal gefuhten habban* 'I shall have fought'
(22) **Ic sceal feohtende gebeon habban* 'I shall have been fighting'

A further restriction is placed on the nonmodal operators: they do not occur in passive formations. Although we find (23) with the passive auxiliary formant (*BE* requiring *PP*) in the environment of *M*, (24) and (25) with passive formants in the environment of perfect and progressive auxiliary verbs respectively are ungrammatical:

(23) *Or*.128.5: *þa Darius geseah þæt he oferwunnen beon wolde* 'When Darius saw that he would be conquered'
(24) * *þæt he oferwunnen geworden hæfde* 'That he had been overcome'
(25) * *þæt he oferwunnen wesende wæs* 'That he was being overcome'

The examples above demonstrate that the word order is very different from that in Modern English. At the end of the ninth century the following patterns are favored, but are by no means exclusive:[10]

(a) In coordinate *and* clauses and in subordinate clauses, especially temporal clauses with time adverbs, the finite verb (*MV* carrying *T*) often occurs at the end. If there are helping verbs, *MV* will usually be

[10] Recent detailed discussion of word-order problems include S. O. Andrew, *Syntax and style in Old English* (Cambridge, 1940); Paul Bacquet, *La structure de la phrase verbale à l'époque Alfrédienne* (Paris, 1962); C. R. Barrett, *Studies in the word-order of Aelfric's Catholic Homilies and Lives of the Saints* (Cambridge, 1953); Charles R. Carlton, *Syntax of the Old English Charters* 170-256 (unpub. doctoral diss., Michigan, 1958); David P. Harris, 'The development of word-order patterns in twelfth-century English' in Albert H. Marckwardt, ed., *Studies in languages and linguistics in honor of Charles C. Fries* 187-98 (University of Michigan, 1964); Bruce Mitchell, 'Syntax and word-order in "The Peterborough Chronicle" 1122-1154', *Neuphilologische Mitteilungen* 65.113-44 (1964).

followed by the nonmodal operators and *M*. The last helping verb will carry *T*. For coordinates see (16), for subordinates (7), (9), (11), (15), (23).[11]

(b) In independent clauses,[12] the finite verb occurs nonfinally except in simple intransitive sentences. If a helping verb is present, *MV* will usually be preceded by *M* or a nonmodal operator, as in (8), (10), (12), (18). When there are two helping verbs, *M* will usually precede *MV*, and the perfect or progressive will follow, as in (19).

Most linguists consider that the order subject *(SU)* – object *(O)* – main verb *(MV)* + auxiliary *(Aux)* which is typical of coordinate and dependent clauses is a 'reversal' of the normal order *SU – Aux – MV – O*. In terms of simplicity of description and explanatory power, however, it is by far the simplest to set up the Old English verb phrase in the order *SU (O) MV + Aux*. This will automatically account for most coordinate and subordinate clauses. A rule will then specify that in independent clauses the last helping verb is moved to position before *MV;* in this way just one rule will account for the fact that if there is one helping verb, it precedes *MV*, but if there are two, only *M* precedes *MV*. Other orders will be accounted for by a stylistic variant rule. Independent motivation for such an analysis is provided by negative constructions formed with *ne*. If the verb is finite, *ne* precedes *MV:*

(26) *Or.*19.10: *He cwæð þæt nan man ne bude be norðan him* 'He said that no man lived north of him'

If there is a helping verb in type-(a) sentences, *ne* precedes the last helping verb, as in (9), (11); in type-(b) sentences it precedes whichever helping verb precedes *MV*. The negative of (19) would therefore be

(27) *Nu ic nille eac þæs maran Alexandres gemunende beon* 'Now I shall also not consider Alexander the Great'

Furthermore, this analysis obviates the necessity of an affix switch rule, a rule which has no independent motivation, especially as *T* never has to be blocked from *MV* in Old English to generate a dummy carrier.

The *Aux* will therefore be optimally generated by[13]

[11] (13), (14), (17) are examples of deviation from this rule.

[12] 'Independent clauses' here include 'demonstrative clauses' introduced by demonstrative adverbs *þa* 'then', *þonne* 'then', *þær* 'there' in which the finite verb or one helping verb usually precedes the subject (cf. Andrew, *Syntax and style in Old English* 3). Both independent clauses with demonstrative adverbs and those without share the main features of verb order under discussion.

[13] The rules are particularly interesting in that they are basically similar to those suggested by Emmon Bach for German, 'The order of elements in a transformational grammar of German', *Lg.* 38.263-9 (1962).

V_{i_x} in Rule 4.4 stands for the class of all V_i that are not $V_{i_{move}}$. It includes verbs homonymous with the members of $V_{i_{move}}$.

4.1 $S \longrightarrow NP - VP$
4.2 $VP \longrightarrow MV + Aux$
4.3 $MV \longrightarrow \begin{Bmatrix} NP - V_t \\ V_i \\ \vdots \end{Bmatrix}$

4.4 $V_i \longrightarrow \begin{Bmatrix} V_{i_{move}} \\ V_{i_x} \end{Bmatrix}$

4.5 $Aux \longrightarrow \left(\begin{Bmatrix} PP - \text{habb, in env. } V_t\ ,\ V_{i_{move}} \\ PP - \text{wes, in env. } V_i \\ (PrP - BE)\ \ (Inf - M) \end{Bmatrix} \right) \qquad T$

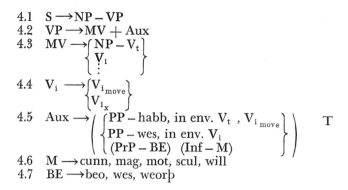

4.6 M ⟶ cunn, mag, mot, scul, will
4.7 BE ⟶ beo, wes, weorþ

5. *Middle English* [14]

By the thirteenth century, the normal word order is similar to that in Modern English. That is, we find *Aux – MV (O)* favored in both independent and dependent clauses. The simplicity criterion therefore requires that this order be generated as basic for Middle English. Such analysis furthermore provides just the kind of information we need to account for the fundamental differences in verb-phrase order between Old and Middle English. Although there is not the independent motivation that *do* provides in Modern English for setting up the members of *Aux* in the order *T (M)* . . . , since no dummy carrier is generable in Middle English, this analysis is simplest, as all other orders can then be derived easily from the basic form. Other constructions can also be neatly accounted for. The negative, for example, is formed during the earlier part of the Middle Engish period by *ne* preceding *T* – first base as in (28); or by *nat* following *T* – first base as in (29) ; or by both *ne* and *nat* as in (30) . By the fifteenth century, negatives are more generally formed by *not* ⌢ *nat* after *T* – first base, as in (31) , (32) :

(28) Ch.*Mel*.2266: *He ne foond neuere womman good* 'He never found a good woman'

(29) Ch.*Mel*.2170: *It aperteneth nat to a wys man* 'It is not suitable for a wise man'

(30) Ch.*Mel*.2220: *Yet ne wolde he nat answere sodeynly* 'Yet he did not want to answer immediately'

(31) *PL*.III.104.22 (1456) : *And uff the maters went not to my maister entent* 'And if the matters did not go according to what my master had planned'

(32) *PL*.III.87.1 (1456) : *and of suche as I will not write* 'And of such things as I will not write about'

[14] Quotations for Middle English are taken from Hans Kurath, Sherman Kuhn, John Reidy, eds., *Middle English dictionary* (Ann Arbor, 1954–) ; James Gairdner, ed., *The Paston letters 1422-1509* (London, 1904) , abbreviated *PL.*, with references to volume, page, and line numbers; and Geoffrey Chaucer, *The text of the Canterbury Tales*, ed. John M. Manly and Edith Rickert (Chicago, 1940) .

As far as the shape of *Aux* is concerned, there has been considerable increase in the complexity of membership, but there is already greater environmental generalization for the perfect participle constructions. The modals are the cognates of the Old English forms and need not concern us here. As in Old English, Early Middle English modals require *Inf,* but owing to a regular late-fourteenth- and early-fifteenth-century rule, this marker is lost and is usually not overtly marked by the mid-fifteenth century. The perfect auxiliary has undergone partial reversal of context restriction: *have – PP* is used for both transitives and intransitives:

(33) *PL*.III.103.24 (1456): *Which Fenn hath promised (V_t) to doo* 'Which Fenn has promised to do'

(34) *PL*.IV.17.10: *Wherfore the people was greved by cauce they had labored (V_i) so often* 'For this reason the people were grieved because they had labored so often'

(35) Ch.*Mel*.3000: *For ye han entred (V_i) in to myn hous by violence* 'For ye have entered my house by violence'

A subset of V_i may also occur with *be – PP;* its members, interestingly enough, are mainly the cognates of exactly those same verbs of movement which in Old English were the only ones that could occur with *habb – PP:*

(36) *PL*.IV.68.13: *But I undrestande ther is comen an other writte to the undrescheryff* 'But I understand that another writ has come to the undersheriff'

(37) Ch.*Mel*.2160: *And by wyndowes ben entred* 'And have entered through the windows'

There is only one progressive formant: the verb *be* requiring *PrP.* More significant for the history of *Aux* is that the perfect occasionally follows the modal and the progressive occasionally appears after the perfect helping verb, instead of being mutually exclusive with it. When this is the case, only *have – PP,* not *be – PP,* precedes the progressive formant. Examples of this complex construction occur mainly in poetry, as in Chaucer's *Knight's Tale*:

(38) Ch.*Kt.T*.929: *We have been waytynge al this fortenyght* 'We have been waiting all this fortnight'

(39) **We been been waytynge al this fortenyght*

Of special interest is the additional use from Early Middle English times of *do* and *gin* as auxiliaries, both requiring *Inf* at their first introduction.[15] Both were originally used only as main verbs; throughout the

[15] Clear loss of identity as *MV* is indicated by the occasional interchange in different MSS of *gin – Inf* and *do – Inf;* cf. *Cursor Mundi,* Göt. 2009 (c. 1400): *A neu liuelad gan he bigin* 'He began a new kind of life', with MS variants *con, cun* (reduced forms of *gan*) and also *dud.* A summary and bibliography of studies on *do* and *gin* is provided in Tauno F. Mustanoja, *A Middle English syntax I: Parts of speech* 600-15 (Helsinki, 1960).

period homonymous verbs *do* 'to cause to' and *gin* 'to begin to' persist as main verbs taking infinitive complement nominalizations; another homonymous verb *do* was a member from Old English times of a small class of substitutive verbs. The auxiliary verbs in question originated in poetry; *do* spread to prose by the late fourteenth century, cf.

(40) *Appeal Usk* in *Bk.Lond.E.*26/101 (1384): *So they diden pursuwe thynges a-yeins the Franchise of london for euer* 'So they pursued matters opposing the franchise of London for ever'

Gin, however, never became established in prose. Only *do* is generated as a formant in the mid-fifteenth-century grammar; a complete version of this grammar would generate *gin* as a deviant member of *Aux,* restricted to poetry. A grammar of Middle English prior to c.1380 would, however, specify restriction to poetry of both *do – Inf* and *gin – Inf* (*Inf* is still marked at this time).[16]

Among examples of auxiliary *do* in the *Paston Letters* are

(41) *PL*.III.2.26 (1454): *As for the prist that dede areste me* 'As for the priest who arrested me'

(42) *PL*.IV.149.37 (1465) *More plainly than I may do wryte at thys tyme* 'More plainly than I may write at this time'

(43) *PL*.IV.143.14 (1465) *Yf they wold do pay such dewts* 'If they would pay such debts'

From (42), (43) and several other passages, it is clear that *do* may occur after *M* and *have – PP*. There is independent motivation for analysing *do* as a second position nonmodal operator mutually exclusive with *be – PrP*: both, for example, fail to occur in passive formation.

The grammar must therefore specify at least the following phrase markers:

$$5.1 \quad \mathrm{S} \longrightarrow \mathrm{NP} - \mathrm{VP}$$

$$5.2 \quad \mathrm{VP} \longrightarrow \mathrm{Aux} - \mathrm{MV}$$

$$5.3 \quad \mathrm{MV} \longrightarrow \left\{ \begin{array}{l} \mathrm{V_t} - \mathrm{NP} \\ \mathrm{V_i} \\ \vdots \end{array} \right\}$$

$$5.4 \quad \mathrm{V_i} \longrightarrow \left\{ \begin{array}{l} \mathrm{V_{i\,move}} \\ \mathrm{V_{i_x}} \end{array} \right\}$$

$$5.5 \quad \mathrm{Aux} \longrightarrow \mathrm{T}\ (\mathrm{M}) \quad \left(\left\{ \begin{array}{l} (\mathrm{have} - \mathrm{PP}) \left(\left\{ \begin{array}{l} \mathrm{be} - \mathrm{PrP} \\ \mathrm{do} \end{array} \right\} \right) \\ \mathrm{be} - \mathrm{PP}, \text{ in env. } — \mathrm{V_{i_{move}}} \end{array} \right\} \right)$$

$$5.6 \quad \mathrm{M} \longrightarrow \text{conn, mow, moot, shal, wol}$$

[16] On some of the problems in accounting for specifically poetic deviance, cf. Samuel R. Levin, 'Poetry and grammaticalness', in Horace Lunt, ed., *Proceedings of the ninth international congress of linguists* 308-15 ('s-Gravenhage, 1964).

6. *Early Modern English* [17]

By the late sixteenth century we find further changes. The chief of these are further development of *have – PP* in the environment of V_i; the spread of *do* as an auxiliary verb; and the appearance of the progressive in passive constructions.

As in Middle English, *do* is not a dummy carrier, but a regular optional member of *Aux*; *do* constructions occur side by side with finite verb constructions in unemphatic assertion, negative, and interrogative sentence types. In one particular, however, the behavior of *do* differs from that of its cognate in Middle English: it invariably occurs without other helping verbs:

(44) *N*.I.191.21–5: *Alledging many examples . . . how studie dooth effeminate a man* 'Alleging there were many examples . . . of how study makes a man effeminate'

(45) **Alledging many examples how study may do effeminate a man.*

(46) *N*.I.158.17: *Thereby I grew to consider how many base men . . . enjoyed content at will* 'From this I came to consider how many base men . . . enjoyed contentment at will'

(47) *N*.I.185.16: *I do not doubt (Doctor Diuell) but you were present* 'I do not doubt (Dr. Devil) that you were present'

(48) *N*.I.208.12: *That loue not to goe in greasie dublets* 'That do not like to walk about in greasy doublets'

(49) *N*.II.314.1: *Why did I enter into anie mention of my owne misusage?* 'Why did I make any mention of the way I myself was misused'

(50) *N*.II.302.5: *Why iest I in such a necessarie perswasiue discourse?* 'Why do I jest in such a necessary persuasive discourse?'

A few Early Modern Northern manuscripts still show use of *do* after other operators, both in prose and in poetry:

(51) *Reg.Manor Scawby Lincolnsh.* (1597): *That the Carrgraues shall doe execute theire office truely* 'That the Cargraves shall execute their duties properly'

(52) *Scot.poems 16th C*.II.189 (1578): *And many other false abusion The Paip hes done invent* 'And the Pope has invented many other false abuses'

Since *do* as a second-position nonmodal operator is restricted to Northern dialects, we may assume that by the sixteenth century in England at least *do* had become an independent helping verb, mutually exclusive with modals, perfect and progressive auxiliaries; it is still incompatible with the passive formant.

[17] Data for Early Modern English are derived from the *Oxford English dictionary;* and Ronald B. McKerrow, ed., *The works of Thomas Nashe* (Oxford, 1958), abbreviated *N.,* with references to volume, line, and page numbers.

In the light of the considerations given above, *Aux* may be set up for Early Modern English by the following rules:

6.1 $S \longrightarrow NP - VP$

6.2 $VP \longrightarrow Aux - MV$

6.3 $MV \longrightarrow \begin{Bmatrix} V_t - NP \\ V_i \\ \vdots \end{Bmatrix}$

6.4 $V_i \longrightarrow \begin{Bmatrix} V_{i_{move}} \\ V_{i_x} \end{Bmatrix}$

6.5 $Aux \longrightarrow T \left(\begin{Bmatrix} (M) \left(\begin{Bmatrix} (have - PP) \ (be - PrP) \\ be - PP, \text{ in env. } — V_{i_{move}} \end{Bmatrix} \right) \\ do \end{Bmatrix} \right)$

6.6 $M \longrightarrow$ can, may, must, shall, will

Of particular interest is the sporadic appearance of the progressive in passive formations. Unlike passive constructions with other members of *Aux,* these passives are not formed with *be – PP.* We find patterns of the kind *The man is seeing by X,* not *The man is being seen by X.*[18]

(53) Deloney, *Gentle Craft* 132.45:[19] *While meat was bringing in* 'While food was being brought in'

The final stages in the development to Modern English consist in the loss of *be – PP* in the environment of most intransitive verbs, the restriction of *do* during the eighteenth and nineteenth centuries to certain explicitly determined environments, and the requirement of *be – PP* in passive constructions, whatever the membership of *Aux.* At the present stage of the language, *Aux* provides the least choices, but is also maximally generalized.

7. *Types of change*

These then are the major mutations in the history of *Aux.* Comparison of the different grammars reveals several types of change, all of which have far-reaching effects on sentence structure. The changes may be summarized as follows:

(a) reversal of order;
(b) loss of class-context restriction;
(c) realignments of existing structures, without radical system change, as when the Old English maximal *Aux* was extended to *T (M)* and two successive optional nonmodal operators;

[18] The latter is a modern construction which did not come into general use until the nineteenth century. The first clear instance of a passive of this type cited by Fernand Mossé, *Histoire de la forme périphrastique être + participe présent II: Moyen-anglais et anglais moderne* par. 263 (Paris, 1938), is from a letter by Robert Southey: *A fellow whose uppermost upper grinder is being torn out by a mutton-fisted barber.* For detailed discussion of the history of the passive progressive, see Mossé, ibid., pars. 231-81.

[19] Thomas Deloney, *Works,* ed. Francis O. Mann (Oxford, 1912).

(d) addition or loss of formants, as when *do* was added, and later when *be – PP* (perfect auxiliary verb) was lost;

(e) and finally, closely related with this, really radical changes of system membership, e.g. when *do,* which was a member of the lexical system, gave rise to an operator in the syntactic system; or later when *do,* which was an optional member of *Aux,* became an obligatory, predictable element, generable as a formative in the transformational component.

8. *Innovations accounting for changes*

It remains to be seen how these changes came about and how they may be considered a paradigm of language change in general.

The minimal change that must be postulated to account for reversal of word order is the growing tendency to favor *SU – Aux – MV (O)* order in all clauses. This tendency, which is amply attested by twelfth-century data, must have developed in two stages: first, preponderance of constructions with a finite verb or one helping verb preceding *O,* as in (19); and second, attraction of a second optional member of *Aux,* if present, to pre-*O* position. The word 'tendency' is used advisedly. All through Old English, both *Aux – MV* and *MV + Aux* patterns existed. What must be accounted for is the fact that the optimal grammar for Old English specifies *MV + Aux* and a rule allowing for certain stylistic switches of auxiliary verbs, but no affix-switch rule. The optimal grammar for Middle English, on the other hand, specifies *Aux – MV,* a rule allowing for certain stylistic switches of auxiliary verbs, and an affix-switch rule. Any synchronic Old English grammar will mirror the two orders for auxiliary verbs. For Middle English we need a new grammar. In other words, the mutations can only be reflected by a different set of rules.[20]

[20] A synchronic grammar cannot account for these changes, except so far as it treats different dialects, or different reflexes of different changes. When Klima says the order in which he describes the rules for pronouns in different dialects reflects the historic order of change, he is actually referring to the order of mutations, not innovations. Each set of rules for each dialect requires different ordering of basically the same rules. Each set has its own unique relationship to the rest in the structure of the language, and cannot be collapsed under the same grammar except as a discrete subset of the grammar. It has been suggested that grammars should provide rules accounting for synchronic relatedness between grammatical systems, such that different systems may be regarded as modifications or extensions of a given basic system. This is essentially what Klima's grammar does for pronouns. In addition, it has been suggested that grammars should provide rules accounting for diachronic relatedness between grammatical systems, also such that the different systems may be regarded as modifications or extensions of a given basic system. Such grammars would reveal with great clarity the similarities and differences between stages of the language, and would provide in simpler, i.e. more compact, form the same information that separate grammars of different stages of the language provide. They cannot, however, specify actual change or provide historical perspective. A grammar of the actual changes would be a kind of algebra accounting in the simplest way possible for all relevant changes, in their chronological order.

The same is true of changes in context restriction of the perfect auxiliary. As OE *habb – PP* came to predominate, it took over the function of *BE – PP*. We might postulate that since those intransitive verbs that were most frequently used (verbs of movement) could occur with both *habb – PP* and *BE – PP*, $V_{i_{move}}$ became a model for other intransitive verbs which, although more numerous, were less frequently used. It is also noteworthy that Middle English was a time when word formation by changes of class membership or extension to new class membership was becoming particularly common; in particular, many new transitives were being formed from intransitives.[21] This meant that class-context restriction was no longer clear, and that ambiguity between the perfect auxiliary formant *be – PP* and the homonymous passive formant could arise.[22]

A further innovation was the extension of the mutually exclusive set of perfect and progressive auxiliaries to two compatible nonmodal operators. Throughout the history of English up to the nineteenth century, and still today in the case of most sentences in which the main verb is the copula *be,* the structure 'base *be* followed by base *be*' has been ungrammatical or at least deviant. Although Modern English sentences of the type *The students are being attacked* are grammatical, *The students are being hungry* is ungrammatical. Strong pressure against such structures must account for the lack of passive progressives with the passive formant in Early Modern English. It also seems to account for the lack of progressives following perfect auxiliaries of the type *be – PP* in Middle English. Unless we are to assume that perfects followed by progressive helping verbs were possible only in transitive verb constructions, we are led to conclude that the two nonmodal operators became compatible AFTER both intransitives and transitives could take *have – PP* as the perfect auxiliary. Once the two became compatible, a mutation arose.

Although I have attempted so far to cover only those changes that took place within the *Aux* rule alone, I have had to mention far-reaching repercussions on the whole system. Change in word order requires, for simplicity of description and explanatory power, the introduction of an affix-switch rule. Behavior of progressive auxiliaries raises the question of the cooccurrence of two *be* bases. Other changes in the *Aux* further demonstrate clear cases of overall system changes. *Do,* which was a main verb requiring infinitive nominalizations, came to be reinterpreted as an auxiliary, presumably because it was followed by an unmarked infinitive. Perhaps pressures of continued association with the main verb *do* (which, as a main verb, could be preceded by auxiliary verbs) countered the tendency to use *do* in modal position; instead it came to fill the same slot as the progressive. This slot was in itself somewhat variable since it

[21] See F. Th. Visser, *An historical syntax of the English language* 93-138 (Leiden, 1963).

[22] Visser, ibid. 131, suggests that this ambiguity was one of the factors leading to the transitivization of intransitives.

was an innovation. The very character of this third position may account for the fact that *do* came to be used more and more as an independent unit which could not tolerate other auxiliary verbs in its environment. Its failure to pattern with other members of *Aux* then further favored the eventual mutation, by Modern English, to non-membership in the regular *Aux* construction, and to restriction to certain predictable environments.

9. *Theory of language change*

Given a knowledge of mutations, such as those in the development of *Aux*, and of the innovations that account for those mutations, can we say that the five proposals for a theory of language change outlined at the beginning of this paper account for syntactic change?

The proposition that language changes by means of a series of individual innovations seems to be fully supported by the history of the *Aux*, in which we can see each step develop individually. The second proposal is that the innovations usually occur at the end of some natural division of the grammar. This must give us pause. Within the syntactic component there are three main points of break: the point where the phrase structure ends and the lexicon begins; the point where the lexicon ends and the transformational subcomponent begins; and finally the point where the syntactic component ends and the morphophonemic begins.[23] Of the changes discussed, the only one that enters at such a break is the affix-switch rule, and this is the result of a mutation, not an innovation giving rise to a mutation; besides, it is largely motivated by simplicity of description rather than by actual language data when it is introduced for Middle English. Changes in context restriction of the perfect and progressive verbs occur within the high-level *Aux* rule, and do not enter at the end of the phrase structure. *Do* extends lexical membership of the category of infinitive complement taking transitives to nonlexical membership of this same high-level *Aux* rule; again, it is not possible to hypothesize that it entered as a low-level phrase-structure subcategory and was then reinterpreted as part of the *Aux*. The third proposal, that innovations are passed on to generation after generation, and the fourth, that mutations occur when the new generation reinterprets a grammar so as to effect radical changes such as restructuring, seem to be well borne out by syntactic evidence. The viability of the fifth proposal, however, that mutations are rare, is doubtful as far as syntactic change is con-

[23] Further subdivisions may or may not be made according to the particular model of grammar adopted. Grammars like Lees's *Grammar of English nominalizations* allow for certain groupings in the phrase structure according to sets of subcategorizations; Charles Fillmore's study 'The position of embedding transformations in a grammar', *Word* 19.208-31 (1963), specifies groupings for two-string vs. one-string transformations. In the latest models, however, such as Chomsky's blocking grammar and Klima's non-blocking grammar (cf. Klima, 'Current developments in generative grammar,' forthcoming in *Kybernetika* I, Prague), the phrase-structure component is minimal and cannot be subject to groupings. Context restrictions and subcategorizations are largely specified in a lexicon in which the only significant groupings are the overall categories *N*, *V*, *Adj*, etc.; only in the filter transformations do we find areas in which the concept 'point of break' is significant for syntax.

cerned. The *Aux,* which is such a small part of the grammar, demonstrates at least six types of mutation. The four different types of pronominal usage which Klima discusses support in a totally unrelated area the observation that mutation in syntax is not rare, although it seems to be relatively infrequent in phonological change.

In view of the factors discussed above it appears that any theory of language change must include the proposals that language changes by means of the additions of single innovations to an adult's grammar, by transmission of these innovations to new generations, and by the reinterpretation of grammars such that mutations occur. Restriction of innovations to points of break seems not to be viable as a generalization for language change, nor does the statement that mutations are rare. Both these proposals must be limited to the area of phonological change.

Suggested Additional Readings for Part IV

[See additional readings for Part I for works cited by author and date only.]

PAUL BACQUET, *La structure de la phrase verbale à l'époque Alfrédienne* (Paris, 1962).

BLOOMFIELD 1933, esp. chapters 10-16, 23.

DINNEEN 1967, esp. chapters 3, 9, 12.

JERRY A. FODOR AND JERROLD J. KATZ, eds., *The Structure of Language* (Englewood Cliffs, 1964), esp. selections 6-8.

DAVID P. HARRIS, "The Development of Word-order Patterns in Twelfth-century English," in Albert H. Marckwardt, ed., *Studies in Languages and Linguistics in Honor of Charles C. Fries* (Ann Arbor, 1964), 187-98.

HOCKETT 1958, esp. chapters 14-31, 50.

LEHMANN 1962, esp. chapter 11.

MALMBERG 1963, esp. chapter 8.

SAMUEL MOORE, "Grammatical and Natural Gender in Middle English," *PMLA* 36.79-103 (1921).

——————, "Loss of Final *n* in Inflectional Syllables of Middle English," *Language* 3.232-59 (1927).

DAVID W. REED, "The History of Inflectional *n* in English Verbs before 1500," *Univ. of California Publications in English* 7:4. 157-328 (1950).

ANN SHANNON, *A Descriptive Syntax of the Parker Manuscript of the Anglo-Saxon Chronicle from 734 to 891* ('s-Gravenhage, 1964).

F. TH. VISSER, *An Historical Syntax of the English Language* (Leiden, 1963).

For additional references to studies of historical English grammar, see HAROLD B. ALLEN, comp., *Linguistics and English Linguistics* (New York, 1966), 41-49.

PART V

Linguistic Variation and Language Contact

At any stage of its development, a language displays internal variation. Modern English, like all other languages, shows variation from one area to another and, within a single area, from one social or professional group to another. It can be assumed that such dialect variation has existed in English from the earliest times forward.

The existence of dialects within a language can be understood in terms of the Saussurian concept of *langue* or structure. For any language there is a fundamental battery of structural rules—the rules of the *langue*—which prescribe its realization, this realization being what de Saussure termed *parole*. Dialects are present when groups of speakers make use of rules beyond those which are common to all speakers of the language. The degree of mutual intelligibility between dialects depends on the degree to which they share rules in addition to the common set. Dialects *A* and *B* may share almost all of their rules, with a correspondingly high degree of mutual intelligibility, while dialects *A* and *C* may share fewer rules, with the degree of mutual intelligibility varying accordingly. Geographically proximate dialects usually share a high percentage of their rules, and linguistic distance tends to increase with geographic distance. When the number of shared rules diverges to the point where mutual intelligibility ceases, speakers are said to employ different languages. Historically, however, different languages from a common source—e.g. Old English, Old High German, Old Icelandic, and Gothic—are often said to be 'dialects' of the source language—in this case, Proto-Germanic.

Not all variation in language is of equal significance. The basic pitch ranges of women's voices are higher than those of men, and some speakers talk louder or faster than others—but this variation generally does not indicate that a speaker belongs or does not belong to a particular dialect community, and as a result, such features are usually ignored by the dialectologist. Phonological, grammatical, or lexical variation, on the other hand, is of interest to the dialectologist since this type of variation signals the dialectal identity of the speaker.

It is not ordinarily possible to determine where dialectal divergence first begins in a language, but investigation has demonstrated that the degree of variation does not remain constant through time and that there is always the possibility of interaction between linguistic systems because of the interaction of the people who use the systems for communication. With the tools of dialectology it becomes possible to examine the status of the variation at various time intervals and, through the exploration of linguistic interaction, to account for the existence of features in a given dialect or language which would otherwise appear to be anomalous.

Linguistic features—like cultural artifacts—tend to be propagated outward from centers of influence and along the lines of communication for such influence. Thus, a feature may appear in areas which are geographically contiguous to the center of influence or in geographically separated areas which for one reason or another have some common cultural orientation. In this way, scientific terminology, for example, may be common to groups of speakers in London, Melbourne, and San Francisco without influencing the speech of non-professional yet geographically more proximate speakers.

In dialectology, centers of influence are generally called 'focal areas' and the perimeters of their influence can often be indicated on maps through the use of imaginary lines called 'isoglosses'. An isogloss borders an area on the map in which an investigator found some feature to occur in the speech of the informants that he interviewed. If isoglosses circle some geographical point, they may indicate the extent to which the features they mark were propagated from that point.

Historically—and metaphorically—isoglosses are said to 'advance' and 'retreat'. That is, if the isoglosses for a particular feature are compared at different points in time, the position of the isogloss may have advanced geographically if more speakers have adopted the feature, or the reverse, if the feature tends to be passing out of use. The advancing of an isogloss is what is usually called 'borrowing', and though the degree of ease with which features are borrowed usually decreases as the structures of the relevant systems diverge, borrowing from one language to another is akin to borrowing from one dialect to another. In the former case, however, the isogloss advances across great bundles of isoglosses which mark major linguistic frontiers. The similarity of words for *tobacco* in the European languages, for example, can be explained in terms of an isogloss which advanced across major linguistic frontiers from some focal point in Europe as the product was introduced from one nation to the next. Even if nothing were known about the early history of tobacco, the principles of dialectology would aid in explaining the appearance of similar vocabulary items in languages of diverse histories.

Since history is short, dialectology has often been the only way to account for the appearance of features which would otherwise obscure the understanding of the internal development of a given language or dialect. The principles of dialectology also make it possible to learn a good deal about the speakers of a language, since the cultural development and historical interaction of peoples tend to be reflected in language. What is known of the speakers of the Indo-European parent language, for example, is known only through an examination of the common features of the descendent dialects. From an examination of the vocabulary, it is conjectured that their tools were of stone, not of metal, since there is a common vocabulary for the former, but not for the latter. And since the descendent dialects have no common terms for *elephant* or *camel,* it can be surmised that these beasts must first have been encountered by Indo-European speakers after the common Indo-European period and that the terms in the individual dialects were borrowed during some later period of interaction with speakers of a language who were familiar with these animals. Where historical records exist, they tend to confirm what could be inferred on the basis of a knowledge of the principles of dialectology. The type and period of borrowings, for example, tell a great deal about the linguistic communities involved and about the nature of their interaction. The fact that the continental Germans borrowed Latin words for *street, wine,* and *cheese* confirms what is known historically about the culture of the mobile, non-agricultural Germanic tribes and about the more stable, highly-integrated commercial culture of the Romans.

From a descriptive point of view, dialectology is the study of linguistic diversity. From a historical point of view, it is the study of the implications and results of diversity and of linguistic interaction, and as such it cannot be divorced from cultural history. In historical dialectology—more than in any other branch of linguistics—one can see both the interrelationship of language and culture and the necessity for viewing language in a cultural framework.

The selections which follow reflect research which has been carried out in the related fields of linguistic variation and language contact. The first two articles exemplify descriptive dialectology. The article by E. Bagby Atwood presents the terminology of dialect investigation and applies the principles of dialectology in a discussion of one widely recognized feature of variation in American English. The article by Albert H. Marckwardt uses similar methodology to outline the characteristics of one major American dialect area—the north central states. Einar Haugen's article is significant for the study of historical dialectology since it presents a theoretical framework for the analysis of features propagated from one linguistic community to another. The article by William Labov considers language contact in terms of socially differentiated varieties of speech and notes the effect of this contact on historical sound change. David DeCamp applies the same principles of variation and contact to the OE period with the result that long-held views on the origin of the OE dialects are called into question. The final article, by Marjorie Daunt, was the original impetus for a re-examination of traditional assumptions about the OE phonological system, and, as such, might also be read with the selections in Part III. An equally important result of the publication of the Daunt article, however, is that it demonstrates that features of writing systems may be adopted by linguistic communities in a manner analogous to the propagation of linguistic features such as lexical or grammatical elements. As a result, borrowed orthographic features, unless properly evaluated, may cloud the interpretation of linguistic history. Since the principles of language contact are fundamental to such an evaluation, the Daunt article is included in this section.

Grease *and* Greasy

A Study of Geographical Variation

E. BAGBY ATWOOD

THE FACT THAT THE VERB *to grease* and the adjective *greasy* are pronounced by some Americans with [s] and by others with [z] has long been well known even to amateur observers of speech.[1] It has also been pretty well accepted that the incidence of [s] or [z] in the words in question is primarily dependent on the geographical location of the speaker rather than on his social or educational level—that [s] is, in general, "Northern," [z] "Southern."

As early as 1896, George Hempl published a study[2] of these two words, based on a rather widely circulated written questionnaire. His returns enabled him to divide the country into four major areas, according to the percentages of [s] in *to grease* and *greasy* respectively. The "North"[3]—extending from New England to the Dakotas—showed 88 and 82 per cent of [s] pronunciations; the "Midland," comprising a

---

Reprinted by permission from *Texas Studies in English* 29.249-60 (1950).

[1] Webster's *New International Dictionary* states that [z] in *grease* is found "esp. Brit. and Southern U.S."; [z] in *greasy* is "perhaps more general in England and the southern U. S. than in the North and East." Kenyon and Knott, *Pronouncing Dictionary* (Springfield, Mass., 1944), give [s] and [z] for the country as a whole, only [z] for the South. *The Century, Funk and Wagnalls New Standard,* and the *American College Dictionary* merely give [s] or [z] for both words. Kenyon and Knott state that "['grizɪ] and [tə griz] are phonetically normal; ['grisɪ] and [tə gris] imitate the noun *grease* [gris]." Certainly many verbs since Middle English times have been distinguished from the corresponding nouns by voicing the final fricative; cf. *house*: *to house, proof*: *to prove, wreath*: *to wreathe, abuse*: *to abuse*—and (with vowel change) *bath*: *to bathe, breath*: *to breathe, grass*: *to graze,* etc. This paper will not be concerned with the origin or history of the feature.

The pronunciation of the vowels is of no significance in our study. For convenience I am using the symbol [i] for both the stressed and the unstressed vowels in *greasy*.

[2] "*Grease* and *Greasy*," *Dialect Notes,* I (1896), 438-44.

[3] In addition to New England, this area includes New Brunswick, Quebec, Ontario, New York, Michigan, Wisconsin, North Dakota, South Dakota, Minnesota, and the northern portions of Pennsylvania, Ohio, Indiana, Illinois, and Iowa.

fairly narrow strip extending from New York City to St. Louis,[4] 42 and 34 per cent; the "South,"[5] 12 and 12 per cent; and the "West"—an ever-widening area extending westward from St. Louis—56 and 47 per cent. The material which Hempl was able to collect was admittedly "insufficient";[6] moreover, he had no means of selecting strictly representative informants;[7] and the answers may not always have been correct, since, it seems to me, an understanding of the questions would have required a certain degree of linguistic sophistication.[8] Still, in spite of these handicaps, Hempl's study has not been greatly improved upon by later writers. Most authorities content themselves by stating that [z] in *to grease* and *greasy* is predominantly Southern, and that either [s] or [z] may occur elsewhere.[9] Few investigators have gathered material that would enable them to draw clearer lines between [s] and [z] than Hempl. . . .[10]

The field records that have been gathered for the *Linguistic Atlas of the United States and Canada*[11] provide us with an excellent basis for

[4] This includes New York City, New Jersey, Delaware, the District of Columbia, southern Pennsylvania, southern Ohio, northern West Virginia, middle Indiana, middle Illinois, and St. Louis, Missouri.

[5] This includes everything to the south of the Midland, as far west as Texas.

[6] *Op. cit.*, p. 438.

[7] For example, he urged his colleagues, especially "teachers of English in colleges, normal schools, and young ladies' seminaries to use the questions as an exercise in English." (*Ibid.*, p. 444.)

[8] Question 45 reads: "In which (if any) of the following does *s* have the sound of *z: 'the grease,' 'to grease,' 'greasy'?"* (Hempl, "American Speech Maps," *Dialect Notes,* I [1896], 317.) Judging from my experience in teaching phonetic transcription to college seniors and graduate students, a considerable proportion of a class would simply not know whether [s] or [z] was used in such words; certainly many students unhesitatingly write [s] in words like *rose* and *has* simply because the *letter s* is used in standard spelling.

[9] See footnote 1. It is sometimes pointed out that the same speaker may use both [ˈgrisi] and [ˈgrizi] with a distinction in meaning. This point will be discussed below.

[10] A. H. Marckwardt was able to draw a fairly clear line through Ohio, Indiana, and Illinois, though on the basis of relatively little data. See "Folk Speech in Indiana and Adjacent States," *Indiana History Bulletin,* XVII (1940), 120-40. Henry L. Smith has long been using the word *greasy* as a test word in his demonstrations of regional variation and to determine the origins of speakers, though he has not published his material. I presume that Dr. Smith's observations are the source of Mario Pei's statement: " 'greazy' . . . would place the speaker south of Philadelphia, while 'greassy' would place him north of Trenton." (*The Story of Language* [Philadelphia and New York, 1949], p. 51.) C. K. Thomas considers the word *greasy* in his survey of the regional speech types, but comes to the strange conclusion that "the choice between [s] and [z] in words like *discern, desolate, absorb, absurd,* and *greasy* seems to be more personal than regional." (*An Introduction to the Phonetics of American English* [New York, 1947], p. 154.) G. P. Krapp is likewise at fault when he states that, in *greasy,* "popular usage and, in general, standard speech have only the form with [z]." (*The Pronunciation of Standard English in America* [New York, 1919], p. 119.)

[11] The New England materials have been published as the *Linguistic Atlas of New England,* ed. Hans Kurath and Bernard Bloch, 3 vols., Providence, R. I., 1939-43. Field records for most of the Middle Atlantic and South Atlantic states were gathered by the late Guy S. Lowman; recently (summer, 1949) Dr. Raven I. McDavid, Jr., completed the work for the eastern seaboard. The records, in an unedited but usable state, are filed at the University of Michigan, where they were made available to me through the courtesy of Professor Kurath.

delimiting the geographical and social spread of speech forms in the eastern United States. A number of features of the *Atlas* methodology[12] are conducive to an accurate picture of native and normal speech. The informants, though relatively few,[13] were carefully chosen, each being both native to and representative of his community. The answers to questions were elicited, so far as possible, in a conversational atmosphere, and thus the occurrence of ungenuine forms was minimized. Finally, the forms were recorded by trained phoneticians, who would be very unlikely to make such errors as to write [s] when the informant actually uttered [z].

A few words should be said regarding the cartographical representation of linguistic atlas data. In such works as the *Atlas Linguistique de la France,*[14] in which each community, or "point" on the map, is represented by a single speaker, it is usually possible to draw lines, or *isoglosses,* separating those communities where a form occurs from those where it does not occur. Often these isoglosses set off a large block of "points," forming a solid area—as, for example, the southern French territory marked by initial [k] in the word *chandelle.*[15] A more complex presentation is sometimes required, as in the case of the northern French occurrences of [k] in this same word: after setting off our solid area we find outside it a number of scattered communities where the feature in question occurs; these must be indicated by additional lines encircling the "points" where the form is found.[16] In still other cases, the communities where a given speech form occurs (for example, *conin* for 'rabbit') are so scattered that it is impossible to connect them; in such cases our isoglosses must consist merely of scattered circles here and there on the map.[17] When this situation obtains we would probably do better to assign a symbol (say, a cross, or a dot, or a triangle) to the scattered form in question, lest the labyrinth of lines become too much for the reader to cope with.

Now, in presenting data from the American *Atlas,* we are faced with all these complications, plus others arising from the fact that more than one informant was chosen to represent each community. That is, at nearly every "point" the American field workers recorded the usage of one elderly, poorly educated informant and one younger, more modern informant. In certain key communities a third type was included—a well educated, or "cultured," speaker who presumably represented the cultivated usage of the area. Thus, at the same point on the map we often

[12] See *Handbook of the Linguistic Geography of New England,* ed. H. Kurath and others (Providence, R. I., 1939), for a complete account of the *Atlas* methodology.

[13] Something like 1600 informants have been interviewed, representing communities from New Brunswick to northern Florida, approximately as far west as Lake Erie.

[14] Ed. J. Gilliéron and E. Edmont, 7 vols., Paris, 1902-10.

[15] See Karl Jaberg, "Sprachgeographie," *Siebenunddreissigstes Jahresheft des Vereins Schweiz. Gymnasiallehrer* (Aarau, 1908), pp. 16-42; also Plate III.

[16] *Ibid.,* Plate III.

[17] *Ibid.,* Plate X.

find such variants as *sot down* (preterite), representing rustic usage, *set* or *sit down,* representing more modern popular usage, and *sat down,* representing cultivated usage.[18] It is obviously impossible to draw isoglosses separating *sot* from *set* or *sat*; it is even impractical to set off the *sot* areas, since the form occurs in about every other community through considerable areas. In other cases, of course, it is quite easy to mark off an area where a certain form is current. *Holp* (for *helped*), for example, occupies a very clear-cut area south of the Potomac.[19] Yet a line marking off this area would by no means constitute a dividing line between *holp* and *helped,* since most of the younger informants within the *holp* area use the standard form *helped.* My point is that an isogloss based on American *Atlas* materials *should in all cases be regarded as an outer limit, not as a dividing line between two speech forms.*

The examples hitherto adduced have, of course, illustrated the incidence of "non-standard" as against "standard" speech forms. What of those instances of two forms which are equally "standard," each within its area? Kurath's map of *pail* and *bucket* provides an example.[20] Here too we must follow the same principle: we must first draw the outer limit of one form, then that of the other. The two lines will lap over each other at some points, enclosing certain communities of mixed usage.[21] Thus, *a dividing line is a double isogloss,* each line being the outer limit of one of the two speech forms in question. The areas of overlapping between the two lines may be wide or narrow, depending on many social, geographical, and historical considerations.

Let us return to *grease* and *greasy.* The variation between [s] and [z] in these words furnishes an almost ideal example of geographical (as against social) distribution. Consider first the verb *grease.* It is unnecessary to describe in detail the incidence of [s] and [z], since the accompanying map tells its own story. The northern line of the [z]-form, it may be observed, takes in the southwestern corner of Connecticut (west of the Housatonic); from there it passes westward just to the north of New Jersey; then it dips sharply southward to Philadelphia, to the west of which it again rises gradually northward to the northwestern corner of Pennsylvania. The transition area (where both [s] and [z] are used) is

[18] In addition, the same informant often uses more than one form; all of these are of course entered at that point on the map. On at least one occasion McDavid picked up from the same informant, as the preterite of *see, I seen, I seed, I see,* and *I saw.*

[19] This verb, as well as the others mentioned, is treated in my *Survey of Verb Forms in the Eastern United States,* to be published soon.

[20] *A Word Geography of the Eastern United States* (Ann Arbor, Mich., 1949), Figure 66.

[21] Even after drawing the lines we would find a good many scattered, or "stray," occurrences of *pail* within the *bucket* area and vice versa. Kurath's lines, which are all outer limits, do not attempt to indicate the presence of stray forms or small patches which occur outside the main area; however, since he also publishes maps on which each occurrence of each word is recorded by a symbol, the reader can easily check and interpret his isoglosses.

relatively narrow to the west of Philadelphia; to the northeast, however, it widens considerably so as to include most of northern New Jersey, as well as New York City and eastern Long Island.

Outside our pair of isoglosses there is a surprisingly small number of "stray" forms. All together, there are only six occurrences of [z] in the [s] area and only six of [s] in the [z] area.[22] (It will be observed, of course, that there is a second area, or island, of [s] along the Ohio River extending northeastward from the vicinity of Marietta, Ohio.) There is no sign whatever of social variation within the solid [s] and [z] areas; cultivated usage is in strict agreement with popular usage.[23] Within the areas of overlapping there is naturally some variation between older and more modern informants—yet the general trend is not at all clear. In the communities of divided usage to the west of Philadelphia the more modern informant uses [s] in six out of eight instances; in such communities to the northeast of Philadelphia the modern preference is for [s] in six instances, for [z] in six others. As for cultured informants within the areas of overlapping, ten use [griz], five use [gris], and one offers both [s] and [z] forms. One might state, very tentatively, that cultivated usage has tended to favor [griz], particularly in New York City and northern New Jersey.

For the adjective *greasy,* the pronunciations [grisi] and [grizi] show almost precisely the same isoglosses as those for [gris] and [griz]. The northern limit of [z] pushes further northward at three points in Pennsylvania;[24] correspondingly, the southern limit of [s] retreats northward at one point in Ohio, three in Pennsylvania, and two in northern New Jersey.[25] Within the [s] area, there are ten stray forms with [z], scattered through New England and the Hudson Valley; six of these occur in the cultured type of informant. Within the [z] area, we again find six stray occurrences of [s]; and precisely the same island of [s] occurs along the Ohio River. In short, a few more eastern informants use [z] in *greasy* than in *grease,* though the difference is not great. Within the areas of overlapping we find almost exactly the same social distribution as in the case of *grease.* Cultured informants prefer [grizi] by eleven to four; this fact, together with the six "stray" northern uses of [z] in the cultured type, inclines us to believe that [z] in *greasy* has penetrated into northeastern cultivated speech a little more palpably than in the case of *grease* —though still to a very slight extent.

[22] This amounts to less than one per cent of the informants. Most of the informants who show exceptional usage also give the "normal" form; that is, they use both [s] and [z] forms.

[23] Although the preterite form of the verb was not called for in the work sheets, Lowman picked up some five instances of *grez* [grɛz] in the [z] area; and a number of other informants reported having heard this form.

[24] Lehigh, Columbia, and Lancaster counties.

[25] Columbia, Armstrong, Blair, Cumberland, Hunterdon, and Morris counties.

After describing the incidence of the speech forms in question, we are still faced with a number of questions, to which our data can provide only partial answers.

What becomes of our isoglosses in the areas west of Pennsylvania? The materials being gathered for the Great Lakes atlas (under the direction of Professor A. H. Marckwardt) will undoubtedly provide an answer. I have not been able to examine the latest of these materials; but judging from preliminary information, as well as from a map already published by Professor Marckwardt,[26] the northern limit of [z] in *greasy* passes through central Ohio, then swings northward so as to take in almost the whole of Indiana, then bends southward through central Illinois in the direction of St. Louis. Whether the areas of transition are wide or narrow we can probably not determine with accuracy, since, in general, only one social type (the elderly, or rustic) is included in the Great Lakes survey.

Why should the isoglosses run where they do? The answer, in part, is relatively simple. Of the two sets of variants, the [s] forms were evidently generalized in the New England colonies, the [z] forms in the Middle and South Atlantic colonies. The westward migrations and settlements of the New Englanders covered New York (State), northern Pennsylvania, Michigan, Wisconsin, and the northern portions of Ohio, Indiana, and Illinois.[27] Many speech features mark off this Northern area from the "Midland"—the area occupied primarily by Pennsylvanians.[28] Most of the northern lines, to be sure, pass further to the north in Pennsylvania than do those of the [s] in *grease* and *greasy*. Yet the penetration of northern forms to the area of Philadelphia is occasionally to be observed in other instances; for example, the line of Northern *clapboards* (as against Midland and Southern *weatherboards*) dips sharply southward so as to take in Philadelphia and northern Delaware. Another explanation for the prevalence of [gris] and ['grisi] in east central Pennsylvania might be the fact that much of the area was occupied in the early 18th century by Palatine Germans, whose native dialect had no [z] phoneme at all[29] and who may, for this reason, have favored [s] in any English words where variation between [s] and [z] occurred.

What is the British practice with regard to the pronunciation of *grease* and *greasy*? No complete survey has been made; but there seems

[26] "Folk Speech of Indiana and Adjacent States," *op. cit.*, p. 128.

[27] Kurath, *Word Geography*, pp. 1-7; see also Lois K. M. Rosenberry, *The Expansion of New England*, Boston and New York, 1909. Even the island of [s] forms around Marietta, Ohio, is to be explained on the basis of early settlement; this area was first settled by New Englanders as early as the 1780's. See Rosenberry, pp. 175ff.

[28] Examples of Northern words (from Kurath) are *whiffletree, pail, darning needle* ('dragonfly'), and *co, boss!* (cow call). Verb forms which I have found to have similar distributions are *hadn't ought* ('oughtn't'), *how be you?, clim* ('climbed'), and *see* as a preterite of *to see*. Note that Kurath's definition of "Midland" does not coincide with that of Hempl; the area, according to the former, extends much farther to the southwestward of Pennsylvania than Hempl indicated. (See *Word Geography*, pp. 27-37.)

[29] See Carroll E. Reed, *The Pennsylvania German Dialect Spoken in the Counties of Lehigh and Berks: Phonology and Morphology* (Seattle, Wash., 1949), pp. 20 and 29.

no doubt that London usage, as well as "Received Standard" usage throughout southern England, is mixed.[30] The questionnaires which Hempl circulated in England (for his study cited above) showed that in London only 25 and 33 per cent of the informants used [s] in *grease* and *greasy;* but that in England exclusive of London the percentages of [s] were 84 and 74.[31] We have no ground, even yet, for rejecting these figures; but it should be pointed out that folk speech in England, just as in the United States, shows its isoglosses. A survey of the linguistic atlas type conducted by Guy S. Lowman in 1934[32] shows that the [z] in *grease* (I have no information on *greasy*) occupies East Anglia and a small adjoining area; that [s] is universal in the remainder of southern England (we are speaking strictly of the rustic type of speaker). Since the line passes through (or very near) London, it is easy to see why the metropolitan area should show a mixture of usage.

Is there any evidence of a differentiation in meaning between ['grisi] and ['grizi]? The *Atlas* provides no answer to this question, since, in the interest of obtaining comparable data, the words were always called for in the same context ("grease the car, axle, etc." and "my hands are greasy"). In general, such differentiations in meaning are characteristic of areas of mixed usage, not of those where one pronunciation or another is definitely established. The distinction usually given in dictionaries is that ['grisi] may mean literally 'covered with grease,' while ['grizi] may be used with less literal, and sometimes unpleasant, connotations.[33] What we can say with confidence is that speakers to the south of our isoglosses do not follow this practice: ['grizi] is universal with the literal meaning 'covered with grease'; whether or not more speakers in the area of overlapping, and to the north of it, would have used ['grizi] had the context been different, we are unable to determine.

How should we evaluate the *Atlas* data as a picture of reality? What is most important to realize is that the *Atlas* makes no attempt whatever to record the usage of non-native speakers, or even of those natives who have resided for long periods outside their home communities. Such speakers are rather uncommon in some communities, fairly numerous

[30] See Daniel Jones, *An English Pronouncing Dictionary,* 9th ed., London, 1948.

[31] Hempl, *op cit.,* pp. 442-43.

[32] Lowman's British field records are filed in an unedited state at the University of Michigan.

[33] Daniel Jones, *English Pronouncing Dictionary*: "Some speakers use the forms . . . with a difference of meaning, ['gri:si] having reference merely to the presence of grease and ['gri:zi] having reference to the slipperiness caused by grease." *Webster's NID* states: ". . . many people in all sections use ['grisi] in some connotations and ['grizi] in others, the first esp. in the literal sense, covered with grease." Cf. Kenyon and Knott: "Some distinguish ['grisi] 'covered with grease' from ['grizi] 'slimy' " *(op. cit.).* G. P. Krapp states: "A distinction is sometimes made in the meaning of ['gri:si] and ['gri:zi], the latter being regarded as a word of unpleasant connotation" *(op. cit.,* p. 119). *Webster's* implies that this distinction is fairly general throughout the country—a very dubious proposition. T. Larsen and F. C. Walker simply prescribe [s] for the meaning 'sticky' and [z] for the meaning 'slippery'—as though this feature were standard and universal. (See *Pronunciation* [Oxford Press, 1931], p. 92.)

in others; in a few of the latter, the *Atlas* may even reflect the usage of a minority of old-timers. In view of this, we might be inclined to wonder whether the percentage method might not give a truer picture of prevalent usage than the isogloss method. The proportion of non-native speech forms in a community would, of course, roughly correspond to the proportion of non-native residents; such data would certainly be valuable, though to collect it on a large enough scale (say, 100 or so informants from each county) would be so difficult as to be practically impossible. Few investigators are qualified to make extensive phonetic observations, and those few must take their informants from such captive groups as college classes, whose usage may or may not be spontaneous or representative. Another feature of the *Atlas* that must be considered is the preponderance of rather old informants. Since the interviews were conducted several years ago, many of the forms shown to be current among the aged may now be rare or even obsolete; moreover, the *Atlas* records would not reflect the most recent trends, fads, and innovations—some of which are rapid, others extremely slow. It seems unlikely to me that the lines on *grease* and *greasy* have shifted radically in the last few years, yet I have no doubt that usage may have changed in certain individual communities.[34] All things considered, the *Linguistic Atlas* offers the most reliable body of data as yet assembled, or likely to be assembled in the near future, on American speech; isoglosses based on it reflect the usage of a highly important segment of our population, and they are, moreover, of the highest value in a study of our cultural and settlement history.

[34] Dr. Smith expresses the opinion that the younger generation in New York City has gone over almost entirely to the [s] in *greasy*.

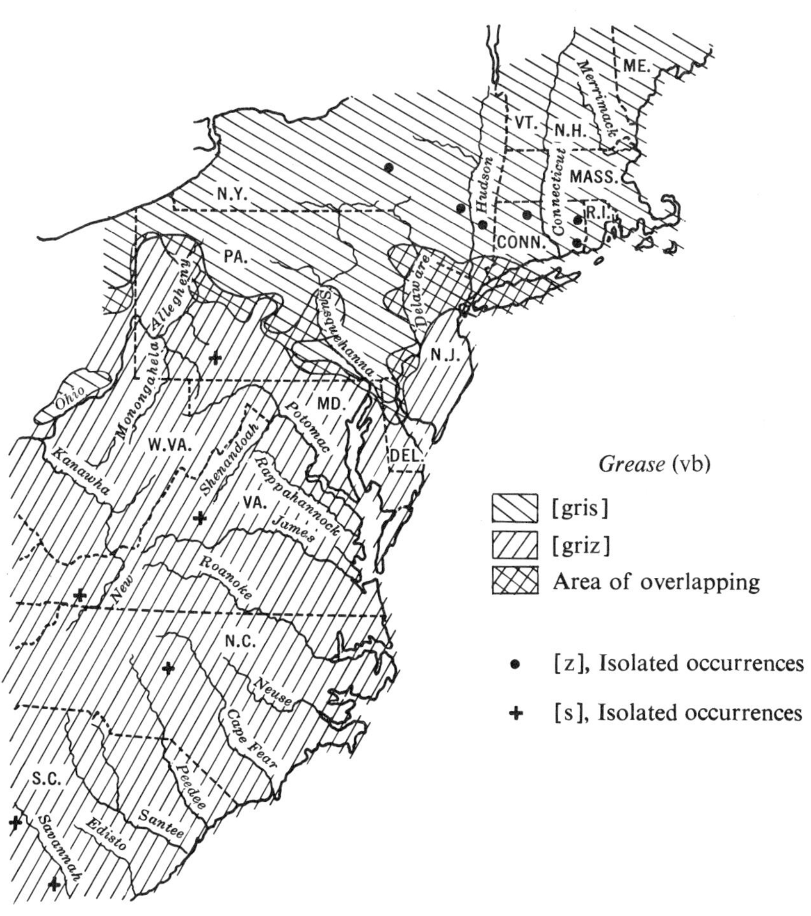

MAP SHOWING THE DISTRIBUTION OF [s] AND [z] IN

GREASE (VERB)

Northern Maine and Eastern Georgia (not shown on the map) show the same usage as the adjoining areas. At the time of this study, no field records were available for Northern New York.

Principal and Subsidiary Dialect Areas in the North-Central States

ALBERT H. MARCKWARDT

WITH THE PUBLICATION of Kurath's *Word Geography of the Eastern United States,*[1] students of American English were provided for the first time with a sound and solidly based concept of the dialect areas to be recognized in this country. There is no need to go into details of his study. It will suffice to say that Kurath disposed once and for all of such negatively conceived catch-all categories as General American. On the positive side he must be credited with the concept of Midland as a specific speech area and type, and with recognizing the essential unity of Northern. This is brief, but it establishes a basis for the present discussion.

It will be recalled that each of Kurath's major dialect regions is divided into a number of sub-areas. Those which are significant for the present purpose are shown on Map 1. The largest single subdivision in the Northern speech area is Kurath's Number 4, consisting of upstate New York and western Vermont. It leads directly into the Western Reserve of Ohio and into the portion of Ontario which is included in the territory covered by the Linguistic Atlas of the North-Central States. The three sub-divisions of the Midland area adjacent to the territory included in the North-Central atlas are numbered 10, 11 and 12 by Kurath. He calls these areas the Upper Ohio Valley, Northern West Virginia and Southern West Virginia respectively. In general the boundary between areas 10 and 11 follows the northern watershed of the Monongahela; that between areas 11 and 12 is the line of the Kanawha Valley.

Reprinted by permission from *Publications of the American Dialect Society,* No. 27, 3-15 (April, 1957).

[1] Hans Kurath, *A Word Geography of the Eastern United States* (Ann Arbor, 1949).

Except for a few scattered places in Kentucky and Indiana, the field records of the Linguistic Atlas of the North-Central States have been completed. They are approximately 350 in number, representing some 175 communities in the six states and the portion of Ontario indicated on Map 2 and those which follow. Preliminary chartings made soon after the beginning of the project indicated that in general the principal boundary between the Northern and Midland speech types would continue westward in such a way that most of Indiana would be included within the Midland area, but that the upper third of Ohio and Illinois would be Northern.[2] All subsequent studies, notably those by Davis[3] and Potter,[4] and numerous incidental observations by McDavid have confirmed this early prognostication.

Now, with virtually all the material necessary for the atlas in hand, it is time to subject this early conclusion to a somewhat more detailed scrutiny and to begin to outline the minor or subsidiary dialect areas on the basis of more complete evidence than Davis had at his disposal. Since the boundaries which Kurath drew between his areas 10 and 11, and between 11 and 12, as they are presented on Map 1, lead directly into the North-Central region, this naturally raises the question as to how they are to be projected. The present study is at least a beginning of an examination of these questions.

Maps 2 and 3 serve to reaffirm the major boundary between the Northern and Midland areas. Map 2 in particular reflects the kind of isogloss that has generally been employed to establish this line: namely, the northernmost extension of typical Midland features. The isoglosses of the four items here represented all have several common characteristics. Three of the four go around the Western Reserve, and even the fourth, though penetrating the Reserve proper, dips below the adjacent Fire Lands. All four cut across the northwestern corner of Ohio, the transition area studied in detail by Potter. Most of Indiana falls below these isoglosses; in one instance, virtually all of it. In three of the four cases, the Illinois boundary terminates in Henderson County, just across the Mississippi River from Burlington, Iowa.

Less frequently have the southern limits of distinctly Northern terms been employed to establish the Northern-Midland boundary. Four of these are indicated on Map 3. It will readily be observed that some of these are somewhat to the south of those items charted on Map 2, the net effect being to create a transition belt, varying in its width but particularly broad in Indiana and the adjacent portions of Illinois and

[2] Hans Kurath, "Dialect Areas, Settlement Areas, and Culture Areas in the United States," in *The Cultural Approach to History,* ed. Caroline F. Ware (New York, 1940).

[3] Alva L. Davis, "A word atlas of the Great Lakes region," unpubl. diss. (University of Michigan, 1948).

[4] Edward E. Potter, "The dialect of northwestern Ohio: a study of a transition area," unpubl. diss. (University of Michigan, 1955).

Ohio. In one instance, that of *stone boat,* there is an additional speech island along the Mississippi, opposite St. Louis.

What we see indicated here is symptomatic of the overlapping spread in the North-Central territory of a number of individual items which maintain a well-defined regional distribution to the east. For example, Kurath's *Word Geography* shows a clear-cut line of demarcation between *sweet corn* and *roasting ear,* following the general direction of the isoglosses separating the North and the Midland.[5] In the North-Central territory, *sweet corn,* though concentrated in the North, is found throughout the area. No state is without an instance of it, and even as far south as Kentucky there were seven occurrences. *Roasting ear* has a complementary distribution, heavy in the south but thinning out as one goes northward. It was not recorded in Ontario, only twice in Wisconsin and once in the Upper Peninsula of Michigan, but it turned up no less than thirteen times in the Michigan Lower Peninsula. Although space does not permit the presentation of additional examples, we now know that many items, between which the line of cleavage was sharp in the East, have invaded each other's territories in the North-Central states, resulting in broad belts of multiple usage. The nature of these items, their general cultural patterning, the extent to which they may have developed distinction in meaning, are all matters for future investigation.

We shall find it convenient to consider next certain of the features whose boundaries in the Eastern United States generally follow the line separating the eleventh and twelfth of Kurath's divisions. Map 4 shows four of these; one is the southern limit of a Northern and North Midland term, *hay mow*. The remaining three isoglosses represent the northern limits of South Midland features. In general the lines follow the Ohio River. On occasion they veer upward, but rarely do they penetrate north of the line of the Old National Road, which connected Wheeling, Columbus, Indianapolis, Vandalia, and St. Louis.

Judging from the general configuration of these isoglosses, we are led to the conclusion that the New England speech island consisting of the area around Marietta, namely the Ohio Company lands, offered an initial obstacle to the introduction of South Midland features. The dips in two of the isoglosses reflect this, and in them there are no significant bulges to the north until they cross Indiana and Illinois. The remaining two items apparently did gain acceptance in the Marietta area, but their spread north of that was prevented by the prior establishment of terms current in Pennsylvania. Nevertheless, they did spread north as far as the line of the Old National Road. At all events, these extensions of the boundary between what Kurath calls the Northern and Southern West Virginia areas do present a fairly clear-cut picture, one which is repeated in other items which have not been charted here.

[5] Kurath, *Word Geography,* Figure 41.

Much less predictable is the behavior of the features which constitute the boundary between the tenth and eleventh of Kurath's subdivisions. A glance at Map 5 will indicate that their behavior is not such as to warrant any general conclusion. The isogloss of *nicker,* though entering Ohio just a little north of Wheeling, quickly rises toward the Western Reserve and follows generally the major boundary between the Northern and Midland speech areas. In addition, we find the term current in the Galena Lead Region, which though mixed in settlement history was originally developed by a Kentuckian. The northern limit of *gutters* follows the Old National Road in Ohio, but upon reaching Indiana again jumps northward almost to the principal Northern-Midland boundary. *Dogbit* as a participial form behaves in a decidedly different fashion. Though not charted by Kurath, this item does appear in Atwood's analysis of verb forms in the Eastern United States.[6] He shows it to be current throughout all of West Virginia and extending into Pennsylvania up to the Monongahela. This isogloss, after following the Old National Road two-thirds of the way across Ohio, suddenly dips toward the Ohio River, and in fact veers considerably below it over a large part of Kentucky.

This raises a question. How are we to account for the erratic behavior of these items? Any explanation undoubtedly can be little more than conjectural, but up to the present there is little ground even for conjecture. It is true, of course, that between the Old National Road and the principal dialect boundary separating the Northern and Midland areas there were no natural barriers, no important pathways of communication and travel, nor patterns of settlement which might have helped to create a second east-west line continuing the division between the tenth and eleventh of Kurath's areas. Moreover, a glance at the last map in the series will suggest that whatever items current in the area between the Monongahela and the Kanawha might have entered Ohio at this point, they would have been in competition with the northern features of the Western Reserve and the Ohio Company lands and also with the Southern or extreme South-Midland features of the Virginia Military District. Consequently, a deflection of these isoglosses either upward or downward is not too surprising.

More important still, perhaps, is the fact that features of the language spreading westward from the West Virginia panhandle and along the Monongahela were thrown into competition with others current throughout Pennsylvania, which were also penetrating the Ohio territory. The general path of this penetration is shown on Map 6. *Spouting,* as the term for gutters or eavestroughs, is now found in a band running all the way across central Ohio, crossing slightly into Indiana. *Run,* as the term for a small stream tributary, covers somewhat more

[6] E. Bagby Atwood, *A Survey of Verb Forms in the Eastern United States* (Ann Arbor, 1953), Figure 3.

territory, with one point heading into southeastern Michigan as well. *Serenade,* as an alternate for *belling, horning,* or *chivaree,* has an even larger radius; it does not go quite as far north as the others but includes the Kentucky bluegrass and part of the hill country. *Fishing worm,* not shown on the map, is more extensive in its coverage than any of those charted.

This points to the fact that in the North-Central area we must reckon with three major population movements and corresponding transmissions of speech features. Heretofore much of our thinking has been primarily in terms of two: the migration from New York and New England into the northern part of the territory, and that from Virginia and the Carolinas into Kentucky and then northward across the Ohio River into southern Ohio and Illinois and most of Indiana. In fact, the census figures for 1870 do explain very satisfactorily the predominance of Northern items in Michigan and Wisconsin, of Midland terms in Indiana, and the division between Northern and Midland in Ohio and Illinois. Convincing and helpful as all of this is, as far as explaining the Hoosier apex is concerned, it does not take into account the migration from Pennsylvania as a third factor, which suggests an historical reason for what may be called an Ohio wedge.

This brief account does not exhaust the possibilities of subsidiary dialect areas which a further examination of our records will enable us to chart. The Northern items entering the area were not all of one piece, and we may confidently expect to find belts or islands in which coastal New England terms are current. We have seen that with respect to at least one feature, the Galena Lead Region constitutes a distinct island. There are others as well, and indeed I am confident that we shall find the movement of settlers up and down the Mississippi River reflected in the distribution of a number of items.

Thus far our analyses do seem to verify the existence of a bundle of isoglosses cutting through our three central states in an apical line, thus constituting the principal dialect boundary between Northern and Midland speech. In general these isoglosses form a relatively broad band, and in many instances they must be interpreted as representing the limits of areas of concentration rather than of actual occurrence. For many terms there is considerable spreading throughout much of the area.

Another band, bounded on the north by the Old National Road and on the south by the Ohio River, constitutes a second transition belt, north of which Southern and South-Midland features fail to penetrate. A third group of South-Midland items, entering the area slightly to the north have failed to establish a well-defined boundary of their own but have either spread as far as the Northern-Midland boundary or have been squeezed behind the subsidiary belt to the south. Finally, a wedge-like intrusion of Pennsylvania terms into and across Ohio have immensely complicated the dialect picture in the latter state.

At this point it is clear that we are dealing with a challenging and highly complex dialect situation: one which will require our drawing upon every available facet of cultural and settlement history to give it meaning and to make it understandable.

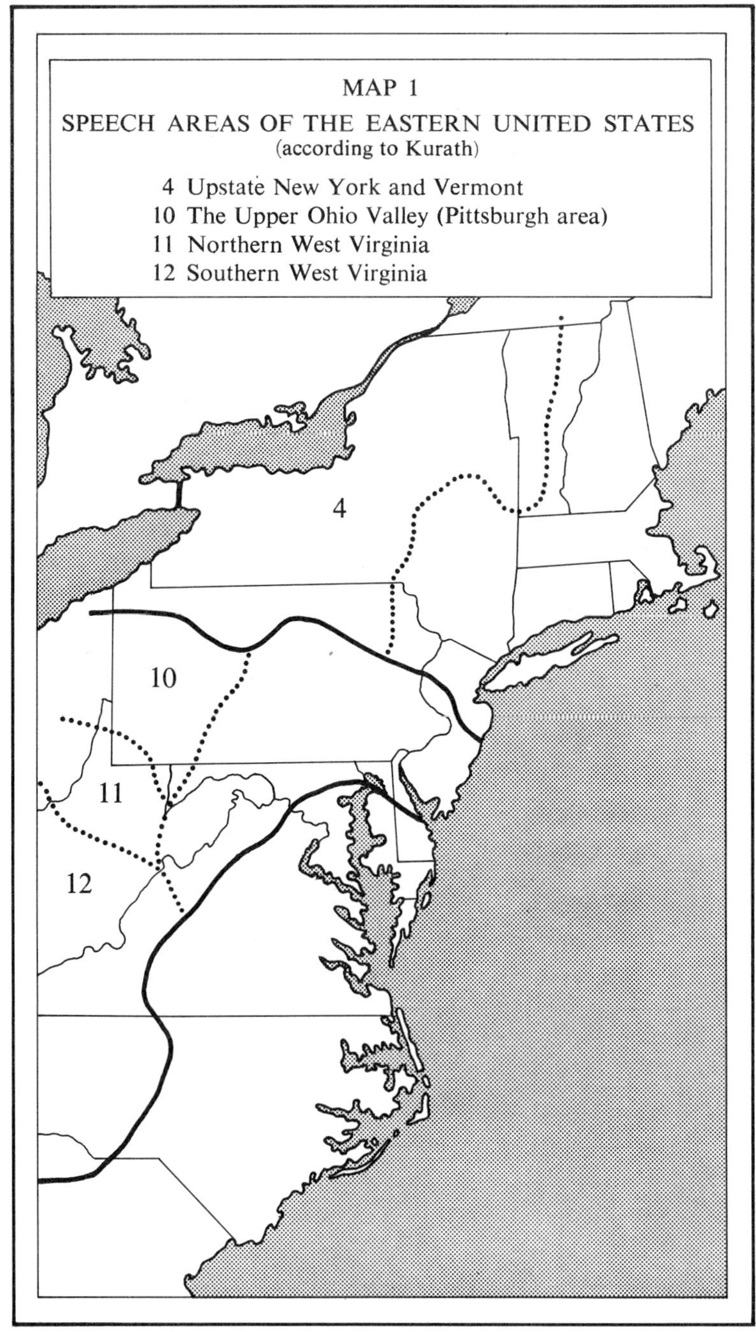
MAP 1
SPEECH AREAS OF THE EASTERN UNITED STATES
(according to Kurath)
4 Upstate New York and Vermont
10 The Upper Ohio Valley (Pittsburgh area)
11 Northern West Virginia
12 Southern West Virginia
4
10
11
12

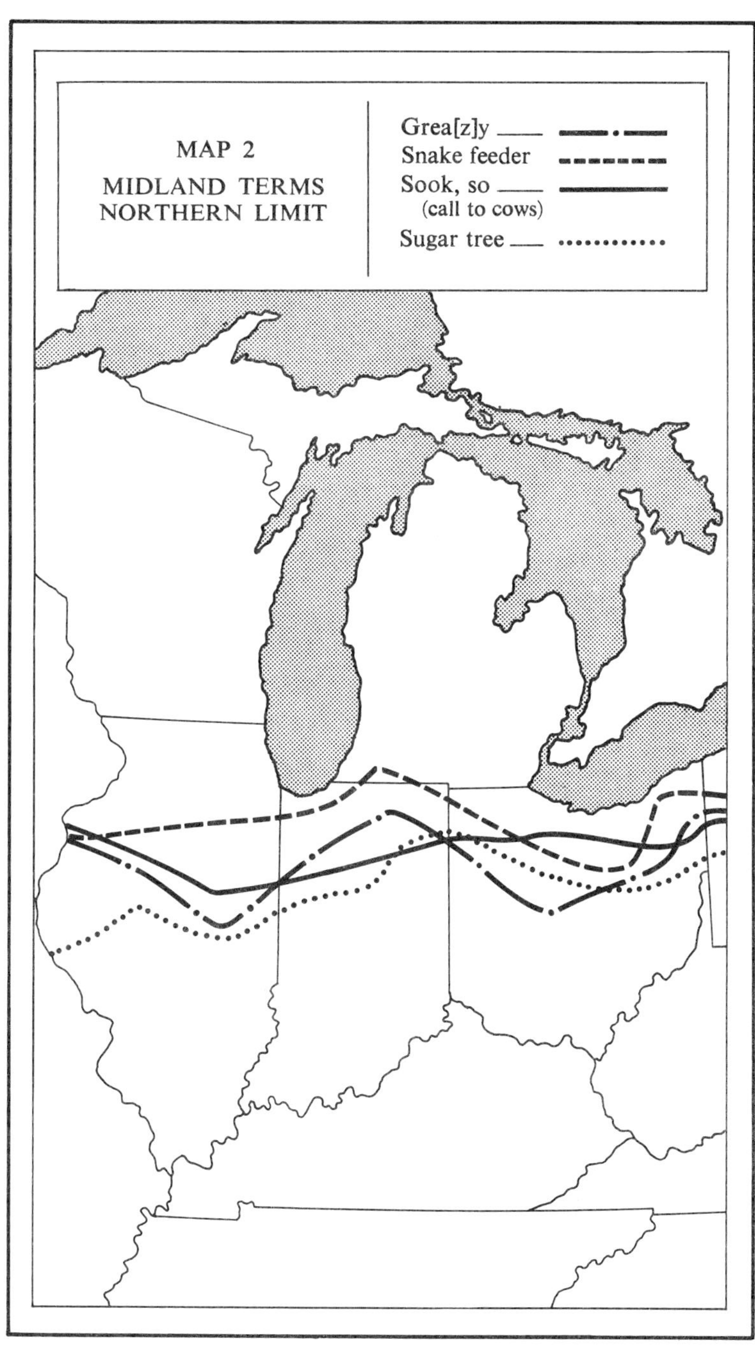
MAP 2
MIDLAND TERMS
NORTHERN LIMIT
Grea[z]y
Snake feeder
Sook, so
(call to cows)
Sugar tree

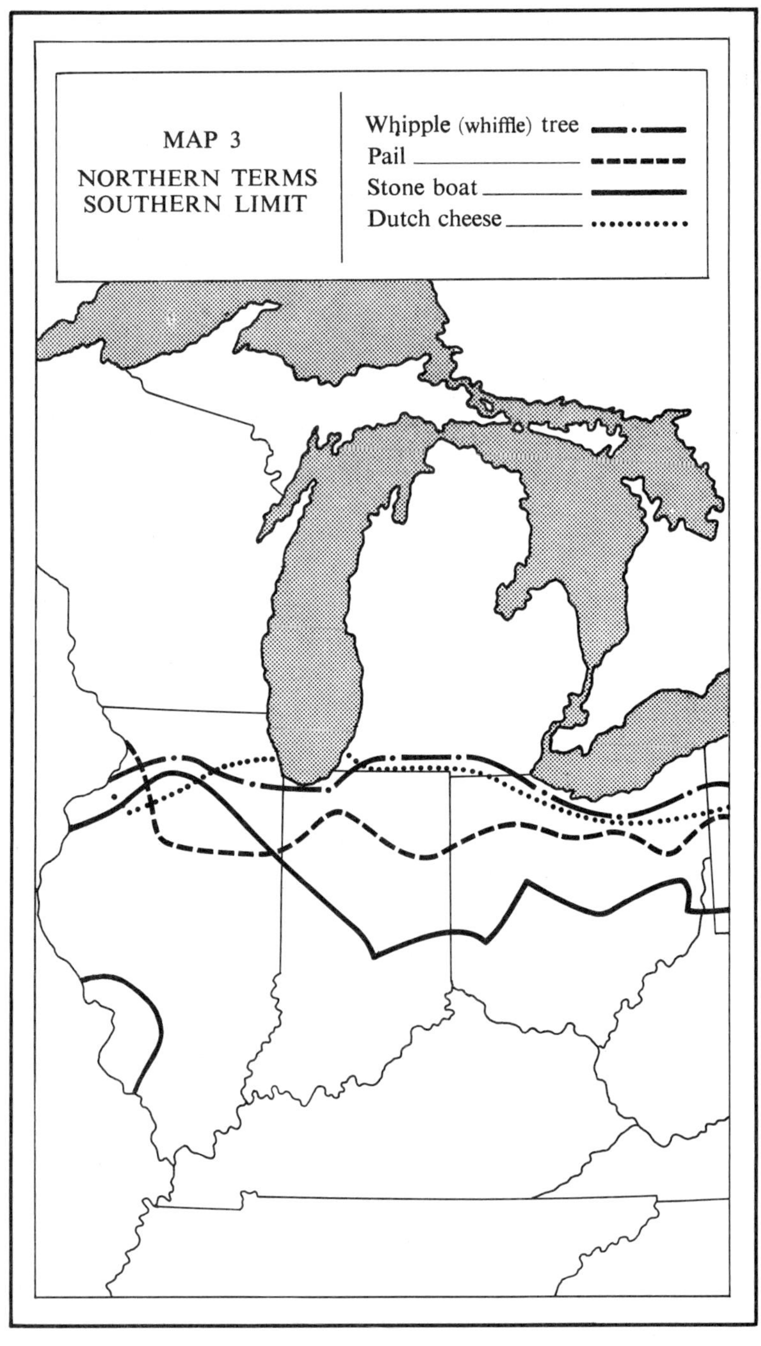
MAP 3
NORTHERN TERMS
SOUTHERN LIMIT
Whipple (whiffle) tree
Pail
Stone boat
Dutch cheese

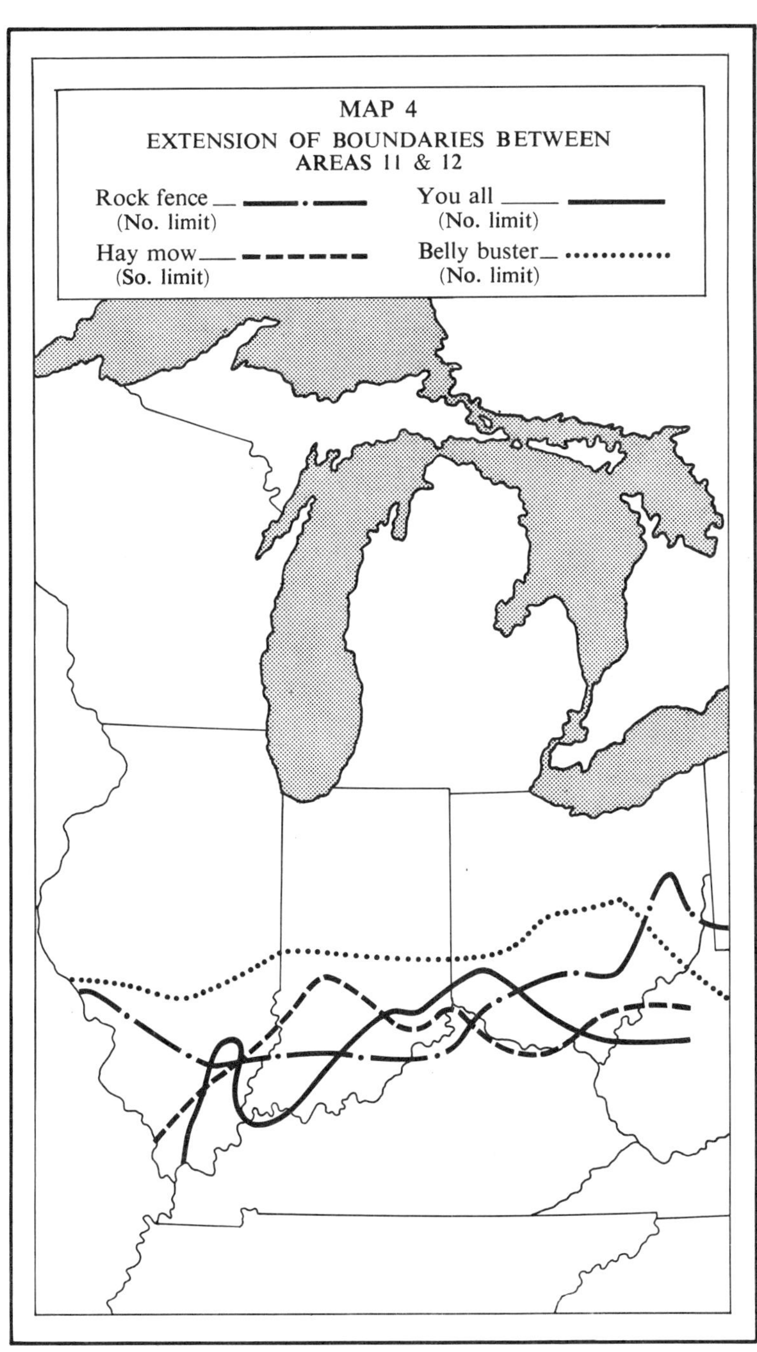
MAP 4
EXTENSION OF BOUNDARIES BETWEEN
AREAS 11 & 12
Rock fence
(No. limit)
You all
(No. limit)
Hay mow
(So. limit)
Belly buster
(No. limit)

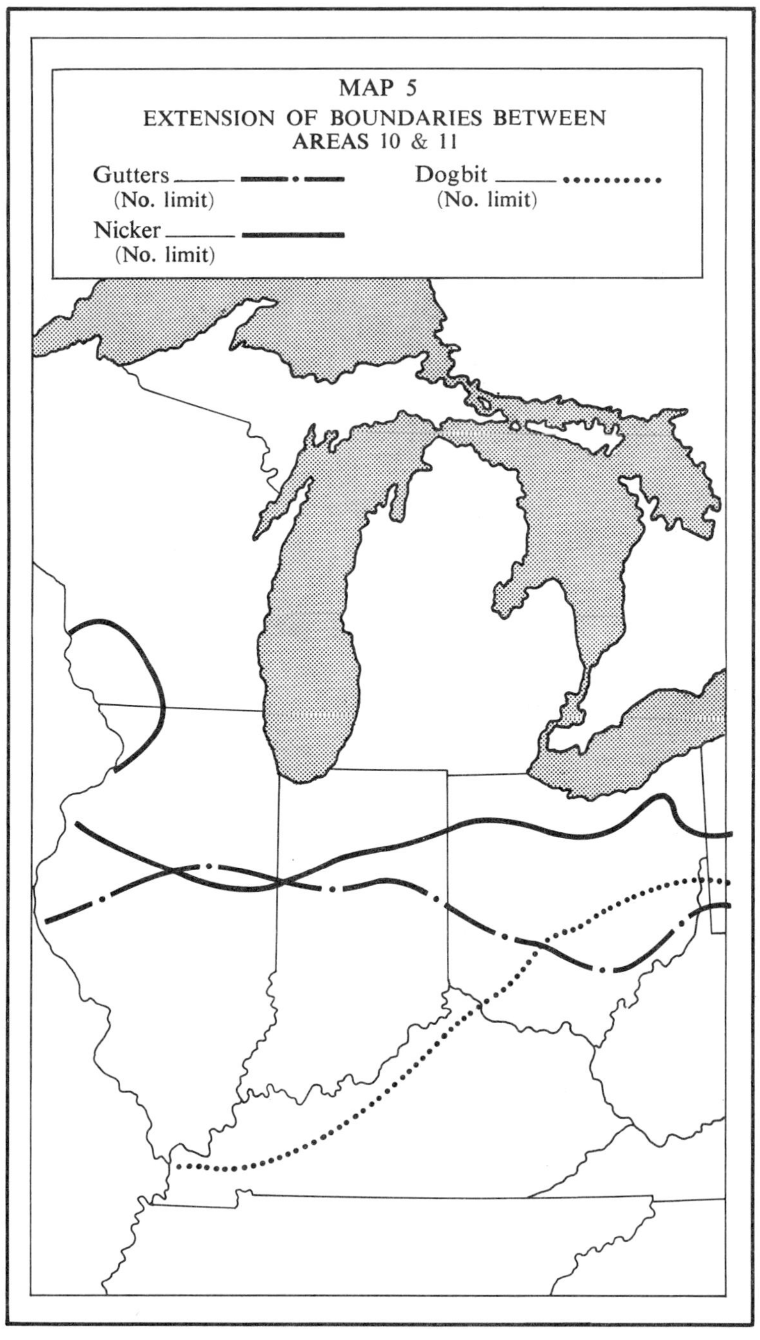
MAP 5
EXTENSION OF BOUNDARIES BETWEEN AREAS 10 & 11
Gutters
(No. limit)
Dogbit
(No. limit)
Nicker
(No. limit)

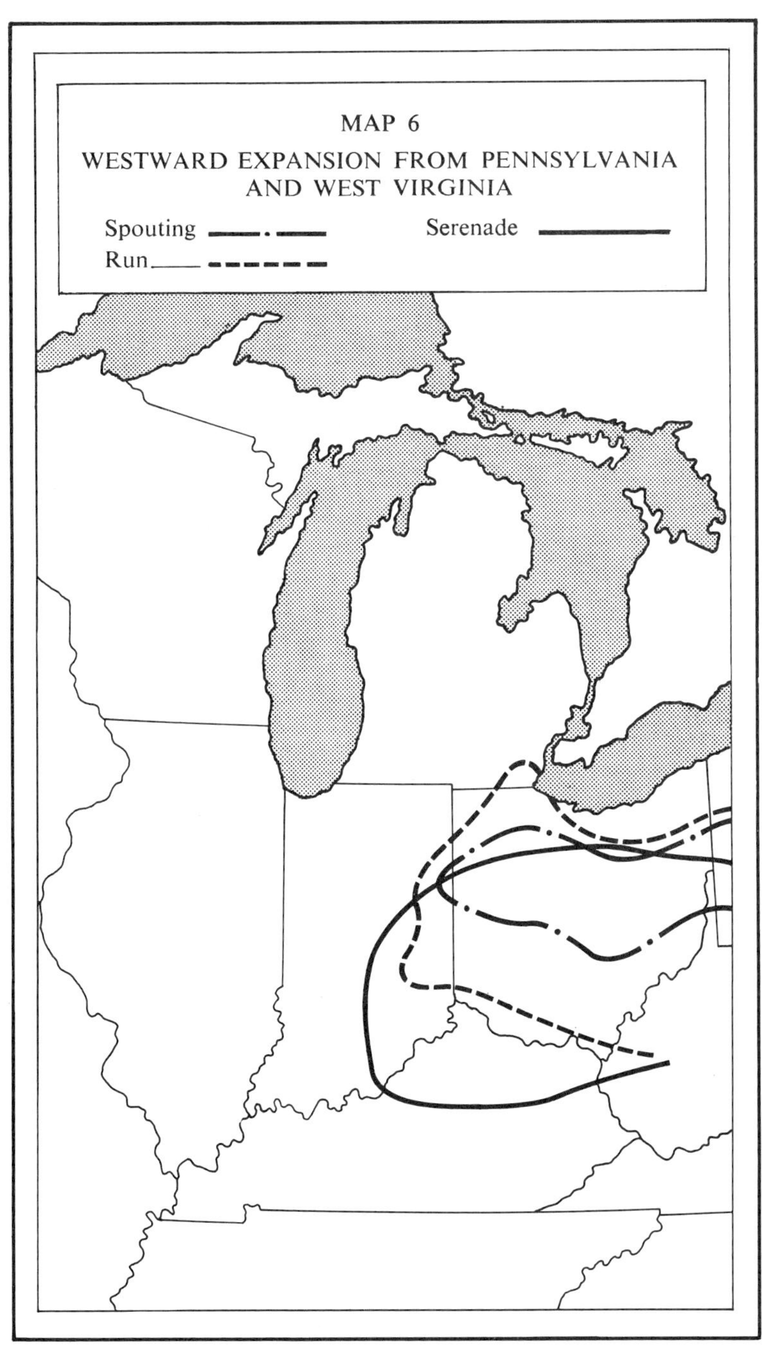
MAP 6
WESTWARD EXPANSION FROM PENNSYLVANIA AND WEST VIRGINIA
Spouting
Serenade
Run

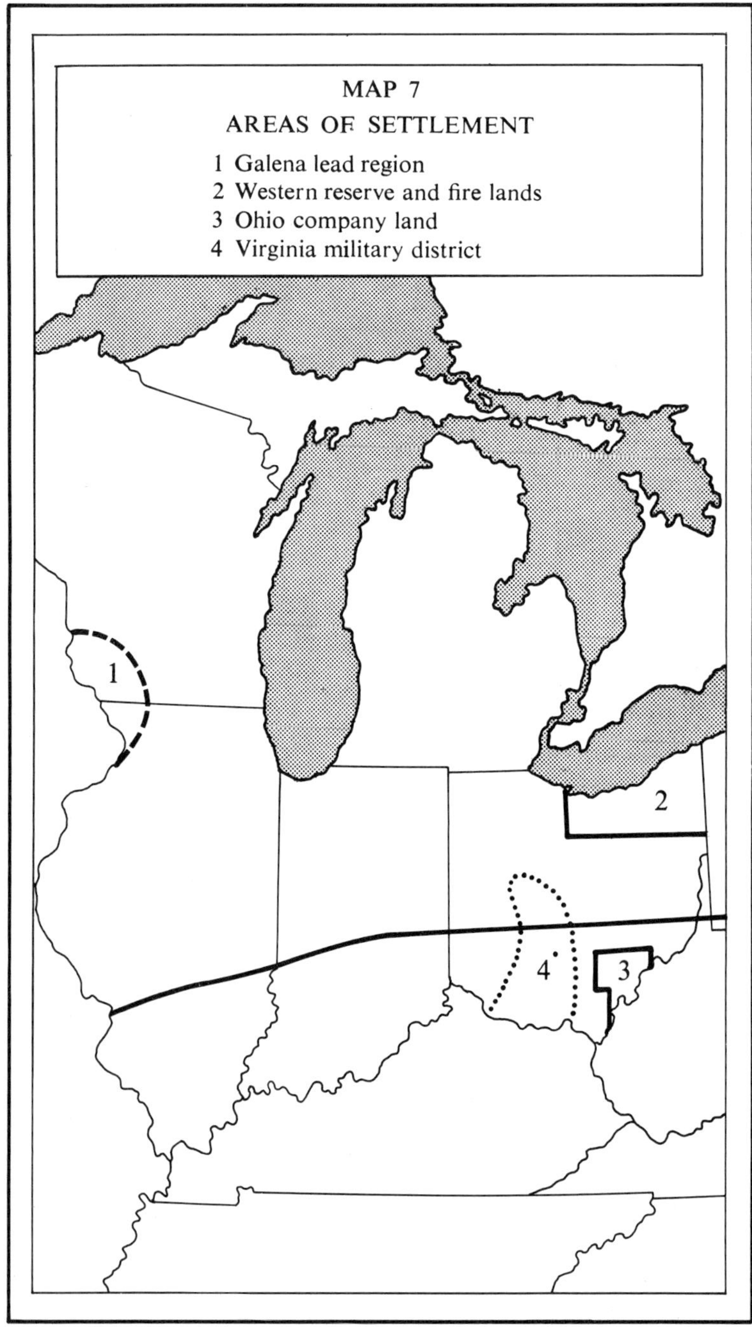
MAP 7
AREAS OF SETTLEMENT
1 Galena lead region
2 Western reserve and fire lands
3 Ohio company land
4 Virginia military district
1
2
3
4

The Analysis of Linguistic Borrowing

EINAR HAUGEN

1. BILINGUALISM AND BORROWING. As early as 1886, Hermann Paul pointed out that all borrowing by one language from another is predicated on some minimum of bilingual mastery of the two languages.[1] For any large-scale borrowing a considerable group of bilinguals has to be assumed. The analysis of borrowing must therefore begin with an analysis of the behavior of bilingual speakers. A vast literature has come into being on the subject of borrowing, particularly in the historical studies of individual languages; but there is still room for discussion of the relationship between the observed behavior of bilingual speakers and the results of borrowing as detected by linguists. Any light that can be thrown on the question by a study of bilingual speakers should be welcome to all students interested in borrowing and in the general linguistic problems associated with this process.[2] In the present article an effort will be made to define more precisely the terminology used in the linguistic analysis of borrowing, and to set up certain hypotheses concerning the process of borrowing. It should then be possible to test these by their usefulness of application to particular studies of bilingualism and borrowing.[3]

Reprinted by permission from *Language* 26.210-31 (1950).

[1] Prinzipien der Sprachgeschichte², Chap. 22 (Halle a. S., 1886).

[2] See the writer's article, Problems of bilingualism, Linqua 2.271-290 (1950), for a discussion of the social pressures that lead to bilingualism, and for some recent studies of the problem.

[3] Languages frequently referred to are abbreviated as follows: E English; N Norwegian; PaG Pennsylvania German; AmG American German; AmN American Norwegian; AmPort. American Portuguese. Other abbreviations are standard or obvious.

Examples from AmN are taken from the writer's own materials, collected chiefly in Wisconsin, under research grants from the Research Committee of the University of Wisconsin (1936, 1937), the Guggenheim Foundation (1942), and the Rockefeller Foundation (1949). The substance of the article was presented to students attending the writer's course Problems and Methods of Research in Bilingualism at the Linguistic Institute (University of Michigan, 1949), and to his colleagues of the Linguistic Circle

2. Mixing the languages. Perhaps the most widely understood term for the phenomena we are here considering is based on the metaphor of 'mixture'. Among speakers of immigrant languages in America it is indeed a popular term; cf. the practice of AmN speakers when they say *han mikser* 'he mixes' or the AmG book title *Gemixte Pickles,* in which the loanword *mix* is at once a description and an example of the process. From popular speech it has passed into the usage of linguists, especially of the older generations; Hermann Paul headed his chapter in the Prinzipien 'Sprachmischung', and the term was regularly used by men like Whitney and Schuchardt. As a description of the process it might seem to have a certain vividness that justifies its use, but on closer inspection it shows disadvantages which have apparently led later linguists, such as Sapir and Bloomfield, to abandon it. Even Paul had to warn against the misunderstanding that it was possible to mix languages 'ungefähr in gleicher menge', as if they could be poured together into a cocktail shaker and result in an entirely new concoction. Except in abnormal cases speakers have not been observed to draw freely from two languages at once. They may switch rapidly from one to the other, but at any given moment they are speaking only one, even when they resort to the other for assistance.[4] The introduction of elements from one language into the other means merely an alteration of the second language, not a mixture of the two. Mixture implies the creation of an entirely new entity and the disappearance of both constituents; it also suggests a jumbling of a more or less haphazard nature. But speakers of e.g. AmN continue to speak a recognizably Norwegian language distinct from their English down to the time when they switch to the latter for good.

So much for the process itself. A further inaccuracy is introduced if the resulting language is called 'mixed' or 'hybrid'. It implies that there are other languages which are 'pure', but these are scarcely any more observable than a 'pure race' in ethnology. The term is ambiguous because it can mean either that the language has adopted elements of foreign origin at some time in the past, or that it shows mutually inconsistent elements in its present-day structure as a result of such adoption. Yet we know that great numbers of words in English which once were adopted are now quite indistinguishable from native words by any synchronic test. Schuchardt insisted that all languages were mixed, but in saying this he gave the word so wide an application that its value for characterizing individual languages would seem to be greatly reduced. In some circles the term 'mixed' or 'hybrid' has actually acquired a pejorative sense, so that reformers have set to work 'purifying'

---

at the University of Wisconsin; the paper has profited from valuable suggestions made by both groups.

The examples from AmPort. are taken from Leo Pap, Portuguese-American speech (New York, 1949).

[4] Paul, Prinzipien 338; Meillet, La méthode comparative 82 (Oslo, 1925); Meillet, Linguistique historique et linguistique générale 76 (Paris, 1921).

the language without seeing clearly what they were about. For the reasons here given, the term 'mixture' is not used in the present discussion. It may have its place in a popularized presentation of the problem, but in technical discussion it is more usefully replaced by the term 'borrowing', which we shall now proceed to define.

3. A DEFINITION OF BORROWING. At first blush the term 'borrowing' might seem to be almost as inept for the process we wish to analyze as 'mixture.' The metaphor implied is certainly absurd, since the borrowing takes place without the lender's consent or even awareness, and the borrower is under no obligation to repay the loan. One might as well call it stealing, were it not that the owner is deprived of nothing and feels no urge to recover his goods. The process might be called an adoption, for the speaker does adopt elements from a second language into his own. But what would one call a word that had been adopted—an adoptee? Anthropologists speak of 'diffusion' in connection with a similar process in the spread of non-linguistic cultural items. We might well speak of linguistic diffusion, though this would suggest the spread of the language itself rather than of elements from it. The real advantage of the term 'borrowing' is the fact that it is not applied to language by laymen. It has therefore remained comparatively unambiguous in linguistic discussion, and no apter term has yet been invented. Once we have decided to retain this well-established linguistic term, we shall simply have to disregard its popular associations, and give it as precise a significance as we can.

(1) We shall assume it as axiomatic that *every speaker attempts to reproduce previously learned linguistic patterns* in an effort to cope with new linguistic situations. (2) *Among the new patterns which he may learn are those of a language different from his own,* and these too he may attempt to reproduce. (3) If he reproduces the new linguistic patterns, *not in the context of the language in which he learned them,* but in the context of another, he may be said to have 'borrowed' them from one language into another. The heart of our definition of borrowing is then *the attempted reproduction in one language of patterns previously found in another.* We shall not here take up the question of what is meant by 'another language'; Bloomfield has adequately pointed out the difficulties involved.[5] The term reproduction does not imply that a mechanical imitation has taken place; on the contrary, the nature of the reproduction may differ very widely from the original, as we shall see.

For our definition it does not matter why the speaker does it, nor whether he is conscious of what he is doing. We shall proceed to analyze what he does by comparing the pattern that he is reproducing with the results that he succeeds in turning out. While it is true that we shall

[5] Language 445 (New York, 1933).

rarely if ever be able to catch a speaker in the actual process of making an original borrowing, it is clear that every loan now current must at some time have appeared as an innovation. Only by isolating this initial leap of the pattern from one language to another can we clarify the process of borrowing.

4. Types of borrowing. Since borrowing has been defined as a process involving reproduction, any attempt to analyze its course must involve a comparison of the original pattern with its imitation. We shall call the original pattern the *model,* and recognize that the loan may be more or less similar to it. It may vary all the way from an imitation satisfactory to a native speaker to one that the native speaker would not recognize at all. Where the loan is (to a native speaker) noticeably different from the model, we are faced with a case of partial learning due to the interference of other factors, as yet unnamed. If we assume, on the basis of common observation, that these factors are the previously established patterns of the speaker's language, we shall be able to separate out two distinct kinds of reproduction. If the loan is similar enough to the model so that a native speaker would accept it as his own, the borrowing speaker may be said to have *imported* the model into his language, provided it is an innovation in that language. But insofar as he has reproduced the model inadequately, he has normally *substituted* a similar pattern from his own language. This distinction between *importation* and *substitution* applies not only to a given loan as a whole but to its constituent patterns as well, since different parts of the pattern may be treated differently. An AmN speaker who tries to reproduce AmE *whip* [hwɪp] will often come out with [hypp-]; he has imported the whole form itself with its meaning, but he has substituted his own high-front-round vowel for the E rounded glide plus lowered-front vowel. If the loan contains patterns that are not innovations in the borrowing language, it becomes impossible to distinguish the two kinds of reproduction. Thus importation and substitution fall together in the initial consonant [h], which are not distinguishable in N and E.

A study of the way these two kinds of reproduction operate in speech suggests that whenever the patterns of the model are new to the borrowing language, a compromise is likely to take place between the two sets of patterns. Some kind of adjustment of habits occurs, whereby the speaker chooses one of his own patterns to stand for a similar one in the model. A study of the results of this normally unconscious procedure indicates that while there are many apparently capricious choices, the overall pattern is not unreasonable. The bilingual speakers who make the first substitutions are in a rough way carrying on an operation of comparative linguistics. That substitution is a common phenomenon under such circumstances has been recognized for phonetics, where the term is well established. That it also applies to elements of inflection, word formation, and syntax has not been so clearly recognized. Yet when an AmPort. speaker substitutes the agent suffix *-o* for English *-er* in *boarder,* producing *bordo,* he is giving evidence that he recognizes the equivalence between the two suffixes. He would not be able to formulate it, but his behavior is evidence of some kind of complex reaction which for brevity's sake we may as well call 'mental', though it can hardly have been conscious. It is the linguist's task to make the speaker's procedures explicit, a task for which he has the advantage of a sophistication that comes from having a vocabulary with which to talk about linguistic behavior. Whether the distinction between importation and substitution can be shown to correspond to mental procedures is uncertain. But it is clear that it is useful in describing the course of borrowing over a period of time, when there is a growing tendency to import rather than substitute as the bilingual command of the languages grows more adequate.

5. THE TERMINOLOGY OF BORROWING. Borrowing as here defined is strictly a process and not a state, yet most of the terms used in discussing it are ordinarily descriptive of its results rather than of the process itself. We shall discuss later the question of the role which loans play within the structure of a language and the extent to which they can be identified without resort to comparative studies. We are here concerned with the fact that the classifications of borrowed patterns implied in such terms as 'loanword', 'hybrid', 'loan translation', or 'semantic loan' are not organically related to the borrowing process itself. They are merely tags which various writers have applied to the observed results of borrowing. We shall illustrate their usual meanings with examples and then try to relate them to the terminology so far proposed and defined.

LOANWORD is the vaguest of the group, since it may include practically any of the others. But it is ordinarily limited to such terms as AmE *shivaree* 'an uninvited serenade of newlyweds' from Fr. *charivari,* in which speakers have imported not only the meaning of the form but also its phonemic shape, though with more or less complete substitution of native phonemes.[6] HYBRID is sometimes used to distinguish loanwords in which only a part of the phonemic shape of the words has been imported, while a native portion has been substituted for the rest. Thus PaG has adopted AmE *plum pie* as [blaʊməpaɪ], in which the morpheme [paɪ] has been imported, but the native [blaʊmə] has been substituted for *plum.*[7] In this case the borrowing speakers must have analyzed the compound into its component morphemes while they were borrowing it, or else they could not have made this partial substitution. This distinction puts the process on a different level from the merely phonemic

[6] On *shivaree* see Alva L. Davis and Raven I. McDavid Jr. in American Speech 24.249-55 (1949).

[7] Paul Schach, Hybrid compounds in Pennsylvania German, American Speech 23.121-34 (1948).

substitution of the preceding type, so that we are required by the evidence to postulate a MORPHEMIC SUBSTITUTION which operates independently of the phonemic.

If we turn now to the LOAN TRANSLATION (known in French as a *calque*), we encounter such examples as the French *presqu'île,* German *Halbinsel,* modeled on Latin *paenīnsula;* or German *Wolkenkratzer,* Fr. *gratte-ciel,* Sp. *rascacielos,* modeled on E *skyscraper.*[8] But are these anything more than an extension of the process observed in the preceding 'hybrid' examples? Instead of substituting only one half of the word, the borrowers have here analyzed and substituted both halves. They have imported a particular structural pattern, viz. the combination of the two constituents into a compound expression with a new meaning of its own not derivable by a simple addition of the two parts.[9] Closely related to this is the SEMANTIC LOAN, which is exemplified by the AmPort. use of *humoroso* with the meaning of the AmE *humorous,* though it meant only 'capricious' in Portugal.[10] Here no formal structural element whatever has been imported, only a meaning, and the substitution of phonemic shape is complete. To call this a 'semantic loan' overlooks the fact that all the loans described above are semantic; it is merely that in this case the new meaning is the only visible evidence of the borrowing. The morphemic substitution is complete. This is true also of phrasal loans, in which syntactic patterns are involved, such as AmN *leggja av* 'discharge', modeled on AmE *lay off.*

If we now try to sum up this discussion, we see that we have succeeded in establishing a division of loans according to their extent of morphemic substitution: none, partial, or complete. Complete morphemic substitution precludes phonemic substitution, but within the morphemic importation there may be a division into more or less phonemic substitution. We thus arrive at the following groupings, based primarily on the relationship between morphemic and phonemic substitution; the terms used to describe them are makeshift expressions, in lieu of an established terminology or better inventions:

(1) LOANWORDS show morphemic importation without substitution. Any morphemic importation can be further classified according to the degree of its phonemic substitution: none, partial, or complete.

(2) LOANBLENDS show morphemic substitution as well as importation. All substitution involves a certain degree of analysis by the speaker of the model that he is imitating; only such 'hybrids' as involve a discoverable foreign model are included here.

(3) LOANSHIFTS show morphemic substitution without importation. These include what are usually called 'loan translations' and 'semantic loans'; the term 'shift' is suggested because they appear in the borrowing language only as functional shifts of native morphemes.

[8] Kr. Sandfeld-Jensen, Die Sprachwissenschaft 69 (Leipzig and Berlin, 1915).
[9] Cf. the apt criticism of the term in Pap 176-7, note 58.
[10] Pap 87-8.

Separate sections will be devoted to the study of each of these types. For all of them it is taken for granted that semantic importation has taken place. It should be noted that the term 'morpheme' does not here include inflectional modifications; when these are applied, they do not affect the grammatical function of the word, but are necessary and therefore non-distinctive accompaniments of its use in the sentence.

6. LOANWORD PHONOLOGY. The simplest and most common substitution is that which takes place when a native sound sequence is used to imitate a foreign one. Complete substitution is characteristic of naive language learners and is heard as a 'foreign accent' by native speakers. However undesirable this may be when one is speaking a foreign language it is normal when reproducing foreign materials in one's own. The results may be almost completely unrecognizable to the speakers of the model language, as when Spanish *virgen* is reproduced in the language of the Taos Indians as [mˈilxiną] or English *spade* is introduced into AmPort. as [ʃiˈpeiro].[11] In many cases the speakers are completely unaware that they have changed the foreign word, as in the story told by Polivanov of the Japanese student who asked his teacher whether *dzurama* or *dorama* was the correct pronunciation of the European word *drama*. When the teacher answered that it was neither one, but *drama,* he nodded and said, 'Ah yes, then it's *dorama*.'[12] Hermann Paul and many writers after him have described this process as one in which the speaker substitutes 'the most nearly related sounds' of his native tongue for those of the other language.[13] But neither the speaker himself nor the linguist who studies his behavior is always certain as to just what sound in his native tongue is most nearly related to the model. Only a complete analysis of the sound system and the sequences in which sounds appear could give us grounds for predicting which sounds a speaker would be likely to substitute in each given case. When the Yaqui Indians reproduce Sp. *estufa* as [ehtúpa], the [h] for [s] is a substitution that occurs only before [t] and [k], where [s] does not occur in their native language; elsewhere they have no trouble with [s]. Polivanov expressed it as follows:[14] 'En entendant un mot inconnu étranger . . . nous tâchons d'y retrouver un complexe de *nos* représentations phonologiques, de les décomposer en des phonèmes propres à *notre* langue maternelle, et même en conformité à *nos* lois de groupement des phonèmes.' Speakers have been trained to react to certain features in the stream of speech and to reproduce these in their own; but they are also trained to reproduce them only in a limited number of combinations and sequences. Loanword phonology is the attempt to recapture the process of analysis that results in phonemic substitution.

[11] George L. Trager, IJAL 10.146 (1944); Pap 94.
[12] TCLP 4.79-96 (1931).
[13] Paul, Prinzipien 340-1; George Hempl, TAPA 29.37; Bloomfield, Language 446.
[14] TCLP 4.80 (1931).

7. Phonological importation. The problem of description is greatly complicated by the fact that the process of learning changes the learner's view of the language. The more he acquires of the new language the less necessary it is for him to interpret its habits in terms of the old language. So he gradually begins to import into his own language those habits of the other which he has mastered and which are not too incompatible with his previously established habits. Linguists have generally assumed that a scale for the time of borrowing can be set up on the basis of phonological form. Early loans are assumed to be the more distorted words, while the late are more similar to their models. Thus Trager in his list of Spanish loans in Taos distinguishes between the 'oldest', the 'more recent', and the 'most recent' largely on the basis of differences in loanword phonology.[15] In general the principle is sound, but we need to make certain reservations. First, there are some words that offer us no criteria, since they do not happen to contain the critical sounds. Second, the difference between the most and the least distorted depends not so much on time as on the degree of bilingualism. Bilingualism may come suddenly or slowly; it may persist over many generations, as among the PaG, and words may come in through various members of the community in several different forms. In AmN communities most loanwords may appear in various forms, with more or with less phonemic substitution; but some substitutions are so widespread that they can hardly have been borrowed recently. It is also possible for bilinguals to touch up the form of an older word and introduce a more 'correct' form if they happen to know it.

Since we cannot follow the fate of individual words and expressions from their earliest introduction, we can only guess at the factors that have influenced the form of any given word. We are entitled, however, to make certain assumptions. First, that *a bilingual speaker introduces a new loanword in a phonetic form as near that of the model language as he can.* Secondly, that *if he has occasion to repeat it, or if other speakers also take to using it, a further substitution of native elements will take place.* Thirdly, that *if monolinguals learn it, a total or practically total substitution will be made.*

In the case of AmN we are dealing very largely with bilinguals, most of whom learned E in childhood, so that many words may vary from a wholly adapted form to one that is almost wholly unadapted. We shall here reckon with certain characteristic stages, while realizing that these are not always chronological:

(1) A pre-bilingual period, in which the loans are made by a relatively small group of bilinguals and spread widely among the monolingual majority; the words show (almost) complete native substitution, with great irregularity in the phonetic results. Some phonemes

[15] IJAL 10.145 (1944).

and phoneme sequences will cause the speakers to vacillate, so that they choose now one, now another of their own as substitutes. In AmN the rhyming words *road* and *load* are reproduced with different N phonemes as /råd/ and /lod/. Such behavior may be called ERRATIC SUBSTITUTION, and is comparable to the scattering of shots over the target of a novice marksman.

(2) A period of ADULT BILINGUALISM, when growing knowledge of E leads to a more SYSTEMATIC SUBSTITUTION, in which the same N phoneme is consistently employed for new E loans. This may often be accompanied by the use of familiar sounds in new positions where they were not found in the native tongue. Thus the initial *v* in E *very, vicious,* and other words of French origin must once have seemed strange to Englishmen who were used to pronouncing it only between vowels. In modern Czech *g* is found initially only in loanwords; elsewhere it is only an allophone of *k*.[16] We shall call this process PHONEMIC REDISTRIBUTION, since it affects the distribution of the phonemes.

(3) A period of CHILDHOOD BILINGUALISM, in which the characteristic process is one of PHONEMIC IMPORTATION, i.e. completely new sound types are introduced. The Yaqui whose first-generation speakers had to substitute *p* for *f* in Spanish *estufa* 'stove', saying [ehtúpa], are by now sufficiently bilingual to produce [fonografo] 'phonograph' without difficulty. AmN speakers acquired E *whip* as /"hyppa/ in the first generation, but as /"wippa/ in the second.

8. THE GRAMMAR OF LOANWORDS. If loanwords are to be incorporated into the utterances of a new language, they must be fitted into its grammatical structure. This means that they must be assigned by the borrower to the various grammatical classes which are distinguished by his own language. Insofar as these are different from those of the model language, an analysis and adjustment will be necessary here as in the case of phonology, and we observe the same predominance of substitution in the early phases, which later yields to a certain degree of importation. The broadest kind of form classes are those that are traditionally known as the 'parts of speech'. In the case of E and N there is no problem at this level, since their structures are closely parallel: E nouns are adopted as AmN nouns, and so forth. It is reported from Chiricahua, an Athabaskan language, that the Spanish adjectives *loco* 'crazy' and *rico* 'rich' are borrowed as verbs.[17] But within the form classes (at least those that have inflections), there are problems for AmN also. N nouns belong to one of three classes known traditionally as masculine, feminine, and neuter, which differ from each other in inflection and syntactical environment. Since E has no corresponding division, an E noun must be assigned to one of these classes on the basis of analogies which are often

[16] V. Mathesius, Englische Studien 70.23 (1935-6).
[17] Harry Hoijer, Lg. 15.110-5 (1939).

difficult to discover both for the speakers and for the analyst. In most languages for which the phenomenon has been studied a clear tendency is seen to assign loanwords to one particular gender unless specific analogies intervene to draw them into other classes. This is even more marked in AmN verbs, where practically every loanword falls into the first class of weak verbs. Such grammatical categories as definiteness, possession, and plurality correspond with sufficient closeness so that little more is involved than a substitution of N forms for E. Again, this would not be true in languages less closely related; the Yaqui have given many loanwords a suffix *-um* with a singular sense though the suffix is plural in Yaqui.[18]

But even in the relation of E and N there are many cases of erroneous analysis, based on special situations, so that e.g. E *-s* (plural) may be borrowed with its stem and treated as if it were part of a singular noun. An example is *kars* 'car', plural *karser;* similarly in AmItalian *pinozzi* 'peanuts'. But the next step, correlated to a bilingual stage of learning, is to import the plural suffix for E loanwords. This becomes such a common thing that the N suffixed article may be added to it, producing a hybrid inflection *-s-* + *-a* 'the', e.g. *kisa* 'the keys'. Adjectives and adverbs may also receive N suffixes, but to a much lesser extent. Here the E influence has frequently led to an importation of zero suffixes, i.e. the abandonment of inflection. Aasta Stene has pointed out that this is promoted by the fact that N also has zero suffixes in some positions.[19] The verbs, on the other hand, have invariably a complete N inflection, with practically no substitution from E. This phenomenon has been noted for several languages, and is sufficiently striking to merit some consideration.[20] Miss Stene stresses the opportunity available to nouns and adjectives of appearing in positions where inflection can be avoided, which is not possible for verbs. While this is true, it should not be overlooked that the function of verb inflections is somewhat different from that of the rest. Tense is a necessary feature of every N (and E) sentence in a way that plurality is not; verbs have no inflectional form with the kind of generalized function that the noun singular has. The noun singular not only refers to individuals of the species, but also to the species itself, and in many cases this is quite sufficient (e.g. *rabbit* as a loanword may refer either to a single rabbit or to rabbits in general). The adjective inflections are even more secondary, since they have no independent meaning but are dependent on the nouns which they modify. Thus the importation of the E lack of inflection is facilitated by the relative unimportance of the corresponding N inflections and we need not assume any deliberate 'avoidance of inflection', at least by the unsophisticated speakers dealt with in this study.

[18] Spicer, Am. Anthr. 45.410-26 (1943).

[19] English loan-words in Modern Norwegian 164 (London and Oslo, 1945).

[20] Stene 163 (her opinion that borrowed verbs are for this reason fewer than nouns seems insufficiently founded); Pap 106.

9. Loanblends. In reproducing the forms of another language speakers will frequently go farther in their adaptation than merely to substitute native sounds and inflections for the foreign ones. They may actually slip in part or all of a native morpheme for some part of the foreign, as in AmPort. *alvachus* 'overshoes', *alvarozes* 'overalls', where the native prefix *al-* has been substituted for the E *o-*.[21] Such substitutions are only discernible when the phonetic results differ from those that derive from phonological substitution. Thus E *-er* is reproduced as AmN /-ər/; only when it is not, can one be sure of a suffix substitution, as in /ˈˈkårrna/ 'corner' (by blending with N *hyrrna* 'corner'). The same would not be true in AmPort., where Eastern AmE *-er* [-ə] is normally reproduced as /-a/. Suffix substitution is obvious in such a word as /ˈbordo/ 'boarder', since /-o/ is a regular agent suffix.[22] The /-a/ is actually ambiguous, since it not only reproduces E *-er,* but is added as a regular suffix to many words which in E end in consonants.[23] In cases like AmN /ˈˈkårrna/, where the suffix is itself meaningless, hardly more than a gender marker, we are dealing with a blended stem. Nearest to this is the blended derivative, in which native suffixes are substituted for the foreign. Thus in PaG *-ig* is often substituted for E *-y,* e.g. *bassig* 'bossy', *fonnig* 'funny', *tricksig* 'tricky'.[24] In AmN it is often hard to distinguish E from N suffixes, since many of them are phonologically equivalent; e.g. E *-y* [-i] is homophonous to N /-i/. Blended compounds constitute the largest class of blends in AmN. Compounds may be borrowed about as freely as simple stems, since the two languages have parallel structures in compounding. But about half of the compounds show substitution of one or both parts. It is conspicuous that in practically every case the substitute closely resembles the foreign term in sound and has a meaning not too remote from it. An example from PaG is *bockabuch* 'pocketbook', where *buch* was substituted for E *book.* The force of the compounding pattern was such that even some phrases which were not compounds in E became so in AmN, e.g. *black walnut* > /ˈblakkvalˌnot/. Only such terms as had direct E models have here been considered loanblends. Independent AmN formations involving E morphemes are here regarded as creations which fall outside the process of borrowing.

10. Loanshifts. Some foreign loans appear in the language only as changes in the usage of native words. Such changes will here be classed as 'shifts', which will be made to include all changes that are not strictly phonological and grammatical. Complete substitution of native morphemes has taken place. When this occurs in simple stems, two possibilities result according to the degree of similarity between the new and the old meanings of the word. If the new meaning has nothing in

[21] Pap 96.
[22] Pap 97.
[23] Pap 101.
[24] Paul Schach, Symposium 3.120 (1949).

common with the old, it may be described as a LOAN HOMONYM. This is the situation when AmPort. has substituted its word *grosseria* 'a rude remark' for E *grocery;* the result is that the word *grosseria* has two homonymous meanings. In a dictionary they would presumably be listed as two distinct words. When there is a certain amount of semantic overlapping between the new and old meanings, one may speak of a LOAN SYNONYM, which only adds a new shade of meaning to the native morpheme. These can in turn be distinguished into SEMANTIC DISPLACEMENTS, in which native terms are applied to novel cultural phenomena that are roughly similar to something in the old culture, and SEMANTIC CONFUSIONS, in which native distinctions are obliterated through the influence of partial interlingual synonymity. It is a semantic displacement when AmPort. uses *pêso* 'weight' (from Span. *peso*) to mean 'dollar'; but it is a semantic confusion when they substitute the native *livraria* 'bookstore, home library' for E *library* instead of using the Port. *biblioteca.*[25] This process may be symbolized as follows: if language A has two words a_1 and a_2 which both overlap some meanings of word b in language B, pressure of B on A will often lead to confusion of a_1 and a_2; if a_1 resembles b phonetically, it may even displace a_2 entirely.

The lack of any satisfactory method of classifying degrees of semantic similarity means that it is not always possible to make the distinctions here suggested. Thus it would be possible to disagree on the classification of AmPort. *crismas* 'Christmas'. It is similar enough to the AmE model so that one might at first imagine it to be a loanword with phonemic substitution; only the fact that a word with exactly this phonemic form already exists in Port. requires us to class it as a loanshift. But is it a loan homonym or a loan synonym? Pap regards its native meaning, 'oil of sacrament', as sufficiently similar to the new meaning to call it the latter ('semantic loan' in his terminology); but one might well feel that there is no common 'area of synonymity' between them, so that it should rather be called a loan homonym.[26] Compounds may also show complete native substitution, as when N *korn* 'grain' + *krubba* 'fodder-rack' are substituted for *corncrib* in the sense of a building for storing unshelled maize. These are the so-called LOAN TRANSLATIONS, which have played a great role in the development of many languages. Thus Gk. *sympátheia,* which was reproduced in E by importation, was reproduced by morpheme substitution in Lat. *compassiō,* G *Mitleid,* Dan. *Medlidenhed,* and Russ. *sobolěžnovanie.*[27] Substitution may equally well extend to complete phrases, whose parts are reproduced as native words; we may call these SYNTACTIC SUBSTITUTIONS, and include such expressions as AmPort. *responder para tras* 'to talk back'.[28]

[25] Pap 79, 88.
[26] Pap 87.
[27] Sandfeld-Jensen 69.
[28] Pap 89.

Loanshifts in general occur most readily when there is both phonetic and semantic resemblance between foreign and native terms. Terms that are interlingually similar will be called ANALOGUES; if the similarity is purely phonetic, they will be called HOMOPHONES, and if it is purely semantic, HOMOLOGUES. All three kinds can become starting-points for a morphemic substitution; in the case of AmN it is noteworthy how strong the force of pure homophony is. The similarity of E and N makes it easy to pour new wine into old bottles—for the old bottles are scarcely distinguishable from the new.

11. CREATION. Loanword lists are often made to include a number of terms whose existence may ultimately be due to contact with a second culture and its language, but which are not strictly loans at all. These did not come into being as direct imitations of a foreign model, but were secondarily created within the borrowing language. An example is the Yaqui term *liósnóoka* 'pray', composed of the loanword *liós* 'God' (from Sp. *dios*) and the native *nóoka* 'speak'.[29] Such formations are sometimes confused with loanblends, since they resemble these in being 'hybrid'. But seen in the light of the borrowing process as here defined, they cannot have come into being as imitations of a foreign model, for there is no Spanish word of the shape *god-speak* meaning 'pray'. A parallel from AmN is *sjærbrukar* 'one who operates a farm for a share of the profits', a technical term much used in the tobacco-raising districts of Wisconsin. The first part is a loanword *sjær* (from AmE *share*), the second is a N *brukar* 'farmer, tenant'. The AmE *sharecropper* is not in use in these districts; a word *shareman* is sometimes heard in English. But neither of these can have suggested the AmN word; its origin must be sought in the N word *gardbrukar* 'farmer (lit. farm-user)', in which the loanword *sjær* was substituted for the native *gard*. This kind of REVERSE SUBSTITUTION, in which loan morphemes are filled into native models, is clearly different from the borrowings previously described and should be distinguished from them. PaG has an interesting series of terms of the type *Gekick* 'habitual kicking or objecting' (e.g. *Gekooks* 'coaxing', *Gepeddel* 'peddling', *Getschäbber* 'jabbering').[30] When classified without regard to the borrowing process, they appear as 'hybrids'; but their starting point is different from such loanblends as *blaumepai* 'plum pie' previously cited. These do not have a specific E model, for English has no words of this type, implying a habitual or even annoying activity. They appear to be secondary derivatives from the borrowed verbs (e.g. *kicken*), and are filled into the pattern of the native words of the type *Gejammer* 'incessant moaning or lamenting'. The only criterion available for deciding whether a term belongs to this class of native creation is that no model exists in the other language. This may

[29] Spicer, Am. Anthr. 45.410-26.
[30] Schach, Symposium 3.115.

be difficult to ascertain without a rather complete knowledge of the language in question. A doubtful case is raised in the AmIt. word *sciainatore* 'boot-black', apparently formed by substituting the loanword *sciainare* 'shine (shoes)' in a native pattern of the type represented by *trovatore* 'troubadour'. But if, as the Italian scholar A. Menarini supposes, there is an AmE word *shiner* meaning 'boot-black', it could be a loanblend, in which the native *-tore* was simply substituted for AmE *-er*.[31] This writer has never heard or seen such a word (except in the sense of a black eye), the usual word being *boot-black,* but he recognizes that it does exist in the compound *shoe-shiner* (also and more commonly *shoe-shine*).

Since the type of creation here discussed needs a name to distinguish it from the kind of creation that consists entirely of native material, we might dub it HYBRID CREATION, thus emphasizing its bilingual nature. But it must be recognized that it is not a part of the borrowing process; rather does it give evidence of an intimate fusion into the language of the borrowed material, since it has become productive in the new language. The number of hybrid creations seems to vary markedly according to circumstances. PaG appears to have great numbers of them, involving such highly productive suffixes as *-erei, -es, -sel, -keet, -meesig, -voll, -weis* and the verbal prefix *var-*.[32] AmN, on the other hand, has relatively few, which may be due to the comparative lack of productive affixes in Norwegian, but also to the briefer period of residence in America. Most hybrid creations are of the type in which loan morphemes have been substituted in the nucleus, while the marginal parts (the affixes) are native. The opposite kind, showing marginal substitution (exemplified by E *talkative*), is not found at all in the AmN materials.

Occasionally one finds reference in loanword studies to a completely native kind of creation, when this has occurred in response to stimuli from another culture. Examples from the Pima Indians have been presented by George Herzog of such newly created descriptive terms as 'having downward tassels' (oats), 'wrinkled buttocks' (elephants), 'dry grapes' (raisins), 'lightning box' (battery), etc.[33] A solitary example from AmN is the word *kubberulla* 'oxcart', from N *kubbe* 'chunk of wood' and *rulla* 'cart' (the wheels were made of slabs of wood).

12. CROSS-CURRENTS OF BORROWING. We may assume that unless a number of individuals borrow a word, it is not likely to attain great currency. If they learn it from the same source, and speak the same dialect and have the same degree of bilingualism, the effect will merely be one of reinforcement of the original form. But the situation is rarely, if ever, as simple as this. The speaker of AmPort. in New Bedford, Mass., is not

[31] A. Menarini, Ai margini della lingua 145-208 (Firenze, 1947); reviewed by Robert A. Hall Jr. in Lg. 24.239-41 (1948).

[32] Schach, Symposium 3.115.

[33] Language, culture, and personality (Essays in memory of Edward Sapir) 66-74 (Menasha, Wis., 1941).

exposed to the same English as the speaker of the same language in California. More important within any one community is the fact that in a bilingual group the same word is liable to variations in reproduction because of the varying degree of bilingualism. The loan is subject to continual interference from the model in the other language, a process which will here be called REBORROWING. It is a commonplace among immigrant groups in America that younger and older speakers will use different forms of the same loanwords. The difference usually consists in the extent of phonological and morphological importation. Some examples from AmN are the following:

MODEL:	whip	tavern	surveyor	Trempealeau	crackers	mocassin	lake
OLDER:	hyppa	tavan	saver	tromlo	krækkis	maggis	lek
YOUNGER:	wippa	tævərn	sørveiər	trempəlo	krækərs	magəsin	leik

The forms acquired will also be differently reproduced when speakers of different dialects attempt them. This follows from our previous definition of borrowing; but the situation becomes almost hopelessly confused when speakers of different dialects live together in the same community, as is the case among immigrants, and the form is passed from speaker to speaker, many of whom may be monolingual at the beginning. It has been possible in the case of AmN dialects to isolate a few instances that seem reasonably certain evidence for the transmission of loanwords within the dialects. At least it is simpler to account for them as INTERDIALECTAL loans than as directly derived from E models. They are listed in the following tabulation:

ENGLISH MODEL	ORIGINAL BORROWING	INTERDIALECTALLY TRANSMITTED FORM
(1) E [dl] > WN [dl] > EN [ll]		
cradle (grain harvester)	krɪdl	krill
middling (coarse flour)	mɪddlɪng	milling
peddler	peddlar	pellar (1 inf.)
(2) E [eɪ] > EN [ei] > WN [ai]		
lake	leik	laik
pail	peil	pail
jail	jeil	jail
frame	freim	fraim
(3) E [ɔu] > EN [å] > WN [ao]		
hoe	hå	hao
(4) E [au] > EN [æu] > Solør [əy] > Røros [ö]		
flour	flæur	fləyr, flör
(5) [ɔ] > EN [å] > Gbr. [öu]		
log	lågg	lougg

In each of these cases the variations within the loanword forms correspond to different reflexes from the same Old Norw. originals, found in a considerable number of native words also. But other loanwords with the same E phonemes have different forms, e.g. *mail* has not become [mail] in the dialects referred to above, but [meil].

A further source of interference with the process of borrowing is the influence of SPELLING. Spelling pronunciations may be suspected wherever the reproduction varies from normal in the direction of a pronunciation traditionally given to a letter in the borrowing language. In any literate community such influence is likely to be present in a number of words which have been brought to the community in writing. Among immigrants this is not true to any considerable extent, but at least in AmN there is a marked tendency to pronounce AmE [æ] as /a/ and [a] as /å/, spelled respectively *a* and *o*.

	bran	*alfalfa*	*saloon*	*tavern*	*lot*	*gallon*	*battery*
ENG. MODEL	[bræn]	[æl ˈfælfə]	[sə ˈlun]	[ˈtævərn]	[lat]	[ˈgælən]	[ˈbæt (ə) ri]
ORAL REPROD.	*bræn	*æl ˈfælfa	*sa ˈlun	ˈtævərn	latt	*gælən	ˈbætri
SPELLING PRON.	brann	ˈˈalfalfa	ˈˈsalon	ˈˈtavan	lått	ˈˈgallan ˈˈgallon	ˈˈbattəri

Such words as *lot* probably come from official documents, *bran* and *alfalfa* from sacks, *saloon* and *tavern* from signs, *gallon* and *battery* from advertisements. The striking part of it is that the spelling pronunciation does not usually affect the entire word, where a choice is possible, so that e.g. *gallon* may have an /a/ in the second syllable, corresponding to the [ə] of the original. A comparison with the E loanwords adopted in N, as reported by Aasta Stene, shows a much higher proportion of spelling pronunciations in the latter, e.g. *buss* 'bus' for AmN *båss, kutte* 'cut' for AmN *katta, hikkori* 'hickory' for AmN *hekkri* (or even *hikkrill*). As one AmN informant commented, when asked for the word for 'battery': 'They just give Norwegian sounds to the English letters.'

13. STRUCTURAL RESISTANCE TO BORROWING. It has long been known that some kinds of linguistic patterns are more likely to be borrowed than others. As long ago as 1881 William Dwight Whitney set up a scale on which he ranged the various patterns according to the freedom with which they are borrowed.[34] Nouns are most easily borrowed, then the various other parts of speech, then suffixes, then inflections, then sounds. He did not deny the possibility of borrowing even members of the last two classes, but contended that they are unusual and generally secondary to the borrowing of vocabulary items. 'The exemption of "grammar" from mixture is no isolated fact; the grammatical apparatus merely resists intrusion most successfully, in virtue of its being the least material and the most formal part of language. In a scale of constantly increasing

[34] W. D. Whitney, On mixture in language, TAPA 12.5-26 (1881).

difficulty it occupies the extreme place.'[35] Emphasis should be laid on Whitney's explanation, viz. that 'whatever is more formal or structural in character remains in that degree free from the intrusion of foreign material.' The same view is expressed by Lucien Tesnière in 1939, apparently without awareness of Whitney's earlier formulation: 'La miscibilité d'une langue est fonction inverse de sa systematisation.'[36]

Whatever the explanation, the facts are abundantly supported by the available lists of loanwords, e.g. for AmN and American Swedish. The following figures show the percentage of each of the traditional parts of speech in the total number of loanwords listed:

	Nouns	Verbs	Adj's	Adv.-Prep.	Interj.
AmN (author's word list)	75.5	18.4	3.4	1.2	1.4
AmN (Flom, Koshkonong Sogning)	71.7	23.0	4.2	0.8	0.5
AmSw. (Johnson, Chisago Lake Småland)	72.2	23.2	3.3	0.4	0.8

It is conspicuous that articles and pronouns do not appear in the lists, though again it would be foolish to deny that they can be borrowed (e.g. English *they* from Scandinavian). All linguistic features can be borrowed, but they are distributed along a SCALE OF ADOPTABILITY which somehow is correlated to the structural organization. This is most easily understood in the light of the distinction made earlier between importation and substitution. Importation is a process affecting the individual item needed at a given moment; its effects are partly neutralized by the opposing force of entrenched habits, which substitute themselves for whatever can be replaced in the imported item. Structural features are correspondences which are frequently repeated. Furthermore, they are established in early childhood, whereas the items of vocabulary are gradually added to in later years. This is a matter of the fundamental patterning of language: the more habitual and subconscious a feature of language is, the harder it will be to change.

This discussion raises the further question whether there is a corresponding difference between languages with respect to borrowing. It would seem that if internal differences exist within a language, similar differences might exist between languages, insofar as these are structurally different. This has frequently been asserted, on the basis of the greater homogeneity of vocabulary in some languages than in others. Typical is the treatment by Otakar Vočadlo, who set up what might be called a SCALE OF RECEPTIVITY among languages, dividing them into the major groups of homogeneous, amalgamate, and heterogeneous.[37] Unfor-

[35] Whitney's statement in Language and the study of language 199 (New York, 1867) to the effect that 'a mixed grammatical apparatus' is a 'monstrosity' and an 'impossibility' has often been quoted, while his later, more considered statement has been overlooked, e.g. by Otto Jespersen in Language 213 (New York, 1922) and by Alf Sommerfelt, Un cas de mélange de grammaires 5 (Oslo, 1926).

[36] TCLP 8.85 (1939).

[37] Otakar Vočadlo, Some observations on mixed languages, Actes du IVe congrès internationale de linguistes 169-76 (Copenhagen, 1938).

tunately Vočadlo excludes in his definition of 'receptivity' the words borrowed from other languages of the same stock, so that he regards e.g. Danish as a 'homogeneous' language. He is also more concerned with practical problems of linguistic purification, so that the basic question of whether structural or social forces are more important does not emerge too clearly. Kiparsky, in commenting on Vočadlo's paper, declared flatly, 'die Fähigkeit der sog. "homogenen" Sprachen, Entlehnungen aufzunehmen, hängt *nicht* von der linguistischen Struktur der Sprache, sondern von der politisch-sozialen Einstellung der Sprecher ab.'[38]

Perhaps one of the most hopeful fields for finding an answer to this question is the situation in the United States. Here a relatively uniform language and culture has exerted a similar pressure on a large number of different languages; much could be learned by comparing the borrowings of immigrant languages of different structures, and by then comparing these with the borrowings of Indian languages, whose structures are even more different than the immigrant languages among themselves. Most of the differences brought out by Vočadlo are not differences in actual borrowing, but in the relationship between importation and substitution, as here defined. Some languages import the whole morpheme, others substitute their own morphemes; but all borrow if there is any social reason for doing so, such as the existence of a group of bilinguals with linguistic prestige.

14. Structural effects of borrowing. Closely related to the preceding is the problem of what borrowing does to a language. The classic instance of English (with which may also be compared Danish) leads one to believe that borrowing is at least a contributory cause of structural reorientation (we avoid as scientifically questionable the term 'simplification'). But if it is true, as pointed out earlier, that the more structural a feature is, the less likely it is to be borrowed, it will be evident that a corollary is that the effects of borrowing on structure are likely to be small. The instances of new inflections actually introduced into wide use in the language are few, cf. the uncertain fate of classical plurals in E words like *phenomena, indices,* etc. In the lexicon the foreign patterns may actually predominate over the native, but the structural elements tend to persist. The chief danger represented by loanwords is the instability of classification which they bring in. They have been shown to vacillate to a statistically higher degree than native words, since they often fail to show criteria that make it possible to classify them immediately in one or another category of gender, number, or the like.[39] The fact that they tend to fall into only one class where there is a choice of several, will strengthen that class at the expense of others. They will often introduce affixes or other bound morphemes that stand in a differ-

[38] Op.cit. 176.
[39] Cf. Stene 5.

ent relation to their stems from that of affixes in native words. While some of these will not be discovered by the borrowing speakers, others will, and may even, as we have seen, become productive.

In phonology the effects may consist exclusively of the filling up of gaps in the native utilization of possible phoneme sequences. Thus when AmN acquires E *street* in the form /strit/, no new phoneme sequence is added: words like *stri* 'stubborn' and *krit* 'chalk' exhibit the same types. But sooner or later loanwords introduce sequences not previously utilized, as when AmFinnish adopted the word *skeptikko* 'sceptic', which then became the only word with *s* before a stop; words like *stove* were reproduced as *touvi*.[40] This type of change has here been called PHONEMIC REDISTRIBUTION, since it will require a different statement concerning the distribution of phonemes and their allophones. There is also the possibility of PHONEMIC IMPORTATION, though the usual rule is that this does not extend beyond bilingual speakers. In English the last sound of *rouge* is limited to words of French origin, but its importation is hardly thinkable if English had not already had it as a 'bound' phoneme occurring after *d* in words like *edge*.

Very little thoroughgoing study has been given so far to the structural effects of borrowing on the phonemic systems, so that we are still uncertain just how to evaluate contentions like those of Pike and Fries concerning the existence of 'conflicting coexistent systems'.[41] Pike's studies of Mazateco have shown that in this language [d] occurs only after nasals and may there be regarded as an allophone of *t*. But the Spanish loanword *siento* 'hundred' is one of a small number of loans in which [t] occurs after nasals, thus setting up a contrast of *t* and *d* not found elsewhere in the language. Yet, as Pike has shown, it contradicts the 'sprachgefühl' of the natives to recognize [d] after nasals as a separate phoneme for this reason. It seems probable, however, that this is a temporary and marginal situation in the language; for according to his own evidence, monolingual speakers tend to nasalize the preceding vowel and drop the *n*, thus restoring the more common native situation. Meanwhile, it is hardly more than a phonemic redistribution which permits voiceless *t* to occur in a position that is otherwise not known in the language, parallel in effect to that which occurred in English when medial *v* was introduced in initial position by the entry of French loanwords. As pointed out by Paul Garvin in commenting on a similar situation in Zoque, no new features of articulation are introduced; but it may happen that they are combined in a new way.[42]

15. THE IDENTIFICATION OF LOANS. So far the identification of loans has been taken for granted, but it must not be inferred from the confidence

[40] J. I. Kolehmainen, Am. Soc. Rev. 2.62-6 (1907).

[41] Fries and Pike, Lg. 25.29-50 (1949).

[42] Paul Garvin, Distinctive features in Zoque phonemic acculturation, SIL 5.13-20 (1947); cf. William Wonderly, IJAL 12.92-5 (1947).

with which such lists are put forward that it is always possible to isolate loan material in each given case. The difficulty, as elsewhere, is that the historical and the synchronic problem have not been clearly distinguished by those who have written about it. Non-scientific writers or speakers show an interesting tendency: if they are monolinguals, they are quite unaware of loans; if they are polylinguals, they suspect them everywhere.

(1) The Historical Problem. As here defined, borrowing is a historical process and therefore to be identified only by historical methods. This means a comparison between earlier and later states of a given language, to detect possible innovations; and thereupon a comparison of the innovations discovered with possible models in other languages. This double comparison is a corollary of our definition of borrowing; its application requires a knowledge of earlier states of the language, as well as of whatever languages may conceivably have exerted the influences in question. As applied specifically to immigrant speech in America, this means a comparison of present-day speech with the speech brought to these shores, and then a comparison of the innovations with AmE as spoken within the areas inhabited by the immigrants. The complete success of this venture depends on a number of factors which will be obvious to the reader, such as the existence of studies of the language in its homeland describing it at the time of immigration. Certain more special problems which the writer has encountered in treating AmN may be less obvious.

(a) Pre-immigration Loans. Some E loanwords penetrated into N speech, even the more remote rural dialects, before immigration. Trade, shipping, and the tourist traffic had led to contacts with the English-speaking world even in those classes that lacked the educational opportunities of acquiring the English language. Some immigrants may even have picked up their first E loanwords from N sailors on board the immigrant ships, not to mention the fact that there were many sailors among the immigrants themselves.[43] An example of a pre-immigration loan is the word *træn* 'train', apparently introduced by the English builders of Norway's first railroad in 1855. In cultivated N usage it was soon replaced by *tog* (a loanshift modeled on G *Zug*), but it is still widely known among dialect speakers.[44] A further complication is introduced by the

[43] Unfortunately no study has been made of E words in the N dialects, parallel to Aasta Stene's for the standard language; anyone who has heard Norwegian sailors speak is aware that they have borrowed heavily from English. Cf. Ivar Alnæs, Bidrag til en ordsamling over sjømandssproget (Christiania, 1902); R. Iversen, Lånord og lønnord hos folk og fant (Trondheim, 1939); A. Larsen and G. Stoltz, Bergens bymål (Christiania, 1912).

[44] Evidence on this point was gathered for the writer from the N dialect archives in Oslo by Magne Oftedal and in Bergen by Olai Skulerud. The related term *rells* 'rails', on the other hand, does not seem to have been known in Norway, though it took root in Sweden; cf. G. Langenfeldt, Språk och Stil 15.88-110 (1915).

fact that returning immigrants brought English words back to the homeland.[45]

(b) International Words. A special category of words is made up of those that are sufficiently common to most west European languages to have a similar spelling and meaning, in spite of widely differing pronunciations. Cultivated people in Norway certainly knew such words as *cigar, district, section* at the time of emigration, so that it becomes uncertain whether they should be regarded as loans even in the rural dialects when they turn up in forms not markedly different from that of the spelling. It is not always possible to say whether given words were current in the dialects; and the spelling pronunciations which they have in AmN might as well have arisen in America as in Norway. This was certainly true of *alfalfa* and *timothy,* which must have been learned in this country since they were the names of American products first met with over here. On the other hand, such words as *music, museum,* and *university* reveal by a highly Americanized pronunciation that the words were not in common use among the immigrants in their Norwegian forms at the time of immigration; yet they can hardly have failed to have heard them in Norway.

(c) Interlingual Coincidences. Where semantic-phonetic similarities exist between two words in different languages, it may be quite impossible to be certain whether borrowing has taken place. Such similarities are of unquestionable importance in causing confusion between two languages spoken by bilinguals. Typical AmN wordshifts are the substitutions of the N *korn* 'grain' for E *corn* 'maize', *grøn* 'food prepared from grain' for E *grain* 'grain other than maize', *brusk* 'tuft of straw' for E *brush* 'thicket'. In each of these cases the fact that we are dealing with the N word in question is confirmed by the variation in phonetic form from dialect to dialect, even though the limited distribution might speak against it in some cases. But when E *crew* is reproduced as N *kru,* we have very little to help us decide whether this is a loanword or a loanshift. The N form is identical with a dialect word *kru* 'crowd, household, multitude'. The AmN word has been identified with this by an AmN writer, Jon Norstog, who asserted that *kru* was not an English word at all, but a Telemark word which he had known from his childhood. The claim must be disallowed, however; for the N word is highly limited in its occurrence and is always neuter in gender, while the AmN word is widespread in all dialects, is mostly feminine, and has nowhere been recorded over here in its N meaning. Similarly with the AmN *travla* 'walk', a widely used word. There is a N dialect term *travla* 'struggle,

[45] The words *river, ticket, coal, surveyor, courthouse,* and *table knife* are reported from Tinn, Norway, as characteristic of returned emigrants by Skulerud, Telemaalet 73 (Christiania, 1918) and Tinnsmaalet (Halle a. S., 1922); cf. similar reports from Sweden and Swedish Finland in Folkmålsstudier 2.137-40 (1934) and Svenskbygden 132.3-5.

labor, slave', found only in remote sections of the country; nowhere does it have the meaning of the AmN word. Yet since its meaning is not identical with that of AmE *travel*, one might be in doubt whether it is a loan at all, were it not for the existence of an English dialect meaning of *travel* 'to walk' (very widespread according to Wright's EDD). Even though this is not at present recorded from Wisconsin, it seems most probable that it was used there and acquired by the N settlers in that state. The E word *cold* with the double meaning of 'a cold spell' and 'an infection' has influenced the meaning of the corresponding N words, which usually meant only 'a cold spell'; yet we find that in some N dialects the N word already had the double meaning.[46] In such cases it has been necessary to weigh the probabilities in the light of our knowledge of the state of the dialects at the time of immigration.

(2) The Synchronic Problem. It appears to be taken for granted, even by some linguists, that a borrowed word somehow occupies a special status within a language. The acute consciousness of the loanword as a 'problem' in certain modern cultures has led to some confusion in the question of what the loanword is and how it is to be regarded in a description of a language at a given time. The rise of synchronic linguistic studies (also called 'descriptive') has led to a renewed consideration of the question whether loanwords can be identified without the kind of double comparison described in the preceding section. Can loanwords be identified by a student who knows nothing of the previous stages of a language?[47] Such a technique, if there is one, would seem to be most useful in dealing with previously unwritten languages; indeed it would be the only one available.

The analyses made so far, however, have applied to languages where the historical facts were at least partially known, and the lists of loanwords to be analyzed have first been determined by historical means. This is true even of Miss Stene's list of E loanwords in modern Norwegian, though she has included in her final list only those words that could be identified by some synchronic criterion as 'not in complete agreement with the linguistic system of Norwegian'. These represent, she believes, the words that 'are felt by the language-conscious speaker to be "foreign" '.[48] She sets up a series of formal characteristics 'by which they reveal the fact that they are aliens in the system'. These are: non-Norwegian orthography, pronunciation, correspondence between spelling and pronunciation, musical accent, dynamic accent, morphology, word-formation, and meaning. Unfortunately no one of these is absolutely decisive (except perhaps the foreign spelling, which is not strictly a linguistic

[46] Cf. Aasen NO² s.v. *kjøld* 'Sogn og fler', but not under *kulde* and the other words.

[47] Cf. V. Mathesius, Zur synchronischen analyse fremden sprachguts, Englische Studien 70.21-35 (1935-6); B. Trnka, Phonological analysis of present-day standard English 49-53 (Prague, 1935); Stene, op.cit.

[48] Stene 5.

matter), since many of them occur also in words of native origin; and some are so common that it seems very doubtful if they are felt as 'foreign' by anyone except the professional linguist.[49] Furthermore, the criteria fail to include some quite obvious loans, such as *drible* 'dribble', *start* 'start', and *streik* 'strike': these have in every respect been assimilated to a common pattern.

Now it would be impossible to deny that, as we have shown in a preceding section, many loanwords have introduced features of arrangement which are numerically less common than certain other features and which sometimes stand in other relationships to the rest of the language than the previously existent patterns. But to identify the results of a historical process like borrowing is simply not possible by a purely synchronic study. What we find when we study a structure without reference to its history is not borrowing or loans, but something that might rather be described as 'structural irregularity'. This is not an absolute thing: word counts have shown that patterns vary in frequency from the extremely common to the extremely rare, with no absolute boundary between the two. Patterns of high frequency are certain not to sound 'queer' to native speakers; just how infrequent must a pattern be before it begins to 'feel foreign'? Very few studies have so far been made in which structural analysis is combined with frequency determinations.[50] Until a language is thus analyzed, any statement about the 'aberrations' of loanwords must remain open to question. Even so it is evident that no synchronic analysis can discover such loanwords as *priest, due, law,* or *skirt* in English. If other words contain sequences that are less common and are found by synchronic analysis to have a different status, they will not thereby be revealed as loanwords, but as something else to which a different name should be given. If confusion is not to be further confounded, the term 'borrowing' and its kinsmen should be limited to the uses of historical linguistics.

This is apparently the conclusion also of Pike and Fries when they state that 'in a purely descriptive analysis of the dialect of a monolingual speaker there are no loans discoverable or describable.'[51] The Germans here make a distinction between the Lehnwort, a historical fact, and the Fremdwort, a contemporary fact.[52] But it does not appear just how the line is to be drawn. None of the languages of modern civilization are so simple in their structure that a single set of categories will exhaustively describe them. Along with their high-frequency habits they exhibit a great number of 'marginal' habits which come into play in given circum-

[49] Cf. the writer's review, Lg. 25.63-8 (1949).

[50] Cf. W. F. Twaddell, A phonological analysis of intervocalic consonant clusters in German, Actes du IVe congrès internationale de linguistes 218-25 (Copenhagen, 1938); Hans Vogt, Structure of Norwegian monosyllables, NTS 12.5-29 (1940).

[51] Lg. 25.31 (1949).

[52] Cf. Eugen Kaufman, Der Fragenkreis ums Fremdwort, JEGP 38.42-63 (1939). Kaufman wishes to eliminate Fremdwörter from German, but not Lehnwörter.

stances, perhaps only in given words. Current phonemic theory seems to assume that the only description of distribution that is relevant in phonology is the phonetic environment. But it seems impossible to get away from the fact that individual words and word groups may have habits of their own, which can only be described in terms of lexical distribution. This does not surprise anyone when speaking of morphological characteristics: thus the first person singular of the verb occurs only in one word in English, viz. *am*. The problem in phonology is not different in kind, only in extent. Rather than to regard such complications as 'coexistent systems', it will probably be best to treat them as systemic fragments occurring under given circumstances—items of LIMITED LEXICAL DISTRIBUTION.

SUMMARY

An attempt has been made in this article to establish a precise definition for the term 'borrowing' by describing it as the process that takes place when bilinguals reproduce a pattern from one language in another. Two kinds of activity which enter into borrowing are distinguished, viz. substitution and importation, which are defined in terms of a comparison between the model and the reproduction. By distinguishing morphemic and phonemic substitution it becomes possible to set up classes of loans: (1) loanwords, without morphemic substitution; (2) loanblends, with partial morphemic substitution; and (3) loanshifts, with complete morphemic substitution. The second of these includes what are more commonly known as 'hybrids', the third the 'loan translations' and 'semantic loans'. Various periods of bilingualism are described, involving erratic and systematic substitution, or importation of phonemes. Loanblends are classified into blended stems, derivatives, and compounds, while loanshifts are divided into loan homonyms and loan synonyms. The process of hybrid creation is so defined as to distinguish it from borrowing, being a reverse substitution, in which the model is to be found in the borrowing language. Among the cross-currents of borrowing, which sometimes confuse the picture, are the procedures called reborrowing, interdialectal loans, and the influence of spelling. The question of structural resistance to borrowing is discussed, and a scale of adoptability is set up, which is shown to have a correlation to the structural organization of the borrowing language. It is shown that the scale of receptivity assumed by some writers is really a difference in the relationship between importation and substitution. The structural effect of borrowing is found to be largely a certain instability in the categories; in phonology it may produce extensive phonemic redistribution, but little phonemic importation. The question of identification of loans is shown to be primarily a historical question, not susceptible to the methods of synchronic analysis. So far as loans are discovered by the latter method, it is not as loans, but as residual structural irregularities, which might rather be called 'systemic fragments' than 'coexistent systems'. The historical problem is difficult enough, fraught as it is with the problems of distinguishing loans made before immigration, international words, and interlingual coincidences from bona-fide loans made during the period of inter-language contact. But the synchronic problem is insoluble without complete analyses of structure which also take into account the relative frequencies of the elements analyzed.

AUTHOR'S POSTSCRIPT (1966)

This article was my first attempt to formulate views on the process of borrowing based on my first-hand experience with American speakers of Norwegian. Among the original contributions made to the general theory of borrowing was my distinction between "importation" and "substitution," and the corresponding distinction between loanwords and "loanshifts," a term I believe I invented. The substance of the article was incorporated in chapter 15, "The Process of Borrowing," in my book The Norwegian Language in America *(2 vols., Philadelphia: University of Pennsylvania Press, 1953).*

In this reworking I changed the classification by making "loanblends" a subclass of loanwords rather than a major class parallel to it, thereby bringing out more clearly the basic distinction between loanword and loanshift. Stimulated by the ideas of the German scholar Werner Betz in his studies of Latin loanwords in Old High German, I worked out a complete classification of borrowings paralleling his German terms by a system of my own. I applied this to a body of unselected letters written by Norwegian immigrants in an article published in Studies in Honor of Albert Morey Sturtevant *(University of Kansas Press, 1952, pp. 76-102). I discussed the problem in reviews of books by Betz's pupils, e.g. one on Old French loans in Middle High German by Emil Öhmann (*Language *28.397-401 (1952)) and one on Latin loans in Old English by Helmut Gneuss (*Language *32.761-66 (1956)). In the latter I still further refined my classification by making a consistently binary division of each class: loanwords were divided into assimilated and unassimilated, loanshifts into creations (exact or approximate replicas of a foreign model) and extensions (homonymous or synonymous replicas).*

In contrast to Betz's system I have attempted to establish a terminology that could be used at all levels of linguistic structure and that was therefore independent of any one of them. This principle was applied in my major statement on this subject, the chapter entitled "Language Contact" in my book Bilingualism in the Americas: A Bibliography and Research Guide *(University of Alabama: American Dialect Society, 1956; Publication No. 26). In this analysis I benefited* *from the work of Uriel Weinreich which had appeared in the meanwhile (*Languages in Contact, *New York, 1953; see my review in* Language *30.380-8. (1954)). I adopted from him the terms "interference" and "interlingual identification," and suggested as units of the latter the terms "diaphone" and "diamorph" which I had proposed in an article on "Problems of Bilingual Description"* (Georgetown University Monograph Series on Languages and Linguistics, *vol. 7, 1954, pp. 9-19). Others have worked further with the problem since 1956, but this is where it stands as far as my contributions have gone.*

Einar Haugen

The Social Motivation of a Sound Change

WILLIAM LABOV

THE WORK WHICH IS REPORTED in the following pages concerns the direct observation of a sound change in the context of the community life from which it stems.[1] The change is a shift in the phonetic position of the first elements of the diphthongs /ai/ and /au/, and the community is the island of Martha's Vineyard, Massachusetts. By studying the frequency and distribution of phonetic variants of /ai/ and /au/ in the several regions, age levels, occupational and ethnic groups within the island, it will be possible to reconstruct the recent history of this sound change; by correlating the complex linguistic pattern with parallel differences in social structure, it will be possible to isolate the social factors which bear directly upon the linguistic process. It is hoped that the results of this procedure will contribute to our general understanding of the mechanism of linguistic change.

The problem of explaining language change seems to resolve itself into three separate problems: the origin of linguistic variations; the spread and propagation of linguistic changes; and the regularity of linguistic change. The model which underlies this three-way division requires as a starting point a variation in one or several words in the speech of one or two individuals.[2] These variations may be induced by the processes of assimilation or differentiation, by analogy, borrowing, fusion, contamination, random variation, or any number of processes in which the language system interacts with the physiological or psychological characteristics of the individual. Most such variations occur only once, and are extinguished

---

Reprinted by permission from *Word* 19.273-309.

[1] An abbreviated version of the present paper was given at the 37th Annual Meeting of the Linguistic Society of America in New York City on December 29, 1962.

[2] See E. Sturtevant. *An Introduction to Linguistic Science*. New Haven: 1947: Ch. VIII: "Why are Phonetic Laws Regular?" The discussion by Martinet in his report, Structural Variation in Language," *Proceedings of the Ninth International Congress of Linguists,* implies a similar model.

as quickly as they arise. However, a few recur, and, in a second stage, they may be imitated more or less widely, and may spread to the point where the new forms are in contrast with the older forms along a wide front. Finally, at some later stage, one or the other of the two forms usually triumphs, and regularity is achieved.

Whereas for the first stage, we are often overwhelmed with an excess of possible explanations, we have quite the reverse situation in attempting to account for the propagation and regularity of linguistic changes. A number of earlier theories which proposed general psychological, physiological or even climatic determinants, have been discarded for some time.[3] The contribution of internal, structural forces to the effective spread of linguistic changes, as outlined by Martinet,[4] must naturally be of primary concern to any linguist who is investigating these processes of propagation and regularization. However, an account of structural pressures can hardly tell the whole story. Not all changes are highly structured, and no change takes place in a social vacuum. Even the most systematic chain shift occurs with a specificity of time and place that demands an explanation.

Widely divergent ideas appear to exist as to what comprises an explanation of the mechanism of change. The usual diachronic procedure, as followed in palaeontology or geology, is to explore the mechanism of change between states by searching for data on intermediate states. It follows that we come closer and closer to an accurate depiction of the mechanism of change as the interval between the two states we are studying becomes smaller and smaller. This is certainly the method followed by such historical linguists as Jespersen, Kökeritz and Wyld, and it is the motivation behind their extensive searches for historical detail. On the other hand, a viewpoint which favors the abstract manipulation of data from widely separated states has been propounded recently by M. Halle;[5] explicit defense of a similar attitude may be found in H. Pilch's study of the vowel systems of Shakespeare, Noah Webster, and present-day America.[6] Neither Halle nor Pilch distinguish the three aspects of change outlined above.

It would seem that the historical approach is more appropriate to an empirical science concerned with change, even over a narrow time span, as this approach leads to statements which are increasingly subject to confirmation or disconfirmation. At the same time, such a close view of historical change makes us increasingly sceptical of the value of limita-

[3] A number of these theories are reviewed by Alf Sommerfelt, "Sur la propagation de changements phonétiques," *Norsk Tidsskrift for Sprogvidenskap* IV (1930), 76-128.

[4] *Economie des changements phonétiques*. Berne: 1955. The empirical confirmation of many of Martinet's ideas to be found in Moulton's investigation of Swiss German dialects has provided strong motivation for some of the interpretations in the present essay. In particular, see "Dialect Geography and the Concept of Phonological Space," *Word* XVIII (1962), 23-32.

[5] "Phonology in a Generative Grammar," *Word* XVIII (1962), 62-72.

[6] "The Rise of the American English Vowel Pattern," *Word* XI (1955), 57-63.

tions on the kinds of data which may be considered: as, for instance, that the linguist explain linguistic events only by other linguistic events. One would expect that the application of structural linguistics to diachronic problems would lead to the enrichment of the data, rather than the impoverishment of it.[7]

The point of view of the present study is that one cannot understand the development of a language change apart from the social life of the community in which it occurs. Or to put it another way, social pressures are continually operating upon language, not from some remote point in the past, but as an immanent social force acting in the living present.

Sturtevant has outlined a concise theory of the spread and consolidation of language changes which consistently views this process in its social dimension. One sentence in particular will serve as an excellent theme for this investigation:

> Before a phoneme can spread from word to word . . . it is necessary that one of the two rivals shall acquire some sort of prestige.[8]

It is hoped that the study of the particular case under discussion will lend support to this general view of the role of social interaction in linguistic change.

1. The island of Martha's Vineyard

The island of Martha's Vineyard, Dukes County, Massachusetts, was chosen as a laboratory for an initial investigation of social patterns in linguistic change.[9] Martha's Vineyard has the advantage of being a self-contained unit, separated from the mainland by a good three miles of the Atlantic Ocean. At the same time, the Vineyard has enough social and geographic complexity to provide ample room for differentiation of linguistic behavior. We are also fortunate in having the records of the *Linguistic Atlas of New England* (henceforth abbreviated LANE) as a background for the present investigation.[10] It is just thirty years since

[7] For a parallel criticism of restrictions on the data imposed by Bloomfieldian linguistics, see W. Diver's review of W. P. Lehmann's *Historical Linguistics, Word* XIX (1963), 100-105.

[8] *Op. cit.*, pp. 74-84. See also H. Hoenigswald's remarks in "Are There Universals of Linguistic Change?" J. S. Greenberg, ed., *Universals of Language*. Cambridge, Mass., 1963. Footnote 8: "Sound changes can apparently not be entirely predicted from internal, systemic stresses and strains, nor can they be explained as the effects of scatter around a target or norm; they have direction and are in that sense specific, much like other happenings in history."

[9] For further details on the social and economic background of Martha's Vineyard, see my 1962 Columbia University Master's Essay, *The Social History of a Sound Change on the Island of Martha's Vineyard, Massachusetts,* written under the direction of Professor Uriel Weinreich.

[10] H. Kurath *et al.* Providence: 1941. Background information on the informants is to be found in H. Kurath, *Handbook of the Linguistic Geography of New England.* Providence: 1939.

Guy Lowman visited Martha's Vineyard; his interviews with four members of the old families of the island give us a firm base from which to proceed, and a time depth of one full generation which adds considerably to the solidity of the conclusions which can be drawn.

Figure 1 shows the general outlines of Martha's Vineyard, and Table 1 gives the population figures from the 1960 Census.

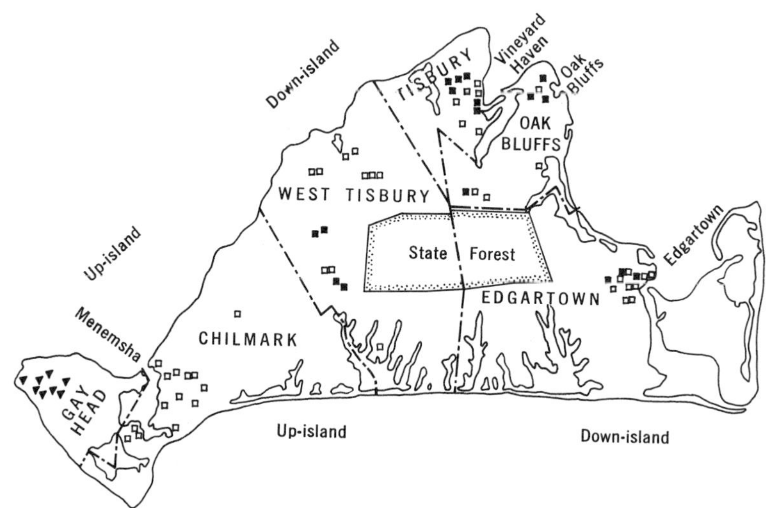

FIGURE 1. Location of the 69 informants on Martha's Vineyard. Ethnic origin of the informants indicated by the following symbols: □ English, ■ Portuguese, ▼ Indian. Symbols placed side by side indicate members of the same family.

The island is divided into two parts by an informal, but universally used distinction between *up-island* and *down-island*. *Down-island* is the region of the three small towns where almost three-fourths of the permanent population live. *Up-island* is strictly rural, with a few villages, farms, isolated summer homes, salt ponds and marshes, and a large central area of uninhabited pine barrens.

As we travel up-island from Vineyard Haven, we come first to the town of West Tisbury, which contains some of the most beautiful farms and fields of the island, now largely untilled and ungrazed. At Chilmark, the ground rises to a series of rolling hills which look out to the Atlantic on one side, and to Vineyard Sound on the other. Chilmark's salt pond is permanently open to the Sound through a narrow channel, and so serves as a permanent harbor for the dozen fishermen who still operate from the docks of the village of Menemsha in Chilmark. Finally, at the southwest corner of the island, there is the promontory of Gay Head, and the houses of the hundred and three Indians who represent the original inhabitants of Martha's Vineyard.

The six thousand native Vineyarders fall into four ethnic groups which are essentially endogamous. First, there are the descendants of the

TABLE 1. *Population of Martha's Vineyard*[11]

Down-island [towns]		3,846
Edgartown	1,118	
Oak Bluffs	1,027	
Vineyard Haven	1,701	
Up-island [rural]		1,717
Edgartown	256	
Oak Bluffs	292	
Tisbury	468	
West Tisbury	360	
Chilmark	238	
Gay Head	103	
Total		5,563

old families of English stock, who first settled the island in the 17th and 18th centuries: the Mayhews, Nortons, Hancocks, Allens, Tiltons, Vincents, Wests, Pooles—all closely related after ten generations of intermarriage. Secondly, there is a large group of Portuguese descent, immigrants from the Azores, Madeira and the Cape Verde Islands. There are Portuguese all along the southeastern New England coast, but the Vineyard has the largest percentage of any Massachusetts county. In 1960, 11% of the population was of first or second generation Portuguese origin; with the third and fourth generation Portuguese, the total would probably come close to 20%.[12]

The third ethnic group is the Indian remnant at Gay Head. The fourth is the miscellaneous group of various origins: English, French Canadian, Irish, German, Polish. Though the sum total of this residual group is almost 15%, it is not a coherent social force, and we will not consider it further in this paper.[13]

Another group which will not be considered directly is the very large number of summer residents, some 42,000, who flood the island in June and July of every year. This tide of *summer people* has had relatively little direct influence on the speech of the Vineyard, although the constant pressure from this direction, and the growing dependence of the island upon a vacation economy, has had powerful indirect effects upon the language changes which we will consider.

The Vineyard is best known to linguists as an important relic area of American English: an island of *r*-pronouncers in a sea of *r*-lessness.

[11] From U.S. Bureau of the Census. *U.S. Census of Population: 1960. Number of Inhabitants. Massachusetts.* Final Report PC(1)—23A. Washington, D.C.: U.S. Government Printing Office, 1962. Table 7, page 23-11.

[12] From U.S. Bureau of the Census, *U.S. Census of Population: 1960. General Social and Economic Characteristics. Massachusetts.* Final Report PC(1)—23c. Washington, D.C.: U.S. Government Printing Office, 1962. Table 89, page 23-260.

[13] There is a sizeable number of retired mainlanders living on the Vineyard as year-round residents. While they are included in the population total, they do not form a part of the social fabric we are considering, and none of the informants are drawn from this group.

With a three-hundred-and-twenty-year history of continuous settlement, and a long record of resistance to Boston ways and manners, the island has preserved many archaic traits which were probably typical of south-eastern New England before 1800. The most striking feature, still strongly entrenched, is the retention of final and pre-consonantal /r/.[14] New England short /o/ is still well represented among the older speakers. Exploratory studies of the Vineyard in 1961 showed that most of the special traits of this island speech shown on the LANE maps may still be found among traditional speakers from 50 to 95 years old.

Lexical survivals of 17th-century English are even clearer indications of the archaic nature of the Vineyard tradition. We find *bannock,* for a fried cake of corn meal, *studdled* for 'dirty, roiled' water, in addition to such items as *tempest* and *buttry* listed in the LANE. Perhaps the most dramatic evidence of the fact that the Vineyard represents an underlying stratum is the presence of *belly-gut,* for a face-down sled ride. In LANE records, this form is shown on the Vineyard and in western New England: in the intervening area, it has been overlaid by three successive layers—*belly-bump, belly-flop,* and currently, no word at all.[15]

As interesting as the structure of Martha's Vineyard English may be, it is not the purpose here to contrast one static system with another. We would like to understand the internal structure of Vineyard English, including the systematic differences which now exist and the changes now taking place within the island. For this purpose, we will select for study a linguistic feature with the widest possible range of variation and the most complex pattern of distribution characteristic of Martha's Vineyard.

2. *Selection of the linguistic variable*

It would be appropriate to ask at this point what are the most useful properties of a linguistic variable to serve as the focus for the study of a speech community. First, we want an item that is *frequent,* which occurs so often in the course of undirected natural conversation that its behavior can be charted from unstructured contexts and brief interviews. Secondly, it should be *structural*: the more the item is integrated into a larger system of functioning units, the greater will be the intrinsic linguistic interest of our study. Third, the distribution of the feature should be highly *stratified*: that is, our preliminary explorations should suggest

[14] On the LANE maps, we find that Guy Lowinan regularly recorded the up-island /r/ as [ɚ] in [wɐɪɚ, hɑɚd, bɑɚn], and down-island /r/ as [ə̣] in the same positions. Essentially the same pattern is to be found among the older speakers today, though not with the regularity that Lowman noted. It is possible that this treatment of /r/ was in fact intended as a broad transcription, for the LANE was much more concerned with vowels than consonants.

[15] See H. Kurath, *A Word Geography of the Eastern United States.* Ann Arbor: 1949. Fig. 162. *Belly-flop* (and the corresponding lexical item in other regions) has generally shifted for the younger generation to denote a flat dive into the water. Coasting is now a less important sport, and its terminology is appropriately impoverished.

an asymmetric distribution over a wide range of age levels or other ordered strata of society.

There are a few contradictory criteria, which pull us in different directions. On the one hand, we would like the feature to be *salient,* for us as well as for the speaker, in order to study the direct relations of social attitudes and language behavior. But on the other hand, we value *immunity from conscious distortion,* which greatly simplifies the problem of reliability of the data.[16]

In the exploratory interviews conducted on the Vineyard in 1961, many structural changes were noted which were plainly parallel to changes taking place on the mainland under the influence of the standard Southeast New England pattern. Changes in phonemic inventory were found: New England short /o/ is rapidly disappearing; the two low back vowels, /ɑ̈/ and /ɔ/ are merging. Important changes in phonemic distribution are occurring: the /or ~ ɔr/ distinction is disappearing: initial /hw/ is giving way to /w/.[17] Shifts in structural lexical systems, all in the direction of regional standards, can be traced. Archaic syntactic features are disappearing. Yet as interesting as these changes may be, there is no reason to think that their distribution will follow a pattern peculiar to the Vineyard.

In the case of tautosyllabic /r/, however, we do have a linguistic variable defined by the geographical limits of the island, which follows a social pattern idiosyncratic to Martha's Vineyard. In some island areas, retroflexion is increasing, and in others, decreasing; as we will note later, the social implications of this fact can not be missed. The variations in /r/ are frequent, salient, and involve far-reaching structural consequences for the entire vowel system.

However, the preliminary exploration of the Vineyard indicated that another variable might be even more interesting: differences in the height of the first element of the diphthongs /ai/ and /au/. Instead of the common Southeast New England standard [aɪ] and [aʊ], one frequently hears on Martha's Vineyard [ɐɪ] and [ɐʊ], or even [əɪ] and [əʊ]. This feature of centralized diphthongs[18] is salient for the linguist, but not for most speakers; it is apparently quite immune to conscious

[16] Many ingenious devices are needed to detect and eliminate deceit on the part of metropolitan informants, whether intended or not. On Martha's Vineyard, this is much less of a problem, but the effects of the interview situation are evident in the careful style of some informants.

[17] The disappearance of New England short /o/ follows the pattern described by W. Avis, "The 'New England Short *o*': a Recessive Phoneme." Language XXXVII (1961), 544-558. Exploratory interviews at other points in southeastern New England (Woods Hole, Falmouth, New Bedford, Fall River, Providence, Stonington) indicate that the loss of the /or ~ ɔr/ and /hw-~w-/ distinctions is parallel to that on Martha's Vineyard.

[18] The terms *centralized diphthongs, centralization,* and *degree of centralization* will be used throughout this study to refer to the various forms of the diphthongs /ai/ and /au/ with first elements higher than [a]. It is not intended that the terms themselves should imply any process or direction of change, except when used with explicit statements to that effect.

distortion, as the native Vineyarders are not aware of it, nor are they able to control it consciously. As far as structure is concerned, we cannot neglect the structural parallelism of /ai/ and /au/; on the other hand these diphthongs are marked by great structural freedom in the range of allophones permitted by the system. These are strictly sub-phonemic differences. Since there are no other up-gliding diphthongs with either low or central first elements in this system, it is not likely that continued raising, or even fronting or backing, would result in confusion with any other phoneme.

The property of this feature of centralization which makes it appear exceptionally attractive, even on first glance, is the indication of a complex and subtle pattern of stratification. This very complexity proves to be rewarding: for when the centralizing tendency is charted in the habits of many speakers, and the influence of the phonetic, prosodic and stylistic environment is accounted for, there remains a large area of variation. Instead of calling this "free" or "sporadic" variation, and abandoning the field, we will pursue the matter further, using every available clue to discover the pattern which governs the distribution of centralized diphthongs.

The problem becomes all the more significant when it becomes apparent that the present trend on Martha's Vineyard runs counter to the long-range movement of these diphthongs over the past two hundred years. And while this sound change is not likely to become a phonemic change in the foreseeable future, it operates in an area where far-reaching phonemic shifts have taken place in the past. It is, in effect, the unstable residue of the Great Vowel Shift.

3. The history of centralized diphthongs

It seems generally agreed that the first element of the diphthong /ai/ was a mid-central vowel in 16th- and 17th-century English.[19] We may assume that when Thomas Mayhew first took possession of his newly purchased property of Martha's Vineyard in 1642, he brought with him the pronunciation /əɪ/ in *right, pride, wine* and *wife*. The later history of this vowel in America indicates that [əɪ] continued to be the favored form well into the 19th century.[20]

[19] See O. Jespersen, *A Modern English Grammar on Historical Principles*, I, London: 1927, page 234, and H. Kökeritz, *Shakespeare's Pronunciation*, New Haven: 1953, p. 216. Among recent historical linguists, H. C. Wyld is a notable exception in positing a front first element in the transition of M.E. *i*: to Mod.E. /ai/, relying on occasional spellings with *ey* and *ei*, but without considering the many other indications of central position. See *A History of Modern Colloquial English*, Oxford: 1920, pages 223-225.

[20] Abundant evidence is given by George Phillip Krapp, *The English Language in America*, II, New York: 1925, pages 186-191.

When we examine the records of the LANE, we find that centralized /ai/ was a healthy survivor in the speech of the Atlas informants.[21] We find it scattered throughout the rural areas of New England, and strongly entrenched in the Genesee Valley of western New York. It had disappeared completely from the Midland, but was quite regular—before voiceless consonants—in both the Upper and Lower South. This differential effect of voiceless and voiced following consonants was only a directing influence in the North, but stood as a regular phonetic rule in the South. On Martha's Vineyard, as on neighboring Nantucket and Cape Cod, centralized /ai/ was frequently recorded.

The history of /au/ differs from that of /ai/ more than our general expectations of symmetry would lead us to predict. There is reason to believe that in England the lowering of /au/ was considerably in advance of /ai/, and it is not likely that the same Thomas Mayhew used /əu/ in *house* and *out*.[22] The American evidence of the late 18th and 19th centuries, as summed up by Krapp, points to [oᴜ] as the conservative, cultured form, giving way to [aᴜ] or [äᴜ], with the rural New England form as [æᴜ] or [ɛᴜ].[23] The Linguistic Atlas records show only a hint of parallelism of /ai/ and /au/.[24] We find [əᴜ] mainly in eastern Virginia, before voiceless consonants, with some small representation in upstate New York, but the principal New England form of [aᴜ] stood out against a background of rural and recessive [æᴜ]. Martha's Vineyard shows very little centralization of /au/ in the LANE maps.

This brief review indicates that the isolated position of /au/ has facilitated phonetic variation on a truly impressive scale. The first element has ranged from [ɨ] to [ä], from [ɛ] to [o] all within the same general structural system. Perhaps one reason why /ai/ has not shown a similar range of variation is the existence of another up-gliding diphthong, /ɔi/.[25] In any case, as the stage is set for our present view of Martha's Vineyard diphthongs, /ai/ is well centralized, but /au/ is not. It may be too strong a statement to say that this represents the phonetic heritage of the seventeenth century Yankee settlers of the island, but we may venture to say that we have no evidence of any intervening events which disturbed the original pattern.

[21] The best view of the distribution of /ai/ may be had from Maps 26-27 in H. Kurath and R. McDavid, *The Pronunciation of English in the Atlantic States*, Ann Arbor: 1962. Centralized diphthongs are well known as a feature of Canadian English, where the effect of the voiceless-voiced consonant environment is quite regular.

[22] Jespersen, *op. cit.*, pages 235-236. Kökeritz, *op. cit.*, pages 144-149. Wyld, *op. cit.*, pages 230-231.

[23] *Op. cit.*, pages 192-196.

[24] Kurath and McDavid, *op. cit.*, Maps 28-29.

[25] The possibility of phonemic confusion with /ɔi/ apparently became a reality in the 17th and 18th century, in both England and America, when both diphthongs had central first elements.

4. The investigation of /ai/ and /au/

The summer visitor to Martha's Vineyard gets only a fleeting impression of the native speech pattern. Seven out of every eight human beings on the island are visitors like himself. But for the Vineyarder, there is no effect of dilution. For him, summer visitors have very little status on the island and their ephemeral nature is convincingly demonstrated on the first week in September of every year, when they disappear even more quickly than the insect population of the summer months. The normal native speech of Martha's Vineyard can then be heard as the dominant sound in public places. A knock on any up-island door will no longer produce a Back Bay stockbroker, but the rightful owner in possession once again. As a rural up-islander he is very likely to use a high degree of centralization of /ai/ and /au/; but in the small town areas of down-island one may also hear this feature, particularly in words such as *right, white, twice, life, wife, like,* but not so much in *while, time, line, I, my, try*. Similarly, one may hear in the streets of Vineyard Haven centralized forms in *out, house, doubt,* but not so much in *now, how,* or *around.*

In order to study this feature systematically, it was necessary to devise an interview schedule which would provide many examples of /ai/ and /au/ in casual speech, emotionally colored speech, careful speech, and reading style. The first of these diphthongs is more than twice as frequent as the second, but even so, several devices were required to increase the concentration of occurrences of both.

1. A lexical questionnaire, using the regional markers shown as most significant in the maps of the LANE, supplemented with recent observations, and concentrating on the following words containing /ai/ and /au/:

spider	rareripe	iodine	dying out
sliding	swipe	quinine	flattening out
		scrimy	dowdy
white bread	nigh		outhouse
white of egg	pie	frying pan	backhouse
nightcrawler	sty	fry pan	crouch
lightning bug	firefly		mow
Italian	shiretown		rowen

2. Questions concerning value judgments, exploring the social orientation of the respondent, were so phrased as to elicit answers containing /ai/ and /au/ forms.[26] Answers to such questions often gave a rich har-

[26] "When we speak of the *right* to *life,* liberty and the pursuit of happiness, what does *right* mean? . . . Is it in *writing?* . . . If a man is successful at a job he doesn't *like,* would you still say he was a successful man?" These questions were generally successful in eliciting the informant's version of the italicized words.

vest of diphthongal forms, with contrasting uses of emotionally stressed and unstressed variants.

3. A special reading, used mainly in the high school, was offered ostensibly as a test of the ability to read a story naturally.[27] Since these readings gave the most exact comparisons between speakers, they were utilized for the spectrographic measurements discussed below.

In addition to the formal interview, observations were made in a great many casual situations: on the streets of Vineyard Haven and Edgartown, in diners, restaurants, bars, stores, docks, and many places where the general sound of public conversation could be noted, if not effectively recorded. But these notations only served as a supplementary check on the tape-recorded interviews. The basic information was gathered in the course of 69 interviews with native island speakers made in three periods: August 1961, late September–October 1961, January 1962. These 69 interviews provide the basis for the discussion to follow.

The sixty-nine speakers, somewhat more than 1% of the population, represent a judgment sample of the community of native residents, and the groups which are important in the social life and value systems of the island. The sampling is proportional to area rather than population: 40 are up-islanders, and only 29 are from down-island, though over 70% of the people live down-island. The most important occupational groups are represented: 14 in fishing, 8 in farming, 6 in construction, 19 in service trades, 3 professionals, 5 housewives, 14 students. The three main ethnic groups are represented: 42 of English descent, 16 Portuguese and 9 Indian.

The locations of the 69 informants are shown on Figure 1, coded by ethnic group. It may be understood that a large proportion of those engaged in fishing are to be found in Chilmark; the farmers are well inland, mainly in West Tisbury; the service trades are heavily concentrated in Edgartown and Vineyard Haven. Of Guy Lowman's four LANE informants, one was in Chilmark, one in West Tisbury, and two in Edgartown.

As a result of these 69 interviews, we have about 3,500 instances of /ai/ and 1,500 instances of /au/ as the basic data for this study.

5. *Scales of measurement*

An important step was to construct a reliable, inter-subjective index to the degree of centralization. In the original transcriptions of the tape-

[27] This two-hundred word reading is constructed as a story told by a teen-age Vineyard boy, of the day he found out his father wasn't always right. An excerpt will show the technique involved: "After the high winds last Thursday, we went down to the mooring to see how the boat was making out. . . . My father started to pump out the bottom, and he told me to find out if the outboard would start. I found out all right. I gave her a couple of real hard pulls but it was no dice. 'Let me try her,' my father said. 'Not on your life,' I told him. 'I've got my pride.' "

recorded interviews[28] a six-point scale of height of the first element was used, ranging from the standard New England form [aɪ] to the fully centralized [əɪ]. Such a transcription was intended to push the distinctions noted to the limits of auditory discrimination. This corresponded to the practice of the LANE, in which the same number of degrees of height can be symbolized. However, it was recognized that such fine distinctions could probably only be reproduced consistently by individuals who had attained a high degree of convergence, and then over a very short time span.

Independent instrumental measurements were used to reduce the scale by objective criteria, and to give a certain degree of objective validity to the entire system of transcription.

Acoustic spectrograms were made of eighty instances of /ai/ as spoken and recorded by seven different Vineyarders.[29] A study of the assembled formant patterns indicated that one particular point in time might be best suited for measuring the degree of height of the first element of the diphthong. This is shown in Figure 2, as the point where the first

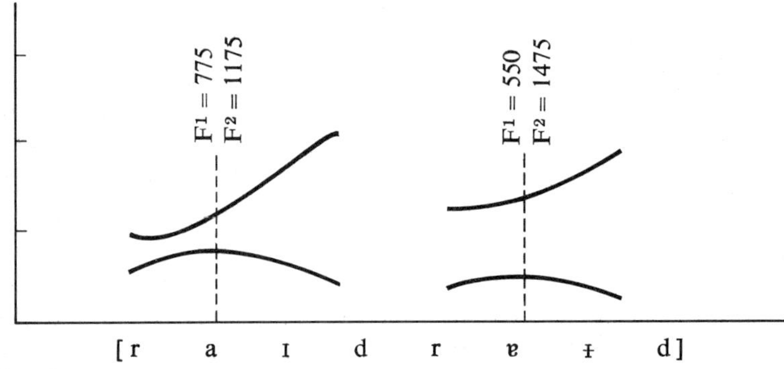

FIGURE 2. Measurement of typical /ai/ diphthongs at first formant maximum.

formant reaches a maximum. Measurements of the first and second formant positions at this point seemed to correspond well to the formant measurements for steady state [a] to [ə] in Peterson and Barney's vowel studies.[30]

The eighty measurements were then plotted on a bi-logarithmic scale, with abscissa and ordinate corresponding to first and second form-

[28] The interviews were recorded at 3¾ inches per second on a Butoba MT-5, using a Butoba MD-21 dynamic microphone. A tape recording of the standard reading, "After the high winds . . ." read by five of the speakers whose formant measurements appear on Figure 3, and other examples of centralized diphthongs used by Vineyard speakers in natural conversation, may be obtained from the writer, Department of Linguistics, Columbia University, New York 27, N.Y.

[29] Spectrograms were made on the Kay Sonograph, using both wide and narrow bands. Seven of these, showing fifteen instances of /ai/ and /au/, are reproduced in the Master's Essay cited above.

[30] G. E. Peterson and H. L. Barney, "Control Methods Used in a Study of the Vowels," *Journal of the Acoustical Society of America* XXIV (1952), 175-184. The de-

ants. The original impressionistic transcriptions were then entered for each measurement, and the result examined for clear separation of impressionistic levels. On the whole, the stratification was good: the impressionistic ratings with more open first elements showed higher first formant and lower second formant readings. However, the separation of grades 2 from 3, and 4 from 5, were not as clear as the others. A reduced four-step scale was then established, and the resulting correlation shown in Figure 3, and the table below.[31]

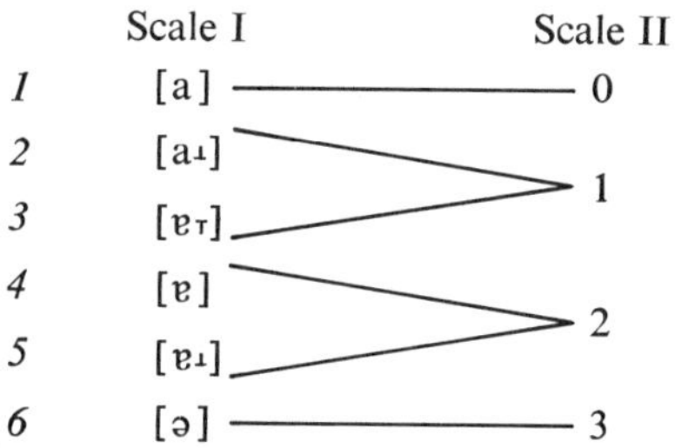

Figure 3 shows the values for Scale II mapped on the bi-logarithmic scale. This is a satisfactory result, with good separation of the four grades of centralization. We have also obtained some justification for the use of the first formant maximum in measuring spectrograms, rather than the second formant minimum. Since the lines separating the four grades parallel the second-formant axis more than the first-formant axis, we have a graphic demonstration that our phonetic impressions are more sensitive to shifts in the first formant than the second.

When this display was originally planned, there was some question as to whether it would be possible to map many different speakers on the same graph. We know that there are significant differences in individual frames of formant reference. Small children, for instance, appear to have vowel triangles organized at considerably higher frequencies than adults. The seven speakers whose readings are displayed in Figure 3 are all male; four are high school students, aged 14 to 15. But the other three are adults, from 30 to 60 years old, with widely different voice qualities.

Ideally, if we were studying the acoustic nature of the /ai/ and /au/ diphthongs, we would want a more uniform group of speakers. Secondly, we would ask for better and more uniform recording conditions: one recording was outdoors, two were in living rooms, four in an empty conference room. However, since the object of the testing was to lend objec-

---

gree of overlap shown in Figure 3 seems roughly comparable to Peterson and Barney's results.

[31] A parallel problem of condensing a finely graded impressionistic scale is discussed in L. Gauchat, J. Jeanjaquet and E. Tappolet, *Tableaux phonétiques des patois suisses romands* (Neuchatel: 1925), p. ix. A seven-level transcription of the mid vowels was reduced to five levels, but without the instrumental justification presented here.

tive confirmation to an impressionistic scale of discrimination, it is only realistic to use a range of recordngs as varied as the body of material on which the entire study is based. Absence of separation of the four grades

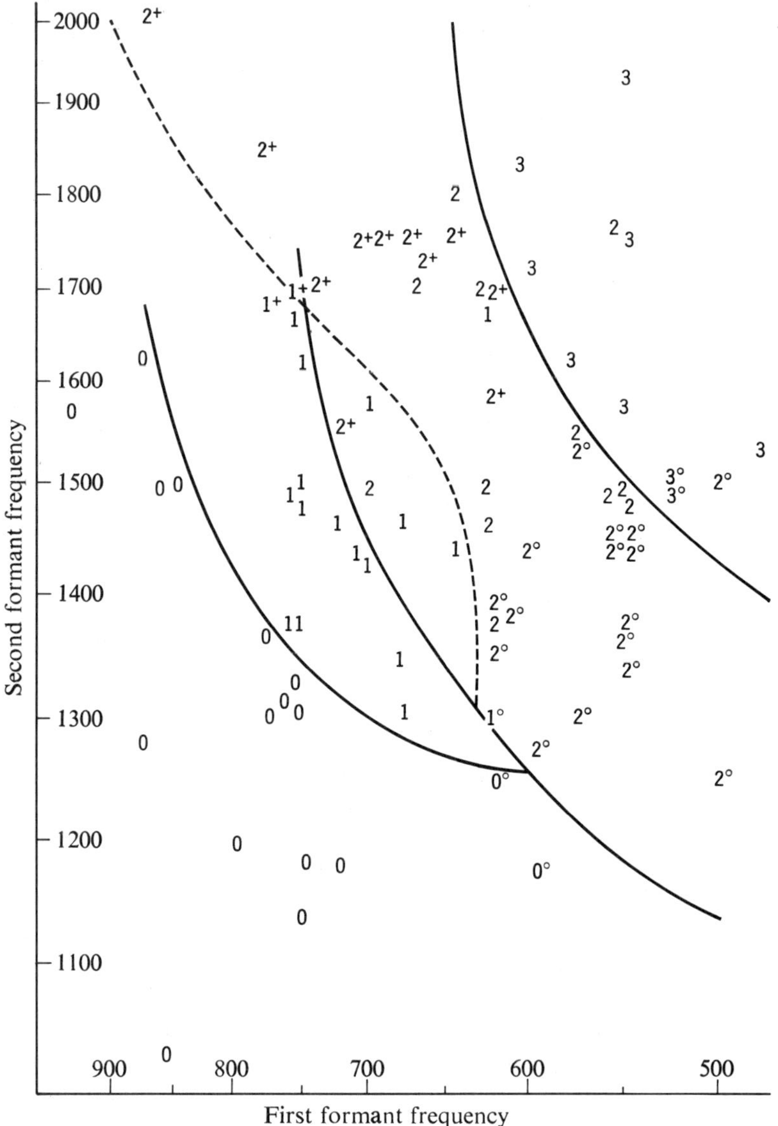

FIGURE 3. Correlation of instrumental measurement and impressionistic ratings of centralization. Numbers 0-3 are the Scale II equivalents of impressionistic ratings of height of first elements of eighty-six /ai/ diphthongs, assigned before spectrographic measurement. Seven different Martha's Vineyard speakers, males ranging from fourteen to sixty years old, are represented here. ° identifies speaker EP, age 31; + identifies speaker GW, age 15.

in Figure 3 might then have indicated only defects in instrumental technique, but a positive result can hardly be derived from such a bias.

It is interesting to note that measurements from no one speaker are distributed over more than half of Figure 3, and some speakers are sharply limited to a narrow sector—still occupying portions of all the grades of centralization. For instance, the highly centralized speaker EP, aged 31, accounts for all of the readings in the lower right portion marked with a ° sign: 0°, 2°, etc. He shows no readings higher than 650 or 1500 cps. On the other hand, speaker DW, aged 15, also highly centralized, accounts for the upper left portion; his readings, marked with a + sign, are all higher than 625 or 1550 cps. Again, speaker GM, aged 15, is limited to a belt from lower left to upper right, filling the space between the two just mentioned. Despite the differences in vowel placement, these seven speakers utilize the same dimension to produce the effect of centralized or open vowels: widely separated formants for centralized vowels, adjacent formants for open vowels. The opposition, though not distinctive, is clearly seen as ranging from compact to (relatively) non-compact.

This display then indicates for us that the reduced impressionistic scale shows good stratification in terms of physical parameters, and we may proceed to employ such ratings with some confidence in their validity.

6. *The linguistic environment*

We can now plot the distribution of centralized forms for each speaker. This is done for each of the 69 interviews on a chart such as is shown in Figure 4. We find that these charts fall into three basic types:

a. uncentralized norms: all words, or almost all, fall into Grade 0, with at most only a few Grade 1's in favored words such as *right* and *out*.

b. centralized norms: most words with Grade 2, and only a few Grade 1's for unfavored forms, such as *time* and *cow*.

c. phonetic conditioning: the influence of the phonetic environment is reflected in a range of values from Grades 0 to 2. Figure 4 is an example of this type.

Such phonetic conditioning is reminiscent of the phonetic regularity found in the southern United States.[32] But on Martha's Vineyard, the distribution is more complex, and nowhere codified with the precision to be found in the South. Before proceeding to chart the various social factors which influence this feature, we should consider the influence of the linguistic environment, and primarily phonetic conditioning.

[32] See Edwin F. Shewmake, *English Pronunciation in Virginia*. Davidson, N.C.: 1927.

FIGURE 4. *Phonetic determination of centralization. Centralization chart for North Tisbury fisherman GB*

Grade	*0*	*1*	*2*	*0*	*1*	*2*	
right	♦♦	♦♦♦♦	♦♦♦♦	♦♦♦♦	♦♦	♦♦♦♦	out
			♦♦	♦			
night	♦♦	♦♦	♦♦	♦	♦		about
white			♦	♦	♦		trout
like		♦♦			♦		house
sight	♦♦♦	♦					
quite	♦			♦♦	♦		south
striped	♦♦			♦	♦♦♦		mouth
swiped		♦		♦	♦		couch
wife	♦♦						
life	♦♦	♦♦♦	♦	♦♦			now
knife	♦		♦	♦♦			how
spider			♦	♦♦			sound
side	♦♦♦♦	♦		♦♦♦♦			down
	♦♦♦			♦♦♦♦			
tide	♦♦♦♦♦	♦		♦♦			
applied	♦			♦♦♦♦			round
characterized	♦			♦			hound
Ivory			♦	♦			ground
live	♦		♦	CI /au/: 0.39			
five		♦					
I've		♦					
by		♦					
fly in			♦				
high	♦						
fryin	♦						
why		♦					
my	♦♦						
try		♦					
I'll	♦						
piles	♦						
while	♦♦♦						
mile	♦						
violence	♦						
shiners	♦						
kind	♦						
iodine		♦					
quinine	♦						
time	♦♦						
line		♦					
I	♦	♦♦♦♦	♦♦♦♦♦				
		♦	♦♦♦♦♦				
fired	♦						
tire	♦						

CI /ai/: 0.75

Segmental Environment. The influence of the following consonant may be indicated by tabulating five general articulatory dimensions:

	Not favoring centralization		Favoring centralization
(a)	sonorants	zero final	obstruents
(b)	nasals		orals
(c)	voiced		voiceless
(d)	velars	labials	apicals
(e)	fricatives		stops

If we apply these oppositions in the order given, from *(a)* to *(e)*, we arrive at a consonant series from most favoring to least favorable to centralization, which seems to conform quite well to the facts:

/t, s: p, f: d, v, z: k, θ, ð: ∅: l, r: n: m/[33]

The *preceding consonant* follows a rather different pattern, almost the reverse, and has considerably less effect. The most favoring initial consonants in centralized syllables are /h, l, r, w, m, n/, with the glottal stop allophone of zero heading the list. Thus the most favored words are *right, wife, night, light, nice, life, house, out.*

Prosodic Factors. Stress regularly increases the degree of centralization for speakers with type *b* and type *c* charts. This is not at all an obvious rule, for the speech of many metropolitan areas shows the opposite tendency: one may note an occasional centralized diphthong in rapid reduced forms, but the same word under full stress is completely uncentralized. This corresponds to the difference between a centralized occurrence and a centralized norm.

A typical case of centralization under stress occurs in this excerpt from a story told by a North Tisbury fisherman:

> Why I could do anything with this dog. I used to drop a [naɪf] or my handkerchief or something, and I'd walk pretty near a quarter of a mile, and I'd stop and I'd turn to the dog: "You go get that! Where'd I lose that [nɐɪf]!"

Stylistic Influence. While we find that most urban speakers have a variety of shifting styles of speech, and that interviews under varying conditions will produce varying counts of phonological features, this is not the case with most Vineyarders. The majority are essentially single-style speakers. Sometimes the conversation will take a livelier tone, or a more formal aspect, but the percentage of centralized forms is not

[33] /ai/ and /au/ are rare before /b, g, ŋ, č, ǰ/; /t/ includes [ʔ]. The non-distinctive [ʔ] variant of zero onset also favors centralization heavily, as in the *1* forms of Figure 3.

significantly affected. Changes in centralization are apparently aspects of a pattern which develops over longer periods of time.[34]

Lexical Considerations. A few special words are given greater centralization than their phonetic form or prosodic position would usually account for. An example is *sliding,* meaning coasting with a small sled. It may be that confusion with an alternant form *sledding* is responsible, or that words which originate in childhood, and are seldom spelled, are more prone to centralization.

7. Distribution by age and time

The over-all degree of centralization for each speaker is expressed by the mean of the numerical values of the grades of each instance listed on the chart. Thus on Figure 4, the centralization index for /ai/ (CI /ai/), is 0.75, and the index for /au/ (CI /au/), is 0.39. We can then find the mean CI for any group of persons by averaging the CI for the members of the group.

We may first wish to see if centralization varies with the age level of the speaker. Table 2 indicates that it does.

TABLE 2. *Centralization indexes by age level*

	CI /ai/	CI /au/
over 75	0.25	0.22
61 to 75	0.35	0.37
46 to 60	0.62	0.44
31 to 45	0.81	0.88
14 to 30	0.37	0.46

Centralization of /ai/ and /au/ appears to show a regular increase in successive age levels, reaching a peak in the 31 to 45 group. We must now consider the reasons for assessing this pattern as evidence for an historical change in the linguistic development of Martha's Vineyard. Is this an example of sound change, or is it merely evidence for a regular change in speaking patterns which is correlated with age?

At this point it is necessary to consider the general question as to whether sound change can be directly observed. The well-known statement of Bloomfield seems to contradict this possibility:

> The process of linguistic change has never been directly observed; we shall see that such observation, with our present facilities, is inconceivable.[35]

[34] One small stylistic influence which appeared was in the standard reading. Those with centralized norms, whose charts were of type *b* and *c,* had slightly higher indexes of centralization for reading than for conversation. The opposite effect was noted for those with uncentralized norms.

[35] *Language* (New York: 1933), p. 347.

When this opinion is viewed in the light of Bloomfield's entire discussion of phonetic change, it appears to be strongly motivated by arguments for the absolute regularity of sound change. Bloomfield wishes to show that such change is quite autonomous, "a gradual favoring of some non-distinctive variants and a disfavoring of others," and quite distinct from the normal fluctuation of non-distinctive forms, "at all times highly variable." Yet since direct observations will always pick up this normal fluctuation, "even the most accurate phonetic record of a language at any one time could not tell us which phonemes were changing."[36] The changes we do observe are likely to be the effects of borrowing and analogic change.

Hockett, while recognizing the possibility of divergent views, has further refined the doctrine of imperceptible changes as a basic mechanism of linguistic change. Movements of the center of the normal distribution of random variations are, for all practical purposes, not subject to direct observation,[37] while the cruder forms of change which are observed must be due to minor mechanisms. Weinreich has pointed out the theoretical limitations of this position;[38] here we may profitably examine the result of applying such neo-grammarian thinking to empirical observations.

The prototype of close studies of sound change in a single community is Gauchat's 1899 investigation of the patois of Charmey, in French-speaking Switzerland.[39] Gauchat observed and tabulated differences in six phonological features in the speech of three generations: speakers over 60 years old, those between 30 and 60, and those under 30. Hermann returned to the scene in 1929, one generation later, to investigate four of these features: his results confirmed the interpretation of Gauchat's data as evidence for historical change, since three of the four had advanced considerably in the same direction. Yet Hermann also showed that real time depth is essential for an accurate view, since the fourth feature had not changed since 1903, and was apparently subject to a number of conflicting influences.[40]

The neo-grammarian viewpoint is that such observable shifts are the results of a series of borrowings, imitations, and random variations.[41]

[36] *Ibid.*, p. 365.

[37] *A Course in Modern Linguistics* (New York: 1958), p. 439.

[38] Review of Hockett, *A Course in Modern Linguistics,* in *Romance Philology* XIII (1959), pp. 329-332. "It is hard to feel comfortable with a theory which holds that the great changes of the past were of one kind, theoretically mysterious and interesting, whereas everything that is observable today is of another kind, transparent and (by implication) of scant theoretical interest."

[39] *L'unité phonétique dans le patois d'une commune.* Halle: 1905.

[40] "Lautveränderungen in der Individualsprache einer Mundart," *Nachrichten der Gesellschaft der Wissenschaften zu Göttingen, Philosophisch-historische Klasse* XI (1929), 195-214.

[41] Such arguments were indeed advanced in some detail to explain Gauchat's results, by P. G. Goidanich, "Saggio critico sullo studio de L. Gauchat," *Archivio Glottologico Italiano* XX (1926), pp. 60-71, [cited by Sommerfelt, *op. cit.*]. As implausible as

These complicated explanations could be applied without contradiction to the present observations on Martha's Vineyard. But we need not make the gratuitous assumption that sound change is something else again, an ineluctable process of drift which is beyond the scope of empirical studies. Here I would like to suggest that the mixed pattern of uneven phonetic conditioning, shifting frequencies of usage in various age levels, areas, and social groups, as we have observed it on Martha's Vineyard, is the process of linguistic change in the simplest form which deserves the name. Below this level, at the point of individual variation, we have events which are sub-linguistic in significance. At the first stage of change, where linguistic changes originate, we may observe many sporadic side-effects of articulatory processes which have no linguistic meaning: no socially determined significance is attached to them, either in the differentiation of morphemes, or in expressive function. Only when social meaning is assigned to such variations will they be imitated and begin to play a role in the language. Regularity is then to be found in the end result of the process, as Sturtevant has argued, and not in the beginning.[42]

If we now accept the evidence we have on hand as adequate in quantity, as reliable and valid, we must still decide if this particular case is an example of a change in community habits of speech. Two aspects of the question seem to make a good case for a positive answer.

First, the records of the LANE show only moderate centralization of /ai/ for the four informants of 1933, aged 56 to 82. It is impossible to calibrate the Lowman transcription against our present scale, especially since his data put more stress on short utterances with stressed, elicited forms. But if we take the LANE symbol /ɐ/ as equivalent to our present [ɐ] of Grade 2, it appears that these speakers had centralized norms for /ai/ averaging about 0.86, as high as the highest point reached in our sample for age level 60 to 90, but only half as high as the highest point for age level 30 to 60. If we weigh their performance against a matched group of present-day speakers, we may conclude that there has been an intervening drop of centralization before the present rise.

Secondly, the question of /au/ is conclusive. The LANE informants had an average rating of 0.06 for CI /au/: that is, for all practical purposes, zero. The record shows a steady rise in centralization of /au/—which we have seen to be a completely new phenomenon in Martha's Vineyard English—reaching indexes of well over 1.00 for most old family, up-island speakers, and going as high as 2.11 in one case. No postulated change in speaking habits with age could account for this rise.

The fact that the amount of centralization for the very old, and the very young speakers, is at a minimum, shows that the effect of age can-

Goidanich's arguments seem, they are quite consistent with Bloomfield's position cited above.

[42] Sturtevant, *op. cit.*, pp. 78-81. See Hoenigswald, *op. cit.*, for further considerations which support this view.

not be discounted entirely, and it may indeed be a secondary factor in this distribution over age levels.

8. Possible explanations for a rise in centralization

So far, our discussion of centralization, the dependent variable under study, has been merely descriptive. As we turn to the problem of explanation, we are faced with the question of what independent variables to examine. Certainly the structural parallelism of /ai/ and /au/ is significant here.[43] Let us assume for the moment that centralization declined to a low point in the late 1930's, and then, after the war, began to rise. At this point we find that a rising first element of /ai/ carries the first element of /au/ with it. Such a change in direction would seem to give us a plausible explanation for the parallelism being called into play at this time, rather than the assumption that it suddenly began to operate after a three hundred year hiatus.

There remains the prior question, that of explaining (or giving a larger context for) the general rise of centralization on the island. Why should Martha's Vineyard turn its back on the history of the English language? I believe that we can find a specific explanation if we study the detailed configuration of this sound change against the social forces which affect the life of the island most deeply.

If we choose a purely psychological explanation, or one based only on phonological paradigms, we have as much as said that social variables such as occupation, income, education, social aspirations, attitudes, are beside the point. We could only prove such a claim by cross-tabulating the independent social variables, one at a time, with the degree of centralization, and showing that any greater-than-chance correlations are spurious.

TABLE 3. *Geographical distribution of centralization*

	CI /ai/	CI /au/	CI /ai/	CI /au/
Down-island			0.35	0.33
Edgartown	0.48	0.55		
Oak Bluffs	0.33	0.10		
Vineyard Haven	0.24	0.33		
Up-island			0.61	0.66
Oak Bluffs	0.71	0.99		
No. Tisbury	0.35	0.13		
West Tisbury	0.51	0.51		
Chilmark	1.00	0.81		
Gay Head	0.51	0.81		

[43] We might wish to construct a rule here which would, in essence, convert [+compact] to [−compact], simpler by one feature than a rule which would merely convert [aɪ] to a centralized form. While such a statement is satisfying in its simplicity and neatness, it should be clear from the following discussion that it would explain only a small part of the mechanism of linguistic change.

TABLE 4. *Centralization by occupational groups*

	CI /ai/	CI /au/
fishermen	1.00	0.79
farmers	0.32	0.22
others	0.41	0.57

TABLE 5. *Centralization by ethnic groups*

Age Level	English CI /ai/	English CI /au/	Portuguese CI /ai/	Portuguese CI /au/	Indian CI /ai/	Indian CI /au/
over 60	0.36–	0.34	0.26–	0.26	0.32–	0.40
46 to 60	0.85–	0.63	0.37–	0.59	0.71–	1.00
31 to 45	1.08–	1.09	0.73–	0.83	0.80–	1.33
under 30	0.35–	0.31	0.34–	0.52	0.47–	0.88
all ages	0.67–	0.60	0.42–	0.54	0.56–	0.90

However, our first attempts reveal some striking social correlations which are not easily explained away. Table 3 shows us the geographical bias of centralization, favoring rural up-island against small-town down-island areas. Table 4 shows the occupational biases, with fishermen at the top and farmers at the bottom. If we add to this the data of Table 5, showing the distribution by ethnic groups, we find ourselves embarrassed with too many explanations. Are these social variables connected in any demonstrable way with the linguistic change? Are they truly independent from one another, or are some of the correlations spurious, the result of some dependency on a larger factor which is logically prior to these? If such a larger pattern exists, we must ask how did it originate, and in what way is it connected with the linguistic events. A simple-minded bookkeeping approach will not answer such questions. We will have to gain some insight into the social structure of the island, and the pressures which motivate the social changes of present-day Martha's Vineyard.

9. *The interaction of linguistic and social patterns*[44]

To understand Martha's Vineyard, we must first realize that this is a very beautiful place, and a very desirable place to live. But it is not an easy place to earn the kind of living which agrees well with the

[44] The information given in the following discussion of social patterns on Martha's Vineyard was derived in part from conversations with the 69 informants. Even more significant, perhaps, was information gained from discussions with community leaders who were in a position to view these patterns as a whole. I am particularly indebted to Mr. Benjamin Morton, head of the Chamber of Commerce, Mr. Henry Beetle Hough, editor of the *Vineyard Gazette,* and Mrs. Charles Davis, superintendent of the Martha's Vineyard Regional High School. Among my informants, I am especially grateful to Mr. Donald Poole of Chilmark, Mr. Benjamin Mayhew, selectman of Chilmark, and Mr. Albert Prada, town clerk of Edgartown.

achievement orientation of modern American society. The 1960 Census shows that it is the poorest of all Massachusetts counties: it has the lowest average income, the highest number of poor people, and the smallest number of rich people.[45] The Vineyard has the highest rate of unemployment: 8.3% as against 4.2% for the state, and it also has the highest rate of seasonal employment. One might think that life on the island is nevertheless easier: perhaps the cost of living is lower. Nothing could be further from the truth: the high cost of ferrying is carried over to a higher price for most consumer goods. As a result, there are more married women with young children working than in any other county: 27.4% as against 17.3% for the state as a whole.

The reason for this economic pressure, and the resulting dependency on the tourist trade, is not hard to find. There is no industry on Martha's Vineyard. The island reached its peak in the great days of the whaling industry; for a time, commercial fishing in the local waters buoyed up the economy, but the run of fish is no longer what it used to be. Large scale fishing is now out of New Bedford on the Grand Banks. Farming and dairying have declined sharply because of the ferry rate, which raises the cost of fertilizer but lowers the profit on milk.

The 1960 Census shows us that the island's labor force of two thousand souls is heavily occupied with service trades. Only 4% are in manufacturing, one seventh of the state average. Five percent are in agriculture, 2.5% in fishing, and 17% in construction; these percentages are five, ten and three times as high as those for the state as a whole.[46]

These economic pressures must be clearly delineated in order to assess the heavy psychological pressures operating on the Vineyarders of old family stock. Increasing dependence on the summer trade acts as a threat to their personal independence. The more far-seeing Vineyarders can envisage the day when they and their kind will be expropriated as surely as the Indians before them. They understand that the vacation business cannot help but unbalance the economy, which produces far too little for the summer trade, but far too much for the winter. Yet it is very hard for the Vineyarder not to reach for the dollar that is lying on the table, as much as he may disapprove of it. We have already noted that many Vineyarders move out of their own homes to make room for summer people.

Those who feel that they truly own this island, the descendants of the old families, have a hard time holding on. Summer people, who have

[45] Table 36 of the 1960 census report PC(1)–23c, cited above in footnote 12, shows some striking contrasts among Massachusetts counties. The median family income for the Vineyard is $4,745, as against $6,272 for the state as a whole. Barnstable County (Cape Cod) and Nantucket are also dependent on a vacation economy, yet they show median incomes of $5,386 and $5,373. The most agricultural county in Massachusetts, Franklin, shows a median of $5,455. The state as a whole has only 12.4% of families with incomes under $3,000; the Vineyard has 23%. The state has 17.0% with incomes over $10,000; the Vineyard has only 6.6%.

[46] See Table 82 of the 1960 census report, as in footnote 45.

earned big money in big cities, are buying up the island. As one Chilmarker said, "You can cross the island from one end to the other without stepping on anything but *No Trespassing* signs." The entire northwest shore has fallen to the outsiders. In Edgartown, the entire row of spacious white houses on the waterfront has capitulated to high prices, with only one exception, and the descendants of the whaling captains who built them have retreated to the hills and hollows of the interior.

This gradual transition to dependency on, and outright ownership by the summer people has produced reactions varying from a fiercely defensive contempt for outsiders to enthusiastic plans for furthering the tourist economy. A study of the data shows that high centralization of /ai/ and /au/ is closely correlated with expressions of strong resistance to the incursions of the summer people.

The greatest resistance to these outsiders is felt in the rural up-island areas, and especially in Chilmark, the only place where fishing is still a major part of the economy.[47] Chilmarkers are the most different, independent, the most stubborn defenders of their own way of living. In order to assess the changing orientation of island groups towards the old family tradition, I included in my interview a battery of questions dealing with the semantics of the word *Yankee*. One question read: "Where on the island would a typical old Yankee be most apt to live?" By far the most common answer was "Chilmark." Chilmarkers were named most often as examples of "typical old Yankees."

Chilmarkers pride themselves on their differences from mainlanders:

> You people who come down here to Martha's Vineyard don't understand the background of the old families of the island . . . strictly a maritime background and tradition . . . and what we're interested in, the rest of America, this part over here across the water that belongs to you and we don't have anything to do with, has forgotten all about . . . .
>
> I think perhaps we use entirely different . . . type of English language . . . think differently here on the island . . . it's almost a separate language within the English language.

To a large extent, this last statement is wishful thinking. Much of the language difference depended upon whaling terms which are now obsolete. It is not unnatural, then, to find phonetic differences becoming stronger and stronger as the group fights to maintain its identity. We have mentioned earlier that the degrees of retroflexion in final and pre-

[47] Despite the low number of Vineyarders listed as fishermen by occupation in the Census, a much larger number of islanders rely upon part-time fishing to supplement their income. In particular, harvesting bay scallops in the salt ponds is a prized source of revenue in the summer months. A great deal of local legislation is designed to protect the professional fishermen from the great number of part-time scallopers taking in too large a share. Much discussion and considerable bitterness develops as a result of this conflict of interest, in which the truly professional Chilmarkers are, psychologically at least, on top.

consonantal /r/ have social significance: at Chilmark, retroflexion is at its strongest, and is steadily increasing among the younger boys.

In Table 3, we note that centralization is higher up-island than down-island, and highest of all in Chilmark. In Table 4, we note that of all occupational groups, fishermen show the highest centralization. Our total number of cases is too small to allow extensive cross tabulations, but if we take the group of Chilmark fishermen in the middle age level, from 30 to 60, we find that these five informants have average indexes of 1.48 for /ai/ and 1.18 for /au/, higher than any other social group which we might select on the island. Conversely, let us list the six speakers with the highest degree of centralization in order of CI /ai/—that is, the upper ten percent:

	CI /ai/	CI /au/
Chilmark fisherman, age 60	1.70	1.11
Chilmark fisherman, age 31	1.65	2.11
Chilmark fisherman, age 55	1.50	1.24
Edgartown fisherman, age 61	1.43	1.07
Chilmark fisherman, age 33	1.33	0.79
Edgartown fisherman, age 52	1.31	1.31

It should be noted here that the two Edgartown fishermen listed are brothers, the last descendants of the old families to maintain their position on the Edgartown waterfront in the face of the encroachment of summer people noted above.

We have now established within reason that the strong upturn in centralization began up-island, among Chilmark fishermen, under the same influence which produced parallel results among the few Edgartown residents who shared their social orientation.

Table 5 shows the developments by age level for each of the three main ethnic groups. All of the examples we have used so far deal with the English group of old family descent; in Chilmark, this is the only group of any size. Let us continue to follow the development of this group through the succeeding age levels, and examine the interaction of social and linguistic patterns.

We see that centralization reaches a peak in the age level from 30 to 45, and that centralization of /au/ has reached or surpassed /ai/ at this point. This age group has been under heavier stress than any other; the men have grown up in a declining economy, after making a more or less deliberate choice to remain on the island rather than leave it. Most of them have been in the armed forces during World War II or in the Korean conflict. Many have been to college, for the English descent group has a strong bent towards higher education. At some point, each of these men elected to make a smaller living on Martha's Vineyard, while many of their contemporaries left to gain more money or more recognition elsewhere.

Severe strains are created in those who are pulled in both directions; the traditional orientation of Martha's Vineyard has long been inward and possessive, yet the pull of modern achievement-oriented America is even greater for some.

> I think actually it's a very hard thing to make that decision. . . . It comes to you later, that you should have made it before. I have another son—Richard—is an aeronautical engineer. He really loves the island. And when he decided to be an aeronautical engineer we discussed it—at length—and I told him at that time: you just can't live on Martha's Vineyard. . . . He works at Grumman, but he comes home every chance he gets and stays just as long as he can.

The speaker is a woman of 55, a descendant of the Mayhew family, who left business school in Boston, and returned to the island to become a real estate agent. Her son made the opposite choice; but another family, of long standing in Chilmark, had this to report about their son:

> . . . we had an idea that he'd go away to school, but he really didn't want to go away. . . . When he was at Chauncey Hall, they tried to get him to go to M.I.T.; but he said no, he didn't want to go anywhere where he had to learn to do something that he couldn't come back to this island.

We can learn a great deal about centralization by studying such histories of particular families. The two speakers who head the list of centralized speakers on page 369 are father and son. The father, a Chilmark lobsterman, is a thoughtful, well-read man with a passionate concern with the history of the whaling industry; he is perhaps the most eloquent spokesman for the older Vineyard tradition, and the author of the quotation on page 368. His son is a college graduate who tried city life, didn't care for it, came back to the island and built up several successful commercial enterprises on the Chilmark docks. He shows a high CI /au/ at 2.11, considerably more centralized than anyone else I have heard at Chilmark. One evening, as I was having dinner at his parents' house, the conversation turned to speech in general, without any specific reference to /ai/ or /au/. His mother remarked, "You know, E. didn't always speak that way . . . it's only since he came back from college. I guess he wanted to be more like the men on the docks. . . ."

Here we see a clear case of hypercorrection at work, and from other evidence as well, it is reasonable to assume that this is a very regular force in implementing the phonetic trend we are studying.

When we come to high school students, we must realize that many of the young people from the old-family group do *not* intend to remain on the island, and this is reflected in the lower average index of Table

5. Comparatively few of the sons of the English descent group will be earning their living on the Vineyard in the next twenty years. In a series of interviews in Martha's Vineyard Regional High School, it was possible to compare speaking habits very closely by means of the standard reading, "After the high winds. . . ." A marked contrast was observed between those who plan to leave the island and those who do not. The latter show strong centralization, while the former show little, if any. To highlight this point, we may take four 15-year old students: the two down-islanders who intend to leave for careers in business and finance, show little or no centralization; the two up-islanders who hope to go to college and return to make their living on the island, show considerable centralization.[48] The indexes speak for themselves:

Down-island, leaving	Up-island, staying
0.00—0.40	0.90—1.00
0.00—0.00	1.13—1.19

One of the down-islanders, from Edgartown, has fallen very much under the influence of the upper class Bostonian visitors. He has lost all constriction in tautosyllabic /r/, and has a fronted low center vowel as well in such words as [ka:], 'car'.

10. Centralization among other ethnic groups

We can now turn to the special position of the Portuguese and Indian ethnic groups, and see if the same approach can account for the distribution of centralized forms among them.

The most common view of the early Portuguese immigration is that the settlers came from an island with a very similar economy, shared the Yankee virtues of thrift and industry, and fitted into the island life almost perfectly. The Azoreans who came first seemed to have a strong inclination for farming and fishing, rather than factory work; in the Vineyard's rather diffuse economy, there was little concentration of the Portuguese into the kinds of industrial pockets we find on the mainland.[49] Even among the tough-minded Chilmarkers, we find a certain grudging acknowledgement of the Yankee-like orientation of the Portuguese:

[48] On the question of leaving the island, one of these boys said: ". . . I can't see myself off island somewhere . . . I like it a lot here, like my father goes lobstering. That's quite a bit of fun . . . as long as I get enough money to live and enjoy myself. I was figuring on . . . going into oceanography because you'd be outdoors: it wouldn't be office work."

[49] In many ways, the Vineyard seems to be more democratic than the mainland. I have heard on the mainland strong expressions of hostility between Portuguese groups from the Azores and those from the Cape Verde Islands, but never on Martha's Vineyard.

> . . . they worked, that's why they were respected. Nobody ever particularly interfered with 'em. You hear somebody make a remark about the dumb Portagee or something, but actually I think they've been pretty well respected because they mind their own business pretty well. They didn't ask for anything.

It took some time, however, for the Portuguese descent group to make its way into the main stream of island life. Intermarriage of Portuguese and Yankee stock occurs, but it is rare. Second-generation Portuguese certainly do not feel at home in every situation: as some Vineyarders put it, these Portuguese have "a defensive attitude." A member of the English group will as a rule speak his mind freely, condemning the summer people and his neighbors with equal frankness. But the second-generation Portuguese never criticizes the summer people in the interview situation, and he is extremely wary of criticizing anyone. When the word *Yankee* is introduced, he shifts uneasily in his chair, and refuses to make any comment at all.

While the speech of the Portuguese second generation is free of any detectable Portuguese influence,[50] it is also lacking the special Vineyard flavor. If we examine the Portuguese age groups over 45 in Table 5, which contain a large proportion of second-generation speakers, we find little or no centralization.

This is not the case with third- and fourth-generation Portuguese speakers. In this group, we find centralization very much on the increase, particularly with /au/. In Table 5, we see that the age group from 31 to 45 has a very high degree of centralization. This age level contains a great many third-generation Portuguese. It is the first Portuguese group which has entered the main stream of island life, occupying positions as merchants, municipal officers, and many other places of secondary leadership. These speakers consider themselves natives of the island, and in response to the term *Yankee,* they either include themselves in, or make fun of the whole idea.

In the youngest age level, the Portuguese descent group shows a very regular use of centralization, whether second or third or fourth generation, and their average centralization index in the table is, at this point, higher than the English group.

One might think that centralization might be on the way to becoming a marker of the ethnic Portuguese on the island, if such a trend continues. But this possibility runs counter to the strongly democratic nature of present-day Vineyard society. Among high school students, for example, there appear to be no social barriers between the ethnic groups, in clubs, at dances, and between friends. This situation is especially shocking to some former mainlanders, who would like to draw a color line against some of the children with Cape Verde backgrounds. But

[50] On the other hand, I have heard a strong Portuguese accent from a second generation Portuguese man, about 40 years old, who was raised on a farm near Taunton, Mass.

despite a few such counter-currents, the unifying, protective nature of Vineyard society shields the island native from the kind of reality which is practised on the outside.[51]

The reason that the youngest Portuguese group shows higher centralization is that a larger percentage identify themselves with the island and the island way of life, than is the case among the English descent group. Whereas almost all of the English group leave the island to go to college, and few return, almost all of the Portuguese group remain. As a result, they are gradually supplanting the English group in the economic life of the island.

It is fair enough to say that the main problem of the Portuguese group has not been to resist the incursions of the summer people but rather to assert their status as native Vineyarders. Their chief obstacle has not been the outsiders, but rather the resistance to full recognition from the English descent group. With full participation in native status, has come full use of the special characteristics of Martha's Vineyard English, including centralized diphthongs.

The Indian descent group is relatively small and homogeneous. The hundred citizens of Gay Head are united in a few closely related families. One would think that these survivors of the aboriginal Wampanoag Indians would have had little trouble in asserting their native status. On the contrary, a long tradition of denigration of the Indian has served, for over a hundred years, to rob him of the dignity which should accompany this feat of survival. The issue revolves around the fact that the declining Indian community has necessarily intermarried with outsiders over the past ten generations. The logic of American society dictated that these outsiders should be Negroes. Thus as early as 1764, the Yankee officials of the Vineyard claimed that only one quarter of the Indians were "of pure blood."[52] In 1870, the Governor of Massachusetts took away the reservation status of Gay Head, on the ground that they really weren't Indians at all, and handed them over to the political ministrations of Chilmark.

For many decades, the Indians were literally second class citizens, and the resentment dating from this period is not entirely gone. On the other hand, we find that a number of Vineyarders, of both English and Portuguese descent, regard the Indians with a mixture of sarcasm and scepticism:

> . . . show me a Gay Head Indian and I'll like to see one.

[51] In several cases, Vineyard youngsters have received rather severe shocks on leaving the island for the armed services or for work in an area where caste restrictions were in force. One boy was put into a Negro regiment on entering the service, though action from Vineyard leaders had him transferred soon afterwards.

[52] A very rich vein of information on this score may be tapped from Richard L. Pease's *Report of the commissioner appointed to complete the examination . . . of all boundary lines . . . at Gay Head.* Boston: 1871. Pease was acting essentially as the hatchet man for the Governor of Massachusetts, to whom he was reporting.

The Indian people are aware of this situation, as shown in this quotation from one of the Indian informants, a woman of 69:

> These island folks, they don't want to mix at all, up this end. . . . They don't like to give the Indian his name, here on the island. I'll tell you that. They like to be dirty with some of their talk.

Despite the great shift in Vineyard ideology over the past three generations, the Indians still feel blocked, geographically and socially, by the Chilmarkers, "up this end." Their attitude toward the Chilmarkers is ambiguous: on the one hand, they resent the Chilmarkers' possessive attitude toward the island, and the traditional hard-fisted, stiff-necked Yankee line. Their reaction to the word *Yankee* is sarcastic and hostile.[53] But their main complaint is that they deserve equal status, and whether they will admit it or not, they would like to be just like the Chilmarkers in many ways.

As far as centralization is concerned, Table 5 indicates that the Indians follow close behind the Chilmarkers. At the same time, they show a greater relative increase of centralization of /au/, similar to the Portuguese development, especially among the young people. Here there are signs of an additional phonetic feature, shared by both Portuguese and Indians: a backed form of /au/, which may be written [ʌu]. It is characteristic of five speakers in the sample, all under 30, all fairly low in socio-economic status. Whether it represents a general trend cannot be determined at this point.

We may note that there has been a revival of Indian culture in the form of pageants staged for the tourist trade, beadwork and other Indian crafts, and with these a revived emphasis on tribal organization. The younger Indians acknowledge that this revival was commercially motivated in its beginnings, but they claim that it is now more than that, and that Indian culture would survive if the vacationers disappeared entirely. The Indian language has been dead for several generations, however, and the ritual formulas must be learned from a book. The Indians are truly traditional speakers of English, and their claim to native status must be expressed in that language.

11. The social meaning of centralization

From the information we now have at hand, there readily emerges the outline of a unifying pattern which expresses the social significance of the centralized diphthongs.

It is apparent that the immediate meaning of this phonetic feature is "Vineyarder." When a man says [rɐɪt] or [hɐʊs], he is unconsciously establishing the fact that he belongs to the island: that he is one of the

[53] "Where they come from—down south somewhere? . . . Lot of 'em come from Jerusalem, you know . . ."

natives to whom the island really belongs. In this respect, centralization is not different from any of the other sub-phonemic features of other regions which are noted for their local dialect. The problem is, why did this feature develop in such a complicated pattern on the Vineyard, and why is it becoming stronger in the younger age levels?

The answer appears to be that different groups have had to respond to different challenges to their native status. And in the past two generations, the challenges have become much sharper through severe economic and social pressures.

The old-family group of English descent has been subjected to pressure from the outside: its members are struggling to maintain their independent position in the face of a long-range decline in the economy and the steady encroachment of the summer people. The member of the tradition-oriented community naturally looks to past generations for his values: these past generations form a reference group for him.[54] The great figures of the past are continually referred to, and those who have died only a few years ago have already assumed heroic stature. "If you could only have been here a few years ago and talked to *N*. He could have told you so many things!"

The sudden increase in centralization began among the Chilmark fishermen, the most close-knit group on the island, the most independent, the group which is most stubbornly opposed to the incursions of the summer people. There is an inherently dramatic character to the fisherman's situation, and a great capacity for self-dramatization in the fisherman himself, which makes him an ideal candidate to initiate new styles in speech. In the early morning, the curtain rises: a solitary figure appears upon the scene. For the course of an entire day, this single actor holds the stage. Then at last, the boat docks; the curtain descends. The play is over, yet the reviews will be read and re-read for generations to come.

> I can remember as a boy, when I first started going to sea with my father, he said to me: remember two things. Always treat the ocean with respect, and remember you only have to make one mistake, never to come back.

Centralized speech forms are then a part of the dramatized island character which the Chilmarker assumes, in which he imitates a similar but weaker tendency in the older generation.

For younger members of the English descent group, we can view the mechanism in greater detail. For them, the old timers and the up-islanders in particular serve as a reference group. They recognize that the Chilmark fishermen are independent, skillful with many kinds of tools and equipment, quick-spoken, courageous and physically strong. Most importantly, they carry with them the ever-present conviction that the island belongs

[54] In the technical sense developed by R. Merton, *Social Theory and Social Structure*. Glencoe, Ill.: 1957.

to them. If someone intends to stay on the island, this model will be ever present to his mind. If he intends to leave, he will adopt a mainland reference group, and the influence of the old-timers will be considerably less. The differential effect in the degree of centralization used is a direct result of this opposition of values.

The Portuguese group is not faced with a dilemma of going or staying. The main challenge to which this group has responded is from the English group, which has certainly served as a reference group for the Portuguese until very recent times. As the number of Portuguese in prominent positions grows, it is no longer urgent to minimize the effects of being Portuguese, but rather to assert one's identity as an islander.

The Gay Head developments are dictated by the antinomy of values which reigns there. On the one hand, the Indian group resents any bar to full participation in the island life, and the Indians have plainly adopted many of the same values as the Chilmarkers. But on the other hand, they would like to insist as well on their Indian identity. Unfortunately, they no longer have linguistic resources for this purpose, and whether they like it or not, they will follow the Chilmark lead.

The role of the Chilmarker, or "old-time typical Yankee" has declined as the reference group which governs the meaning of "islander" and has shifted away from that which governs "Yankee." Even among the Chilmarkers, the more far-sighted members of the community recognize that the term *Yankee* no longer fits the island. Whereas this word may still be a rallying cry in some parts of New England, it has outlived its usefulness on Martha's Vineyard. In emphasizing descent status rather than native status, *Yankee* summons up invidious distinctions which are no longer good currency on the island.

> People don't make so much about it as they used to when I was young. People would make that statement: "I'm a Yankee! I'm a Yankee!" But now you very seldom—mostly, read it in print.[55]

In summary, we can then say that the meaning of centralization, judging from the context in which it occurs, is *positive orientation towards Martha's Vineyard.* If we now overlook age level, occupation, ethnic group, geography, and study the relationship of centralization to this one independent variable, we can confirm or reject this conclusion. An examination of the total interview for each informant allows us to place him in one of three categories: *positive*—expresses definitely positive feelings towards Martha's Vineyard; *neutral*—expresses neither positive nor negative feelings towards Martha's Vineyard; *negative*—indicates desire to live elsewhere. When these three groups are rated for mean centralization indexes, we obtain the striking result of Table 6.

[55] The speaker is one of the Mayhews, a retired Chilmark fisherman, who has as much claim to be a "typical old Yankee" as any person on Martha's Vineyard.

TABLE 6. *Centralization and orientation toward Martha's Vineyard*

Persons		CI/ai/	CI/au/
40	Positive	0.63	0.62
19	Neutral	0.32	0.42
6	Negative	0.09	0.08

The fact that this table shows us the sharpest example of stratification we have yet seen, indicates that we have come reasonably close to a valid explanation of the social distribution of centralized diphthongs.

12. The intersection of social and linguistic structures

The following abstract scheme may serve to summarize the argument which has been advanced so far to explain the spread and propagation of this particular linguistic change.

1. A language feature used by a group A is marked by contrast with another standard dialect.
2. Group A is adopted as a reference group by group B, and the feature is adopted and exaggerated as a sign of social identity in response to pressure from outside forces.
3. Hypercorrection under increased pressure, in combination with the force of structural symmetry, leads to a generalization of the feature in other linguistic units of Group B.
4. A new norm is established as the process of generalization levels off.
5. The new norm is adopted by neighboring and succeeding groups for whom group B serves as a reference group.

There remains a gap in the logic of the explanation: in what way do social pressures and social attitudes come to bear upon linguistic structures? So far we have assembled a convincing series of correlations: yet we still need to propose a rational mechanism by which the deep-seated elements of structure enter such correlations.

It has been noted that centralized diphthongs are not salient in the consciousness of Vineyard speakers. They can hardly therefore be the direct objects of social affect. The key to the problem may lie in the fact that centralization is only one of many phonological features which show the same general distribution, though none may be as striking or as well stratified as /ai/ and /au/. There are no less than fourteen phonological variables which follow the general rule that the higher, or more constricted variants are characteristic of the up-island, "native" speakers, while the lower, more open variants are characteristic of down-island speakers under mainland influence.[56] We can reasonably assume that this

[56] In the following list of variables in question, the up-island form is given first. PHONEMIC INVENTORY: /o/—/ou/ in *road, toad, boat, whole* . . . PHONEMIC DISTRIBUTION: /ɛ/ only before intersyllabic /r/ instead of both /ɛ/ and /æ/; /r/—/ə/ in tautosyllabic position. PHONEMIC INCIDENCE: /ɪ ⁀ ɛ/ in *get, forget, when, anyway, can* . . . ; /ɛ ⁀ æ/ in

"close-mouthed" articulatory style is the object of social affect. It may well be that social evaluation interacts with linguistic structures at this point, through the constriction of several dimensions of phonological space. Particular linguistic variables would then be variously affected by the overall tendency towards a favored articulatory posture, under the influence of the social forces which we have been studying. Evidence for such an hypothesis must come from the study of many comparable developments, in a variety of English dialects and other languages. It is enough to note here that it is a plausible mechanism for socio-linguistic interaction which is compatible with the evidence which has been gathered in this investigation.

13. Limitations of this study

We noted earlier that one limitation of this study stems from the fact that the variable selected is not salient. This limitation, coupled with the small size of the Vineyard population, made it impractical to explore thoroughly the subjective response of native speakers to centralized diphthongs. Other shortcomings of the technique used on Martha's Vineyard may be seen in the sampling method, which was far from rigorous.[57] The statements made about developments through various age levels among the Portuguese and Indians are based on an inadequate number of cases. The sample is particularly weak in the down-island area, especially in Oak Bluffs, and the picture of down-island trends is correspondingly weaker than up-island developments. Finally, it may be noted that the interviewing technique was not as firmly controlled as it might have been: a number of changes in the interview structure were made as the study progressed.

With these reservations, we can say that the findings give good confirmation of the main theme of the study: the correlation of social patterns with the distributional pattern of one linguistic variable.[58] The reliability of the index used was tested in several cases where the same informant was interviewed twice, with good results.[59] Indexes for read-

---

have, had, that; /ʌ⁀ɑ/ in *got.* PHONETIC REALIZATION: [ɐɪ⁀aɪ] and [ɐʊ⁀aʊ]; [r̩⁀ɚ]; [ɨr⁀ər] in *work, person . . . ;* [ə⁀ʌ] in *furrow, hurry . . . ;* [o˔ʊ⁀oʊ] in *go, no . . . ;* [ii ∼ ɪi] and [uu⁀ʊu]; [ɪᵊ⁀ɪ] and [ɛᵊ⁀ɛ].

[57] The problem of sampling technique for linguistic variables is a difficult one at the moment. While we are sure that linguistic behavior is more general than the behavior usually traced by survey methods, we do not know how much more general it is, nor can we estimate easily how far we may relax the sampling requirements, if at all.

[58] In addition to the positive correlations discussed above, the explanation given is reinforced by certain negative results of alternate explanations. The education level of the informants is not correlated significantly with degree of centralization. The distribution of sub-standard or archaic grammar does not correspond to the distribution of centralized forms.

[59] For example, two interviews with Ernest Mayhew, Chilmark fisherman, age 83, showed these results: first interview, CI /ai/ 0.67, CI /au/ 0.58; second interview, CI /ai/ 0.59, CI /au/ 0.40. The count for /au/ is based on about one-third as many items as for /ai/.

ing style did not diverge sharply from the other portions of the interview. The validity of the scale of measurement was well established by instrumental methods, and the validity of the whole seems to be reinforced by the unitary nature of the final interpretation.

The techniques developed on Martha's Vineyard are presently being refined and applied to a much more complex situation in the urban core of New York City. Here multiple-style speakers are the rule, not the exception; instead of three ethnic groups we have a great many; mobility and change are far more rapid; and the population is huge. Here the sampling requirements must be far more rigid; and the techniques used to assess the social meaning of linguistic cues must be more subtle and complex. Yet the basic approach, of isolating the socially significant variables, and correlating them with the patterns of general social forces, is the same as that which has been used on Martha's Vineyard. It is hoped that such methods will give us further insight into the mechanism of linguistic change.

The Genesis of the Old English Dialects: A New Hypothesis

DAVID DeCAMP

1. Introduction. THE OLD ENGLISH DIALECTS have traditionally been viewed as mere extensions of the dialects of the continental Germanic tribes before their migration to Britain. Following Bede's famous division of the fifth-century invaders into Jutes, Angles, and Saxons, writers have postulated three corresponding dialects: Kentish, Anglian, and Saxon. In this paper I shall develop the hypothesis that the origins of the English dialects lie not in pre-migration tribal affiliations but in certain social, economic, and cultural developments which occurred after the migration was completed. This does not imply that the continental Germanic dialects are irrelevant to the genesis of English dialects; indeed the influence of Frisian is central to my hypothesis. Only those influences, however, which were felt after the migrations were relevant to formation of the English dialects; for I believe that these dialects originated not on the continent but on the island of Britain.

The striking similarities between Frisian and the Kentish (south-eastern) dialect of Old English have long been noticed. More than fifty years ago, Theodor Siebs[1] postulated a special Kentish-Frisian branch of the Anglo-Frisian limb of his Germanic family tree, insisting that Kentish was 'genetically' more closely related to Frisian than were Anglian and Saxon—that Kentish speech was, in fact, merely the Frisian spoken by the fifth-century invaders of Kent. Favoring this hypothesis are the linguistic similarities, numerous Kentish-Frisian cultural affinities to be discussed later in this paper, and the sixth-century account of Procopius

Reprinted by permission from *Language* 34.232-44 (1958).

[1] Theodor Siebs, *Geschichte der friesischen Sprache* (Strassburg, 1901); *Zur Geschichte der englisch-friesischen Sprache* (Halle, 1889).

of Caesarea, who divided the Germanic inhabitants of Britain into *Angiloi* and *Frissones*.[2] Because the Jutes are not mentioned by Tacitus (their origin and even their existence are disputed by modern writers) and because they never appear in Kentish place names or early written traditions, Siebs assumed that Bede had erroneously substituted Jutes for Frisians. Though no one now doubts that there were Frisians, among others, in Kent, Siebs' hypothesis can be refuted in two ways. First, the evidence summarized in §3 of this paper indicates that all the Kentish-Frisian linguistic similarities probably did not develop until after the migrations; it is certain that some of these similarities did not appear until the eighth or ninth century. These can hardly prove a common ancestor in the fifth century.[3] Second, as will be demonstrated in §4, modern historians have shown that the accounts of both Bede and Procopius were greatly oversimplified, that there were no migrations of entire tribes, rather that Kent was colonized by a mixture of continental peoples.

Siebs' argument was circular. Bede, aware in the eighth century of different political and cultural areas with rapidly developing linguistic characteristics, assumed corresponding tribal units in the fifth. Siebs then based his argument for continental origin of dialects on these same tribal names. Siebs, working strictly in the Stammbaum tradition of historical linguistics, did not accept any means for the transfer of linguistic features from one area to another except mass migration of speakers. Many linguists have been similarly bound by these Stammbaum preconceptions. Even Alois Brandl, though he recognized the importance of the church and state as additional formative influences, stated,[4] 'Es ist denknotwendig, dass der Dialekt ursprünglich am Stamme hängt', and declared[5] his first criterion for determining Old English dialect boundaries to be 'Direkte Berichte über die Siedlungen der Germanenstämme in Britannien, denn auf der Verschiedenheit jener Stämme beruhte naturgemäss die ursprüngliche Verschiedenheit der Mundarten.' Subsequent writers have echoed Brandl's assumption, without proof but with an implied or expressed 'naturgemäss'.

I do not accept the continental origin hypothesis and believe that I have evidence to refute it. I propose to approach the Frisian-Old English problem with the methods of modern linguistic geography. I assume that linguistic features can move from one area to another without mass migration of the speakers, through imitation of the speech of

[2] *De bello gotthico* iv.19.

[3] This argument was used by H. Munro Chadwick, *The origin of the English nation* 67-71 (Cambridge, 1907).

[4] Alois Brandl, *Zur Geographie der altenglischen Dialekte* 29 (Berlin, 1915). ['It is necessary to believe that the dialect depends originally upon the tribe.' *Eds.*]

[5] Ibid. 5. ['. . . direct reports concerning the settlements of the Germanic tribes in Britain, for the original diversity of the dialects rests naturally on the diversity of those tribes.' *Eds.*]

one area by speakers from another. Usually innovations travel from a superior to an inferior culture, following the routes of communication and trade. My plan will be (1) to establish the approximate boundaries of the dialect areas with which I will deal; (2) to present the evidence for dating the development of these dialects as post-migration; (3) to outline the political, social, and economic developments in England which conditioned the linguistic changes; and finally, (4) to describe a series of linguistic changes resulting from linguistic diffusion, changes which can account for the most basic features of the Old English dialect distribution.

2. *The isophones.* My discussion will center on what are probably the oldest and most basic isophones of Old English. These are presented in Figure 1. North of Line A, OE *ǣ* (< WGmc. *ā*) was raised to *ē*: *strēt/strǣt, dēd/dǣd.* This isophone, sometimes known as 'Pogatscher's Line', was established on the basis of the distribution of place names containing the element *stret-/strat-*, e.g. *Stretford/Stratford.*[6] Line B

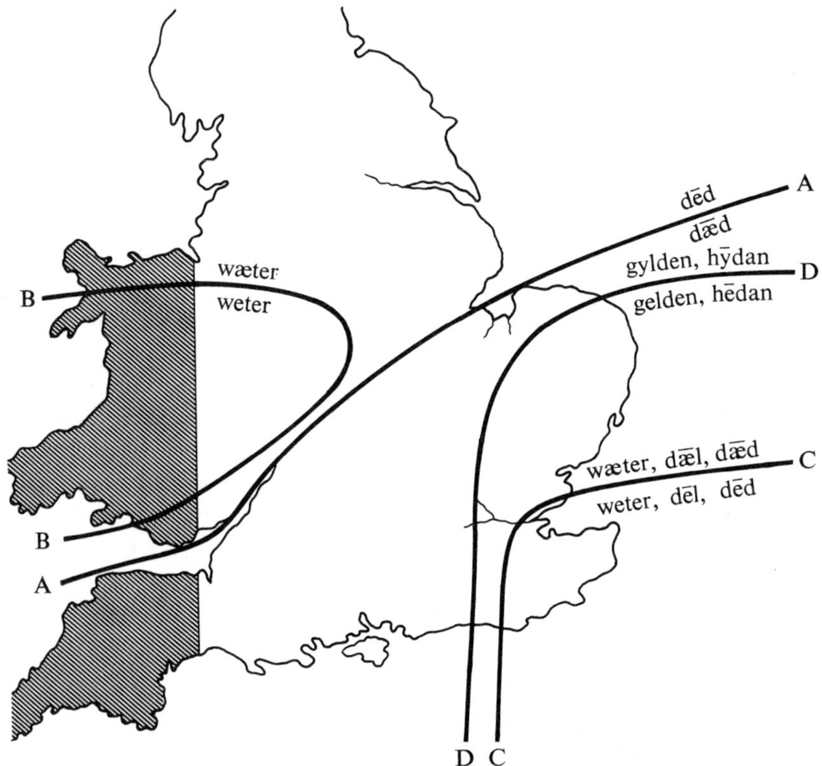

FIGURE 1

roughly defines a southwest Midland area in which OE short *æ* was also raised to *e: weter/wæter, feder/fæder.* This *e* was still characteristic of southwest Midland speech in Middle English, and at least one Old English text in which it appears regularly, the Vespasian Psalter, can be localized with reasonable certainty.[7] Line C indicates the Kentish area, in which *æ̆̄* (regardless of origin) was raised to *ĕ̄*. This innovation also appears regularly in Frisian. Thus we find *dēd* in the north and southwest Midland and also in Kentish-Frisian, but *dǣd* in an intervening conservative belt extending from Devonshire northeast to the old East Anglia (Norfolk and Suffolk). We find *weter* in the southwest Midland and in Kentish-Frisian, but *wæter* in the same intervening belt and also in the North. Only in Kentish-Frisian was the long *ǣ* which resulted from umlaut of early OE *ā* (< Gmc. *ai*) raised to *ē;* thus, the Gmc. *i*-stem noun **dailiz* appears as *dēl* in Kentish-Frisian, but as *dǣl* elsewhere in England. The linguistic geographer will immediately recognize the peculiarity of this distribution. A well-known rule of thumb in dialectology states that lateral areas are usually conservative, central areas innovating, for changes usually spread through the center of an area, leaving isolated unchanged patches at the sides. Here, however, the central area is conservative, cutting off innovating areas to the northwest and southeast.

Line D indicates the area in which the *ȳ̆*, resulting from umlaut of *ū̆*, was unrounded and lowered to *ĕ̄: gelden/gylden* (< **guldin*), *hēdan/hȳdan* (< **hūdjan*). The *ĕ̄* forms appear in Frisian and in the southeastern counties from Kent to Suffolk. This line has been well established on the basis of place names containing such elements as *hell-/hill-* or *hull-,* and *mel-/mil-* or *mul-*.[8]

The exact location of these isophones is uncertain. Few if any Old English texts can be localized with precision and certainty. Most texts are of the ninth century or later, with very few before 800 A.D., almost none before 700. Most early texts are not originals but later copies, which may well have been altered in copying. Generally place name evidence is more reliable than textual evidence. Consequently, no comprehensive linguistic atlas, such as that provided for Middle English by Moore, Meech, and Whitehall, is possible here.[9] Our increased knowledge of Middle English aids the student of Old English dialects. Extrapolation from the linguistic geography of Middle English confirms the approximate location of the isophones in Figure 1. My lines, however, are not such precise boundaries; I do not believe the evidence warrants precision. My hypothesis depends only on the general geographical relationships

[6] Alois Pogatscher, *Anglia* 23.302-9 (1901); modified by Otto Ritter, *Anglia* 37.269-75 (1913), and Brandl 31-42.

[7] Sherman Kuhn, *Speculum* 18.458-83 (1943), 23.591-629 (1948).

[8] Henry Cecil Wyld, *Englische Studien* 47.1-58, 145-66 (1913); modified by Brandl 42-74.

[9] *Essays and studies* (Univ. of Michigan) 13.1-60 (1935).

of the areas to one another. It is sufficient, for example, to establish that an area of indeterminate size and boundaries existed in the southwest Midland in which early OE *æ* was raised to *e*.

3. The age of the isophones. The raising of early OE *ǣ̆* (<WGmc. *ā̆*) to *ē̆* has traditionally been dated very early. For example, Luick writes:[10] 'Offenbar liegt ein gemein-anglofriesischer Vorgang vor, dessen Anfänge mindestens in die Zeit der Nachbarschaft der beiden Stämme auf dem Kontinent fallen.' Though he gives some phonological evidence, successfully refuted by Kuhn,[11] his principal reason seems to be his assumption that Anglo-Frisian similarities must either be coincidental or must prove a 'gemein-anglofriesischer Vorgang' and therefore must be pre-invasion.

The best evidence for a later date is the frequent, sometimes preponderant appearance of *ǣ̆* (spelled *ae, æ,* or *ę*) beside *ē* in early texts from the *ē̆*-areas. In the earliest Kentish documents, *ē* for *ǣ̆* is relatively rare. Variants of *æðel-* as an element in personal names are regular, whereas there is only one occurrence of the *eðel-* type. For example, the name *aedilmaeri* (*Æðelmǣr*) in MS Cott. Aug. ii.2 illustrates the seventh-century retention of both long and short *æ*.[12] These forms were long ago noticed by Chadwick and by Weightman.[13] Luick and Sievers-Brunner acknowledged them, but refused to draw from them the inference that the *ǣ̆* > *ē̆* change was still incomplete in the seventh and eighth centuries. Sievers-Brunner merely commented on these texts,[14] 'doch ist deren Sprache vielleicht nicht rein kentisch.' Kuhn has dealt with a similar problem in the eighth-century Mercian Corpus Gloss. In Corpus, forms with *æ* outnumber those with *e* by a ratio of five to one. Kuhn refuted the traditional interpretation of dialect mixture and demonstrated that this text illustrates a sound change not yet completed.[15] Because there is no sound evidence, other than the Frisian similarities, for a fifth-century date, we must conclude that these changes were taking place in the seventh century in Kent and perhaps as late as the early ninth century for short *ă̈* > *ĕ* in the Midland.

No one now questions the late date of the Kentish and Frisian raising to *ē* of the long *ǣ* which resulted from umlaut, for *i*-umlaut occurred in the seventh century. Similarly the southeast Midland, Kentish, and Frisian appearance of *ē̆* (as opposed to *ȳ̆*) as the umlaut of *ū̆* is recog-

[10] Karl Luick, *Historische Grammatik der englischen Sprache* 1. §118 (Leipzig, 1921). ['Evidently there is a common Anglo-Frisian model, whose origins fall at least within the time of the geographical proximity of the two tribes on the continent.' *Eds.*]

[11] Kuhn, *PMLA* 54.1-19 (1939).

[12] In Henry Sweet, *The oldest English texts* 427-8 (London, 1885), and in John Earle, *A hand-book to the land-charters and other Saxonic documents* 10 (Oxford, 1888). This is the only seventh-century charter of which the original is preserved.

[13] Chadwick 67; Jane Weightman, *Englische Studien* 35.337-49 (1905).

[14] Eduard Sievers (rev. by Karl Brunner), *Altenglische Grammatik* §2, Anm. 5 (Halle, 1951). ['. . . indeed their language is perhaps not pure Kentish.' *Eds.*]

[15] Kuhn, *PMLA* 54.1-19 (1939).

nized as later than the seventh century. These two Anglo-Frisian similarities must either be discounted as coincidence or recognized as the result of post-migration influences. If we accept the latter alternative, we are denying the Stammbaum basis of the traditional argument for pre-migration dating. There would then be no reason to object to a post-migration date for the development of all the Old English dialect characteristics, even if we did not have the positive textual evidence I have outlined. If one denied the validity of all the texts, he would only be faced with two unprovable alternative assumptions and with these two unshakable precedents for Anglo-Frisian similarities developed after the migrations. And though admittedly scanty, the textual evidence cannot be ignored. We may conclude that the English dialects developed in England between the sixth and the ninth century.

Linguistic geography provides many examples of the continuing influence of one dialect upon another, even after the two have been geographically separated. Among the most striking is the loss of postvocalic retroflexion in the speech of the eastern United States. This '*r*-dropping' originated in England considerably after the establishment of the English colonies in America. The innovation was carried across the Atlantic, and its geographical distribution reflects the extent of British influence, with western New England and certain isolated localities such as Martha's Vineyard generally retaining strong retroflexion. Even an undeveloped conjecture that similar processes produced the similar features in Frisian, Kentish, and various northerly dialects would be at least as believable as the unproved assumption of continental origin. I hope to demonstrate further that historical events could have conditioned such linguistic diffusion, and to present a hypothetical but consistent sequence of developments which could have produced precisely these similarities and their approximate distribution.

4. Frisia, Kent, and the settlement history of England. The myth of three Germanic tribes dividing Britain among them originates in Bede's well-known account:[16]

> Now the strangers had come from three of the more mighty nations in Germany, that is, the Saxons, the Angles, and the Jutes. Of the Jutes came the people of Kent and the settlers in Wight, that is, those who hold the Isle of Wight, and those in the province of the West Saxons who are called unto this day the nation of the Jutes, directly opposite the Isle of Wight. From the Saxons, that is, those from that region which now is called the land of the Old Saxons, descended the East Saxons, the South Saxons, and the West Saxons. Further, from the Angles, that is, those from that country which is called Angeln and from that time to this is said to stand deserted between the provinces of the Jutes and the Saxons, descend the East Angles, the Midland Angles [Mediterranei Angli], the Mercians, and all the progeny of the

[16] *Historia ecclesiastica* i.15.

> Northumbrians, that is, of that race which inhabits the north side of the river Humber, and the other nations of the Angles.

Until recently, this account was generally accepted by historians. It still appears, with little or no qualification, in a number of Old English grammars and histories of the English language.

In the first place, however, this paragraph is the sole authority for the tripartite division of the Germanic invaders. All other such accounts, including the entry in the Anglo-Saxon Chronicle, were clearly derived from it. Gildas, only a century after the event and two centuries earlier than Bede, called all the invaders Saxons.[17] Procopius called them Angles and Frisians.[18] Furthermore, Bede immediately abandons his classification of the invaders, never again mentions the Jutes, and seems to equate the Angles and the Saxons. He criticizes the Britons for never preaching the gospel to the 'genti Saxonum sive Anglorum'—not 'gentibus Saxonum et Anglorum'.[19] The 'Anglorum sive Saxonum gens'—not 'Anglorum et Saxonum gentes'—arrive in three long ships.[20] He quotes Gregory's letter addressing Aethelbert of Kent as 'regi Anglorum'.[21]

Other evidence would refute Bede's classification even if he had not himself discounted it. The name *Jute* never appears in Kentish place names or personal names, and there is no evidence that the Kentish ever called themselves by that name, despite Bede's claim.[22] Archeology has indicated that migrants from Jutland were probably not even represented in the mixed group that settled in Kent.[23] Finally, the archeological evidence from Essex is similar to that from Kent and has little in common with that from Wessex.[24] Bede's assertion that Essex, Wessex, and Sussex were settled by one common race, the Saxons, simply cannot be accepted.

Modern historians agree that the conquest of Britain was not a transfer of entire continental nations, each with its own culture and language. Rather, it was a slow colonization by numerous bands representing many continental tribes, which did not themselves differ significantly from one another. Whatever tenuous tribal affiliations the invaders had had in the fifth century were soon mostly lost or confused. People migrated not as Angles, Saxons, or Frisians, but as individual adventurer-leaders, with small and heterogeneous followings.[25]

[17] *De excidio et conquestu Britanniae.*

[18] *De bello gotthico* iv.19.

[19] *Hist. eccl.* i.22.

[20] Ibid. i.15.

[21] Ibid. i.32.

[22] R. G. Collingwood and J. N. L. Myres, *Roman Britain and the English settlements* 346 (Oxford, 1937).

[23] R. H. Hodgkin, *A history of the Anglo-Saxons* 92 (Oxford, 1939).

[24] Ibid. 146.

[25] Ibid. 155; Collingwood and Myres 347-8; Peter Hunter Blair, *Anglo-Saxon England* 10-11 (Cambridge, 1956); F. M. Stenton, *Anglo-Saxon England* 6-10 (Oxford, 1947).

The striking variations in Kentish graves indicate that Kent especially was settled by such mixed groups. All attempts to relate the Kentish evidence to that from any one area on the continent have failed.[26] We must agree with Jerrold[27] that 'The Jutish race and civilization, as described by Bede and as we know it from the graves of the late fifth and sixth centuries, was made in Kent.'

During the reign of Aethelbert (c. 560–616), Kent achieved tremendous cultural and political dominance. It is no accident that Augustine's success was in Kent. In wealth and prestige, in its legal system, in learning, and in cosmopolitan outlook, Kent far surpassed anything known in England since Roman days. As Hodgkin says,[28] 'Kent might seem barbarous to the Romans but to the peoples of Britain it was a center of civilization.'

The fifth-century invaders may have inherited some of the culture of Roman Britain, for the principal Roman-British centers of population—Dover, Canterbury, Faversham, and Rochester—were also among the principal Germanic settlements.[29] Primarily, however, this Kentish supremacy may be attributed to Kent's unique position on the old trade route with the continent. The Kentish were the traders of England from the beginning and were exposed to all manner of continental influences. Judging from the great number of early English coins found on the sites of Frisian settlements, probably most of this overseas trade was in Frisian hands, though there may have been some trading directly with the Franks.[30] Evidence of these Frankish-Frisian influences is abundant. Augustine's mission in Kent was aided by the fact that Aethelbert had married the Christian daughter of the Frankish King Hariberht. Many sixth- and seventh- century *trientes,* small gold coins of Frankish pattern, have been found in Kent.[31] The nature of much of the magnificent ceramic work and jewelry which marks Aethelbert's day indicates that the Kentish received through the Frisians and the Franks many remnants of the dying Roman civilization in western Europe. Hodgkin has conjectured that the long-necked vases found in Kentish graves were wine vessels in which Rhenish wine was imported.[32] Aerial photography has revealed the outlines of the early fields; the open-field system in Kent and adjacent east Midland areas, as opposed to the strip cultivation practiced elsewhere in England, suggests Rhineland influence.[33] Early Kentish laws are more similar to the Frisian than to the West Saxon, in that there was no evidence of the West Saxon division of the nobility into two classes, whereas the dependent and servile classes were more elab-

[26] Hodgkin 92-7.
[27] Douglas Jerrold, *An introduction to the history of England* 214 (Cambridge, 1952).
[28] Hodgkin 262.
[29] Jerrold 214.
[30] Hodgkin 98-100; Stenton 219.
[31] Chadwick 17.
[32] Hodgkin 91.
[33] Jerrold 214.

orately classified. One of these classes, the *laet,* is clearly identical with the *litus* or *lazzus* of the Frisian, Frankish, and Old Saxon laws.[34] This evidence, though not proving a Kentish-Frisian racial identity, as once was maintained, does prove a continuing Frisian influence throughout the Anglo-Saxon period.

Aethelbert's immediate kingdom, his *regnum,* was small—little more than modern Kent and Surrey. But his *imperium* extended north to the Humber, and he probably wielded considerable influence over the independent kingdoms of Bernicia and Deira north of the Humber.[35] This prestige early extended the Kentish-Frisian trade route northward at least as far as Yorkshire. According to Bede, in 679 a Northumbrian named Imma was sold as a slave to a Frisian merchant somewhere in the neighborhood of the river Trent. The Frisian took Imma to London, possibly for shipment to the continent. However, Hlothere, king of Kent, learning that Imma was really a captured thane rather than a commoner, paid a ransom to the Frisian so that Imma could return home to Northumbria.[36] The old Deiran cemeteries have yielded archeological material strikingly similar to that from Kentish and Frisian graves.[37] The Sutton Hoo treasure, found in Suffolk in 1939, contains a purse of gold Frankish coins of the seventh century.[38] X-ray photography has recently revealed that the blade of the sword in this treasure was of the pattern-welded Rhenish type, though the jewels which decorated its sword-knot were of East Anglian workmanship.[39] The open-field system of cultivation extended northward from Kent as far as the Wash, though not west into West Saxon territory.[40] That literary traditions followed this trade route is illustrated by the Finn tale in *Beowulf,* which authorities agree originated among the Ingvaeonic peoples and was carried from Friesland both to Upper Germany and to the Mercian and Northumbrian areas of England.[41] Kentish education was also imitated. Bede tells us[42] that the East Anglian King Sigbert (631–634) 'set up a school in which boys should be instructed in letters, by the help of bishop Felix whom he had gotten from Kent, and who appointed them masters and teachers after the manner of the men of Kent [iuxta morem Cantuariorum].' Myres notes a tradition in *Historia Brittonum* that the first Teutonic leaders in Northumbria were a son and nephew of the Kentish Hengist; this probably represents a later attempt by the Northumbrians to connect their genealogy with that of the prestigious Kentish.[43]

[34] Hodgkin 94; Chadwick 77-8.
[35] Hodgkin 261.
[36] *Hist. eccl.* iv.22.
[37] Collingwood and Myres 412.
[38] Jerrold 223.
[39] Blair 283.
[40] Hodgkin 174.
[41] Fr. Klaeber, ed., *Beowulf* 235 (New York, 1941).
[42] *Hist. eccl.* iii.18.
[43] Collingwood and Myres 412.

We may conclude that it was along this route from the continent to Kent and then northward to Mercia and Northumbria that cultural innovations generally passed: trade goods, Christianity, education, and literature. In early years the Southwest of England remained a rather backward area, comparatively isolated from these influences.

5. Frisian linguistic innovations in England. I suggest that between the sixth and the eighth century, a series of five phonological innovations followed this route from Frisia to Kent and that the extent of their penetration to other parts of England accounts for part (not all) of the dialect pattern in the East of England. The diffusion of these innovations

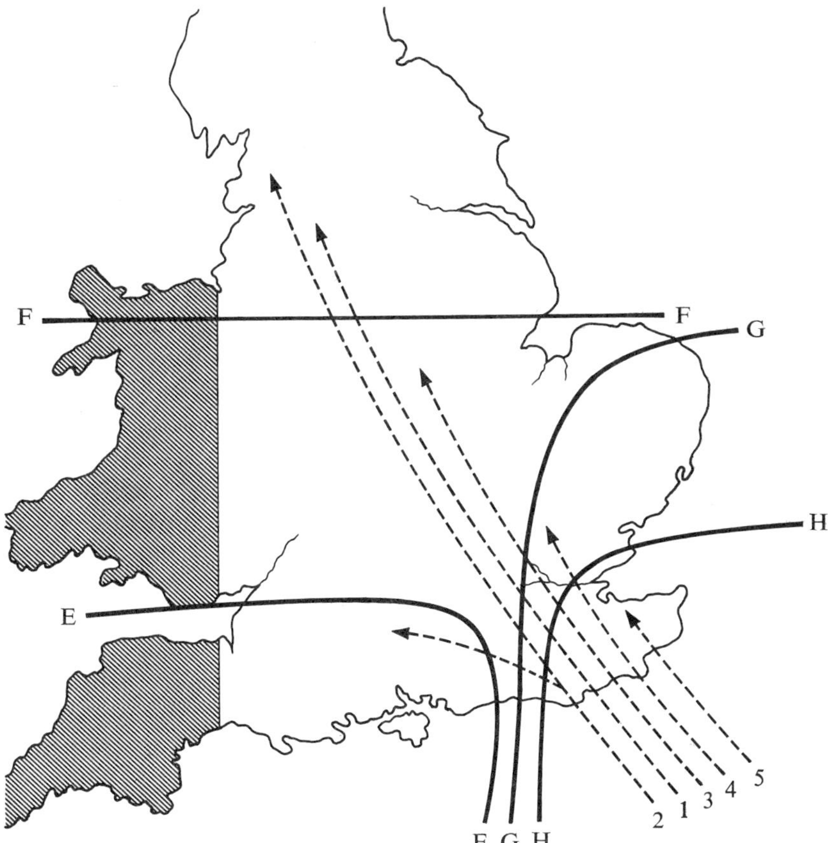

FIGURE 2

is illustrated in Figure 2. First is the raising of long *ǣ* (< WGmc. *ā*) to *ē* (*dēd/dǣd*). Originating in Frisia some time in the sixth or early seventh century, this innovation soon was adopted in Kent and spread northward, eventually covering all of Germanic speaking England except the

Southwest, thus producing the isophone indicated by Line E. The later reinstatement of the conservative *ǣ* in the east Midland area will be discussed below.

Not long afterward, the innovation known as *i*-umlaut, which had originated somewhere in southern Germany and had spread northward to the Frisians, was similarly carried from Frisia to Kent, and then, probably during the first half of the seventh century, spread throughout England. In the area southwest of Line E, the long *ǣ* which resulted from the umlaut of early OE *ā* (e.g. *dǣl* < **dāli*) fell in with earlier long *ǣ* (WGmc. *ā*). Hence *dǣl* and *dǣd* with the same vowel in the Southwest. Elsewhere, however, including Frisia, the older *ǣ* had already closed to *ē* and the two vowels remained phonemically distinct (*dǣl, dēd*).

The third innovation, like the first, probably originated in Frisian: the raising of the short *ǣ̆* to *ĕ* (*weter/wæter*). This was carried to Kent in the late seventh century and spread northward. By this time, however, Kentish influence had diminished in the North. Kent had ceased to be a great military and political power, and had been increasingly dominated by Mercia. Kent still maintained considerable cultural prestige, but this waning influence was probably insufficient to carry the third innovation farther north than the Wash (Line F). I have already pointed out that forms containing this *ĕ* occasionally occur in Kentish texts as early as the late seventh century and that Kuhn found them to be comparatively rare (a ratio of about one to five) in a Mercian text of the late eighth. This indicates that the northward diffusion of *ĕ* must have been very slow.

Even the cultural supremacy of Kent was soon challenged. Under a succession of competent rulers in the seventh century, the northern kingdoms of Bernicia and Deira were united to form Northumbria, which became a major power, even defeating the Mercians in battle in 654. The monastery of Lindisfarne, founded in 635 by Aidan, grew in stature until the Celtic church in the North seriously rivaled the Roman church centered at Canterbury. When the apostate Mercians were reconverted to Christianity, it was by missionaries from Lindisfarne. Though the Synod of Whitby in 664 decided in favor of Rome and Canterbury, still Lindisfarne, Wearmouth, and Jarrow were the centers of learning until the Danish invasions. Consequently the northward diffusion of eighth-century Frisian innovations was increasingly restricted.

The fourth innovation illustrated in Figure 2 was the lowering and unrounding to *ē̆* of the *ȳ̆* which had recently resulted from the umlaut of *ū̆*; e.g. *gelden/gylden* (< **guldin*), *hēdan/hȳdan* (< **hūdjan*). This *ē̆* spread northward into most of East Anglia (Line G), but its appearance was probably only sporadic as far north as the Wash. The fifth Frisian innovation was the raising to *ē* of the long *ǣ* resulting from umlaut of *ā* (< Gmc. *ai*); thus *dǣl* (< Gmc. **dailiz*) became *dēl*, just as *dǣd* had become *dēd* more than a century before. This probably did not spread much beyond the old boundaries of Kent itself (Line H).

According to my hypothesis, eastern England in the late eighth century was a dialect transition area, as shown in Figure 2, marked by a series of east-west isoglosses indicating the northernmost extent of the Kentish-Frisian influences moving up from the Southeast. The Southwest had remained untouched by these innovations, with the exception of *i*-umlaut. Kent and Frisia had participated in all of them.

6. The restoration of ǣ̆ in the southeast Midland. If this pattern of isophones had remained unchanged, this explanation would certainly have been thought of long ago. Certain events in the ninth and tenth centuries, however, altered and partially obscured the pattern. Under a series of remarkably competent and successful rulers, Wessex rapidly became the leading state in England. In 825, according to the Anglo-Saxon Chronicle, the East Angles, in revolt against the domination of Beornwulf of Mercia, placed themselves under the protection of King Egbert, and the entire southeast Midland area was soon under West Saxon control. With the destruction of the northern monasteries by the Vikings, the Southwest became the dominant area in learning as well.

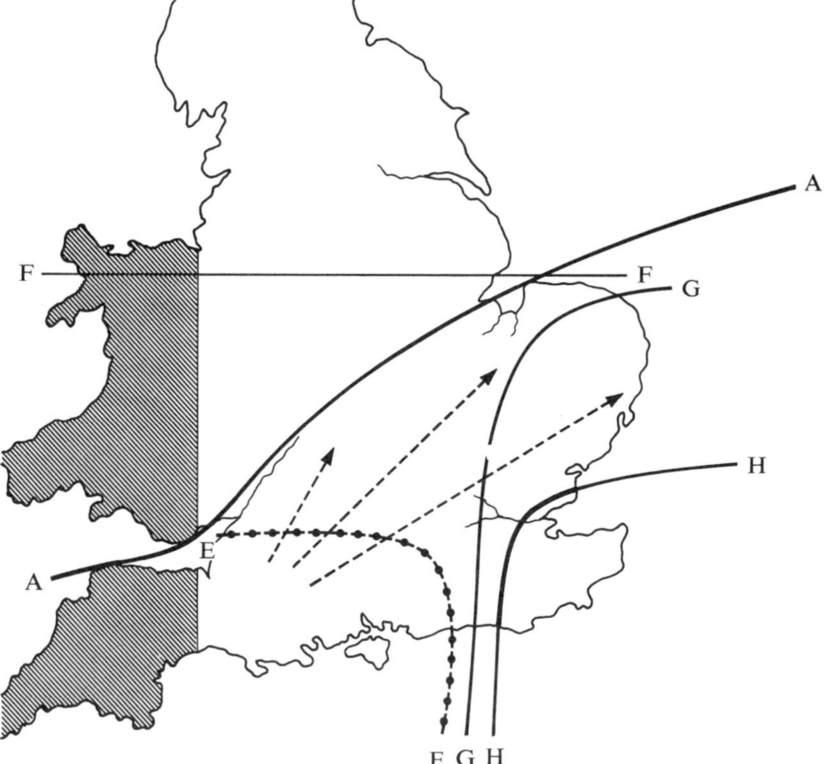

FIGURE 3

According to my hypothesis, the southeast Midland area had adopted many of the Kentish-Frisian innovations; but this new West Saxon influence, moving in from the Southwest, tended to reintroduce the older conservative forms, relatively uninfluenced by earlier Kentish-Frisian developments. As is indicated in Figure 3, a wedge of conservative West Saxon was driven into the dialect pattern of eastern England, separating the lateral areas of Kentish-Frisian influence in the Northwest and Southeast. Thus the dialectal principle that lateral areas are usually conservative still holds here, for the conservative ǣ̆ of West Saxon was really an innovation in the East, intruding into an area in which the earlier innovations had become standard.

This eastward diffusion of West Saxon ǣ̆ resulted from east Midland imitation of West Saxon, which by the tenth century had become recognized as the standard language of England. Wyld writes,[44]

> The fact is that all O. E. documents of the later period, with very few exceptions, are written in a common form which in all essential features is W. Saxon . . . so much so that it is commonly assumed that after Ælfred's time the prestige of Wessex in Government, Arms, and Letters, was such that the dialect of that area became a literary *koinē* in universal use in written documents.

In an article on the inconsistent use of *e* and *æ* in Farman's Mercian glosses,[45] Kuhn demonstrates the eagerness of tenth-century Mercian scribes to imitate West Saxon, even to the point of hyperurbanism. The Rushworth[1] glosses and the Worcester version of the Anglo-Saxon Chronicle, though written in areas where *ǣ̆* had earlier been raised to *ĕ*, contain relatively few *e* spellings for these words. In Rushworth[1] the West Saxon *æ* outnumbers *e* by a ratio of about twenty-five to two. Furthermore, *æ* is also substituted for *e* in more than a third of the words which etymologically represent Germanic *e* and which should have had *e* both in East Mercian and also in West Saxon, e.g. *stæfne, ðægnum, wæg,* for *stefna, ðegnum, weg.* If we accept Kuhn's hypothesis, we can see in this scribal imitation the northeastward movement of West Saxon *æ* actually in progress. What better evidence of linguistic imitation can we ask than hyperurbanism?

Unfortunately there is practically no direct textual evidence from the east Midland area which could verify the presence of the Kentish-Frisian forms before they were obliterated by West Saxon influence. There is only one very early East Saxon charter (MS Cott. Aug. ii.29), from the late seventh century, written in Latin but containing English personal and local names.[46] These show preponderantly *e* spellings, e.g.

[44] Henry Cecil Wyld, *A history of modern colloquial English* 49 (Oxford, 1936).

[45] Kuhn, *PMLA* 60.631-69 (1945).

[46] In Sweet 426, Earle 13. It is described in Chadwick 70. Recent scholarship has shown that this is not an original, as Chadwick and Earle thought, but a copy made at

hedilburge (*Æthelburh*). Though this text is comparatively well localized, being a grant by an East Saxon to an East Saxon abbess of land for an East Saxon abbey, I agree that this is evidence too slim for conclusive verification. Yet I know of no textual evidence to refute the hypothesis.

This restoration of the conservative *ǣ̆* in the East, following the five processes illustrated in Figure 2, accounts for the dialect distribution shown in Figure 1. Line A (Pogatscher's Line) is now seen to be the northern boundary of the northeastward movement of the West Saxon *ǣ̆*. Lines C and D are essentially identical with Lines G and H respectively. The southwest Midland area bounded by Line B, characterized by the Kentish-Frisian *ĕ* in *weter* and *feder,* may be recognized in Figure 3 as the area between Lines F and A. Line E, no longer the boundary of West Saxon *ǣ̆,* remained the boundary of various other linguistic features which can best be considered West Saxon innovations. Some of these remained confined to the Southwest, but others later spread eastward into Kent or northward into the Mercian area.

I cannot explain why it was the *ǣ̆* and not other West Saxon features which were carried eastward in the ninth and tenth centuries. Parallels are available in modern linguistic geography: many Americans emulate the eastern New England pronunciation of *aunt, dance, calf,* and *path* with a lowered vowel (even to the point of hyperurbanisms like [hat] for *hat*) without also adopting the intrusive *r* in *law-r-and order.* We can only conclude that the *ǣ̆* became a shibboleth of the standard West Saxon dialect, and so was more widely imitated than were other West Saxon features.

A major advantage of the hypothesis presented in this paper is that it more closely parallels the formation of modern dialects as discovered by both American and European linguistic geographers. It is doubtful that the basic processes of dialect formation—innovation and diffusion—have radically changed since the fifth century. My hypothesis accounts not only for the similarities between Frisian and Kentish, but also for those between Kentish, Frisian, and various northerly dialects—similarities which have generally been ignored or dismissed as coincidental. It recognizes the evidence which led Siebs to believe, quite rightly, that Frisian was of prime importance in the formation of the Old English dialects, but avoids the inconsistencies in Siebs' theory. Finally, and perhaps most important, it is consistent with the modern conception of early English history as interpreted by the leading historians. Even the language of fifteen hundred years ago does not exist in a vacuum but is a feature of a cultural complex. Toward its historical interpretation the discovery of a sword or a purse of coins in an old burial mound can be as significant as the discovery of new texts.

---

the same abbey in the late eighth century; see Dorothy Whitelock, ed., *English historical documents* 1.446-8 (London, 1955). The language could therefore be a mixture of seventh- and eighth-century forms.

Old English Sound-Changes Reconsidered in Relation to Scribal Tradition and Practice

MARJORIE DAUNT

OLD ENGLISH PHONOLOGY, as it is at present formulated, mainly rests on two assumptions, that Anglo-Saxon scribes were not highly skilled orthographers using a traditional method, but simple scribes who to the best of their ability wrote what they said, so that a change in spelling in most cases indicates a change in pronunciation; and, secondly, that, with a few exceptions, they recorded their speech on the one-sound one-letter plan. Luick says: "Für jeden Laut wurde in der Regel nur ein Zeichen gebraucht (obwohl zum Teil dasselbe wie für einen Anderen)."[1]

The results of accepting these premises are far-reaching. An elaborate system of Sound-changes has been built up, the stages of which can be approximately dated, so that in respect of any given word-form it is possible to say that certain earlier developments must have taken place; and Luick's great *Grammatik* shows how every writing in the Anglo-Saxon manuscripts can be explained from the point of view of its sound value. Some of the results, however, are not entirely convincing, and among the doubtful points are (1) the phonetic improbability (if the facts of living speech are taken into consideration) of some of the processes of "Sound-development" described; and (2) the group of "Sound-Laws" connected with the development and elimination of glides; above all, the classification among Old English vowels of both long and short diphthongs. An example of the first of these results is provided by the WSax *fiellan*, in the development of which the following

---

Reprinted by permission (with the author's emendations) from *Transactions of the Philological Society 1939* (1939), pp. 108-37.

[1] *Historische Grammatik* § 53. ['For every sound only one symbol was used, as a rule (although at times the same one [was used] for another [sound]).' *Eds.*]

stages are traced: **falljan* > **fæll(j)an,* by isolated fronting of [ɑ] to [æ], **feall(j)an* by development of a back glide between the front vowel and the dark *ll,* then *fiellan* by palatalization of the diphthong before *j.* It is, however, very unlikely that *ll* would have remained dark in such very close proximity to [j], so dark as to have a distinctly velar on-glide. Why then is the **feall(j)an* stage inserted? Because *feallan* is found for the verb of which *fiellan* is a derivative; a Sound-change, known as Breaking, has been built on *ea* and *l* and a consonant, and similar writings; lastly this sound-change has been given a chronological position and therefore "must have taken place". To take another instance, in some texts the forms *deaȝas* and *dæȝas* are found, and the explanation given is that the first contains a diphthong which has been monophthongized in the second, in the same circumstances that caused the development of the said diphthong. It is true that a change in the consonant is suggested, but there appears to be no reason why the consonant should have been fronted in this setting. There are many other cases where a mathematical application of definite "Sound-Laws" in so-called chronological order produces a beautifully dovetailed result, but one which requires extraordinary unanimity on the part of large groups of Old English speakers.

In the second case, that of the 'sound-laws' dealing with glides, we find that certain spellings, *ea, eo, io, ie,* are said to represent diphthongs which exist in two quantities, and are phonemic yet only distinguished by the quantity of one of their elements, e.g. [e:o] and [eo], [ɛ:ɑ], and [ɛɑ], etc., a highly improbable state of affairs. It is in the highest degree unlikely that Old English contained two sets of diphthongs, differing only in quantity, and a sharp distinction should be made between a "real" diphthong which has phonemic value in the vowel system, and a contextual variant of a simple vowel, which might be called a "conditioned" diphthong, in which a short vowel acquires a slightly diphthongal sound in combination with the off- or on-glide of a preceding or following consonant, and in that context only, e.g. NE [ei] in *gate, safe,* or *made,* is plainly not dependent for its diphthongal value on the neighbouring sounds, nor probably was the sound represented by the OE writing *ea* in such words as *dream, eac, beatan,* but NE *field* is often pronounced [fɪəɫd], [fɪuɫd], or even [fɪɒɫd], and these are contextual variants of [i:] produced in combination with [ɫ], and belong to the [i:] phoneme. Sievers points out[2] that these contextual variants in place of short vowels occur, and he describes them as "short diphthongs" or "Breakings", but he adds inverted commas, and also the remark: "Reducierte Diphthonge haben . . . nur die Zeitdauer gewöhnlicher kurzer Vocale." He quotes the "diphthongs" of this kind found in the Westphalian dialect, and compares them with the Old English

[2] E. Sievers, *Grundzüge der Phonetik* § 507. ['Reduced diphthongs have . . . only the duration of the usual short vowels.' *Eds.*]

"Breakings". But the Westphalian variant of [e], and [o], namely [ie] and [uɑ], in such words as *Piepper* (Pfeffer) and *Kualle* (Kohle), even if it can be regarded as parallel to the Old English Breakings, which does not seem certain, is not complicated by the presence in Westphalian of a long [i:e] and [u:ɑ].[3] It is the existence of the *two* phonemes in Old English which is so unlikely.

It is true that Luick talks of "unecht" [i.e., false] diphthongs,[4] but he says in the next breath, "Die kurzen [Diphthonge] unterscheiden sich von ihnen [den langen] nur durch die Quantität." But in existing Indo-European languages there is, so far as my knowledge and information go, no example of "long" and "short" diphthongs, differentiated only by quantity, being phonemic, and it seems very unlikely that Old English had what is now non-existent.

Sweet says, "Of course it is possible to make the glide element of a diphthong so short that the whole combination can be regarded as the equivalent of a short vowel, as in OE *ea, eo*.[5] The words containing "short" *eo, ea,* in their later development, behave as if they contained the simple vowel only, and it is very likely that the sounds implied by *ea, eo* writings in certain conditions should be grouped, not with what are called "long" *ea, eo,* but with [æ] and [e]; in fact they are contextual variants of the *æ* and *e* phonemes; but if so, what becomes of the "Sound-Changes", built up on them, viz. Breaking, Palatal Diphthongization, Back-Mutation, and the "Smoothing" or Monophthongization of these diphthongs?

If the results achieved by building on the two basic assumptions are unsatisfactory, perhaps the assumptions themselves are unsound, and it might be well to reconsider them. What do we know about the Anglo-Saxon schools of writing? What can we gather about the possible training of the scribes as orthographers? Do they show any signs of careful representation of sound? Is there any evidence that they could distinguish fine shades of speech sounds? And do they show any sign of grouping sounds on any sort of scientific basis? To answer these questions it is necessary to go rather far afield.

Fortunately the few things that we do know about the Anglo-Saxon scribes, which may help to solve the present problem, are certain. We know that the Northumbrians and Mercians were first taught to write Latin letters by Irishmen, and we know that before that they used runes, and we can see what alterations they made in their runes to meet changes in the language.

At this point it might be well to face the difficulty of manuscripts and standards. For the purpose of this paper the general practices of

[3] J. Reis, *Die deutschen Mundarten* 115.

[4] *Hist. Gram.* § 133. ['The short [diphthongs] are distinguished from [the long diphthongs] only through quantity.' *Eds.*]

[5] *History of English Sounds* § 73.

scribes are more important than isolated spellings, the professional intention rather than the individual variation or mistake, and the writings specially in question appear in many manuscripts. It is not taking too much for granted to accept as a foundation a Northumbrian early school of writing, of Irish-Latin tradition, of which the *Caedmon Hymn* in the Moore manuscript is the best relic and of which the Durham *Liber Vitae* and the *Lindisfarne Gospels* are later descendants; a Mercian school, which was famous and closely connected with the Northumbrian, but to which it is not safe to give the *Vespasian Psalter*, so that this school can only be suggested as a possible link in the Irish-Anglo-Saxon tradition; finally a West-Saxon school, best represented, it is generally agreed, by the MSS Hatton 20, and Cotton Tib. B. xi, of the *Hierdeboc*,[6] the Parker *Chronicle*, and the Lauderdale *Orosius*. Too much doubt has been cast on the *Charter of Aeþelwulf* for it to be used as definite West Saxon of an earlier date than Alfred. Any statements made here are based on this group in the first place, and the distinction between Northumbrian and West Saxon is not as essential as might appear, since the question is chiefly one of general relationship, and concerns writings whose widespread existence is not questioned.

The Irish influence on the Northumbrian scribes must have lasted on till a late date, if the Irish ornamentation of the *Lindisfarne Gospels* is any guide, and there is every reason why Irish influence should be strong on Alfred's school. Where could he get his teachers except from Ireland, Wales, or the Continent? On the Continent Irish teachers were to be found in numbers. Although Alfred says there were not many good scholars north of the Thames, there were fewer still south of it, and the preface to the *Cura Pastoralis* says: *Ælfred Kyning . . . me his writerum sende suð & norð*.[7] If Alfred got any teachers from the north, and certainly Plegmund was a Mercian, he must have got men trained in the Irish-Latin tradition. If he sent to Wales, and Asser was a Welshman, he might well meet the same tradition there. Hodgkin[8] says that Alfred is not known to have drawn any of his helpers direct from Ireland, but, as the tradition of English writing was almost certainly established to a large extent before Alfred's time, and only re-established by him, there is no necessity to labour the point of direct Irish contact. W. Keller[9] points out that no trace of continental influence can be seen in the handwriting of the West-Saxon school for thirty years after the king's death, which makes much fresh Continental influence on the orthography unlikely.

The traditional methods of the Latin teachers, and of the Irish, are not often mentioned in connexion with the Anglo-Saxon scribes, yet

[6] H. Sweet, *Gregory's Pastoral Care*, E.E.T.S.; Luick, *Hist. Gram.;* C. L. Wrenn, "Standard Old English," *Trans. Phil. Soc.* 1933, 65-88.

[7] H. Sweet, *Past. Care* 9.

[8] R. H. Hodgkin, *History of the Anglo-Saxons* II. 641.

[9] W. Keller, *Angelsächsische Palæographie* 22.

these seem extremely relevant, since respect would make the Anglo-Saxons follow them as far as possible. The many Latin Grammars known to have been in the country, and used by such men as Bede and Alcuin,[10] always have a section devoted to sounds and their writing, vowels, consonants, diphthongs, diacritics, and the rest. Isidore of Seville's *Etymologiae,* which was certainly used by Bede, contains a section *De Orthographia,* which is typical of many others. The whole of this section would make any scribe think hard. In the section *De Litteris Latinis* Isidore gives quite a good definition of vowel and consonant: "Vocales sunt quae directo hiatu faucium sine ulla conlisione varie emittuntur. Et dictae vocales quod per se vocem inpleant, et per se syllabam faciant nulla adhaerente consonante. Consonantes sunt, quae diverso motu linguae vel inpressione labrorum efficiuntur. Et vocatae consonantes quia per se non sonant, sed iunctis vocalibus consonant."[11] The last statement, the non-sonority of consonants, occurs in almost every grammar, it is repeated by Alcuin, and indeed it persisted in many English grammars to quite recent times. It is important here because it might confirm in the mind of an Anglo-Saxon orthographer the idea that a consonant which he perceived to be specially resonant must have a vowel attached to it in writing. Another important section of the *Etymologiae* deals with "barbarisms", and under the heading of *De barbarismo,* what must not be written or said, the attention of Anglo-Saxon writers would be drawn to distinctions of kinds of speech and the need of care in recording it: "Barbarismus autem fit scripto et pronuntiatione."[12] And in view of the writing of Old English consonants the attention he draws to change of value, in *De Orthographia,* is useful: "C et G (litterae) quandam cognationem habent. Nam dum dicimus 'centum' (et) 'trecentos', postea dicimus 'quadringentos' G ponentes pro C."[13]

Alcuin's sprightly *Grammatica,* with its conversations between MAGISTER and SAXO and FRANCO, contains much the same material and refers expressly to Donatus. Franco says to the Magister: "Ut reor, in Donato legimus, tria accidisse litteris; nomen, figuram, potestatem. De nominibus et figuris non est opus dicere, sed de potestate velim dicas."[14] It must be remembered that *littera* has a special meaning. "FRANCO:

[10] J. D. A. Ogilvy, *Books known to Anglo-Saxon Writers from Bede to Alcuin* (Med. Acad. Am.).

[11] ['Vowels are those which are uttered by means of a direct opening of the throat without any coming together in any way. The spoken vowels may produce sound by themselves, and they may form a syllable alone without any adjoining consonant. The consonants are those which are produced by a different motion of the tongue or physical pressure of the lips. And they are called consonants because they do not sound by themselves, but resound together with vowels.' *Eds.*]

[12] ['The greatest "barbarism", however, is done in writing and pronunciation.' *Eds.*]

[13] ['C and G (letters) have a certain connection. For, while we say "centum" (and) "trecentos", afterwards we say "quadringentos", placing G for C.' *Eds.*]

[14] ['As I believe, we read in Donatus that there are three properties for letters: the name, the shape, the power. Of the names and shapes, it is not necessary to speak, but about the power I desire discussion.' *Eds.*]

Da definitionem quoque. SAXO: Littera est pars minima vocis articulatae."[15] Similar passages can be found in many Latin Grammars known to the Anglo-Saxons, and the interest here lies in the fact that the training of the native scribes almost certainly was based on a careful consideration of "how we ought to write". Their first idea would surely be to apply the Latin rules in recording English speech in Latin letters, but a glance at these Latin Grammars will show that, however useful the principles suggested there might be, they could not supply the details needed for Old English writing. Where else would the Anglo-Saxons naturally turn?

The Irish had early established a school and tradition for the writing of their vernacular, and it would be natural for the Anglo-Saxons to follow that orthographic tradition, in writing Old English, when the Latin instructions failed them. In the first instance, the Irish teachers, listening as foreigners to a strange tongue and trying to write it down, would hear shades of pronunciation which the English speakers would not have heard in themselves, and the Anglo-Saxons would probably try to follow their example and establish an orthographic method and tradition, for native English writing, on their lines. What were the Irish lines likely to be?

All experts on Old Irish agree as to the difficulty of dating and grading the existing manuscripts, most of which are found on the Continent. Vendryès,[16] agreeing with Zimmer, puts the earliest hand in the *Würzburg Glosses* at the end of the seventh century, while Pokorny[17] dates the *Würzburg Glosses* "about A.D. 770 to 780", and puts the *Cambray Homile* "about A.D. 700". In any case, the earliest existing Irish remains predate the Anglo-Saxon manuscripts, and there is agreement among Irish scholars as to the early date at which the Irish scribal tradition was probably established, so that if the earliest Irish teachers did not write exactly as the surviving manuscripts indicate, still the main points of Old Irish orthography are definitely established at a date early enough to have preceded any surviving Anglo-Saxon manuscripts. However, the similarity between Old Irish and Anglo-Saxon orthography in many points is too marked to be safely ignored, and as the aim here is to stress the common principle in view of the social contact, it would not really matter if the cases had been reversed and the Anglo-Saxons had taught the Irish, as it is quite possible that in some points they did. The chief features of Old Irish orthography[18] (some of which are obviously adopted from Late Latin) are:—

[15] ['FRANCO: Give the definition too. SAXO: A letter is the smallest part of articulated sound.' *Eds.*]

[16] J. Vendryès, *Grammaire du vieil-irlandais.*

[17] J. Pokorny, *A Historical Reader of Old Irish.*

[18] J. Pokorny, *A Concise Old Irish Grammar.*

1. Long vowels are frequently written double, e.g. OIr *baan* 'white'; *ee* 'he'. This is common in the *Würzburg Glosses,* though limited to final or monosyllables, and is frequent in Old English manuscripts.

2. The letter *æ* is used, as in Late Latin, as the equivalent of *e;* e.g. *æclis,* or *eclis* 'church', are both in the *Würzburg Glosses.* While in the West-Saxon manuscripts the signs *æ* and *e* are usually separated, there are, even there, frequent confusions. In the *Lindisfarne Gospels, cwæþ* and *cweþ* occur within a few lines; and such forms as *wellæ, æhteða* (*ęahteða*), *meæssa, siæ, onduæardra* (*ondueardra*), bear out the suggestion that in the use of *æ* phonetic fact and what Isidore calls "discipline" are mixed.

3. *ch, th* are often used in Old Irish for the fricatives, and these appear irregularly in Anglo-Saxon manuscripts, e.g. *Ealchere* in the *Parker Chronicle; chwæm* 'cui', in *Lindisfarne Gospels.*

4. The diphthongs with *a,* e.g. *aí, aé,* can interchange in writing with those in *o, oí, oé,* so that the same word can be spelt *aís, aés, oís,* or *oés* 'people', in the same manuscript. There are traces of this in the *Würzburg Glosses.*[19] (Is this the origin of the confusion between *eo, ea* writings in Northumbrian and other Anglian texts?)

5. Every consonant can be aspirated in Old Irish, and only *c* and *t* show it in writing, so *b* and *d,* etc., can be both plosive and voiced fricative. Such Old English forms as *heben* in *Caedmon's Hymn,* and the many cases of variation of *ð* and *d,* e.g. *madmas, maðmas,* are of course obvious.

6. All these points are of minor importance compared with the chief feature of Old Irish orthography, the indication of consonant colour, and the consequent appearance of "false" diphthongs beside the "true". All the Old Irish grammars give the same warning, that it is important to distinguish "real" diphthongs from the cases where a short simple vowel is followed by a writing intended to show the articulation of the following consonant, e.g. *ia* from *i* + *a* + a consonant. Vendryès[20] says that there are two sorts of vowels to be distinguished: those which have a syllabic value in pronunciation, and those which serve to indicate graphically, like an accent or sign of sorts, the exact position of the consonants. There were three values of consonant in Old Irish, those with *i, a,* and *u* resonance, e.g., OIr *tua(ith), dig(la)e,* and *fi(ur).*[21] In the case of the false diphthongs, the true vowel retains its natural quantity. Vendryès calls this on-glide writing a "voyelle d'infection", and says it is difficult to determine exactly what it corresponded to in pronunciation. It was apparently a "phonème de liaison ou de passage", short enough not to affect the quantity of the word at all, slight enough to be suppressed without any drawback to the script, and yet clear

[19] R. Thurneysen, *Handbuch des alt-irischen Grammatik* § 62.
[20] *Grammaire du viel-irlandais* § 74.
[21] The brackets enclose the complete consonant.

enough to be perceptible to the speaker. In general the infection of *i* is alone noted in a systematic fashion, even in cases where the orthography of the word does not make it necessary. It is regularly noted in the *Würzburg Glosses*. The *a* quality is not shown in the earliest Old Irish except in a few cases. The *u* quality is generally noted because its value is morphologically significant. A very clear exposition of Old Irish consonant colour is to be found in O. J. Bergin's article on "Palatalization".[22] He takes his examples from the *Milan* and *St. Gall Glosses* since they show consonant quality better than the *Würzburg*. The colouring of *a* represents a neutral position; for *u* the tongue is drawn back and the lips protruded. In modern Irish the *a* and *u* qualities are classed together as "non-palatal" as against "palatal", because *u* quality no longer plays the part it did in the inflexional system, and does not thrust itself on the notice of the grammarian. Thus OIr nom. *fer*, gen. *fir*, dat. *fiur*, have been reduced to *fear, fir, fear*. Bergin, however, makes it plain that in Modern Irish it would be a mistake from a phonetic point of view to ignore *u* quality, but even in Old Irish the difference between *u* and *a*, over the whole range of consonants, was not so marked as the difference of either from *i*. Earlier Old Irish writes *tene, cene*, with nothing to mark the pronunciation of *n*, but in the *Milan Glosses* a non-palatal glide is inserted, *cenae* (39[9] 3). From all this, certain facts emerge, which are important for the understanding of the tradition in which the Anglo-Saxons were probably trained by the Irish:

(1) that the morphological significance of consonant colour in Irish led to its expression in writings, which even then were tending to become traditional;
(2) that diphthongal writings, in many cases, represented only a simple vowel in a definite phonetic context;
(3) that, where no confusion was likely to follow in the spoken language, a certain amount of ambiguity of writing was accepted;
(4) that a distinction between "clear" and "dark" was recognized by the Irish in the case of all consonants, and that vowel letters were used as diacritics, and could be put either before or after the consonant they distinguished.

The next two questions that arise are: How far is there any sign that the Anglo-Saxons were capable of noticing fine distinctions of consonant sound, even if their attention had been drawn to them? and How far is there any evidence that they followed the Irish methods of orthography? The answer to the first of these questions is that there is very good reason to think that the Anglo-Saxons could perceive consonant sound very well indeed. Length of consonant was phonemic in Old English, and the difference between *cwelan* and *cwellan*, or *mēte* and *mētte*, rested on [l] or [l:], [t] or [t:]. They were also, like the Irish,

[22] *Eriu* iii. 50.

alliterators in poetry, and this alliteration was not merely a literary device known to a few cultured people, but a means of poetic ornament employed and enjoyed even by the humblest man who sang a charm. The well-known facts of Old English alliteration show a strong sense of consonant quality in the people:—

1. As in Old Irish poetry, any vowel could alliterate with any other vowel, probably because it was the absence of consonant that was felt to alliterate.

2. ʒ = [j] could alliterate with ʒ = [γ]. In this case it seems that it was the friction that was felt to be the alliterating element; and, indeed, the changed place of articulation does not obscure the similarity of manner of articulation of these consonants. It has been said that this was a kind of "eye-alliteration", traditional and accepted, but not sound. That this is unlikely, and an incomplete explanation, and that the poet must have intended the combination, is indicated by two facts. The Religious Epics, which have no traditional poems behind them, might have shown a modification of the traditional alliteration if, in this particular point, it had been weak; for, as the vast majority of people would hear, but never read the poems, there would be no reason to continue a weak alliteration; also in *Maldon,* written at a time when [γ] had become [g] initially, the alliteration is either [j] or [g], and only one doubtful line occurs, l. 100, and in this it is possible to keep to the proper consonant if one stress was not intended to alliterate, as is very probable, since *Maldon* frequently has only one alliterating stress in each half-line. Even the recognition of *st, sp,* and *sc* as each "one thing", not to be confused with each other or *s*, shows a keenness of perception. There is certainly good reason to think that their powers of hearing sounds were not to be despised.

How far is there any sign that the Anglo-Saxons followed the possible instructions of the Irish? There is plenty of evidence of their use of vowel letters as diacritics, and, while this has often been admitted in individual cases, not enough allowance has been made for it as possibly a fundamental principle of their training. They certainly show, even in their practice of runic writing, that diacritics were in their methods. The early futhark of twenty-four letters was increased to twenty-eight by about A.D. 700, which is the present dating of the Thames knife. This covers the period when learning and handwriting were being established and brought to a high standard in Northumbria and Mercia. Among the added runes two are specially significant, ᚢ [u] was altered to express the new sound [y] by the insertion of *i* to show its fronted quality, ᚣ. (The same thing was done when it was necessary to adapt the Late Latin alphabet to the Old English sounds. In Latin V an *i* was inserted to produce [y], and this V is found in the coin of Eanred of Northumbria, 807-841.[23] To represent the sound which developed from Germanic [au], and which is written in the manuscripts *ea*, a new rune was made which looks like the *e* rune balanced precariously on the stroke of the *a* rune, ᛠ . In both these cases the adaptation is made by means of a diacritic, and, in both, this diacritic seems to be a vowel. In this connexion it might be noted that the rune ᛠ is not found used for "short" *ea* till a date much later than that at which the orthographic tradition might be expected to be established, when it would obviously be a copy of the orthography. In the earliest examples of "short" *ea* in inscriptions, it appears in Roman letters in mixed Roman and runic carvings.

It is even safe to go a step further. It has long been generally accepted that, in many cases, *i*, *e*, and even *ȝ* denote a palatalized consonant, and examples of this are *secean, heriȝeas* or *herias* or *herȝas, dæiȝ*. These writings are frequent in West Saxon, but in the Northumbrian manuscripts they are common. The *Lindisfarne Gospels* show frequent forms such as *ðeiȝn, ceiȝendo, deiȝlice* (beside *deȝlice*), *neirxna wonga, seisto, ȝebreinȝendum, reihtniss*. Is it the Irish tradition which the Northumbrian writer is following here? It has not yet been suggested that another set of diphthongs *ei, æi*, etc., should be added to the Old English vowel system on the basis of these writings, and they are usually accepted as denoting the front, or fronted consonant. Why should a distinction be made thus between a front *i* diacritic and a back, or *u/o/a* one? Surely there is no point in a scribe's marking one kind of sound unless another is possible? Is it unreasonable to assume that the Anglo-Saxon scribes used *u, o, a* in some cases to show dark quality as well as *i* to show clear, and that in so doing they were trying to follow the instructions originally given them and the tradition laid down? If, as seems probable, the principle of dark colour writing of consonants came into Anglo-Saxon orthography early, then we are not forced to think that every later scribe analysed every consonant he wrote, for he would learn the traditional spelling, and only deviate from it when it became glaringly inaccurate. That this traditional spelling was a strong influence is shown by the fact that OScand *kalla*, when it first appears in *Maldon*, is given the traditional, but scarcely at that date phonetic, spelling *ceallian*. The most helpful and convincing evidence would be, and is, that of the language itself. Are the facts more easily explained on this hypothesis? Are later forms more comprehensible? In short, is Old English Phonology more scientific, and in line with what we know of speech, if we assume that the Anglo-Saxon scribes had a definite training in orthography, and that they grouped their sounds? Some sort of grouping of sounds is implied in any form of orthography, and the important question which has not yet been answered is whether the Anglo-Saxons grouped *ea, eo*, and *io* in special conditions with *æ, e*, and *i*. Let us take it that the Anglo-Saxon scribes knew very well what they were writing, or at least that the leaders

[23] H. Arntz, *Handbuch der Runenkunde* 148.

among them did, and that one sound was not necessarily represented by one letter, but that they used *u/o/a* as diacritics for consonants, as well as *i* and *e*. Thus "Breaking", "Palatal Diphthongization", and "Back-Mutation", as "Sound-Laws" in the accepted sense of the word, should be omitted from any account of the sounds of Old English, and replaced by phoneme grouping and a study of orthography.

II

If there is any truth in the suggestion already put forward, that dark and clear consonants were both indicated by vowel diacritics, then the forms of words in Old English manuscripts should be more easily explained on this hypothesis, both in relation to each other, and also in relation to forms found in later stages of the language. The scribal writings whose usual interpretation is questioned here are of two kinds:

(1) those connected with back or velar sounds, e.g. *eo, io, ea,* found before *r* and *l* when followed by another consonant, *h,* and before single consonants with a back vowel following it, e.g. *weorpan, eald, feohtan, beadu,* etc., and also in some cases in connexion with *w*. In each case we are told that a back-glide "developed" and that the result is a "diphthong" which can be removed from its setting for the purposes of classification and called "short".

(2) those connected with front consonants, e.g. *ea, ie,* where the stock explanation is that a front glide is developed between the consonant and a front vowel and again a "short" diphthong is the result.

If these glide writings are due to the consonant, or belong to it, then the nature of the consonant in each case is of vital importance. *l* presents the least difficulty; when it follows *i* [i], there is never any diphthongal writing, cf. *cild, wilde,* which implies a clear *l;* when it follows *e, eo* writings are only found if it is supported by *c* or *h* or occasionally *f,* cf. *seolc, seolh, seolf,* evidently because the [ɫ] was kept dark by the following velars, and in the case of *f* the lip-consonant may have rounded and darkened the *l*; after [æ] the *l* seems to have been dark in all cases, cf. *eall,* etc., so dark as often to counteract the [ɑ̈ > æ] tendency, and so we find Anglian *ald,* etc. *h* is usually accepted as being a breath fricative after vowels, and the writing *ch* for it supports this idea. Where and when it was fronted, and how far, is not so easy to decide. It does not necessarily follow that combination with a front vowel produced [ç] from [χ] or [x], for the Scottish *brecht* has [x]. Considerable variation between [χ], [x], and [ç] might have existed at the same time. The voiced [γ] undoubtedly was fronted to [j] before and after front vowels, and it is very probable that the breath [χ] and [x] underwent a similar fronting, though its survival till the fourteenth century, when [j] had long passed to the vowel [i], suggests that it was never so far forward in the Old English period. The point to be emphasized is the possibility of variant forms ranging from [χ], [x] to [ç] existing at the same time.

Most writers on Old English phonology say that *r* was a point trill. But was it? Sievers[24] suggests a totally different sound: "Das *r* des ags. war wahrscheinlich cerebral, d.h. wurde mit stark zurückgebogener Zungenspitze gesprochen, wie z.t. noch heute im englischen. Nur so nämlich erklärt sich phonetisch die Brechung vor *r*." By *Brechung* Sievers means a very slight glide pronunciation, as is clear from his remarks on "short diphthongs" quoted already. H. C. Wyld supports the suggestion of an "inverted" *r* for the "Breaking" conditions but suggests that in all other cases OE *r* was a trill.[25] Whatever sound we assume the Old English *r* to have been, certain facts have to be accounted for; first, the sound must have had, in certain conditions, a marked syllabic and 'dark' quality; secondly, this quality came out most strongly when followed by another consonant, less strongly when followed by a back vowel; thirdly, it was sometimes written before and sometimes after the vowel in accented syllables, and this is taken to represent a real variation of sound, Metathesis. Of the *r* sounds existing at the present time, only three are likely to have been in general use in Old English. There is the lingual trill [r], the alveolar fricative [ɹ], and the frictionless retroflex sound which will be denoted here by [ɻ], and which is the most important of the three. How does [r] fit in with what we know of Old English *r*? It was, we know, the *r* in general use among the Latin and Celtic races, as it still is, but it does not, as we know it, have a strongly-marked dark colour in certain conditions, nor is its resonance markedly increased by a following consonant, nor does metathesis, if that is a sound-change at all, appear among speakers using it. Such pronunciations as Scottish [modrən], [sauðrən], for 'modern', 'southern', are the result of the Scandinavian influence (cf. OScand *suþrænn,* etc.). Old Irish has practically no trace of metathesis at all, only one word showing a change of position of *r*; *bérle* 'speech', once appears for *bélre,*[26] and here, if it is not a scribe's mistake, it still is not a question of relationship to the vowel. Lastly, the [r] does not, and has not, changed to a fricative in the countries where it is used, so that if it were the general and only Old English *r,* as is usually stated, the present day [ɹ] and [ɻ] have still to be accounted for. It seems very unlikely that Old English *r* was always [r]. Of the other possible *r* sounds, [ɻ] fits in better than [ɹ], but there is a possibility that [ɹ]

[24] E. Sievers, *Angelsächsische Grammatik* § 178. For his definition of *cerebral* see *Grundzüge der Phonetik* § 297. ['The *r* of Anglo-Saxon was probably cerebral, that is, spoken with the apex of the tongue sharply turned back, as it is to some extent still today in English. Only in this way is the breaking before *r* to be explained phonetically.' *Eds.*]

[25] H. C. Wyld, *A Short History of English* §§ 85, 102.

[26] R. Thurneysen, *Handbuch des alt-irischen* § 179.

existed in some conditions. While we cannot in all cases be sure of the values intended by the Germanic peoples in the use of the Roman letters they borrowed, the comparative uniformity of *s* [s], in all Latin languages, makes it likely that the voiced version of it as written *z* was something pretty near [z]. It is accepted that Germanic *z* passed to *r* in West Germanic; the relationship of OE *ceosan, coren,* shows that something which was voiced *s* has been grouped by the Anglo-Saxons with the IE *r,* as in *beran.* It is not easy to see how a [z] could produce a lingual trill, but a slight dropping of the jaw will turn [z] into an alveolar fricative [ɹ], and a slight retraction of the tongue will produce the retroflex [ɻ] from [z]. Both these *r*-sounds must have originated somewhere, and the [ɻ] is found before a consonant in Norway as well as in England. In the West Country, and large parts of the rest of England, the alveolar fricative [ɹ] is heard initially, and varying forms of the retroflex [ɻ] after vowels. The retroflex [ɻ] also has a strong on-glide which is intensified when another consonant follows so that there seems good reason why the on-glide should sometimes be recorded, but not at all why a lingual trill, after a front vowel, should show a back on-glide, as "Breaking" requires. With regard to metathesis, it is noticeable that writings which suggest the transposed position of *r* and vowel are extremely frequent in the part of the country occupied by the Scandinavians, but it is not altogether safe to deduce more from this than an additional piece of evidence against OE *r* [r]. Professor Daniel Jones suggests that metathesis was probably not a "change" at all, but an attempt to write the frictionless retroflex with a strong sonant quality of a special vowel, e.g. vowel and consonant said together, as it is heard in Somerset to-day, so that when faced with [θɻd:ɑ̈] or [gɻs], the scribes might, and did, write *þridda,* or *þirda, gærs* or *græs,* and the two forms mean exactly the same thing, and if in later development, a separate vowel emerged it might appear before or after the consonant. Whichever view is taken of metathesis, a change or no change, the evidence to be drawn from it is entirely in favour of [ɻ]. The fact that when metathesis is found in a word like *irnan,* sometimes no back vowel writing appears, and sometimes *iornan,* could be explained as a retention of the traditional writing in some cases, as in *gærs, ærn,* while in others the consonant was grouped in its proper setting, as in *iornan.* The conclusion seems to be that Sievers was right, and that medially after vowels, and finally, OE *r* was probably [ɻ], initially possibly [ɹ], and the lingual trill, if it had ever been the natural *r* of the Germanic people, was displaced.

By the assumption that "Breaking", "Palatal Diphthongization", and "Back-Mutation" were developments which can be dated within limits, a system of "sound-changes" has been built up, which in some cases may be purely fictitious, in others only part of a long-drawn-out process. The so-called breaking of *e* to *eo* before *lc,* or *r* and a consonant, must have "happened" just whenever [e] came in contact with [ɫ], or a suitable *r*. The recognition of the on-glide in writing provides no evidence whatever as to the moment of development, nor is the fact that similar "breakings" are found in Old Frisian any proof that this "sound-change" happened in a common Anglo-Frisian period, since the Frisians were converted and taught from England, and may have adopted orthographic methods from this country.

Let us examine the phonetic implications of the forms found for OE *seah* 'saw', as a typical example. The development usually described is:

WGerm	**sah*.
Early OE	**sæh,* with fronting of *a* to *æ,* an isolative change, *seah* "breaking" by "development" or a back glide before h [x],
Late OE	*sæh* "Monophthongization" of the "diphthong" again before *h,* now fronted to [ç],
	seh a further palatalization,
ME	*sauh* where [æ] has become [ä] and an *u*-glide developed before the back consonant,
	seih where an *i*-glide developed,
	sih, sy, with complete palatalization of the vowel, and presumably consonant.

Surely it is plain that the important fact here is progressive palatalization, a steady fronting of the consonant and vowel, from [χ], [x], to [ç], and from [ä] to [æ] to [e] and in some cases in ME to [i]; but which sound affected which at any given point is surely hard to say. In some districts the vowel might be ahead of the consonant, while at the same time the reverse might be true in others. The so-called Anglian *seh* and *sæh,* contemporary with WSax *seah,* is a case in point. There is no necessity to assume that there has ever been a diphthong here. If the consonant colour was sometimes indicated in writing, then *sæh* and *seah* could perfectly well represent exactly the same form [sæx], and *seh* a slight variant. In the case of ME *sauh,* obviously the [χ], or [x], remained, and quite probably [ä] may have remained unfronted, as in the common OE spelling *sah*. It is extremely likely that [säx], [sæx], [sæç], [seç][27] were all in existence at the same time. It would be daring to assign any one value to a spelling, and until the friction was lost it is not safe to say that ME *seih* or *sauh* were any more diphthongs than OE *sæh, seh,* or *sah*. The whole series from early Old English to Middle English must have contained the following forms, but in what order, [säx], [sax], [sæx], [sæc], [sex], [seç]? What then does the *seah* writing mean in this series more than that the consonant still had dark quality, and that at a time when [x] and [ç], or something like them, were both in existence, this was [x]in a position where its darkness was more palpable?

[27] Not to mention other possible variants with [a] and [ɛ].

Again, in the case of the *l* groups in "Breaking", the distinction made in writing after *i* and *e* and *æ,* referred to above, shows how sharply the qualities of *l* were differentiated. Even when such writings as *beadu, sweostor,* appear, it need not mean more than that velarization of other consonants than *r, l,* and *h* was heard in non-West Saxon districts, and sometimes even in Wessex; thus OE *weorþan, liomu, scearon, feaht, beoran, feadur,* are much more simple if we regard them as conventionalized writings of [weɹpan], [lim̶u], [scæ:ɹɒn], [fæxt] or [fæχt], [beɹan], [fæd̶ur]. It is not necessary to make an elaborate "sound change" out of such forms as *beadu, feadur,* and say that Back-Mutation "took place" in the Anglian districts before other consonants than in West Saxon; it is surely enough to note that the dark quality of these consonants is recorded in such and such a manuscript, and that the Anglian scribes keep closely to the Irish tradition.

A supporting reason in favour of regarding the writings of *eo* and *ea* as only variants of [e] and [æ], in certain conditions, is that in the overwhelming majority of cases the forms to be traced in Middle English show exactly the development to be expected of [e] and [æ], e.g. OE *earm,* ME *erm, arm;* in OE *eorþe* the vowel must have become lengthened in late OE before this consonant group, as is indicated by Orm's writing *erþe,* and then shortened again, or a short type may have survived; a lengthened form in early NE is suggested by the NE spelling, but *ea* in a NE word usually points back to ME [ɛ:] or [æ:], as far as can be judged by other words, and *eorþe,* if the vowel had been lengthened in OE to [e:o], would have been likely to give ME [e:], NE **eerth* (cf. OE *deor,* NE *deer*). If it be argued that *r* has a lowering effect on preceding vowels and so [e:] was lowered to [ɛ:] in this case, that does not apply to *seolh* 'seal', gen. *seoles,* which shows in NE the *ea* spelling pointing to ME [ɛ:], the normal result of OE [e][28] in an open accented syllable, but not the normal result of [e:o]. A late OE stage *æ* and *e* or *i* is always allowed in established phonology for earlier *ea, eo,* and accounted for as a monophthongization; but the point is sufficiently clear that in the great majority of cases, the apparently descended forms are no different from those descended from the simple vowel in each case. In general the so-called "short" diphthongs leave no trace.[29]

When "Breaking" combinations are followed by *i* or *j,* it is suggested that the "diphthong" is palatalized to another diphthong, but in every dialect except West Saxon the result is a simple vowel, and that result is the same as if the accented vowel were [æ] or [i], e.g. WSax *ierming,*

[28] It is usually accepted that OE *e* was [e] and was lowered to [ɛ] in early Middle English, but in some cases, as in the opening accented syllable, *e* may have been [ɛ] in Old English. It would be a contextual variant of [e], or, more likely, [ɛ] was the principal phone and [e] before *ld, mb, nd,* etc., the variant. There is nothing to prove which was the value of the sound in any one context since it might have been raised or lowered before Middle English.

[29] Special cases will be dealt with later.

Angl *erming;* where the *i*-mutation is supposed to affect a diphthong *io* in WSax, we are told that this diphthong is not affected in Anglian, but forms like *wiorpeð* probably show [i] or [ɪ] in a special context and *o* as a diacritic to *r* and WSax *hierde* need not be explained in any other way than that the *i* [i], which appeared in Germanic as a raising of [e] before [j], here appears under special conditions. The curious series of forms offered as an explanation of *fiellan* has already been examined. It requires us to believe that [ɫɫj] could still remain so dark that a back on-glide developed, and then that shortly afterwards the "short" diphthong was palatalized. The same peculiar explanation is put forward that in WSax *hliehhan,* [x] remained velar, and so developed a short diphthong in time to be palatalized. Where it can be traced, however, [j] has a distinctly fronting influence on a preceding consonant, as in *drencan* or *secgan,* so that it is the more unreasonable to assume that its palatalizing influence remained dormant so long. It is probably safest to conclude that a word containing [i] or [j] never had exactly the same phonetic stages as a simple form of its root, and that something like [hlɑ̈x:(j)an], [hlæx:(j)an], [hlæç:an], [hleç:an], [hliç:an], was the probable series.

These forms are supported by WSax *hlihhan,* Angl *hlæhhan* or *hlehhan;* ME *lyhe, liȝe.* The common forms with [x] and [γ], OE *hlōh, hlōȝon,* would account for infinitive forms with that consonant, as is implied in ME *lauhen, lauȝe,* etc.

An interesting point to be noticed in connexion with these *eo, ea* writings, is that the experience of practical phoneticians, dealing with living languages, shows that any consonant glide occurring after close [e] tends to be on the same level and to be slightly rounded, while [ɛ] and [æ] usually have [ɑ̈] glides after them. This tendency in existing speech is widespread, and there is no reason to suppose it to be modern. Thus, as WGerm [au] went through the fronting stage to OE [æu], if it worked that way, its natural glide would be [ɑ̈], and *ea,* which is plainly a tidying up of *æa,* so frequently found, might at first have been a phonetic writing for the long diphthong. In the "Breaking" cases the natural on-glides of the dark consonants would be in the region of [o] and [ɑ̈], and the fact that the writings *ea* and *eo* are used, shows, I would suggest, not that the real and the conditioned diphthongs were alike except for quantity, but that they were so different as never to be confused.

A few words about the much-discussed *ie* writings might be suitable here. Putting aside the cases where *ie* is a variant of [e] or [e:] after *c, ȝ,* or *sc,* which are comparatively few in number and present little difficulty, the majority of cases of *ie* represent the *i*-mutation of either a long diphthong or a so-called "short" one. In each case the result in late West Saxon is the same, [i] or [i:]; and it seems very arbitrary to say that *ie* is a diphthong, which is later monophthongized, in view of the facts that Anglian and Kentish show a monophthong in every case, and that even in the best manuscripts *ie* and *i* occur together,[30] and that *ie* is soon abandoned. Two possible explanations might be added to the many already in circulation. If in Wessex the root vowels reached [i:] and [i] early, then for a time a palatalized on-glide of the consonant might have been heard, and written, and the natural palatal on-glide after *i* would be *e*. But the uncertainty of the writings *ie* and *i* suggests that if a glide intepretation is to be accepted, the writing should be regarded as a piece of over-carefulness, introduced for a period but never consistently followed, and the vowel should be counted as [i], [i:]. But quite another explanation might be true. In a large number of cases where *ie* occurs, the vowel has come up from a lower level, and it seems quite possible that for a time there were two values of *i*, a high front [i] or [i:] in words like *cild, fisc, wilde, ridan,* and a lower form [ɪ:] and [ɪ], which was in every case the result of palatalization in words like *ieldra, ierming, hiehþo, cierran,* where [ä], [æ], [ɛ], [e], [i], were the probable stages. A nice point in favour of this is that the non-West Saxon texts show *e* in almost all such cases, *erming, hehþu, cerran,* etc., and [e] is very closely related to [ɪ][31] and is used to help French speakers to get modern English [ɪ] in *bid, hit,* etc. This second explanation seems the more likely to be the true one. [i] and [ɪ] are quite possible vowels to find in the same vowel system; they occur together to-day, nor is it unreasonable to suggest that some scribes distinguished them for a time, though never very exactly, and that they used the method, common enough, of vowel diacritics.

Before the suggestions put forward in this paper can be accepted, certain aspects of the questions must be considered. These concern Old English forms which do not at first sight fall into line, or later forms which might be quoted as evidence for the existence of earlier "short" diphthongs. These difficulties can be grouped under various headings:—

1) Shifting of Accent

In a number of cases the later language shows a main vowel apparently derived from what has been described here as the slight on-glide of the consonant, e.g. *York* from *Eoforwic*. Here the accent must have shifted on to the on-glide of the consonant, which naturally increased into a full vowel, and as the [jo], [ja] forms of this type are commonest in parts of the country where the Danes were, the North Country, the Scandinavian *ja, jo* forms should probably be taken as strongly influencing the native ones. In any case a later development of the consonant glide is no proof that it was exceptionally prominent three or four hundred years before.

[30] Cf. *Cotton* (*i*), and *Hatton* MSS of *Pastoral Care.*

[31] H. Sweet, *History of English Sounds* 43, 44.

2) *Lengthened and Contracted Forms*

The on-glide is sometimes developed as the friction of the consonant lessens, e.g. *feoh* [fex], may go through a stage [feo] before reaching ME *fe* [fe:], but the diphthong need only be established as the consonant friction was lost, just as in New England a form of *field,* [fɪɔ•d], is found, with the accent on the second element of the vowel and no consonant contact for *l* at all. In the case of *seolh, seoles,* as has been pointed out before, while certainty is impossible, it is likely that the root vowel was [ɛ] in both cases and so remained till early ME, when vowels were lengthened in open accented syllables, since OE *eo,* so-called "long", usually shows NE spelling *ie,* or *ee,* whereas *seal* shows the *ea* which usually indicates ME [ɛ:], often the result of [ɛ] having been so lengthened. Probably in this case lengthening of the vowel did not occur in OE with the loss of *h,* because the loss of friction may have been very slight, and any increase of energy possibly slipped into the *l.* Contracted forms like *sēon, slēan,* are covered by this explanation, for [seχan], [sexan], could develop into [seo^ʌ^an] as the friction of the consonant lessened, and the diphthong then developed could absorb the unaccented final vowel. For *slēan,* a stage [slæxan] has to be assumed in any case and this could produce *ǣa, ēa,* and the Northumbrian *slan* shows the development normally to be expected.

3) *Rounding*

Words like *beorn, eorþe,* often show later forms with rounding of the vowel, in certain areas, e.g. ME *burn, urþe.* These much later forms can hardly affect the question of the OE writing; late West Saxon showed a tendency to round [e] after [w], which might have spread, and many of the cases quoted have labials initially or following the vowel. A similar rounding is found in Northumbrian. Even if the on-glide developed naturally, and rounded the preceding vowel to [y], or [œ], this was obviously a local tendency, since all the cases where *e* appears are more numerous than those with rounding. As far as place-names can be traced the *e* forms are as old as the rounded ones, in many cases older.

III

Finally, a number of conclusions need emphasizing, and the first is that the phenomena connected with "glides" were much less important and much more indefinite than they have been considered, that there were, in the true sense of the word, no "short diphthongs", and that no such sound-changes as "Breaking", "Palatal Diphthongization", or "Back Mutation" ever "took place"; but that certain tendencies were continuously at work, and that the outstanding fact is the progressive palatalization, which went on for hundreds of years, and affected vowels and consonants so intricately, that it is a mistake to cut it up into sections and give them titles and dates. The various writings of *ea, io, ie,* could be quite effectively covered by a detailed section on orthography.

Secondly, not nearly enough has been done in grouping the sounds, and therefore the writings, of Old English phonemically. Some kind of mental grouping is implicit in any ordered orthography, and there is no doubt that the writing of the Anglo-Saxon scribes would be definitely affected by the mental grouping of their sounds. That they classed [f] and [v], [s] and [z], and [θ] and [ð] together as three groups, is plain, but the grouping of other sounds is not made so clear. If we consider all the words which in pre-Old English would have had, as we suppose [ɑ̈], the normal Old English letter which appears in West Saxon is *æ,* which is found in all but a few phonetic contexts, and which might be regarded as the principal member of the phoneme, probably either [a] or [æ] in value. This is borne out by the fact that the old [ɑ̈] rune ᚨ in the Anglo-Saxon runes is [æ], and a special form ᚫ is adapted for [ɑ̈]. In special contexts, *a, o* (before a nasal), and *ea* appear, and these can be regarded as subsidiary members of the phoneme, in so far as they really represent a variation of sound, which has to be established. Now it seems to be of real importance that these groupings should be carefully made, since the writers, or the founders of the Old English orthography must have made such a grouping, and we may thus get a clue as to what sounds they considered the same, and so wrote by one symbol; or, conversely, considered so different as never to be confusable and so wrote with one letter, or group of letters. Where vowels are concerned, the question of relative distance of one from another is pertinent, since a harmony of vowels tends to even up the distance between them in any one form of speech, and if some can be ascertained with any certainty, it gives an assurance as to the likely places of the others.

Thirdly, a phonetic overhauling of the possible sounds of Old English in relation to those of Old Irish and Late Latin, might yield valuable results even now. The difference between [æ] and [a], or [i] and [ɪ], or [χ] and [x], or [t] and [th] are linguistically very important, but are not suggested by the very hard-and-fast "keys" to pronunciation of Old English usually given. No work on Old English with which I am acquainted, begins with a chapter like the first of Sturtevant's "The Pronunciation of Greek and Latin", where the evidence for the phonetic value of Greek and Latin letters is weighed point by point, comparatively. When we consider that the Anglo-Saxons were taught their script by Irish teachers, who themselves had learnt Latin sounds, and by Latin missionaries, whose pronunciation, from the Roman point of view, might be distinctly "provincial", it may be that the guides to pronunciation given us are generally too simple. Sturtevant points out[32] that Greek ε

[32] E. H. Sturtevant, *The Pronunciation of Greek and Latin* 3.

was identified with Latin *i,* e.g. *piper, citrus,* which shows that Latin *i* was probably rather an open sound. How open was the Old English sound represented by *i*? This question has been shown to be important, since the acoustic relations of [i] are different from those of [ɪ], and this may have a bearing on the question of *ie.*

Fourthly, I would suggest that in the interpretation of Old English scribal writings, too strong a bias in favour of vowels has often been shown, and that the whole field could well be re-examined with more attention to consonants, since the facts that they were members of a race whose poetry was alliterative, and taught by men in whose native speech fine shades of consonant pronunciation were phonemic, might lead the Anglo-Saxons to show special care and discrimination in writing consonants, or at least to attempt it, and this is not reflected in the proportion of space usually given to vowel and consonant in Old English Grammars.

Lastly, a new formulation of Old English phonology would be interesting on some such lines as the following:—

(a) SCRIPT

(b) ORTHOGRAPHY, (1) Writing of Consonants
(2) Writing of Vowels

This section would cover the writing of consonant colour and the "true" and "false" diphthongs.

(c) PALATALIZATION. This should be the most important section, and should trace processes but not be too much cut up into "changes".
(1) Palatalization of Consonants, e.g. [γ] to [j], [χ] to [ç], [k] to [tʃ]
(2) Palatalization of Vowels
Isolative Changes, *i*-mutation.

(d) NASALIZATION

(e) ROUNDING

(f) LOSS OF SOUNDS AND CONTRACTION
(1) Consonants
(2) Vowels

(g) OTHER MINOR PHENOMENA

Two great advantages appear from the recognition of consonant colour writings, and the resulting eclipse of glides. The first is that West Saxon and Anglian are brought much nearer together in form, and as recent archæological research has tended to break down the strict line between Angle and Saxon,[33] this is all to the good. Jespersen, long ago, suggested that the Anglian and West Saxon forms were probably much

[33] Hodgkin, *History of the Anglo-Saxons* I. 117.

nearer to each other in actual pronunciation than they appeared in writing.

The last and perhaps best result is that it may break down much of the system which has been built up, and which seems to offer an explanation for every possible writing. This paper has no claim to be regarded as anything but a plea for a reconsideration of the field, the case for the prosecution, and I am quite sure of one thing only, that in linguistic analysis a complete system must be partly wrong.[34]

AUTHOR'S POSTSCRIPT (1966)

In 1945 Professor F. Mossé published similar views to those in the above article, cf. Manuel de l'anglais du Moyen Âge, I Vieil-anglais *§§ 8, 12, 22, 33, etc. He only discovered our similar views in 1947. He arrived in Old English from Old Irish and I reversed the journey.*

Marjorie Daunt

[34] [*Eds.*: The author has a further defense of her paper in "Some Notes on Old English Phonology," *Transactions of the Philological Society 1952* (1953), pp. 48-54.]

Suggested Additional Readings for Part V

[See additional readings for Part I for works cited by author and date only.]

E. Bagby Atwood, *A Survey of Verb Forms in the Eastern United States* (Ann Arbor, 1953).

________________, "The Methods of American Dialectology," *Zeitschrift für Mundartforschung* 30.1-29 (1963).

Bloomfield 1933, esp. chapters 19, 25-27.

John C. Catford, "The Linguistic Survey of Scotland," *Orbis* 6.105-21 (1957).

John L. Fischer, "Social Influences in the Choice of a Linguistic Variant," *Word* 14.47-56 (1958).

W. Nelson Francis, "Graphemic Analysis of Late Middle English Manuscripts," *Speculum* 37.32-47 (1962).

Ignace J. Gelb, *A Study of Writing*, 2nd ed. (Chicago, 1963). Also Phoenix P109.

Hockett 1958, esp. chapters 38-40, 46-49, 56.

Hans Kurath, *Handbook of the Linguistic Geography of New England* (Providence, R. I., 1939).

________________, *Word Geography of the Eastern United States* (Ann Arbor, 1949).

________________ and Raven I. McDavid, Jr., *The Pronunciation of English in the Atlantic States* (Ann Arbor, 1961).

William Labov, "Phonological Correlates of Social Stratification," in John J. Gumperz and Dell Hymes, eds., *The Ethnography of Communication* (Menasha, Wis., 1964), 164-76.

Lehmann 1962, esp. chapters 8, 13.

RAVEN I. McDAVID, JR., "American English Dialects," in W. Nelson Francis, *The Structure of American English* (New York, 1958), 480-543.

______________, "Postvocalic /-r/ in South Carolina: A Social Analysis," *American Speech* 23.194-203 (1948).

ANGUS McINTOSH, "The Analysis of Written Middle English," *Transactions of the Philological Society 1956* (1957), 26-55.

______________, "A New Approach to Middle English Dialectology," *English Studies* 44.1-11 (1963).

FERNAND MOSSÉ, *A Handbook of Middle English,* trans. James A. Walker (Baltimore, 1952).

WILLIAM G. MOULTON, "Dialect Geography and the Concept of Phonological Space," *Word* 18.23-32. (1962).

HAROLD ORTON AND EUGEN DIETH, *Survey of English Dialects: Introduction* (Leeds, 1962).

M. L. SAMUELS, "Some Applications of Middle English Dialectology," *English Studies* 44.81-94 (1963).

ROBERT P. STOCKWELL, "Structural Dialectology: A Proposal," *American Speech* 34.258-68 (1959).

______________ AND WESTBROOK BARRITT, "Scribal Practice: Some Assumptions," *Language* 37.75-82 (1961).

URIEL WEINREICH, *Languages in Contact: Findings and Problems* (New York, 1953).

______________, "Is a Structural Dialectology Possible?" *Word* 10.388-400 (1954).

Index